S0-APN-265

MASS MEDIA:
A BIBLIOGRAPHY WITH INDEXES

Mass Media: A Bibliography With Indexes

James B. Martin (Editor)

Nova Science Publishers, Inc.
New York

Senior Editors: Susan Boriotti and Donna Dennis
Coordinating Editor: Tatiana Shohov
Office Manager: Annette Hellinger
Graphics: Wanda Serrano
Editorial Production: Jennifer Vogt, Matthew Kozlowski and Maya Columbus
Circulation: Ave Maria Gonzalez, Indah Becker Raymond Davis and Vladimir Klestov
Communications and Acquisitions: Serge P. Shohov
Marketing: Cathy DeGregory

Library of Congress Cataloging-in-Publication Data
Available Upon Request

ISBN 1-59033-262-8.

400 Oser Ave, Suite 1600
Hauppauge, New York 11788-3619
Tele. 631-231-7269 Fax 631-231-8175
e-mail: Novascience@earthlink.net
Web Site: http://www.novapublishers.com

Printed in the United States of America

CONTENTS

PREFACE

Mass media has become an integral part of the human experience. News travels around the world in a split second effecting people in other countries in untold ways. Although being on top of the news may be good, at least for news junkies, mass media also transmits values or the lack thereof, condenses complex events and thoughts to simplified sound bites and often ignores the essence of an event or story. The selective bibliography gathers the books and magazine literature over the previous ten years while providing access through author, title and subject indexes.

General

1990 Philippine media profile. Published/Created: [Quezon City?]: Philippine Information Agency, Media Studies Division , [1991] Related Authors: Philippine Information Agency. Media Studies Division. Description: 54 p.: maps; 21 cm. Subjects: Mass media--Philippines--Directories. LC Classification: P92.P5 A16 1991

A Handbook of qualitative methodologies for mass communication research / edited by Klaus Bruhn Jensen and Nicholas W. Jankowski. Published/Created: London; New York: Routledge, 1991. Related Authors: Jensen, Klaus. Jankowski, Nick. Description: xiv, 272 p.; 23 cm. ISBN: 0415054044 0415054052 (pbk.) Notes: Includes bibliographical references (p. [232]-259) and indexes. Subjects: Mass media--Research--Humanities--Social sciences--Methodology. LC Classification: P91.3 .H35 1991 Dewey Class No.: 302.23/072 20

Adams, Paul. Writing right for today's mass media: a textbook and workbook with language exercises / Paul Adams. Published/Created: Chicago: Nelson-Hall Publishers, c1998. Description: ix, 450 p.: ill.; 28 cm. ISBN: 0830414568 (pbk.) Subjects: Journalism--Mass media--Authorship. Report writing. Reporters and reporting. LC Classification: PN4781 .A25 1998 Dewey Class No.: 808/.06607 21

Alexander, David. How you can manipulate the media: guerrilla methods to get your story covered by TV, radio, and newspapers / David Alexander. Published/Created: Boulder, Colo.: Paladin Press, c1993. Description: xii, 98 p.: ill.; 21 cm. ISBN: 0873647297 Subjects: Mass media. Press and propaganda. Manipulative behavior. LC Classification: P91 .A427 1993 Dewey Class No.: 659 20

An Integrated approach to communication theory and research / edited by Michael B. Salwen and Don W. Stacks. Published/Created: Mahwah, N.J.: Erlbaum, 1996. Related Authors: Salwen, Michael Brian. Stacks, Don W. Description: xiii, 600 p.; 26 cm. ISBN: 0805816305 (alk. paper) 0805816313 (pbk.: alk. paper) Notes: Includes bibliographical references and indexes. Subjects: Communication--Mass media--Methodology. Series: LEA's communication series LC Classification: P91 .I558 1996 Dewey Class No.: 302.2/01 20

Arnold, George T. Media writer's handbook: a guide to common writing and editing problems / George T. Arnold. Edition Information: 2nd ed. Published/Created: Boston: McGraw-Hill, c2000. Description: xxi, 257 p.; 24 cm. ISBN: 0697355012 (pbk.) Notes: Includes index. Subjects: Journalism--Style manuals--Mass media--Authorship. Series: The McGraw-Hill series in mass communication and journalism LC Classification: PN4783 .A76 2000 Dewey Class No.: 808/.027 21

Audiencemaking: how the media create the audience / editors, James S. Ettema and D.

Charles Whitney. Published/Created: Thousand Oaks, Calif.: Sage Publications, c1994. Related Authors: Ettema, James S. Whitney, D. Charles (David Charles), 1946- Description: 242 p.; 23 cm. ISBN: 0803946252 (cl) 0803946260 (pb) Notes: Includes bibliographical references and index. Subjects: Mass media--Audiences--Economic aspects. Series: Sage annual reviews of communication research; v. 22 LC Classification: P96.A83 A95 1994 Dewey Class No.: 302.23 20

Bagdikian, Ben H. The media monopoly / Ben H. Bagdikian. Edition Information: 3rd ed. Published/Created: Boston: Beacon Press, 1990. Description: xxiii, 288 p.; 21 cm. ISBN: 080706159X Notes: Includes bibliographical references (p. 253-275) and index. Subjects: Mass media--Economic aspects--Monopolies--United States. LC Classification: P96.E252 U625 1990 Dewey Class No.: 338.4/730223/0973 20

Bagdikian, Ben H. The media monopoly / Ben H. Bagdikian. Edition Information: 4th ed. Published/Created: Boston: Beacon Press, 1992. Description: xxxi, 288 p.; 21 cm. ISBN: 0807061573 Notes: Includes bibliographical references (p. 253-275) and index. Subjects: Mass media--Economic aspects--Monopolies--United States. LC Classification: P96.E252 U625 1992 Dewey Class No.: 338.4/730223/0973 20

Barnouw, Erik, 1908- Media marathon: a twentieth-century memoir / Erik Barnouw. Published/Created: Durham: Duke University Press, c1996. Description: viii, 264 p.: ill.; 24 cm. ISBN: 0822317281 (cloth: alk. paper) 0822317389 (pbk.: alk. paper) Notes: Includes bibliographical references and index. Subjects: Barnouw, Erik, 1908- Mass media specialists--United States--Biography. LC Classification: P92.5.B37 A3 1996 Dewey Class No.: 302.23/092 B 20

Baughman, James L., 1952- The republic of mass culture: journalism, filmmaking, and broadcasting in America since 1941 / James L. Baughman. Published/Created: Baltimore: John Hopkins University Press, c1992. Description: xvii, 257 p.; 24 cm. ISBN: 080184276X (alk. paper) 0801842778 (pbk.: alk. paper) Notes: Includes bibliographical references and index. Subjects: Mass media--United States--History. Series: The American moment LC Classification: P92.U5 B345 1992 Dewey Class No.: 302.23/0973 20

Baughman, James L., 1952- The republic of mass culture: journalism, filmmaking, and broadcasting in America since 1941 / James L. Baughman. Edition Information: 2nd ed. Published/Created: Baltimore: Johns Hopkins University Press, 1997. Description: xvii, 287 p.; 24 cm. ISBN: 0801855209 (acid-free paper) 0801855217 (pbk.: acid-free paper) Notes: Includes bibliographical references (p. 251-274) and index. Subjects: Mass media--United States--History. Series: The American moment LC Classification: P92.U5 B345 1997 Dewey Class No.: 302.23/0973 20

Becker, Samuel L. Discovering mass communication / Samuel L. Becker, Churchill Roberts. Edition Information: 3rd ed. Published/Created: New York: HarperCollins, c1992. Related Authors: Roberts, Churchill Lee, 1940- Description: xviii, 541 p.: ill.; 24 cm. ISBN: 067346119X Notes: Includes bibliographical references and index. Subjects: Mass media. LC Classification: P90 .B343 1992 Dewey Class No.: 302.23 20

Beckert, Christine. Getting started in mass media / Christine Beckert. Published/Created: Lincolnwood, Ill.: National Textbook Co., c1992. Description: vii, 120 p.; 28 cm. ISBN: 0844256501 Notes: Includes index. Subjects: Mass media. LC Classification: P90 .B3434 1992

Bell, Allan. The language of news media / Allan Bell. Published/Created: Oxford, UK; Cambridge, MA: Blackwell, 1991. Description: xv, 277 p.: ill.; 24 cm. ISBN: 0631164340: 0631164359 (pbk.): Notes: Includes bibliographical references (p. [254]-268) and index. Subjects: Mass media and language. Broadcast journalism--Language. Newspapers--Language. Sociolinguistics. Series: Language in society (Oxford, England); 16. Variant Series: Language in society; 16 LC Classification: P96.L34 B45 1991 Dewey Class No.: 302.23/014 20

Benarde, Melvin A. You've been had?: how the media and environmentalists turned Americans in to a nation of hypochondriacs / Melvin A. Benarde. Published/Created: New Brunswick, NJ: Rutgers University Press, 2002. Projected Pub. Date: 0205 Description: p. cm. ISBN: 0813530504 (cloth: alk. paper) Notes: Includes bibliographical references and index. Subjects: Environmental health. Environmental health--Responsibility. Quacks and quackery. Consumer education. Mass media in health education. LC Classification: RA440.5 .B46 2002 Dewey Class No.: 615.9/02 21

Benthall, Jonathan. Disasters, relief and the media / Jonathan Benthall. Published/Created: London; New York: I.B. Tauris, 1993. Description: xiii, 267 p.: ill.; 23 cm. ISBN: 1850437378 (pbk.) 1850436428 Notes: Includes bibliographical references and index. Subjects: Disaster relief. Disasters--Press coverage. Mass media. Disaster relief--Public relations. LC Classification: HV553 .B47 1993

Berger, Arthur Asa, 1933- Essentials of mass communication theory / Arthur Asa Berger. Published/Created: Thousand Oaks: Sage Publications, c1995. Description: x, 208 p.: ill.; 24 cm. ISBN: 080397356X 0803973578 (pbk.) Notes: Includes bibliographical references (p. 192-196) and indexes. Subjects: Mass media--Philosophy--United States. LC Classification: P90 .B413 1995 Dewey Class No.: 302.23/0973 20

Berger, Arthur Asa, 1933- Media analysis techniques / Arthur Asa Berger. Edition Information: Rev. ed. Published/Created: Newbury Park: Sage Publications, c1991. Description: xiii, 143 p.: ill.; 23 cm. ISBN: 080394361X 0803943628 (pb) Notes: Includes bibliographical references and indexes. Subjects: Mass media--Methodology. Mass media criticism. Series: The Sage commtext series; v. 10 LC Classification: P91 .B43 1991 Dewey Class No.: 302.23/01 20

Berger, Arthur Asa, 1933- Media and communication research methods: an introduction to qualitative and quantitative approaches / Arthur Asa Berger. Published/Created: Thousand Oaks, Calif.: Sage Publications, 2000. Description: xix, 295 p.: ill.; 24 cm. ISBN: 0761918523 (alk. paper) 0761918531 (pbk.: alk. paper) Notes: Includes bibliographical references (p. 265-268) and indexes. Subjects: Mass media--Research--Methodology. Communication--Research--Methodology. LC Classification: P91.3 .B385 2000 Dewey Class No.: 302.23/07/2 21

Berger, Arthur Asa, 1933- Media research techniques / Arthur Asa Berger. Edition Information: 2nd ed. Published/Created: Thousand Oaks: Sage Publications, c1998. Description: viii, 175 p.: ill.; 24 cm. ISBN: 0761915362 (acid-free paper) 0761915370 (pbk.: acid-free paper) Notes: Includes bibliographical references (p. 167-168) and indexes. Subjects: Mass media--Research--Methodology. LC Classification: P91.3 .B386 1998 Dewey Class No.: 302.23/072 21

Berger, Arthur Asa, 1933- Media research techniques / Arthur Asa Berger. Published/Created: Newbury Park, Calif.: Sage Publications, c1991. Description: vii, 148 p.: ill.; 23 cm. ISBN: 080394179X 0803941803 (pbk.) Notes: Includes bibliographical references (p. 142-143) and indexes. Subjects: Mass media--Research--Methodology. LC Classification: P91 .B44 1991 Dewey Class No.: 302.23/072 20

Berger, Arthur Asa, 1933- Narratives in popular culture, media, and everyday life / Arthur Asa Berger. Published/Created: Thousand Oaks: Sage Publications, c1997. Description: xiii, 200 p.: ill.; 21 cm. ISBN: 0761903445 (cloth; acid-free paper)

0761903453 (pbk.: acid-free paper) Notes: Includes bibliographical references (p. 186-188) and indexes. Subjects: Discourse analysis, Narrative. Narration (Rhetoric) Mass media and language. LC Classification: P302.7 .B43 1997 Dewey Class No.: 401/.41 20

Biagi, Shirley. Facing difference: race, gender, and mass media / Shirley Biagi, Marilyn Kern-Foxworth. Published/Created: Thousand Oaks, Calif.: Pine Forge Press, c1997. Related Authors: Kern-Foxworth, Marilyn. Description: xxi, 285 p.: ill.; 24 cm. ISBN: 0803990944 (p: alk. paper) Notes: Includes bibliographical references and index. Subjects: Mass media and minorities--United States. Series: Journalism and communication for a new century LC Classification: P94.5.M552 U626 1997 Dewey Class No.: 302.23/086/930973 21

Biagi, Shirley. Media impact: an introduction to mass media / Shirley Biagi. Edition Information: 2nd ed. Published/Created: Belmont, Calif.: Wadsworth Pub., c1992. Description: xxiv, 564 p.: ill. (some col.); 24 cm. ISBN: 0534162428 (acid-free paper) Notes: Includes bibliographical references and index. Subjects: Mass media. LC Classification: P90 .B489 1992 Dewey Class No.: 302.23 20

Biagi, Shirley. Media/impact: an introduction to mass media / Shirley Biagi. Edition Information: Updated 1st ed. Published/Created: Belmont, Calif.: Wadsworth, c1990. Description: xx, 411 p.: ill.; 24 cm. ISBN: 053412660X Notes: Includes bibliographical references (p. 391-403). Subjects: Mass media. LC Classification: P90 .B489 1990 Dewey Class No.: 302.23 20

Biagi, Shirley. Media/impact: an introduction to mass media / Shirley Biagi. Edition Information: 5th ed. Published/Created: Australia; Belmont, CA: Wadsworth Pub., c2001. Description: xxvii, 425 p.: col. ill.; 26 cm. ISBN: 0534575102 (pbk.) 0534575110 (instructor's ed.) Notes: Includes bibliographical references and index. Subjects: Mass media. LC Classification: P90 .B489 2001 Dewey Class No.: 302.23 21

Biagi, Shirley. Media/impact: an introduction to mass media / Shirley Biagi. Edition Information: 4th ed. Published/Created: Belmont, CA: Wadsworth Pub. Co., c1999. Description: xxvii, 428 p.: ill. (some col.); 29 cm. ISBN: 0534548105 (pbk.: alk. paper) Notes: Includes bibliographical references (p. 405-412) and index. Subjects: Mass media. LC Classification: P90 .B489 1999 Dewey Class No.: 302.23 21

Biagi, Shirley. Media/impact: an introduction to mass media / Shirley Biagi. Edition Information: Updated 3rd ed. Published/Created: Belmont, CA: Wadsworth Pub., c1998. Description: xxiv, 413 p.: ill. (some col.); 26 cm. ISBN: 0534504825 (pbk.) Notes: Includes bibliographical references (p. 390-400) and index. Subjects: Mass media. LC Classification: P90 .B489 1998 Dewey Class No.: 302.23 21

Biagi, Shirley. Media/impact: an introduction to mass media / Shirley Biagi. Edition Information: 3rd ed. Published/Created: Belmont, Calif.: Wadsworth Pub. Co., c1996. Description: xxiv, 411 p.: col. ill.; 26 cm. ISBN: 0534217443 Notes: Includes bibliographical references (p. 390-400) and index. Subjects: Mass media. LC Classification: P90 .B489 1996 Dewey Class No.: 302.23 20

Biagi, Shirley. Media/impact: an introduction to mass media / Shirley Biagi. Edition Information: Updated 2nd ed. Published/Created: Belmont, Calif.: Wadsworth Pub. Co., c1994. Description: xxiv, 564 p.: ill. (some col.); 24 cm. ISBN: 0534201849 Notes: Includes bibliographical references and index. Subjects: Mass media. LC Classification: P90 .B489 1993 Dewey Class No.: 302.23 20

Biagi, Shirley. Media/impact: an introduction to mass media / Shirley Biagi. Edition

Information: Updated 1st ed. Published/Created: Belmont, Calif.: Wadsworth, c1990. Description: xx, 411 p.: ill.; 24 cm. ISBN: 053412660X Notes: Includes bibliographical references (p. 391-403). Subjects: Mass media. LC Classification: P90 .B489 1990 Dewey Class No.: 302.23 20

Bignell, Jonathan. Media semiotics: an introduction / Jonathan Bignell. Edition Information: 2nd ed. Published/Created: Manchester; New York: Manchester University Press: Distributed exclusively in the USA by Palgrave, 2002. Projected Pub. Date: 0203 Description: p. cm. ISBN: 0719062055 (pbk.) Notes: Includes bibliographical references and index. Subjects: Mass media--Semiotics. LC Classification: P96.S43 B54 2002 Dewey Class No.: 302.23/01/4 21

Bishop, Carol Keiser. Under the lens: a look at the American media / Carol Keiser Bishop. Published/Created: Ann Arbor: University of Michigan Press, c1997. Description: xx, 165 p.: ill.; 26 cm. ISBN: 0472084038 (pbk.) Subjects: Mass media--United States--Problems, exercises, etc. English language--Textbooks for foreign speakers. Readers--Mass media. Series: Alliance (Ann Arbor, Mich.) Variant Series: Alliance LC Classification: PE1127.M28 B57 1997 Dewey Class No.: 302.23/0973 21

Bittner, John R., 1943- Mass communication / John R. Bittner. Edition Information: 6th ed. Published/Created: Boston: Allyn & Bacon, c1996. Description: xxx, 514 p.: ill. (some col.); 26 cm. ISBN: 0135607981 Notes: Includes bibliographical references (p. 489-498) and index. Subjects: Mass media. LC Classification: P90 .B515 1996 Dewey Class No.: 302.23 20

Black, Jay. Introduction to media communication / Jay Black, Jennings Bryant, Susan Thompson. Edition Information: 5th ed. Published/Created: Boston, Mass.: McGraw-Hill, c1998. Related Authors: Bryant, Jennings. Thompson, Susan, 1957- Description: xvi, 432 p.: ill. (some col.); 28 cm. ISBN: 0697327159 (pbk.) Notes: Includes bibliographical references and index. Subjects: Mass media. LC Classification: P90 .B519 1998 Dewey Class No.: 302.23 21

Black, Jay. Introduction to media communication: understand the past, experience the present, marvel at the future. Edition Information: 4th ed. / Jay Black, Jennings Bryant. Published/Created: Madison: Brown & Benchmark, c1995. Related Authors: Bryant, Jennings. Black, Jay. Introduction to mass communication. Description: xviii, 606 p.: ill. (some col.); 26 cm. ISBN: 0697201244 Notes: Rev. ed. of: Introduction to mass communication / Jay Black, Frederick C. Whitney. 2nd ed. c1988. Includes bibliographical references and index. Subjects: Mass media--United States. LC Classification: P92.U5 B4 1995 Dewey Class No.: 302.23/0973 21

Blain, Neil, 1951- Sport and national identity in the European media / Neil Blain, Raymond Boyle, and Hugh O'Donnell. Published/Created: Leicester; New York: Leicester University Press; New York, NY, USA: Distributed in the U.S. and Canada by St. Martin's Press, 1993. Related Authors: Boyle, Raymond, 1966- O'Donnell, Hugh, 1949- Description: vii, 209 p.: ill.; 23 cm. ISBN: 0718514513 Notes: Includes bibliographical references (p. [200]-203) and index. Subjects: Mass media and sports--Europe. Sports--Social aspects--Europe. Sports and state--Europe. Series: Sport, politics, and culture LC Classification: GV742 .B53 1993 Dewey Class No.: 070.4/49796 20

Block, Eleanor S. Communication and the mass media: a guide to the reference literature / Eleanor S. Block, James K. Bracken. Published/Created: Englewood, Colo.: Libraries Unlimited, 1991. Related Authors: Bracken, James K., 1952- Description: xii, 198 p.; 25 cm. ISBN: 0872878104: Notes: Includes indexes. Subjects: Communication--Reference books--Bibliography. Mass media Reference books--Bibliography.

Communication--Bibliography. Mass media--Bibliography. Series: Reference sources in the humanities series LC Classification: Z5630 .B54 1991 P90 Dewey Class No.: 016.3022 20

Blum, Eleanor. Mass media bibliography: an annotated guide to books and journals for research and reference / Eleanor Blum and Frances Goins Wilhoit. Edition Information: 3rd ed. Published/Created: Urbana: University of Illinois Press, c1990. Related Authors: Wilhoit, Frances Goins. Blum, Eleanor. Basic books in the mass media. Description: viii, 344 p.; 29 cm. ISBN: 0252017064 (alk. paper) Notes: Rev. ed. of: Basic books in the mass media. 2nd ed. 1980. Subjects: Mass media--Bibliography. LC Classification: Z5630 .B55 1990 P90 Dewey Class No.: 016.30223 20

Bogart, Leo. Commercial culture: the media system and the public interest / Leo Bogart. Published/Created: New York: Oxford University Press, 1995. Description: 384 p.; 25 cm. ISBN: 0195090985 Notes: Includes bibliographical references (p. 328-369) and index. Subjects: Mass media--Economic aspects--United States. Mass media and culture--United States. Mass media policy--United States. LC Classification: P96.E252 U627 1995 Dewey Class No.: 338.4/730223 20

Bogart, Leo. Commercial culture: the media system and the public interest / Leo Bogart, with a new preface by the author. Published/Created: New Brunswick, N.J.: Transaction Publishers, c2000. Description: xxvi, 384 p.; 23 cm. ISBN: 0765806053 (pbk.: alk. paper) Notes: Originally Published: New York: Oxford University Press, 1995. With new introd. Includes bibliographical references (p. 328-369) and index. Subjects: Mass media--Economic aspects--United States. Mass media and culture--United States. Mass media policy--United States. LC Classification: P96.E252 U627 2000 Dewey Class No.: 302.23/0973 21

Bolter, J. David, 1951- Remediation: understanding new media / Jay David Bolter and Richard Grusin. Published/Created: Cambridge, Mass.: MIT Press, c1999. Related Authors: Grusin, Richard. Description: xi, 295 p.: ill. (some col.); 24 cm. ISBN: 0262024527 (hardcover: alk. paper) Notes: Includes bibliographical references (p. [276]-284) and index. Subjects: Mass media--Technological innovations. LC Classification: P96.T42 B59 1998 Dewey Class No.: 302.2223 21

Borchers, Timothy A. Persuasion in the media age / Timothy A. Borchers. Published/Created: Boston: McGraw-Hill, c2002. Description: xxiv, 472 p.: ill.; 24 cm. ISBN: 0767415418 (pbk.) Notes: Includes bibliographical references (p. 446-456) and index. Subjects: Persuasion (Rhetoric) Mass media. LC Classification: P301.5.P47 B67 2002 Dewey Class No.: 302.23/01 21

Bower, Tom. Maxwell, the outsider / Tom Bower. Published/Created: New York: Viking, 1992. Description: xix, 539 p., [8] p. of plates: ill.; 24 cm. ISBN: 0670846546: Notes: Includes index. Subjects: Maxwell, Robert, 1923- Publishers and publishing--Great Britain--Biography. Newspaper publishing--History--20th century. Mass media. LC Classification: Z325.M394 B69 1992 Dewey Class No.: 070.5/0941 20

Bower, Tom. Maxwell: the final verdict / Tom Bower Published/Created: London: HarperCollins, 1995. Description: xxii, 478 p., [16] p. of plates: ill.; 24 cm. ISBN: 0002555646 Notes: Includes index. Subjects: Maxwell, Robert, 1923- Publishers and publishing--Great Britain--Biography. Newspaper publishing--Great Britain--History--20th century. Mass media--Great Britain. LC Classification: Z325.M394 B68 1995 Dewey Class No.: 070.5/092 B 21

Boyle, Raymond, 1966- Power play: sport, the media, and popular culture / Raymond Boyle and Richard Haynes.

Published/Created: New York: Longman, 2000. Projected Pub. Date: 0001 Related Authors: Haynes, Richard. Description: p. cm. ISBN: 0582369398 (alk. paper) Notes: Includes bibliographical references and index. Subjects: Mass media and sports--Social aspects--Great Britain. Mass media and sports--Economic aspects--Great Britain. LC Classification: GV742 .B69 2000 Dewey Class No.: 306.4/83 21

Braden, Maria, 1946- Getting the message across: writing for the mass media / Maria Braden with Richard L. Roth. Published/Created: Boston, MA: Houghton Mifflin, c1997. Related Authors: Roth, Richard L. Description: xxi, 330 p.: ill.; 28 cm. Cancelled ISBN: 0395716233 Notes: Includes bibliographical references and index. Subjects: Mass media--Authorship. LC Classification: P96.A86 B73 1997 Dewey Class No.: 808/.066302 21

Branch, Melville Campbell, 1913- Telepower, planning, and society: crisis in communication / Melville C. Branch. Published/Created: Westport, Conn.: Praeger, 1994. Description: xi, 203 p.; 25 cm. ISBN: 0275945995 (hardcover: alk. paper) Notes: Includes bibliographical references (p. [195]-197) and index. Subjects: Planning. Mass media. Telecommunication. LC Classification: HD87.5 .B733 1994 Dewey Class No.: 384/.068 20

Branston, Gill. The media student's book / Gill Branston and Roy Stafford. Published/Created: London; New York: Routledge, 1996. Related Authors: Stafford, Roy. Description: x, 394: ill.; 26 cm. ISBN: 0415114055 (hbk) 0415114063 (pbk.) Notes: Includes bibliographical references (p. 367-371) and indexes. Subjects: Mass media. LC Classification: P90 .B6764 1996 Dewey Class No.: 302.23 20

Branston, Gill. The media student's book / Gill Branston and Roy Stafford. Edition Information: 2nd ed. Published/Created: London: New York: Routledge, 1999 Related Authors: Stafford, Roy. Description: xii, 468 p.: ill.; 25 cm. ISBN: 0415173078 0415173086 (pbk.) Notes: Includes bibliographical references (p. 452-460) and index. Subjects: Mass media. LC Classification: P90 .B6764 1999 Dewey Class No.: 302.23 21

Branwyn, Gareth. Jamming the media: a citizen's guide: reclaiming the tools of communication / by Gareth Branwyn. Published/Created: San Francisco: Chronicle Books, c1997. Description: 353 p.: ill.; 24 cm. ISBN: 0811817954 Notes: Includes bibliographical references and index. Subjects: Mass media--Data processing. Technology and civilization. Multimedia systems. LC Classification: P96.D36 B73 1997 Dewey Class No.: 302.23/0285 21

Brawley, Edward Allan. Human services and the media: developing partnerships for change / Edward Allan Brawley. Published/Created: Australia: Harwood Academic Publishers, c 1995. Related Authors: Brawley, Edward Allan. Mass media and human services. Description: viii, 379 p.: ill.; 24 cm. ISBN: 3718605945 (hardcover) 3718605740 (softcover) Notes: "This book is a substantially revised and updated version of a volume originally Published in 1983 as Mass media and human services by Sage Publications, Newbury Park, California, USA"--T.p. verso. Includes bibliographical references (p. 329-347) and index. Subjects: Mass media and social service--United States. Social service--Public relations--United States. Series: Applied social problems and intervention strategies, 1070-6585; v. 2 LC Classification: HV42 .B68 1995

Briggs, Asa, 1921- A social history of the media: from Gutenberg to the Internet / Asa Briggs and Peter Burke. Published/Created: Malden, MA: Blackwell, 2001. Projected Pub. Date: 0111 Related Authors: Burke, Peter. Description: p. cm. ISBN: 0745623743 0745623751 (pbk.) Notes: Includes bibliographical references (p.) and index. Subjects: Mass media--History. Mass media--Social aspects. LC Classification:

P90 .B695 2001 Dewey Class No.: 302.23/09 21

Brooker, Will, 1970- Batman unmasked: analysing a cultural icon / Will Brooker. Published/Created: New York: Continuum, 2001. Description: vii, 358 p.: ill.; 23 cm. ISBN: 0826449492 Notes: Includes bibliographical references (p. 334-352) and index. Subjects: Batman (Fictitious character) in mass media--History. LC Classification: P96.B37 B76 2001 Dewey Class No.: 700/.451 21 National Bib. No.: GBA0-X0505

Browne, Donald R. Electronic media and indigenous peoples: a voice of our own? / Donald R. Browne. Edition Information: 1st ed. Published/Created: Ames: Iowa State University Press, 1996. Description: xiii, 301 p.; 24 cm. ISBN: 0813823161 (alk. paper) Notes: Includes bibliographical references (p. 253-284) and index. Subjects: Ethnic mass media. Mass media and minorities. Mass media and language. LC Classification: P94.5.M55 B76 1996 Dewey Class No.: 302.23/0994 20

Bruck, Connie. Master of the game: Steve Ross and the creation of Time Warner / Connie Bruck. Published/Created: New York: Simon & Schuster, 1994. Description: 395 p.: ill.; 25 cm. ISBN: 0671725742: Notes: Includes bibliographical references (p. [367]-369) and index. Subjects: Ross, Steve, 1927-1992. Time Warner, Inc. Mass media--United States--Biography. LC Classification: P92.5.R67 M37 1994 Dewey Class No.: 302.23/4/092 B 20

Burkhart, Ford N. Media, emergency warnings, and citizen response / Ford N. Burkhart. Published/Created: Boulder: Westview Press, 1991. Description: viii, 152 p.: ill.; 23 cm. ISBN: 0813383900: Notes: Includes bibliographical references (p. [129]-139) and index. Subjects: Emergency management--United States. Emergency communication systems--United States. Disasters--Press coverage--United States. Mass media--United States--Psychological aspects. Social networks--United States--Psychological aspects. LC Classification: HV551.3 .B87 1991 Dewey Class No.: 363.3/472 20

Burton, Graeme. More than meets the eye: an introduction to media studies / Graeme Burton. Published/Created: London; New York: E. Arnold: Distributed in the USA by Routledge, Chapman and Hall, c1990. Description: xi, 191 p., [1] leaf of plates: ill.; 24 cm. ISBN: 0340504099 Summary: An introduction to media studies covering such areas as media institutions, analyses of media products and messages, and a study of the media's effect on audiences. Notes: Includes bibliographical references (p. [183]-189) and index. Subjects: Mass media. LC Classification: P90 .B86 1990 Dewey Class No.: 302.23 20

Camenson, Blythe. Great jobs for communications majors / Blythe Camenson; series developers and contributing authors Stephen E. Lambert, Julie Ann DeGalan. Published/Created: Lincolnwood, Chicago, Ill.: VGM Career Horizons, c1995. Related Authors: Lambert, Stephen E. DeGalan, Julie. Description: xiii, 210 p.; 23 cm. ISBN: 0844243558: Notes: Includes index. Subjects: Communication--Mass media--Vocational guidance. LC Classification: P91.6 .C36 1995 Dewey Class No.: 302.2/023/73 20

Cappella, Joseph N. Spiral of cynicism: the press and the public good / Joseph N. Cappella, Kathleen Hall Jamieson. Published/Created: New York: Oxford University Press, 1997. Related Authors: Jamieson, Kathleen Hall. Description: viii, 325 p.: ill.; 21 cm. ISBN: 0195090632 (alk. paper) 0195090640 (pbk.: alk. paper) Notes: Includes bibliographical references (p. [281]-320) and index. Subjects: Congress--Reporters and reporting. Press and politics--Government and the press--United States. Mass media--Influence. LC Classification: PN4888.P6 C37 1997 Dewey Class No.: 071/.3 20

Chenoweth, Neil. Virtual Murdoch: reality wars on the information highway / Neil Chenoweth. Published/Created: London:

Secker & Warburg, 2001. Description: xvi, 399 p.; 24 cm. ISBN: 0436233894 Notes: Includes bibliographical references (p. [384]-386) and index. Subjects: Murdoch, Rupert, 1931- Newspapers--Ownership. Publishers and publishing--Australia--Biography. Mass media.

Chowla, N. L. (Nand Lal), 1921-1989. Listening and viewing: writings on mass media / by N.L. Chowla; edited by M.V. Desai. Published/Created: New Delhi: Sanchar Pub. House in association with NAMEDIA Foundation, 1991. Related Authors: Desai, M. V., 1922- NAMEDIA (Foundation). Description: xii, 273 p.; 22 cm. ISBN: 8172030029: Notes: Includes index. Subjects: Mass media. LC Classification: P91.25 .C555 1991 Dewey Class No.: 302.23 20

Christians, Clifford G. Good news: social ethics and the press / Clifford G. Christians, John P. Ferré, P. Mark Fackler. Published/Created: New York: Oxford University Press, 1993. Related Authors: Ferré, John P. Fackler, Mark. Description: xvi, 265 p.; 24 cm. ISBN: 0195074319 (acid-free paper) 0195084322 (pbk.: acid-free paper) Notes: Includes bibliographical references (p. 235-255) and index. Subjects: Journalistic ethics--United States--History--20th century. Foreign news--United States--History--20th century. Journalism--Objectivity--United States. Mass media--Moral and ethical aspects--United States. Mass media--Political aspects--United States--History 20th century. LC Classification: PN4888.P6 C47 1993 Dewey Class No.: 174/.9097/0973 20

Cities, class and communication: essays in honour of Asa Briggs / edited by Derek Fraser. Published/Created: London: Harvester Wheatsheaf, 1990. Related Authors: Briggs, Asa, 1921- Fraser, Derek. Description: 264 p.: ill.; 24 cm. ISBN: 0745006531: Notes: Includes bibliographical references and index. Subjects: Briggs, Asa, 1921- --Bibliography. Sociology, Urban--Great Britain. Social classes--Great Britain. Mass media--Great Britain. Great Britain--Social conditions. LC Classification: HN385 .C527 1990 Dewey Class No.: 909/.0982/1082 20

Clare, John, 1955-. John Clare's guide to media handling / John Clare. Published/Created: Aldershot, England; Burlington, Vt., USA: Gower, c2001. Description: xxi, 138 p.: ill.; 25 cm. ISBN: 0566082985 (hardcover) Notes: Includes index. Subjects: Public relations. Mass media and business. Industrial publicity. LC Classification: HD59 .C53 2001 Dewey Class No.: 659.2 21

Cohen, Jeff, 1951- Through the media looking glass: decoding bias and blather in the news / Jeff Cohen and Norman Solomon. Published/Created: Monroe, Me.: Common Courage Press, c1995. Related Authors: Solomon, Norman, 1951- Description: x, 275 p.: ill.; 20 cm. ISBN: 1567510493 1567510485 (pbk.) Notes: Includes index. Subjects: Journalism--Objectivity. Mass media--Objectivity. Journalistic ethics. Mass media--Moral and ethical aspects. LC Classification: PN4784.O24 C64 1995 Dewey Class No.: 302.23/0973/09045 20

Cohn, Robin. The PR crisis bible: how to take charge of the media when all hell breaks loose / Robin Cohn. Edition Information: 1st ed. Published/Created: New York: St. Martin's Press, c2000. Description: xii, 340 p.: ill.; 22 cm. ISBN: 0312252307 Notes: "Truman Talley books." Includes index. Subjects: Crisis management. Corporations--Public relations. Mass media and business. Disasters--Press coverage. LC Classification: HD49 .C64 2000 Dewey Class No.: 659.2 21

Collins, Richard, 1946- New media, new policies: media and communications strategies for the future / Richard Collins and Cristina Murroni. Published/Created: Cambridge, MA: Published by Polity Press in association with Blackwell, 1996. Related Authors: Murroni, Cristina. Description: ix, 243 p.; 24 cm. ISBN: 0745617859 (alk. paper) 0745617867 (pbk.: alk. paper) Notes: "This study was undertaken in the Media and Communication Programme at the Institute for Public Policy Research (IPPR) in London between 1994 and 1996"--Pref. Includes bibliographical references and index. Subjects: Mass media--Great Britain--Planning. Mass media policy--Great Britain. LC Classification: P95.815 .C65 1996 Dewey Class No.: 302.23/0941 20

Collins, Ronald K. L. The death of discourse / Ronald K.L. Collins & David M. Skover. Published/Created: Boulder, Colo.: Westview Press, 1996. Projected Pub. Date: 9601 Related Authors: Skover, David M., 1951- Description: p. cm. ISBN: 0813327229 (alk. paper) 0813327237 (pbk.: alk. paper) Notes: Includes bibliographical references and index. Subjects: Freedom of speech--United States--Popular works. Freedom of speech--Social aspects. Mass media--United States--Language. Popular culture--United States--Language. LC Classification: KF4772.Z9 C65 1996 Dewey Class No.: 342.73/0853 347.302853 20

Communicating uncertainty: media coverage of new and controversial science / edited by Sharon M. Friedman, Sharon Dunwoody, Carol L. Rogers. Published/Created: Mahwah, N.J.: L. Erlbaum Associates, 1999. Related Authors: Friedman, Sharon M. Dunwoody, Sharon. Rogers, Carol L. Description: xiv, 277 p.: ill.; 24 cm. ISBN: 0805827277 (cloth: alk. paper) 0805827285 (pbk.: alk. paper) Notes: Includes bibliographical references and indexes. Subjects: Science in mass media. Science news. Mass media--Audiences. Discoveries in science. Series: LEA's communication series LC Classification: P96.S33 C66 1999 Dewey Class No.: 500 21

Communication for a new world: Brazilian perspectives / edited by José Marques de Melo. Published/Created: São Paulo, Brasil: School of Communication and Arts, University of São Paulo, 1993. Related Authors: Melo, José Marques de. Universidade de São Paulo. Escola de Comunicações e Artes. International Association for Mass Communication Research. Description: 383 p.: ill.; 23 cm. ISBN: 8572050337 Notes: "IAMCR/AIERI, ALAIC, INTERCOM, ECA-USP"--P. [4] of cover. Papers presented by ECA-USP and other Brazilian institutions to the XVIII IAMCR Scientific Conference, Guarujá, São Paulo, 1992. Abstracts also in French, Spanish, and Portuguese. Includes bibliographical references. Subjects: Communication--Congresses. Mass media--Congresses. Communication--Brazil--Congresses. LC Classification: P87.2 .I17 1992 Dewey Class No.: 302.2 20

Communication in history: technology, culture, society / [edited by] David Crowley, Paul Heyer. Published/Created: New York, N.Y.: Longman, c1991. Related Authors: Crowley, D. J. (David J.), 1945- Heyer, Paul, 1946- Description: xiv, 290 p.: ill.; 24 cm. ISBN: 0801305985 Notes: Includes bibliographical references and index. Subjects: Communication--History. Mass media--History. LC Classification: P90 .C62945 1991 Dewey Class No.: 302.2/09 20

Compaine, Benjamin M. Who owns the media?: competition and concentration in the mass media industry / Benjamin M. Compaine, Douglas Gomery. Edition Information: 3rd ed. Published/Created: Mahwah, N.J.: L. Erlbaum Associates, 2000. Related Authors: Gomery, Douglas. Related Titles: Who owns the media? Description: xxii, 604 p.: ill.; 26 cm. ISBN: 0805829350 (alk. paper) 0805829369 (pbk.: alk. paper) Notes: Rev. ed. of: Who owns the media? / Benjamin M. Compaine ... [et al.]. 2nd ed. 1982. Includes bibliographical references and indexes. Subjects: Mass media--Economic aspects--United States. Mass media--Political aspects--United States. Mass media--Ownership--United States. Series: LEA's communication series LC Classification: P96.E252 U68 2000 Dewey Class No.: 302.23/0973 21

Condit, Celeste Michelle, 1956- The meanings of the gene: public debates about human heredity / Celeste Michelle Condit. Published/Created: Madison: University of Wisconsin Press, c1999. Description: xi, 325 p.; 24 cm. ISBN: 0299163601 (cloth: alk. paper) 0299163644 (paper: alk. paper) Notes: Includes bibliographical references (p. 296-313) and index. Subjects: Genetics--Social aspects--United States--History--20th century.. Genetics--Public opinion--History--20th century. Genetics in mass media--History--20th century. Series: Rhetoric of the human sciences LC Classification: QH438.7 .C65 1999 Dewey Class No.: 304.5 21

Conners, Gail A. Good news!: how to get the best possible media coverage for your school / Gail A. Conners. Published/Created: Thousand Oaks, Calif.: Corwin Press, c2000. Description: xii, 116 p.: ill.; 29 cm. ISBN: 0761975063 (alk. paper) 0761975071 (pbk.: alk. paper) Notes: Includes bibliographical references (p. 116). Subjects: Schools--Public relations--United States. Community and school--United States. Education in mass media. LC Classification: LB2847 .C65 2000 Dewey Class No.: 659.2/9371 21

Conquest, John, 1943- Trouble is their business: private eyes in fiction, film, and television, 1927-1988 / John Conquest. Published/Created: New York: Garland Pub., 1990. Description: liii, 497 p.; 23 cm. ISBN: 0824059476 (alk. paper) Notes: Includes bibliographies and index. Subjects: Detectives in mass media. Series: Garland reference library of the humanities; vol. 1151 LC Classification: P96.D4 C66 1990 Dewey Class No.: 016.30223/0883632 20

Cook, Deborah, 1954- The culture industry revisited: Theodor W. Adorno on mass culture / Deborah Cook. Published/Created: Lanham, Md.: Rowman & Littlefield Publishers, c1996. Description: xiv, 190 p.; 24 cm. ISBN: 0847681548 (cloth: alk. paper) 0847681556 (pbk.: alk. paper) Notes: Includes bibliographical references (p. 171-184) and index. Subjects: Adorno, Theodor W., 1903-1969. Popular culture--History--20th century. Popular culture--Economic aspects. Mass media--History--20th century. Mass media--Economic aspects. LC Classification: CB427 .C626 1996 Dewey Class No.: 909.82 20

Couldry, Nick. The place of media power: pilgrims and witnesses of the media age / Nick Couldry. Published/Created: London; New York: Routledge, 2000. Description: xii, 238 p.: ill.; 25 cm. ISBN: 0415213142 0415213150 (pbk.) Notes: Includes bibliographical references (p. 213-230) and index. Subjects: Mass media--Influence. Mass media--Social aspects. Series: Comedia LC Classification: P94 .C63 2000 Dewey Class No.: 302.23 21 National Bib. No.: GB99-U7659

Crainer, Stuart. Business the Rupert Murdoch way: 10 secrets of the world's greatest deal maker / by Stuart Crainer. Published/Created: New York: AMACOM, c1999. Description: xi, 154 p.; 23 cm. ISBN: 0814470343 Notes: Includes bibliographical references and index. Subjects: Murdoch, Rupert, 1931- --Views on industrial management. Industrial management. Mass media--Management. Series: The business way series LC Classification: HD31 .C685 1999 Dewey Class No.: 658 21

Croteau, David. The business of media: corporate media and the public interest / David Croteau, William Hoynes. Published/Created: Thousand Oaks, Calif.: Pine Forge Press, c2001. Related Authors: Hoynes, William. Description: xv, 302 p.: ill.; 23 cm. ISBN: 0761986405 (pbk.: acid-free paper) Notes: Includes bibliographical references (p. 271-281) and index. Subjects: Mass media--Economic aspects--United States. Mass media policy--United States. Mass media--Social aspects--United States. LC Classification: P96.E252 U634 2001 Dewey Class No.: 302.23/0973 21

Dale, Elizabeth. The rule of justice: the people of Chicago versus Zephyr Davis / Elizabeth Dale. Published/Created:

Columbus: Ohio State University Press, c2001. Description: vii, 158 p.: ill.; 24 cm. ISBN: 0814208673 (cloth: alk. paper) 0814250688 (pbk.: alk. paper) Notes: Includes bibliographical references (p. 143-154) and index. Subjects: Davis, Zephyr, d. 1888. Criminal justice, Administration of--Illinois--Chicago History--Case studies. Criminal justice, Administration of--Illinois--Chicago Public opinion--History. Trials (Murder)--Illinois--Chicago--History--Case studies. Mass media and crime--Illinois--Chicago--History--Case studies. Mass media and public opinion--Illinois--Chicago--History Case studies. Series: The history of crime and criminal justice series LC Classification: HV9956.C47 D35 2001 Dewey Class No.: 364.15/23/0977311 21

Dayan, Daniel, 1943- Media events: the live broadcasting of history / Daniel Dayan, Elihu Katz. Published/Created: Cambridge, Mass.: Harvard University Press, 1992. Related Authors: Katz, Elihu, 1926- Description: xi, 306 p.; 22 cm. ISBN: 067455955X (alk. paper) Notes: Includes bibliographical references (p. 275-293) and index. Subjects: Television broadcasting of news. Mass media--Social aspects. History, Modern--1945- LC Classification: PN4784.T4 D38 1992 Dewey Class No.: 070.1/95 20

Deeter, William R., 1946- Working with the press: a practical "How to" for achieving a competitive advantage / William R. Deeter; with contributions from Kirk Deeter, Jonathan Diamond, and Murray H. Morse Jr.; illustrators by James P. Grady. Published/Created: Austin, Tex.: Keel Publications, 1995. Projected Pub. Date: 9508 Related Authors: Deeter, Kirk D. Description: p. cm. ISBN: 0945609175 (pbk.) Subjects: Public speaking. Press conferences. Interviewing in journalism. Interviewing in the mass media. LC Classification: PN4193.P73 D44 1994 Dewey Class No.: 659.2 20

DeFleur, Melvin L. (Melvin Lawrence), 1923- Understanding mass communication: a liberal arts perspective / Melvin L. DeFleur, Everette E. Dennis. Edition Information: 6th ed. Published/Created: Boston: Houghton Mifflin, c1998. Related Authors: Dennis, Everette E. Description: xviii, 587 p.: ill. (some col.); 24 cm. ISBN: 0395871123 Notes: Includes bibliographical references (p. [549]-563) and index. Subjects: Mass media. LC Classification: P90 .D443 1998 Dewey Class No.: 302.23/0973 21

DeFleur, Melvin L. (Melvin Lawrence), 1923- Understanding mass communication / Melvin L. DeFleur, Everette E. Dennis. Edition Information: 4th ed. Published/Created: Boston: Houghton Mifflin, c1991. Related Authors: Dennis, Everette E. Description: xiv, 637 p.: ill.; 26 cm. ISBN: 0395472725 Notes: Includes bibliographical references and index. Subjects: Mass media--United States. LC Classification: P92.U5 D42 1991 Dewey Class No.: 001.51/0973 19

DeFleur, Melvin L. (Melvin Lawrence), 1923- Understanding mass communication: a liberal arts perspective / Melvin L. DeFleur, Everette E. Dennis. Edition Information: Updated 1996 ed. Published/Created: Boston: Houghton Mifflin, c1996. Related Authors: Dennis, Everette E. Description: x, 646 p.: ill. (some col.); 24 cm. ISBN: 0395764920 (examination copy) 0395746817 (student text) Notes: Includes bibliographical references and index. Subjects: Mass media. LC Classification: P90. .D443 1996 Dewey Class No.: 302.23/0973 20

DeFleur, Melvin L. (Melvin Lawrence), 1923- Understanding mass communication: a liberal arts perspective/ Melvin L. DeFleur, Everette E. Dennis. Edition Information: 5th ed. Published/Created: Boston: Houghton Mifflin, c1994. Related Authors: Dennis, Everette E. Description: x, 646 p.: ill.; 26 cm. ISBN: 0395674042 (student text) 0395690714(examination text) Notes: Includes bibliographical references and index. Subjects: Mass media--United States. LC Classification: P92.U5 D42 1994

DeLuca, Kevin Michael. Image politics: the new rhetoric of environmental activism / Kevin Michael DeLuca. Published/Created: New York: Guilford Press, 1999. Description: xvi, 203 p.: ill.; 24 cm. ISBN: 1572304618 (hc.) Notes: Includes bibliographical references and index. Subjects: Environmentalism. Mass media and the environment. Rhetoric. Series: Revisioning rhetoric LC Classification: GE195 .D45 1999 Dewey Class No.: 363.7/0525 21

Dennis, Everette E. Media debates: great issues for the digital age / Everette E. Dennis, John C. Merrill. Edition Information: 3rd ed. Published/Created: Australia; Belmont, CA: Wadsworth Thomson Learning, 2001. Projected Pub. Date: 1111 Related Authors: Merrill, John Calhoun, 1924- Description: p. cm. ISBN: 0534579337 Notes: Includes bibliographical references and index. Subjects: Mass media--United States. Journalism--United States. LC Classification: P92.U5 D445 2001 Dewey Class No.: 302.23/0973 21

Dennis, Everette E. Media debates: issues in mass communication / Everette E. Dennis, John C. Merrill. Published/Created: New York: Longman, c1991. Related Authors: Merrill, John Calhoun, 1924- Description: xi, 228 p.; 24 cm. ISBN: 0801304369 Notes: Includes bibliographical references and index. Subjects: Mass media--United States. Journalism--United States. LC Classification: P92.U5 D445 1991 Dewey Class No.: 302.23/0973 20

Dennis, Everette E. Of media and people / Everette E. Dennis. Published/Created: Newbury Park, CA: Sage Pub., c1992. Description: vii, 187 p.; 23 cm. ISBN: 0803947461 080394747X (pbk.) Notes: Includes bibliographical references (p. 179-180) and index. Subjects: Mass media. Journalism. LC Classification: P91 .D447 1992 Dewey Class No.: 302.23 20

Dewdney, Christopher, 1951- Last flesh: life in the transhuman era / Christopher Dewdney. Edition Information: 1st ed. Published/Created: Toronto: HarperCollins, c1998. Description: 204 p.; 22 cm. ISBN: 0006384722 Notes: Includes index. Includes bibliographical references: p. 189-193. Subjects: Technology--Social aspects. Mass media--Social aspects. Computers and civilization. Civilization, Modern--20th century. Technologie--Aspect social. LC Classification: HM221 .D49 1998 Dewey Class No.: 303.48/3 21

Dijck, José van. Imagenation: popular images of genetics / José Van Dijck. Published/Created: New York, N.Y.: New York University Press, 1998. Description: vii, 235 p.; 23 cm. ISBN: 0814787967 (hbk.) 0814787975 (pbk.) Notes: Includes bibliographical references (p. 219-227) and index. Subjects: Genetics in mass media. LC Classification: P96.G45 D55 1998 Dewey Class No.: 576.5 21

Dijk, Jan van. The network society: social aspects of new media / Jan van Dijk; translated by Leontine Spoorenberg. Published/Created: London; Thousand Oaks, Calif.: Sage Publications, c1999. Description: 267 p.: ill.; 25 cm. ISBN: 0761962816 0761962824 (pbk.) Notes: Includes bibliographical references (p. [252]-264) and index. Subjects: Mass media--Technological innovations. Mass media--Social aspects. LC Classification: P96.T42 D5513 1999 Dewey Class No.: 302.23 21

Directori espanyol d'investigació en comunicació = Directorio español de investigación en comunicación = Spanish directory on mass communication research. Edition Information: 2a. ed. Published/Created: [Barcelona]: Generalitat de Catalunya, Centre d'Investigació de la Comunicació, 1995. Related Authors: Catalonia (Spain). Centre d'Investigació de la Comunicació. Description: 589 p.; 30 cm. ISBN: 8439335075 Subjects: Mass media--Spain--Directories. Mass media--Research--Spain. Series: Obres de referència; 3 LC Classification: P88.8 .D56 1995 Dewey Class No.: 302.23/025/46 21

Dizard, Wilson P. Old media, new media: mass communications in the information age / Wilson Dizard, Jr. Edition Information: 3rd ed. Published/Created: New York: Longman, c2000. Description: xv, 233 p.; 24 cm. ISBN: 080133277X (alk. paper) Notes: Includes bibliographical references (p. 211-220) and index. Subjects: Mass media--United States--Technological innovations. LC Classification: P96.T422 U634 2000 Dewey Class No.: 302.23/0973 21

Dizard, Wilson P. Old media/new media: mass communications in the information age / Wilson Dizard. Jr.. Published/Created: New York: Longman, c1994. Description: xviii, 215 p.: ill.; 24 cm. ISBN: 0801311519 Notes: Includes bibliographical references (p. 201-206) and index. Subjects: Mass media--United States--Technological innovations. LC Classification: P96.T422 U634 1994 Dewey Class No.: 302.23/0973 20

Dizard, Wilson P. Old media/new media: mass communications in the information age / Wilson Dizard, Jr. Edition Information: 2nd ed. Published/Created: New York: Longman, c1997. Description: xx, 242 p.: ill.; 24 cm. ISBN: 0801317436 Notes: Includes bibliographical references (p. 227-234) and index. Subjects: Mass media--United States--Technological innovations. LC Classification: P96.T422 U634 1997 Dewey Class No.: 302.23/0973 20

Dizard, Wilson P. Old media/new media: mass communications in the information age / Wilson Dizard. Jr.. Published/Created: New York: Longman, c1994. Description: xviii, 215 p.: ill.; 24 cm. ISBN: 0801311519 Notes: Includes bibliographical references (p. 201-206) and index. Subjects: Mass media--United States--Technological innovations. LC Classification: P96.T422 U634 1994 Dewey Class No.: 302.23/0973 20

Dominick, Joseph R. The dynamics of mass communication / Joseph R. Dominick. Edition Information: 5th ed., International ed. Published/Created: New York: McGraw-Hill, c1996. Description: xxiii, 599 p.: ill. (some col.); 26 cm. ISBN: 0070179964 (acid-free paper) Notes: Includes bibliographical references and index. Subjects: Mass media. Series: McGraw-Hill series in mass communication LC Classification: P90 .D59 1996 Dewey Class No.: 302.23 20

Dominick, Joseph R. The dynamics of mass communication / Joseph R. Dominick. Edition Information: 6th ed. Published/Created: Boston: McGraw Hill, c1999. Description: xxiii, 568 p.: ill. (some col.); 26 cm. ISBN: 007290478X (acid-free paper) 0071156852 (International ed.) Notes: Includes bibliographical references and index. Subjects: Mass media. Series: McGraw-Hill series in mass communication LC Classification: P90 .D59 1999 Dewey Class No.: 302.23 21

Dominick, Joseph R. The dynamics of mass communication / Joseph R. Dominick. Edition Information: Updated 1994 ed. Published/Created: New York: McGraw-Hill, 1994. Description: xxii, 616 p.: ill. (some col.); 26 cm. ISBN: 0070178828 Notes: Includes bibliographical references and index. Subjects: Mass media. LC Classification: P90 .D59 1994 Dewey Class No.: 302.23 20

Dominick, Joseph R. The dynamics of mass communication/ Joseph R. Dominick. Edition Information: 4th ed. Published/Created: New York: McGraw-Hill, c1993. Description: xxii, 616 p.: ill. (some col.); 26 cm. ISBN: 0070178054 Notes: Includes bibliographical references and index. Subjects: Mass media. Series: McGraw-Hill series in mass communication LC Classification: P90 .D59 1993 Dewey Class No.: 302.23 20

Dominick, Joseph R. The dynamics of mass communication: media in the digital age / Joseph R. Dominick. Edition Information: 7th ed. Published/Created: Boston, MA.: McGraw-Hill, c2002. Description: xxxii, 528 p.: ill.; 25 cm. ISBN: 0072407662 (alk. paper) Notes: Includes bibliographical reference (p. 515) and index. Subjects:

Mass media. Series: McGraw-Hill series in mass communication LC Classification: P90 .D59 2002 Dewey Class No.: 302.23 21

Donnelly, William J. Planning media: strategy and imagination / William J. Donnelly. Published/Created: Upper Saddle River, N.J.: Prentice Hall, c1996. Description: xvi, 333 p.: ill., map; 25 cm. ISBN: 0135678358 Notes: Includes bibliographical references and index. Subjects: Mass media--Planning. Marketing--Planning. LC Classification: P95.815 .D66 1996 Dewey Class No.: 659 20

Downing, John. Radical media: rebellious communication and social movements / by John D.H. Downing; with Tamara Villarreal Ford, Genève Gil, and Laura Stein. Published/Created: Thousand Oaks, Calif.: Sage Publications, c2001. Description: xiv, 426 p.; 24 cm. ISBN: 0803956983 (alk. paper) 0803956991 (pbk.: alk. paper) Notes: Includes bibliographical references (p. 396-421) and index. Subjects: Radicalism in mass media. Social movements. LC Classification: P91 .D67 2001 Dewey Class No.: 302.23/4 21

Eastham, Scott, 1949- The media matrix: deepening the context of communication studies / Scott Eastham. Published/Created: Lanham: University Press of America, c1990. Description: 127 p.: ill.; 23 cm. ISBN: 0819177148 (alk. paper) 0819177156 (pbk.: alk. paper) Notes: Includes bibliographical references (p. 117-126). Subjects: Mass media. LC Classification: P90 .E24 1989 Dewey Class No.: 302.23 20

Eberts, Marjorie. Careers for talkative types & others with the gift of gab / Marjorie Eberts and Margaret Gisler. Published/Created: Lincolnwood, IL: VGM Career Horizons, 1998. Related Authors: Gisler, Margaret. Description: 153 p.; 23 cm. ISBN: 0844222860 (cloth) 0844222879 (pbk.) Subjects: Vocational guidance--United States. Professions--Vocational guidance--United States. Public relations--Vocational guidance--United States. Mass media--Vocational guidance--United States. Sales personnel--Vocational guidance--United States. Series: VGM careers for you series LC Classification: HF5382.5.U5 E24 1998 Dewey Class No.: 331.7/02 21

Eisenhart, Douglas M. Publishing in the information age: a new management framework for the digital era / Douglas M. Eisenhart. Published/Created: Westport, Conn.: Quorum Books, 1994. Description: xiv, 296 p.: ill.; 25 cm. ISBN: 0899308473 (alk. paper) Notes: Includes bibliographical references (p. [277]-282) and index. Subjects: Publishers and publishing--United States. Mass media--United States. LC Classification: Z471 .E55 1994 Dewey Class No.: 070.5/0973 20

Emery, Michael C. The press and America: an interpretive history of the mass media / Michael Emery, Edwin Emery. Edition Information: 7th ed. Published/Created: Englewood Cliffs, N.J.: Prentice Hall, c1992. Related Authors: Emery, Edwin. Description: xiv, 715 p.: ill.; 24 cm. ISBN: 013739277X Notes: Includes bibliographical references (p. 631-695) and index. Subjects: Press--United States--History. Journalism--United States--History. Mass media--United States--History. American newspapers--History. LC Classification: PN4855 .E6 1992 Dewey Class No.: 071/.3 20

Emery, Michael C. The press and America: an interpretive history of the mass media / Michael Emery, Edwin Emery, Nancy L. Roberts. Edition Information: 9th ed. Published/Created: Boston: Allyn & Bacon, c2000. Related Authors: Emery, Edwin. Roberts, Nancy L., 1954- Description: xxi, 698 p.: ill.; 24 cm. ISBN: 0205295576 Notes: Includes bibliographical references (p. 607-679) and index. Subjects: Press--United States--History. Journalism--United States--History. Mass media--United States--History. American newspapers--History. LC Classification: PN4855 .E6 2000 Dewey Class No.: 071/.3 21

Emery, Michael C. The press and America: an interpretive history of the mass media / Michael Emery, Edwin Emery, with Nancy L. Roberts. Edition Information: 8th ed. Published/Created: Boston: Allyn and Bacon, c1996. Related Authors: Emery, Edwin. Roberts, Nancy L., 1954- Description: xii, 724 p.: ill.; 25 cm. ISBN: 0205183891 Notes: Includes bibliographical references (p. 643-712) and index. Subjects: Press--United States--History. Journalism--United States--History. Mass media--United States--History. American newspapers--History. LC Classification: PN4855 .E6 1996 Dewey Class No.: 071/.3 20

Environmentalism and the mass media: the North--South divide / Graham Chapman ... [et al.]. Published/Created: London; New York: Routledge, 1997. Related Authors: Chapman, Graham. Description: xviii, 327 p.: ill., maps; 25 cm. ISBN: 0415155045 (cloth) 0415155053 (pbk.) Notes: "Global Environmental Change Programme." "Indian Institute of Advanced Study, Shimla." Includes bibliographical references and index. Subjects: Mass media and the environment--Great Britain. Environmentalism--Great Britain. Mass media and the environment--India. Environmentalism--India. Economic development. Series: Global environmental change series LC Classification: P96.E572 G744 1997 Dewey Class No.: 333.7 20

Epskamp, C. P. On printed matter and beyond: media, orality and literacy / Kees Epskamp; [translated by the Language Lab]. Published/Created: The Hague: Center for the Study of Education in Developing Countries, c1995. Description: 136 p.: ill.; 24 cm. ISBN: 9064432104 Notes: "This paperback is an anthology of essays written in the period of 1982-1994. Some of the essays have been Published at an earlier date."--p. 10. "A number of the chapters in this book were originally written in Dutch and translated by Richard de Nooy and Ping Cleton of The Language Lab."--p. 14-15. Subjects: Mass media and language. Mass media in education. Written communication. Oral tradition. Mass media and culture. Narration (Rhetoric) Mass media--Developing countries. Series: CESO paperback; no. 23 LC Classification: P96.L34 E67 1995

European Workshop on Approaches in Communicating Space Applications to Society: proceedings, ESTEC, Noordwijk, The Netherlands, 14-15 May 1995 / [edited by T.D. Guyenne & B. Battrick]; European Space Agency = Agence Spatiale Europeenne. Published/Created: Noordwijk, The Netherlands: ESA Publications Division, c1995. Related Authors: Guyenne, T. D., ed. Battrick, B., 1946- ed. European Space Agency. Description: 51 p.: ill.; 30 cm. ISBN: 9290922192 Notes: "July 1995." Includes bibliographical references (p. 30). Subjects: Astronautics in mass media--Congresses. Astronautics and state--Europe--Congresses. Astronautics--Social aspects--Europe--Congresses. Communication planning--Europe--Congresses. Series: ESA SP; 384 LC Classification: P96.A792 E854 1995

Evans, Andrew. This virtual life: escapism and simulation in our media world / Andrew Evans. Published/Created: London: Vision, c2001. Description: xii, 275 p.: ill.; cm. ISBN: 1901250598 (pbk.) Notes: Includes bibliographical references (p. 258-267) and index. Subjects: Virtual reality. Mass media.

Fairclough, Norman, 1941- Media discourse / Norman Fairclough. Published/Created: London; New York: E. Arnold, 1995. Projected Pub. Date: 9508 Description: p. cm. ISBN: 0340632224 0340588896 Notes: Includes bibliographical references (p.) and index. Subjects: Mass media and language. LC Classification: P96.L34 F35 1995 Dewey Class No.: 302.23 20

Farrar, Ronald T. Mass communication: an introduction to the field / Ronald T. Farrar. Edition Information: 2nd ed., annotated intructor's ed. Published/Created: Madison: Brown & Benchmark, c1996. Description: 1 v. (various pagings): ill.; 28 cm. ISBN: 0697259870 Notes: Includes bibliographical references and index. LC Classification: P90 .F28 1996 Dewey Class No.: 302.23 20

Federman, Joel. Media ratings: design, use and consequences / by Joel Federman, with the assistance of Stephanie Carbone, Linda and Evans. Published/Created: Studio City, Calif.: Mediascope, c1996. Description: 153 p.; 23 cm. ISBN: 1889162000 (pbk.) Subjects: Mass media--Ratings--Audiences. LC Classification: P96.R36 F43 1996 Dewey Class No.: 302.23 21

Ferguson, Sherry Devereaux. Researching the public opinion environment: theories and methods / Sherry Devereaux Ferguson. Published/Created: Thousand Oaks, Calif.: Sage Publications, c2000. Description: xvi, 296 p.; 24 cm. ISBN: 0761915303 (hc: acid-free) 0761915311 (pb: acid free) Notes: Includes bibliographical references (p. 263-282) and index. Subjects: Public opinion. Public opinion polls. Mass media and public opinion. Series: Sage series in public relations LC Classification: HM1236 .F47 2000 Dewey Class No.: 303.3/8 21

Fidler, Roger F. Mediamorphosis: understanding new media / Roger Fidler. Published/Created: Thousand Oaks, Calif.: Pine Forge Press, c1997. Description: xviii, 302 p.: ill.; 23 cm. ISBN: 0803990863 (alk. paper) Notes: Includes bibliographical references and index. Subjects: Mass media--History--Technological innovations--Forecasting. Series: Journalism and communication for a new century LC Classification: P91 .F467 1997 Dewey Class No.: 302.23/09 21

Fink, Conrad C. Inside the media / Conrad C. Fink. Published/Created: New York: Longman, c1990. Description: xviii, 398 p.: ill.; 24 cm. ISBN: 0801302579: Notes: Includes bibliographical references (p. 371-380) and indexes. Subjects: Mass media--United States. LC Classification: P92.U5 F56 1990 Dewey Class No.: 302.23/0973 20

Foerstel, Herbert N. From Watergate to Monicagate: ten controversies in modern journalism and media / Herbert N. Foerstel. Published/Created: Westport, Conn.: Greenwood Press, 2001. Description: 279 p.: ill.; 24 cm. ISBN: 0313311633 (alk. paper) Notes: Includes bibliographical references (p. [267]-268) and index. Subjects: Journalism. Mass media. LC Classification: PN4731 .F58 2001 Dewey Class No.: 070.4 21

Folkerts, Jean. The media in your life: an introduction to mass communication / Jean Folkerts, Stephen Lacy. Edition Information: 2nd ed. Published/Created: Boston, MA: Allyn and Bacon, c2001. Related Authors: Lacy, Stephen. Description: xxii, 520 p.: col. ill.; 26 cm. ISBN: 0205317820 Notes: Includes bibliographical references (p. 475-489) and index. Subjects: Mass media. LC Classification: P90 .F628 2001 Dewey Class No.: 302.23 21

Folkerts, Jean. The media in your life: an introduction to mass communication / Jean Folkerts, Stephen Lacy, Lucinda Davenport. Published/Created: Boston: Allyn and Bacon, c1998. Related Authors: Lacy, Stephen, 1948- Davenport, Lucinda. Description: xxxii, 558 p.: ill. (some col.); 26 cm. + 1 computer laser optical disk (4 3/4 in.) ISBN: 020515414X (pbk.: alk. paper) Notes: Includes bibliographical references (p. 527-540) and index. System requirements for accompanying computer disk: Macintosh and Windows. Subjects: Mass media. LC Classification: P90 .F628 1998 Dewey Class No.: 302.23 21

Folkerts, Jean. Voices of a nation: a history of mass media in the United States / Jean Folkerts, Dwight L. Teeter, Jr. Edition Information: 4th ed. / with chapter biographies by Keith Kincaid. Published/Created: Boston: Allyn and Bacon, c2002. Projected Pub. Date: 0111 Related Authors: Teeter, Dwight L. Kincaid, Keith. Description: p. cm. ISBN: 0205335462 (alk. paper) Notes: Includes bibliographical references and index. Subjects: Mass media--United States--

History. LC Classification: P92.U5 F58 2002 Dewey Class No.: 302.23/0973 21

Folkerts, Jean. Voices of a nation: a history of mass media in the United States / Jean Folkerts, Dwight L. Teeter, Jr. Edition Information: 2nd ed. Published/Created: New York: Macmillan College; Toronto: Maxwell Macmillan Canada; New York: Maxwell Macmillan International, c1994. Related Authors: Teeter, Dwight L. Description: xviii, 570 p.: ill.; 24 cm. ISBN: 0023386517 Notes: Includes bibliographical references and index. Subjects: Mass media--United States--History. LC Classification: P92.U5 F58 1994 Dewey Class No.: 302.23/0973 20

Forum on the Role of the Media in Racial Stereotyping: February 26, 1990, Telecommunications Theatre, Healey Library, University of Massachusetts/Boston, Harbor Campus / presented by William Monroe Trotter Institute, University of Massachusetts/Boston. Published/Created: Boston: The Institute, [1990] Related Authors: William Monroe Trotter Institute. Related Titles: Racial stereotyping. Description: iii, 29 p.; 28 cm. Notes: Cover Racial stereotyping. Includes bibliographical references. Subjects: African Americans in mass media--Congresses. Stereotype (Psychology) in mass media--Congresses. Mass media--United States. LC Classification: P94.5.A37 F67 1990 Dewey Class No.: 305.8/96073 20

Fox, James Alan. How to work with the media / James Alan Fox, Jack Levin. Published/Created: Newbury Park, Calif.: Sage Publications, c1993. Related Authors: Levin, Jack, 1941- Description: viii, 93 p.: ill.; 23 cm. ISBN: 0803950888 (cl.) 0803950896 (pbk.) Subjects: Mass media and educators--United States. Universities and colleges--Public relations--United States. Series: Survival skills for scholars; v. 2 LC Classification: LB2342.8 .F69 1993 Dewey Class No.: 659.2/937878 20

Fox, Roy F. Mediaspeak: three American voices / Roy F. Fox. Published/Created: Westport, Conn.: Praeger, c2001. Description: xv, 225 p.: ill.; 24 cm. ISBN: 0275961931 (alk. paper) Notes: Includes bibliographical references (p. [211]-220) and index. Subjects: Mass media--Social aspects--United States. Advertising--United States. United States--Social conditions--1980- LC Classification: HN90.M3 F69 2001 Dewey Class No.: 302.23 21

Friedmann, Anthony. Writing for visual media / Anthony Friedmann. Published/Created: Boston: Focal Press, c2001. Description: xiii, 250 p.; 26 cm. computer optical disc (4 3/4 in.) ISBN: 0240803876 (pbk.: alk. paper) Notes: Includes bibliographical references (p. [237]-241) and index. Subjects: Mass media--Authorship. LC Classification: P96.A86 F75 2001 Dewey Class No.: 8058/.066302 21

Ghosh, Subir, 1945- Mass communication today: in the Indian context / Subir Ghosh. Published/Created: Calcutta: Profile Publishers: Distributors, Rupa & Co., 1996. Description: 342 p.; 23 cm. ISBN: 8185550085 Notes: Includes bibliographical references and index. Subjects: Mass media--India. Mass media policy--India. Communication--Social aspects--India. LC Classification: P92.I7 G46 1996 Dewey Class No.: 302.23/0954 21

Ghosh, Subir, 1945- Mass media today: in the Indian context / Subir Ghosh. Published/Created: Calcutta: Profile Publishers: Distributors, Rupa & Co., 1991. Description: xii, 224 p.: ill.; 23 cm. ISBN: 8185550026: Notes: Includes bibliographical references. Subjects: Mass media--Social aspects--India. LC Classification: HN690.Z9 M323 1991 Dewey Class No.: 302.23/0954 20

Gifford, Clive. Media & communications / written by Clive Gifford. Edition Information: 1st American ed. Published/Created: New York: A.A. Knopf; New York: Distributed by Random

House, 1999. Description: 59 p.: ill. (chiefly col.): 29 cm. ISBN: 0375802231 (tr) 0375902236 (glb) Notes: Includes index. Subjects: Communication--History. Mass media--History. Variant Series: Eyewitness books LC Classification: P90 .G474 1999 Dewey Class No.: 302.2 21

Ginneken, Jaap van, 1943- Understanding global news: a critical introduction / Jaap van Ginneken. Published/Created: London; Thousand Oaks: Sage, 1998. Description: viii, 239 p.: ill., maps; 24 cm. ISBN: 0761957081 076195709X (pbk.) Notes: Includes bibliographical references (p. [228]-234) and index. Subjects: Foreign news. Mass media. LC Classification: PN4784.F6 G5513 1998 Dewey Class No.: 070.4/332 21

Gitlin, Todd. Media unlimited: the torrent of sounds and images in modern life / Todd Gitlin. Edition Information: 1st ed. Published/Created: New York: Metropolitan Books, 2002. Projected Pub. Date: 0203 Description: p. cm. ISBN: 0805048987 (hb) Notes: Includes index. Subjects: Mass media. LC Classification: P90 .G4778 2002 Dewey Class No.: 302.23 21

Glasgow Media Group reader / edited by John Eldridge. Published/Created: New York: Routledge, 1995. Related Authors: Eldridge, J. E. T. (John Eric Thomas) Philo, Greg. Description: x, 399 p.: ill.; 25 cm. ISBN: 0415127297 (v. 1: alk. paper) 0415127300 (pbk.: v. 2: alk. paper) 0415130360 (v. 1: alk. paper) 0415130379 (pbk.: v. 2: alk. paper) Notes: Vol. 2: edited by Greg Philo. Includes bibliographical references and index. Subjects: Mass media--Influence. Reporters and reporting. Press. Series: Communication and society (Routledge (Firm)) Variant Series: Communication and society LC Classification: P94 .G58 1995 Dewey Class No.: 302.23 20

Glasgow University Media Group. Getting the message: news, truth and power / Glasgow University Media Group; edited by John Eldridge. Published/Created: London; New York: Routledge, 1993. Related Authors: Eldridge, J. E. T. (John Eric Thomas) Description: viii, 358 p.: ill., ports.; 24 cm. ISBN: 0415079837 (pbk.) Notes: Includes bibliographical references and index. Subjects: Mass media. Journalism. Series: Communication and society (Routledge (Firm)) Variant Series: Communication and society LC Classification: P91.25 .G57 1993 Dewey Class No.: 302.23 20

Godfrey, Donald G. Reruns on file: a guide to electronic media archives / compiled by Donald G. Godfrey. Published/Created: Hillsdale, N.J.: Lawrence Erlbaum Associates, c1992. Description: xlix, 322 p.; 25 cm. ISBN: 080581146X 0805811478 (pbk.) Notes: Includes indexes. Subjects: Mass media--United States--Archival resources Directories. Mass media--Canada--Archival resources--Directories. Mass media--Great Britain--Archival resources Directories. Series: Communication textbook series. Broadcasting LC Classification: P96.A722 U54 1992 Dewey Class No.: 302.23/02573 20

Goldberg, Robert Getting the talk right / Robert Goldberg. Published/Created: Knoxville, Tenn.: Whittle Books, c1993. Description: 86 p.: ill. (some col.), ports.; 26 cm. ISBN: 1879736195: Subjects: Corporations--Public relations. Mass media and business. Corporate image. Series: The chief executive press, 1060-8923 LC Classification: HD59 .G58 1993 Dewey Class No.: 659.2/85 20

Goodwin, Craufurd D. W. Talking to themselves: the search for rights and responsibilities of the press and mass media in four Latin American nations / Craufurd D. Goodwin, Michael Nacht. Published/Created: New York, NY: Institute of International Education, c1995. Related Authors: Nacht, Michael. Description: 112 p.; 23 cm. ISBN: 087206221X Notes: Discusses the media in Argentina, Brazil, Chile, and Mexico. Includes bibliographical references (p. 101-102). Subjects: Mass media--Latin America. Journalism--Latin America

Series: IIE research report; no. 26 LC Classification: P92.L3 G63 1995

Gottfried, Ted. The American media / Ted Gottfried. Published/Created: New York: F. Watts, c1997. Description: 160 p.: ill.; 24 cm. ISBN: 0531113159 Summary: Surveys the history of American media, covering such aspects as yellow journalism, the syndicates, and radio news. Notes: Includes bibliographical references (p. 147-155) and index. Subjects: Mass media--Press--United States--History. Variant Series: An Impact book LC Classification: P92.U5 G64 1997 Dewey Class No.: 302.23/0973 20

Gourley, Catherine, 1950- Media wizards: a behind-the-scene look at media manipulations / Catherine Gourley. Published/Created: Brookfield, Conn.: Twenty-First Century Press, c1999. Description: 128 p.: ill.; 26 cm. ISBN: 0761309675 (lib. bdg.) Summary: Explores the various tools advertisers, broadcasters, and others involved in the media use to impart messages to the public, describing both historical and contemporary media events and phenomena. Notes: Includes bibliographical references (p. 123-126) and index. Subjects: Manipulative behavior. Mass media. LC Classification: P90 .G65 1999 Dewey Class No.: 302.23 21

Graber, Doris A. (Doris Appel), 1923- Processing the news: how people tame the information tide / Doris A. Graber. Edition Information: 2nd ed. Published/Created: Lanham, Md.: University Press of America, [1993] Description: x, 300 p.: ill.; 23 cm. ISBN: 0819190985 (acid-free paper) Notes: Originally Published: New York: Longman, 1988. Includes bibliographical references (p. 269-293) and index. Subjects: Public opinion--Political socialization--Mass media--Political aspects--United States--Case studies. Human information processing--Case studies. Democracy. LC Classification: HM261 .G78 1993 Dewey Class No.: 306.2 20

Greater Philadelphia Cultural Alliance. Cultural resource directory / Greater Philadelphia Cultural Alliance. Published/Created: Philadelphia, PA: Greater Philadelphia Cultural Alliance, 1998- Description: v.: ill.; 22 cm. 25th ed. (1998)- Current Frequency: Annual Continues: Greater Philadelphia Cultural Alliance. Membership directory and resource guide 1095-8398 (OCoLC)37604985 (DLC)sn 97004568 ISSN: 1097-5063 Cancel/Invalid LCCN: sn 98000012 Notes: A membership directory and guide to cultural organizations in the greater Philadelphia area. SERBIB/SERLOC merged record Subjects: Arts facilities--Mass media--Pennsylvania--Philadelphia Region Directories. LC Classification: F158.18 .G74a Dewey Class No.: 974.8/11/0025 21

Green, John O., 1945- The new age of communications / John O. Green; foreword by Paul Gilster. Edition Information: 1st ed. Published/Created: New York: Henry Holt, 1997. Description: 144 p.: ill.; 22 cm. ISBN: 0805040277 (alk. paper) 0805040269 (alk. paper) Notes: Includes bibliographical references (p. 140) and index. Subjects: Communication--Social aspects. Mass media--Social aspects. Series: A scientific American focus book LC Classification: HM258 .G695 1997 Dewey Class No.: 302.2 21

Greenslade, Roy. Maxwell: the rise and fall of Robert Maxwell and his empire / Roy Greenslade. Published/Created: New York: Carol Pub. Group, c1992. Description: vii, 376 p.: ill.; 24 cm. ISBN: 1559721235: Notes: "A Birch Lane Press book." Includes bibliographical references (p. 360-366) and index. Subjects: Maxwell, Robert, 1923- Newspaper publishing--Great Britain--History--20th century. Publishers and publishing--Great Britain--Biography. Mass media--Great Britain. LC Classification: Z325.M394 G73 1992 Dewey Class No.: 070.5/092 B 20

Greh, Deborah. Untangling the Web: a guide to mass communication on the Web / Deborah Greh. Edition Information: 2nd ed. Published/Created: Boston: Bedford/St.

Martin's, c2000. Description: 39 p.: ill.; 23 cm. ISBN: 0312250142 Notes: Includes bibliographical references (p. 34-35). Subjects: Mass media--Computer network resources. World Wide Web. LC Classification: P91.28 .G74 2000 Dewey Class No.: 025.06/30223 21

Gunter, Barrie. Media research methods: measuring audiences, reactions and impact / Barrie Gunter. Published/Created: London; Thousand Oaks, Calif.: Sage Publications, 2000. Description: 314 p.; 24 cm. ISBN: 0761956581 076195659X (pbk.) Notes: Includes bibliographical references (p. [280]-307) and index. Subjects: Mass media--Research--Methodology. LC Classification: P91.3 .G86 2000 Dewey Class No.: 302.23/07/2 21 National Bib. No.: GBA0-10129

Haggerty, Mike. The headline vs. the bottom line: mutual distrust between business and the news media / by Mike Haggerty and Wallace Rasmussen. Published/Created: Nashville, TN: The Freedom Forum First Amendment Center at Vanderbilt University, [1994]. Related Authors: Rasmussen, Wallace. Description: 104 p.: ill.; 28 cm. Notes: Includes bibliographical references and index. Subjects: Mass media and business--United States. Journalism, Commercial--United States. LC Classification: P96.B872 H34 1994

Hanclosky, Walter V. Principles of media development / Walter V. Hanclosky. Published/Created: White Plains, NY: Knowledge Industry Publications, c1995. Description: xi, 212 p.: ill.; 28 cm. ISBN: 086[illegible] Subjects: Mass media. Communication. LC Classification: P90 .H28[illegible] Dewey Class No.: 302.23 20

Hand, [illegible] an mass media through 200 y[illegible]d. Published/Created: [illegible]W]: Kangaroo Press, [1990] [illegible] p.: ill.; 19 x 21 cm. ISBN: 08[illegible] [illegible]jects: Mass media--Au[illegible] Series: 200 years in pic[illegible]cation: P92.A76 H33 19[illegible]o.: 302.23/0994 20

Handbook of the media in Asia / edited by Shelton A. Gunaratne. Published/Created: New Delhi; Thousand Oaks, Calif.: Sage Publications, 2000. Related Authors: Gunaratne, Shelton A. Description: x, 722 p.: map; 25 cm. ISBN: 0761994270 Notes: Includes bibliographical references and indexes. Subjects: Mass media--Asia--Handbooks, manuals, etc. LC Classification: P92.A7 H36 2000 Dewey Class No.: 302.23/095 21

Handbook on mass media in the United States: the industry and its audiences / edited by Erwin K. Thomas and Brown H. Carpenter. Published/Created: Westport, Conn.: Greenwood Press, 1994. Related Authors: Thomas, Erwin Kenneth. Carpenter, Brown H. Description: xv, 325 p.: ill.; 25 cm. ISBN: 0313278113 (hardcover: alk. paper) Notes: Includes bibliographical references (p. [309]-313) and index. Subjects: Mass media--United States--Handbooks, manuals, etc. LC Classification: P92.U5 H36 1994 Dewey Class No.: 302.23/0973 20

Hardt, Hanno. Interactions: critical studies in communication, media, and journalism / Hanno Hardt. Published/Created: Lanham, Md.: Rowman & Littlefield, 1998. Projected Pub. Date: 9806 Description: p. cm. ISBN: 0847688879 (cloth: alk. paper) 0847688887 (pbk.: alk. paper) Notes: Most chapters are essays, edited for this publication, which were previously Published in various sources, 1972-1996. Includes bibliographical references and index. Subjects: Communication. Mass media. Journalism. Series: Critical media studies LC Classification: P90 .H324 1998 Dewey Class No.: 302.2 21

Harless, James D. Mass communication: an introductory survey / James D. Harless. Edition Information: 2nd ed. Published/Created: Dubuque, IA: Wm. C. Brown Publishers, c1990. Description: xiii, 575 p.: ill.; 23 cm. ISBN: 0697014681 Notes: Includes bibliographical references and index. LC Classification: P90 .H327 1990 Dewey Class No.: 302.23 20

Harrie, Eva, 1967- The Nordic media market 2000: Denmark, Finland, Iceland, Norway, Sweden media companies and business activities / compiled by Eva Harrie. Published/Created: Göteborg: NORDICOM, 2000. Related Authors: Nordicom. Description: 81 p.; 30 cm. ISBN: 9189471008 Notes: Includes bibliographical references (p. 80). Subjects: Mass media--Economic aspects--Scandinavia. Series: Nordic media trends, 1401-0410; 5 LC Classification: P96.E252 S344 2000 Dewey Class No.: 338.4/730223/0948 21

Hart, Andrew. Understanding the media: a practical guide / Andrew Hart. Published/Created: London; New York: Routledge, 1991. Description: xvi, 267 p.: ill.; 24 cm. ISBN: 0415057124 0415057132 (pbk.) Notes: Includes bibliographical references (p. 253-257) and index. Subjects: Mass media. LC Classification: P90 .H3346 1991 Dewey Class No.: 302.23 20

Hausman, Carl, 1953- Crafting the news for electronic media: writing, reporting and producing / Carl Hausman. Published/Created: Belmont, Calif.: Wadsworth Pub. Co., c1992. Description: x, 290 p.: ill.; 25 cm. ISBN: 053414358X Notes: Includes bibliographical references (p. 283-285) and index. Subjects: Broadcast journalism. Television broadcasting of news. Mass media--Authorship. Television authorship. Radio authorship. Report writing. LC Classification: PN4784.B75 H38 1992 Dewey Class No.: 070.1/9 20

Herman, Edward S. Beyond hypocrisy: decoding the news in an age of propaganda: including A doublespeak dictionary for the 1990s / by Edward S. Herman; illustrations by Matt Wuerker. Published/Created: Boston, MA: South End Press, c1992. Description: 239 p.: ill.; 23 cm. ISBN: 0896084361 (cloth: acid-free): 0896084353 (paper: acid-free): Notes: Includes bibliographical references (p. 189-227) and index. Subjects: Mass media and language--United States. Mass media--Political aspects--United States. Press and propaganda--United States. English language--Terms and phrases. United States--Politics and government--1981-1989. United States--Politics and government--1989-1993. LC Classification: P96.L342 U55 1992 Dewey Class No.: 302.23/014 20

Hiebert, Ray Eldon. Exploring mass media for a changing world / by Ray Eldon Hiebert and Sheila Jean Gibbons. Published/Created: Mahwah, N.J.: Lawrence Erlbaum Associates, 2000. Related Authors: Gibbons, Sheila Jean, 1951- Description: xx, 349 p.: ill.; 25 cm. ISBN: 0805829164 (pbk.: alk. paper) Notes: Includes bibliographical references and indexes. Subjects: Mass media. LC Classification: P90 .H478 1999 Dewey Class No.: 302.23 21

Hiebert, Ray Eldon. Mass media VI: an introduction to modern communication / Ray Eldon Hiebert, Donald F. Ungurait, Thomas W. Bohn. Published/Created: New York: Longman, c1991. Related Authors: Ungurait, Donald F. Bohn, Thomas W. Related Titles: Mass media 6. Mass media six. Description: xix, 666 p.: ill. (some col.); 26 cm. ISBN: 0801304539 Notes: Includes bibliographical references and index. Subjects: Mass media. Communication. LC Classification: P90 .H4793 1990 Dewey Class No.: 302.23 20

Hilliard, Robert L., 1925- Writing for television, radio, and new media / Robert L. Hilliard. Edition Information: 7th ed. Published/Created: Belmont, CA: Wadsworth Thomson Learning, 2000. Related Authors: Hilliard, Robert L., 1925- Writing for television and radio. Description: xiii, 466 p.: ill.; 24 cm. ISBN: 0534561241 Notes: Rev. ed. of: Writing for television and radio. 6th ed. Includes bibliographical references (p. 457-459) and index. Subjects: Broadcasting--Authorship. Mass media--Authorship. LC Classification: PN1990.9.A88 H55 2000 Dewey Class No.: 808.2/2 21

Hispanic media directory of the Americas / Latin American Journalism Program, School of Journalism and Mass Communication, Florida International University = Guía de medios en español de las Américas / Programa Latinoamericano de Periodismo, Escuela de Periodismo y Medios de Comunicación, Universidad Internacional de la Florida. Published/Created: North Miami, FL: Latin American Journalism Program, School of Journalism and Mass Communication, Florida International University, [1996] Related Authors: Florida International University. Latin American Journalism Program. Description: 1 v.: ill., maps; 23 cm. 1996. Current Frequency: Annual Continued by: Latin American media directory plus United States and Canada 1094-298X (DLC) 98655032 (OCoLC)36689848 ISSN: 1094-2971 Cancel/Invalid LCCN: sn 97036360 Notes: In English and Spanish. SERBIB/SERLOC merged record Subjects: Mass media--Latin America--Directories. Hispanic American mass media--Directories. LC Classification: P88.8 .H57 Dewey Class No.: 302.23/025 21

History of the mass media in the United States: an encyclopedia / edited by Margaret A. Blanchard; commissioning editor Carol J. Burwash. Published/Created: Chicago: Fitzroy Dearborn, c1998. Related Authors: Blanchard, Margaret A. Description: xxxii, 752 p.: ill., 29 cm. ISBN: 1579580122 Notes: Includes bibliographical references (p. xxxi-xxxii) and index. Subjects: Mass media--United States--History--Encyclopedias. LC Classification: P92.U5 H55 1998 Dewey Class No.: 302.23/0973/03 21

Hitchcock, John R. (John Robert) Sportscasting / John R. Hitchcock. Published/Created: Boston: Focal Press, c1991. Description: xii, 107 p.: forms; 24 cm. ISBN: 0240800621 (pbk.) Subjects: Mass media and sports--Vocational guidance Television broadcasting of sports--Vocational guidance. Radio broadcasting of sports--Vocational guidance. Series: Electronic media guides LC Classification: GV742 .H58 1991 Dewey Class No.: 070.4/49796023 20

Hollis, Daniel Webster, 1942- The ABC-CLIO companion to the media in America / Daniel Webster Hollis, III. Published/Created: Santa Barbara, Calif.: ABC-CLIO, c1995. Description: xiii, 352 p.: ill.; 27 cm. ISBN: 087436776X (cloth: alk. paper) Notes: Includes bibliographical references (p. 327-333) and index. Subjects: Mass media--United States--History--Handbooks, manuals, etc. Series: ABC-CLIO companions to key issues in American history and life LC Classification: P92.U5 H58 1995 Dewey Class No.: 302.23/0973 20

Hoover's guide to media companies. Published/Created: Austin, Tex.: Hoover's Business Press, c1996. Description: xv, 522 p.: ill.; 23 cm. ISBN: 1878753967 Notes: "Advertising, books, cd-rom, film, Internet, magazines, newspapers, online, radio/TV"--Cover. Subjects: Mass media--United States--Directories. Computer industry--United States--Directories. Multimedia systems industry--United States--Directories. Communication--United States--Directories. Corporations--United States--Directories. LC Classification: P88.8 .H66 1996 Dewey Class No.: 302.23/025/73 21

Horgan, John, 1940- Irish media: a critical history, 1922-2000 / John Horgan. Published/Created: London; New York: Routledge, 2001. Projected Pub. Date: 0102 Description: p. cm. ISBN: 0415216400 (alk. paper) 0415216419 (pbk. :alk. paper) Notes: Includes bibliographical references and index. Subjects: Mass media--Ireland--History--20th century. LC Classification: P92.I76 H67 2000 Dewey Class No.: 302.23/09417/0904 21

Howard, Carole, 1945- On deadline: managing media relations / Carole M. Howard, Wilma K. Mathews. Edition Information: 3rd ed. Published/Created: Prospect Heights, Ill.: Waveland Press, c2000. Related Authors: Mathews, Wilma, 1945- Description: xix, 347 p.; 23 cm. ISBN:

1577660862 Notes: Includes bibliographical references (p. 335-336) and index. Subjects: Mass media and business. Public relations. LC Classification: HD59 .H64 2000 Dewey Class No.: 659.2 21

Howard, Carole, 1945- On deadline: managing media relations / Carole M. Howard, Wilma K. Mathews. Edition Information: 2nd ed. Published/Created: Prospect Heights, Ill.: Waveland Press, c1994. Related Authors: Mathews, Wilma, 1945- Description: xviii, 239 p.; 23 cm. ISBN: 088133801X Notes: Includes bibliographical references (p. 231-232) and index. Subjects: Mass media and business. Public relations. LC Classification: HD59 .H64 1994 Dewey Class No.: 659.2 20

Hunt, Todd, 1938- Mass communication: producers and consumers / Todd Hunt, Brent D. Ruben. Published/Created: New York, NY: HarperCollins College Publishers, c1993. Related Authors: Ruben, Brent D. Description: xxi, 506 p.: ill. (some col.); 26 cm. ISBN: 0065000528 Notes: Includes bibliographical references and indexes. Subjects: Mass media. LC Classification: P90 .H83 1993 Dewey Class No.: 302.23 20

Hutchison, Earl R., 1926- Writing for mass communication / Earl R. Hutchison, Sr. Edition Information: 2nd ed. Published/Created: White Plains, N.Y.: Longman Publishers USA, c1996. Description: xvii, 382 p.: ill.; 28 cm. ISBN: 0801312353 Notes: Includes bibliographical references (p.) and index. Subjects: Mass media--Authorship. Journalism--Authorship. LC Classification: P96.A86 H88 1996 Dewey Class No.: 808/.066302 20

Images in language, media, and mind / edited by Roy F. Fox. Published/Created: Urbana, Ill.: National Council of Teachers of English, c1994. Related Authors: Fox, Roy. F. Description: xiii, 246 p.: ill.; 26 cm. ISBN: 0814122817: Notes: Includes bibliographical references and index. Subjects: Visual communication. Psycholinguistics. Imagery (Psychology) Mass media--Psychological aspects. LC Classification: P93.5 .I47 1994 Dewey Class No.: 302.2/22 20

Imaging the city: continuing struggles and new directions / edited by Lawrence J. Vale and Sam Bass Warner Jr. Published/Created: New Brunswick, NJ: Center for Urban Policy Research, c2001. Related Authors: Vale, Lawrence J., 1959- Warner, Sam Bass, 1928- Description: xxiii, 519 p.: ill.; 26 cm. ISBN: 0882851691 (cloth: alk. paper) 0882851705 (pbk.: alk. paper) Notes: Includes bibliographical references (p. 455-488) and index. Subjects: City planning--History--20th century. City planning--Social aspects. Cities and towns in mass media. LC Classification: NA9095 .I46 2001 Dewey Class No.: 711/.4/09 21

Impact of mass media: current issues / edited by Ray Eldon Hiebert. Edition Information: 4th ed. Published/Created: New York: Longman, c1999. Related Authors: Hiebert, Ray Eldon. Description: ix, 482 p.; 24 cm. ISBN: 0801331986 Notes: Includes bibliographical references and index. Subjects: Mass media--United States. Mass media--Influence. Mass media--Social aspects. LC Classification: P92.U5 I46 1999 Dewey Class No.: 302.23/0973 21

Impact of mass media: current issues / edited by Ray Eldon Hiebert; with a foreword by Carol Reuss. Edition Information: 3rd ed. Published/Created: White Plains, N.Y.: Longman Pub. Group, c1995. Related Authors: Hiebert, Ray Eldon. Description: xv, 472 p.; 24 cm. ISBN: 0801308380 Notes: Includes bibliographical references and index. Subjects: Mass media--United States. Mass media--Influence. Mass media--Social aspects. Series: Longman series in public communication LC Classification: P92.U5 I46 1995 Dewey Class No.: 302.23/0973 20

Information sources for the press and broadcast media / editor, Sarah Adair. Edition Information: 2nd ed. Published/Created: London; New Providence, NJ: Bowker-Saur, 1999. Projected Pub. Date: 9909

Related Authors: First ed. edited by Selwyn Eagle. Adair, Sarah. Description: p. cm. ISBN: 1857392612 Notes: Includes bibliographical references and index. Subjects: Mass media--Information services--Research. Internet. Series: Guides to information sources (London, England) Variant Series: Guides to information sources LC Classification: P96.I47 I5 1999 Dewey Class No.: 302.23/072 21

Inglis, Fred. Media theory: an introduction / Fred Inglis. Published/Created: Oxford, UK; Cambridge, Mass., USA: B. Blackwell, 1990. Description: viii, 212 p.: ill.; 24 cm. ISBN: 0631159177 0631159185 (pbk.) Notes: Includes bibliographical references and index. LC Classification: P90 .I485 1990 Dewey Class No.: 302.23 20

International communications in North-East Asia / edited by Hyeon-Dew Kang. Published/Created: Seoul, Korea: NANAM Pub. House; Columbia, Mo.: NANAM International Publications, 1994. Related Authors: Kang, Hyon-du. Description: 493 P.: ill.; 23 cm. ISBN: 8930060188 (pbk.) Notes: Reprint of "Changing international order in North-East Asia and communication policies" Published in 1992. Includes bibliographical references and index. Subjects: Telecommunication--Mass media--East Asia--Congresses. LC Classification: HE8410.5 .I58 1994

International mass media communications review: the quarterly refereed interdisciplinary journal of the Center for the Study of Social Sciences and Humanities Related Authors: Center for the Study of Social Sciences and Humanities (Anacortes, Wash.) Description: v.; 20 cm. Current Frequency: Quarterly ISSN: 1092-6747 Cancel/Invalid LCCN: sn 97000126 Notes: Description based on: Vol. 10, no. 1 (May 1997); title from cover. SERBIB/SERLOC merged record Subjects: Mass media--Periodicals. LC Classification: P87 .I549 Dewey Class No.: 302 12

Itule, Bruce D., 1947- News writing and reporting for today's media / Bruce D. Itule, Douglas A. Anderson. Edition Information: 3rd ed. Published/Created: New York: McGraw-Hill, c1994. Related Authors: Anderson, Douglas A. Description: xxx, 716 p.: ill.; 24 cm. ISBN: 0070324158 (acid-free paper): Notes: Includes index. Subjects: Reporters and reporting. Journalism--Mass media--Authorship. Report writing. LC Classification: PN4781 .I78 1994 Dewey Class No.: 070.4/3 20

Itule, Bruce D., 1947- News writing and reporting for today's media / Bruce D. Itule, Douglas A. Anderson. Edition Information: 5th ed. Published/Created: Boston: McGraw-Hill College, c2000. Related Authors: Anderson, Douglas A. Description: xx, 471 p.: ill.; 24 cm. ISBN: 0073654981 Notes: Includes index. Subjects: Reporters and reporting. Journalism--Mass media--Authorship. Report writing. LC Classification: PN4781 .I78 2000 Dewey Class No.: 070.4/3 21

Itule, Bruce D., 1947- News writing and reporting for today's media / Bruce D. Itule, Douglas A. Anderson. Edition Information: 2nd ed. Published/Created: New York: McGraw-Hill, c1991. Related Authors: Anderson, Douglas A. Description: xxiv, 711 p.: ill.; 24 cm. ISBN: 007557263X Notes: Includes bibliographical references (p. 695-696) and index. Subjects: Reporters and reporting. Journalism--Mass media--Authorship. Report writing. LC Classification: PN4781 .I78 1991 Dewey Class No.: 070.4/3 20

Jacobsen, Clay, 1956- Circle of seven / Clay Jacobsen. Published/Created: Nashville, Tenn.: Broadman & Holman Publishers, c2000. Description: viii, 392 p.; 23 cm. ISBN: 0805422838 Subjects: Investigative reporting--Fiction. Public opinion polls--Conspiracies--Journalists--Mass media--Fiction. Genre/Form: Christian fiction. Political fiction. LC Classification: PS3560.A2584 C57 2000 Dewey Class No.: 813/.54 21

Jawitz, William. Understanding mass media / William Jawitz. Edition Information: 5th ed. Published/Created: Lincolnwood, Ill.: National Textbook Co., c1996. Related Authors: Schrank, Jeffrey. Understanding mass media. Description: xv, 512 p.: ill. (some col.); 25 cm. ISBN: 0844258318 Notes: Rev. ed. of: Understanding mass media / Jeffrey Schrank. 4th ed. 1991. Includes bibliographical references and index. Subjects: Mass media. LC Classification: P90 .J344 1996 Dewey Class No.: 302.23 20

Jeffres, Leo W. Mass media processes / Leo W. Jeffres. Edition Information: 2nd ed. Published/Created: Prospect Heights, Ill.: Waveland Press, c1994. Related Authors: Jeffres, Leo W. Mass media. Description: xiii, 519 p.: ill.; 23 cm. ISBN: 0881337609 Notes: Rev. ed. of: Mass media: processes and effects, c1986. Includes bibliographical references (p. 377-500) and index. Subjects: Mass media. LC Classification: P90 .J345 1994 Dewey Class No.: 302.23 20

Jensen, Joli. Redeeming modernity: contradictions in media criticism / Joli Jensen. Published/Created: Newbury Park, Calif.: Sage Publications, c1990. Description: 221 p.; 23 cm. ISBN: 0803934769 0803934777 (pbk.) Notes: Includes bibliographical references (p. 202-206) and index. Subjects: Mass media. Popular culture. Mass media--Social aspects. Mass media--United States. Series: Communication and human values (Newbury Park, Calif.) Variant Series: Communication and human values LC Classification: P91 .J47 1990 Dewey Class No.: 302.23/0973 20

Jensen, Klaus. The social semiotics of mass communication / Klaus Bruhn Jensen. Published/Created: London; Thousand Oaks, Calif.: Sage Pubs., 1995. Description: vi, 228 p.: ill.; 24 cm. ISBN: 080397809X 0803978103 (pbk.) Notes: Includes bibliographical references (p. [207]-220) and index. Subjects: Mass media--Semiotics. Semiotics--Social aspects. Mass media--Social aspects. Mass media--Research. LC Classification: P91 .J475 1995 Dewey Class No.: 302.23/01 20

Jensen, Robert, 1958- Writing dissent: taking radical ideas from the margins to the mainstream / Robert Jensen. Published/Created: New York: P. Lang, c2001. Description: x, 150 p.; 23 cm. ISBN: 0820456519 (alk. paper) Notes: Includes bibliographical references (p. [149]-150). Subjects: Journalism--Political aspects. Radicalism in mass media. Series: Media & culture (New York, N.Y.); v. 5. Variant Series: Media & culture; vol. 5 LC Classification: PN4751 .K46 2001 Dewey Class No.: 302.23 21

Johnston, Carla B. Global news access: the impact of new communications technologies / Carla Brooks Johnston. Published/Created: Westport, Conn.: Praeger, 1998. Description: 269 p.: ill., map; 24 cm. ISBN: 0275957748 (alk. paper) Notes: Includes bibliographical references (p. [247]-251) and index. Subjects: Mass media policy. Mass media--Technological innovations. Mass media--Influence. Democracy. LC Classification: P95.8 .J64 1998 Dewey Class No.: 303.48/33 21

Johnston, Carla B. Screened out: how the media control us and what we can do about it / Carla Brooks Johnston. Published/Created: Armonk, N.Y.: M.E. Sharpe, c2000. Description: xiii, 216 p.; 23 cm. ISBN: 0765604884 (hardcover: alk. paper) Notes: Includes bibliographical references (p. 193-203) and index. Subjects: Mass media--Influence. Mass media and propaganda. Mass media--Ownership. Media literacy. Mass media--United States. Series: Media, communication, and culture in America LC Classification: P94 .J638 2000 Dewey Class No.: 302.23 21

Journalism & communication monographs. Published/Created: Columbia, SC: Association for Education in Journalism and Mass Communication, c1999- Related Authors: Association for Education in Journalism and Mass Communication. Description: v.; 23 cm. Vol. 1, no. 1

(spring 1999)- Current Frequency: Quarterly Continues: Journalism & mass communication monographs 1077-6966 (DLC) 95660817 (OCoLC)30858169 ISSN: 1522-6379 Subjects: Journalism--Periodicals. Mass media--Periodicals. LC Classification: PN4722 .J6 Dewey Class No.: 070/.5 19

Journalism & mass communication educator. Published/Created: Columbia, SC: Association for Education in Journalism and Mass Communication in cooperation with the Association of Schools of Journalism and Mass Communication, c1995- Related Authors: Association for Education in Journalism and Mass Communication. Association of Schools of Journalism and Mass Communication. Description: v.; 23 cm. 50/1 (spring 1995)- Current Frequency: Quarterly Continues: Journalism educator 0022-5517 (DLC) 66097803 (OCoLC)1783227 ISSN: 1077-6958 Cancel/Invalid LCCN: sn 94002794 Notes: Title from cover. SERBIB/SERLOC merged record Subjects: Communication--Study and teaching (Higher)--United States Periodicals. Journalism--Study and teaching (Higher)--United States Periodicals. Mass media--Study and teaching (Higher)--United States Periodicals. LC Classification: PN4788 .J63 Dewey Class No.: 302.2/071/173 20

Journalism & mass communication quarterly. Published/Created: Columbia, SC: Association for Education in Journalism and Mass Communication, c1995- Related Authors: Association for Education in Journalism and Mass Communication. Description: v.: ill.; 23 cm. Vol. 72, no. 1 (spring 1995)- Current Frequency: Quarterly Continues: Journalism quarterly 0196-3031 (DLC) 28013599 (OCoLC)5002442 ISSN: 1077-6990 Cancel/Invalid LCCN: sn 94002796 CODEN: JMCQFA Notes: Title from cover. Each issue has also a distinctive title. Has occasional special supplement. SERBIB/SERLOC merged record Subjects: Journalism--Periodicals. Mass media--Periodicals. Communication--Periodicals. Journalism--United States--Periodicals. Journalism--Bibliography--Periodicals. LC Classification: PN4700 .J7 Dewey Class No.: 070 12

Kahane, Howard, 1928- Logic and contemporary rhetoric: the use of reason in everyday life / Howard Kahane. Edition Information: 7th ed. Published/Created: Belmont, Calif.: Wadsworth Pub. Co., c1995. Description: xvii, 350 p.: ill.; 23 cm. ISBN: 0534254640 Notes: Includes bibliographical references (p. 327-341) and indexes. Subjects: Reasoning. Fallacies (Logic) Judgment (Logic) Mass media. Textbooks. LC Classification: BC177 .K34 1995 Dewey Class No.: 160 20

Kahane, Howard, 1928- Logic and contemporary rhetoric: the use of reason in everyday life / Howard Kahane. Edition Information: 6th ed. Published/Created: Belmont, Calif.: Wadsworth Pub. Co., c1992. Description: xvi, 350 p.: ill.; 24 cm. ISBN: 0534168965 Notes: Includes bibliographical references (p. 331-339) and indexes. Subjects: Reasoning. Fallacies (Logic) Judgment (Logic) Mass media. LC Classification: BC177 .K34 1992 Dewey Class No.: 160 20

Kahane, Howard, 1928- Logic and contemporary rhetoric: the use of reason in everyday life / Howard Kahane, Nancy Cavender. Edition Information: 9th ed. Published/Created: Australia; Belmont, CA: Wadsworth Thomson Learning, [2001] Related Authors: Cavender, Nancy. Description: xv, 393 p.: ill.; 24 cm. ISBN: 053453578X Notes: Includes bibliographical references (p. 372-377) and indexes. Subjects: Reasoning. Fallacies (Logic) Judgment (Logic) Mass media. LC Classification: BC177 .K34 2001 Dewey Class No.: 160 21

Kahane, Howard, 1928- Logic and contemporary rhetoric: the use of reason in everyday life / Howard Kahane, Nancy Cavender. Edition Information: 8th ed. Published/Created: Belmont, Calif.: Wadsworth Pub., c1998. Related Authors: Cavender, Nancy. Description: xii, 369 p.;

ill.; 23 cm. ISBN: 0534524702 (pbk.) Notes: Includes bibliographical references (p. 347-357) and indexes. Subjects: Reasoning. Fallacies (Logic) Judgment (Logic) Mass media. LC Classification: BC177 .K34 1998 Dewey Class No.: 160 21

Kaniss, Phyllis C. Making local news / Phyllis Kaniss. Published/Created: Chicago: University of Chicago Press, 1991. Description: x, 260 p.: ill., maps; 24 cm. ISBN: 0226423476 (alk. paper) Notes: Includes bibliographical references (p. 235-253) and index. Subjects: Journalism--Social aspects--United States. Local mass media--United States. Journalism--Political aspects--United States. Local government and the press--United States. City planning and the press. LC Classification: PN4749 .K35 1991 Dewey Class No.: 302.23/0973 20

Katz, Helen E. The media handbook / Helen Katz. Published/Created: Lincolnwood, Ill., USA: NTC Business Books, c1995. Description: xiv, 163 p.; 24 cm. ISBN: 0844235164 Notes: Includes bibliographical references (p. 158) and index. Subjects: Advertising media planning. Mass media and business. Marketing channels. LC Classification: HF5826.5 .K38 1995 Dewey Class No.: 659 20

Keating, Michael, 1943- Covering the environment: a handbook on environmental journalism / by Michael Keating; [foreward by Peter Desbarats]. Published/Created: Ottawa: National Round Table on the Environment and the Economy, c1993. Related Authors: National Round Table on the Environment and the Economy (Canada) Description: x, 164 p.: ill.; 24 cm ISBN: 1895643201 Notes: Issued also in French under Reportages sur l'environnement. " Published in conjunction with the Graduate School of Journalism, the University of Western Ontario"--Cover. Includes bibliographical references (p. 154-157) and index. Subjects: Environmental protection--Press coverage--Canada. Mass media and the environment--Canada. Pollution--Environmental aspects--Canada. Pollution--Environmental aspects. Environmental protection--Canada--Directories. Series: National Round Table series on sustainable development; 10 LC Classification: PN4914.E64 K43 1993 Dewey Class No.: 070.4/493637 21

Kerchner, Kathy. SoundBites: a business guide for working with the media / by Kathy Kerchner. Edition Information: 1st ed. Published/Created: Superior, WI: Savage Press, c1997. Description: 283 p.; 22 cm. ISBN: 1886028303 Notes: Includes index. Subjects: Mass media and business--United States. Public relations--United States. LC Classification: HD59.6.U6 K47 1997 Dewey Class No.: 659.2 21

Kessler, Lauren. Mastering the message: media writing with substance and style / Lauren Kessler and Duncan McDonald. Edition Information: 2nd ed. Published/Created: Dubuque, Iowa: Kendall/Hunt, c1999. Related Authors: McDonald, Duncan, 1945- Description: xvi, 319 p.: ill.; 23 cm. Notes: Includes index. Subjects: Mass media--Authorship. Report writing. LC Classification: P96.A86 K47 1999 Dewey Class No.: 808/.066302 21

Kessler, Lauren. The search: information gathering for the mass media / Lauren Kessler, Duncan McDonald. Published/Created: Belmont, Calif.: Wadsworth Pub. Co., c1992. Related Authors: McDonald, Duncan, 1945- Kessler, Lauren. Uncovering the news. Description: xiv, 241 p.; 23 cm. ISBN: 0534162789 Notes: Rev. ed. of: Uncovering the news. 1st ed. c1987. Includes bibliographical references and index. Subjects: Mass media--Research--Methodology. Mass media--Authorship. LC Classification: P91.3 .K45 1992 Dewey Class No.: 028.7/08/8097 20

Kessler, Lauren. When words collide: a media writer's guide to grammar and style / Lauren Kessler, Duncan McDonald. Edition Information: 4th ed. Published/Created: Belmont: Wadworth

Pub. Co., c1996. Related Authors: McDonald, Duncan, 1945- Description: xii, 221 p.; 23 cm. ISBN: 0534257402 (acid-free paper) Notes: Includes index. Subjects: English language--Grammar. Journalism--Style manuals. Mass media--Authorship. LC Classification: PE1112 .K435 1996 Dewey Class No.: 808/.042 20

Kessler, Lauren. When words collide: a media writer's guide to grammar and style / Lauren Kessler, Duncan McDonald. Edition Information: 5th ed. Published/Created: Belmont, CA: Wadsworth, c2000. Related Authors: McDonald, Duncan, 1945- Description: x, 230 p.; 23 cm. ISBN: 0534561330 0534561365 (instructor's ed.) Notes: Includes index. Subjects: English language--Grammar. Journalism--Style manuals. Journalism--Mass media--Authorship. LC Classification: PE1112 .K435 2000 Dewey Class No.: 808/.042 21

Kessler, Lauren. When words collide: a media writer's guide to grammar and style / Lauren Kessler, Duncan McDonald. Edition Information: 3rd ed. Published/Created: Belmont, Calif.: Wadsworth Pub. Co., c1992. Related Authors: McDonald, Duncan, 1945- Description: xiii, 242 p.; 23 cm. ISBN: 0534170285 Notes: Includes index. Subjects: English language--Grammar. Journalism--Style manuals. Mass media--Authorship. LC Classification: PE1112 .K435 1991 Dewey Class No.: 808/.042 20

Kilpatrick, William, 1940- The family new media guide: a parents' guide to the very best choices in values-oriented media, including videos, CD-ROMs, audiotapes, computer software, and on-line services / William Kilpatrick, Gregory Wolfe, and Suzanne M. Wolfe. Published/Created: New York, NY: Simon & Schuster, c1997. Related Authors: Wolfe, Gregory. Wolfe, Suzanne M. Description: 268 p.; 22 cm. ISBN: 068481322X Notes: "A Touchstone book." Subjects: Mass media--Handbooks, manuals, etc. LC Classification: P90 .K459 1997 Dewey Class No.: 302.23 21

Klaidman, Stephen. Health in the headlines: the stories behind the stories / Stephen Klaidman. Published/Created: New York: Oxford University Press, 1991. Description: 249 p.; 22 cm. ISBN: 0195052986 (acid-free paper): Notes: Includes bibliographical references and index. Subjects: Health risk assessment--Press coverage--United States. Health risk communication--United States. Social medicine--United States. Health in mass media. LC Classification: PN4784.M4 K55 1991 Dewey Class No.: 070.4/49613 20

Koppett, Leonard. Sports illusion, sports reality: a reporter's view of sports, journalism, and society / Leonard Koppett. Published/Created: Urbana: University of Illinois Press, c1994. Description: xiv, 295 p.; 23 cm. ISBN: 0252064151 (paper: acid-free paper) Notes: Originally Published: Boston: Houghton Mifflin, 1981. With new pref. Subjects: Sports--Social aspects--United States. Sports journalism--United States. Mass media--Social aspects--Canada. Sports journalism--Canada. Mass media--Social aspects--Canada. LC Classification: GV706.5 .K67 1994 Dewey Class No.: 306.4/83/0973 20

Kovarik, Bill. Web design for the mass media / Bill Kovarik. Published/Created: Boston: Allyn and Bacon, 2002. Description: xiv, 316 p.: ill.; 24 cm. ISBN: 0801332834 (pbk.) Notes: Includes index. "Glossary and bibliogrphy are found on the book's web site"--P. ix. Subjects: Web sites--Design. Web site development. Mass media.

Kranch, Douglas A. Automated media management systems / Douglas A. Kranch. Published/Created: New York: Neal-Schuman, c1991. Description: x, 282 p.: ill.; 23 cm. ISBN: 1555700918 Notes: Includes bibliographical references (p. 275-277) and index. Subjects: Information storage and retrieval systems--Audio-visual materials. Information storage and retrieval systems--Nonbook materials. Cataloging of nonbook materials--Data processing. Audio-visual library service Data processing. Media programs

(Education)--Automation. Libraries and mass media--Automation. LC Classification: Z699.5.A9 K7 1991 Dewey Class No.: 025.3/4/0285 20

Krupin, Paul J. The U.S. all media e-mail directory: communicate via electronic mail with magazine, newspaper, tv and radio media and contacts nationwide / by Paul J. Krupin. Published/Created: Kennewick, Wash.: Direct Contact Pub., 1997. Description: 229 p.; 28 cm. ISBN: 1885035039 Notes: Includes index. Subjects: Mass media--United States--Directories. Electronic mail systems--Directories. LC Classification: P88.8 .K78 1997 Dewey Class No.: 302.23/025/73 21

Kumar, Keval J. Media education, communication, and public policy: an Indian perspective / Keval J. Kumar. Edition Information: 1st ed. Published/Created: Bombay: Himalaya Pub. House, 1995. Description: xxii, 425 p.: maps; 22 cm. ISBN: 8174931805 Notes: Includes bibliographical references (p. [297]-321). Subjects: Mass media in education--India. Communication in education--India. LC Classification: LB1043.2.I4 K86 1995 Dewey Class No.: 371.3/58 21

Kurian, George Thomas. Encyclopedia of medical media & communications / George Thomas Kurian. Published/Created: Gaithersburg, Md.: Aspen Publishers, 1996. Description: viii, 985 p.; 26 cm. ISBN: 0834206854 Notes: Includes bibliographical references and index. Subjects: Communication in medicine. Health in mass media. Medicine--Periodicals--Bibliography. LC Classification: R118 .K87 1996 Dewey Class No.: 610/.14 20

Kusanthan, T. Zambia urban sexual behaviour and condom use survey 1999 / T. Kusanthan, Keiji Suzuki. Published/Created: [Washington, D.C]: Research Dept., PSI: Lusaka: Society for Family Health, 2000. Related Authors: Suzuki, Keiji. Population Services International. Research Division. Society for Family Health (Zambia) Description: xi, 182 leaves: ill.; 30 cm. Notes: Includes bibliographical references (leaf 159). Subjects: Birth control--Zambia--Public opinion. Condoms--Zambia--Public opinion. Mass media in birth control--Zambia. Public opinion--Zambia. LC Classification: HQ766.5.Z3 K87 1999 Dewey Class No.: 363.9/6/096894 21

Lacey, Nick, 1961- Image and representation: key concepts in media studies / Nick Lacey. Published/Created: New York: St. Martin's Press, 1998. Description: x, 256 p.: ill.; 23 cm. ISBN: 031221202X (hbk.: alk. paper) 0312212038 (pbk.: alk. paper) Notes: Includes bibliographical references (p. 247-251) and index. Subjects: Mass media. Imagery (Psychology) Semiotics. Mental representation. LC Classification: P91 .L29 1998 Dewey Class No.: 302.23 21

Lacey, Nick, 1961- Media institutions and audiences: key concepts in media studies / Nick Lacey. Published/Created: New York: Palgrave, 2002. Projected Pub. Date: 0202 Description: p. cm. ISBN: 0333658698 (cloth) Notes: Includes bibliographical references and index. Subjects: Mass media. Mass media--Audiences. LC Classification: P91 .L294 2002 Dewey Class No.: 302.23 21

Lacy, Stephen, 1948- Media management: a casebook approach / Stephen Lacy, Ardyth B. Sohn, Jan LeBlanc Wicks; contributing authors, George Sylvie, Angela Powers, Nora J. Rifon. Published/Created: Hillsdale, N.J.: :L. Earlbaum Associates, 1993. Related Authors: Sohn, Ardyth Broadrick, 1946- Wicks, Jan LeBlanc. Description: xiv, 391 p.; 25 cm. ISBN: 0805806598 (cloth) 080581308X (pbk.) Notes: Includes bibliographical references (p. 372-383) and indexes. Subjects: Mass media--Management--Case studies. Series: Communication textbook series LC Classification: P96.M34 M4 1993 Dewey Class No.: 302.23/068 20

Lakoff, Robin Tolmach. The language war / Robin Tolmach Lakoff. Published/Created:

Berkeley: University of California Press, 2000. Description: x, 322 p.; 24 cm. ISBN: 0520222962 (alk. paper) Notes: Includes bibliographical references (p. 283-312) and index. Subjects: Sociolinguistics--United States. Mass media and language--United States. Power (Social sciences)--United States. United States--Languages--Political aspects. LC Classification: P40.45.U5 L35 2000 Dewey Class No.: 306.44/0973 21

Lancaster, Kent M. Strategic media planning: a complete text with integrated software / Kent M. Lancaster, Helen E. Katz. Edition Information: 2nd ed. Published/Created: Lincolnwood, Ill., USA: NTC Business Books, c1995. Projected Pub. Date: 9502 Related Authors: Katz, Helen E. Description: p. cm. ISBN: 0844235377 Notes: Includes bibliographical references and index. Subjects: Mass media--Planning--Handbooks, manuals, etc. Mass media--Planning--Software. LC Classification: P95.815 .L36 1995 Dewey Class No.: 659.1/11 20

Langley, Stephen. Jobs in arts and media management / Stephen Langley, James Abruzzo. Edition Information: 1992-1993 ed. Published/Created: New York: ACA Books: Allworth Press; Saint Paul, MN: Distributor to the trade in the U.S., Consortium Book Sales & Distribution, [1992?], c1990. Related Authors: Abruzzo, James. Description: xvi, 279 p.; 23 cm. ISBN: 0915400995: Subjects: Arts--Management--Mass media--Management--Vocational guidance--United States. LC Classification: NX765 .L36 1992 Dewey Class No.: 700/.68 20

Langley, Stephen. Jobs in arts and media management: what they are and how to get one!: / Stephen Langley, James Abruzzo. Published/Created: New York, N.Y.: ACA Books, c1990. Related Authors: Abruzzo, James. Description: xiv, 281 p.; 23 cm. ISBN: 0915400804: Subjects: Arts--Mass media--Management--Vocational guidance--United States. LC Classification: NX765 .L36 1989 Dewey Class No.: 700/.68 20

Language industries atlas / edited by P.M. Hearn and D.F. Button. Published/Created: Amsterdam; Washington: IOS Press, 1994. Related Authors: Hearn, P. M. (Paul M.) Button, D. F. (Diana F.) Description: xviii, 406 p.: ill., maps; 25 cm. ISBN: 9051991487 Notes: Includes bibliographical references and indexes. Subjects: Language services--Directories. Linguistics--Societies, etc.--Directories. Mass media--Directories. LC Classification: P40.5.L36 L36 1994 Dewey Class No.: 402/.5 21

Latin looks: images of Latinas and Latinos in the U.S. media / edited by Clara E. Rodríguez. Published/Created: Boulder, Colo.: Westview Press, 1997. Related Authors: Rodriguez, Clara E., 1944- Description: viii, 288 p.: ill.; 24 cm. ISBN: 0813327652 (alk. paper) 0813327660 (pbk.: alk. paper) Notes: Includes bibliographical references (p. 271-274) and index. Subjects: Hispanic Americans and mass media. LC Classification: P94.5.H582 U65 1997 Dewey Class No.: 305.868/073 21

Lee, Martin A. Unreliable sources: a guide to detecting bias in news media / Martin A. Lee and Norman Solomon. Published/Created: New York, NY: Carol Pub. Group, c1990. Related Authors: Solomon, Norman, 1951- Description: xiv, 419 p.: ill.; 24 cm. ISBN: 081840521X (cloth): Notes: "A Lyle Stuart book." Includes bibliographical references (p. 373-403) and index. Subjects: Journalism--Objectivity--Mass media--Objectivity--United States. LC Classification: PN4888.O25 L44 1990 Dewey Class No.: 302.23/0973 20

Lee, Mary Price. Drugs and the media / Mary Price Lee, Richard S. Lee. Edition Information: 1st ed. Published/Created: New York: Rosen Pub. Group, 1994. Related Authors: Lee, Richard S. (Richard Sandoval), 1927- Description: 64 p.: ill. (some col.); 25 cm. ISBN: 0823915379 Notes: Includes bibliographical references (p. 62) and index. Subjects: Drugs and mass media--Substance abuse--United

States--Juvenile literature. Series: The Drug abuse prevention library LC Classification: HV5825 .L434 1994 Dewey Class No.: 070.4/4936229/0973 20

Lent, John A. Bibliographic guide to Caribbean mass communication / compiled by John A. Lent. Published/Created: Westport, Conn.: Greenwood Press, 1992. Description: xi, 301 p.; 24 cm. ISBN: 0313282102 (alk. paper) Notes: Includes indexes. Subjects: Mass media--Caribbean Area--Bibliography. Series: Bibliographies and indexes in mass media and communications, 1041-8350; no. 5 LC Classification: Z5634.C37 L45 1992 P92.C33 Dewey Class No.: 016.30223/09729 20

Levinson, Paul. Digital McLuhan: a guide to the information millennium / Paul Levinson. Published/Created: New York: Routledge, 1999. Description: xiv, 226 p.; 24 cm. ISBN: 041519251X (hardcover) Notes: Includes bibliographical references (p. [204]-211) and index. Subjects: McLuhan, Marshall, 1911- Mass media. LC Classification: P90 .L413 1999 Dewey Class No.: 302.23 21

Levinson, Paul. Digital McLuhan: a guide to the information millenium / Paul Levinson. Published/Created: New York: Routledge, 2001. Projected Pub. Date: 0103 Description: p. cm. ISBN: 0415249910 Notes: Originally Published: 1999. Includes bibliographical references (p.) and index. Subjects: McLuhan, Marshall, 1911- Mass media. LC Classification: P90 .L413 2001 Dewey Class No.: 302.23 21

Linsky, Marty. The view from the top: conversations with 14 people who will be running journalism organizations into the 21st century / by Marty Linsky. Published/Created: St. Petersburg, Fla.: Poynter Institute for Media Studies, 1997. Description: 44 p.: ill.; 23 cm. Subjects: Mass media--United States--Management. Series: The Poynter papers; no. 10 LC Classification: P96.M342 U65 1997 Dewey Class No.: 070.4/068 21

Lipschultz, Jeremy Harris, 1958- Free expression in the age of the Internet: social and legal boundaries / Jeremy Harris Lipschultz. Published/Created: Boulder, Colo.: Westview Press, 2000. Description: xv, 331 p.: ill.; 24 cm. ISBN: 0813391083 (hc: alk. paper) 081339113X (pbk.: alk. paper) Notes: Includes bibliographical references (p. 309-319) and index. Subjects: Freedom of speech--United States. Internet. Mass media--Social aspects. LC Classification: KF4772 .L57 2000 Dewey Class No.: 342.73/0853 21

Living in the information age: a new media reader / edited by Erik P. Bucy. Published/Created: Belmont, CA: Wadsworth Thomson Learning, 2001. Projected Pub. Date: 1111 Related Authors: Bucy, E. Page, 1963- Description: p. cm. ISBN: 0534590497 (pbk.) Notes: Includes bibliographical references and index. Subjects: Mass media. Information society. Series: Wadsworth series in mass communication and journalism LC Classification: P91.25 .L58 2001 Dewey Class No.: 302.23 21

Logan, Robert A. Social responsibility and science news: four case studies / Robert A. Logan with Lillie M. Fears and Nancy Fraser Wilson. Published/Created: Washington, D.C.: Media Institute, c1997. Related Authors: Fears, Lillie M. Wilson, Nancy Fraser. Media Institute (Washington, D.C.) Description: vi, 248 p.; 28 cm. ISBN: 0937790532 Notes: Includes bibliographical references (p. 235-248). Subjects: Journalistic ethics--Case studies. Science news--Case studies. Mass media--Social aspects--Case studies. LC Classification: PN4756 .L64 1997 Dewey Class No.: 174/.9097 21

Low, Linda. Economics of information technology and the media / Linda Low. Published/Created: Singapore; New Jersey: World Scientific; Singapore: Singapore University Press, National University of Singapore, c2000. Description: xvii, 335 p.: ill.; 22 cm. ISBN: 9810238444 (pbk.) 9810238436 (hard) Notes: Includes bibliographical references (p. 317-332) and index. Subjects: Information technology--Mass media--Economic aspects. LC Classification: HC79.I55 L68 2000

Lowe, Barry. Media mythologies / Barry Lowe. Published/Created: Sydney, NSW: University of New South Wales Press, 1995. Description: 165 p.; 22 cm. ISBN: 0868400068 Notes: Includes bibliographical references (p. 157-162) and index. Subjects: Mass media--Social aspects--Australia. LC Classification: P91 .L68 1995 Dewey Class No.: 302.23 20

Lowenstein, Ralph Lynn, 1930- Macromedia--mission, message, and morality / Ralph L. Lowenstein, John C. Merrill. Published/Created: New York: Longman, c1990. Related Authors: Merrill, John Calhoun, 1924- Description: x, 309 p.; 23 cm. ISBN: 0801304717 Notes: Includes bibliographical references (p. 185-298) and index. Subjects: Mass media. LC Classification: P90 .L69 1990 Dewey Class No.: 302.23 20

Lowery, Shearon. Milestones in mass communication research: media effects / Shearon A. Lowery, Melvin L. DeFleur. Edition Information: 3rd ed. Published/Created: White Plains, N.Y.: Longman Publishers USA, c1995. Related Authors: DeFleur, Melvin L. (Melvin Lawrence), 1923- Description: xv, 415 p.: ill.; 24 cm. ISBN: 0801314372 Notes: Includes bibliographical references and index. Subjects: Mass media. Mass society. LC Classification: HM258 .L68 1995 Dewey Class No.: 302.23 20

Luhmann, Niklas. The reality of the mass media / Niklas Luhmann; translated by Kathleen Cross. Published/Created: Stanford, Calif.: Stanford University Press, 2000. Description: 154 p.; 24 cm. ISBN: 0804740763 0804740771 (pbk.) Notes: "First Published in German as Die Realität der Massenmedien, Westdeutscher Verlag, 1996 (second, enlarged edition)"--T.p. verso. Includes bibliographical references (p. [123]-149) and index. Subjects: Mass media--Communication--Social aspects. Mass media--Audiences. Series: Cultural memory in the present LC Classification: HM1206 .L8513 2000 Dewey Class No.: 302.23 21

Lyle, Jack. Communication, media, and change / Jack Lyle, Douglas B. McLeod. Published/Created: Mountain View, Calif.: Mayfield Pub. Co., c1993. Related Authors: McLeod, Douglas B. (Douglas Birmingham), 1958- Description: xix, 264 p.: ill.; 24 cm. ISBN: 0874849357 Notes: Includes bibliographical references (p. 252-257) and index. Subjects: Communication--Mass media--Technological innovations. LC Classification: P96.T42 L95 1993 Dewey Class No.: 302.2 20

Maddoux, Marlin. Free speech or propaganda?: how the media distorts the truth / Marlin Maddoux. Published/Created: Nashville: T. Nelson, c1990. Description: 224 p.; 21 cm. ISBN: 0840772386 Notes: Includes bibliographical references (p. 223-224). Subjects: Journalism--Mass media--Objectivity--United States. LC Classification: PN4888.O25 M34 1990 Dewey Class No.: 071/.3 20

Making the local news: local journalism in context / edited by Bob Franklin and David Murphy. Published/Created: London; New York: Routledge, 1998. Related Authors: Franklin, Bob, 1949- Murphy, David. Description: xi, 273 p.; 25 cm. ISBN: 0415168023 (alk. paper) 0415168031 (pbk.: alk. paper) Notes: Includes bibliographical references and index. Subjects: Journalism—History--Journalism, Regional--Local mass media--Great Britain. LC Classification: PN5124.L65 M36 1998 Dewey Class No.: 072 21

Malawi. Board of Censors. Guidelines to censorship / Board of Censors. Edition Information: Rev. [ed.]. Published/Created: Limbe [Malawi]: The Board, [1991] Description: 8 p.; 21 cm. Notes: "January, 1991"--Foreword. Subjects: Mass media--Censorship--Malawi. LC Classification: P96.C42 M316 1991

Managing in the media / Peter Block ... [et al.]. Published/Created: Boston, MA: Focal Press, 2001. Projected Pub. Date: 0102 Related Authors: Block, Peter. Description: p. cm. ISBN: 0240515994 (alk. paper) Notes: Includes bibliographical references and index. Subjects: Mass media--Management. Mass media--Great Britain--Management. LC Classification: P96.M34 M36 2001 Dewey Class No.: 302.23/068 21

Maney, Kevin, 1960- Megamedia shakeout: the inside story of the leaders and the losers in the exploding communications industry / Kevin Maney. Published/Created: New York: J. Wiley, c1995. Description: ix, 358 p.: ill.; 25 cm. ISBN: 0471107190 (acid-free paper) Subjects: Mass media--United States--Finance. Mass media--Technological innovations. Corporations, American. LC Classification: P96.E252 U648 1995 Dewey Class No.: 338.4/730223/0973 20

Manovich, Lev. The language of new media / Lev Manovich. Edition Information: 1st MIT Press pbk. ed. Published/Created: Cambridge, Mass.: MIT Press, 2002. Description: xxxix, 354 p.: ill.; 23 cm. ISBN: 0262133741 (hc.: alk. paper) Notes: Includes bibliographical references and index. Subjects: Mass media--Technological innovations. Series: Leonardo (Series) (Cambridge, Mass.) Variant Series: Leonardo LC Classification: P96.T42 M35 2000 Dewey Class No.: 302.2 21

Marconi, Joe. Image marketing: using public perceptions to attain business objectives / Joe Marconi. Published/Created: Lincolnwood, Ill., USA: NTC Business Books; Chicago, Ill.: American Marketing Association, c1996. Description: xviii, 232 p.: ill.; 24 cm. ISBN: 0844235040 (alk. paper) Notes: Includes bibliographical references (p. 217-219) and index. Subjects: Corporate image. Advocacy advertising. Public relations. Mass media and business. LC Classification: HD59.2 .M37 1996 Dewey Class No.: 659.2 20

Margaret Gee's Australian media guide Published/Created: Melbourne: Information Australia/Margaret Gee Media, 1991- Related Authors: Gee, Margaret, 1954- Description: v.: maps; 27 cm. 36th ed. (Mar./July 1991)- Current Frequency: Three no. a year Continues: Margaret Gee's media guide (OCoLC)37170839 ISSN: 1036-9201 Additional Form Avail.: Also available on CD-ROM. Subjects: Mass media--Australia--Directories. LC Classification: P88.8 .M357

Marketer's guide to media. Published/Created: New York, NY: Adweek, Inc., c1992- Description: v.; 22 cm. Vol. 15, no. 1 (spring/summer 1992)- Current Frequency: Annual, <1997-98- Former Frequency: Semiannual, 1992-<1994 Continues: Mediaweek's guide to media 1057-1280 (DLC) 93646375 (OCoLC)23763994 ISSN: 1061-7159 Cancel/Invalid LCCN: sn 92003174 Notes: Title from cover. SERBIB/SERLOC merged record Subjects: Advertising media planning--United States--Periodicals. Advertising--United States--Costs--Periodicals. Advertising--United States--Rates--Periodicals. Mass media--United States--Periodicals. LC Classification: HF5826.5 .M45 Dewey Class No.: 338.4/76591/097305 20

Marmo, Michael. More profile than courage: the New York City transit strike of 1966 / Michael Marmo. Published/Created: Albany: State University of New York, c1990. Description: ix, 333 p.: ill.; 24 cm. ISBN: 0791402614 0791402622 (pbk.) Notes: Includes index. Bibliography: p. 281-326. Subjects: Transport Workers' Strike, New York, N.Y., 1966. Strikes and lockouts--Transport workers--New York (State) New York--History--20th century. Collective bargaining--Effect of mass media on--New York (State)--New York. Series: SUNY series in American labor history LC Classification: HD5325.T72 1966 .N48 1990 Dewey Class No.: 331.89/2813884/09747109046 20

Marsh, Harry D. Creating tomorrow's mass media / Harry Marsh. Published/Created: Fort Worth, Tex.: Harcourt Brace College Publishers, c1995. Description: x, 181 p.: ill.; 24 cm. ISBN: 0155019481 (pbk.) Notes: Includes bibliographical references and index. Subjects: Mass media--United States. Mass media--United States--Technological innovations. Mass media and technology--United States. LC Classification: HN90.M3 M36 1995 Dewey Class No.: 302.23 20

Masindo's Indonesian media guide. Published/Created: Jakarta: Citra Buana Masindo; Singapore: Gold Group Asia/Pacific, c2000- Related Authors: Citra Buana Masindo, PT. Gold Group Asia/Pacific Ltd. Description: v.: ill.; 28 cm. Ed. 1 (2000)- Subjects: Mass media--Indonesia--Directories LC Classification: P88.8 .M365

Mass communication & society. Published/Created: Mahwah, NJ: Lawrence Erlbaum Associates, c1998- Related Authors: Association for Education in Journalism and Mass Communication. Mass Communications and Society Division. Description: v.; 23 cm. Some issues combined. Vol. 1, no. 1/2 (winter/spring 1998)- Current Frequency: Two to 4 times a year Continues: Mass comm review 0193-7707 (DLC) 94660546 (OCoLC)3489331 ISSN: 1520-5436 Cancel/Invalid LCCN: sn 98000824 Notes: Title from cover. Official journal of the Mass Communication & Society Division of the Association for Education in Journalism and Mass Communication. SERBIB/SERLOC merged record Additional Form Avail.: Also available via World Wide Web; OCLC FirstSearch Electronic Collections Online; Subscription required for access to abstracts and full text. Subjects: Mass media--Communication--Journalism--Social aspects--Periodicals. Mass media and culture--Communication and culture--Periodicals. LC Classification: P95.54 M37 Dewey Class No.: 302.23/05 21

Mass communication and public health: complexities and conflicts / Charles Atkin, Lawrence Wallack, editors. Published/Created: Newbury Park: Sage Publications, c1990. Related Authors: Atkin, Charles K. Wallack, Lawrence Marshall. Description: 198 p.; 23 cm. ISBN: 0803939248 (C) 0803939256 (P) Notes: Includes bibliographical references (p. 182-191) and index. Subjects: Mass media in health education. Variant Series: Sage focus editions; v. 121 LC Classification: RA440.5 .M37 1990 Dewey Class No.: 362.1/014 20

Mass communication research methods / Anders Hansen ... [et al.]. Published/Created: New York: New York University Press, 1998. Related Authors: Hansen, Anders. Description: viii, 350 p.; 23 cm. ISBN: 0814735711 (clothbound) 081473572X (paperback) Notes: Includes bibliographical references (p. 320-331) and index. Subjects: Mass media--Research--Methodology. LC Classification: P91.3 .M366 1998 Dewey Class No.: 302.23/07/2 21

Mass communication research: on problems and policies: the art of asking the right questions: in honor of James D. Halloran / edited by Cees J. Hamelink, Olga Linné. Published/Created: Norwood, N.J.: Ablex Pub. Corp., c1994. Related Authors: Hamelink, Cees J., 1940- Linné, Olga, 1941- Halloran, James D. (James Dermot) Description: xviii, 417 p.: ill.; 34 cm. ISBN: 0893917389 0893919519 (pbk.) Notes: Publications by James D. Halloran: p. 399-406. Includes bibliographical references and indexes. Subjects: Mass media--Research. LC Classification: P91.3 .M367 1994 Dewey Class No.: 302.23 20

Mass communication: concepts and essays / edited by Bassey Bassey Daniel. Published/Created: Calabar, Nigeria: Wusen Press, c1997. Related Authors: Daniel, Bassey Bassey. Description: viii, 225 p.: ill.; 21 cm. ISBN: 978228632X Notes: Includes bibliographical references (p. 188 215) and indexes. Subjects: Mass media. Mass media--Nigeria. LC

Classification: P90 .M287 1997 Dewey Class No.: 302.23 21

Mass communication: issues and perspectives / edited by Robert Abelman, Robin Ross. Edition Information: 2nd ed. Published/Created: Needham Heights, MA: Ginn Press, c1992. Related Authors: Abelman, Robert. Ross, Robin. Description: xiv, 340 p.; 28 cm. ISBN: 0536581827 Subjects: Mass media. LC Classification: P90 .M165 1992 Dewey Class No.: 302.23 20

Mass communications research resources: an annotated guide / edited by Christopher H. Sterling, James K. Bracken, and Susan M. Hill; with contributions from Louise Benjamin ... [et al.]. Published/Created: Mahwah, N.J.: Erlbaum, 1998. Related Authors: Sterling, Christopher H., 1943- Bracken, James K., 1952- Hill, Susan M. Description: xv, 208 p.; 24 cm. ISBN: 0805820248 (alk. paper) Notes: Includes bibliographical references and index. Subjects: Telecommunication--Bibliography. Mass media--Bibliography. Series: LEA's communication series LC Classification: Z7164.T28 M37 1998 HE7631 Dewey Class No.: 016.384 21

Mass media & society / Alan Wells, Ernest A. Hakanen, editors. Published/Created: Greenwich, Conn.: Ablex Pub. Corp., c1997. Related Authors: Wells, Alan, 1940- Hakanen, Ernest A. Description: xii, 613 p.: ill.; 24 cm. ISBN: 1567502881 (cloth) 156750289X (paper) Notes: Includes bibliographical references and indexes. Subjects: Mass media--Social aspects--United States. Mass media--United States. Series: Contemporary studies in communication, culture & information. Variant Series: Contemporary studies in communication, culture & information series LC Classification: HM258 .M26578 1997 Dewey Class No.: 302.23 20

Mass media and health: opportunities for improving the nation's health: a report to the Office of Disease Prevention and Health Promotion and Office for Substance Abuse Prevention. Published/Created: [Washington, D.C.]: U.S. Dept. of Health and Human Services, Public Health Service, Office of Disease Prevention and Health Promotion, [1991] Related Authors: United States. Office of Disease Prevention and Health Promotion. Description: xiv, 56 p.; 23 cm. Notes: Shipping list no.: 91-394-P. Item 485-B "Spring 1991." Includes bibliographical references (p. 56). Subjects: Mass media in health education--United States. Health education--United States. Health promotion--United States. Mass media--United States. Health Policy--United States. Series: Monograph series (United States. Office of Disease Prevention and Health Promotion) Variant Series: Monograph series LC Classification: RA440.5 .M4 1991 Dewey Class No.: 362.1 20 Govt. Doc. No.: HE 20.34:M 38

Mass media and rural development in Nigeria: proceedings of a national seminar organised by the Directorate of Food, Roads, and Rural Infrastructures, the Presidency, Lagos / edited by E.O. Akeredolu-Ale. Published/Created: Ibadan: Spectrum Books, 1993. Related Authors: Akeredolu-Ale, E. O. Lagos State (Nigeria). Directorate of Food, Roads and Rural Infrastructures. Description: ix, 270 p.: ill.; 25 cm. ISBN: 9782462268 Notes: Includes bibliographical references and index. Subjects: Rural development--Nigeria--Congresses. Mass media and community development--Nigeria--Congresses. LC Classification: HN831.Z9 C655 1993

Mass media in 2025: industries, organizations, people, and nations / edited by Erwin K. Thomas and Brown H. Carpenter. Published/Created: Westport, Conn.: Greenwood Press, 2001. Related Authors: Thomas, Erwin Kenneth. Carpenter, Brown H. Description: vi, 202 p.; 24 cm. ISBN: 0313313989 (alk. paper) Notes: Includes bibliographical references (p. [191]-194) and index. Subjects: Mass media--Forecasting. Series: Contributions to the study of mass media and communications, 0732-4456; no. 62 LC

Classification: P96.F67 M37 2001 Dewey Class No.: 302.23/01/12 21

Mass media in the information age / Thomas M. Pasqua ... [et al.]. Published/Created: Englewood Cliffs, N.J.: Prentice Hall, [1990] Projected Pub. Date: 1111 Related Authors: Pasqua, Thomas M. Description: p. cm. ISBN: 0135603927 Notes: Includes index. Subjects: Mass media. LC Classification: P90 .M295 1990 Dewey Class No.: 302.23 20

Mass media issues / compiled & edited by George Rodman. Edition Information: 4th ed. Published/Created: Dubuque, Iowa: Kendall/Hunt Pub. Co., c1993. Related Authors: Rodman, George R., 1948- Description: xiv, 514 p.: ill.; 23 cm. ISBN: 0840367570 Notes: Includes bibliographical references and index. Subjects: Mass media--United States. LC Classification: P92.U5 M29 1993 Dewey Class No.: 302.23/0973 20

Mass media issues: analysis and debate / compiled and edited by Denis Mercier. Edition Information: 5th ed. Published/Created: Dubuque, Iowa: Kendall/Hunt Pub. Co., c1996. Related Authors: Mercier, Denis. Description: xvi, 491 p.: ill.; 24 cm. ISBN: 0787205079 Notes: Includes bibliographies and index. Subjects: Mass media--United States. LC Classification: P92.U5 M29 1996 Dewey Class No.: 302.23/0973 20

Mass media writing: an introduction / Gail Baker-Woods ... [et al.]. Published/Created: Scottsdale, Ariz.: Gorsuch Scarisbrick, c1997. Related Authors: Baker-Woods, Gail. Description: xvii, 350 p.: ill.; 24 cm. ISBN: 0897874250 (alk. paper) Notes: Includes bibliographical references (p. 339-340) and index. Subjects: Mass media--Authorship. Report writing. LC Classification: P96.A86 M36 1997 Dewey Class No.: 808/.066302 20

Mass media, social control, and social change: a macrosocial perspective / edited by David Demers and K. Viswanath. Edition Information: 1st ed. Published/Created: Ames: Iowa State University Press, 1999. Related Authors: Demers, David P. Viswanath, K. (Kasisomayajula) Description: xiii, 454 p.: ill.; 24 cm. ISBN: 0813826829 (acid-free paper) Notes: Includes bibliographical references and index. Subjects: Social change. Mass media--Influence. Social control. Mass media--Social aspects. LC Classification: HM101 .M336 1999 Dewey Class No.: 302.23 21

Mass media. Published/Created: Guilford, Conn.: Dushkin Pub. Group., c1994- Description: v.: ill.; 28 cm. 1st ed. (94/95)- Current Frequency: Annual ISSN: 1092-0439 Notes: SERBIB/SERLOC merged record Subjects: Mass media--United States--Periodicals. Series: Annual editions LC Classification: P92.U5 M275 Dewey Class No.: 302.23/0973/04 20

Mass media: opposing viewpoints / Byron L. Stay, book ed. Published/Created: San Diego, Calif.: Greenhaven Press, c1999. Related Authors: Stay, Byron L., 1947- Description: 203 p.: ill.; 22 cm. ISBN: 0737700556 (lib. bdg.: alk. paper) 0737700548 (pbk.: alk. paper) Notes: Includes bibliographical references (p. 195-197) and index. Subjects: Mass media. Series: Opposing viewpoints series (Unnumbered) Variant Series: Opposing viewpoints series LC Classification: P90 .M2926 1999 Dewey Class No.: 302.23 21

Mass media: opposing viewpoints / William Barbour, book editor. Published/Created: San Diego, CA: Greenhaven Press, c1994. Related Authors: Barbour, William, 1963- Description: 306 p.: ill.; 23 cm. ISBN: 1565101073 (lib. bdg.: alk. paper): 1565101065 (pbk.: alk. paper): Notes: Includes bibliographical references (p. 296-299) and index. Subjects: Mass media. Series: Opposing viewpoints series (Unnumbered) Variant Series: Opposing viewpoints series LC Classification: P91.25 .M27 1994 Dewey Class No.: 302.23 20

Mattelart, Armand. Rethinking media theory: signposts and new directions / Armand Mattelart + Michèle Mattelart; translated by James A. Cohen and Marina Urquidi. Published/Created: Minneapolis: University of Minnesota Press, c1992. Related Authors: Mattelart, Michèle. Description: xii, 219 p.; 23 cm. ISBN: 0816619085 (hc: acid-free paper) 0816619107 (pb: acid-free paper) Notes: Translation of: Penser les médias. Includes bibliographical references (p. 193-209) and index. Subjects: Communication. Mass media. Series: Media & society; 5 LC Classification: P90 .M34413 1992 Dewey Class No.: 302.2 20

Maxwell, Elisabeth, 1921- A mind of my own: my life with Robert Maxwell / Elisabeth Maxwell. Edition Information: 1st ed. Published/Created: New York: HarperCollins, c1994. Description: xiii, 536 p.: ill.; 25 cm. ISBN: 0060171049: Subjects: Maxwell, Elisabeth, 1921- Maxwell, Robert, 1923- Publishers' spouses--Great Britain--Biography. Publishers and publishing--Great Britain--Biography. Newspaper publishing--Great Britain--History--20th century. Politicians--Great Britain--Biography. Mass media--Great Britain--History--20th century. LC Classification: Z325.M392 A3 1994 Dewey Class No.: 070.5/092 B 20

Mayeux, Peter E. Writing for the electronic media / Peter E. Mayeux. Edition Information: 2nd, [rev.] ed. Published/Created: Madison, Wis.: Brown & Benchmark Publishers, c1994. Related Authors: Mayeux, Peter E. Writing for the broadcast media. Description: xiv, 449 p.: ill.; 24 cm. ISBN: 0697143996 Notes: Rev. ed. of: Writing for the broadcast media. 1985. Includes bibliographical references (p. 417-422) and index. Subjects: Broadcasting--Authorship. Mass media--Authorship. Report writing. LC Classification: PN1990.9.A88 M39 1994 Dewey Class No.: 808/.066791 20

Mbozi, Parkie Shakantu. The study of the impact of the HIV/AIDS billboards on knowledge of and attidutes [sic] about HIV/AIDS among urban student[s] in Zambia / Parkie Shakantu Mbozi. Published/Created: Lusaka: Study Fund, Social Recovery Project, [1997]. Description: ix, 75 leaves: ill., maps; 30 cm. Notes: Cover title. "January 1997." Includes bibliographical references (leaves 41-[43]). Subjects: AIDS (Disease)--Zambia--Prevention. AIDS (Disease)--Zambia--Public opinion. Mass media in health education--Zambia. Series: Serial (World Bank. Social Recovery Fund. Study Fund Committee); no. 33. Variant Series: Serial; no. 33 LC Classification: RA643.86.Z33 M36 1997 Dewey Class No.: 362.1/969792/0096894 21

McAdams, Katherine C. Reaching audiences: a guide to media writing / Katherine C. McAdams, Jan Johnson Elliott. Published/Created: Boston: Allyn and Bacon, c1996. Related Authors: Yopp, Jan Johnson. Description: xii, 383 p.; 23 cm. ISBN: 0023783516 Notes: Includes bibliographical references and index. Subjects: Mass media--Authorship. Mass media--Audiences. Report writing. LC Classification: P96.A86 M38 1996 Dewey Class No.: 808/.066302 20

McCullagh, Ciaran. Media power: a sociological introduction / Ciaran McCullagh; consultant editor, Jo Campling. Published/Created: New York: Palgrave, 2002. Projected Pub. Date: 0206 Related Authors: Campling, Jo. Description: p. cm. ISBN: 0333643402 0333643410 (pbk.) Notes: Includes bibliographical references and index. Subjects: Mass media--Social aspects. LC Classification: HM1206 .M38 2002 Dewey Class No.: 302.23 21

McKean, David. Media coverage of the drug crisis: a report from the forum held on April 1, 1992 at the Annenberg Washington Program / by David McKean. Published/Created: Washington, D.C.: Annenberg Washington Program, c1992. Related Authors: Northwestern University (Evanston, Ill.). Annenberg Washington Program in Communications Policy Studies. Description: 15 p.; 28 cm. Notes:

Includes bibliographical references. Subjects: Drugs and mass media--United States--Congresses. Drug abuse--United States--Congresses. LC Classification: HV5825 .M365 1992

McKeone, Dermot H. Measuring your media profile / Dermot McKeone. Published/Created: Aldershot, Hampshire, England; Brookfield, Vt.: Gower, c1995. Description: xiii, 235 p.: ill.; 24 cm. ISBN: 0566075784 Notes: Includes bibliographical references (p. 227) and index. Subjects: Mass media--Methodology. Mass media criticism. Public relations. LC Classification: P91 .M374 1995 Dewey Class No.: 302.23/01 20

McLoughlin, Linda, 1957- The language of magazines / Linda McLoughlin. Published/Created: London; New York: Routledge, 2000. Description: xii, 115 p.: ill.; 25 cm. ISBN: 0415214246 (alk. paper) Notes: Includes bibliographical references (p. 114-115) and index. Subjects: Mass media and language. Periodicals. Discourse analysis. Series: Intertext (London, England) Variant Series: Intertext LC Classification: P96.L34 M367 2000 Dewey Class No.: 302.23/01/4 21

McLuhan, Marshall, 1911- The medium is the massage: an inventory of effects / Marshall McLuhan, Quentin Fiore; produced by Jerome Agel. Published/Created: San Francisco, CA: HardWired, c1996. Related Authors: Fiore, Quentin. Agel, Jerome. Description: 159 p.: ill.; 18 cm. ISBN: 188886902X Notes: Originally Published: New York: Random House, 1967. Subjects: Mass media--History. Technology and civilization. LC Classification: P90 .M258 1996 Dewey Class No.: 302.23/09 21

McLuhan, Marshall, 1911- Understanding media: the extensions of man / Marshall McLuhan; introduction by Lewis H. Lapham. Edition Information: 1st MIT Press ed. Published/Created: Cambridge, Mass.: MIT Press, 1994. Related Titles: Extensions of man. Description: xxiii, 365 p.; 23 cm. ISBN: 0262631598: Notes: Includes bibliographical references (p. 361-365). Subjects: Mass media. Communication. Communication and technology. LC Classification: P90 .M26 1994 Dewey Class No.: 302.23 20

McLuhan, Marshall, 1911- War and peace in the global village: an inventory of some of the current spastic situations that could be eliminated by more feedforward / [by] Marshall McLuhan, Quentin Fiore; produced by Jerome Agel. Published/Created: San Francisco, CA: HardWired, [1997?], c1968. Related Authors: Fiore, Quentin. Description: 190 p.: ill.; 18 cm. ISBN: 1888869070 Subjects: Technology and civilization. War and civilization. Mass media--Social aspects. Information society. LC Classification: CB478 .M24 1997 Dewey Class No.: 303.48/3 21

McQuail, Denis. Audience analysis / Denis McQuail. Published/Created: Thousand Oaks, Calif.: Sage Publications, c1997. Description: x, 166 p.: ill.; 24 cm. ISBN: 0761910018 (cloth: acid-free paper) 0761910026 (pbk.: acid-free paper) Notes: Includes bibliographical references (p. 151-161) and index. Subjects: Mass media--Audiences. LC Classification: P96.A83 M39 1997 Dewey Class No.: 302.23 21

McQuail, Denis. Mass communication theory: an introduction / Denis McQuail. Edition Information: 3rd ed. Published/Created: London; Thousand Oaks: Sage Publications, 1994. Description: xiv, 416 p.: ill.; 24 cm. ISBN: 0803977840 Notes: Includes bibliographical references (p. [385]-407) and index. Subjects: Mass media. LC Classification: P90 .M35 1994 Dewey Class No.: 302.23 20

McQuail, Denis. McQuail's mass communication theory / [Denis McQuail]. Edition Information: 4th ed. Published/Created: London; Thousand Oaks: Sage Publications, 2000. Description: x, 542 p.: ill.; 26 cm. ISBN: 0761965467 0761965475 (pbk.) Notes: Includes bibliographical references (p.

[505]-535) and index. Subjects: Mass media. LC Classification: P90 .M35 2000 Dewey Class No.: 302.23 21

McQuail, Denis. Media performance: mass communication and the public interest / Denis McQuail. Published/Created: London; Newbury Park, Calif.: Sage Publications, 1992. Description: xvii, 350 p.: ill.; 24 cm. ISBN: 0803982941 080398295X (pbk.) Notes: Includes bibliographical references (p. [317]-345) and index. Subjects: Mass media. LC Classification: P90 .M36 1992 Dewey Class No.: 302.23 20

Meadow, Charles T. Ink into bits: a web of converging media / Charles T. Meadow. Published/Created: Lanham, Md.: Scarecrow Press, 1998. Description: xvi, 292 p.; 23 cm. ISBN: 081083507X (cloth: alk. paper) 0810835088 (pbk.: alk. paper) Notes: Includes bibliographical references (p. [259]-282) and index. Subjects: Mass media--Technological innovations. Information technology. Books and reading. LC Classification: P96.T42 M4 1998 Dewey Class No.: 302.23 21

Media & public life / edited by Everette E. Dennis & Robert W. Snyder. Published/Created: New Brunswick, N.J.: Transaction Publishers, c1997. Related Authors: Dennis, Everette E. Snyder, Robert W., 1955- Description: xv, 190 p.; 23 cm. ISBN: 1560008741 (paper: alk. paper) Notes: Originally Published as vol. 9, no. 1 of Media studies journal, Winter 1995. Includes bibliographical references (p. [183]-184) and index. Subjects: Mass media--United States. Mass media--Social aspects--United States. LC Classification: P92.U5 M39 1997 Dewey Class No.: 302.23/0973 20

Media advocacy and public health: power for prevention / Lawrence Wallack ... [et al.]; foreword by Michael Pertschuk. Published/Created: Newbury Park: Sage Publications, c1993. Related Authors: Wallack, Lawrence Marshall. Description: xiii, 226 p.; 24 cm. ISBN: 0803942885 0803942893 (pbk.) Notes: Includes bibliographical references (p. 210-217) and index. Subjects: Mass media in health education. Health promotion. LC Classification: RA440.5 .M427 1993 Dewey Class No.: 362.1/014 20

Media and communication: readings in methodology, history and culture / edited by Helge Rønning and Knut Lundby. Published/Created: Oxford; New York: Norwegian University Press, c1991. Related Authors: Rønning, Helge. Lundby, Knut. Description: 382 p.: ill.; 24 cm. ISBN: 8200213528: 8200213536 (pbk.) Notes: Includes bibliographical references (p. [361]-374) and index. Subjects: Mass media. Communication. LC Classification: P90 .M366 1991 Dewey Class No.: 302.23 20

Media and Environment Workshop: Harare, August 3-8, 1992. input by Musa Zondi. Published/Created: [Harare?: s.n., 1992?] Related Authors: Zondi, Musa. Description: 1 v. (various pagings); 30 cm. Notes: "Input by Musa Zondi." Subjects: Mass media and the environment--Congresses. LC Classification: P96.E57 M44 1992

Media and market forces: challanges and opportunities: proceedings of the regional seminars and national colloquium / edited by V.S. Gupta, Rajeshwar Dyal. Published/Created: Published for AMIC, Friedrich Ebert Stiftung by Concept Pub. Co., 1997. Related Authors: Gupta, V. S. Dyal, Rajeshwar. Asian Mass Communication Research and Information Centre. Friedrich-Ebert-Stiftung. Description: 266 p.; 22 cm. ISBN: 8170226988 Summary: Contributed research papers of various seminars organized by Asian Mass Communication Research and Information Centre and Friedrich-Ebert-Stiftung. Notes: Includes bibliographical references and index. Subjects: Mass media--Communication--Social aspects--Telecommunications--India--Congresses. LC Classification: P92.I7 M395 1997 Dewey Class No.: 302.23/0954 21

Media and mental health / Glasgow Media Group; edited by Greg Philo. Published/Created: London; New York: Longman, 1996. Related Authors: Philo, Greg. Glasgow University Media Group. Description: xv, 135 p.; 24 cm. ISBN: 0582292190 (alk. paper) Notes: Includes bibliographical references (p. 115-118) and index. Subjects: Mental illness in mass media. Mass media--Social aspects. LC Classification: P96.M45 M43 1996 Dewey Class No.: 362.2 20

Media courses UK. Published/Created: London: British Film Institute, 1993- Related Authors: British Film Institute. Description: v.; 20 x 21 cm. 1993- Current Frequency: Annual Notes: SERBIB/SERLOC merged record Subjects: Mass media--Study and teaching--Great Britain Directories. Universities and colleges--Great Britain--Curricula Directories. LC Classification: P91.5.G7 M43

Media economics: theory and practice / edited by Alison Alexander, James Owers, and Rod Carveth. Published/Created: Hillsdale, N.J.: L. Erlbaum Associates, 1993. Related Authors: Alexander, Alison. Owers, James. Carveth, Rod. Description: xii, 391 p.; 25 cm. ISBN: 080580434X (c) 0805813071 (p) Notes: Includes bibliographical references and indexes. Subjects: Mass media--Economic aspects. LC Classification: P96.E25 M4 1993 Dewey Class No.: 338.4/730223 20

Media economics: theory and practice / edited by Alison Alexander, James Owers, Rodney Carveth. Edition Information: 2nd ed. Published/Created: Mahwah, N.J.: L. Erlbaum Associates, 1998. Related Authors: Alexander, Alison. Owers, James. Carveth, Rod. Description: ix, 304 p.; 23 cm. ISBN: 0805818421 (paper: alk. paper) Notes: Includes bibliographical references and indexes. Subjects: Mass media--Economic aspects. LC Classification: P96.E25 M4 1998 Dewey Class No.: 338.4/730223 21

Media firms: structures, operations, and performance / Robert G. Picard, editor. Published/Created: Mahwah, N.J.: Erlbaum, 2002. Projected Pub. Date: 0205 Related Authors: Picard, Robert G. Description: p. cm. ISBN: 0805841652 (alk. paper) Notes: Conference held May 2002. Includes bibliographical references and index. Subjects: Mass media--Economic aspects--Congresses. Corporations--Congresses. LC Classification: P96.E25 W67 2002 Dewey Class No.: 338.4/730223 21

Media Seminar on Health for All through Primary Health Care: report: convened by the Regional Office for the Western Pacific of the World Health Organization, Harbin City, Heilongjiang Province, People's Republic of China, 29 August-4 September 1989. Published/Created: Manila, Philippines: The Office, [1990] Related Authors: World Health Organization. Regional Office for the Western Pacific. Description: 106 p.: ill., maps, port.; 29 cm. Notes: "(WP)P10/ICP/IEH/002-E." "English only." "January 1990." Subjects: Public health--Congresses. Mass media in health education--Congresses. Primary Health Care--congresses Public Relations--congresses Mass Media--congresses LC Classification: MLCM 93/04969 (R)

Media texts, authors and readers: a reader / edited by David Graddol and Oliver Boyd-Barrett. Published/Created: Clevedon, England; Philadelphia: Multilingual Matters in association with The Open University, c1994. Related Authors: Graddol, David. Boyd-Barrett, Oliver. Description: xiii, 282 p.: ill.; 25 cm. ISBN: 185359220X: 1853592196 (pbk.): Notes: "Language and literacy in social context." Includes bibliographical references and index. Subjects: Mass media and language. Discourse analysis. Mass media--Authorship. Mass media--Audiences. LC Classification: P96.L34 M38 1994 Dewey Class No.: 302.2 20

Media/reader: perspectives on mass media industries, effects, and issues / [edited by] Shirley Biagi. Edition Information: 2nd ed.

Published/Created: Belmont, Calif.: Wadsworth Pub. Co.: c1993. Related Authors: Biagi, Shirley. Description: xvi, 340 p.: ill.; 24 cm. ISBN: 0534190863 (alk. paper) Notes: Includes index. LC Classification: P91.25 .M374 1993 Dewey Class No.: 302.23 20

Mehta, D. S. (Dalpat Singh), 1924- Mass communication and journalism in India / D.S. Mehta. Edition Information: Rev. and enl. ed. Published/Created: New Delhi: Allied Publishers, 1992. Description: xix, 403 p.; 22 cm. ISBN: 8170233534: Notes: Includes index. Includes bibliographical references (p. [369]-396). Subjects: Mass media--Journalism--India. LC Classification: P92.I7 M47 1992 Dewey Class No.: 302.23/0954 20

Mencher, Melvin. Basic media writing / Melvin Mencher. Edition Information: 6th ed. Published/Created: Boston: McGraw-Hill College, c1999. Description: xvi, 512 p.: ill.; 24 cm. ISBN: 0697353680 (alk. paper) Notes: Includes bibliographical references and indexes. Subjects: Journalism--Style manuals. Writing. Mass media. LC Classification: PN4783 .M4 1999 Dewey Class No.: 808/.06607 21

Mencher, Melvin. Basic media writing / Melvin Mencher. Edition Information: 5th ed. Published/Created: Madison [Wis.]: Brown & Benchmark, c1996. Description: xviii, 488 p.: ill.; 24 cm. ISBN: 0697270017 Notes: Includes bibliographical references and indexes. Subjects: Journalism--Style manuals. Writing. Mass media. LC Classification: PN4783 .M4 1996 Dewey Class No.: 808/.06607 20

Mencher, Melvin. Basic media writing / Melvin Mencher. Edition Information: 4th ed. Published/Created: Madison, Wis.: Brown & Benchmark, c1993. Description: xvii, 457 p.: ill.; 24 cm. ISBN: 069708664X Notes: Includes bibliographical references and indexes. Subjects: Journalism--Style manuals. Writing. Mass media. LC Classification: PN4783 .M4 1993 Dewey Class No.: 808/.06607 20

Merrill, John Calhoun, 1924- Modern mass media / John C. Merrill, John Lee, Edward Jay Friedlander. Edition Information: 2nd ed. Published/Created: New York, NY: HarperCollins College Pub., c1994. Related Authors: Lee, John, 1931- Friedlander, Edward Jay. Description: xvii, 445 p.: ill.; 24 cm. ISBN: 0060444703 0673990257 (pbk.) Notes: Includes bibliographical references and index. LC Classification: P90 .M453 1994 Dewey Class No.: 302.23 20

Midwinter, Eric C. Out of focus: old age, the press, and broadcasting / Eric Midwinter. Published/Created: London: Centre for Policy on Ageing in association with Help the Aged, 1991. Related Authors: Help the Aged (Organization) Description: viii, 64 p.: ill.; 30 cm. ISBN: 0904139816 Notes: Includes bibliographical references. Subjects: Journalism--Great Britain--Social aspects. Aged in mass media. Aged on television. LC Classification: PN5124.S6 M53 1991 Dewey Class No.: 305.26 20

Miller, Peter G. Media power: how your business can profit from the media / Peter G. Miller. Published/Created: Dearborn: Financial Pub., c1991. Description: viii, 172 p.; 24 cm. ISBN: 0793102693: Notes: Includes index. Subjects: Industrial publicity--Mass media and business--United States. Marketing--Management. LC Classification: HD59.6.U6 M55 1991 Dewey Class No.: 659 20

Mitgang, Lee D., 1949- Big Bird and beyond: the new media and the Markle Foundation / Lee D. Mitgang. Edition Information: 1st ed. Published/Created: New York: Fordham University Press, 2000. Related Authors: John and Mary R. Markle Foundation. Description: xxii, 292 p.; 24 cm. ISBN: 0823220400 0823220419 (pbk.) Notes: Includes bibliographical references (p. [273]-279) and index. Subjects: John and Mary R. Markle Foundation--History. Mass media--Research--United States--History. LC Classification: P87 .M55 2000 Dewey Class No.: 384.55/06/573 21

Moffitt, Mary Anne, 1944- Campaign strategies and message design: a practitioner's guide from start to finish / Mary Anne Moffitt. Published/Created: Westport, Conn.: Praeger, 1999. Description: xi, 207 p.: ill.; 25 cm. Use/Repro. Advisory: Includes bibliographical references (p. [201]-203) and index. ISBN: 0275955923 (acid-free paper) 0275964701 (pbk.: acid-free paper) Subjects: Publicity. Mass media--Social aspects. Corporate image. LC Classification: HM263 .M54 1999 Dewey Class No.: 659 21

Mogel, Leonard. Careers in communications and entertainment / by Leonard Mogel Published/Created: Sydney; New York: Simon & Schuster, 2000. Description: vii, 374 p.: ill.; 28 cm. ISBN: 0684870177 Notes: "Over 250 detailed job descriptions; expert advice on job hunting, career planning, internships, and more; candid interviews with industry insiders"--Cover. "Kaplan Books"--T.p. verso. Includes bibliographical references. Subjects: Communication--Vocational guidance. Mass media--Vocational guidance. LC Classification: P91.6 .M59 2000 Dewey Class No.: 302.23/023 21

Moisy, Claude. The foreign news flow in the information age / by Claude Moisy. Published/Created: [Cambridge, Mass.]: Joan Shorenstein Center, Press, Politics, Public Policy, Harvard Unviersity, John F. Kennedy School of Government, c1996. Related Authors: Joan Shorenstein Center on the Press, Politics, and Public Policy. Description: 16 p.; 28 cm. Notes: Cover title. "November 1996." Includes bibliographical references (p. 16). Subjects: Foreign news--United States. Foreign news--United States--Public opinion. Journalism--Mass media--Technological innovations. Series: Discussion paper (Joan Shorenstein Center on the Press, Politics, and Public Policy); D-23. Variant Series: Discussion paper; D-23 LC Classification: PN4888.F69 M58 1996 Dewey Class No.: 070.4/332 21

Montonen, Marjatta. Alcohol and the media / by Marjatta Montonen. Published/Created: Copenhagen: World Health Organization, Regional Office for Europe, c1996. Description: iii, 165 p.; 24 cm. ISBN: 9289013265 Notes: Bibliography: p. 144-165. Subjects: Alcoholism--Prevention. Alcoholism--Study and teaching. Alcoholism in mass media. Advertising--Alcoholic beverages. Alcohol drinking. Alcoholism--Prevention and control. Mass media. Health policy. Health education. Alcoholism--Prevention. Mass media. Medical policy. Health education. Series: Publication series of the European alcohol action plan WHO regional publications. European series, 0378-2255; no. 62 LC Classification: HV5035 .M65 1996

Moore, David W. (David William), 1940- The superpollsters: how they measure and manipulate public opinion in America / David W. Moore. Edition Information: 2nd ed. Published/Created: New York: Four Walls Eight Windows, c1995. Description: xiii, 426 p.: ill.; 24 cm. ISBN: 1568580231 Notes: Includes index. Subjects: Public opinion--United States. Public opinion polls. Mass media--United States--Influence. Election forecasting--United States. LC Classification: HN90.P8 M66 1995 Dewey Class No.: 303.3/8/0973 20

Moore, David W. (David William), 1940- The superpollsters: how they measure and manipulate public opinion in America / David W. Moore. Published/Created: New York: Four Walls Eight Windows, c1992. Description: xi, 388 p.: ill.; 24 cm. ISBN: 0941423743: Notes: Includes index. Subjects: Public opinion--United States. Public opinion polls. Mass media--United States--Influence. Election forecasting--United States. LC Classification: HN90.P8 M66 1992 Dewey Class No.: 303.3/8 20

Moores, Shaun. Interpreting audiences: the ethnography of media consumption / Shaun Moores. Published/Created: London; Thousand Oaks [Calif.]: Sage, 1993. Description: 154 p.; 24 cm. ISBN: 0803984464: 0803984472 (pbk.) Notes: Includes bibliographical references (p. [141]-151) and index. Subjects: Mass media--Audiences. Mass media--Research-

-History. Mass media Audiences Series: Media, culture, and society series. Variant Series: The Media, culture & society series LC Classification: P96.A83 M66 1993 Dewey Class No.: 302.23 20

Moores, Shaun. Interpreting audiences: the ethnography of media consumption / Shaun Moores. Published/Created: London; Thousand Oaks [Calif.]: Sage, 1993. Description: 154 p.; 24 cm. ISBN: 0803984464: 0803984472 (pbk.) Notes: Includes bibliographical references (p. [141]-151) and index. Subjects: Mass media--Audiences--Research--History. Series: Media, culture, and society series. Variant Series: The Media, culture & society series LC Classification: P96.A83 M66 1993 Dewey Class No.: 302.23 20

Moores, Shaun. Media and everyday life in modern society / Shaun Moores. Published/Created: Edinburgh: Edinburgh University Press, c2000. Description: viii, 168 p.; 24 cm. ISBN: 0748611797 Notes: Includes bibliographical references (p. 151-162) and index. Subjects: Mass media--Social aspects. LC Classification: HM1206 .M65 2000 Dewey Class No.: 302.23 21

Mora, Anthony. The alchemy of success / Anthony Mora. Published/Created: New York: Dunhill Pub. Co., 1997. Projected Pub. Date: 9704 Description: p. cm. ISBN: 093501621X (pbk: alk. paper) Subjects: Advertising. Mass media. Public relations. LC Classification: HF5823 .M57 1997 Dewey Class No.: 659 21

Morley, David, 1949- Home territories: media, mobility, and identity / David Morley. Published/Created: New York: Routledge , 2000. Projected Pub. Date: 0010 Description: p. cm. ISBN: 0415157641 (alk. paper) 041515765X (pbk.: alk. paper) Notes: Includes bibliographical references and index. Subjects: Mass media--Social aspects. Population geography. Group identity. Postmodernism--Social aspects. LC Classification: HM1206 .M67 2000 Dewey Class No.: 306 21

Morris, John L. A study of attitudes toward audience interaction in journalism / John L. Morris. Published/Created: Lewiston, N.Y.: E. Mellen Press, 2002. Projected Pub. Date: 1111 Description: p. cm. ISBN: 0773473084 Notes: Includes bibliographical references and index. Subjects: Reporters and reporting--United States--Public opinion. Mass media--United States--Public opinion. Series: Mellen studies in journalism; v. 1 LC Classification: PN4867 .M67 2002 Dewey Class No.: 302.23/0973 21

Murdoch, David Hamilton, 1937- The American West: the invention of a myth / David H. Murdoch. Published/Created: Reno: University of Nevada Press, c2001. Description: xii, 136 p.; 22 cm. ISBN: 0874173698 (pbk.) Notes: Includes bibliographical references (p. [121]-129) and index. Subjects: Frontier and pioneer life--West (U.S.)--Public opinion. Myth--Social aspects--United States--History--20th century. National characteristics, American. Public opinion--United States--History--20th century. West (U.S.)--Civilization--20th century--Public opinion. West (U.S.)--In mass media. LC Classification: F595 .M94 2001 Dewey Class No.: 978/.033 21

Murray, John A., 1954- Mythmakers of the west: shaping America's imagination / by John A. Murray. Published/Created: Flagstaff, Ariz.: Northland Pub., 2001. Projected Pub. Date: 0106 Description: p. cm. ISBN: 0873587723 Notes: Includes bibliographical references and index. Subjects: Regionalism--West (U.S.) West (U.S.)--Civilization. Legends--West (U.S.) Landscape--West (U.S.) West (U.S.)--Intellectual life. West (U.S.)--In mass media. LC Classification: F591 M93 2001 Dewey Class No.: 978 21

Navarrete, Lisa. Out of the picture, Hispanics in the media / prepared by Lisa Navarrete, with Charles Kamasaki. Published/Created: Washington, D.C.: Policy Analysis Center, Office of Research Advocacy and Legislation, National Council of La Raza, c1994. Related Authors: Kamasaki,

Charles. Description: iii, 43 p.: ill.; 28 cm. Notes: Includes bibliographical references. Subjects: Hispanic Americans in mass media. Mass media--United States. Mass media--Social aspects--United States. Series: State of Hispanic America (National Council of La Raza); 1994. Variant Series: State of Hispanic America; 1994 LC Classification: E184.S75 S735 1994 P94.5.H58

Negt, Oskar. Public sphere and experience: toward an analysis of the bourgeois and proletarian public sphere / Oskar Negt and Alexander Kluge; foreword by Miriam Hansen; translated by Peter Labanyi, Jamie Owen Daniel, and Assenka Oksiloff. Published/Created: Minneapolis: University of Minnesota Press, c1993. Related Authors: Kluge, Alexander, 1932- Description: xlix, 305 p.; 24 cm. ISBN: 0816620318 (alk. paper) Notes: Includes bibliographical references and index. Subjects: Mass media--Social aspects. Public relations and politics. Social classes. Series: Theory and history of literature; v. 85 LC Classification: HM258 .N4313 1993 Dewey Class No.: 302.23 20

Neill, S. D. (Samuel D.), 1928- Clarifying McLuhan: an assessment of process and product / S.D. Neill. Published/Created: Westport, Conn.: Greenwood Press, 1993. Description: xiv, 151 p.: ill.; 25 cm. ISBN: 031328444X (alk. paper) Notes: Includes bibliographical references (p. [131]-141) and indexes. Subjects: McLuhan, Marshall, 1911- Mass media. Series: Contributions to the study of mass media and communications, 0732-4456; no. 37 LC Classification: P92.5.M3 N4 1993 Dewey Class No.: 302.23/092 20

Nelson, Joyce. Sultans of sleaze: public relations and the media / Joyce Nelson. Published/Created: Monroe, Me.: Common Courage Press, [1992], c1989. Description: 160 p.; 24 cm. ISBN: 1567510035 1567510027 (pbk.) Notes: "First Published by Between the Lines, Toronto, Ontario, Canada"--T.p. verso. Includes bibliographical references. Subjects: Mass media--Economic aspects. Public relations. Publicity. LC Classification: P96.E25 N45 1992 Dewey Class No.: 338.4/730223 20

Neuzil, Mark. Mass media & environmental conflict: America's green crusades / Mark Neuzil. Published/Created: Thousand Oaks, Calif.: Sage Publications, c1996. Related Authors: Kovarik, William. Description: xxvii, 243 p.: ill.; 24 cm. ISBN: 0761903321 (cloth) 076190333X (pbk.) Notes: Includes bibliographical references (p. 213-228) and indexes. Subjects: Mass media and the environment--United States. Mass media--Social aspects--United States. United States--Environmental conditions. United States--Social conditions--1980- LC Classification: P96.E572 U66 1996 Dewey Class No.: 363.7/00973 20

Nevitt, Barrington. Who was Marshall McLuhan?: exploring a mosaic of impressions / Barrington Nevitt, with Maurice McLuhan; editors, Frank Zingrone, Wayne Constantineau, Eric McLuhan. Published/Created: Toronto, Canada: Stoddart, 1995. Related Authors: McLuhan, Maurice. Zingrone, Frank. Constantineau, Wayne. McLuhan, Eric. Description: 323 p.; 24 cm. ISBN: 0773757686 Notes: Originally Published: Comprehensivist Publications, 1994. Includes bibliographical references (p. 299-308) and index. Subjects: McLuhan, Marshall, 1911- Mass media specialists--Canada--Biography. LC Classification: P92.5.M3 N47 1995 Dewey Class No.: 302.23/092 B 21

Newsworkers: toward a history of the rank and file / Hanno Hardt and Bonnie Brennen, editors. Published/Created: Minneapolis: University of Minnesota Press, c1995. Related Authors: Hardt, Hanno. Brennen, Bonnie. Description: xiii, 237 p.; 24 cm. ISBN: 0816627061 (hc) 081662707X (pb) Notes: Includes bibliographical references and index. Subjects: Press--Mass media--History. Press--Mass media--United States--History. Reporters and reporting--United States--History. LC Classification: PN4781 .N37 1995 Dewey Class No.: 070.9 20

Nichols, John. It's the media, stupid / John Nichols and Robert W. McChesney. Published/Created: New York: Seven Stories Press, c2000. Related Authors: McChesney, Robert Waterman, 1952- Description: 127 p.; 18 cm. ISBN: 1583220291 (pbk.) Subjects: Mass media--United States. Mass media--Social aspects. Communication, International. Series: The open media pamphlet series; 17 LC Classification: P92.U5 N53 2000 Dewey Class No.: 302.23/0973 21

Nichols, William. Media relations in sport / William Nichols ... [et al.]. Published/Created: Morgantown, WV: Fitness Information Technology, c2002. Description: xvi, 291 p.: ill.; 29 cm. ISBN: 1885693222 Notes: Includes bibliographical references (p. 279-283) and index. Subjects: Mass media and sports. Series: Sport management library LC Classification: GV742 .N53 2002 Dewey Class No.: 070.4/49796 21

Nightingale, Virginia. Studying audiences: the shock of the real / Virginia Nightingale. Published/Created: London; New York: Routledge, 1996. Description: xi, 172 p.; 24 cm. ISBN: 0415024471 0415143985 (pbk.) Notes: Includes bibliographical references (p. [153]-162) and index. Subjects: Mass media--Audiences--Research--History. Television viewers--Research--History. Mass media criticism. Mass media and culture. LC Classification: P96.A83 N54 1996 Dewey Class No.: 302.23 21

Niven, David, 1971- Tilt?: the search for media bias / David Niven. Published/Created: Westport, Conn.: Praeger, 2002. Projected Pub. Date: 0209 Description: p. cm. ISBN: 0275975770 (alk. paper) Notes: Includes bibliographical references and index. Subjects: Journalism--Objectivity--United States. Mass media--Objectivity--United States. LC Classification: PN4888.O25 N58 2002 Dewey Class No.: 071/.3 21

Noronha, Shonan F. R. Careers in communications / Shonan F.R. Noronha. Edition Information: 3rd ed. Published/Created: Lincolnwood, Chicago, Ill., U.S.A.: VGM Career Horizons, c1999. Description: xvii, 181 p.; 24 cm. ISBN: 0844263176 0844263184 (paper) Notes: Includes bibliographical references. Subjects: Communication--Vocational guidance--United States. Mass media--Vocational guidance--United States. Series: VGM professional careers series LC Classification: P91.6 .N67 1999 Dewey Class No.: 302.2/23/73 21

Noronha, Shonan F. R. Careers in communications / Shonan F.R. Noronha. Published/Created: Lincolnwood, Ill., USA: VGM Career Horizons, c1994. Description: xv, 155 p.; 25 cm. ISBN: 0844241822 0844241830 (pbk.) Notes: Includes bibliographical references. Subjects: Communication--Vocational guidance--United States. Mass media--Vocational guidance--United States. Series: VGM professional careers series LC Classification: P91.6 .N67 1994 Dewey Class No.: 302.2/023/73 20

Nuessel, Frank H. The image of older adults in the media: an annotated bibliography / Frank Nuessel. Published/Created: Westport, Conn.: Greenwood Press, c1992. Description: xxiv, 181 p.; 25 cm. ISBN: 0313280185 (alk. paper) Notes: Includes indexes. Subjects: Aged in mass media--Bibliography. Series: Bibliographies and indexes in gerontology, 0743-7560; no. 18 LC Classification: Z5633.A39 N84 1992 P94.5.A38 Dewey Class No.: 305.26 20

O'Neill, John, 1933- Plato's cave: desire, power, and the specular functions of the media / John O'Neill. Published/Created: Norwood, N.J.: Ablex Pub. Corp., c1991. Description: xi, 206 p.: ill.; 24 cm. ISBN: 0893917222 (cl) Notes: Includes bibliographical references and indexes. Subjects: Mass media. Series: Communication and information science LC Classification: P90 .O49 1991 Dewey Class No.: 302.23 20

O'Neill, John, 1933- Plato's cave: television and its discontents / John O'Neill. Edition Information: Rev. ed. Published/Created:

Cresskill, NJ: Hampton Press, 2002. Projected Pub. Date: 0202 Description: p. cm. ISBN: 1572733896 157273390X Notes: Includes bibliographical references and index. Subjects: Mass media. Television. Series: The Hampton Press communication series. Critical bodies LC Classification: P90 .O49 2002 Dewey Class No.: 302.23/45 21

Oppenheim, Frank M., 1925- Behind the bits: managing the media maze / Frank M. Oppenheim, Helen C. Swift. Published/Created: Lanham: University Press of America, c1998. Related Authors: Swift, Helen. Description: ix, 226 p.; 22 cm. ISBN: 0761811702 (pbk.: alk. paper) Notes: Includes bibliographical references (p. [195]-218) and index. Subjects: Mass media. LC Classification: P90 .O66 1998 Dewey Class No.: 302.23 21

Oriard, Michael, 1948- King Football: sport and spectacle in the golden age of radio and newsreels, movies and magazines, the weekly and the daily press / Michael Oriard. Published/Created: Chapel Hill: University of North Carolina Press, 2001. Projected Pub. Date: 1111 Description: p. cm. ISBN: 0807826502 (cloth: alk. paper) Notes: Includes bibliographical references and index. Subjects: Football--History--20th century. Mass media and sports--History--20th century. LC Classification: GV950 .O73 2001 Dewey Class No.: 796.332/09/041 21

Orlik, Peter B. Electronic media criticism: applied perspectives / Peter B. Orlik. Edition Information: 2nd ed. Published/Created: Mahwah, NJ: L. Erlbaum Associates, 2001. Description: xviii, 405 p.: ill.; 26 cm. ISBN: 0805836411 (pbk.: alk. paper) Notes: Includes bibliographical references and index. Subjects: Mass media criticism. LC Classification: P96.C76 O76 2001 Dewey Class No.: 302.23/7 21

Orlik, Peter B. Electronic media criticism: applied perspectives / Peter B. Orlik. Published/Created: Boston: Focal Press, c1994. Description: xvi, 335 p.: ill.; 26 cm. ISBN: 0240801628 (acid-free paper): Notes: Includes bibliographical references and index. Subjects: Mass media criticism. LC Classification: P96.C76 O76 1994 Dewey Class No.: 302.23 20

Orlik, Peter B. The electronic media: an introduction to the profession / Peter B. Orlik. Published/Created: Needham, Mass.: Allyn and Bacon, c1992. Description: xix, 491 p.: ill.; 24 cm. ISBN: 0205130321 Notes: Includes bibliographical references p. ([471]-480) and index. Subjects: Mass media. LC Classification: P90 .O74 1992 Dewey Class No.: 302.23 20

O'Sullivan, Tim, 1952- Studying the media: an introduction / Tim O'Sullivan, Brian Dutton, Philip Rayner. Edition Information: 2nd ed. Published/Created: London: Arnold; New York: Co- Published in the USA by Oxford University Press, c1998. Related Authors: Dutton, Brian, 1952- Rayner, Philip, 1947- Description: 384 p.: ill. (some col.); 25 cm. ISBN: 034067685X Notes: Includes bibliographical references (p. [357]-369) and index. Subjects: Mass media. LC Classification: P90 .O84 1998 Dewey Class No.: 302.23 21

O'Sullivan, Tim, 1952- Studying the media: an introduction / Tim O'Sullivan, Brian Dutton, Philip Rayner. Published/Created: London; New York, NY: Edward Arnold; New York, NY: Distributed in the USA by Routledge, Chapman, and Hall, 1994. Related Authors: Dutton, Brian, 1952- Rayner, Philip, 1947- Description: xi, 308 p.: ill.; 25 cm. ISBN: 034059828X: Notes: Includes bibliographical references (p. [297]-303) index. Subjects: Mass media. LC Classification: P90 .O84 1994 Dewey Class No.: 302.23 20

Out of bounds: sports, media, and the politics of identity / edited by Aaron Baker and Todd Boyd. Published/Created: Bloomington: Indiana University Press, c1997. Related Authors: Baker, Aaron. Boyd, Todd. Description: xviii, 206 p.: ill.; 24 cm. ISBN: 0253332281 (cl: alk. paper) 025321095X (pa: alk. paper) Notes:

Includes bibliographical references and index. Subjects: Mass media and sports--Sports--Social aspects--United States. LC Classification: GV742 .O88 1997 Dewey Class No.: 070.4/49796 20

Owen, Bruce M. The Internet challenge to television / Bruce M. Owen. Published/Created: Cambridge, Mass.: Harvard University Press, 1999. Description: xii, 372 p.: ill.; 24 cm. ISBN: 0674872991 (alk. paper) Notes: Includes bibliographical references (p. 352-365) and index. Subjects: Television broadcasting--Digital television--Economic aspects--Digital video--Economic aspects--Telecommunication--United States--Forecasting. Mass media--Audiences. World Wide Web. Convergence LC Classification: HE8700.8 .O826 1999 Dewey Class No.: 384.55/0973 21

Owen, Diana Marie. Media messages in American presidential elections / Diana Owen. Published/Created: New York: Greenwood Press, 1991. Description: xxi, 198 p.: ill.; 24 cm. ISBN: 0313263620 Notes: Includes bibliographical references ([177]-193) and index. Subjects: Presidents--United States--Election. Mass media--Political aspects--United States. Political campaigns--United States. Series: Contributions to the study of mass media and communications, 0732-4456; no. 25 LC Classification: JK524 .O94 1991 Dewey Class No.: 324.7/3/0973 20

Paietta, Ann Catherine, 1956- Animals on screen and radio: an annotated sourcebook / by Ann C. Paietta and Jean L. Kauppila. Published/Created: Metuchen, N.J.: Scarecrow Press, 1994. Related Authors: Kauppila, Jean L., 1957- Description: xi, 385 p.; 23 cm. ISBN: 0810829398 (alk. paper) Notes: Includes bibliographical references (p. 327-336) and indexes. Subjects: Animals in mass media--Film catalogs. Animals in mass media--Discography. LC Classification: Z5633.A53 P35 1994 P96.A53 Dewey Class No.: 016.79143/66 20

Parsigian, Elise K. Proposal savvy: creating successful proposals for media projects / Elise K. Parsigian. Published/Created: Thousand Oaks, Calif.: Sage Publications, c1996. Description: xxii, 264 p.; 24 cm. ISBN: 0761900268 (acid-free paper) 0761900276 (pbk.: acid-free paper) Notes: Includes bibliographical references and index. Subjects: Mass media--Authorship. Mass media--Research--Methodology. Proposal writing in business. Business communication. LC Classification: P96.A86 P375 1996 Dewey Class No.: 808/.066302 20

Pavlik, John V. (John Vernon) New media technology and the information superhighway / John V. Pavlik; foreword by Everette E. Dennis. Published/Created: Boston: Allyn and Bacon, c1996. Description: xiv, 434 p.; 23 cm. ISBN: 0205162487 (pbk.) 0205163009 (casebound) Notes: Includes bibliographical references (p. 409-425) and index. Subjects: Mass media--Technological innovations. Mass media--Economic aspects. Mass media--Social aspects. LC Classification: P96.T42 P38 1996 Dewey Class No.: 302.23 20

Pavlik, John V. (John Vernon) New media technology: cultural and commercial perspectives / John V. Pavlik; foreword by Everette E. Dennis. Edition Information: 2nd [rev.] ed. Published/Created: Boston: Allyn and Bacon, c1998. Related Authors: Pavlik, John V. (John Vernon). New media technology and the information superhighway. Description: xiv, 400 p.; 23 cm. ISBN: 020527093X Notes: Rev. ed. of: New media technology and the information superhighway. 1996. Includes bibliographical references (p. 379-394) and index. Subjects: Mass media--Technological innovations. Mass media--Social aspects. Mass media--Economic aspects. Mass media--United States. LC Classification: P96.T42 P38 1998 Dewey Class No.: 302.23 21

Pei, Minxin. From reform to revolution: the demise of communism in China and the Soviet Union / Minxin Pei.

Published/Created: Cambridge, Mass.: Harvard University Press, 1994. Description: 253 p.: ill.; 25 cm. ISBN: 067432563X (alk. paper) Notes: Includes bibliographical references (p. [213]-243) and index. Subjects: Communism--China. Communism--Soviet Union. Mass media--China. Mass media--Soviet Union. China--Economic conditions--1976- Soviet Union--Economic conditions--1985-1991. LC Classification: HX418.5 .P43 1994 Dewey Class No.: 321.9/2/0947 20

Pember, Don R., 1939- Mass media in America / Don R. Pember. Edition Information: 6th ed. Published/Created: New York: Macmillan, c1992. Description: vii, 536 p.: ill. (some col.); 25 cm. ISBN: 0023937807 (pbk.) Notes: Includes bibliographical references and index. Subjects: Mass media--United States. LC Classification: P92.U5 P4 1992 Dewey Class No.: 302.23/0973 20

Perlmutter, David D., 1962- Policing the media: street cops and public perceptions of law enforcement / David D. Perlmutter. Published/Created: Thousand Oaks, California: Sage Publications, c2000. Description: xv, 159 p.: ill.; 24 cm. ISBN: 0761911049 (alk. paper) 0761911057 (pbk.: alk. paper) Notes: Includes bibliographical references (p. [149]-157) and index. Subjects: Saint Louis Park (Minn.) Police Dept. Police--United States--Public opinion. Police--United States--Attitudes. Police in mass media. Cop shows--Social aspects--United States. LC Classification: HV8138 .P45 2000 Dewey Class No.: 363.2/0973 21

Perse, Elizabeth M. Media effects and society / Elizabeth M. Perse. Published/Created: Mahwah, NJ: L. Erlbaum Associates, 2001. Description: xiv, 331 p.; 24 cm. ISBN: 0805825053 (alk. paper) Notes: Includes bibliographical references (p. 260-303) and indexes. Subjects: Mass media--Influence--Social aspects. Series: LEA's communication series LC Classification: P94 .P384 2001 Dewey Class No.: 302.23 21

Persky, Stan, 1941- Mixed media, mixed messages / Stan Persky; [editor, Audrey McClellan]. Published/Created: Vancouver: New Star Books, 1991. Related Authors: McClellan, Audrey. Description: ii, 206 p.; 22 cm. ISBN: 092158623X Notes: The articles reprinted in this book originally appeared in the Vancouver Sun's Saturday Review, the Globe and Mail, Books in Canada, and the Canadian Forum. Includes index. Subjects: Mass media--Moral and ethical aspects. LC Classification: P94 .P385 1991 Dewey Class No.: 302.23 20

Persuasive communication and drug abuse prevention / edited by Lewis Donohew, Howard E. Sypher, William J. Bukoski. Published/Created: Hillsdale, N.J.: L. Erlbaum Associates, 1991. Related Authors: Donohew, Lewis. Sypher, Howard E. Bukoski, William J. National Institute on Drug Abuse. University of Kentucky. Center for Prevention Research. Description: xxi, 349 p.: ill.; 24 cm. ISBN: 0805806938 (c) Notes: Papers delivered at a symposium sponsored by the National Institute on Drug Abuse and University of Kentucky's Center for Prevention Research; held in the spring of 1989. Includes bibliographical references and indexes. Subjects: Drug abuse--United States--Prevention--Congresses. Drugs and mass media--United States--Congresses. Narcotics, Control of--United States--Congresses. Persuasion (Rhetoric)--Congresses. Series: Communication (Hillsdale, N.J.) Variant Series: Communication LC Classification: HV5825 .P375 1991 Dewey Class No.: 362.29/17/0973 20

Pesmen, Sandra. Writing for the media / Sandra Pesmen. Published/Created: Chicago, Ill: NYC Business Books, 1998. Projected Pub. Date: 9811 Description: p. cm. ISBN: 0844230766 Subjects: Mass media--Authorship. Public relations. Report writing. Journalism. LC Classification: HM263 .P46 1998 Dewey Class No.: 659.2 21

Picard, Robert G. The economics and financing of media companies / Robert G. Picard. Edition Information: 1st ed. Published/Created: Fordham University Press: New York, 2002. Projected Pub. Date: 0203 Description: p. cm. ISBN: 0823221741 082322175X (pbk.) Notes: Includes bibliographical references and index. Subjects: Mass media--Economic aspects. Mass media--Finance. Series: Business, economics, and legal studies series; 1 LC Classification: P96.E25 P528 2002 Dewey Class No.: 338.4/730223 21

Picturing the past: media, history, and photography / edited by Bonnie Brennen and Hanno Hardt. Published/Created: Urbana: University of Illinois Press, c1999. Related Authors: Brennen, Bonnie. Hardt, Hanno. Description: 263 p.: ill.; 24 cm. ISBN: 0252024656 (cloth: alk. paper) 025206769X (pbk.: alk. paper) Notes: Includes bibliographical references and index. Subjects: Photojournalism--History. Photography--Social aspects. Mass media--History--20th century. Series: The history of communication LC Classification: TR820 .P555 1999 Dewey Class No.: 070.4/9/09 21

Pinskey, Raleigh. You can hype anything / Raleigh Pinskey. Edition Information: Carol Publishing Group ed. Published/Created: Secaucus, NJ: Carol Pub. Group, 1995. Related Authors: Pinskey, Raleigh. Zen of hype. Description: viii, 172 p.; 21 cm. ISBN: 0806516305 (pbk.): Notes: "A Citadel Press book." "Originally Published as: The zen if hype"--T.p. verso. Subjects: Public relations. Industrial publicity. Mass media and business. LC Classification: HD59 .P526 1995 Dewey Class No.: 659 20

Poindexter, Paula Maurie. Research in mass communication: a practical guide / Paula M. Poindexter, Maxwell E. McCombs. Published/Created: Boston: Bedford/St. Martin's, c2000. Related Authors: McCombs, Maxwell E. Description: xxxvii, 451 p.: ill.; 24 cm. ISBN: 0312191626 Notes: Includes bibliographical references (p. 435-440) and index. Subjects: Mass media--Research--Methodology. LC Classification: P91.3 .P64 2000 Dewey Class No.: 302.23/072 21

Pollack, Martin. Washington, D.C. media directory / Martin Pollack, editor. Published/Created: Ft. Lauderdale, Fla.: Alliance Publishers, [199-] Description: 149 p.: ill.; 28 cm. ISBN: 0936836156: Subjects: Press--Washington (D.C.)--Directories. Mass media--Washington (D.C.)--Directories. American newspapers--Washington (D.C.)--Directories. American periodicals--Washington (D.C.)--Directories. LC Classification: PN4899.W3 P65 1990z Dewey Class No.: 302.23/025/753 20

Poster, Mark. The second media age / Mark Poster. Published/Created: Cambridge, MA: Polity Press, 1995. Projected Pub. Date: 9505 Description: p. cm. ISBN: 0745613950 (cloth: alk. paper) 0745613969 (pbk.: alk. paper) Notes: Includes index. Subjects: Mass media--Technological innovations. Mass media--Social aspects. Mass media and technology. Human-machine systems. LC Classification: P96.T42 P67 1995 Dewey Class No.: 302.23 20

Priest, Susanna Hornig. Doing media research: an introduction / Susanna Hornig Priest; illustrations by Scott McCullar. Published/Created: Thousand Oaks, Calif.: Sage Publications, c1996. Description: xxviii, 265 p.: ill.; 25 cm. ISBN: 080397292X (cloth: alk. paper) 0803972938 (pbk.: alk. paper) Notes: Includes bibliographical references (p. 235-236) and index. Subjects: Mass media--Research--Methodology. Social sciences--Methodology. LC Classification: P91.3 .P75 1996 Dewey Class No.: 302.23/072 20

Proceedings of National Seminar on Role of Mass Communication in Nation Building Process. Published/Created: Madras: United Writers' Association, 1990. Related Authors: United Writers' Association (Madras, India) Description: 75 p., [3] leaves of plates: ill.; 26 cm. Notes: Cover title. Subjects: Communication--India--Congresses. Mass media--Social aspects--India--Politics and government--1977- --Congresses. Communication in economic development--India--Congresses. LC Classification: P92.I7 N38 1990

Puette, William. Through jaundiced eyes: how the media view organized labor / William J. Puette. Published/Created: Ithaca, N.Y.: ILR Press, c1992. Description: viii, 228 p.: ill.; 24 cm. ISBN: 0875461840 (alk. paper) 0875461859 (pbk.: alk. paper) Notes: Includes bibliographical references (p. [206]-219) and indexes. Subjects: Labor unions and mass media--United States. Labor unions--Press coverage--United States. Industrial relations--Press coverage--United States. Employees--United States--Public opinion. Labor unions--United States--Public opinion. LC Classification: P96.T7 P84 1992 Dewey Class No.: 331.88/0973 20

Questioning the media: a critical introduction / [edited by] John Downing, Ali Mohammadi, Annabelle Sreberny-Mohammadi. Published/Created: Newbury Park, Calif.: Sage Publications, c1990. Related Authors: Downing, John. Mohammadi, Ali. Sreberny, Annabelle. Description: 385 p.: ill.; 24 cm. ISBN: 0803936427 0803936435 (pbk.) Notes: Includes bibliographical references (p. 373-382). Subjects: Mass media. LC Classification: P90 .Q48 1990 Dewey Class No.: 302.23 20

Questioning the media: a critical introduction / editors, John Downing, Ali Mohammadi, Annabelle Sreberny-Mohammadi. Edition Information: 2nd ed. Published/Created: Thousand Oaks, Calif.: Sage Publications, c1995. Related Authors: Downing, John. Mohammadi, Ali. Sreberny, Annabelle. Description: xxix, 511 p.: ill.; 24 cm. ISBN: 0803971966 (alk. paper: acid-free paper) 0803971974 (pbk.: acid-free paper) Notes: Includes bibliographical references (p. 494-506). LC Classification: P90 .Q48 1995 Dewey Class No.: 302.23 20

Ray, Dixy Lee. Trashing the planet: how science can help us deal with acid rain, depletion of the ozone, and nuclear waste (among other things) / Dixy Lee Ray and Lou Guzzo. Published/Created: Washington, D.C.: Regnery Gateway; Lanham, MD: Distributed by National Book Network, c1990. Related Authors: Guzzo, Louis R., 1919- Description: x11, 206 p.; 23 cm. ISBN: 0895265443 (alk. paper): Notes: Includes bibliographical references (p. 173-198) and index. Subjects: Pollution. Environmental protection. Human ecology. Mass media and the environment. Communication in science. LC Classification: TD174 .R39 1990 Dewey Class No.: 363.73 20

Ray, Dixy Lee. Trashing the planet: how science can help us deal with acid rain, depletion of the ozone, and nuclear waste (among other things) / Dixy Lee Ray with Lou Guzzo. Edition Information: 1st HarperPerennial ed. Published/Created: New York, NY: HarperPerennial, 1992. Related Authors: Guzzo, Louis R., 1919- Description: xii, 206 p.; 21 cm. ISBN: 0060974907 (paper): Notes: Originally Published: Washington, D.C.: Regnery Gateway; Lanham, MD: Distributed by National Book Network, c1990. Includes bibliographical references (p. 173-198) and index. Subjects: Pollution. Environmental protection. Human ecology. Mass media and the environment. Communication in science. LC Classification: TD174 .R39 1992 Dewey Class No.: 363.73 20

Rayner, Philip, 1947- Media studies: the essential introduction / Philip Rayner, Pete Wall, and Stephen Kruger. Published/Created: London; New York: Routledge, 2001. Projected Pub. Date: 0108 Related Authors: Wall, Peter. Kruger, Stephen, 1951- Description: p. cm. ISBN: 041523610X 0415236118 (pbk.) Notes: Includes bibliographical references and index. Subjects: Mass media. LC Classification: P90 .R345 2001 Dewey Class No.: 302.23 21

Redmond, James. Balancing on the wire: the art of managing media / James Redmond and

Robert Trager. Published/Created: Boulder, CO.: Coursewise, c1998. Related Authors: Trager, Robert. Description: ix, 468 p.: ill.; 25 cm. ISBN: 039593849X Notes: Include bibliographical references (p. 429-446) and index. Subjects: Mass media--Management. LC Classification: P96.M34 R43 1998 Dewey Class No.: 302.23/068 21

Reeves, Byron, 1949- The media equation: how people treat computers, television, and new media like real people and places / Byron Reeves & Clifford Nass. Published/Created: Stanford, Calif.: CSLI Publications; New York: Cambridge University Press, c1996. Related Authors: Nass, Clifford Ivar. Description: xiv, 305 p.; 25 cm. ISBN: 157586052X Notes: Includes bibliographical references (p. [257]-298) and index. Subjects: Mass media--Audiences. Mass media--Influence. Mass media--Psychological aspects. LC Classification: P96.A83 R44 1996 Dewey Class No.: 302.23 20

Ricks, Charles W. The military-news media relationship: thinking forward / Charles W. Ricks. Published/Created: [Carlisle Barracks, PA]: Strategic Studies Institute, U.S. Army War College, [1993] Related Authors: Army War College (U.S.). Strategic Studies Institute. Related Titles: Military news media relationship. Description: vii, 40 p.; 23 cm. Notes: "December 1, 1993." Includes bibliographical references (p. 36-40). Subjects: Journalism, Military--United States. Armed Forces and mass media--United States. United States--Armed Forces--Public relations. LC Classification: P96.A75 R53 1993 Dewey Class No.: 355.3/42/0973 20

Ridgway, Judith, 1939- Practical media relations / Judith Ridgway. Edition Information: 2nd ed. Published/Created: Aldershot; Brookfield, Vt., USA: Gower, c1996. Related Authors: Ridgway, Judith, 1939- Successful media relations. Description: ix, 222 p.; 22 cm. ISBN: 0566077027 (pbk.) Notes: Rev. ed. of: Successful media relations. 1984. Includes bibliographical references (p. 217) and index. Subjects: Mass media and business. Public relations. LC Classification: HD59 .R48 1996 Dewey Class No.: 659.2 20

Riffe, Daniel. Analyzing media messages: using quantitative content analysis in research / Daniel Riffe, Stephen Lacy, Frederick G. Fico. Published/Created: Mahwah, N.J.: Erlbaum, 1998. Related Authors: Lacy, Stephen, 1948- Fico, Frederick. Description: x, 208 p.: ill.; 24 cm. ISBN: 0805820183 (cloth: alk. paper) 0805820191 (pbk.: alk. paper) Notes: Includes bibliographical references (p. 193-200) and indexes. Subjects: Content analysis (Communication) Mass media--Research--Methodology. Mass media--Statistical methods. Series: LEA's communication series LC Classification: P93 .R54 1998 Dewey Class No.: 302.23/01/4 21

Riha, Bob. National Media guide for emergency & disaster incidents / [Bob Riha, Jr., David Handschuh]. Edition Information: 1st ed. Published/Created: [Durham, NC: National Press Photographers Association, 1995] Related Authors: Handschuh, David. National Press Photographers Association (U.S.) Description: iv, 81 p.: ill.; 28 cm. Notes: "A special report by the National Press Photographers Association." Includes bibliographical references. Subjects: Disasters--Press coverage--United States. Government and the press--United States. Emergency management--United States. Mass media--United States. LC Classification: PN4888.D57 R55 1995 Dewey Class No.: 070.4/49904 20

Rivers, Caryl. Slick spins and fractured facts: how cultural myths distort the news / Caryl Rivers. Published/Created: New York: Columbia University Press, c1996. Description: xv, 250 p.: ill.; 24 cm. ISBN: 023110152X (acid-free paper) Notes: Includes bibliographical references (p. [225]-240) and index. Subjects: Journalism--Objectivity. Mass media--Objectivity. Journalistic ethics. Mass media--Moral and ethical aspects. LC

Classification: PN4784.O24 R58 1996 Dewey Class No.: 302.23 20

Rodman, George R., 1948- Making sense of media: an introduction to mass communication / George Rodman. Edition Information: [1st ed.]. Published/Created: Boston: Allyn & Bacon, c2001. Description: xxx, 530 p.: col. ill.; 25 cm. ISBN: 0801332060 (pbk.) Notes: Includes bibliographical references (p. 493-514) and index. Subjects: Mass media--United States. LC Classification: P92.U5 R57 2001 Dewey Class No.: 302.23 21

Roos, Johan. Managing strategy processes in emergent industries: the case of media firms / Johan Roos and Georg Von Krogh with Peggy Simcic Brønn. Published/Created: Basingstoke: Macmillan Business, 1996. Related Authors: Von Krogh, George. Simcic Brønn, Peggy. Description: xii, 178 p.: ill.; 22 cm. ISBN: 0333665732 Notes: Includes bibliographical references and index. Subjects: Strategic planning. Business planning. Mass media industry LC Classification: HD30.28 .R662 1996 National Bib. No.: GB97-2478

Ross, Jeff. The semantics of media / by Jeff Ross. Published/Created: Dordrecht; Boston: Kluwer Academic Publishers, c1997. Description: vii, 137 p.: ill.; 24 cm. ISBN: 0792343891 (hc: alk. paper) Notes: Includes bibliographical references (p. 133-134) and index. Subjects: Mass media and language. Semantics. Semantics (Philosophy) Content analysis (Communication) Series: Studies in linguistics and philosophy; v. 64 LC Classification: P96.L34 R67 1997 Dewey Class No.: 302.23//01/4 21

Rowe, David, 1954- Sport, culture, and the media: the unruly trinity / David Rowe. Published/Created: Buckingham [England]; Philadelphia: Open University Press, c1999. Description: xii, 193 p.: ill.; 23 cm. ISBN: 0335202039 (hbk) 0335202020 (pbk) Notes: Includes bibliographical references (p. [176]-189) and index. Subjects: Mass media and sports--Social aspects. Sports--Anthropological aspects. Series: Issues in cultural and media studies LC Classification: GV742 .R69 1999 Dewey Class No.: 306.4/83 21

Ruben, Douglas H. Publicity for mental health clinicians: using TV, radio, and print media to enhance your public image / Douglas H. Ruben. Published/Created: Binghamton, NY: Haworth Press, c1995. Description: xvii, 216 p.: ill.; 23 cm. ISBN: 1560249536 Notes: Includes bibliographical references and index. Subjects: Mass media in mental health education. Mental health services--Marketing. Radio in publicity. Television in publicity. Series: Haworth marketing resources LC Classification: RA790.87 .R83 1995 Dewey Class No.: 362.2/068/8 20

Ruddock, Andy. Understanding audiences: theory and method / Andy Ruddock. Published/Created: London; Thousand Oaks [Calif.]: SAGE, 2001. Description: 201 p.; 24 cm. ISBN: 0761963448 0761963456 (pbk.) Notes: Includes bibliographical references (p. [182]-197) and index. Subjects: Mass media--Audiences. Mass media--Influence. LC Classification: P96.A83 R83 2001 Dewey Class No.: 302.23 21 National Bib. No.: GBA0-X6111

Ruthless criticism: new perspectives in U.S. communication history / William S. Solomon, Robert W. McChesney, editors. Published/Created: Minneapolis: University of Minnesota Press, c1993. Related Authors: Solomon, William Samuel. McChesney, Robert Waterman, 1952- Description: ix, 389 p.: ill.; 23 cm. ISBN: 0816621691 (alk. paper) 0816621705 (pbk.: alk. paper) Notes: Includes bibliographical references and index. Subjects: Communication--United States--History. Mass media--United States--History. LC Classification: P92.U5 R87 1993 Dewey Class No.: 302.23/0973 20

Salmon, Richard, 1965- Henry James and the culture of publicity / Richard Salmon. Published/Created: Cambridge; New York: Cambridge University Press, 1997. Description: viii, 233 p.; 24 cm. ISBN: 052156249X (hardback) Notes: Includes bibliographical references (p. 218-228) and index. Subjects: James, Henry, 1843-1916 --Political and social views. Literature and society--United States--History--19th century. Literature and society--United States--History--20th century. Authorship--Social aspects--United States--History. Civilization, Modern--Historiography. Mass media--United States--History. Publicity--United States--History. Criticism--United States--History. LC Classification: PS2127.P6 S25 1997 Dewey Class No.: 813/.52 21

Salzman, Jason. Making the news: a guide for nonprofits and activists / Jason Salzman. Published/Created: Boulder, Colo.: Westview Press, 1998. Description: xv, 289 p.: ill.; 19 cm. ISBN: 0813368987 (alk. paper) Notes: Includes bibliographical references (p. 279-280) and index. Subjects: Publicity--Fund raising--Endowments--Social service--Public relations--United States. Nonprofit organizations--United States--Finance. Endowments--United States--Management. Special events. Mass media and social service--United States. LC Classification: HM263 .S247 1998 Dewey Class No.: 659/.0973 21

Sanders, Barry, 1938- A is for ox: violence, electronic media, and the silencing of the written word / Barry Sanders. Edition Information: 1st ed. Published/Created: New York: Pantheon Books, c1994. Description: xiii, 269 p.; 22 cm. ISBN: 0679417117: Notes: Includes bibliographical references (p. 245-256) and index. Subjects: Oral communication--Social aspects. Literacy. Mass media and youth. Mass media--Social aspects. Children and violence. LC Classification: P95 .S26 1994 Dewey Class No.: 302.2/242 20

Sawant, P. B., 1930- Mass media in contemporary society / P.B. Sawant. Published/Created: New Delhi: Capital Foundation Society, c1998. Description: 220 p.; 22 cm. ISBN: 8185298122 Subjects: Mass media--India. Mass media--Social aspects--India. Mass media--Political aspects--India. Communication--India. LC Classification: P92.I7 S39 1998 Dewey Class No.: 302.23/0954 21

Scodari, Christine. Media criticism: journeys in interpretation / Christine Scodari, Judith Mosier Thorpe. Published/Created: Dubuque, Iowa: Kendall/Hunt Pub. Co., c1992. Related Authors: Thorpe, Judith Mosier. Description: xi, 198 p.; 24 cm. ISBN: 0840370768 Notes: Includes bibliographical references and indexes. Subjects: Mass media criticism. LC Classification: P96.C76 S35 1992 Dewey Class No.: 302.23 20

Scollon, Ronald, 1939- Mediated discourse as social interaction: a study of news discourse / Ron Scollon. Published/Created: London; New York: Longman, 1998. Projected Pub. Date: 9804 Description: p. cm. ISBN: 0582327261 0582327253 (pbk.) Notes: Includes bibliographical references (p.) and index. Subjects: Mass media. Social interaction. Journalism. Mass media--Audiences. Discourse analysis. LC Classification: P91 .S365 1998 Dewey Class No.: 302.23 21

Seguin, James A. Media career guide: preparing for jobs in the 21st century / James Seguin. Published/Created: New York: St. Martin's Press, c1998. Description: vi, 87 p.; 23 cm. ISBN: 0312179626 Notes: Includes bibliographical references (p. 80-81) and index. Subjects: Mass media--Vocational guidance. Communication--Vocational guidance. LC Classification: P91.6 .S44 1998 Dewey Class No.: 302.23/023 21

Seiden, Martin H. Access to the American mind: the impact of the new mass media / Martin H. Seiden. Published/Created: New York: Shapolsky Publishers, c1991. Description: xiii, 234 p.; 24 cm. ISBN:

0944007716: Notes: Includes bibliographical references (p. 229-234). Subjects: Mass media--United States. LC Classification: P92.U5 S45 1990 Dewey Class No.: 302.23/0973 20

Seminar on Media Research Meets the Future: how new challenges promote new media uses and media research, Lisbon (Portugal) 2nd-4th April 1992. Published/Created: Amsterdam, Netherlands: ESOMAR, [1992] Related Authors: Esomar. Description: v, 324 p.: ill., maps; 23 cm. ISBN: 9283111842 Notes: Includes bibliographical references. Subjects: Mass media--Planning--Research--Congresses. LC Classification: P95.815 .S43 1992 Dewey Class No.: 302.23/072 20

Severin, Werner J. (Werner Joseph) Communication theories: origins, methods, and uses in the mass media / Werner J. Severin, James W. Tankard, Jr. Edition Information: 4th ed. Published/Created: New York: Longman, c1997. Related Authors: Tankard, James W. Description: xiv, 424 p.: ill.; 24 cm. ISBN: 0801317037 Notes: Includes bibliographical references and index. Subjects: Mass media. Communication. LC Classification: P90 .S4414 1997 Dewey Class No.: 302.23 20

Severin, Werner J. (Werner Joseph) Communication theories: origins, methods, and uses in the mass media / Werner J. Severin, James W. Tankard, Jr. Edition Information: 3rd ed. Published/Created: New York: Longman, c1992. Related Authors: Tankard, James W. Description: xii, 364 p.: ill.; 24 cm. ISBN: 0801304636 Notes: Includes bibliographical references and index. LC Classification: P90 .S4414 1991 Dewey Class No.: 302.23 20

Severin, Werner J. (Werner Joseph) Communication theories: origins, methods, and uses in the mass media / Werner Severin, James Tankard, Jr. Edition Information: 5th ed. Published/Created: New York: Addison Wesley Longman, 2000. Projected Pub. Date: 0006 Related Authors: Tankard, James W. Description: p. cm. ISBN: 0801333350 (alk. paper) Notes: Includes bibliographical references and index. LC Classification: P90 .S4414 2000 Dewey Class No.: 302.23 21

Shane, Ed. Selling electronic media / Ed Shane; foreword and discussion points by Michael C. Keith. Published/Created: Boston: Focal Press, c1999. Description: xx, 462 p.: ill., maps; 26 cm. ISBN: 0240803272 (pbk.: alk. paper) Notes: Includes bibliographical references and index. Subjects: Selling--Mass media. LC Classification: HF5439.M267 S49 1999 Dewey Class No.: 384.5/068/8 21

Shaver, Mary Alice. Make the sale!: how to sell media with marketing / by Mary Alice Shaver. Edition Information: 1st ed. Published/Created: Chicago, IL: Copy Workshop, c1995. Description: 295 p.; 23 cm. ISBN: 0962141569 Notes: Includes bibliographical references. Subjects: Mass media--Marketing. LC Classification: P96.M34 S48 1995 Dewey Class No.: 302.23/068/8 20

Shea, David J. Media isn't a four letter word: a guide to effective encounters with the members of the fourth estate / by David J. Shea and John F. Gulick. Published/Created: Washington, DC: Electronic Industries Association, c1994. Related Authors: Gulick, John F. Description: 51 p.: ill.; 23 cm. Subjects: Public relations. Mass media and business. LC Classification: HD59 .S5417 1994 Dewey Class No.: 659.2 20

Shearer, Ann, 1943- Survivors and the media / Ann Shearer. Published/Created: London: J. Libbey, c1991. Description: v, 73 p.; 25 cm. ISBN: 0861963326 Notes: Includes bibliographical references. Subjects: Disasters--Press coverage. Journalistic ethics. Mass media--Moral and ethical aspects. Series: Research monograph series (Broadcasting Standards Council (Great Britain)); 2. Variant Series: Research monograph series / Broadcasting Standards Council, 0956-9073; 2 LC Classification: PN4784.D57 S44 1991

Shimkin, David. State of the art: issues in contemporary mass communication / David Shimkin, Harold Stolerman, Helene O'Connor. Published/Created: New York: St. Martin's Press, 1992. Related Authors: Stolerman, Harold. O'Connor, Helene. Description: xvii, 406 p.: ill.; 24 cm. ISBN: 0312055439 Notes: Includes index. Subjects: Mass media. LC Classification: P90 .S446 1992 Dewey Class No.: 302.23 20

Shining in the media spotlight: a communications handbook for tourism professionals. Edition Information: 1995-96 ed. Published/Created: Madrid, Spain: World Tourism Organization, c1995. Related Authors: World Tourism Organization. Description: 17 p., 101 leaves; 30 cm. ISBN: 928440133X Notes: "Preview copy"--T.p. verso. Subjects: Tourism. Mass media in business. LC Classification: G155.A1 S488 1995 Dewey Class No.: 338.4/791 21

Shoemaker, Pamela J. Mediating the message: theories of influences on mass media content / Pamela J. Shoemaker, Stephen D. Reese. Edition Information: 2nd ed. Published/Created: White Plains, N.Y.: Longman, c1996. Related Authors: Reese, Stephen D. Description: xiv, 313 p.; 24 cm. ISBN: 0801312515 Notes: Includes bibliographical references (p. 273-302) and index. Subjects: Mass media. Content analysis (Communication) LC Classification: P91 .S46 1996 Dewey Class No.: 302.23 20

Shoemaker, Pamela J. Mediating the message: theories of influences on mass media content / Pamela J. Shoemaker, Stephen D. Reese. Published/Created: New York: Longman, c1991. Related Authors: Reese, Stephen D. Description: x, 233 p.: ill.; 23 cm. ISBN: 0801303079 Notes: Includes bibliographical references and index. Subjects: Mass media. Content analysis (Communication) LC Classification: P91 .S46 1991 Dewey Class No.: 302.23 20

Shrivastava, K. M Media issues / K.M. Shrivastava. Published/Created: New Delhi: Sterling Publishers, c1992. Description: 168 p.; 23 cm. ISBN: 8120714709: Summary: Study in the Indian context. Notes: Includes index. Subjects: Mass media. LC Classification: P90 .S46 1992 Dewey Class No.: 302.23 20

Silk, Catherine, 1946- Racism and anti-racism in American popular culture: portrayals of African-Americans in fiction and film / Catherine Silk and John Silk. Published/Created: Manchester; New York: Manchester University Press; New York, NY, USA: Distributed exclusively in the USA and Canada by St. Martin's Press, c1990. Related Authors: Silk, John, 1942- Description: x, 186 p.; 23 cm. ISBN: 0719030706 Notes: Includes bibliographical references and index. Subjects: Afro-Americans in mass media. Popular culture--United States--History--20th century. Mass media--United States--History--20th century. LC Classification: P94.5.A372 U57 1990 Dewey Class No.: 813.009/3520396073 20

Simmonds, Diana. Squidgie dearest: the making of a media goddess: Australia's love affair with Princess Diana / Diana Simmonds. Published/Created: Leichhardt, NSW: Pluto Press Australia, 1995. Description: 152 p.: ill.; 22 cm. ISBN: 1864030224 Subjects: Diana, Princess of Wales, 1961- --Windsor, House of--Public opinion. Princesses--Monarchy--Great Britain--Public opinion. Public opinion--Mass media--Australia. LC Classification: DA591.A45 S56 1995 Dewey Class No.: 941.085/092 20

Singletary, Michael W., 1938- Mass communication research: contemporary methods and applications / Michael Singletary. Published/Created: New York: Longman, c1994. Description: xix, 473 p.: ill.; 25 cm. ISBN: 0801308828 Notes: Includes bibliographical references and index. Subjects: Mass media—Research-Methodology. LC Classification: P91.3 .S53 1994 Dewey Class No.: 302.23/072 20

Sloan, W. David (William David), 1947- Perspectives on mass communication history / Wm. David Sloan. Published/Created: Hillsdale, N.J.: L. Erlbaum Associates, 1991. Description: xii, 379 p.; 24 cm. ISBN: 0805808353 (c) 0805808639 (p) Notes: Includes bibliographical references and index. Subjects: Mass media--United States--History. Series: Communication textbook series. General communication theory and methodology LC Classification: P92.U5 S56 1991 Dewey Class No.: 302.23/0973 20

Smith, Anthony, 1938- Software for the self: technology and culture / Anthony Smith. Published/Created: New York: Oxford University Press, c1996. Description: xi, 128; 21 cm. ISBN: 0195039009 Notes: Includes bibliographical references (p. 121-128). Subjects: Information technology--Social aspects. Mass media--Social aspects. LC Classification: T58.5 .S64 1996 Dewey Class No.: 303.48/33 21

Smith, Anthony, 1938- The age of behemoths: the globalization of mass media firms / by Anthony Smith. Published/Created: New York: Priority Press Publications, 1991. Description: vii, 83 p.; 23 cm. ISBN: 0870783254: Notes: "A Twentieth Century Fund paper." Includes bibliographical references (p. 79-80) and index. Subjects: Mass media--United States--Social aspects. Mass media--Social aspects. Mass media--Ownership--United States. Mass media--Ownership. Consolidation and merger of corporations--United States. Consolidation and merger of corporations. LC Classification: HN90.M3 S63 1991 Dewey Class No.: 302.23/0973 20

Smith, Joel, 1925- Understanding the media: a sociology of mass communication / Joel Smith. Published/Created: Cresskill, N.J.: Hampton Press, c1995. Description: xxiv, 392 p.: ill.; 24 cm. ISBN: 1572730048 1572730056 (pbk.) Notes: Includes bibliographical references (p. 323-370) and indexes. Subjects: Mass media--Social aspects. Series: The Hampton Press communication series. Mass communications and journalism LC Classification: HM258 .S538 1995 Dewey Class No.: 302.23 20

Smith, Ronald A. (Ronald Austin), 1936- Play-by-play: radio, television, and big-time college sport / Ronald A. Smith. Published/Created: Baltimore, Md.: Johns Hopkins University Press, 2001. Projected Pub. Date: 0111 Description: p. cm. ISBN: 0801866863 (hardcover: alk. paper) Notes: Includes bibliographical references and index. Subjects: Mass media and sports--United States. College sports--United States. LC Classification: GV742 .S64 2001 Dewey Class No.: 796.04/3/0973 21

Society and the media: a collection of essays / edited by Marilyn J. Carter. Published/Created: New York: HarperCollins College Publishers, c1996. Related Authors: Carter, Marilyn J. Description: 192 p.; 24 cm. ISBN: 0673975150 Notes: Includes bibliographical references. Subjects: Mass media--Social aspects--United States. LC Classification: HN90.M3 S68 1996 Dewey Class No.: 302.23 21

Solomon, Norman, 1951- The habits of highly deceptive media: decoding spin and lies in mainstream news / Norman Solomon. Published/Created: Monroe, Me.: Common Courage Press, c1999. Description: 294 p.: ill.; 20 cm. ISBN: 1567511554 (cloth) 1567511546 (pbk.) Notes: Includes index. Subjects: Journalism--Objectivity. Mass media--Objectivity. Journalistic ethics. Mass media--Moral and ethical aspects. LC Classification: PN4784.O24 S655 1999 Dewey Class No.: 302.23 21

Solomon, Norman, 1951- Wizards of media Oz: behind the curtain of mainstream news / Norman Solomon and Jeff Cohen. Published/Created: Monroe, Me.: Common Courage Press, c1997. Related Authors: Cohen, Jeff, 1951- Description: 294 p.: ill.; 20 cm. ISBN: 156751118X (paper: alk. paper) 1567511198 (cloth: alk. paper) Notes: Includes index. Subjects: Journalism--Objectivity. Mass media--Objectivity. Journalistic ethics. Mass media--Moral and ethical aspects. LC Classification: PN4784.O24 S66 1997 Dewey Class No.: 302.23 21

Sommerville, C. John (Charles John), 1938- How the news makes us dumb: the death of wisdom in an information society / C. John Sommerville. Published/Created: Downers Grove, Ill.: InterVarsity Press, c1999. Description: 155 p.; 21 cm. ISBN: 0830822011 0830822038 Notes: Includes bibliographical references (p. [153]-155). Subjects: Journalism--United States--Objectivity. Mass media--United States--Objectivity. Press and politics--United States. LC Classification: PN4888.O25 S66 1999 Dewey Class No.: 302.23/0973 21

Sorlin, Pierre. Mass media / Pierre Sorlin. Published/Created: London; New York: Routledge, 1994. Description: 158 p.; 21 cm. ISBN: 0415110238: 0415072093 (pbk.): Notes: Includes bibliographical references (p. [151]-153) and index. Subjects: Mass media. Series: Key ideas LC Classification: P90 .S637 1994 Dewey Class No.: 302.23 20

Soruco, Gonzalo R., 1943- Cubans and the mass media in South Florida / Gonzalo R. Soruco. Published/Created: Gainesville: University Press of Florida, c1996. Description: xv, 151 p.: ill.; 24 cm. ISBN: 0813013798 (acid-free paper) Notes: Includes bibliographical references (p. 133-142) and index. Subjects: Hispanic Americans and mass media--Florida. Cuban Americans--Florida--Social life and customs. LC Classification: P94.5.C83 S67 1996 Dewey Class No.: 302.23/089687291073 20

Spaeth, Merrie. Marketplace communication / Merrie Spaeth. Published/Created: New York: Mastermedia Limited, c1996. Description: xx, 292 p.: ill.; 22 cm. ISBN: 1571010327 Subjects: Communication in management. Mass media and business LC Classification: HD30.3 .S662 1996 Dewey Class No.: 658.4/5 21

Sparks, Glenn Grayson. Media effects research: a basic overview / Glenn G. Sparks. Published/Created: Belmont, CA: Wadsworth/Thomson Learning, c2002. Description: xv, 221 p.: ill.; 24 cm. ISBN: 0534545866 (pbk.: alk. paper) Notes: Includes bibliographical references and index. Subjects: Mass media--Social aspects. Mass media--Research--Methodology. Series: Wadsworth series in mass communication and journalism LC Classification: HM1206 .S66 2002 Dewey Class No.: 302.23 21

Split image: African Americans in the mass media / edited by Jannette L. Dates and William Barlow. Edition Information: 2nd ed. Published/Created: Washington, D.C.: Howard University Press, 1993. Related Authors: Dates, Jannette Lake, 1937- Barlow, William, 1943- Description: 574 p.: ill.; 24 cm. ISBN: 0882581783 (acid-free paper): 0882581791 (pbk.: acid-free paper): Notes: Includes bibliographical references (p. 545-549) and index. Subjects: African Americans and mass media. LC Classification: P94.5.A372 U574 1993 Dewey Class No.: 302.23/089/96073 20

SPREP Regional Environmental Media Training Workshop (Apia, Western Samoa, 2-13 July 1990): report / organised by the South Pacific Regional Environment Programme (SPREP) and the South Pacific Commission (SPC) Regional Media Centre; hosted by the Environment Division, Department of Lands and Environment, Government of Western Samoa. Published/Created: Noumea, New Caledonia: The Commission, c1990. Related Authors: South Pacific Regional Environment Programme. South Pacific Commission. Regional Media Centre. Description: iii, 21 p.; 30 cm. ISBN: 9822031866 Notes: "October 1990." Subjects: Environmental education--Oceania--Congresses. Mass media and the environment--Oceania--Congresses. LC Classification: QH541.2 .S69 1990

Stally, Aulora. SAfAIDS' regional media needs assessment / [Aulora Stally, Michele Fleet, and Kate Mhambi]. Published/Created: Avondale, Harare, Zimbabwe: SAfAIDS, [1999] Related Authors: Fleet, Michele. Mhambi, Kate. Southern Africa AIDS Information Dissemination Service. Description: 29 p.; 30 cm. Notes: "March 1999." Subjects: Southern Africa AIDS Information Dissemination Service. AIDS (Disease) and mass media--Africa, Southern. Mass media surveys--Africa, Southern. LC Classification: P96.A392 A3567 1999 Dewey Class No.: 070.4/493621969792 21

Stamm, Keith R. The mass communication process: a behavioral and social perspective / Keith R. Stamm, John E. Bowes. Published/Created: Dubuque, Iowa: Kendall/Hunt Pub. Co., c1990. Related Authors: Bowes, John E. Description: viii, 244 p.: ill.; 24 cm. ISBN: 0840360452 Notes: Includes bibliographical references and indexes. Subjects: Communication--Social aspects. Mass media--Social aspects. Communication--Social aspects--United States. Mass media--Social aspects--United States. LC Classification: HM258 .S678 1990 Dewey Class No.: 302.23 20

State of the media in Ghana / Ghana Journalists Association; in cooperation with Friedrich Ebert Stiftung. Published/Created: Ghana: Anasesem Publications, c1994. Related Authors: Ghana Journalists Association. Friedrich-Ebert-Stiftung. Description: iii, 73 p.; 24 cm. ISBN: 9988552041 Subjects: Mass media--Journalism--Mass media--Political aspects--Ghana--Congresses. LC Classification: P92.G48 S73 1994 Dewey Class No.: 302.23/09667 21

Stauffer, Dennis. Mediasmart: how to handle a reporter, by a reporter / Dennis Stauffer. Published/Created: Minneapolis: MinneApple Press, c1994. Description: 284 p.; 24 cm. ISBN: 0964042908 Notes: Includes bibliographical references (p. 277-278) and index. Subjects: Interviewing in mass media. Interviewing in journalism. Reporters and reporting. LC Classification: PN4784.I6 S78 1994

Steinbock, Dan. Triumph and erosion in the American media and entertainment industries / Dan Steinbock. Published/Created: Westport, Conn.: Quorum Books, 1995. Description: xv, 328 p.; 25 cm. ISBN: 0899309143 (alk. paper) Notes: Includes bibliographical references (p. [277]-310) and index. Subjects: Mass media--Economic aspects--United States. LC Classification: P96.E252 U67 1995 Dewey Class No.: 384/.0973 20

Stevenson, Nick. Understanding media cultures: social theory and mass communication / Nick Stevenson. Published/Created: London; Thousand Oaks, Calif.: Sage, 1995. Description: 238 p.; 25 cm. ISBN: 0803989318 (pbk.) Notes: Includes bibliographical references (p. [218]-229) and index. Subjects: Communication--Social aspects. Mass media--Social aspects. LC Classification: HM258 .S753 1995 Dewey Class No.: 302.23 20

Stovall, James Glen. Writing for the mass media / James Glen Stovall. Edition Information: 3rd ed. Published/Created: Englewood Cliffs, N.J.: Prentice Hall, c1994. Description: viii, 311 p.: ill.; 28 cm. ISBN: 0130979651 Notes: Includes bibliographical references and index. Subjects: Mass media--Authorship. Report writing. LC Classification: P96.A86 S8 1994 Dewey Class No.: 808/.06602 20

Stovall, James Glen. Writing for the mass media / James Glen Stovall. Edition Information: 2nd ed. Published/Created: Englewood Cliffs, NJ: Prentice Hall, c1990. Description: x, 293 p.: ill.; 28 cm. ISBN: 0139708987 Notes: Includes index. Subjects: Mass media--Authorship. Report writing. LC Classification: P96.A86 S8 1990 Dewey Class No.: 808/.066302 19

Stovall, James Glen. Writing for the mass media / James Glen Stovall. Edition Information: 4th ed. Published/Created: Boston: Allyn and Bacon, c1998. Description: 410 p.: ill.; 28 cm. ISBN: 020527837X Notes: Includes bibliographical references and index.

Subjects: Mass media--Authorship. Report writing. LC Classification: P96.A86 S8 1998 Dewey Class No.: 808/.066302 21

Straubhaar, Joseph D. Media now: communications media in the information age / Joseph Straubhaar, Robert LaRose. Edition Information: 2nd ed. Published/Created: Belmont, Calif.: Wadsworth Pub. Co., 2000. Projected Pub. Date: 1111 Related Authors: LaRose, Robert. Straubhaar, Joseph D. Communications media in the information society. Description: p. cm. ISBN: 0534548288 Notes: Rev. ed. of: Communications media in the information society. Updated ed. c1997. Subjects: Telecommunication--United States. Information technology--United States. Mass media--United States. LC Classification: HE7775 .S79 2000 Dewey Class No.: 384/.0973 21

Symposium on Information Technologies in the Media and Entertainment Industries: their impact on employment, working conditions and labour-management relations / International Labour Organization, Sectoral Activities Programme. Published/Created: Geneva: ILO, 2000. Related Authors: International Labour Organisation. Sectoral Activities Programme. Description: ix, 95 p.: ill.; 30 cm. ISBN: 9221119254 Notes: Includes bibliographical references. Subjects: Entertainers--Effect of technological innovations on Congresses. Mass media--Employees--Effect of technological innovations on--Congresses. Communication and technology--Congresses. Information technology--Economic aspects--Congresses. LC Classification: HD6331.18.E65 S96 2000

Talking to strangers: meditated therapeutic communication / Gary Gumpert and Sandra L. Fish, editors. Published/Created: Norwood, NJ: Ablex Pub. Corp., c1990. Related Authors: Gumpert, Gary. Fish, Sandra L. Description: x, 255 p.; 24 cm. ISBN: 0893914908 (cloth) 0893916269 (pbk.) Notes: Includes bibliographical references and indexes. Subjects: Mass media in counseling. Series: Communication and information science LC Classification: RC466.3 .T35 1990 Dewey Class No.: 616.89/14 20

Taylor, Robert L., 1942- Health fact, health fiction: getting through the media maze / Robert L. Taylor. Published/Created: Dallas, Tex.: Taylor Pub., c1990. Description: vii, 158 p.; 24 cm. ISBN: 0878336834: Notes: Includes bibliographical references (p. 151-158). Subjects: Mass media in health education--United States. Health promotion--United States. Advertising--Medicine--United States. Health behavior. Consumer education--United States. LC Classification: RA440.5 .T39 1990 Dewey Class No.: 613/.0973 20

Telephony, the Internet, and the media: selected papers from the 1997 Telecommunications Policy Research Conference / edited by Jeffrey K. MacKie-Mason and David Waterman. Published/Created: Mahwah, N.J.: Lawrence Erlbaum Associates, Publishers, 1998. Related Authors: Waterman, David. MacKie-Mason, Jeffrey K. Description: xxiv, 297 p.: ill.; 24 cm. ISBN: 0805831517 (hardcover: alk. paper) 0805831525 (pbk.: alk. paper) Notes: Includes bibliographical references and indexes. Subjects: Telecommunication policy--Congresses. Telephone--Congresses. Internet--Congresses. Mass media--Congresses. Series: Telecommunications (Mahwah, N.J.) Variant Series: Telecommunications LC Classification: HE7645 .T45 1997 Dewey Class No.: 384 21

The Daily creation: the Washington Post media companion / Washington Post Writers Group. Published/Created: Boston: Allyn and Bacon, c1991. Related Authors: Washington Post Writers Group. Description: xi, 282 p.; 23 cm. ISBN: 0205130879 Subjects: Mass media. LC Classification: P91.25 .D35 1991 Dewey Class No.: 302.23 20

The journal of African communications. Published/Created: Bowie, MD:

Department of Communications, Bowie State University, c1996- Related Authors: Bowie State University. Dept. of Communications. Description: v.; 22 cm. Cover of v. 1, no. 1 gives date as spring 1996. Vol. 1, no. 1 (fall 1996)- Current Frequency: Semiannual ISSN: 1084-8142 Cancel/Invalid LCCN: sn 96032238 sn 95006252 Notes: SERBIB/SERLOC merged record Subjects: Communication--Africa--Periodicals. Africans--Communication--Periodicals. African diaspora--Periodicals. Africa--In mass media--Periodicals. LC Classification: P92.A4 J68 Dewey Class No.: 302.2/096/05 21

The Mass media in OIC countries / General Secretariat of the Organization of the Islamic Conference [and] Statistical, Economic and Social Research and Training Centre for Islamic Countries. Edition Information: Rev. ed. Published/Created: Ankara, Turkey: The Centre, 1990. Related Authors: Organization of Islamic Conference. General Secretariat. Statistical, Economic, and Social Research and Training Centre for Islamic Countries. Description: xv, 307 p.; 28 cm. ISBN: 9290471204 Subjects: Mass media--Islamic countries--Directories. Series: Directory series in OIC member countries; 6. Variant Series: Directory series; 6 LC Classification: P92.I77 M37 1990

The media & the public / edited by Casey Ripley, Jr. Published/Created: New York: H.W. Wilson, 1994. Related Authors: Ripley, Casey. Related Titles: Media and the public. Description: 219 p.; 19 cm. ISBN: 0824208560 Notes: Includes bibliographical references (p. 211-212). Subjects: Mass media and public opinion--United States. Journalism--United States. Public opinion--United States. Mass media--Social aspects--United States. Mass media--Technological innovations. Series: The reference shelf; v. 66, no. 5 LC Classification: P96.P832 U66 1994 Dewey Class No.: 302.23/0973 20

The media and the twenty-first century / [edited by Nick Dazang.]. Published/Created: Lagos: NUJ, Abuja Coucil, [1996?] Related Authors: Dazang, Nick. Nigeria Union of Journalists. Abuja Council. Description: xv, 149 p.; 26 cm. ISBN: 978342520X Notes: "Papers compiled and edited...are the outcome of the 1996 Press Week/Founders' Day Celebration organised by the Nigeria Union of Journalists, Abuja Council, which took place from Monday, March 11, 1996, to Friday, March 15, 1996"--P. xiii. Includes bibliographical references. Subjects: Mass media--Nigeria--Congresses. LC Classification: P92.N5 M43 1996 Dewey Class No.: 302.23/09669 21

The Media in Western Europe: the Euromedia handbook / Euromedia Research Group; editor, Bernt Stubbe Østergaard. Published/Created: London; Newbury Park, Calif.: Sage Publications, 1992. Related Authors: Østergaard, Bernt Stubbe. Euromedia Research Group. Description: xi, 265 p.; 23 cm. ISBN: 0803985754 0803985762 (pbk.) Notes: Includes index. Subjects: Mass media--Europe--Handbooks, manuals, etc. Series: Sage communications in society LC Classification: P92.E9 M4 1992 Dewey Class No.: 302.23/094 20

The media market in the Netherlands & Flanders: a statistical guide / [edited by Tom Herpers, Marja Hageman, Hans Prins]. Published/Created: The Hague: NBLC; Rotterdam: Boekblad, c1993. Related Authors: Herpers, Tom. Hageman, Marja Prins, Hans. Description: 144 p.; 21 cm. ISBN: 9074864023 (Boekblad BV) 9054830166 (NBLC) Subjects: Mass media--Netherlands--Marketing--Statistics. Mass media--Flanders--Marketing--Statistics. LC Classification: P96.M362 N41413 1993 Dewey Class No.: 381/.4530223/09492021 21

The media: an introduction / edited by A. Briggs & P. Cobley. Edition Information: 2nd ed. Published/Created: New York: Pearson Education, 2002. Projected Pub. Date: 0202 Related Authors: Briggs,

Adam. Cobley, Paul, 1963- Description: p. cm. ISBN: 0582423465 Notes: Includes bibliographical references and index. Subjects: Mass media. LC Classification: P90 .M364 2002 Dewey Class No.: 302.23 21

The Significance of the media in American history / James D. Startt and Wm. David Sloan, editors. Published/Created: Northport, Ala.: Vision Press, c1994. Related Authors: Startt, James D., 1932- Sloan, W. David (William David), 1947- Description: xi, 382 p.; 23 cm. ISBN: 0963070045 Notes: Includes bibliographical references and index. Subjects: Mass media--United States--History. United States--History. LC Classification: P92.U5 S54 1994 Dewey Class No.: 302.23/0973 20

Thompson, Gary, 1950- Rhetoric through media / Gary Thompson. Published/Created: Boston: Allyn and Bacon, c1997. Description: xiii, 657 p.: ill.; 23 cm. ISBN: 0205189180 Notes: Includes bibliographical references (p. 643-649) and index. Subjects: Mass media--Authorship. Rhetoric. Mass media criticism. LC Classification: P96.A86 T48 1997 Dewey Class No.: 808/.042 20

Thompson, John B. (John Brookshire) Ideology and modern culture: critical social theory in the era of mass communication / John B. Thompson. Published/Created: Stanford, Calif.: Stanford University Press, 1990. Description: viii, 362 p.: ill.; 24 cm. ISBN: 0804718458 Notes: Includes bibliographical references (p. [332]-351) and index. Subjects: Culture. Ideology. Mass media. LC Classification: HM101 .T5133 1990 Dewey Class No.: 306 20

Thompson, John B. (John Brookshire) The media and modernity: a social theory of the media / John B. Thompson. Published/Created: Stanford, CA: Stanford Univeristy Press, 1995. Description: viii, 314 p.: ill.; 24 cm. ISBN: 0804726787 (cloth) Notes: Includes bibliographical references (p. [266]-297) and index. Subjects: Mass media--Social aspects. Communication--Social aspects. LC Classification: HM258 .T465 1995 Dewey Class No.: 302.23 20

Thompson, Kenneth, 1937- Moral panics / Kenneth Thompson. Published/Created: London; New York: Routledge, 1998. Description: ix, 157 p.; 21 cm. ISBN: 0415119766 0415119774 (pbk.) Notes: Includes bibliographical references (p. [143]-148) and indexes. Subjects: Deviant behavior--Public opinion. Deviant behavior in mass media. Social problems--Public opinion. Social problems in mass media. Moral conditions. Hysteria (Social psychology) Moral panics Series: Key ideas LC Classification: HM291 .T46 1998 Dewey Class No.: 302.5/42 21

Thunborg, Annika. Public and non-profit interaction: U.S. assistance to eastern European media, 1989-1995 / Annika Thunborg. Published/Created: Lund, Sweden: Lund University Press; Bromley, Kent, England: Chartwell-Bratt, c1997. Description: ix, 266 p.: ill.; 23 cm. ISBN: 9179664199 0862384818 Notes: Includes bibliographical references (p. 243-266). Subjects: Economic assistance, American. Technical assistance, American. Press--Europe, Eastern. Mass media--Europe, Eastern. Series: Lund political studies; 100 LC Classification: ACQUISITION IN PROCESS (COPIED)

Tidman, Peter, 1924- Tidman's media interview technique: handling the media and getting your point across on TV, radio, and within your organization / Peter Tidman, H. Lloyd Slater. Published/Created: London; New York: McGraw-Hill, c1992. Related Authors: Slater, H. Lloyd, 1951- Related Titles: Media interview technique. Description: viii, 151 p.; 23 cm. ISBN: 0077075773 Notes: Includes index. Subjects: Interviewing in mass media. LC Classification: P96.I54 T53 1992 Dewey Class No.: 302.23 20

Tolson, Andrew. Mediations: text and discourse in media studies / Andrew Tolson. Published/Created: New York: Arnold, c1996. Projected Pub. Date: 9604

Description: p. cm. ISBN: 0340574895 Notes: Includes bibliographical references and index. Subjects: Mass media and language. Discourse analysis. LC Classification: P96.L34 T65 1996 Dewey Class No.: 401/.41 21

Towards a civic society: the Baltic media's long road to freedom: perspectives on history, ethnicity and journalism / edited by Svennik Høyer, Epp Lauk and Peeter Vihalemm. Published/Created: Tartu: Baltic Association for Media Research: Nota Baltica Ltd, 1993. Related Authors: Høyer, Svennik, 1931- Lauk, E. Vihalemm, Peeter. Description: 366 p.: maps; 22 cm. ISBN: 9985600142 Notes: Includes bibliographical references. Subjects: Mass media--Baltic States--History. Press--Baltic States--History. Journalism--Baltic States--History. LC Classification: P92.B29 T68 1993 Dewey Class No.: 302.23/0947/4 20

Trow, George W. S. My pilgrim's progress: media studies, 1950-1998 / George W.S. Trow. Edition Information: 1st ed. Published/Created: New York: Pantheon Books, 1999. Description: 278 p.; 22 cm. ISBN: 0375401342 Subjects: Mass media--United States--History--20th century. LC Classification: P92.U5 T74 1999 Dewey Class No.: 302.23/0973/09045 21

Turner, Marcia Layton. How to think like the world's greatest new media moguls / Marcia Layton Turner. Published/Created: New York: McGraw-Hill, c2001. Description: vi, 216 p.; 21 cm. ISBN: 0071360697 Notes: Includes bibliographical references and index. Subjects: Mass media--Technological innovations. World Wide Web. Series: The leader's edge LC Classification: P96.T42 T87 2001 Dewey Class No.: 302.23 21

Turnock, Robert. Interpreting Diana: television audiences and the death of a princess / Robert Turnock. Published/Created: London: British Film Institute, 2000. Description: v, 138 p.; 24 cm. ISBN: 0851707882 0851707890 (pbk.) Notes: Includes bibliographical references (p. [129]-134) and index. Subjects: Diana, Princess of Wales, 1961- --Death and burial--Press coverage. Diana, Princess of Wales, 1961- --In mass media. Mass media and public opinion--Great Britain. Television--Social aspects--Great Britain. Television viewers--Great Britain. LC Classification: DA591.A45 D5374 2000 Dewey Class No.: 941.085/092 21

Turow, Joseph. Media systems in society: understanding industries, strategies, and power / Joseph Turow. Published/Created: New York: Longman, c1992. Description: xvi, 265 p.: ill.; 25 cm. ISBN: 0801305993 Notes: Includes bibliographical references and index. Subjects: Mass media. LC Classification: P90 .T87 1992 Dewey Class No.: 302.23 20

Turow, Joseph. Media systems in society: understanding industries, strategies, and power / Joseph Turow. Edition Information: 2nd ed. Published/Created: New York: Longman, c1997. Description: xvii, 298 p.; 24 cm. ISBN: 0801317045 Notes: Includes bibliographical references and index. Subjects: Mass media. LC Classification: P90 .T87 1997 Dewey Class No.: 302.23 20

Turow, Joseph. Media today: an introduction to mass communication / Joseph Turow. Published/Created: Boston: Houghton Mifflin Co., c1999. Description: xviii, 490 p.: ill. (some col.); 26 cm. ISBN: 0395870771 Notes: Includes bibliographical references and index. Subjects: Mass media. LC Classification: P90 .T874 1999 Dewey Class No.: 302.23 21

Van Nostran, William. The media writer's guide: writing for business and educational programs / by William Van Nostran. Published/Created: Boston: Focal Press, c2000. Related Authors: Van Nostran, William. Scriptwriter's handbook. Description: vii, 242 p.: ill.; 28 cm. ISBN: 0240803167 (alk. paper) Notes: Rev. ed. of: The scriptwriter's handbook. 1989. Includes bibliographical references (p. 231-233) and index. Subjects: Television authorship. Industrial television--Video recordings--Mass media--Authorship. Television in education. Business writing. LC Classification: PN1992.7 .V36 2000 Dewey Class No.: 808.2/25 21

Van Nostran, William. The scriptwriter's handbook / William J. Van Nostran. Published/Created: Boston: Focal Press, c1996. Related Authors: Van Nostran, William. Nonbroadcast television writer's handbook. Description: ix, 403 p.: ill.; 26 cm. ISBN: 0240802527 (acid-free paper) Notes: Rev. ed. of: The nonbroadcast television writer's handbook. 1983. Includes bibliographical rferences (p. 395-397). Subjects: Television authorship. Industrial television--Video recordings--Mass media--Authorship. Television in education. Business writing. LC Classification: PN1992.7 .V36 1996 Dewey Class No.: 808.2/25 20

Venturi, Robert. Two responses to some immediate issues / Robert Venturi and Denise Scott Brown. Published/Created: Philadelphia: Institute of Contemporary Art, c1993. Related Authors: Scott Brown, Denise, 1931- University of Pennsylvania. Institute of Contemporary Art. Description: 12 p.; 36 cm. ISBN: 0884540707 Notes: "Published on the occasion of the exhibition 'About architecture: an installation by Venturi, Scott Brown and Associates' organized by the Institute of Contemporary Art, Philadelphia, and presented February 12-April 18, 1993"--P. 12. Subjects: Kahn, Louis I., 1901-1974 --Appreciation. Venturi Scott Brown and Associates. Mass media and architecture--United States. LC Classification: NA2543.M37 V46 1993 Dewey Class No.: 720/.1/05 20

Vivian, John. The media of mass communication / John Vivian. Edition Information: 6th ed. Published/Created: Boston: Allyn and Bacon, 2002. Projected Pub. Date: 1111 Description: p. cm. ISBN: 0205335403 Notes: Includes index. LC Classification: P90 .V53 2002 Dewey Class No.: 302.23 21

Vivian, John. The media of mass communication / John Vivian. Edition Information: 5th ed. Published/Created: Boston: Allyn and Bacon, 1998. Projected Pub. Date: 9810 Description: p. cm. ISBN: 0205287395 (alk. paper) Notes: Includes bibliographical references and index. Subjects: Mass media. LC Classification: P90 .V53 1998 Dewey Class No.: 302.23 21

Vivian, John. The media of mass communication / John Vivian. Edition Information: 3rd ed. Published/Created: Boston: Allyn and Bacon, c1995. Description: xxxi, 496 p.: ill. (some col.); 26 cm. ISBN: 0205164528 Notes: Includes bibliographical references and indexes. Subjects: Mass media. LC Classification: P90 .V53 1995 Dewey Class No.: 302.23 20

Vivian, John. The media of mass communication / John Vivian. Published/Created: Boston: Allyn and Bacon, c1991. Description: xix, 411 p.: ill. (some col.); 26 cm. ISBN: 0205125417 Notes: Includes bibliographical references and index. Subjects: Mass media. LC Classification: P90 .V53 1991 Dewey Class No.: 302.23 20

Wade, John. Dealing effectively with the media / John Wade. Published/Created: Los Altos, Calif.: Crisp Publications, c1992. Description: iv, 83 p.: ill.; 26 cm. ISBN: 1560521163 (pbk.) Notes: Series statement from publisher's listing on p. 87. Includes bibliographical references (p. 83). Subjects: Interviewing in mass media. Series: Fifty-Minute series LC Classification: P96.I54 W33 1992 Dewey Class No.: 302.23 20

Wahl, Otto F. Media madness: public images of mental illness / Otto F. Wahl. Published/Created: New Brunswick, NJ: Rutgers University Press, c1995. Description: xiv, 220 p.: ill.; 24 cm. ISBN: 0813522129 (acid-free paper) Notes: Includes bibliographical references (p. 195-208) and index. Subjects: Mental illness in mass media. Mass media--United

States. LC Classification: P96.M452 U68 1995 Dewey Class No.: 362.2 20

Wahlstrom, Billie J. Perspectives on human communication / Billie J. Wahlstrom. Published/Created: Dubuque, Iowa: Wm. C. Brown, c1992. Description: xvii, 398 p.: ill.; 24 cm. ISBN: 0697107043 Notes: Includes bibliographical references and indexes. Subjects: Communication. Mass media. LC Classification: P90 .W214 1992 Dewey Class No.: 302.2

Ward, Jean (Jean W.) Search strategies in mass communication / Jean Ward, Kathleen A. Hansen. Edition Information: 3rd ed. Published/Created: New York: Longman, c1997. Related Authors: Hansen, Kathleen A. Description: xii, 371 p.: ill., map; 24 cm. ISBN: 080131755X Notes: Includes index. Subjects: Mass media--Research--Methodology. Communication--Research--Methodology. LC Classification: P91.3 .W37 1997 Dewey Class No.: 302.23/072 20

Ward, Jean (Jean W.) Search strategies in mass communication / Jean Ward, Kathleen Hansen. Edition Information: 2nd ed. Published/Created: New York: Longman, c1993. Related Authors: Hansen, Kathleen A. Description: xvi, 296 p.: ill.; 24 cm. ISBN: 0801310350 Notes: Includes bibliographical references and indexes. Subjects: Mass media--Research--Methodology. Communication--Research--Methodology. LC Classification: P91.3 .W37 1992 Dewey Class No.: 302.23/072 20

Ward, Sue. Getting the message across: public relations, publicity, and working with the media / Sue Ward. Published/Created: London; Boulder, Colo.: Journeyman, 1992. Description: x, 237 p.; 22 cm. ISBN: 1851720421 185172043X (pbk) Notes: Includes index. Subjects: Publicity. Public relations. Mass media. LC Classification: HM263 .W29 1992 Dewey Class No.: 302.23 20

Weber, Samuel M. Mass mediauras: form, technics, media / Samuel Weber; edited by Alan Cholodenko. Published/Created: Sydney: Power Publications, c1996. Related Authors: Cholodenko, Alan. Description: 247 p.; 22 cm. ISBN: 0909952221 Notes: Includes bibliographical references and index. Subjects: Mass media criticism. Aesthetics. LC Classification: P96.C76 W44 1996 Dewey Class No.: 302.23 21

Webster, James G. The mass audience: rediscovering the dominant model / by James G. Webster, Patricia F. Phalen. Published/Created: Mahwah, N.J.: Erlbaum, 1997. Related Authors: Phalen, Patricia F. Description: xv, 158 p.: ill.; 24 cm. ISBN: 0805823042 (acid-free paper) 0805823050 (pbk.: acid-free paper) Notes: Includes bibliographical references (p. 135-150) and indexes. Subjects: Mass media--Audiences. Series: LEA's communication series LC Classification: P96.A83 W43 1997 Dewey Class No.: 302.23 20

Whitaker, Wayne R., 1940- Mediawriting: print, broadcast, and public relations / W. Richard Whitaker, Janet E. Ramsey, Ronald D. Smith. Published/Created: New York: Longman, c2000. Related Authors: Ramsey, Janet E. Smith, Ronald D., 1948- Description: xx, 373 p.; 24 cm. ISBN: 0321011376 (pbk.) 0321018443 (teacher's ed.) Notes: Includes bibliographical references and index. Subjects: Mass media--Authorship. Broadcast journalism--Authorship. Public relations--Authorship. Journalism--Authorship. LC Classification: P96.A86 W48 2000 Dewey Class No.: 808/.066/302 21

Wicks, Robert H. Understanding audiences: learning to use the media constructively / Robert H. Wicks. Published/Created: Mahwah, N.J.: L. Erlbaum Associates, 2001. Description: xv, 241 p.: ill.; 23 cm. ISBN: 0805836470 (pbk.: alk. paper) Notes: Includes bibliographical references (p. 201-228) and indexes. Subjects: Mass media--Audiences. LC Classification: P96.A83 W53 2001 Dewey Class No.: 302.23 21

Wilcox, Dennis L. Public relations writing and media techniques / Dennis L. Wilcox, Lawrence W. Nolte; foreword by Patrick Jackson. Edition Information: 2nd ed. Published/Created: New York: HarperCollins College Publishers, c1995. Related Authors: Nolte, Lawrence W. Description: xxii, 514 p.: ill.; 24 cm. ISBN: 0065011066 Notes: Includes bibliographical references and index. Subjects: Public relations--United States. Public relations--United States--Authorship. Mass media--Authorship. Business writing. LC Classification: HM263 .W494 1995 Dewey Class No.: 659.2 20

Wilcox, Dennis L. Public relations writing and media techniques / Dennis L. Wilcox, Lawrence W. Nolte; foreword by Patrick Jackson. Published/Created: New York: Harper & Row, c1990. Related Authors: Nolte, Lawrence W. Description: xiv, 461 p.: ill.; 24 cm. ISBN: 0060471050 Notes: Includes bibliographical references. Subjects: Public relations--United States. Public relations--United States--Authorship. Mass media--Authorship. Business writing. LC Classification: HM263 .W49 1990 Dewey Class No.: 659.2 20

Willis, William James, 1946- New directions in media management / Jim Willis, Diane B. Willis. Published/Created: Boston: Allyn and Bacon, c1993. Related Authors: Willis, Diane B. Description: xii, 403 p.: ill.; 25 cm. ISBN: 0205139744 Notes: Includes bibliographical references (p. 395-396) and index. Subjects: Mass media--Management. LC Classification: P96.M34 W55 1993 Dewey Class No.: 302.23/068 20

Willis, William James, 1946- Reporting on risks: the practice and ethics of health and safety communication / Jim Willis with Albert Adelowo Okunade. Published/Created: Westport, Conn.: Praeger, 1997. Related Authors: Okunade, Albert Adelowo. Description: x, 229 p.; 24 cm. ISBN: 0275952967 (hc: alk. paper) 0275952983 (pb: alk. paper) Notes: Includes bibliographical references (p. [221]-224) and index. Subjects: Health risk communication. Health in mass media. LC Classification: RA423.2 .W55 1997 Dewey Class No.: 614.4/4 21

Willis, William James, 1946- The age of multimedia and turbonews / Jim Willis. Published/Created: Westport, Conn.: Praeger, 1994. Description: xi, 239 p.; 25 cm. ISBN: 0275943771 (alk. paper) 027594378X (pbk.) Notes: Includes bibliographical references (p. [229]-233) and index. Subjects: Multimedia systems. Mass media. LC Classification: QA76.575 .W55 1994 Dewey Class No.: 302.23/0285/66 20

Willis, William James, 1946- The shadow world: life between the news media and reality / Jim Willis. Published/Created: New York: Praeger, 1991. Description: 260 p.; 25 cm. ISBN: 0275934241 (alk. paper) 027593425X (pbk.: alk. paper) Notes: Includes bibliographical references (p. [251]-253) and index. Subjects: Reporters and reporting. Journalism--Objectivity. Mass media--Objectivity. Reporters and reporting--United States. Journalism--Objectivity--United States. LC Classification: PN4797 .W528 1991 Dewey Class No.: 070.4/3 20

Wimmer, Roger D. Mass media research: an introduction / Roger D. Wimmer, Joseph R. Dominick. Edition Information: 3rd ed. Published/Created: Belmont, Calif.: Wadsworth Pub. Co., c1991. Related Authors: Dominick, Joseph R. Description: xv, 478 p.: ill.; 25 cm. ISBN: 0534139620 Notes: Includes bibliographical references and indexes. Subjects: Mass media--Research. Series: Wadsworth series in mass communication LC Classification: P91.3 .W47 1991 Dewey Class No.: 302.23/072 20

Wimmer, Roger D. Mass media research: an introduction / Roger D. Wimmer, Joseph R. Dominick. Edition Information: 4th ed. Published/Created: Belmont, Calif.: Wadsworth Pub. Co., 1994. Related Authors: Dominick, Joseph R. Description:

xiv, 497 p.: ill.; 24 cm. ISBN: 0534174728: Notes: Includes bibliographical references and index. Subjects: Mass media--Research. Series: Wadsworth series in mass communication LC Classification: P91.3 .W47 1994 Dewey Class No.: 302.23/072 20

Windahl, Swen, 1942- Using communication theory: an introduction to planned communication / Sven Windahl and Benno H. Signitzer, with Jean T. Olson. Published/Created: London; Newbury Park, Calif.: Sage Publications, 1992. Related Authors: Signitzer, Benno. Olson, Jean T. Description: 248 p.: ill.; 25 cm. ISBN: 0803984308 0803984316 (pbk.) Notes: Includes bibliographical references (p. [223]-242) and index. Subjects: Communication planning. Mass media--Planning. LC Classification: P95.815 .W56 1992 Dewey Class No.: 302.2 20

Winston, Brian. Media technology and society: a history: from the telegraph to the Internet / Brian Winston. Published/Created: London; New York: Routledge, 1998. Related Authors: Winston, Brian. Misunderstanding media. Description: xiv, 374 p.; 25 cm. ISBN: 0415142296 (alk. paper) 041514230X (pbk.: alk. paper) Notes: Rev. ed. of: Misunderstanding media. 1986. Includes bibliographical references (p. 343-360) and index. Subjects: Mass media--Technological innovations--History. Communication--Technological innovations--History. Communication--Social aspects. Mass media--Social aspects. LC Classification: P96.T42 W49 1998 Dewey Class No.: 302.23 21

Winston, Brian. Technologies of seeing: photography, cinematography and television / Brian Winston. Published/Created: London: British Film Institute, 1996. Description: viii, 143 p.; 25 cm. ISBN: 0851706010 0851706029 (pbk.) Notes: Includes bibliographical references (p.119-137) and index. Subjects: Mass media--Technological innovations--History. LC Classification: P96.T42 W53 1996 Dewey Class No.: 302.23 21

Wood, Donald N., 1934- Post-intellectualism and the decline of democracy: the failure of reason and responsibility in the twentieth century / Donald N. Wood; foreword by Neil Postman. Published/Created: Westport, Conn.: Praeger, 1996. Description: xvii, 302 p.: ill.; 24 cm. ISBN: 0275954218 (alk. paper) 027595661X (pbk.: alk. paper) Notes: Includes bibliographical references (p. [269]-283) and index. Subjects: Mass media--Social aspects--Social problems--Democracy--United States. LC Classification: HN90.M3 W63 1996 Dewey Class No.: 301 20

Wurman, Richard Saul, 1935- Information anxiety 2 / Richard Saul Wurman; with additional research & writing by Loring Leifer & David Sume; Karen Whitehouse, editor; Michael J. Nolan, information designer. Published/Created: Indianapolis, Ind.: Que, c2001. Related Authors: Leifer, Loring. Sume, David. Whitehouse, Karen. Description: 308 p.: ill.; 24 cm. ISBN: 0789724103 Notes: Includes index. Subjects: Communication. Mass media. LC Classification: P90 .W8 2001 Dewey Class No.: 302.2 21

Wurman, Richard Saul, 1935- Information anxiety: what to do when information doesn't tell you what you need to know / Richard Saul Wurman. Published/Created: New York: Bantam, c1990. Description: 358 p.: ill.; 24 cm. ISBN: 0553348566: Notes: Includes bibliographical references (p. 339-348) and index. Subjects: Communication. Mass media. LC Classification: P90 .W8 1990 Dewey Class No.: 302.23/4 20

INTERNATIONAL MASS MEDIA

Bebyk, Valerii. The mass media of post-communist Ukraine / by Valeriy Bebyk and Oleksander Sydorenko. Published/Created: Kyiv: Innovation and Development Centre, 1998. Related Authors: Sydorenko, O. I. Description: 84 p.; 20 cm. ISBN: 9667345076 Notes: Includes bibliographical references (p. [80]-81). Subjects: Mass media--Ukraine. Post-communism--Ukraine. LC Classification: P92.U38 B427 1998 Dewey Class No.: 302.23/09477/09049 21

Berry, Eleanor. Robert Maxwell as I knew him: a black comedy / Eleanor Berry. Published/Created: Braunton Devon [England]: Merlin Books, 1993. Description: 139 p.; 21 cm. ISBN: 0863036538 Subjects: Maxwell, Robert, 1923- Publishers and publishing--Great Britain--Biography. Newspaper publishing--Great Britain--History--20th century. Mass media--Great Britain. Newspapers Production LC Classification: Z325.M394 B47 1993 Dewey Class No.: 070.5/092 20

Blain, Neil, 1951- Sport and national identity in the European media / Neil Blain, Raymond Boyle, and Hugh O'Donnell. Published/Created: Leicester; New York: Leicester University Press; New York, NY, USA: Distributed in the U.S. and Canada by St. Martin's Press, 1993. Related Authors: Boyle, Raymond, 1966- O'Donnell, Hugh, 1949- Description: vii, 209 p.: ill.; 23 cm. ISBN: 0718514513 Notes: Includes bibliographical references (p. [200]-203) and index. Subjects: Mass media and sports--Europe. Sports--Social aspects--Europe. Sports and state--Europe. Series: Sport, politics, and culture LC Classification: GV742 .B53 1993 Dewey Class No.: 070.4/49796 20

Boeren, A. J. J. M. In other words--: the cultural dimension of communication for development / Ad Boeren. Published/Created: The Hague, Netherlands: Centre for the Study of Education in Developing Countries, c1994. Description: 229 p.: ill.; 24 cm. Cancelled ISBN: 906443140x Notes: Includes bibliographical references (p. 211-227) Subjects: Communication--Mass media--Communication planning--Developing countries.Communication and culture. Series: CESO paperback; no. 19 LC Classification: P92.2 .B64 1994 Dewey Class No.: 302.2/09172/4 20

Bourgault, Louise Manon. Mass media in sub-Saharan Africa / Louise M. Bourgault. Published/Created: Bloomington: Indiana University Press, c1995. Description: xv, 294 p.: map; 25 cm. ISBN: 0253312507 (alk. paper) 0253209382 (pbk.: alk. paper) Notes: Includes bibliographical references (p. 270-287) and index. Subjects: Mass media--Africa, Sub-Saharan. LC Classification: P92.A46 B68 1995 Dewey Class No.: 302.23/0967 20

Brennan, Patrick H. Reporting the nation's business: press-government relations during the Liberal years, 1935 1957 /

Patrick H. Brennan. Published/Created: Toronto; Buffalo: University of Toronto Press, c1994. Description: xiv, 250 p., [12] p. of plates: ill.; 24 cm. ISBN: 0802029779 Notes: Includes bibliographical references and index. Subjects: Liberal Party of Canada--History--20th century. Government and the press--Mass media--Political aspects--Canada. LC Classification: PN4748.C3 B74 1994 Dewey Class No.: 071/.1/0904 20

Browne, Donald R. Electronic media and industrialized nations: a comparative study / Donald R. Browne. Edition Information: 1st ed. Published/Created: Ames: Iowa State University Press, 1999. Description: xiii, 561 p.; 24 cm. ISBN: 0813804221 Notes: Includes bibliographical references (p. 527-533) and index. Subjects: Broadcasting--Mass media--Europe. LC Classification: PN1990.6.E85 B76 1999 Dewey Class No.: 384.54/094 21

Caspi, Dan, 1946- The in/outsiders: the media in Israel / Dan Caspi, Yehiel Limor. Published/Created: Cresskill, N.J.: Hampton Press, c1999. Related Authors: Limor, Yehiel. Description: xix, 342 p.; 24 cm. ISBN: 1572731737 1572731745 Notes: Includes bibliographical references (p. 311-326) and indexes. Subjects: Mass media--Israel. Series: The Hampton Press communication series LC Classification: P92.I79 C37 1999 Dewey Class No.: 302.23/095694 21

Civic discourse: intercultural, international, and global media / coedited by Michael H. Prosser and K.S. Sitaram. Published/Created: Stamford, Conn.: Ablex Pub. Corp., c1999. Related Authors: Prosser, Michael H., 1936- Sitaram, K. S. Description: xiv, 508 p.: ill.; 24 cm. ISBN: 1567504167 1567504175 (paper) Notes: "Volume 2"--Cover. Includes bibliographical references and indexes. Subjects: Intercultural communication--Social aspects. Series: Civic discourse for the third millennium LC Classification: HM258 .C5347 1999 Dewey Class No.: 302.23 21

Cohen, Akiba A. Holocaust trials in the German and Israeli press / Akiba A. Cohen ... [et al.]. Published/Created: Cresskill, NJ: Hampton Press, 2001. Projected Pub. Date: 1111 Description: p. cm. ISBN: 157273387X 1572733888 (pbk.) Notes: Includes biblographical references (p.) and index. Subjects: Holocaust, Jewish (1939-1945)--Mass media and the Holocaust. Holocaust, Jewish (1939-1945)--War crime trials--Press coverage--Germany. Holocaust, Jewish (1939-1945)--War crime trials--Press coverage--Israel. Series: The Hampton Press communication series LC Classification: D804.3 .C62 2001 Dewey Class No.: 940.53/18 21

Communication & development / edited by Anjan Kumar Banerji. Published/Created: Varanasi: UGC-Special Assistance Programme, Dept. of Journalism & Mass Communication, Banaras Hindu University, 1995. Related Authors: Banerji, Anjan Kumar. Banaras Hindu University. Dept. of Journalism & Mass Communication. UGC-Special Assistance Programme. Description: 135 p.; 22 cm. Summary: Collection of contributed papers at different seminars with special reference to India. Subjects: Mass media--India. Mass media policy--India. Mass media in community development--India. 92-13 LC Classification: P92.I7 C596 1995 Dewey Class No.: 302.23/0954 21

Communication in Latin America: journalism, mass media, and society / Richard R. Cole, editor. Published/Created: Wilmington, Del.: Scholarly Resources, 1996. Related Authors: Cole, Richard R. Description: xx, 260 p.; 24 cm. ISBN: 0842025588 (cloth: alk. paper) 0842025596 (paper: alk. paper) Notes: Includes bibliographical references (p. 253-258). Filmography: p. 259-260. Subjects: Mass media--Latin America. Journalism--Latin America. Series: Jaguar books on Latin America; no. 14 LC Classification: P92.L3 C54 1996 Dewey Class No.: 302.23/098 20

Communication, values, and society / [edited by] Crispin C. Maslog; foreword by Teodoro Benigno. Published/Created:

Quezon City, Philippines: Philippine Association of Communication Educators, c1992. Related Authors: Maslog, Crispin C. Philippine Association of Communication Educators. Description: viii, 386 p.: ill.; 22 cm. ISBN: 971870308X Notes: Includes bibliographical references. Subjects: Mass media. Mass media--Philippines. LC Classification: P91 .C562 1992 Dewey Class No.: 302.23 20

Communications in Bangladesh. Part 1 [microform]. Published/Created: New Delhi: Library of Congress Office; Washington, D.C.: Library of Congress Photoduplication Service, 1999. Description: 5 microfiches. Notes: A collection of pamphlets Published during 1994-1997. Contents list arranged alphabetically by title. Collected and organized by the Library of Congress Office, New Delhi. Master microform held by: DLC. Subjects: Communication--Bangladesh. Mass media--Bangladesh. Series: South Asia ephemera collection. Bangladesh; B-CLR-84.1 LC Classification: Microfiche 98/62006 (P)

Converging media? Converging regulation? / edited by Richard Collins. Published/Created: London: Institute for Public Policy Research, IPPR, c1996. Related Authors: Collins, Richard, 1946- Description: 70 p.: ill.; 22 cm. ISBN: 186030026X Notes: Includes bibliographical references. Subjects: Mass media policy--Great Britain. Communication policy--Great Britain. Series: Media (London, England) Variant Series: Media LC Classification: P95.82.G7 C66 1996 Dewey Class No.: 302.23/0941 21

Cooper-Chen, Anne. Mass communication in Japan / Anne Cooper-Chen with Miiko Kodama. Edition Information: 1st ed. Published/Created: Ames, Iowa: Iowa State University Press, 1997. Related Authors: Kodama, Miiko, 1942- Description: xi, 263 p.: ill.; 24 cm. ISBN: 0813827108 (acid-free paper) Notes: Includes bibliographical references (p. 233-245) and index. Subjects: Mass media--Japan. LC Classification: P92.J3 C67 1997 Dewey Class No.: 302.23/0952 21

Crone, Tom. Law and the media: an everyday guide for professionals / Tom Crone. Edition Information: 2nd ed. Published/Created: Oxford [England]; Boston: Butterworth-Heinemann, 1991. Description: xii, 214 p.; 24 cm. ISBN: 0750602163 Notes: Includes index. Subjects: Mass media--Law and legislation--Libel and slander--Great Britain. LC Classification: KD2870 .C76 1991 Dewey Class No.: 343.4109/9 344.10399 20

Cultural difference, media memories: Anglo-American images of Japan / edited by Phil Hammond. Published/Created: London; Herndon, VA: Cassell, 1997. Related Authors: Hammond, Phil, 1962- Description: xxv, 229 p.; 23 cm. ISBN: 0304701106 0304701114 (pbk.) Notes: Includes bibliographical references and index. Subjects: Public opinion--Japan in mass media--United States. Japan in mass media--Great Britain. Japan--Foreign public opinion, American. Japan--Foreign public opinion, British. LC Classification: DS849.U6 C85 1997 Dewey Class No.: 303.3/8/0973 21

Dajani, Nabil H. Disoriented media in a fragmented society: the Lebanese experience / Nabil H. Dajani. Published/Created: [Beirut]: American University of Beirut, c1992. Description: 191 p.; 23 cm. Notes: Includes bibliographical references (p. 187-191). Subjects: Mass media--Social aspects--Lebanon. LC Classification: HN659.Z9 M34 1994 Dewey Class No.: 302.23/095692 20

Das Gupta, Achintya. State-of-the-art of media campaigns [microform]: a comprehensive search of literature: final report / Achintya Das Gupta, Anish K. Barua. Published/Created: Dhaka, Bangladesh: United Nations Development Program: World Bank, 1992. Related Authors: United Nations Development Programme.

Description: 67, 24 leaves; 29 cm. Summary: With special reference to Bangladesh. Notes: Master microform held by: DLC. Microfiche. New Delhi: Library of Congress Office; Washington, D.C.: Library of Congress Photoduplication Service, 1996. 2 microfiches. Subjects: Mass media--Social aspects--Communication in community development--Bangladesh. B-21; B-25 LC Classification: Microfiche 96/62026 (H)

DeLuca, Anthony R. Politics, diplomacy, and the media: Gorbachev's legacy in the West / Anthony R. DeLuca. Published/Created: Westport, Conn.: Praeger, 1998. Description: x, 165 p.; 25 cm. ISBN: 0275959686 (alk. paper) Notes: Includes bibliographical references (p. [155]-158) and index. Subjects: Gorbachev, Mikhail Sergeevich, 1931- Communication in politics--Public relations and politics--Mass media and public opinion--Soviet Union--Politics and government--1985-1991. LC Classification: DK288 .D45 1998 Dewey Class No.: 947.085 21

Demers, David P. Global media: menace or Messiah? / David Demers, with a foreword by Melvin DeFleur. Edition Information: Rev. ed. Published/Created: Creskill, N.J.: Hampton Press, c2002. Description: xxv, 209 p.; 23 cm. ISBN: 1572734310 (pbk.) Notes: Includes bibliographical references (p. 179-195) and index. Subjects: Mass media--Ownership. Communication, International--Social aspects. Series: The Hampton Press communication series LC Classification: P96.E25 D46 2001 Dewey Class No.: 302.23 21

Dimkpa, Prince. Media management in Nigeria / [Prince Dimkpa]. Published/Created: Lagos: Org Communication Consultants, [1997] Description: viii, 195 p.; 24 cm. ISBN: 978019018X Notes: Includes bibliographical references. Subjects: Mass media--Nigeria--Management. LC Classification: P96.M342 N643 1997 Dewey Class No.: 302.23/09669 21

Dynamics of media politics: broadcasts and electronic media in Western Europe / edited by Karen Siune and Wolfgang Truetzschler for the Euromedia Research Group. Published/Created: London; Newbury Park: Sage Publications, 1992. Related Authors: Siune, Karen. Truetzschler, Wolfgang. Euromedia Research Group. Description: xii, 206 p.; 23 cm. ISBN: 0803985738 0803985746 (pbk.) Notes: Includes bibliographical references and index. Subjects: Mass media policy--Europe. Series: Sage communications in society LC Classification: P95.82.E85 D9 1992 Dewey Class No.: 302.23/094 20

Ebo, Stella-Joan. Mass media and society: an introduction / Stella-Joan Ebo. Published/Created: Enugu; Los Angeles: ACENA Publishers, 1996. Description: 108 p.; 21 cm. ISBN: 9782114235 Notes: Includes bibliographical references (p. 100-104) and index. Subjects: Mass media--Social aspects--Nigeria. LC Classification: HN831.Z9 M32 1996 Dewey Class No.: 302.23/09669 21

Ellis, Frank, 1953- From glasnost to the Internet: Russia's new infosphere / Frank Ellis. Published/Created: New York: St. Martin's Press, 1999. Description: xxiii, 259 p.; 23 cm. ISBN: 031221765X (cloth) Notes: Includes full text of the 1992 Russian mass media law in English. Includes bibliographical references (p. 240-250) and index. Subjects: Mass media--Internet--Russia (Federation) LC Classification: P92.R9 E45 1999 Dewey Class No.: 302.2/0947 21

Exploring the limits: Europe's changing communication environment: European Communication Council report 1997. Published/Created: Berlin; New York: Springer, c1997. Related Authors: European Communication Council. Description: 368 p.: ill.; 26 cm. ISBN: 3540626379 Notes: Includes bibliographical references. Subjects: Communication--Mass media--Europe. LC Classification: P92.E9 E98 1997 Dewey Class No.: 320.2/094 21

Fathi, Asghar. Canadian studies in mass communication / Asghar Fathi. Published/Created: Toronto: Canadian Scholars' Press, 1990. Description: vii, 117 p.; 23 cm. ISBN: 0921627475 Notes: Includes bibliographical references. Subjects: Mass media--Canada. LC Classification: P92.C3 F37 1990 Dewey Class No.: 302.23/71 20

Federation of Cameroon Media Professionals. Constitution of the Federation of Cameroon Media Professionals. Published/Created: [Cameroon?: s.n., 1995?] Description: 39 p.; 21 cm. Subjects: Federation of Cameroon Media Professionals. Mass media--Cameroon--Societies, etc. LC Classification: P92.C17 F43 1995 Dewey Class No.: 302.23/06/06711 21

France and the mass media / edited by Brian Rigby, Nicholas Hewitt. Published/Created: Houndmills, Basingstoke, Hampshire: Macmillan, 1991. Related Authors: Rigby, Brian. Hewitt, Nicholas. Description: xi, 238 p.; 23 cm. ISBN: 0333512812: Notes: "Based on papers given at the conference 'L'Avènement des mass-media dans la France de l'après-guerre: culture et culture populaire,' held at the Maison Française d'Oxford from 17 to 19 February 1989, under the auspices of the Maison Française and the European Humanities Research Centre at the University of Warwick"--P. viii. Includes bibliographical references (p. 220-227) and index. Subjects: Popular culture--France--History--20th century Congresses. Mass media--France--Influence--Congresses. France--Civilization--1945- --Congresses. Series: Warwick studies in the European humanities, 0956-5108 LC Classification: DC33.7 .F678 1991

Frederikse, Julie. None but ourselves: masses vs media in the making of Zimbabwe / Julie Frederikse; with photographs by Biddy Partridge. Edition Information: 10th anniversary of independence ed. Published/Created: Harare: Oral Traditions Association of Zimbabwe in association with Anvil Press, 1990. Related Authors: Partridge, Biddy. Description: xii, 371 p.: ill., maps; 30 cm. ISBN: 0797409610 Notes: Includes bibliographical references (p. [351]-365) and index. Subjects: Press and propaganda--Zimbabwe. Propaganda, Zimbabwean. Zimbabwe--History--Chimurenga War, 1966-1980--Mass media and the war Zimbabwe--History--Chimurenga War, 1966-1980--Press coverage. Zimbabwe--History--Chimurenga War, 1966-1980--Propaganda. LC Classification: P96.C45 F74 1990 Dewey Class No.: 302.23/096891/09046 20

Ghosh, Subir, 1945- Mass communication today: in the Indian context / Subir Ghosh. Published/Created: Calcutta: Profile Publishers: Distributors, Rupa & Co., 1996. Description: 342 p.; 23 cm. ISBN: 8185550085 Notes: Includes bibliographical references and index. Subjects: Mass media policy--India. Communication--Social aspects--India. LC Classification: P92.I7 G46 1996 Dewey Class No.: 302.23/0954 21

Ghosh, Subir, 1945- Mass media today: in the Indian context / Subir Ghosh. Published/Created: Calcutta: Profile Publishers: Distributors, Rupa & Co., 1991. Description: xii, 224 p.: ill.; 23 cm. ISBN: 8185550026: Notes: Includes bibliographical references. Subjects: Mass media--Social aspects--India. LC Classification: HN690.Z9 M323 1991 Dewey Class No.: 302.23/0954 20

Giorgi, Liana. The post-socialist media: what power the West?: the changing media landscape in Poland, Hungary, and the Czech Republic / Liana Giorgi; with a foreword by Philip Schlesinger and with the collaboration of Ronald J. Pohoryles. Published/Created: Aldershot, England; Brookfield, Vt.: Avebury, c1995. Related Authors: Pohoryles, Ronald J. Description: x, 151 p.; 23 cm. ISBN: 1856286541 Notes: Includes bibliographical references (p. 150-151). Subjects: Mass media--Poland. Mass media--Hungary. Mass media--Czech Republic. Post-communism-

-Europe, Central. Media Poland Hungary Czech Republic Series: Contemporary trends in European social sciences LC Classification: P92.P6 G56 1995 Dewey Class No.: 302.23/0943 20

Global media news. Published/Created: Pullman, WA: Center for Global Media Studies, 1999- Related Authors: Center for Global Media Studies. Description: v.; 28 cm. Vol. 1, no. 1 (summer 1999)- Current Frequency: Quarterly ISSN: 1524-7783 Subjects: Mass media--Periodicals. LC Classification: IN PROCESS Dewey Class No.: 302 13

Globalization, communications, and Caribbean identity / edited by Hopeton S. Dunn. Edition Information: 1st ed. Published/Created: New York: St. Martin's Press, 1995. Related Authors: Dunn, Hopeton S. Description: xviii, 228 p.: ill.; 24 cm. ISBN: 0312127642 Notes: Includes bibliographical references. Subjects: Mass media--Caribbean Area. Communication, International. Mass media and culture--Caribbean Area. Mass media and technology--Caribbean Area. Mass media policy--Caribbean Area. LC Classification: P92.C33 G58 1995 Dewey Class No.: 302.23/09729 20

González Manet, Enrique. Informatics and society: the new challenges / Enrique González-Manet; translated by Laurien Alexandre. Published/Created: Norwood, N.J.: Ablex Pub., c1992. Description: xii, 201 p.; 24 cm. ISBN: 0893917761 (cloth) 089391777X (pbk.) Notes: Translated from Spanish. Includes bibliographical references (p. 181-192) and indexes. Subjects: Mass media. Mass media--Latin America. Series: The Communication and information science series LC Classification: P91 .G63 1992 Dewey Class No.: 302.23/098 20

Gordon, W. Terrence, 1942- Marshall McLuhan: escape into understanding: a biography / W. Terrence Gordon. Published/Created: New York: Basic Books, c1997. Related Authors: McLuhan, Marshall, 1911- Description: xiv, 465 p.: ill.; 25 cm. ISBN: 0465005497 Notes: Includes bibliographical references (p. [436]-454) and index. Subjects: McLuhan, Marshall, 1911- Mass media specialists--Canada--Biography. LC Classification: P92.5.M3 G67 1997 Dewey Class No.: 302.23/092 B 21

Government media, autonomy and after / edited by G.S. Bhargava. Published/Created: New Delhi: Institute of Social Sciences and Concept Pub. Co., 1991. Related Authors: Bhargava, G. S., 1925- Institute of Social Sciences (New Delhi, India) Description: xii, 134 p.; 22 cm. ISBN: 8170223660: Notes: Papers presented at a seminar organized by the Institute of Social Sciences, on 28 April 1990, at the Parliament House Annexe, New Delhi. Includes index. Includes bibliographical references. Subjects: Mass media policy--India--Congresses. LC Classification: P95.82.I4 G68 1991 Dewey Class No.: 302.23/0954 20

Great Britain. Dept. of National Heritage. Media ownership: the Government's proposals; presented to Parliament / by the Secretary of State for National Heritage by command of Her Majesty, May 1995. Published/Created: London: HMSO, [1995] Description: 35 p.; 30 cm. Subjects: Mass media--Ownership--Great Britain. Mass media policy--Great Britain. Series: Cm (Series) (Great Britain. Parliament); 2872. Variant Series: Cm; 2872 LC Classification: P96.E252 G73 1995 Dewey Class No.: 384.54/3 21

Gunasekara, H. M. Media as bridge maker / H.M. Gunasekara; research assistants, M.C. Mathupala, Nalaka Gunawardene. Published/Created: Colombo: Friedrich-Ebert-Stiftung, 1993. Related Authors: Mathupala, M. C. Gunawardene, Nalaka. Friedrich-Ebert-Stiftung (Sri Lanka) Coordinating Group for Studies on South Asian Perspectives. Description: x, 107 p.; 22 cm. ISBN: 9556070109 Notes: At head of Coordinating Group for Studies on South Asian Perspectives. Includes bibliographical references (p. 96). Subjects: Mass media--South Asia.

Communication--International cooperation. LC Classification: P92.S64 G86 1993 Dewey Class No.: 302.23/0954 20

Gupta, V. S. Third revolution in Indian perspective: contemporary issues and themes in communication / V.S. Gupta. Published/Created: New Delhi: Concept Pub. Co., 1995. Description: 200 p.; 23 cm. ISBN: 8170225590 Notes: Includes bibliographical references (p. [193]-197) and index. Subjects: Communication--India. Mass media--Social aspects--India. Mass media--India--Influence. Communication in rural development--India. LC Classification: P92.I7 G87 1995 Dewey Class No.: 302.2/0954 20

Gusau, Nababa Sanda. The mass media in Nigeria / by Nababa Sanda Gusau. Published/Created: [Nigeria: s.n., 1994] Description: iii, 89 p.; 24 cm. Subjects: Mass media--Nigeria. LC Classification: P92.N5 G87 1994 Dewey Class No.: 302.23/09669 21

Hamm, Donald. New opportunities in new media: Saskatchewan's arts and cultural industries / prepared by Donald Hamm for Saskatchewan Municipal Government; in partnership with the Department of Canadian Heritage and Industry Canada; with the participation of Saskfilm Published/Created: [Saskatchewan?: s.n., 1994] Related Authors: Saskatchewan. Saskatchewan Municipal Government. Arts, Cultural Industries, and Multiculturalism Branch. Canada. Canadian Heritage. Canada. Industry Canada. Saskfilm. Description: 85 p.: ill.; 28 cm. Notes: Cover title. Prepared for the Arts, Cultural Industries, and Multiculturalism Branch of Saskatchewan Municipal Government. "October, 1994"--Cover. Includes bibliographical references (p. 70-72). Subjects: Mass media--Saskatchewan--Marketing. Cultural industries--Saskatchewan. LC Classification: P96.M342 C224 1994 Dewey Class No.: 384/.041 21

Hiebert, Ray Eldon. Exploring mass media for a changing world / by Ray Eldon Hiebert and Sheila Jean Gibbons. Published/Created: Mahwah, N.J.: Lawrence Erlbaum Associates, 2000. Related Authors: Gibbons, Sheila Jean, 1951- Description: xx, 349 p.: ill.; 25 cm. ISBN: 0805829164 (pbk.: alk. paper) Notes: Includes bibliographical references and indexes. Subjects: Mass media. LC Classification: P90 .H478 1999 Dewey Class No.: 302.23 21

Images and empires: visuality in colonial and postcolonial Africa / Paul S. Landau and Deborah Kaspin, editors. Published/Created: Berkeley: University of California Press, c2002. Projected Pub. Date: 0210 Related Authors: Landau, Paul Stuart, 1962- Kaspin, Deborah, 1953- Description: p. cm. ISBN: 0520229487 (cloth: alk. paper) 0520229495 (paper: alk. paper) Notes: Includes bibliographical references and index. Subjects: Visual anthropology--Africa. Visual sociology--Africa. Africa--Colonization. Postcolonialism--Africa. Africa in art. Africa in literature. Africa in mass media. LC Classification: GN645 .I43 2002 Dewey Class No.: 301/.096 21

Images of Germany in the American media / edited by Jim Willis. Published/Created: Westport, Conn.: Praeger, 1999. Related Authors: Willis, William James, 1946- Description: xii, 193 p.; 25 cm. ISBN: 0275959635 (alk. paper) Notes: Includes bibliographical references (p. [187]-188) and index. Subjects: Mass media--United States. Germany--In mass media. LC Classification: P96.G48 I47 1999 Dewey Class No.: 302.23/0973 21

In search of boundaries: communication, nation-states and cultural identities / edited by Joseph M. Chan and Bryce T. McIntyre. Published/Created: Westport, CT: Ablex Pub., 2001. Projected Pub. Date: 0201 Related Authors: Chan, Joseph Man. McIntyre, Bryce Telfer. Description: p. cm. ISBN: 1567505708 (alk. paper) 1567505716 (pbk.: alk. paper) Notes: Includes bibliographical references. Subjects: Mass media. Group identity. Boundaries. Globalization. Series:

Advances in communication and culture LC Classification: HM1206 .I5 2001 Dewey Class No.: 302.23 21

Internews. Indonesian broadcast media in the post-Suharto period / a report prepared for OTI by Internews Network, Inc.; principal investigators, Kathleen Reen and Eric S. Johnson. Published/Created: [Jakarta]: The Network, [1998?] Related Authors: Reen, Kathleen. Johnson, Eric S., 1967- National Institute of Standards and Technology (U.S.). Office of Technology Innovation. Description: 40 leaves; 30 cm. Subjects: Broadcast journalism--Indonesia. Mass media surveys--Indonesia. LC Classification: PN5449.I5 I58 1998 Dewey Class No.: 302.23/09598 21

Jakubowicz, Karol. Conquest or partnership?: East-West European integration in the media field / Karol Jakubowicz. Published/Created: [D¨sseldorf, Germany]: European Institute for the Media, c1996. Related Authors: European Institute for the Media. Description: vii, 49 p.; 30 cm. Notes: "December 1996"--Cover. Includes bibliographical references (p. 27-28). Subjects: Mass media--Europe, Eastern. European cooperation. Series: Mediafact LC Classification: P92.E95 J35 1996 Dewey Class No.: 302.23/0947 21

Janas, Justyna. History of the mass media in Ethiopia / Justyna Janas. Published/Created: Warsaw: Warsaw University, Institute of Oriental Studies, Dept. of African Languages and Cultures, 1991. Description: 83 p.; 30 cm. Notes: Includes bibliographical references (p. 77-83). Subjects: Mass media--Ethiopia--History. Series: Studies of the Department of African Languages and Cultures LC Classification: P92.E8 J36 1991 Dewey Class No.: 302.23/0963 21

Jeffres, Leo W. Mass media effects / Leo W. Jeffres, with Richard M. Perloff. Edition Information: 2nd ed. Published/Created: Prospect Heights, Ill.: Waveland Press, c1997. Related Authors: Perloff, Richard M. Jeffres, Leo W. Mass media. Description: ix, 494 p.: ill.; 23 cm. ISBN: 0881339628 (pbk.) Notes: Rev. ed.: of Mass media: processes and effects, c1986. Includes bibliographical references (p. 387-476) and index. Subjects: Mass media. LC Classification: P90 .J345 1997 Dewey Class No.: 302.23 21

Joseph, Joni C. Mass media and rural development / Joni C. Joseph. Published/Created: Jaipur: Rawat Publications, c1997. Description: 240 p.: maps; 23 cm. Cancelled ISBN: 817033410X Summary: Case study of Kerala, India. Notes: Includes bibliographical references (p. [221]-233) and index. Subjects: Rural development--India. Mass media--India--Social aspects. Mass media--India--Economic aspects. Communication in rural development--India. LC Classification: HN683.5 .J586 1997 Dewey Class No.: 307.1/412/0954 21

Journal of communication studies. Published/Created: Varanasi: National Council of Development Communication, 2000- Related Authors: National Council of Development Communication (India) Description: v.; 25 cm. Some no. combined. Vol. 18, no. 1-2 (2000)- Current Frequency: Two no. a year Continues: Interaction (V¯ar¯anas¯i, India). Interaction (DLC) 88912947 (OCoLC)19619501 ISSN: 0970-5554 Notes: Title from cover. Subjects: Mass media--India--Periodicals. Mass media in agricultural extension work--India Periodicals. Mass media in community development--India--Periodicals. LC Classification: HN690.Z9

Junaid, Shahwar. Communications media and public policy / Shahwar Junaid. Published/Created: Rawalpindi, Pakistan: Publishing Consultants, 1995. Description: 198 p.; 22 cm. Notes: Includes bibliographical references (p. [197]-198). Subjects: Communication, International. Mass media--Technological innovations. Mass media--Social aspects. Political planning. LC Classification: P96.I5 J86 1995 Dewey Class No.: 302.2 21

Kasoma, Francis Peter, 1943- Communication policies in Zambia / Francis P. Kasoma. Published/Created: Tampere [Finland]: Tampereen yliopisto, 1990. Description: ii, 104 p.; 21 cm. ISBN: 9514425669 Notes: Includes bibliographical references (p. 104). Subjects: Communication policy--Zambia. Mass media--Zambia. Series: Julkaisuja (Tampereen yliopisto. Tiedotusopin laitos). Sarja B; 30. Variant Series: Julkaisuja. Sarja B / Tampereen yliopisto, Tiedotusopin laitos = Publications. Series B / University of Tampere, Dept. of Journalism and Mass Communication, 0358-4151; 30 LC Classification: P95.82.Z33 K37 1990

Kazan, Fayad E. Mass media, modernity, and development: Arab states of the Gulf / Fayad E. Kazan; foreword by Frederick Frey. Published/Created: Westport, Conn.: Praeger, 1993. Description: xxiii, 291 p.: ill., map; 25 cm. ISBN: 0275945332 (alk. paper) Notes: Includes bibliographical references (p. [269]-279) and index. Subjects: Mass media--Social aspects--Arabian Peninsula. Mass media in community development--Arabian Peninsula. Progress. LC Classification: HN662.Z9 M35 1993 Dewey Class No.: 302.23/0953 20

Khan, M. I. (Mohammad Ikram), 1916- Studies in modern mass-media: issues, problems, and prospects / M.I. Khan, Kaushal Kumar. Published/Created: Delhi: Kanishka Publishers Distributors, 1993. Related Authors: Kumar, Kaushal, 1945- Description: 3 v.; 23 cm. ISBN: 8185475822 (set): 8185475830 8185475849 8185475857 Notes: Includes bibliographical references (v. 1, p. [353]-367) and indexes. Subjects: Mass media--India. Mass media--Social aspects--India. Communication--Social aspects--India. LC Classification: P92.I7 K48 1993 Dewey Class No.: 302.23 20

Kivikuru, Ullamaija. Changing mediascapes?: a case study in nine Tanzanian villages / by Ullamaija Kivikuru in collaboration with William Lobulu and Gervas Moshiro. Published/Created: Helsinki: University of Helsinki, Institute of Development Studies, [1994]. Related Authors: Lobulu, William. Moshiro, Gervas. Description: 1 v. (various pagings): ill.; 25 cm. ISBN: 9514569083 Notes: Includes bibliographical references (p. [195-201]). Subjects: Mass media--Tanzania. Communication in rural development--Tanzania. Series: Report. B (Helsingin yliopisto. Kehitysmaainstituutti); 94/28. Variant Series: Report B.,0353-9493; 28/1994 LC Classification: P92.T34 K58 1994 Dewey Class No.: 302.23/09678 21

Kolar-Panov, Dona. Video, war, and the diasporic imagination / Dona Kolar-Panov. Published/Created: London; New York: Routledge, 1997. Description: xvi, 270 p.; 24 cm. ISBN: 0415148804 Notes: Includes bibliographical references (p. 240-262) and index. Subjects: Mass media—Australia. Bosnians--Croats--Australia--Ethnic identity. Mass media & minorities--Australia. Yugoslav War, 1991-1995--Mass media & the war. Series: Routledge research in cultural and media studies LC Classification: P96.A832 A85 1997 Dewey Class No.: 302.23/0994 20

Kuhn, Raymond. The media in France / Raymond Kuhn. Published/Created: London; New York: Routledge, 1995. Description: xiii, 284 p.; 24 cm. ISBN: 0415014581 (pbk.) 041501459X Notes: Includes bibliographical references (p. [268]-275) and index. Subjects: Mass media--France. LC Classification: P92.F8 K84 1995 Dewey Class No.: 302.23/0944 20

Kunczik, Michael, 1946- Media giants: ownership concentration and globalisation / Michael Kunczik. Published/Created: Bonn: Friedrich-Ebert-Stiftung, c1997. Related Authors: Simon, Diet. Friedrich-Ebert-Stiftung. Abteilung Internationale Entwicklungszusammenarbeit. Description: 213 p.: ill.; 22 cm. Notes: "Communication manual"--Cover. " Published by the Division for International Development Cooperation of Friedrich-Ebert-Stiftung (FES)--T.p. verso. Includes bibliographical references (p. 203-213).

"Translated from the German by Diet Simon"--T.p. verso. Subjects: Mass media--Ownership. Communication, International. Mass media and culture. LC Classification: P96.E25 K86 1997 Dewey Class No.: 302.23 21

Lent, John A. Bibliography of Cuban mass communications / compiled by John A. Lent. Published/Created: Westport, Conn.: Greenwood Press, 1992. Description: xi, 357 p.; 24 cm. ISBN: 0313284555 (alk. paper) Notes: Includes indexes. Subjects: Mass media--Cuba--Bibliography. Series: Bibliographies and indexes in mass media and communications, 1041-8350; no. 6 LC Classification: Z5634.C9 L46 1992 P92.C9 Dewey Class No.: 016.30223/097291 20

Lent, John A. Mass communications in the Caribbean / John A. Lent. Edition Information: 1st ed. Published/Created: Ames: Iowa State University Press, 1990. Description: xiii, 398 p.: ill.; 24 cm. ISBN: 0813811821 (alk. paper) Notes: Includes bibliographical references (p. 347-375) and index. Subjects: Mass media--Caribbean Area. LC Classification: P92.C33 L46 1990 Dewey Class No.: 302.23/09729 20

Lohmann, Robin. Images of old age in German and American print media: empirical investigations into defining principles and patterns of visual representation / Robin Lohmann. Published/Created: Aachen: Shaker, 1997. Description: 199 p.: ill.; 21 cm. ISBN: 3826521684d Notes: Originally presented as the author's thesis (doctoral)--Universität Kiel, 1992. Includes bibliographical references (p. 172-187).d Some ill. in German. Subjects: Aged in mass media. Mass media--Germany. Mass media--United States. Content analysis (Comnmunication) Series: Sprache & Kultur, 1430-7782 LC Classification: P94.5.A38 L65 1997 Dewey Class No.: 302.23/084/6 21

Lorimer, Rowland, 1944- Mass communication in Canada / Rowland Lorimer and Jean McNulty. Edition Information: 3rd ed. Published/Created: Toronto: New York: Oxford University Press, 1996. Related Authors: McNulty, Jean, 1942- Description: xvi, 398 p.: ill.; 23 cm. ISBN: 0195412087 (alk. paper) Notes: Includes bibliographical references (p. [374]-388) and index. Subjects: Mass media--Canada. Communication--Canada. LC Classification: P92.C3 L67 1996 Dewey Class No.: 302.23/0971 21

Lorimer, Rowland, 1944- Mass communication in Canada / Rowland Lorimer, Mike Gasher. Edition Information: 4th ed. Published/Created: [Don Mills, Ont.; New York]: Oxford University Press, [2001] Related Authors: Gasher, Mike, 1954- Description: xii, 359 p.: ill.; 23 cm. ISBN: 0195415280 Notes: Includes bibliographical references (p. [336]-349) and index. Subjects: Mass media--Canada. Communication--Canada.

Lynch, Daniel C. After the propaganda state: media, politics, and "thought work" in reformed China / Daniel C. Lynch. Published/Created: Stanford, CA: Stanford University Press, c1999. Description: viii, 327 p.; 24 cm. ISBN: 0804734615 (cloth: alk. paper) Notes: Includes bibliographical references. Subjects: Mass media--Communication--Social aspects--China. Social change--China. Political participation--China. LC Classification: HN740.Z9 M35 1999 Dewey Class No.: 302.2 21

Manning, Paul, 1955- Spinning for labour: trade unions and the new media environment / Paul Manning. Published/Created: Aldershot, Hants, England; Brookfield, Vt.: Ashgate, c1998. Description: xii, 401 p.; 23 cm. ISBN: 1840143398 Notes: Includes bibliographical references (p. 380-397) and index. Subjects: Labor unions and mass media--Great Britain. LC Classification: P96.T72 G745 1998 Dewey Class No.: 331.88/0941 21

Marchand, Philip, 1946- Marshall McLuhan: the medium and the messenger: a biography / Philip Marchand; [with a new foreword by Neil Postman]. Edition Information: 1st MIT Press ed.

Published/Created: Cambridge, Mass.: MIT Press, 1998. Description: xiii, 322 p.: ill.; 23 cm. ISBN: 0262631865 Notes: Originally Published: New York: Ticknor & Fields, 1989. Includes bibliographical references (p. [309]-314) and index. Subjects: McLuhan, Marshall, 1911- Mass media specialists--Canada--Biography. LC Classification: P92.5.M3 M34 1998 Dewey Class No.: 302.23/092 B 21

Markets and myths: forces for change in the media of Western Europe / [edited by] Anthony Weymouth and Bernard Lamizet. Published/Created: London; New York: Longman, 1996. Related Authors: Weymouth, Tony, 1938- Lamizet, Bernard. Description: xxiv, 255 p.: ill., map; 24 cm. ISBN: 0582275652 Notes: Discusses media in Britain, France, Germany, Italy, and Spain. Includes bibliographical references (p. 222-232) and index. Subjects: Mass media--Europe, Western--History--20th century. LC Classification: P92.E9 M37 1996 Dewey Class No.: 302.23/094 20

Marshall, Ian. Media realities: the news media and power in Australian society / Ian Marshall, Damien Kingsbury. Published/Created: South Melbourne, Australia: Longman, 1996. Related Authors: Kingsbury, Damien. Description: vi, 226 p.; 24 cm. ISBN: 0582808200 Notes: Includes bibliographical references (p. 213-220) and index. Subjects: Mass media--Australia. Mass media--Social aspects--Australia. Journalism--Social aspects--Australia. Power (Social sciences) LC Classification: P92.A76 M37 1996 Dewey Class No.: 302.23/0994 21

Maslog, Crispin C. Philippine mass communication: (a mini-history) / by Crispin C. Maslog. Published/Created: Quezon City: New Day Publishers, 1990. Description: vi, 52 p.; 23 cm. ISBN: 971100383X Notes: Includes bibliographical references (p. 50-52) Subjects: Mass media--Philippines--History. LC Classification: P92.P5 M374 1990

Mass media and the Caribbean / edited by Stuart H. Surlin and Walter C. Soderlund. Published/Created: New York: Gordon and Breach, c1990. Related Authors: Surlin, Stuart H. Soderlund, Walter C. Description: xviii, 471 p.: ill., map; 23 cm. ISBN: 2881244475 (hardcover) 2881244483 (softcover) Notes: Includes bibliographical references and indexes. Subjects: Mass media--Social aspects--Caribbean Area. Series: Caribbean studies; v. 6 LC Classification: HN195.2.M3 M36 1990 Dewey Class No.: 302.23/09729 20

Mass media for the nineties: the South African handbook of mass communication / editor, A.S. De Beer. Edition Information: 1st ed. Published/Created: Pretoria: J.L. van Schaik, 1993. Related Authors: De Beer, A. S. (Arrie) Description: 426 p.: ill.; 25 cm. ISBN: 0627018378 Notes: Includes bibliographical references and index. Subjects: Mass media--South Africa. LC Classification: P92.S58 M37 1993 Dewey Class No.: 302.23/0968 20

Mass media in the Asian Pacific / edited by Bryce T. McIntyre. Published/Created: Clevedon; Philadelphia: Multilingual Matters, c1998. Related Authors: McIntyre, Bryce Telfer. Description: 101 p.: ill.; 26 cm. ISBN: 1853593974 (alk. paper) Notes: Includes bibliographical references. Subjects: Mass media--Pacific Area. Mass media--China. Mass media--China--Hong Kong. Mass media--Taiwan. Series: Monographs on Asian Pacific communication Multilingual matters (Series) Variant Series: Multilingual matters LC Classification: P92.P16 M37 1998 Dewey Class No.: 302.23/09182/3 21

Mass media, towards the millennium: the South African handbook of mass communication / A.S. de Beer, editor. Edition Information: 2nd ed. Published/Created: Pretoria: J.L. van Schaik, 1998. Related Authors: De Beer, A.S. (Arrie) Related Titles: Mass media for the nineties. Description: vii, 530 p.: ill.; 25 cm. ISBN: 062702324X Notes: Second ed. of Mass media for the nineties. 1st ed. 1993. Includes bibliographical references and index. Subjects: Mass media--South Africa. LC Classification: P92.S58 M37 1998 Dewey Class No.: 302.23/0968 21

Mass media, towards the millennium: the South African handbook of mass communication / A.S. de Beer, editor. Edition Information: 2nd ed. Published/Created: Pretoria: J.L. van Schaik, 1998. Related Authors: De Beer, A.S. (Arrie) Related Titles: Mass media for the nineties. Description: vii, 530 p.: ill.; 25 cm. ISBN: 062702324X Notes: Second ed. of Mass media for the nineties. 1st ed. 1993. Includes bibliographical references and index. Subjects: Mass media--South Africa. LC Classification: P92.S58 M37 1998 Dewey Class No.: 302.23/0968 21

Mayer, Henry, 1919- Mayer on the media: issues and arguments / Henry Mayer; edited by Rodney Tiffen. Published/Created: North Ryde, NSW: AFTRS; St. Leonards, NSW: Allen & Unwin, 1994. Related Authors: Tiffen, Rodney. Description: xxi, 201 p.; 22 cm. ISBN: 1863736255 (Allen & Unwin) Notes: Chiefly previously Published material. Includes bibliographical references (p. 192-196) and index. Subjects: Mass media--Australia. LC Classification: P92.A76 M39 1994 Dewey Class No.: 302.23/0994 20

McGuinness, P. P. (Padraic Pearse) The media crisis in Australia: ownership of the media and democracy / Padraic P. McGuinness. Published/Created: Melbourne, Vic.: Schwartz & Wilkinson, c1990. Description: 110 p.; 22 cm. ISBN: 1863370366: Subjects: Mass media--Ownership. Mass media policy--Australia. LC Classification: P96.E252 A86 1990 Dewey Class No.: 302.23/0994 20

Media and communications in the Third World / edited by Zahid Hussain, Vanita Ray. Published/Created: New Delhi: Kanishka Publishers, Distributors, 2000. Related Authors: Zaidi, Z. H. (Zahid Hussain), 1942- Ray, Vanita. Academy of Third World Studies. Description: xix, 249 p.; 22 cm. ISBN: 8173913331 Summary: Papers presented at a seminar organized by Academy of Third World Studies. Notes: "In association with Academy of Third World Studies, New Delhi." Includes bibliographical references and index. Subjects: Communication--Social aspects--Developing countries. Mass media--Political aspects--Developing countries. Mass media--Religious aspects--Developing countries. LC Classification: HN980 .M33 2000

Media and development: themes in communication and extension / edited by M.R. Dua, V.S. Gupta. Published/Created: New Delhi: Har-Anand Publications, c1994. Related Authors: Dua, M. R. Gupta, V. S. Regional Seminar on "Media and Development" (1993: Hisar, India) Description: 176 p.: ill.; 22 cm. ISBN: 8124101914: Summary: Papers presented at the Regional Seminar on "Media and Development" held in March 1993, at Hisar. Notes: Includes bibliographical references. Subjects: Mass media in community development--India. Mass media policy--India. LC Classification: HN690.Z9 M357 1994 Dewey Class No.: 302.23/0954 20

Media and market forces: challanges and opportunities: proceedings of the regional seminars and national colloquium / edited by V.S. Gupta, Rajeshwar Dyal. Published/Created: Published for AMIC, Friedrich Ebert Stiftung by Concept Pub. Co., 1997. Related Authors: Gupta, V. S. Dyal, Rajeshwar. Asian Mass Communication Research and Information Centre. Friedrich-Ebert-Stiftung. Description: 266 p.; 22 cm. ISBN: 8170226988 Summary: Contributed research papers of various seminars organized by Asian Mass Communication Research and Information Centre and Friedrich-Ebert-Stiftung. Notes: Includes bibliographical references and index. Subjects: Mass media--Communication--Mass media--Social aspects--Telecommunication--India--Congresses. LC Classification: P92.I7 M395 1997 Dewey Class No.: 302.23/0954 21

Media and politics in Asia: trends, problems, and prospects / edited by Carolina G. Hernandez, Werner Pfennig. Published/Created: [Diliman, Quezon City, Philippines]: U.P. Center for Integrative and Development Studies; [Manila]: National Institute for Policy Studies: Friedrich Naumann Foundation, c1991. Related Authors: Hernandez, Carolina G. Pfennig, Werner, 1944- University of the Philippines. Center for Integrative and Development Studies. National Institute for Policy Studies (Philippines) Friedrich-Naumann-Stiftung. Description: ix, 236 p.: ill.; 23 cm. ISBN: 9718797009 Notes: Based on a conference of the same name held Mar. 1990, Manila, Philippines. Subjects: Mass media--Political aspects--Asia--Congresses. LC Classification: P92.A7 M42 1991 Dewey Class No.: 302.23/095 20

Media and rural development / ed. by C.M. Jain, Thomas Can Published/Created: Jaipur: University Book House, c1995. Related Authors: Jain, C. M. Cangan, Thomas. National Seminar on Media and Rural Development (1995?: Jaipur, India) Description: 151 p.; 23 cm. ISBN: 8185488487: Summary: Contributed research articles of the National Seminar on Media and Rural Development held recently at Jaipur; with special reference to India. Notes: Includes bibliographical references. Subjects: Rural development--India--Jaipur--Congresses. Mass media--India--Jaipur--Social aspects--Congresses. Communication in rural development--India--Jaipur Congresses. LC Classification: HN690.I86 M4 1995 Dewey Class No.: 307.1/412/0954 20

Media audiences in Ireland: power and cultural identity / edited by Mary J. Kelly, Barbara O'Connor. Published/Created: Dublin, Ireland: University College Dublin Press, 1997. Related Authors: Kelly, Mary J., 1952- O'Connor, Barbara, M.A. Description: vi, 280 p.: ill.; 24 cm. ISBN: 1900621096 Notes: Includes bibliographical references and index. Subjects: Mass media--Ireland--Audiences. Mass media--Social aspects--Ireland. LC Classification: P96.A832 I746 1997 Dewey Class No.: 302.23/09417 21

Media-use patterns for social mobilization in Ethiopia. Published/Created: Addis Ababa: UNICEF, [1990] Related Authors: UNICEF Ethiopia. Description: 1 v. (various foliations); 29 cm. Notes: "January 1990." Includes bibliographical references. Subjects: Mass media--Social aspects--Ethiopia. Mass media in community development--Ethiopia. Mass media in social service--Ethiopia. LC Classification: HN789.Z9 M36 1990

Meier, Werner A., 1948- Media-landscape Switzerland / Werner A. Meier, Michael Schanne; [English translation, Eileen Walliser-Schwarzbart]. Edition Information: 1st ed. Published/Created: Zürich: Pro Helvetia Documentation-Information-Press, 1995. Related Authors: Schanne, Michael. Description: 127, [2] p.: ill.; 21 cm. ISBN: 3908102243 Notes: "Pro Helvetia Arts Council of Switzerland Information"--Cover. One col. map laid in. Includes bibliographical references (p. [129]). Subjects: Mass media--Switzerland. LC Classification: P92.S95 M4513 1995 Dewey Class No.: 302.23/09494 21

Melencio, Hernan S. The media activist: a media worker's handbook on unionism / Hernan S. Melencio, Carlos Antonio Q. Añonuevo. Edition Information: [1st ed.]. Published/Created: [Metro Manila, Philippines]: Published by the Kapisanan ng mga Manggagawa sa Media ng Pilipinas in cooperation with Friedrich Ebert Stiftung, [1990] Related Authors: Añonuevo, Carlos Antonio Q. Kapisanan ng mga Manggagawa sa Media ng Pilipinas. Friedrich-Ebert-Stiftung. Description: 148 p.: ill.; 22 cm. Notes: Includes bibliographical references. Subjects: Mass media--Philippines. Mass media--Employees--Labor unions--Philippines. LC Classification: P92.P5 M45 1990

Midwinter, Eric C. Out of focus: old age, the press, and broadcasting / Eric Midwinter. Published/Created: London: Centre for

Policy on Ageing in association with Help the Aged, 1991. Related Authors: Help the Aged (Organization) Description: viii, 64 p.: ill.; 30 cm. ISBN: 0904139816 Notes: Includes bibliographical references. Subjects: Journalism--Great Britain--Social aspects. Aged in mass media. Aged on television. Mass media--Great Britain. LC Classification: PN5124.S6 M53 1991 Dewey Class No.: 305.26 20

Monograph on development communication: proceedings of the First National Congress on Development Communication held on November 18-22, 1990 at Communication Foundation for Asia, Media Group, Manila, Philippines / edited by Fely Imperial-Soledad. Published/Created: Manila: Communication Foundation for Asia, Media Group, [1990] Related Authors: Soledad, Fely Imperial-Communication Foundation for Asia. Media Group. Description: 121 p.; 23 cm. Notes: Includes bibliographical references. Subjects: Communication in economic development--Philippines Congresses. Mass media--Philippines--Congresses. LC Classification: HD76 .N38 1990

Mulay-Parakh, Regina. S.A.V.E.: communication for cooperation / Regina Mulay-Parakh. Published/Created: New Delhi: Mudrit, c1998. Description: xxi, 282 p.; 23 cm. ISBN: 8187129034 Notes: Includes bibliographical references (p. [267]-270) and index. Subjects: South Asian Association for Regional Cooperation. Mass media--South Asia. LC Classification: P92.S64 M85 1998 Dewey Class No.: 302.23/0954 21

Oblas, Peter B. Perspectives on race and culture in Japanese society: the mass media and ethnicity / Peter B. Oblas. Published/Created: Lewiston: E. Mellen Press, c1995. Description: viii, 220 p.; 24 cm. ISBN: 077348986X (hard) Notes: Includes bibliographical references (p. [197]-216) and index. Subjects: Ethnology-- Mass media--Japan--History--To 645. LC Classification: DS830 .O25 1995 Dewey Class No.: 305.8/00952 20

Ongoing research in communication and media in Finland 1996 / editor, Eija Poteri. Published/Created: Tampere, Finland: University of Tampere Dept. of Journalism and Mass Communication, 1996. Related Authors: Poteri, Eija. Description: 141 p.; 21 cm. ISBN: 9514439716 Notes: Includes indexes. Subjects: Communication--Research--Finland. Mass media--Research--Finland. LC Classification: P91.5.F5 O53 1996

Osborne, G (Graeme) Communication traditions in Australia: packaging the people / Graeme Osborne, Glen Lewis. Edition Information: 2nd ed. Published/Created: Melbourne; New York: Oxford University Press, 2001. Related Authors: Lewis, Glen, 1943- Osborne, G. (Graeme) Communication traditions in 20th-century Australia. Description: x, 246 p.; 22 cm. ISBN: 0195514653 Notes: First Published 1995. Includes bibliographical references (p. 218-236) and index. Subjects: Communication--Social aspects--Australia. Communication--Australia--History. Mass media--Social aspects--Australia. Australia--Civilization.

Osborne, G. (Graeme) Communication traditions in 20th-century Australia / Graeme Osborne, Glen Lewis. Published/Created: Melbourne; New York: Oxford University Press, 1995. Related Authors: Lewis, Glen, 1943- Description: x, 195 p.; 22 cm. ISBN: 0195535111 Notes: Includes bibliographical references (p. 173-186) and index. Subjects: Mass media--Social aspects--Australia. Communication--Social aspects--Australia. Communication--Australia--History--20th century. Australia--Civilization--20th century. Series: Australian retrospectives LC Classification: HN850.Z9 M375 1995 Dewey Class No.: 305.2/0994 20

Perry, Nick (Nick H.) The dominion of signs: television, advertising, and other New Zealand fictions / Nick Perry. Published/Created: Auckland: Auckland University Press, 1994. Description: xi, 162 p.: ill.; 22 cm. ISBN: 186940100X Notes: Includes bibliographical references

(p. 152-158) and index. Subjects: Popular culture--Mass media--Advertising--Social aspects--New Zealand. New Zealand--Civilization. LC Classification: DU418 .P47 1994 Dewey Class No.: 993 20

Pokharapurkar, Raja, 1946- Rural development through community television / Raja Pokharapurkar. Published/Created: New Delhi: Concept Pub. Co., 1993. Description: 243 p.: ill., maps; 23 cm. ISBN: 8170224500: Notes: Includes bibliographical references (p. [228]-238) and index. Subjects: Television in rural development--India. Mass media in community development--India. Rural development--India. LC Classification: HN690.Z9 C67467 1993

Proceedings of National Seminar on Role of Mass Communication in Nation Building Process. Published/Created: Madras: United Writers' Association, 1990. Related Authors: United Writers' Association (Madras, India) Description: 75 p., [3] leaves of plates: ill.; 26 cm. Notes: Cover title. Subjects: Communication--India--Congresses. Mass media--Social aspects--India--Congresses. India--Politics and government--1977- --Congresses. Communication in economic development--India--Congresses. LC Classification: P92.I7 N38 1990

Quist-Adade, Charles. In the shadows of the Kremlin and the White House: Africa's media image from communism to post-communism / Charles Quist-Adade. Published/Created: Lanham, Md.: University Press of America, 2000. Projected Pub. Date: 0012 Description: p. cm. ISBN: 0761819134 (cloth: alk. paper) Notes: Includes bibliographical references (p.) and index. Subjects: Mass media--Soviet Union--Russia (Federation)--United States. Africans--Racism--Russia--History. LC Classification: P96.A372 R876 2000

Rantanen, Terhi. The global and the national: media and communication in post-Communist Russia / Terhi Rantanen. Published/Created: Lanham: Rowman & Littlefield, 2002. Projected Pub. Date: 0203 Description: p. cm. ISBN: 0742515672 (alk. paper) 0742515680 (pbk.: alk. paper) Notes: Includes bibliographical references and index. Subjects: Mass media--Russia (Federation) Communication--Russia (Federation) Series: Critical media studies LC Classification: P92.R9 R36 2002 Dewey Class No.: 302.23/0947 21

Rao, Vepa. A curve in the hills: communication and development / Vepa Rao. Published/Created: Shimla: Indian Institute of Advanced Study, 1997. Description: 98 p.; 22 cm. ISBN: 8185952418 Summary: Study of three villages in Nahan Block, in Sirmaur District. Notes: Includes bibliographical references (p. [95]-98) Subjects: Mass media--Social aspects--India--Nahan (Block) Mass media in community development--India--Nahan (Block) LC Classification: HN690.Z9 M36 1997 Dewey Class No.: 302.23/0954/52 21

Reeves, Geoffrey W., 1945- Communications and the 'Third World' / Geoffrey Reeves. Published/Created: London; New York: Routledge, 1993. Description: xii, 277 p.; 22 cm. ISBN: 0415047617 0415047625 (pbk.) Notes: Includes bibliographical references (p. 257-272) and index. Subjects: Mass media--Developing countries. Mass media--Research--Developing countries. Series: Studies in culture and communication LC Classification: P92.2 .R4 1993 Dewey Class No.: 302.23/09172/4 20

Reimer, Bo. The most common of practices on mass media use in late modernity / Bo Reimer. Published/Created: Stockholm, Sweden: Almqvist & Wiksell, 1994. Description: 250 p.; 25 cm. ISBN: 9122016228 Notes: "Ph. D. dissertation, Department of Journalism and Mass Communication, Göteborg University, Sweden." Includes bibliographical references. Subjects: Mass media--Sweden--Audiences. Series: Göteborgsstudier i journalistik och masskommunikation; 4. Variant Series: Gothenburg studies in journalism and mass communication, 1101-4652; 4 LC

Classification: P96.A832 S87 1994 Dewey Class No.: 302.23/09485 20

Report of six Seminars on "Autonomy of the Electronic Media" / organized by NAMEDIA Foundation, March 1990; seminars at Ahmedabad, March 4 ... [etc.]. Published/Created: New Delhi: NAMEDIA, [1990] Related Authors: NAMEDIA (Foundation). Description: 45 leaves; 30 cm. Subjects: Broadcasting policy--India--Congresses. Mass media policy--India--Congresses. LC Classification: HE8689.2 .S47 1990

Review of Norwegian assistance to IPS / by COWI. Published/Created: Oslo, Norway: Ministry of Foreign Affairs, [1997] Related Authors: COWIconsult (Firm) Description: 58 p.; 30 cm. ISBN: 8271774867 Notes: Includes bibliographical references (p. 65-72). Subjects: Inter Press Service. Mass media--Developing countries. Communication--International cooperation. Norway--Foreign economic relations. Series: Evaluation report (Oslo, Norway); 97.10. Variant Series: Evaluation report; 10.97 LC Classification: P92.2 .R48 1997 Dewey Class No.: 302.23/09172/4 21

Robertson, Alexa. National prisms and perceptions of dissent: the Euromissile controversy reflected in opinion and the news in the UK and FRG, 1980-83 / Alexa Robertson. Published/Created: Stockholm: University of Stockholm, Dept. of Political Science, c1992. Description: xii, 295 p.: ill.; 25 cm. ISBN: 9171530703 Notes: Thesis (Ph.D.)--Stockholm universitet, 1992. Includes bibliographical references (p. 283-295). Subjects: North Atlantic Treaty Organization--Armed Forces--Public opinion. Cruise missiles--Public opinion. Intermediate-range ballistic missiles--Public opinion. Public opinion--Great Britain. Public opinion--Germany (West) Mass media--Great Britain. Mass media--Germany (West) Series: Stockholm studies in politics, 0346-6620; 45 LC Classification: UA646.3 .R59 1992 Dewey Class No.: 355/.031090821 20

Rohm, Wendy Goldman. The Murdoch mission: the digital transformation of a media empire / Wendy Goldman Rohm. Published/Created: New York: J. Wiley, c2002. Description: xiv, 288 p.; 24 cm. ISBN: 0471383600 (alk. paper) Notes: Includes bibliographical references (p. 267-277) and index. Subjects: Murdoch, Rupert, 1931- Mass media--Australia--Biography. LC Classification: P92.5.M87 R64 2001 Dewey Class No.: 070/.092 B 21

Rosario-Braid, Floranel. Social responsibility in communication media / by Florangel Rosario-Braid. Published/Created: Quezon City: Katha Pub., c1993. Description: xi, 159 p.; 26 cm. Notes: Includes bibliographical references. Subjects: Mass media--Social aspects--Philippines. LC Classification: HN720.Z9 M37 1993 Dewey Class No.: 302.23/09599 20

Salam, Shaikh Abdus. Mass media in Bangladesh: newspaper, radio and television / Shaikh Abdus Salam. Published/Created: Dhaka: South Asian News Agency, c1997. Description: 149 p.: map; 22 cm. ISBN: 9843002962 Notes: Includes bibliographical references (p. 147-149). Subjects: Mass media--Bangladesh. Communication--Social aspects--Bangladesh. LC Classification: P92.B36 S25 1997 Dewey Class No.: 302.23/095492 21

Sharma, S. K. (Sanjeev Kumar), Dr. Political communication and local newsmedia / S.K. Sharma. Published/Created: Almora, India: Shree Almora Book Depot, 1992. Description: viii, 115 p.; 22 cm. Cancelled ISBN: ISBN (invalid) 8190020996: Summary: Study, with particular reference to Meerut District, Uttar Pradesh. Notes: Revision of the author's thesis (Ph. D.--Meerut University, 1989). Includes bibliographical references (p. [105]-112) and index. Subjects: Local mass media--India--Meerut (District) Community newspapers--India--Meerut (District) Communication--Political aspects--India. LC Classification: P96.L62 I537 1992 Dewey Class No.: 302.23/09542 20

Sharma, Sita Ram, 1932- Educational development in India: the role of media in education / Sita Ram Sharma. Edition Information: 1st ed. Published/Created: New Delhi: Anmol Publications, 1990. Description: vi, 349 p.; 22 cm. ISBN: 8170412862: Notes: Includes bibliographical references. Subjects: Mass media in education--Communication in education--Education--India--History. LC Classification: LB1043.2.I5 S53 1990 Dewey Class No.: 370/.954 20

Shawcross, William. Murdoch / William Shawcross. Edition Information: 1st Simon & Schuster ed. Published/Created: New York: Simon & Schuster, 1993. Description: 492 p., [16] p. of plates: ill.; 25 cm. ISBN: 0671673270: Notes: Originally Published: Great Britain: Chatto and Windus, c1992. Includes bibliographical references (p. [462]-466) and index. Subjects: Murdoch, Rupert, 1931- Mass media--Australia--Biography. LC Classification: P92.5.M87 S5 1993 Dewey Class No.: 070/.092 B 20

Shawcross, William. Rupert Murdoch: ringmaster of the information circus / William Shawcross. Published/Created: London: Chatto & Windus, 1992. Description: xiii, 616 p., [16] p. of plates; 24 cm. ISBN: 0701134518: Notes: Includes bibliographical references (p. 589-592) and index. Subjects: Murdoch, Rupert, 1931- Journalism LC Classification: P92.5.M87 S53 1992 Dewey Class No.: 070/.092 B 20

Simmonds, Diana. Squidgie dearest: the making of a media goddess: Australia's love affair with Princess Diana / Diana Simmonds. Published/Created: Leichhardt, NSW: Pluto Press Australia, 1995. Description: 152 p.: ill.; 22 cm. ISBN: 1864030224 Subjects: Diana, Princess of Wales, 1961- --Windsor, House of--Public opinion. Princesses--Monarchy--Great Britain--Public opinion. Public opinion--Mass media--Australia. LC Classification: DA591.A45 S56 1995 Dewey Class No.: 941.085/092 20

Social work, the media, and public relations / edited by Bob Franklin and Nigel Parton. Published/Created: London; New York: Routledge, 1991. Related Authors: Franklin, Bob, 1949- Parton, Nigel. Description: x, 242 p.; 23 cm. ISBN: 0415050022 0415050030 (pbk.) Notes: Includes bibliographical references (p. [227]-236) and index. Subjects: Social service--Great Britain. Mass media and social service--Great Britain. Social service--Public relations--Great Britain. LC Classification: HV245 .S6237 1990 Dewey Class No.: 361.941 20

Soong, Roland. Latin American media: a pan-regional perspective / Roland Soong, Paul J. Donato, Pablo Verdin. Published/Created: New York (650 Avenue of the Americas, New York 10011): Audits & Surveys Worldwide, [1995?] Related Authors: Donato, Paul J. Verdin, Pablo. Description: 357 p.: ill., map; 29 cm. Notes: "This book originated from the research study known as Los medios y mercados de Latinoamérica: a multi-media planning system"--P. 1. Includes bibliographical references (p. 306-357). Subjects: Mass media--Latin America. LC Classification: P92.L3 S66 1995 Dewey Class No.: 302.23/098 20

Sophokleous, Andreas Kl., 1940- Mass media in Cyprus / [text, Andreas Cl. Sophocleous, Panayiotis Papademetris]. Published/Created: Nicosia, Cyprus: Press and Information Office, Republic of Cyprus, 1991. Related Authors: Papad¯em¯etr¯es, Panagi¯ot¯es. Cyprus. Grapheio Typou kai Pl¯erophori¯on. Description: 54 p.: ill. (some col.); 25 cm. ISBN: 9963380379 Subjects: Mass media--Cyprus. LC Classification: P92.C93 S67 1991 Dewey Class No.: 302.23/095693 20

Sorenson, John, 1952- Imagining Ethiopia: struggles for history and identity in the Horn of Africa / John Sorenson. Published/Created: New Brunswick, N.J.: Rutgers University Press, 1993. Description: xii, 216 p.: map; 24 cm. ISBN: 0813519721: 081351973X (pbk.) Notes: Includes bibliographical references

(p. [193]-207) and index. Subjects: Famines--Ethiopia--History--20th century. Famines in mass media--History--20th century. Ethiopia--Politics and government--1889-1974--Public opinion. Ethiopia--Politics and government--1974-1991--Public opinion. Ethiopia--Foreign public opinion. LC Classification: DT387 .S67 1993 Dewey Class No.: 963/.05 20

Souchou, Yao. Mahathir's rage: mass media and the West as transcendental evil / Yao Souchou. Published/Created: [Australia]: National Library of Australia, [1994] Description: 17 p.; 30 cm. ISBN: 0869053736 Notes: "The views presented in this paper are those of the author(s) and do not necessarily reflect those of the Asia Research Centre or Murdoch University." "November 1994." Includes bibliographical references (p. 17). Subjects: Mass media--Asia, Southeastern. Series: Working paper (Murdoch University. Asia Research Centre); no. 45. Variant Series: Working paper, 1037-4612; no. 45 LC Classification: P92.A725 S68 1994

Stevenson, Robert L. Communication, development, & the Third World: the global politics of information / Robert L. Stevenson. Published/Created: Lanham, Md.: University Press of America, 1993. Description: xv, 223 p.; 23 cm. ISBN: 0819184888 (pbk.: alk. paper) Notes: Originally Published: New York: Longman, c1988, in Series: Communications. Includes bibliographical references (p. 193-214) and index. Subjects: Communication--Developing countries. Mass media--Developing countries. Communication--International cooperation. Communication, International. LC Classification: P92.2 .S7 1993 Dewey Class No.: 302.2/09172/4 20

Sun, Wanning, 1963- Leaving China: media, migration, and transnational imagination / Wanning Sun. Published/Created: Lanham: Rowman & Littlefield, 2002. Projected Pub. Date: 0207 Description: p. cm. ISBN: 0742517969 (alk. paper) 0742517977 (pbk.: alk. paper) Subjects: Mass media--China. Migration, Internal--China. Chinese--Foreign countries--Communication. China--Emigration and immigration. Series: Asian voices (Rowman and Littlefield, inc.) Variant Series: Asian voices LC Classification: P92.C5 S86 2002 Dewey Class No.: 302.23/0951 21

Taras, David, 1950- Power and betrayal in the Canadian media / David Taras. Edition Information: Updated ed. Published/Created: Peterborough, Ont., Canada; Orchard Park, NY: Broadview Press, c2001. Description: viii, 262 p.; 23 cm. ISBN: 155111464X Notes: Includes bibliographical references (p. 241-262). Subjects: Mass media--Canada. LC Classification: P92.C3 T37 2001 Dewey Class No.: 302.23/0971 21

Taras, David, 1950- Power and betrayal in the Canadian media / David Taras. Published/Created: Peterborough, Ont.; Orchard Park, NY: Broadview Press, c1999. Description: viii, 247 p.; 23 cm. ISBN: 1551111411 Notes: Includes bibliographical references (p. 227-247). Subjects: Mass media--Canada. LC Classification: P92.C3 T37 1999 Dewey Class No.: 302.23/0971 21

The European citizen and the media: European media policy: should it exist?: proceedings of the colloquium, the Council Chamber, BBC Broadcasting House, London, June 4, 1993. Published/Created: Düsseldorf: European Institute for the Media, c1993. Related Authors: European Institute for the Media. Description: 65 p.; 30 cm. ISBN: 392967307X Notes: Includes bibliographical references. Subjects: Mass media policy--Europe--Congresses. European cooperation--Congresses. Series: Mediafact, 1021-5700; no. 15 LC Classification: P95.82.E85 E94 1993

The European citizen and the media: European media policy: should it exist?: proceedings of the colloquium, the Council Chamber, BBC Broadcasting House, London, June 4, 1993. Published/Created: Düsseldorf: European Institute for the Media, c1993.

Related Authors: European Institute for the Media. Description: 65 p.; 30 cm. ISBN: 392967307X Notes: Includes bibliographical references. Subjects: Mass media policy--Europe-- European cooperation. Series: Mediafact, 1021-5700; no. 15 LC Classification: P95.82.E85 E94 1993

The global village: dead or alive? / edited by Ray B. Browne and Marshall W. Fishwick. Published/Created: Bowling Green, OH: Bowling Green State University Popular Press, c1999. Related Authors: Browne, Ray Broadus. Fishwick, Marshall William. Description: 223 p.: ill.; 24 cm. ISBN: 0879727713 0879727721 (pbk.) Notes: Includes bibliographical references. Subjects: McLuhan, Marshall, 1911- Global village. Social history--1970- Internationalism. Mass media-- Communication--Information technology-- Social aspects. LC Classification: HN17.5 .G57 1999 Dewey Class No.: 302.23/4 21

The global village: dead or alive? / edited by Ray B. Browne and Marshall W. Fishwick. Published/Created: Bowling Green, OH: Bowling Green State University Popular Press, c1999. Related Authors: Browne, Ray Broadus. Fishwick, Marshall William. Description: 223 p.: ill.; 24 cm. ISBN: 0879727713 0879727721 (pbk.) Notes: Includes bibliographical references. Subjects: McLuhan, Marshall, 1911- Global village. Social history--1970- Internationalism. Mass media-- Communication--Information technology-- Social aspects. LC Classification: HN17.5 .G57 1999 Dewey Class No.: 302.23/4 21

The media & communications in Australia / edited by Stuart Cunningham & Graeme Turner. Published/Created: Crows Nest, N.S.W.: Allen & Unwin, 2002. Related Authors: Cunningham, Stuart. Turner, Graeme. Description: xvii, 382 p.; 23 cm. ISBN: 1865086746 Notes: Includes bibliographical references (p. 344-369) and index. Subjects: Mass media--Australia. Communication--Australia. LC Classification: P92.A76 M4 2002

The media and the twenty-first century / [edited by Nick Dazang.]. Published/Created: Lagos: NUJ, Abuja Coucil, [1996?] Related Authors: Dazang, Nick. Nigeria Union of Journalists. Abuja Council. Description: xv, 149 p.; 26 cm. ISBN: 978342520X Notes: "Papers compiled and edited...are the outcome of the 1996 Press Week/Founders' Day Celebration organised by the Nigeria Union of Journalists, Abuja Council, which took place from Monday, March 11, 1996, to Friday, March 15, 1996"--P. xiii. Includes bibliographical references. Subjects: Mass media--Nigeria. LC Classification: P92.N5 M43 1996 Dewey Class No.: 302.23/09669 21

The Media in Australia: industries, texts, audiences / edited by Stuart Cunningham and Graeme Turner. Edition Information: 1st ed. Published/Created: St. Leonards, N.S.W.: Allen & Unwin, 1993. Related Authors: Cunningham, Stuart. Turner, Graeme. Description: xvi, 414 p.; 23 cm. ISBN: 1863733434 Notes: Includes bibliographical references (p. [369]-390) and index. Subjects: Mass media-- Australia. LC Classification: P92.A76 M43 1993

The media in Britain: current debates and developments / edited by Jane Stokes and Anna Reading. Published/Created: Houndmills, Basingstoke, Hampshire: Macmillan; New York: St. Martin's Press, 1999. Related Authors: Stokes, Jane C. Reading, Anna. Description: xxi, 316 p.; 24 cm. ISBN: 0312225288 (cloth) Notes: Includes bibliographical references and index. Subjects: Mass media--Great Britain. Mass media policy--Great Britain. Popular culture--Great Britain. LC Classification: P92.G7 M43 1999 Dewey Class No.: 302.23/0941 21

Trivedi, Harshad R. Mass media and new horizons: impact of TV and video on urban milieu / Harshad R. Trivedi; foreword by R.S. Trivedi. Published/Created: New Delhi: Concept Pub. Co., 1991. Related Authors: Indian Space Research Organization. Development and

Educational Communication Unit. Related Titles: Mass media & new horizons. Impact of TV and video on urban milieu. Description: 192 p.: ill., 1 map; 23 cm. ISBN: 8170223237: Notes: Spine Mass media & new horizons. Copyright: Development and Educational Communication Unit, Space Application Centre, Ahmedabad. Study conducted in Ahmad¯ab¯ad City, Gujarat. Includes index. Subjects: Mass media--Social aspects--India--Ahmad¯ab¯ad. Mass media--Influence. Series: Concepts in communication, informatics & librarianship; 27 LC Classification: HN690.Z9 M38 1991

Tunstall, Jeremy. Media moguls / Jeremy Tunstall, Michael Palmer. Published/Created: London; New York: Routledge, 1991. Related Authors: Palmer, Michael, 1946- Description: 258 p.; 24cm. ISBN: 0415054672 (HB) 0415054680 (PB) Notes: Includes bibliographical references (p. 223-243) and index. Subjects: Mass media--Europe. Mass media--Biography. Communication, International. Series: Communication and society (Routledge (Firm)) Variant Series: Communication and society LC Classification: P92.E9 T8 1991 Dewey Class No.: 302.23/09224 20

Tunstall, Jeremy. The Anglo-American media connection / Jeremy Tunstall and David Machin. Published/Created: New York: Oxford University Press, 1999. Related Authors: Machin, David. Description: viii, 286 p.; 24 cm. ISBN: 0198715226 (pbk.) 0198715234 Notes: Includes bibliographical references (p. [276]-280) and index. Subjects: Mass media--Great Britain. Mass media--United States--Influence. Mass media--Europe. LC Classification: P92.G7 T857 1999 Dewey Class No.: 302.23/0941 21

Turner, Graeme. British cultural studies: an introduction / Graeme Turner. Edition Information: 2nd ed. Published/Created: London; New York: Routledge, 1996. Description: vi, 258 p.: ill.; 21 cm. ISBN: 0415129303 (pbk.: alk. paper) Notes: Includes bibliographical references (p. [241]-252) and index. Subjects: Popular culture--Great Britain--History--20th century. Mass media--Great Britain--History--20th century. Great Britain--Civilization--20th century. LC Classification: DA589.4 .T87 1996 Dewey Class No.: 306.4/0941 20

Turner, Graeme. Fame games: the production of celebrity in Australia / Graeme Turner, Frances Bonner, P. David Marshall. Published/Created: Cambridge; New York: Cambridge University Press, 2000. Related Authors: Bonner, Frances. Marshall, P. David. Description: xi, 196 p.: ill.; 24 cm. ISBN: 0521791472 (alk. paper) 0521794862 (pbk.: alk. paper) Notes: Includes bibliographical references (p. 179-188) and index. Subjects: Mass media and publicity--Australia. Celebrities--Australia. LC Classification: P96.P852 A878 2000 Dewey Class No.: 302.23/0994 21

Usha Rani, N. Folk media for development: a study of Karnataka's traditional media / N. Usha Rani. Edition Information: 1st ed. Published/Created: Bangalore: Karnataka Book Publishers, 1996. Description: 171 p.: ill.; 22 cm. Notes: Includes bibliographical references and index. Subjects: Mass media--Folklore--Mass media in community development--India--Karnataka. Karnataka (India)--Social life and customs. LC Classification: P92.I7 U78 1996 Dewey Class No.: 302.23/0954/87 21

Velacherry, Joseph 1930- Social impact of mass media in Kerala / Joseph Velacherry. Published/Created: Delhi: Published for the CISRS, Bangalore by ISPCK, 1993. Description: 260 p.; 22 cm. ISBN: 8172140649: Notes: Includes bibliographical references (p. [258]-260). Subjects: Mass media--Social aspects--India--Kerala. Mass media--Influence. Kerala (India)--Social conditions. Series: Social research series (Bangalore, India); no. 20. Variant Series: Social research series; 20 LC Classification: P92.I7 V45 1993 Dewey Class No.: 302.23/0954/83 20

Veljanovski, C. G. The media in Britain today: the facts, the figures / prepared by Cento Veljanovski; with a foreword by Sir Alan Peacock. Published/Created: London: News International, 1990. Description: 91 p.: ill. (some col.); 30 cm. ISBN: 0951563408 Notes: GB91-#2150 14 AUGUST 1991 Includes bibliographical references (p. 90-91). Subjects: Mass media--Economic aspects--Great Britain. LC Classification: P96.E252 G78 1990 Dewey Class No.: 338.4/730223 20

Venturelli, Shalini. Liberalizing the European media: politics, regulation, and the public shere / Shalini Venturelli. Published/Created: Oxford: New York: Clarendon Press, 1998. Description: 316 p.; 24 cm. ISBN: 0198233795 Notes: Includes bibliographical references (p. [285]-308) and index. Subjects: Mass media policy--Europe. Communication policy--Europe. LC Classification: P95.82.E85 V46 1998 Dewey Class No.: 302.2/094 21

Vijaya Lakshmi, K. P. Communications across the borders: the U.S., the non-aligned and the new information order / K.P. Vijaya Lakshmi. Published/Created: New Delhi, India: Radiant Publishers, c1993. Description: xii, 202 p.; 22 cm. ISBN: 8170272041: Notes: Includes bibliographical references (p. [180]-197) and index. Subjects: Communication--Developing countries. Mass media policy--Developing countries. Communication--United States--International cooperation. Communication--Political aspects. LC Classification: P92.2 .V55 1993

Vipond, Mary, 1943- The mass media in Canada / Mary Vipond. Edition Information: 3rd ed. Published/Created: Toronto: James Lorimer, 2000. Description: 193 p.; 23 cm. ISBN: 1550287141 Notes: Includes bibliographical references (p. [174]-185) and index. Subjects: Mass media--Canada--History. LC Classification: P92.C3 V56 2000 Dewey Class No.: 302.23/0971 21

Wadia, Angela. Communication and media: studies in ideas, initiatives, and institutions / Angela Wadia. Published/Created: New Delhi: Kanishka Publishers, Distributors, 1999. Description: vi, 324 p.; 23 cm. ISBN: 8173912823 Notes: Includes bibliographical references and index. Subjects: Mass media--India. Communication--India. LC Classification: P92.I7 W33 1999

Walsh, Gretchen. The media in Africa and Africa in the media: an annotated bibliography / Gretchen Walsh; with an introductory essay by Keyan G. Tomaselli. Published/Created: London; New Providence, NJ: H. Zell Publishers, 1996. Description: xxv, 291 p.; 24 cm. ISBN: 1873836813 (acid-free paper) Notes: Includes indexes. Subjects: Mass media--Afric. LC Classification: Z5634.A4 W35 1996 P92.A4 Dewey Class No.: 016.30223/096 20

Westoff, Charles F. Mass media and reproductive behavior in Africa / Charles F. Westoff, Akinrinola Bankole. Published/Created: Calverton, Md.: Macro International Inc., [1997] Related Authors: Bankole, Akinrinola. Macro International. Institute for Resource Development. Demographic and Health Surveys. Description: ix, 39 p.: ill.; 28 cm. Notes: "April 1997." Includes bibliographical references (p. 39). Subjects: Mass media in birth control--Africa. Birth control--Africa. Sexual behavior surveys--Africa. Series: Demographic and Health Surveys analytical reports; no. 2 LC Classification: HQ766.5.A3 W47 1997

Wickremaratne, Dharman. Media guide of Sri Lanka / [compiled by Dharman Wickremaratne]. Edition Information: Year 2000 ed. Published/Created: Nugegoda: Sri Lanka Environmental Journalists Forum, 2000. Related Authors: Sri Lanka Environmental Journalists Forum. Description: 240 p.; 23 cm. ISBN: 9559161172 Summary: Directory that lists about 250 names and addresses of media from all over Sri Lanka. Notes: Page 240 is left blank for notes. Includes index.

Subjects: Mass media--Sri Lanka. LC Classification: P92S75 W+

Williams, Kevin, 1955- Get me a murder a day!: the history of mass communication in Britain / Kevin Williams. Published/Created: New York: Arnold, 1997. Projected Pub. Date: 9709 Description: p. cm. ISBN: 0340691581 (hb) 0340614668 (pb) Notes: Includes bibliographical references and index. Subjects: Mass media--Great Britain--History. LC Classification: P92.G7 W49 1997 Dewey Class No.: 302.23/0941 21

Zaharopoulos, Thimios. Mass media in Greece: power, politics, and privatization / Thimios Zaharopoulos and Manny E. Paraschos. Published/Created: Westport, Conn.: Praeger, 1993. Related Authors: Paraschos, Manny. Description: xx, 214 p.: ill.; 25 cm. ISBN: 027594106X (alk. paper) Notes: Includes bibliographical references (p. [191]-206) and index. Subjects: Mass media--Greece. LC Classification: P92.G75 Z34 1993 Dewey Class No.: 302.23/09495 20

Zaki, Bello Muhammad. Western media & Nigerian development / Bello Muhammad Zaki. Published/Created: Kano [Nigeria]: Hadiza-Giwa Press, c1998. Description: ii, 132 p.; 21 cm. ISBN: 9780278109 (pbk.) Notes: Includes bibliographical references (p. 131-132). Subjects: Mass media--Nigeria. LC Classification: P92.N5 Z35 1998 Dewey Class No.: 302.23/09669 21

Zha, Jianying. China pop: how soap operas, tabloids, and bestsellers are transforming a culture / Jianying Zha. Published/Created: New York: New Press: Distributed by W.W. Norton, c1995. Description: x, 210 p.; 22 cm. ISBN: 1565842499 Subjects: Mass media--Social aspects--China. Social change--China. LC Classification: P92.C5 Z43 1995 Dewey Class No.: 302.23/0951 20

Zhao, Yuezhi, 1965- Media, market, and democracy in China: between the party line and the bottom line / Yuezhi Zhao. Published/Created: Urbana: University of Illinois Press, c1998. Description: x, 255 p.; 24 cm. ISBN: 0252023757 (alk. paper) 0252066782 (pbk.: alk. paper) Notes: Includes bibliographical references (p. [235]-243 and index. Subjects: Press--China--History. Government and the press--China. Mass media policy--China. Series: The history of communication LC Classification: PN5364 .Z48 1998 Dewey Class No.: 079/.51/09 21

Ziegler, Dhyana. Thunder and silence: the mass media in Africa / Dhyana Ziegler and Molefi Kete Asante. Published/Created: Trenton, N.J.: Africa World Press, c1992. Related Authors: Asante, Molefi K., 1942- Related Titles: Thunder & silence. Description: vi, 205 p.; 23 cm. ISBN: 0865432503 (HB): 0865432511 (PB): Notes: Title on cover and spine: Thunder & silence. Includes bibliographical references (p. 195-199) and index. Subjects: Mass media--Africa. LC Classification: P92.A4 Z54 1992 Dewey Class No.: 302.23/096 20

LAW AND MASS MEDIA

Armstrong, Mark. Media law in Australia / Mark Armstrong, David Lindsay, Ray Watterson. Edition Information: 3rd ed. Published/Created: Melbourne; New York: Oxford University Press, 1995. Related Authors: Lindsay, David. Watterson, Ray. Description: xi, 307 p.: ill.; 23 cm. ISBN: 0195536037 Notes: Includes bibliographical references and index. Subjects: Mass media--Law and legislation--Australia. LC Classification: KU1064.5 .A97 1995 Dewey Class No.: 343.9409/9 349.40399 20

Bensman, Marvin R., 1937- Broadcast/cable regulation / Marvin R. Bensman. Published/Created: Lanham, MD: University Press of America, c1990. Related Authors: Bensman, Marvin R., 1937- Broadcast regulation. Description: 211 p.; 23 cm. ISBN: 0819176613 (alk. paper) Notes: Rev. ed. of: Broadcast regulation. 2nd ed. c1985. Includes index. Subjects: Broadcasting--Law and legislation--United States--Digests. Mass media--Law and legislation--United States--Digests. Cable television--Law and legislation--United States Digests. LC Classification: KF2763.36 .B46 1990 Dewey Class No.: 343.7309/945/02638 347.303994502638 20

Bollinger, Lee C., 1946- Images of a free press / Lee C. Bollinger. Published/Created: Chicago: University of Chicago Press, 1991. Description: xii, 209 p.; 22 cm. ISBN: 0226063488 (alk. paper) Notes: Includes bibliographical references and index. Subjects: Freedom of the press--Freedom of speech--Mass media--Law and legislation--United States. LC Classification: KF4774 .B65 1991 Dewey Class No.: 342.73/0853 347.302853 20

Botein, Michael. Regulation of the electronic mass media: law and policy for radio, television, cable, and the new video technologies / by Michael Botein. Edition Information: 3rd ed. Published/Created: St. Paul, Minn.: West Group, 1998. Related Authors: Ginsburg, Douglas H., 1946- Regulation of the electronic mass media. Description: xxv, 605 p.; 26 cm. ISBN: 0314211225 (alk. paper) Notes: Rev. ed. of: Regulation of the electronic mass media / by Douglas H. Ginsburg, Michael Botein, and Mark D. Director. 2nd ed. c1991. Includes index. Kept up to date by supplements. Subjects: Broadcasting--Radio--Television--Cable television--Mass media--Law and legislation--United States--Cases. Series: American casebook series LC Classification: KF2804 .G56 1998 Dewey Class No.: 343.7309/94 21

Burns, Yvonne. Media law / Yvonne Burns. Published/Created: Durban: Butterworths, c1990. Description: xix, 420 p.; 24 cm. ISBN: 0409013420 Notes: Includes bibliographical references and index. Subjects: Mass media--Law and legislation--South Africa. Freedom of the press--South Africa. LC Classification: KTL3482 .B87 1990 Dewey Class No.: 343.6809/9 346.80399 20

Burrows, J. F. (John Frederick), 1939- Media law in New Zealand / John Burrows,

Ursula Cheer. Edition Information: 4th ed. Published/Created: Oxford [England]; New York: Oxford University Press, 1999. Related Authors: Cheer, Ursula. Burrows, J. F. (John Frederick), 1939- News media law in New Zealand. Description: lxix, 480 p.; 24 cm. ISBN: 0195583655 Notes: Rev. ed. of: News media law in New Zealand / J.F. Burrows. 3rd ed. 1990. Includes bibliographical references (p. 468-469) and index. Subjects: Mass media--Law and legislation--New Zealand. Press law--New Zealand. Journalists--Legal status, laws, etc.--New Zealand. LC Classification: KUQ1064.5 .B87 1999

Butler, D. A. (Des A.) Australian media law / Des Butler, Sharon Rodrick; with contributions by Lawrence McNamara, Anne Fitzgerald. Edition Information: 1st ed. Published/Created: Sydney: LBC Information Services; Holmes Beach, Fla.: Gaunt [distributor], 1999. Related Authors: Rodrick, Sharon. McNamara, Lawrence. Fitzgerald, Anne, barrister. Description: xxii, 569 p.; 24 cm. ISBN: 0455216754 Notes: Includes bibliographical references (p. 547-550) and index. Subjects: Press law--Australia. Freedom of the press--Australia. Freedom of information--Australia. Mass media--Law and legislation--Australia. LC Classification: KU1065 .B88 1999 Dewey Class No.: 343.9409/9 21

Campbell, Douglas S. The Supreme Court and the mass media: selected cases, summaries, and analyses / Douglas S. Campbell. Published/Created: New York: Praeger, 1990. Description: 242 p.; 24 cm. ISBN: 0275935493 (pbk.: alk. paper) 0275934217 (hard: alk. paper) Notes: Includes bibliographical references (p. [234]-237) and index. Subjects: Mass media--Law and legislation--United States--Digests. LC Classification: KF2750.A59 C36 1990 Dewey Class No.: 343.73/099 347.30399 20

Carey, Peter, LL. M. Media and entertainment: the law and business / Peter Carey, Richard Verow. Published/Created: Bristol: Jordans, 1998. Related Authors: Verow, Richard. Description: xlviii, 557 p.; 25 cm. ISBN: 0853084491 Notes: Includes bibliographical references (p. [527]) and index. Subjects: Mass media--Law and legislation--Great Britain. Press law--Great Britain. Performing arts--Law and legislation--Great Britain. LC Classification: KD2870 .C37 1998 Dewey Class No.: 343.4109/9 21

Carey, Peter, LL. M. Media law / by Peter Carey. Edition Information: 2nd ed. Published/Created: London: Sweet & Maxwell, 1999. Description: xxvii, 390 p.; 22 cm. ISBN: 0421673303 Notes: Includes index. Subjects: Mass media--Law and legislation--Great Britain. LC Classification: KD2870 .C373 1999 Dewey Class No.: 343.4109/9 21

Carey, Peter, LL. M. Media law / by Peter Carey. Published/Created: London: Sweet & Maxwell, 1996. Description: xix, 246 p.: ill.; 25 cm. ISBN: 0421571403 Notes: Includes index. Subjects: Mass media--Law and legislation--Great Britain. LC Classification: KD2870 .C37 1996

Carter, T. Barton. Mass communication law in a nutshell / by T. Barton Carter, Juliet Lushbough Dee, Harvey L. Zuckman. Edition Information: 5th ed. Published/Created: St. Paul, Minn.: West Group, 2000. Related Authors: Dee, Juliet Lushbough. Zuckman, Harvey L. Related Titles: Mass communication law in a nutshell. Description: lxi, 622 p.; 19 cm. ISBN: 031423831X (alk. paper) Notes: Rev. ed. of: Mass communication law in a nutshell / by T. Barton Carter ... [et al.]. 4th ed. 1994. Includes index. Subjects: Mass media--Law and legislation--United States. Series: Nutshell series. Variant Series: West nutshell series LC Classification: KF2750.Z9 M37 2000 Dewey Class No.: 343.7309/9 21

Carter, T. Barton. The First Amendment and the fourth estate: the law of mass media / by T. Barton Carter, Marc A. Franklin, Jay B. Wright. Edition Information: 7th ed. Published/Created: Westbury, N.Y.: Foundation Press, 1997. Related Authors:

Franklin, Marc A. Wright, Jay B. Description: xxxix, 1080 p.; 27 cm. ISBN: 1566625432 (hard-cover: alk. paper) Notes: Includes index. Subjects: Mass media--Law and legislation--United States--Cases. Press law--United States--Cases. Journalists--Legal status, laws, etc.--United States Cases. LC Classification: KF2750.A7 F73 1997 Dewey Class No.: 343.7309/9 21

Carter, T. Barton. The First Amendment and the fourth estate: the law of mass media / by T. Barton Carter, Marc A. Franklin, Jay B. Wright. Edition Information: 5th ed. Published/Created: Westbury, N.Y.: Foundation Press, 1991. Related Authors: Franklin, Marc A. Wright, Jay B. Description: xxxiii, 921 p.; 26 cm. + teacher's manual. ISBN: 0882778692 Notes: Includes index. Subjects: Mass media--Law and legislation--United States--Cases. Press law--United States--Cases. Journalists--Legal status, laws, etc.--United States Cases. LC Classification: KF2750.A7 F73 1991 Dewey Class No.: 343.7309/9 347.30399 20

Carter, T. Barton. The First Amendment and the fourth estate: the law of mass media / by T. Barton Carter, Marc A. Franklin, Jay B. Wright. Edition Information: 8th ed. Published/Created: New York: Foundation Press, 2001. Related Authors: Franklin, Marc A. Wright, Jay B. Description: xlvii, 1146 p.; 27 cm. ISBN: 1587780569 (alk. paper) Notes: Includes index. Subjects: Mass media--Law and legislation--United States--Cases. Press law--United States--Cases. Journalists--Legal status, laws, etc.--United States Cases. LC Classification: KF2750.A7 F73 2001 Dewey Class No.: 343.7309/9 21

Carter, T. Barton. The First Amendment and the fourth estate: the law of mass media / by T. Barton Carter, Marc A. Franklin, Jay B. Wright. Edition Information: 6th ed. Published/Created: Westbury, N.Y.: Foundation Press, 1994. Related Authors: Franklin, Marc A. Wright, Jay B. Description: xxxv, 1006 p.; 27 cm. ISBN: 156662147X (alk. paper) Notes: Accompanied by: Teacher's manual (ix, 118 p.). Includes index. Subjects: Mass media--Law and legislation--United States--Cases. Press law--United States--Cases. Journalists--Legal status, laws, etc.--United States Cases. LC Classification: KF2750.A7 F73 1994 Dewey Class No.: 343.7309/9 347.30399 20

Carter, T. Barton. The First Amendment and the fourth estate: the law of mass media / by T. Barton Carter, Marc A. Franklin, Jay B. Wright. Edition Information: 5th ed. Published/Created: Westbury, N.Y.: Foundation Press, 1991. Related Authors: Franklin, Marc A. Wright, Jay B. Description: xxxiii, 921 p.; 26 cm. + teacher's manual. ISBN: 0882778692 Notes: Includes index. Subjects: Mass media--Law and legislation--United States--Cases. Press law--United States--Cases. Journalists--Legal status, laws, etc.--United States Cases. LC Classification: KF2750.A7 F73 1991 Dewey Class No.: 343.7309/9 347.30399 20

Cohen, Jeremy, 1949- Social research in communication and law / Jeremy Cohen, Timothy Gleason. Published/Created: Newbury Park, Calif.: Sage Publications, c1990. Related Authors: Gleason, Timothy W. Description: 140 p.; 23 cm. ISBN: 0803932669 0803932677 (pbk.) Notes: Includes bibliographical references. Subjects: Mass media--Law and legislation--United States. Series: Sage commtext series; v. 23. Variant Series: The Sage commtext series; 23 LC Classification: KF2750 .C64 1990 Dewey Class No.: 343.7309/9 347.30399 20

Communication development and human rights in Asia / edited by Cees J. Hamelink and Achal Mehra. Published/Created: Singapore: Asian Mass Communication Research and Information Centre, c1990. Related Authors: Hamelink, Cees J., 1940- Mehra, Achal. Seminar on Communication Development and Human Rights (1988: Bangalore, India) Description: xxvi, 194 p.; 22 cm. ISBN: 9971905396: Notes: "Seminar on Communication Development and Human Rights in Bangalore from 9-11

May 1988"--P. vii. Includes bibliographical references. Subjects: Civil rights--Developing countries--Congresses. Human rights--Developing countries--Congresses. Mass media--Developing countries--Congresses. LC Classification: JC599.D44 C65 1990

Communication law and policy: the journal of the Law Division of the Association for Education in Journalism and Mass Communication. Published/Created: Mahwah, N.J.: Lawrence Erlbaum Associates, c1996- Related Authors: Association for Education in Journalism and Mass Communication. Law Division. Lawrence Erlbaum Associates. Description: v.; 25 cm. Vol. 1, no. 1 (winter 1996)- Current Frequency: Quarterly ISSN: 1081-1680 Cancel/Invalid LCCN: sn 95001504 CODEN: CLPOFJ Notes: Title from cover. SERBIB/SERLOC merged record Additional Form Avail.: Also available via World Wide Web; OCLC FirstSearch Electronic Collections Online; Subscription required for access to abstracts and full text. Subjects: Mass media--Law and legislation--United States Periodicals. Freedom of speech--United States--Periodicals. Mass media policy--United States--Periodicals. LC Classification: K3 .O388 Dewey Class No.: 343 12

Crawford, Michael G. The journalist's legal guide / Michael G. Crawford. Edition Information: 2nd ed. Published/Created: Toronto: Carswell, 1990. Description: 323 p.; 24 cm. ISBN: 0459338676 0459338773 (pbk.) Notes: Includes bibliographical references and index. Subjects: Press law--Canada. Mass media--Law and legislation--Canada. Broadcasting--Law and legislation--Canada. LC Classification: KE2550 .C7 1990 Dewey Class No.: 343.7109/98 347.103998 20

Creech, Kenneth. Electronic media law and regulation / by Kenneth C. Creech. Edition Information: 2nd ed. Published/Created: Boston: Focal Press, c1996. Description: xxv, 502 p.: ill., forms; 24 cm. ISBN: 0240802160 (pbk. acid-free paper) Notes: Includes bibliographical references (p. 475-480) and index. Subjects: Television--Law and legislation--Radio--Law and legislation--Mass media--Law and legislation--United States. LC Classification: KF2805 .C74 1996 Dewey Class No.: 343.7309/9 347.30399 20

Creech, Kenneth. Electronic media law and regulation / Kenneth C. Creech. Published/Created: Boston: Focal Press, c1993. Description: xxiii, 404 p.: forms; 24 cm. ISBN: 024080130X (acid free pb.): Notes: Includes bibliographical references (p. 381-385) and index. Subjects: Television--Law and legislation--United States. Radio--Law and legislation--United States. Mass media--Law and legislation--United States. LC Classification: KF2805 .C74 1993 Dewey Class No.: 343.7309/9 347.30399 20

Creech, Kenneth. Electronic media law and regulation / Kenneth Creech. Edition Information: 3rd ed. Published/Created: Boston: Focal Press, c2000. Description: xxv, 369 p.: forms; 24 cm. ISBN: 0240803590 (pbk.: alk. paper) Notes: Includes bibliographical references (p. 355-360) and index. Subjects: Television--Radio--Law and legislation--United States. Mass media--Law and legislation--United States. LC Classification: KF2805 .C74 2000 Dewey Class No.: 343.7309/9 21

Crone, Tom. Law and the media: an everyday guide for professionals / Tom Crone. Edition Information: 3rd ed. Published/Created: Oxford [England]; Boston: Focal Press, 1995. Description: xii, 235 p.; 24 cm. ISBN: 0750620080 Notes: Includes index. Subjects: Mass media--Law and legislation--Great Britain. Press law--Great Britain. Libel and slander--Great Britain. Series: Focal Press media series Journalism media manual LC Classification: KD2870 .C76 1995 Dewey Class No.: 343.4109/9 344.10399 20

Crone, Tom. Law and the media: an everyday guide for professionals / Tom Crone. Edition Information: 2nd ed.

Published/Created: Oxford [England]; Boston: Butterworth-Heinemann, 1991. Description: xii, 214 p.; 24 cm. ISBN: 0750602163 Notes: Includes index. Subjects: Mass media--Law and legislation--Press law--Libel and slander--Great Britain. LC Classification: KD2870 .C76 1991 Dewey Class No.: 343.4109/9 344.10399 20

Detroit College of Law entertainment & sports law forum. Published/Created: Detroit, Mich.: Detroit College of Law Entertainment & Sports Law Society, c1994. Related Authors: Detroit College of Law. Entertainment & Sports Law Society. Description: 1 v.; 24 cm. Vol. 1, no. 1 (spring 1994). Current Frequency: Annual Continued by: Detroit College of Law at Michigan State University entertainment & sports law journal (DLC)sn 97033021 (OCoLC)35104886 ISSN: 1079-4557 Cancel/Invalid LCCN: sn 94005330 Notes: SERBIB/SERLOC merged record Subjects: Performing arts--Law and legislation--Mass media--Law and legislation--Sports--Law and legislation--United States--Periodicals. LC Classification: K4 .E739 Dewey Class No.: 344.73/097 347.30497 20

Dickerson, Donna Lee, 1948- Florida media law / Donna Lee Dickerson. Edition Information: 2nd ed. Published/Created: Tampa: University of South Florida Press, c1991. Description: xv, 262 p.; 23 cm. ISBN: 081301039X 0813010357 Notes: Includes bibliographical references and index. Subjects: Press law--Florida. Freedom of the press--Florida. Mass media--Law and legislation--Florida. LC Classification: KFF316 .D52 1991 Dewey Class No.: 342.759/0853 347.5902853 20

Earthtalk: communication empowerment for environmental action / edited by Star A. Muir and Thomas L. Veenendall. Published/Created: Westport, Conn.: Praeger, 1996. Related Authors: Muir, Star A. Veenendall, Thomas Lee. Description: xviii, 233 p.; 24 cm. ISBN: 027595370X (alk. paper) Notes: Includes bibliographical references (p. [207]-223) and index. Subjects: Environmental sciences--Information services. Mass media. Environmental policy. Series: Praeger series in political communication, 1062-5623 LC Classification: GE25 .E27 1996 Dewey Class No.: 363.7/0014 20

Emord, Jonathan W., 1961- Freedom, technology, and the First Amendment / by Jonathan W. Emord. Published/Created: San Francisco, Calif.: Pacific Research Institute for Public Policy, c1991. Related Authors: Pacific Research Institute for Public Policy. Description: xv, 335 p.; 24 cm. ISBN: 0936488387: Cancelled ISBN: 0936588379 (hard): Notes: Includes bibliographical references and index. Subjects: Freedom of the press--Telecommunication--Law and legislation--Mass media--Law and legislation--United States. LC Classification: KF4774 .E46 1991 Dewey Class No.: 342.73/0853 347.302853 20

Feintuck, Mike, 1961- Media regulation, public interest, and the law / Mike Feintuck. Published/Created: Edinburgh: Edinburgh University Press, c1999. Description: ix, 230 p.; 23 cm. ISBN: 0748609970 (pbk.) Notes: Includes bibliographical references (p. 217-223) and index. Subjects: Mass media--Law and legislation--Great Britain. Mass media--Law and legislation. LC Classification: KD2870 .F45 1999 Dewey Class No.: 343.4109/9 21

Finlay, Marike. The social discourses of law and policy on communication / Marike Finlay. Published/Created: Montreal: Discours social/Social Discourse, 1991. Description: vii, 261 p.; 23 cm. ISBN: 0771702337: Notes: Cover title. Includes bibliographical references (p. 249-261). Subjects: Telecommunication--Law and legislation--Social aspects. Mass media policy--Social aspects. Discourse analysis. LC Classification: K4305.4 .F56 1991 Dewey Class No.: 302.23 20

Forlizzi, Lori. The boundaries of free speech: how free is too free? Edition Information: Abridged ed. / [writer, Lori Forlizzi]. Published/Created: Dubuque, Iowa:

Kendall/Hunt Pub. Co., [c1991] Related Authors: Piazza, Thomas Leonard. Boundaries of free speech. Description: 28 p.: ill.; 28 cm. ISBN: 0840369271 Notes: Cover title. Abridged ed. of: The boundaries of free speech by Tom Piazza and Keith Melville. Includes bibliographical references (p. 27). Subjects: Freedom of speech--Mass media--Censorship--United States. Series: National issues forum. Variant Series: National issues forums LC Classification: KF4772.Z9 F67 1991 Dewey Class No.: 342.73/0853 347.302853 20

Francois, William E. Mass media law and regulation / William E. Francois. Edition Information: 6th ed. Published/Created: Prospect Heights, Ill.: Waveland Press, c1994. Description: xx, 651 p.: map; 24 cm. + yearbook. ISBN: 0881337463 Notes: Includes bibliographical references and indexes. Subjects: Press law--Mass media--Law and legislation--United States. LC Classification: KF2750 .F7 1994 Dewey Class No.: 343.7309/9 347.30399 20

Francois, William E. Mass media law and regulation / William E. Francois. Edition Information: 5th ed. Published/Created: Ames: Iowa State University Press, 1990. Description: xxv, 698 p.; 24 cm. ISBN: 0813809681 (alk. paper) Notes: Includes bibliographical references and indexes. Subjects: Press law--Mass media--Law and legislation--United States. LC Classification: KF2750 .F7 1990 Dewey Class No.: 343.73/099 347.30399 20

Franklin, Marc A. Cases and materials [on] mass media law / by Marc A. Franklin, David A. Anderson, Fred H. Cate. Edition Information: 6th ed. Published/Created: New York: Foundation Press, 2000. Related Authors: Anderson, David A., 1939- Cate, Fred H. Description: xxxvii, 787 p.; 26 cm. ISBN: 1566628946 (alk. paper) Notes: Includes index. Subjects: Mass media--Law and legislation--United States--Cases. Series: University casebook series LC Classification: KF2750.A7 F7 2000 Dewey Class No.: 343.7309/9 21

Franklin, Marc A. Cases and materials on mass media law / by Marc A. Franklin, David A. Anderson. Edition Information: 5th ed. Published/Created: Westbury, N.Y.: Foundation Press, 1995. Related Authors: Anderson, David A., 1939- Description: xlv, 802 p.; 26 cm. ISBN: 1566622565 (hardcover: alk. paper) Notes: Includes index. Kept up to date by supplements. Subjects: Mass media--Law and legislation--United States--Cases. Series: University casebook series LC Classification: KF2750.A7 F7 1995 Dewey Class No.: 343.73/099 347.30399 20

Franklin, Marc A. Cases and materials on mass media law / by Marc A. Franklin, David A. Anderson. Edition Information: 4th ed. Published/Created: Westbury, N.Y.: Foundation Press, 1990. Related Authors: Anderson, David A., 1939- Related Titles: Mass media law. Description: lxi, 951 p.; 27 cm. ISBN: 0882777785 Notes: Cover Mass media law. Kept up to date by supplements. Subjects: Mass media--Law and legislation--United States--Cases. Series: University casebook series LC Classification: KF2750.A7 F7 1990 Dewey Class No.: 343.73/099 347.30399 20

From massacres to genocide: the media, public policy, and humanitarian crises / Robert I. Rotberg, Thomas G. Weiss, editors. Published/Created: Washington, D.C.: Brookings Institution, c1996. Related Authors: Rotberg, Robert I. Weiss, Thomas George. Description: x, 203 p.; 24 cm. ISBN: 0815775903 (alk. paper) 081577589X (pbk.: alk. paper) Notes: Includes bibliographical references and index. Subjects: Disaster relief. International relief. Disasters--Press coverage. Mass media. Disaster relief--Public relations. Human rights. LC Classification: HV553 .F76 1996 Dewey Class No.: 363.3/4526 20

Fundamentals of mass communication law / Donald M. Gillmor ... [et al.]. Published/Created: Minneapolis/St. Paul: West Pub. Co., c1996. Related Authors: Gillmor, Donald M. Description: xxxi, 428 p.: ill., maps; 26 cm. ISBN: 0314062386 (hard: alk. paper) Notes: Includes bibliographical references and index. Subjects: Press law--Mass media--Law and legislation--United States. LC Classification: KF2750 .F86 1996 Dewey Class No.: 343.7309/9 347.30399 20

Gallant, Simon. Media law: a practical guide to managing publication risks / by Simon Gallant, Jennifer Epworth. Published/Created: London: Sweet & Maxwell, 2001. Related Authors: Epworth, Jennifer. Description: xlix, 442 p.; 26 cm. + 1 computer laser optical disc (4 3/4 in.) ISBN: 0421598204 Notes: Includes index. Subjects: Mass media--Law and legislation--Great Britain. Press law--Great Britain. Libel and slander--Great Britain. Risk management--Great Britain. LC Classification: KD2870 .G35 2001

Garry, Patrick M. Scrambling for protection: the new media and the First Amendment / Patrick M. Garry. Published/Created: Pittsburgh: University of Pittsburg Press, c1994. Description: vi, 198 p.; 23 cm. ISBN: 0822937980 (cloth: acid-free paper) Notes: Includes bibliographical references (p. 173-195) and index. Subjects: Freedom of the press--Mass media--Law and legislation--United States. Series: Pitt series in policy and institutional studies LC Classification: KF4774 .G373 1994 Dewey Class No.: 342.73/0853 347.302853 20

Geller, Henry. 1995-2005: regulatory reform for principal electronic media / by Henry Geller. Published/Created: Washington, DC: Annenberg Washington Program, Communications Policy Studies, Northwestern University, c1994. Related Authors: Northwestern University (Evanston, Ill.). Annenberg Washington Program in Communications Policy Studies. Related Titles: Regulatory reform for principal electronic media. Description: 38 p.; 28 cm. Summary: This paper outlines policies that Congress should adopt for the principal electronic media...from approximately 1995-2005. Notes: "Position paper" "November 1994" Includes bibliographical references. Subjects: Broadcasting--Law and legislation--Telecommunication--Law and legislation--Broadcasting policy--Mass media--Law and legislation--United States.

Gibbons, Thomas. Regulating the media / Thomas Gibbons. Edition Information: 2nd ed. Published/Created: London: Sweet & Maxwell, 1998. Description: xix, 326 p.; 22 cm. ISBN: 0421606606 Notes: Includes bibliographical references and index. Subjects: Mass media--Law and legislation--Great Britain. Series: Modern legal studies LC Classification: KD2870.G53 1998 Dewey Class No.: 343.4109/9 21

Ginsburg, Douglas H., 1946- Regulation of the electronic mass media: law and policy for radio, television, cable, and the new video technologies / by Douglas H. Ginsburg, Michael Botein, and Mark D. Director. Edition Information: 2nd ed. Published/Created: St. Paul, Minn.: West Pub., c1991. Related Authors: Botein, Michael. Director, Mark D. Ginsburg, Douglas H., 1946- Regulation of broadcasting. Description: xlviii, 657 p.; 26 cm. ISBN: 0314829466 Notes: Rev. ed. of: Regulation of broadcasting. 1979. Includes bibliographical references and index. Subjects: Broadcasting--Law and legislation--United States--Cases. Radio--Law and legislation--United States--Cases. Television--Law and legislation--United States--Cases. Cable television--Law and legislation--United States Cases. Mass media--Law and legislation--United States--Cases. Series: American casebook series LC Classification: KF2804 .G56 1991 Dewey Class No.: 343.73/09945 347.3039945 20

Ginsburg, Douglas H., 1946- Statutory supplement to regulation of the electronic mass media: law and policy for radio, television, cable, and the new video technologies / by Douglas H. Ginsburg, Michael H. Botein, Mark D. Director. Edition Information: 2nd ed. Published/Created: St. Paul, Minn.: West Pub., Co., 1991. Related Authors: Botein, Michael. Director, Mark D. Ginsburg, Douglas H., 1946- Regulation of the electronic mass media. Description: 69 p.; 25 cm. Subjects: Broadcasting--Radio--Television--Cable television--Mass media--Law and legislation--United States. Series: American casebook series LC Classification: KF2804 .G56 1991 Suppl. Dewey Class No.: 343.7309/945 347.3039945 20

Goldberg, David. EC media law and policy / David Goldberg, Tony Prosser, Stefaan Verhulst. Published/Created: London; New York: Longman, 1998. Related Authors: Prosser, Tony. Verhulst, Stefaan (Stefaan G.) Description: xix, 137 p.; 22 cm. ISBN: 0582312663 (pbk.) Notes: Includes bibliographical references (p. 130-133) and index. Subjects: Mass media--Law and legislation--European Union countries. Series: European law series LC Classification: KJE6946 .G65 1998 Dewey Class No.: 341.7/57/094 21

Haltom, William. Reporting on the courts: how the mass media cover judicial actions / William Haltom. Published/Created: Chicago: Nelson-Hall Publishers, 1998. Description: ix, 351 p.; 23 cm. ISBN: 0830414053 (alk. paper) Notes: Includes bibliographical references (p. 329-342) and index. Subjects: Journalism, Legal--Mass media--United States. LC Classification: KF8725 .H35 1998 Dewey Class No.: 343.7309/9 21

Harris, Nicholas. The media and the law: a handbook of law and ethics for media practice / by Nicholas Harris. Edition Information: Rev. Published/Created: Katoomba, NSW, Australia: Harris Johnsson Report, 1995. Description: 94 p.; 30 cm. ISBN: 1875616004 Notes: Includes index. Subjects: Mass media--Law and legislation--Australia. Journalistic ethics--Australia. Courts--Australia--Popular works. LC Classification: KU1064.5 .H37 1995 Dewey Class No.: 343.9409/9 21

Hemmer, Joseph J. Communication law: the Supreme Court and the First Amendment / Joseph J. Hemmer, Jr. Published/Created: Lanham, MD: University Press of America, 2000. Projected Pub. Date: 0007 Description: p. cm. ISBN: 157292151X (hbk.: alk. paper) 1572921501 (pbk.: alk. paper) Notes: Includes index. Subjects: Mass media--Law and legislation--Press law--Freedom of speech--Constitutional law--United States. Freedom of expression LC Classification: KF2750 .H46 2000 Dewey Class No.: 342.73/0853 21

Hindman, Elizabeth Blanks, 1962- Rights vs. responsibilities: the Supreme Court and the media / Elizabeth Blanks Hindman. Published/Created: Westport, Conn.: Greenwood Press, 1997. Description: 189 p.; 25 cm. ISBN: 0313299226 (alk. paper) Notes: Includes bibliographical references (p. [175]-180) and index. Subjects: United States. Supreme Court. Freedom of the press--Mass media--Law and legislation--Journalistic ethics--Journalism--Objectivity--United States. Series: Contributions to the study of mass media and communications, 0732-4456; no. 50 LC Classification: KF4774 .H56 1997 Dewey Class No.: 342.73/0853 347.302853 20

Holding the media accountable: citizens, ethics, and the law / edited by David Pritchard. Published/Created: Bloomington: Indiana University Press, c2000. Related Authors: Pritchard, David Hemmings. Description: viii, 203 p.; 24 cm. ISBN: 0253336627 (cloth: alk. paper) 0253213576 (pbk.: alk. paper) Notes: Includes bibliographical references and index. Subjects: Mass media--Moral and ethical aspects--Journalistic ethics--Mass media and public opinion--United States. Mass media--Law and legislation. Responsibility. LC Classification: P94 .H65 2000 Dewey Class No.: 174/.9097 21

Holsinger, Ralph L. Media law / Ralph L. Holsinger, Jon Paul Dilts. Edition Information: 4th ed. Published/Created: New York: McGraw-Hill, c1997. Related Authors: Dilts, Jon. Description: xvii, 693 p.: ill.; 25 cm. ISBN: 007029710X (alk. paper) Notes: Includes bibliographical references and indexes. Subjects: Mass media--Law and legislation--Press law--United States. Series: McGraw Hill series in mass communication LC Classification: KF2750 .H65 1997 Dewey Class No.: 343.7309/9 347.30399 20

Holsinger, Ralph L. Media law / Ralph L. Holsinger, Jon Paul Dilts. Edition Information: 3rd ed. Published/Created: New York: McGraw-Hill, c1994. Related Authors: Dilts, Jon. Description: xxi, 707 p.: ill.; 25 cm. ISBN: 0070296731 (acid-free paper) Notes: Includes bibliographical references and indexes. Subjects: Mass media--Law and legislation--Press law--United States. Series: McGraw-Hill series in mass communication LC Classification: KF2750 .H65 1994 Dewey Class No.: 343.7309/9 347.30399 20

Holsinger, Ralph L. Media law / Ralph L. Holsinger. Edition Information: 2nd ed. Published/Created: New York: McGraw-Hill, c1991. Description: xviii, 670 p.: ill.; 24 cm. ISBN: 0070296472 Notes: Includes bibliographical references and index. Subjects: Mass media--Law and legislation--United States. Press law--United States. LC Classification: KF2750 .H65 1991 Dewey Class No.: 343.7309/9 347.30399 20

Importing the first amendment: freedom of expression in American, English and European law / edited by Ian Loveland. Published/Created: Oxford: Hart Pub.; Evanston, Illinois. Distributed in the United States by Northwestern University Press, 1998. Related Authors: Loveland, Ian. Description: xxii, 198 p.; 24 cm. ISBN: 1901362280 (acid-free paper) Notes: Includes bibliographical references and index. Subjects: Freedom of speech--Great Britain. Freedom of speech--European Union countries. Mass media--Law and legislation--Great Britain. Mass media--Law and legislation--European Union countries. Law--Great Britain--American influences. LC Classification: KD4110 .I47 1998 Dewey Class No.: 342.41/0853 21

International media liability: civil liability in the information age / editor, Christian Campbell. Published/Created: Chichester; New York: Wiley, 1997. Related Authors: Campbell, Christian T. Center for International Legal Studies. Description: xxxiv, 424 p.; 25 cm. ISBN: 0471965782 Notes: "Published under the auspices of the Center for International Legal Studies, Salzburg, Austria." Includes index. Subjects: Mass media--Law and legislation. Libel and slander. Press law--Criminal provisions. LC Classification: K4240 .I56 1997 Dewey Class No.: 346.03/4 21

Interrogating popular culture: deviance, justice, and social order / edited by Sean E. Anderson, Gregory J. Howard. Published/Created: Guiderland, NY: Harrow and Heston, 1997. Projected Pub. Date: 9712 Related Authors: Anderson, Sean E. Howard, Gregory J. Related Titles: Journal of criminal justice and popular culture. Description: p. cm. ISBN: 0911577424 (alk. paper) Notes: The papers originally appeared in the Journal of criminal justice and popular culture. Includes bibliographical references and index. Subjects: Crime in popular culture--Crime in mass media. Mass media and criminal justice--Criminology--United States. LC Classification: HV6791 .I587 1997 Dewey Class No.: 364.973 21

Iris: legal observations of the European Audiovisual Observatory. Published/Created: Strasbourg: The Observatory, [1995- Related Authors: European Audiovisual Observatory. Description: v.; 30 cm. Vol. 1, no. 1 (Jan. 1995)- Current Frequency: Monthly ISSN: 1023-8565 Notes: SERBIB/SERLOC merged record Subjects: Mass media--Law and legislation--Europe--. LC Classification: KJC6946.A13 I75

Is regulation still an option in a digital universe: papers from the 30th University of Manchester International Broadcasting Symposium, 1999 / editors, Tim Lees, Sue Ralph and Jo Langham Brown. Published/Created: Luton: University of Luton Press, 2000. Related Authors: Lees, Tim ed. Ralph, Sue ed. Brown, Jo Langham ed. University of Manchester

International Broadcasting Symposium (30th: : Manchester` 1999) Description: xii, 326 p.; 24 cm. ISBN: 1860205747 (pbk.) Subjects: Mass media--Law and legislation--Congresses. Series: Current debates in broadcasting, 0963-6544; 9

Jordan, Michael, Dr. Media law: cases and materials / Michael Jordan; editing assistant, Scott Broadway. Published/Created: Dubuque, Iowa: Kendall/Hunt Pub. Co., c1998. Related Authors: Broadway, Scott. Description: viii, 523 p.; 28 cm. ISBN: 0787251747 Subjects: Mass media--Law and legislation--United States--Cases. LC Classification: KF2750.A7 J67 1998 Dewey Class No.: 343.7309/9 21

Kang, Hyon-du. Media culture in Korea / by Hyeon-dew Kang. Published/Created: [Seoul]: Seoul National University Press, c1991. Description: ix, 222 p.; 23 cm. Notes: Includes bibliographical references and index. Subjects: Mass media--Korea. Popular culture--Korea. Series: Korean studies series (Soul Taehakkyo. Sahoe Kwahak Yon'guso); no. 12. Variant Series: Korean studies series; no. 12 LC Classification: P92.K6 K36 1991 Dewey Class No.: 302.23/09519 20

Kang, Jerry, 1968- Communications law and policy: cases and materials / Jerry Kang. Published/Created: Gaithersburg, MD: Aspen Law & Business, c2001. Description: xx, 665 p.: ill.; 25 cm. ISBN: 0735519927 Notes: Includes index. Subjects: Mass media--Law and legislation--United States--Cases. LC Classification: KF2750.A7 K36 2001 Dewey Class No.: 343.7309/9 21

Kaplar, Richard T. Cross ownership at the crossroads: the case for repealing the FCC's newspaper/broadcast cross ownership ban / Richard T. Kaplar; with an introduction by Laurence H. Winer. Published/Created: Washington, D.C.: Media Institute, c1997. Description: xi, 77 p.; 23 cm. ISBN: 0937790559 Notes: Includes bibliographical references (p. 61-73) and index. Subjects: Press monopolies--Press law--Broadcasting--Law and legislation--American newspapers--Ownership. Restraint of trade--United States. Series: Media policy series LC Classification: KF2750 .K36 1997

Kedrowski, Karen M. Media entrepreneurs and the media enterprise in the U.S. Congress / Karen M. Kedrowski. Published/Created: Cresskill, N.J.: Hampton Press, c1996. Description: xii, 238 p.: ill.; 24 cm. ISBN: 1572730129 (cloth) 1572730137 (pbk.) Notes: Includes bibliographical references (p. 221-227) and indexes. Subjects: Legislators--Communication in politics--Mass media--Political aspects--United States. Series: The Hampton Press communication series. Political communication LC Classification: JK1140 .K43 1996 Dewey Class No.: 328.73/07 20

Law relating to cinemas, videos, computers, and telephones / [compiled] by R.N. Choudhry, S.P. Singh. Edition Information: 1st ed. Published/Created: New Delhi: Orient Pub. Co., 1997. Related Authors: Choudhry, R. N., Advocate. Singh, S. P., Advocate. Description: xxxii, 1039 p.; 25 cm. Notes: Includes bibliographical references and indexes. Subjects: Mass media--Motion pictures--Telecommunication--Law and legislation--India. LC Classification: KNS1065 .A28 1997 Dewey Class No.: 343.5409/9 21

Legal guide to audiovisual media in Europe: recent legal developments in broadcasting, film, telecommunications, and the global information society in Europe and neighboring states / [edited by the European Audiovisual Observatory]. Published/Created: Strasbourg: The Observatory, 1999. Related Authors: European Audiovisual Observatory. Council of Europe. Description: 205 p.; 30 cm. ISBN: 9287141614 Notes: "Council of Europe"--Cover. The list of members to the Advisory Committee laid in. Subjects: Mass media--Telecommunication--Computer networks--Law and legislation--Europe. LC Classification: KJC6946+

Legal problems of the functioning of media in a democratic society. Published/Created: Ljubljana: University of Ljubljana, Faculty of Law; [Strasbourg]: Council of Europe, 1995. Related Authors: Univerza v Ljubljani. Pravna fakulteta. Council of Europe. Description: 178 p.; 24 cm. Notes: At head of University of Ljubljana, Faculty of Law, Council of Europe/Conseil de l'Europe, European Media Law Forum. Includes bibliographical references. Subjects: Mass media--Law and legislation--European Union countries Congresses. Freedom of speech--European Union countries--Congresses. LC Classification: KJE6946 .A85 1994

Lensen, Anton. Concentration in the media industry: the European Community and mass media regulation / by Anton Lensen. Published/Created: Washington, D.C.: Annenberg Washington Program [in] Communications Policy Studies, Northwestern University, c1992. Related Authors: Northwestern University (Evanston, Ill.). Annenberg Washington Program in Communications Policy Studies. Description: 38 p.; 28 cm. Notes: Includes bibliographical references (p. 34-38). Subjects: Mass media--Ownership--Europe. Mass media--Law and legislation--Europe. European communities. LC Classification: P96.E252 E8515 1992 Dewey Class No.: 302.23/094 20

Libel and the media: the chilling effect / Eric Barendt ... [et al.]. Published/Created: Oxford: Clarendon Press; New York: Oxford University Press, 1997. Related Authors: Barendt, E. M. Description: vii, 211 p.; 23 cm. ISBN: 0198262272 (acid-free paper) 0198262345 (pbk.) Notes: Includes bibliographical references and index. Subjects: Libel and slander--Great Britain. Mass media--Law and legislation--Great Britain. Freedom of the press--Great Britain. LC Classification: KD1960 .L53 1997 Dewey Class No.: 342.41/0853 21

Lively, Donald E., 1947- Essential principles of communications law / Donald E. Lively. Published/Created: New York: Praeger, 1992. Description: xiv, 360 p.; 25 cm. ISBN: 027593912X (alk. paper) Notes: Includes bibliographical references and index. Subjects: Mass media--Law and legislation--Press law--Telecommunication--Law and legislation--United States. LC Classification: KF2750 .L58 1991 Dewey Class No.: 343.7309/9 347.30399 20

Lively, Donald E., 1947- Modern communications law / Donald E. Lively. Published/Created: New York: Praeger, c1991. Description: xiv, 571 p.; 25 cm. ISBN: 0275937356 (lib. bdg.: alk. paper) Notes: Includes bibliographical references and index. Subjects: Mass media--Law and legislation--United States--Cases. Press law--United States--Cases. Telecommunication--Law and legislation--United States Cases. LC Classification: KF2750.A7 L58 1991 Dewey Class No.: 343.7309/9 347.30399 20

Lutzker, Arnold P. Copyrights and trademarks for media professionals / Arnold P. Lutzker. Published/Created: Boston: Focal Press, c1997. Description: x, 194 p.: ill.; 24 cm. ISBN: 0240802764 (pbk.: alk. paper) Notes: Includes index. Subjects: Copyright--Trademarks--Law and legislation--Mass media--Law and legislation--United States. Series: Broadcasting & cable series. Variant Series: Broadcast & cable series LC Classification: KF2994 .L88 1997 Dewey Class No.: 346.7304/82 21

Making trouble: cultural constructions of crime, deviance, and control / Jeff Ferrell and Neil Websdale, editors. Published/Created: New York: Aldine de Gruyter, c1999. Related Authors: Ferrell, Jeff. Websdale, Neil. Description: xiii, 376 p.; 24 cm. ISBN: 0202306178 (alk. paper) 0202306186 (pbk.: alk. paper) Notes: Includes bibliographical references and index. Subjects: Criminology. Deviant behavior. Criminal behavior. Crime in mass media. Social control. Series: Social problems and social issues LC Classification: HV6001 .M35 1999 Dewey Class No.: 364 21

Martin, Robert, 1939- Media law / Robert Martin. Published/Created: Concord, Ont.: Irwin Law, 1997. Description: ix, 193 p.; 23 cm. ISBN: 1552210049 Notes: Includes bibliographical references and index. Subjects: Mass media--Law and legislation--Canada. Press law--Canada. Freedom of information--Canada. Freedom of speech--Canada. Freedom of the press--Canada. Series: Essentials of Canadian law LC Classification: KE2460 .M37 1997 Dewey Class No.: 342.71/0853 21 National Bib. No.: C96-931598-8

Mass communication law in a nutshell / by T. Barton Carter ... [et al.]. Edition Information: 4th ed. Published/Created: St. Paul, Minn.: West Pub. Co., 1994. Related Authors: Carter, T. Barton. Description: xlvii, 520 p.; 19 cm. ISBN: 0314040811 (acid-free paper) Notes: Includes index. Subjects: Mass media--Law and legislation Series: Nutshell series. Variant Series: West nutshell series LC Classification: KF2750.Z9 M37 1994 Dewey Class No.: 343.7309/9 347.30399 20

Mass media laws and regulations in India / compiled by K.S. Venkateswaran. Published/Created: Singapore: Asian Mass Communication Research and Information Centre, c1993. Related Authors: Venkateswaran, K. S. Asian Mass Communication Research and Information Centre. Description: xiii, 665 p.; 24 cm. ISBN: 9971905442 Notes: Includes bibliographical references (p. 74-76). Subjects: Mass media--Law and legislation--India. LC Classification: KNS1064.5 .M37 1993 Dewey Class No.: 343.5409/99 345.403999 20

Mass media laws and regulations in Malaysia / compiled by Shad Saleem Faruqui and Sankaran Ramanathan. Published/Created: Singapore: Asian Media Information and Communication Centre, 1998. Related Authors: Shad Saleem Faruqui. Ramanathan, Sankaran. Asian Media, Information and Communication Centre. Description: 318 p.; 23 cm. ISBN: 9971905701 Notes: Includes bibliographical references (p. [319]). Subjects: Mass media--Law and legislation--Malaysia. Press law--Malaysia. LC Classification: KPG1065 .A28 1998

Mass media laws and regulations in Nepal / compiled by Gokul Prasad Pokhrel, Bharat Dutta Koirala. Published/Created: Kathmandu: Nepal Press Institute, and Asian Mass Communication Research and Information Centre, Singapore, 1995. Related Authors: Pokhrel, Gokul Prasad. Koirala, Bharat Dutta. Nepal Press Institute. Asian Mass Communication Research and Information Centre. Description: xi, 183 p.; 23 cm. ISBN: 997190554X Notes: Includes bibliographical references (p. 183). Subjects: Mass media--Law and legislation--Nepal. LC Classification: KPK108.5 .M37 1995

Mass media laws and regulations in Singapore / compiled by Ang Peng Hwa and Yeo Tiong Min. Published/Created: Singapore: Asian Media Information and Communication Centre, c1998. Related Authors: Ang, Peng H. Yeo, Tiong Min. Asian Media Information and Communication Centre. Description: vi, 575, [1] p.; 23 cm. ISBN: 9971905698 Notes: Includes bibliographical references (p. [576]). Subjects: Mass media--Law and legislation--Singapore. LC Classification: KPP108.35 .A28 1998 +

Mass media laws and regulations in Thailand / compiled by Vitit Muntarbhorn. Published/Created: Singapore: Asian Media Information and Communication Centre, c1998. Related Authors: Withit Mantaphon. Asian Media Information and Communication Centre. Description: viii, 174 p.; 23 cm. ISBN: 997190571X Subjects: Mass media--Law and legislation--Thailand. Press law--Thailand. LC Classification: KPT3482 .A28 1998 Dewey Class No.: 343.59309/9 21

McGonagle, Marie. A textbook on media law / Marie McGonagle. Published/Created: Dublin: Gill & Macmillan, c1996. Description: xxxvi, 314 p.; 24 cm. ISBN: 071712312X Notes: Includes bibliographical references and index. Subjects: Freedom of the press--Ireland. Press law--Ireland. Mass media--Law and legislation--Ireland. LC Classification: KDK1262 .M32 1996

Media, culture, and the modern African American freedom struggle / edited by Brian Ward. Published/Created: Gainesville: University Press of Florida, 2001. Related Authors: Ward, Brian, 1961- Description: viii, 312 p.; 24 cm. ISBN: 0813020743 (cloth: alk. paper) Notes: Includes bibliographical references and index. Subjects: African Americans and mass media. African Americans--Civil rights. Mass media--United States--Ethnic relations. LC Classification: P94.5.A372 U56 2001 Dewey Class No.: 302.23/089/96073 21

Middleton, Kent. Key cases in the law of public communication / Kent R. Middleton, Bill F. Chamberlin. Published/Created: White Plains, N.Y.: Longman, c1995. Related Authors: Chamberlin, Bill F., 1944- Description: xiii, 310 p.; 24 cm. ISBN: 0801313872 Subjects: Press law--United States--Cases. Mass media--Law and legislation--United States--Cases. Freedom of the press--United States--Cases. Free press and fair trial--United States--Cases. LC Classification: KF2750.A7 M53 1995 Dewey Class No.: 343.7309/98 347.303998

Middleton, Kent. The law of public communication / Kent R. Middleton, Robert Trager, Bill F. Chamberlin. Edition Information: 5th ed. Published/Created: New York: Longman, c2000. Related Authors: Trager, Robert. Chamberlin, Bill F., 1944- Description: x, 624 p.: ill., 1 map; 24 cm. ISBN: 0801332117 Notes: Includes indexes. Subjects: Press law--Law and legislation--Freedom of the press--United States. LC Classification: KF2750 .M53 2000 Dewey Class No.: 343.7309/98 21

Middleton, Kent. The law of public communication / Kent R. Middleton, Bill F. Chamberlin. Edition Information: 3rd ed. Published/Created: New York: Longman, c1994. Related Authors: Chamberlin, Bill F., 1944- Description: xiii, 625 p.; 24 cm. ISBN: 0801311888 Notes: Includes bibliographical references and index. Kept up to date by supplements. Subjects: Press law--Mass media--Law and legislation--Freedom of the press--Free press and fair trial--United States. LC Classification: KF2750 .M53 1994 Dewey Class No.: 345.73/0853 347.305853 20

Middleton, Kent. The law of public communication / Kent R. Middleton, Robert Trager, Bill F. Chamberlin. Edition Information: 5th ed., 2001 update ed. Published/Created: New York: Longman, c2001. Related Authors: Trager, Robert. Chamberlin, Bill F., 1944- Description: xiii, 624 p.; 23 cm. ISBN: 0321087577 Notes: Includes indexes. Subjects: Press law--Mass media--Law and legislation--Freedom of the press--United States.

Middleton, Kent. The law of public communication. Edition Information: 4th ed. / Kent R. Middleton, Bill F. Chamberlin, Matthew D. Bunker. Published/Created: New York: Longman, c1997. Related Authors: Chamberlin, Bill F., 1944- Bunker, Matthew D. Description: x, 676 p.: ill.; 24 cm. ISBN: 0801317150 Notes: Includes indexes. Subjects: Press law--Mass media--Law and legislation--Freedom of the press--Free press and fair trial--United States. LC Classification: KF2750 .M53 1997 Dewey Class No.: 343.7309/98 347.303998 20

Middleton, Kent. The law of public communication. Edition Information: 4th ed. / Kent R. Middleton, Bill F. Chamberlin, Matthew D. Bunker. Published/Created: New York: Longman, c1997. Related Authors: Chamberlin, Bill F., 1944- Bunker, Matthew D. Description: x, 676 p.: ill.; 24 cm. ISBN: 0801317150 Notes: Includes indexes. Subjects: Press law--Mass media--Law and legislation--Freedom of the press--Free press and fair trial--United States. LC Classification: KF2750 .M53 1997 Dewey Class No.: 343.7309/98 347.303998 20

Moore, Roy L. Mass communication law and ethics / Roy L. Moore. Edition Information: 2nd ed. Published/Created: Mahwah, N.J.: L. Erlbaum Associates, 1999. Description: xvi, 678 p.: ill., forms, map; 26 cm. ISBN: 0805825991 (alk. paper) Notes: Includes bibliographical references and index. Subjects: Mass media--Law and legislation--Journalistic ethics--United States. Law and ethics. Series: LEA's communication series LC Classification: KF2750 .M66 1999 Dewey Class No.: 343.7309/9 21

Moore, Roy L. Mass communication law and ethics / Roy L. Moore. Edition Information: 2nd ed. Published/Created: Mahwah, N.J.: L. Erlbaum Associates, 1999. Description: xvi, 678 p.: ill., forms, map; 26 cm. ISBN: 0805825991 (alk. paper) Notes: Includes bibliographical references and index. Subjects: Mass media--Law and legislation--Journalistic ethics. Series: LEA's communication series LC Classification: KF2750 .M66 1999 Dewey Class No.: 343.7309/9 21

Moore, Roy L. Mass communication law and ethics / Roy L. Moore. Edition Information: 2nd ed. Published/Created: Mahwah, N.J.: L. Erlbaum Associates, 1999. Description: xvi, 678 p.: ill., forms, map; 26 cm. ISBN: 0805825991 (alk. paper) Notes: Includes bibliographical references and index. Subjects: Mass media--Law and legislation--Journalistic ethics. Series: LEA's communication series LC Classification: KF2750 .M66 1999 Dewey Class No.: 343.7309/9 21

Moore, Roy L. Mass communication law and ethics / Roy L. Moore. Published/Created: Hillsdale, N.J.: Erlbaum, 1994. Description: viii, 610 p.: ill.; 25 cm. ISBN: 0805802401 (acid-free paper) Notes: Includes bibliographical references (p. 528-570) and index. Subjects: Mass media--Law and legislation--Journalistic ethics--United States. Law and ethics. Series: LEA's communication series LC Classification: KF2750 .M66 1994 Dewey Class No.: 343.7309/9 347.30399 20

Moore, Roy L. Mass communication law and ethics: a casebook / Roy L. Moore. Published/Created: Mahwah, N.J.: L. Erlbaum Associates, 1999. Description: vii, 339 p.; 26 cm. ISBN: 0805832785 Subjects: Mass media--Law and legislation--United States--Cases. Mass media--Moral and ethical aspects--Case studies. LC Classification: KF2750.A7 M66 1999 Dewey Class No.: 343.7309/9 21

Moore, Roy L. Mass communication law and ethics: a casebook / Roy L. Moore. Published/Created: Mahwah, N.J.: L. Erlbaum Associates, 1999. Description: vii, 339 p.; 26 cm. ISBN: 0805832785 Subjects: Mass media--Law and legislation--Moral and ethical aspects--United States—Cases. LC Classification: KF2750.A7 M66 1999 Dewey Class No.: 343.7309/9 21

Osinbajo, Yemi. Nigerian media law / by Yemi Osinbajo, Kedinga Fogam. Published/Created: Lagos: Gravitas Publishments, 1991. Related Authors: Fogam, P. Kedinga. Description: xxix, 385 p.: forms; 23 cm. ISBN: 9783120905 (pbk.) 9783120913 (case) Notes: Includes bibliographical references and index. Subjects: Mass media--Law and legislation--Press law--Libel and slander--Nigeria. LC Classification: KTA1064.5 .O84 1991 Dewey Class No.: 343.66909/98 346.6903998 20

Pakistan. Mass media laws and regulations in Pakistan, and a commentary from a historical perspective / chief compiler, Javed Jabbar; co-compiler, Qazi Faez Isa. Published/Created: Singapore: Asian Media Information and Communication Centre (AMIC), 1997. Related Authors: Javed Jabbar, 1945- Faez Isa, Qazi. Description: xxvi, 940 p.; 23 cm. ISBN: 9971905647 Notes: Includes bibliographical references (p. 938-939). Subjects: Mass media--Law and legislation--Press law--Pakistan. LC Classification: KPL1064.5 .A28 1997 Dewey Class No.: 343.549109/9/02632 21

Paraschos, Manny. Media law and regulation in the European Union: national, transnational, and U.S. perspectives / Emmanuel E. Paraschos. Edition Information: 1st ed. Published/Created: Ames, Iowa: State University Press, 1998. Description: xiii, 274 p.; 24 cm. ISBN: 0813828074 (alk. paper) Notes: Includes bibliographical references (p. 255-262) and index. Subjects: Mass media--Law and legislation--European Union countries. Mass media--Law and legislation--United States. LC Classification: KJE6946 .P37 1998 Dewey Class No.: 341.7/57/094 21

Pearson, Mark, 1954- The journalist's guide to media law / Mark Pearson. Published/Created: St. Leonards, NSW, Australia: Allen & Unwin, 1997. Description: viii, 272 p.; 22 cm. ISBN: 1864484349 Notes: Includes bibliographical references (p. 259-261) and index. Subjects: Mass media--Law and legislation--Australia. Press law--Australia. Journalists--Legal status, laws, etc.--Australia. LC Classification: KU1065 .P43 1997 Dewey Class No.: 343.9409/9 21

Price, Monroe Edwin, 1938- Media and sovereignty: law, identity, and technology in a global environment / Monroe E. Price. Published/Created: Cambridge, Mass.: MIT Press, 2002. Projected Pub. Date: 0210 Description: p. cm. ISBN: 0262162113 (alk. paper) Notes: Includes bibliographical references and index. Subjects: Mass media--Law and legislation. LC Classification: K4240 .P75 2002 Dewey Class No.: 343.09/9 21

Rajapakshe, Wijeyadasa. Media freedom and responsibility / Wijeyadasa Rajapakshe. Published/Created: [Nugegoda]: W. Rajapakshe, 2000. Description: 165 p.; 22 cm. ISBN: 9559701312 Summary: An overview of the media case laws and practice, their concepts, ethics and traditions in Sri Lanka. Subjects: Mass media--Law and legislation--Sri Lanka. Press law--Freedom of the press--Sri Lanka. LC Classification: KPS1064.5 .R35 2000 Dewey Class No.: 342.5493/0853 21

Rayudu, C. S., 1946- Mass media laws and regulations / C.S. Rayudu, S.B. Nageswara Rao. Edition Information: 1st ed. Published/Created: Bombay: Himalaya Pub. House, 1995. Related Authors: Nageswara Rao, S. B. Description: 293 p.; 23 cm. ISBN: 8174930515: Subjects: Mass media--Law and legislation--India. LC Classification: KNS1064.5 .R39 1995 Dewey Class No.: 343.5409/9 345.40399 20

Regulating the changing media: a comparative study / edited by David Goldberg, Tony Prosser, and Stefaan Verhulst. Published/Created: Oxford: Clarendon Press; New York: Oxford University Press, 1998. Related Authors: Goldberg, David. Prosser, Tony. Verhulst, Stefaan (Stefaan G.) Description: xvi, 321 p.; 24 cm. ISBN: 0198267819 (alk. paper) Notes: Includes bibliographical references and index. Subjects: Mass media--Law and legislation. LC Classification: K4240 .R44 1998 Dewey Class No.: 343.09/9 21

Robertson, Geoffrey. Media law / Geoffrey Robertson and Andrew Nicol. Edition Information: 4th ed. Published/Created: London: Sweet & Maxwell, 2002. Related Authors: Nicol, Andrew. Description: xxxviii, 908 p.; 26 cm. ISBN: 0752005197 Subjects: Mass media--Law and legislation--Great Britain.

Ruggles, Myles Alexander. The audience reflected in the medium of law: a critique of the political economy of speech rights in the United States / by Myles Alexander Ruggles. Published/Created: Norwood, N.J.: Ablex Pub. Corp., c1994. Description: xx, 185 p.; 23 cm. ISBN: 0893918814 (cloth) 0893919934 (pbk.) Notes: Includes bibliographical references (p. 165-174) and index. Subjects: Freedom of speech--Mass media--Law and legislation--United States. Freedom of speech--Economic aspects. LC Classification: KF4772 .R84 1994 Dewey Class No.: 342.73/0853 347.302853 20

Sableman, Mark, 1951- More speech, not less communications law in the information age

/ Mark Sableman; with a foreword by Paul Simon. Published/Created: Carbondale: Southern Illinois University Press, c1997. Description: xx, 277 p.; 24 cm. ISBN: 0809320711 (cloth: alk. paper) 0809321351 (pbk.: alk. paper) Notes: Includes bibliographical references (p. 273-277). Subjects: Mass media--Law and legislation--Press law--Telecommunication--Law and legislation--United States. LC Classification: KF2750 .S33 1997 Dewey Class No.: 343.7309/9 21

Saunders, Kevin W. Violence as obscenity: limiting the media's First Amendment protection / Kevin W. Saunders. Published/Created: Durham: Duke University Press, 1996. Description: viii, 246 p.; 24 cm. ISBN: 0822317583 (cloth: alk. paper) 0822317672 (pbk.: alk. paper) Notes: Includes bibliographical references and index. Subjects: Mass media--Law and legislation--Violence in mass media--Law and legislation--Obscenity (Law)--Freedom of the press--United States. Series: Constitutional conflicts LC Classification: KF2750 .S38 1996 Dewey Class No.: 343.7309/9 347.30399 20

Siegel, Paul, 1954- Communication law in America / Paul Siegel. Published/Created: Boston, MA: Allyn and Bacon, 2002. Projected Pub. Date: 0107 Description: p. cm. ISBN: 0205289878 (alk. paper) Notes: Includes index. Subjects: Mass media--Law and legislation--Press law--Freedom of speech--United States. LC Classification: KF2750 .S53 2002 Dewey Class No.: 343.7309/9 21

Study on new media and copyright: final report / prepared by NGL Nordicity Group Ltd. Published/Created: [Ottawa]: Industry Canada, New Media, Information Technologies Industry Branch, c1994. Rclatcd Authors: NGL Nordicity Group Ltd. Canada. New Media. Description: iv, 83 p.; 28 cm. ISBN: 0662224930 Notes: Issued also in French under Etude sur les nouveaux médias et le droit d'auteur. Includes bibliographical references. Subjects: Copyright--Canada. Copyright and electronic data processing--Canada. Intellectual property--Canada. Multimedia systems--Law and legislation--Canada. Mass media--Law and legislation--Canada. LC Classification: KE2799 .S78 1994 Dewey Class No.: 346.7104/82 20 Govt. Doc. No.: DSS Cat. no. C2-240/1994E National Bib. No.: C95-700070-7

Swaziland. Parliament. House of Assembly. Media Council Bill Select Committee. A report of the Media Council Bill Select Committee: Bill no. 9, 1997. Published/Created: [Mbabane?]: House of Assembly, [1998] Description: 1 v. (various pagings); 29 cm. Subjects: Mass media--Law and legislation--Swaziland. Press law--Swaziland. Journalistic ethics--Swaziland. LC Classification: KTR108.5 .A23 1998 Dewey Class No.: 343.688709/9 21

Talbott, James N. New media: intellectual property, entertainment, and technology law / by James N. Talbott. Published/Created: New York: Clark Boardman Callaghan, 1997. Projected Pub. Date: 9712 Description: p. cm. ISBN: 0836611322 (alk. paper) Subjects: Mass media--Law and legislation--Multimedia systems--Law and legislation--United States. LC Classification: KF2750 .T35 1997 Dewey Class No.: 343.7309/9 21

Teeter, Dwight L. Law of mass communications: freedom and control of print and broadcast media / by Dwight L. Teeter, Jr., Bill Loving. Edition Information: 10th ed. Published/Created: New York, N.Y.: Foundation Press, 2001. Related Authors: Loving, Bill. Description: xvii, 983 p.; 26 cm. ISBN: 1587781352 (alk. paper) Notes: Includes bibliographical references (p. 919-925) and index. Subjects: Press law--Mass media--Law and legislation--United States.

The celling of America: an inside look at the U.S. prison industry / edited by Daniel Burton-Rose with Dan Pens and Paul Wright. Edition Information: 1st ed. Published/Created: Monroe, Me.: Common Courage Press, c1998. Related Authors:

Burton-Rose, Daniel. Pens, Dan. Wright, Paul, 1965- Description: v, 263 p.; 20 cm. ISBN: 1567511406 1567511414 (alk. paper) Notes: "A Prison legal news book." Includes bibliographical references and index. Subjects: Prisons--Government policy--Criminal justice, Administration of--Prisoners--Social conditions. Prisoners--Legal status, laws, etc.--Convict labor--United States. Prisons in mass media. Prison administration--United States. LC Classification: HV9469 .C46 1998 Dewey Class No.: 365/.973 21

The First Amendment and the media: an assessment of free speech and a free press / by the Media Institute and its First Amendment Advisory Council. Published/Created: Washington, D.C.: The Institute, 1997- Related Authors: Media Institute (Washington, D.C.) First Amendment Advisory Council. Description: v.; 28 cm. 1997- Current Frequency: Annual Cancel/Invalid LCCN: 96080247 Notes: SERBIB/SERLOC merged record Subjects: Freedom of speech--United States--Periodicals. Freedom of the press--United States--Periodicals. Mass media--Law and legislation--United States Periodicals. LC Classification: KF4772 .F567 Dewey Class No.: 342.73/0853 21

The Media and criminal justice policy: recent research and social effects / edited by Ray Surette. Published/Created: Springfield, Ill., U.S.A.: C.C. Thomas, c1990. Related Authors: Surette, Ray. Description: xx, 312 p.: ill.; 27 cm. ISBN: 0398056870 Notes: Includes bibliographical references. Subjects: Mass media and criminal justice. Criminal justice, Administration of. Mass media--Social aspects. LC Classification: P96.C74 M4 1990 Dewey Class No.: 302.23 20

Watkins, John J., 1949- The mass media and the law / John J. Watkins. Published/Created: Englewood Cliffs, N.J.: Prentice Hall, c1990. Description: xiv, 642 p.; 25 cm. ISBN: 0135588189: Notes: Includes bibliographical references (p. 620-630) and index. Subjects: Mass media--Law and legislation--United States. LC Classification: KF2750 .W37 1990 Dewey Class No.: 343.7309/9 347.30399 20

Weiler, Paul C. Entertainment, media, and the law: text, cases, problems / by Paul C. Weiler. Published/Created: St. Paul, Minn.: West, 1997. Description: xxxi, 1024 p.; 26 cm. ISBN: 0314211519 (alk. paper) Notes: Supplements Published: West Group (2000-). Includes bibliographical references and indexes. Kept up to date by supplements. Subjects: Performing arts--Law and legislation--United States Cases. Entertainers--Legal status, laws, etc.--United States Cases. Mass media--Law and legislation--United States--Cases. Series: American casebook series LC Classification: KF4290.A7 W45 1997 Dewey Class No.: 344.73/099 21

Zelezny, John D., 1955- Communications law: liberties, restraints, and the modern media / John D. Zelezny. Edition Information: 3rd ed. Published/Created: Belmont, CA: Wadsworth/Thomson Learning, c2001. Description: xiii, 546 p.: ill.; 23 cm. ISBN: 053451331X Notes: Includes indexes. Subjects: Mass media--Law and legislation--United States. Press law--United States. Freedom of speech--United States. Libel and slander--United States. Obscenity (Law)--United States. LC Classification: KF2750 .Z45 2000 Dewey Class No.: 343.7309/9 21

Zelezny, John D., 1955- Communications law: liberties, restraints, and the modern media / John D. Zelezny. Edition Information: 2nd ed. Published/Created: Belmont, Calif.: Wadsworth Pub. Co., c1997. Description: xvii, 541 p.: ill; 25 cm. ISBN: 053451264X (alk. paper) Notes: Includes bibliographical references and index. Subjects: Mass media--Law and legislation--United States. Press law--United States. Freedom of speech--United States. Libel and slander--United States. Obscenity (Law)--United States. Series: Wadsworth series in mass communication and journalism LC Classification: KF2750 .Z45 1997 Dewey Class No.: 343.7309/9 347.30399 20

Zelezny, John D., 1955- Communications law: liberties, restraints, and the modern media / John D. Zelezny. Published/Created: Belmont, Calif.: Wadsworth Pub. Co., c1993. Description: xviii, 540 p.: ill.; 24 cm. ISBN: 0534134521 (acid-free paper) Notes: Includes bibliographical references and indexes. Subjects: Mass media--Law and legislation--United States. Press law--United States. Freedom of the press--United States. Libel and slander--United States. Copyright--United States. Series: The Wadsworth series in mass communication and journalism LC Classification: KF2750 .Z45 1993 Dewey Class No.: 343.7309/9 347.30399 20

Zilber, Jeremy, 1966- Racialized coverage of Congress: the news in black and white / Jeremy Zilber and David Niven. Published/Created: Westport, Conn.: Praeger, 2000. Related Authors: Niven, David, 1971- Description: x, 141 p.; 22 cm. ISBN: 0275968413 (alk. paper) Notes: Includes bibliographical references (p. [129]-136) and index. Subjects: United States. Congress--Press coverage. Afro-American legislators. Afro-Americans in mass media. Press and politics--United States. United States--Race relations--Political aspects. LC Classification: E185.615 .Z55 2000 Dewey Class No.: 328.73/008996073 21

Culture and Mass Media

A Cultural studies reader: history, theory, practice / edited by Jessica Munns and Gita Rajan; with the British section edited and introduced by Roger Bromley. Published/Created: London; New York: Longman, 1995. Related Authors: Munns, Jessica, 1949- Rajan, Gita, 1952- Bromley, Roger. Description: x, 694 p.: ill.; 24 cm. ISBN: 0582214106 (csd) 0582214114 (ppr) Notes: Includes bibliographical references and index. Subjects: Popular culture--Culture--Study and teaching--United States. Popular culture--Culture--Study and teaching--Great Britain. Criticism--United States--Great Britain. Mass media--United States--Great Britain. LC Classification: E169.04 .C85 1995 Dewey Class No.: 306 20

A Manual on ethnic reporting / [edited by] Crispin C. Maslog, Alice Colet-Villadolid. Published/Created: Intramuros, Manila: Philippine Press Institute, [1991] Related Authors: Maslog, Crispin C. Villadolid, Alice Colet- Maslog, Crispin C. Manual on peace reporting in Mindanao. 1990. Related Titles: Manual on peace reporting in Mindanao. Description: vii, 195 p.; 22 cm. ISBN: 9718703020 (v. 1) 9711100827 (v. 2) Notes: Includes: A manual on peace reporting in Mindanao / Crispin C. Maslog. Includes bibliographical references. Subjects: Mass media and minorities--Philippines. Mass media and race relations--Philippines. Ethnic press--Philippines. Philippines--Ethnic relations. LC Classification: P94.5.M552 P65 1991

A night in at the opera: media representations of opera / edited by Jeremy Tambling. Published/Created: London: J. Libbey, c1994. Related Authors: Tambling, Jeremy. Description: iii, 310 p.: ill.; 24 cm. ISBN: 0861964667 Notes: Includes bibliographical references. Subjects: Opera. Operas--Film and video adaptations. Mass media and music. Music--Philosophy and aesthetics. LC Classification: ML3858 .N54 1994 Dewey Class No.: 792.5

Afrocentric visions: studies in culture and communication / edited by Janice D. Hamlet. Published/Created: Thousand Oaks, Calif.: Sage Publications, c1998. Related Authors: Hamlet, Janice D. Description: xiv, 266 p.; 24 cm. ISBN: 0761908102 (acid-free paper) 0761908110 (pbk.: acid-free paper) Notes: Includes bibliographical references and index. Subjects: African Americans--Ethnic identity. African Americans--Communication. Afrocentrism--United States. African American arts. African Americans in mass media. LC Classification: E185.625 .A388 1998 Dewey Class No.: 305.896/073 21

Aging and identity: a humanities perspective / edited by Sara Munson Deats and Lagretta Tallent Lenker. Published/Created: Westport, Conn.: Praeger, 1999. Related Authors: Deats, Sara Munson. Lenker, Lagretta Tallent. Description: x, 256 p.; 24 cm. ISBN: 0275964795 (alk. paper) Notes: Includes bibliographical references (p [229]-246), filmography and index.

Subjects: Aged in popular culture. Old age in literature. Aged in art. Aged in mass media. Aging in literature. Aging in art. LC Classification: HQ1061 .A444 1999 Dewey Class No.: 305.26 21

Aldrich, Leigh Stephens. Covering the community: a diversity handbook for media / by Leigh Stephens Aldrich. Published/Created: Thousand Oaks, Calif.: Pine Forge Press, c1999. Projected Pub. Date: 9903 Description: p. cm. ISBN: 0761985131 (acid-free paper) Notes: Includes bibliographical references (p.) and index. Subjects: Mass media and culture--Handbooks, manuals, etc. Pluralism (Social sciences)--Handbooks, manuals, etc. Series: A diversity stylebook for media LC Classification: P94.6 .A43 1999 Dewey Class No.: 302.23 21

Bachman, John F., 1948- In the news tonight: meditations by a TV news anchor / John F. Bachman. Published/Created: Minneapolis: Augsburg, c1990. Description: 64 p.; 18 cm. ISBN: 0806624655 (alk. paper): Subjects: Meditations. Mass media--Religious aspects--Christianity--Meditations. LC Classification: BV4832.2 .B252 1990 Dewey Class No.: 242 20

Bankole, Akinrinola. The role of mass media in family planning promotion in Nigeria / Akinrinola Bankole. Published/Created: Calverton, Md.: Macro International, [1994] Description: 24 p.: ill.; 28 cm. Notes: "April 1994." Includes bibliographical references (p. 24). Subjects: Mass media in birth control--Nigeria. Birth control clinics--Utilization--Nigeria. Mass media in health education--Nigeria. Family Planning--education--Nigeria. Mass Media--Nigeria. Nigeria--Population. Series: DHS working papers; no. 11 LC Classification: HQ766.5.N5 B35 1994 Dewey Class No.: 363.9/6/09669 20

Benjamin, Ionie. The Black press in Britain / Ionie Benjamin. Published/Created: Stoke-on-Trent, Staffordshire, England: Trentham Books, 1995. Description: viii, 134 p.: ill.; 25 cm. ISBN: 1858560284 (pbk.) Notes: Includes bibliographical references (p. 121) and index. Subjects: Black newspapers--Great Britain--History. Blacks in mass media--History. Mass media and race relations--Great Britain--History. LC Classification: PN5124.B55 B46 1995 Dewey Class No.: 072/.089/96 21

Bensley, Lillian Southwick. Video games and real-life aggression: a review of the literature / Lillian Bensley, Juliet Van Eenwyk. Published/Created: Olympia, Wash.: Washington State Dept. of Health, [2000] Related Authors: VanEenwyk, Juliet. Washington (State). Dept. of Health Description: 47 p.; 28 cm. Notes: "May 2000." Includes bibliographical references (p. 33-38). Subjects: Video games. Violence in mass media. Aggressiveness Aggressiveness in children. LC Classification: HQ784.V53 B45 2000

Berger, Arthur Asa, 1933- Manufacturing desire: media, popular culture, and everyday life / Arthur Asa Berger. Published/Created: New Brunswick, N.J.: Transaction Publishers, c1996. Description: x, 258 p.; 24 cm. ISBN: 1560002263 (alk. paper) Notes: Includes bibliographical references (p. 235-248) and indexes. Subjects: Mass media and culture--United States. Popular culture--United States. LC Classification: P94.6 .B47 1996 Dewey Class No.: 302.23/0973 20

Berger, Arthur Asa, 1933- Popular culture genres: theories and texts / Arthur Asa Berger. Published/Created: Newbury Park: Sage Publications, c1992. Description: xix, 171 p.; 23 cm. ISBN: 0803947259 (cloth) 0803947267 (pbk.) Notes: Includes bibliographical references (p. 160-162) and indexes. Subjects: Mass media. Popular culture. Literary form. Series: Foundations of popular culture; vol. 2 LC Classification: P91 .B445 1992 Dewey Class No.: 302.23 20

Bertrand, Claude Jean. Media ethics & accountability systems / by Claude-Jean Bertrand. Published/Created: New Brunswick, N.J.: Transaction Publishers, c2000. Description: x, 164 p.; 23 cm.

ISBN: 1560004207 Notes: Includes bibliographical references (p. 157-164). Subjects: Mass media--Moral and ethical aspects. LC Classification: P94 .B47 2000 Dewey Class No.: 175 21

Between the sheets, in the streets: queer, lesbian, and gay documentary / Chris Holmlund and Cynthia Fuchs, editors. Published/Created: Minneapolis: University of Minnesota Press, c1997. Related Authors: Holmlund, Chris. Fuchs, Cynthia. Description: x, 274 p.: ill.; 26 cm. ISBN: 0816627746 (hardcover: alk. paper) 0816627754 (pbk.: alk. paper) Notes: Includes bibliographical references and index. Filmography: p. 241-263. Subjects: Documentary mass media--United States. Gays in popular culture--United States. Series: Visible evidence; v. 1 LC Classification: P96.D622 U63 1997 Dewey Class No.: 306.76/6 21

Bh¯arat¯i, 'Sa'si, 1950- Glossary of drama, theatre, and electronic media: English-Hindi / Shashi Bharati. Published/Created: Delhi: B.R. Pub. Corp., c1996. Description: 142 p.; 25 cm. ISBN: 8170188547 Subjects: Theater--Dictionaries. Drama--Mass media--English language--Dictionaries--Hindi. 22; 23-90 LC Classification: PN2035 .B43 1996 Dewey Class No.: 792/.03 21

Blackman, Lisa, 1965- Mass hysteria: critical psychology and media studies / Lisa Blackman and Valerie Walkerdine. Published/Created: Houndmills [Eng.]; New York: PALGRAVE, 2001. Related Authors: Walkerdine, Valerie. Description: viii, 216 p.; 23 cm. ISBN: 0333647815 Notes: Includes bibliographical references (p. 197-206) and index. Subjects: Mass media--Psychological aspects. Social psychology. LC Classification: P96.P75 B58 2001 Dewey Class No.: 302.23/01/9 21

Blanchard, Robert O. (Robert Okie), 1934- Media education and the liberal arts: a blueprint for the new professionalism / Robert O. Blanchard, William G. Christ. Published/Created: Hillsdale, N.J.: L. Erlbaum Associates, 1993. Related Authors: Christ, William G. Description: xiii, 187 p.: ill.; 24 cm. ISBN: 0805804889 Notes: Developed from a symposium held at Trinity University in Feb. 1987. Includes bibliographical references (p. 162-174) and indexes. Subjects: Study and teaching (Higher) Series: Communication (Hillsdale, N.J.) Variant Series: Communication LC Classification: P91.3 .B55 1993 Dewey Class No.: 302.23/071/1 20

Blauner, Peter. Man of the hour: a novel / by Peter Blauner. Edition Information: 1st ed. Published/Created: Boston: Little, Brown, c1999. Description: 424 p.; 24 cm. ISBN: 0316038172 Subjects: Heroes--Fiction. Bombers (Terrorists)--Fiction. Terrorism--Fiction. Mass media and crime--Fiction. New York (N.Y.)--Fiction. Genre/Form: Adventure stories. LC Classification: PS3552.L3936 M36 1999 Dewey Class No.: 813/.54 21

Boafo, S. T. Kwame. Bibliography of teaching and study materials on African media and communication systems / compiled by S.T. Kwame Boafo. Published/Created: Nairobi, Kenya: African Council for Communication Education, 1991. Description: 11 p.; 30 cm. ISBN: 9966450041 Subjects: Mass media--Africa--Bibliography. Communication--Africa--Bibliography. Series: Communication teaching and study materials; 5 LC Classification: Z5635.A35 B63 1991 P92.A4

Booth, John E. (John Erlanger) The critic, power, and the performing arts / John E. Booth. Published/Created: New York: Columbia University Press, c1991. Related Authors: Twentieth Century Fund. Description: xx, 225 p.; 24 cm. ISBN: 0231074603 (alk. paper) Notes: "A Twentieth Century Fund essay." Includes bibliographical references (p. 211-215) and index. Subjects: Performing arts--United States. Criticism. Mass media and the arts--United States. LC Classification: PN2266.5 .B66 1991 Dewey Class No.: 791/.0973 20

Botha, Wilna. The role of the media in education: a discussion document: research findings and recommendations / by Wilna Botha. Published/Created: Johannesburg: EduSource, c1993. Description: 89 p.; 30 cm. ISBN: 062017336X Notes: "March 1993." Includes bibliographical references (p. 85-89). Subjects: Media programs (Education)--South Africa. Mass media in education--South Africa. Series: EduSource (Series); 93/01. Variant Series: EduSource; 93/01 LC Classification: LB1028.4 .B68 1993 Dewey Class No.: 371.3/35 20

Brake, Laurel, 1941- Print in transition, 1850-1910: studies in media and book history / Laurel Brake. Published/Created: Houndmills, Basingstoke, Hampshire; New York: Palgrave, 2001. Description: xv, 341 p.: ill.; 23 cm. ISBN: 0333770471 Notes: Includes bibliographical references (p. 307-320) and index. Subjects: Pater, Walter, 1839-1894 --Career in publishing. Publishers and publishing--Great Britain--History--19th century. Publishers and publishing--Great Britain--History--20th century. English periodicals--History--19th century. English periodicals--History--20th century. Sex in mass media--Great Britain--History--19th century. Sex in mass media--Great Britain--History--20th century. LC Classification: Z325 .B738 2001 Dewey Class No.: 070.5/0941/09034 21

Brasch, Walter M., 1945- Enquiring minds and space aliens: wandering through the mass media and popular culture / by Walt Brasch. Published/Created: Elmwood, Ill.: Mayfly Productions, c1996. Description: xxvii, 194 p.; 24 cm. ISBN: 0962461342 Subjects: Mass media and culture--United States. Popular culture--United States. LC Classification: P94.65.U6 B7 1996 Dewey Class No.: 302.23/0973 20

Brasch, Walter M., 1945- Sex and the single beer can: probing the media and American culture / by Walt Brasch. Published/Created: Elmwood, Ill.: Mayfly Productions, c1997. Description: xvii, 237 p.; 23 cm. ISBN: 0962461369 Notes: Collection of newspaper columns, most of which have been rev. for this publication. Subjects: Mass media and culture--United States. Popular culture--United States. LC Classification: P94.65.U6 B73 1997 Dewey Class No.: 302.23/0973 21

Bridges, Joe. An Internet guide for mass communication students / Joe Bridges. Published/Created: Madison WI: Brown & Benchmark, c1997. Description: vii, 124 p.: ill.; 23 cm. ISBN: 0697352730 Notes: Includes bibliographical references (p. 123-124). Subjects: Internet--Handbooks, manuals, etc. Mass media--Study and teaching (Higher)--Computer network resources. LC Classification: TK5105.875.I57 B745 1997

Brooks, Daniel, 1958- The Noam Chomsky lectures / Daniel Brooks and Guillermo Verdecchia. Published/Created: Toronto: Coach House Press, c1991. Related Authors: Verdecchia, Guillermo. Description: 93 p.: ill.; 22 cm. ISBN: 0889104131 Notes: Includes bibliographical references (p. 91-93). Subjects: Chomsky, Noam--Drama. Mass media--Moral and ethical aspects--Drama. LC Classification: PR9199.3.B69715 N63 1991 Dewey Class No.: 812/.54 20

Brown, Susan. Development of a mass media school in Namibia: feasibility, demand, curriculum, and budget estimate / a report prepared for UNESCO Namibia by Susan Brown. Published/Created: [Windhoek]: Namibian Institute for Social and Economic Research, University of Namibia, [1991] Related Authors: UNESCO Namibia. Description: 34 leaves; 30 cm. Notes: "September 1991." Subjects: Mass media--Study and teaching--Namibia. LC Classification: P91.5.N3 B76 1991

Budde, Michael L. The (magic) kingdom of God: Christianity and global culture industries / Michael Budde. Published/Created: Boulder, Colo.: Westview Press, 1997. Description: viii, 177 p.; 24 cm. ISBN: 0813330750 (cloth: alk. paper) Notes: Includes bibliographical references (p. 153-168) and index

Subjects: Catholic Church--Membership. International business enterprises--Religious aspects Christianity. Advertising. Mass media. Marketing. Christianity and culture. Identification (Religion) Evangelistic work. Christian education. Cultural industries. LC Classification: BR115.E3 B83 1997 Dewey Class No.: 261 21

Bugeja, Michael J. Living ethics: developing values in mass communication / Michael J. Bugeja. Published/Created: Boston, Mass.: Allyn and Bacon, c1996. Description: xix, 344 p.: ill.; 23 cm. ISBN: 0205173233 Notes: Includes bibliographical references and index. Subjects: Mass media--Moral and ethical aspects. LC Classification: P94 .B84 1996 Dewey Class No.: 302.23 20

Bunt, Gary R. Virtually Islamic: computer-mediated communication and cyber Islamic environments / Gary R. Bunt. Published/Created: Cardiff: University of Wales Press, c2000. Description: [x], 189 p.; 22 cm. ISBN: 0708316123 0708316115 (pbk) Notes: Includes bibliographical references (p. 167-181) and index. Subjects: Islam in mass media. Islam--Computer network resources. LC Classification: P96.I84 B86 2000 Dewey Class No.: 297 21 National Bib. No.: GBA0-40401

Burkhart, Ford N. Media, emergency warnings, and citizen response / Ford N. Burkhart. Published/Created: Boulder: Westview Press, 1991. Description: viii, 152 p.: ill.; 23 cm. ISBN: 0813383900: Notes: Includes bibliographical references (p. [129]-139) and index. Subjects: Emergency management--United States. Emergency communication systems--United States. Disasters--Press coverage--United States. Mass media--United States--Psychological aspects. Social networks--United States--Psychological aspects. LC Classification: HV551.3 .B87 1991 Dewey Class No.: 363.3/472 20

Burton, Graeme. More than meets the eye: an introduction to media studies / Graeme Burton. Edition Information: 2nd ed. Published/Created: London; New York: Arnold; New York: Distributed exclusively in the USA by St. Martin's Press, 1997. Description: xi, 240 p.: ill.; 25 cm. ISBN: 0340676639 Notes: Includes bibliographical references (p. [232]-238) and index. Subjects: Mass media--Study and teaching. LC Classification: P91.3 .B79 1997 Dewey Class No.: 302.23/07 21

Calvert, Clay. Voyeur nation: media, privacy, and peering in modern culture / Clay Calvert. Published/Created: Boulder, Colo.: Westview Press, 2000. Description: v, 274 p.; 22 cm. ISBN: 0813366275 (alk. paper) Notes: Includes bibliographical references and index. Subjects: Mass media. Voyeurism. Privacy, Right of. Series: Critical studies in communication and in cultural industries series Variant Series: Critical studies in communication and in the cultural industries LC Classification: P91 .C28 2000 Dewey Class No.: 302.23 21

Campbell, Christopher P. Race, myth and the news / Christopher P. Campbell. Published/Created: Thousand Oaks, Calif.: Sage Publications, c1995. Description: viii, 173 p.; 23 cm. ISBN: 0803958714 (cloth: alk. paper) 0803958722 (pbk.: alk. paper) Notes: Includes bibliographical references (p. 159-165) and index. Subjects: Racism in the press--United States. Mass media and race relations--United States. Television broadcasting of news--Political aspects--United States. Television broadcasting of news--Social aspects--United States. LC Classification: PN4888.R3 C36 1995 Dewey Class No.: 305.8 20

Campbell, Richard, 1949- Media & culture: an introduction to mass communication / Richard Campbell, Christopher R. Martin, Bettina Fabos. Edition Information: 3rd ed. Published/Created: Boston: Bedford/St. Martin's, c2002. Related Authors: Martin, Christopher R. Fabos, Bettina. Campbell, Richard, 1949- Media and culture. Description: xxiii, 613 p.: ill. (some col.); 28 cm. ISBN: 031239070X Notes: Rev. ed of: Media and culture. 2nd ed. c2000

Includes bibliographical references (p. 575-562) and index. Subjects: Mass media and culture--United States. Popular culture--United States. LC Classification: P94.65.U6 C36 2002 Dewey Class No.: 302.23/0973 21

Campbell, Richard, 1949- Media and culture: an introduction to mass communication / Richard Campbell, with Christopher R. Martin and Bettina Fabos. Edition Information: 2nd ed. Published/Created: Boston: Bedford/St. Martin's, c2000. Related Authors: Martin, Christopher R. Fabos, Bettina. Description: xxxiii, 555 p.: ill. (some col.); 26 cm. ISBN: 0312202008 Notes: Includes bibliographical references (p. 519-526) and index. Subjects: Mass media and culture--United States. Popular culture--United States. LC Classification: P94.65.U6 C36 2000 Dewey Class No.: 302.23/0973 21

Campbell, Stan. Mind over media: the power of making sound--entertainment choices / Stan Campbell, Randy Southern. Published/Created: Wheaton Ill.: Tyndale, c2001. Related Authors: Southern, Randy. Description: 165 p.: ill.; 22 cm. ISBN: 1561798703 (pbk.) Subjects: Christian teenagers--Religious life. Mass media--Religious aspects--Christianity. Mass media. Christian life. LC Classification: BV4531.3 .C36 2001 Dewey Class No.: 241/.65 21

Carroll, Noël (Noël E.) A philosophy of mass art / Noël Carroll. Published/Created: Oxford: Clarendon Press; New York: Oxford University Press, 1998. Description: xii, 425 p.; 24 cm. ISBN: 0198711298 (hard: alk. paper) 0198742371 (pbk.: alk. paper) Notes: Includes bibliographical references and index. Subjects: Mass media and the arts. Popular culture. LC Classification: NX180.M3 C37 1998 Dewey Class No.: 700/.1/03 21

Cashmore, Ernest. The Black culture industry / Ellis Cashmore. Published/Created: London; New York: Routledge, 1997. Description: 203 p.; 26 cm. ISBN: 0415120829 0415120837 (pbk.) Notes: Includes bibliographical references (p. 182-186) and index. Subjects: Afro-Americans--Race identity. Racism--United States--History--20th century. Afro-American arts. Afro-Americans in mass media. United States--Race relations. LC Classification: E185.615 .C352 1997 Dewey Class No.: 305.896/073 21

Cawelti, John G. The six-gun mystique sequel / John G. Cawelti. Published/Created: Bowling Green, OH: Bowling Green State University Popular Press, c1999. Description: xi, 215 p.; 24 cm. ISBN: 0879727853 (clothbound) 0879727861 (pbk.) Notes: Includes bibliographical references and filmographies (p. 167-2150. Subjects: Western stories--History and criticism. Western films--History and criticism. West (U.S.)--In mass media. LC Classification: P96.W48 C393 1999 Dewey Class No.: 700/.4278 21

Chabon, Michael. The amazing adventures of Kavalier and Clay: a novel / Michael Chabon. Published/Created: New York: Random House, c2000. Description: 639 p.; 25 cm. ISBN: 0679450041 (acid-free paper) Subjects: Comic books, strips, etc.--Authorship--Fiction. Heroes in mass media--Fiction. Czech Americans--Fiction. Young men--Fiction. Cartoonists--Fiction. New York (N.Y.)--Fiction. Genre/Form: Humorous stories. Bildungsromane. LC Classification: PS3553.H15 A82 2000 Dewey Class No.: 813/.54 21

Charles, Gerard, 1946- The media of the republic / Gerard Charles. Published/Created: Greensborough, Vic.: Steele Wilson Books, 1999. Description: 287 p.; 24 cm. ISBN: 1876262060 Notes: Includes bibliographical references (p. [285]-287). Subjects: Diana, Princess of Wales, 1961- --Death and burial--Press coverage. Diana, Princess of Wales, 1961- --In mass media. Mass media--Australia--Moral and ethical aspects. Mass media criticism--Australia. LC Classification: DA591.A45 D5285 1999 Dewey Class No.: 941.085/092 21

Charles, Gerard, 1946- The telecard affair: diary of a media lynching / Gerard Charles. Published/Created: Greensborough, Vic.: Steele Wilson Books, 2001. Description: 230 p.; 22 cm. ISBN: 1876262109 Subjects: Reith, Peter, 1950- --In mass media. Mass media--Australia. Mass media--Moral and ethical aspects--Australia. Journalistic ethics--Australia. Dewey Class No.: 079/.4 21

Chesebro, James W. Analyzing media: communication technologies as symbolic and cognitive systems / James W. Chesebro, Dale A. Bertelsen. Published/Created: New York: Guilford Press, c1996. Related Authors: Bertelsen, Dale A. Description: ix, 228 p.; 24 cm. ISBN: 1572301546 Notes: Includes bibliographical references (p. 189-217) and index. Subjects: Mass media criticism. Communication and technology. Communication and culture. Series: Revisioning rhetoric LC Classification: P96.C76 C48 1996 Dewey Class No.: 302.23 20

Christians, Clifford G. Media ethics: cases & moral reasoning / Clifford G. Christians, Kim B. Rotzoll, Mark Fackler. Edition Information: 3rd ed. Published/Created: New York: Longman, c1991. Related Authors: Rotzoll, Kim B. Fackler, Mark. Description: xviii, 445 p.: ill.; 23 cm. ISBN: 0801306507 (pbk.) 0801306663 (csd.) Notes: Includes bibliographical references (p. 427-434) and index. Subjects: Mass media--Moral and ethical aspects. Series: Communications (Annenberg School of Communications (University of Pennsylvania)) Variant Series: Communications LC Classification: P94 .C45 1990 Dewey Class No.: 170 20

Christians, Clifford G. Media ethics: cases & moral reasoning / Clifford G. Christians, Mark Fackler, Kim B. Rotzoll. Edition Information: 4th ed. Published/Created: New York: Longman, c1995. Related Authors: Fackler, Mark. Rotzoll, Kim B. Description: xiv, 350 p.: ill.; 24 cm. ISBN: 0801311861 Notes: Includes bibliographical references (p. 335-342) and index. Subjects: Mass media--Moral and ethical aspects. LC Classification: P94 .C45 1995 Dewey Class No.: 170 20

Claussen, Dane S., 1963- Anti-intellectualism in American media: magazines & higher education / Dane S. Claussen. Published/Created: New York: P. Lang, 2002. Projected Pub. Date: 0206 Description: p. cm. ISBN: 0820457213 (pbk.: alk. paper) Notes: Includes bibliographical references and index. Subjects: Mass media and culture--United States. Education, Higher--United States. United States--Intellectual life--20th century. Series: Higher ed; v. 11 LC Classification: P94.65.U6 C58 2002 Dewey Class No.: 302.23/0973 21

Cohen, Jason. Generation Ecch! / Jason Cohen and Michael Krugman; comix [sic] by Evan Dorkin. Published/Created: New York: Simon & Schuster, c1994. Related Authors: Krugman, Michael. Dorkin, Evan. Description: 218 p.: ill.; 23 cm. ISBN: 0671886940: Notes: "A Fireside book." Subjects: Mass media and young adults--United States--Humor. Popular culture--United States--Humor. LC Classification: P94.5.Y68 C65 1994 Dewey Class No.: 305.23/5/0973 20

Cohl, H. Aaron. Are we scaring ourselves to death?: how pessimism, paranoia, and a misguided media are leading us toward disaster / H. Aaron Cohl. Edition Information: 1st St. Martin's Griffin ed. Published/Created: New York: St. Martin's Griffin, 1997. Description: vi, 151 p.; 21 cm. ISBN: 0312150563 Notes: "A Thomas Dunne book"--T.p. verso. Subjects: Mass media--United States--Psychological aspects. Social psychology--United States. Risk perception--United States. Risk communication--United States. Sensationalism in journalism--United States. LC Classification: HN90.M3 C64 1997 Dewey Class No.: 302 20

Coldrick, Jack. Dr. Marie Stopes and press censorship of birth-control: the story of the Catholic campaign against newspaper advertising in Ireland and Britain / by Jack

Coldrick. Published/Created: Belfast: Athol books, 1992. Related Titles: Doctor Marie Stopes and press censorship of birth-control. Description: 23 p.: ill.; 21 cm. Cancelled ISBN: 0085034616 Subjects: Stopes, Marie Carmichael, 1880-1958. Birth control--Religious aspects--Catholic Church. Freedom of the press--Great Britain. Freedom of the press--Ireland. Mass media in birth control--Great Britain. Mass media in birth control--Ireland. LC Classification: HQ764.S7 C65 1992 Dewey Class No.: 613.9/4 20

Communication and culture in war and peace / edited by Colleen Roach; preface by Johan Galtung. Published/Created: Newbury Park: Sage Publications, c1993. Related Authors: Roach, Colleen A. Description: xxv, 274 p.: ill.; 23 cm. ISBN: 0803950624 (cloth) 0803950632 (pbk.) Notes: Includes bibliographical references and index. Subjects: Communication and culture. Mass media--Social aspects. Peace. Series: Communication and human values (Newbury Park, Calif.) Variant Series: Communication and human values LC Classification: P91 .C539 1993 Dewey Class No.: 302.2 20

Communication in history: technology, culture, society / [edited by] David Crowley & Paul Heyer. Edition Information: 2nd ed. Published/Created: White Plains, N.Y.: Longman Publishers USA, c1995. Related Authors: Crowley, D. J. (David J.), 1945- Heyer, Paul, 1946- Description: xvi, 368 p.: ill.; 24 cm. ISBN: 0801312507 Notes: Includes bibliographical references (p. 359-362) and index. Subjects: Communication--History. Mass media--History. LC Classification: P90 .C62945 1995 Dewey Class No.: 302.2/09 20

Conquest, John, 1943- Trouble is their business: private eyes in fiction, film, and television, 1927-1988 / John Conquest. Published/Created: New York: Garland Pub., 1990. Description: liii, 497 p.; 23 cm. ISBN: 0824059476 (alk. paper) Notes: Includes bibliographies and index. Subjects: Detectives in mass media. Series: Garland reference library of the humanities; vol. 1151 LC Classification: P96.D4 C66 1990 Dewey Class No.: 016.30223/0883632 20

Continental shift: globalisation and culture / edited by Elizabeth Jacka. Published/Created: Double Bay, N.S.W.: Local Consumption Publications, c1992. Related Authors: Jacka, Elizabeth. Continental Shift Conference (1991: Sydney, N.S.W.) Description: 160 p.: ill.; 21 cm. ISBN: 0949793248 Notes: Book derives from papers of the Continental Shift Conference held April 1991. School of Humanities, University of Technology, Sidney gave support in mounting the conference. Includes bibliographical references. Subjects: Communication, International--Congresses. Communication--International cooperation--Congresses. Mass media and technology--Congresses. Mass media and culture--Congresses. LC Classification: P96.I5 C69 1992 Dewey Class No.: 302.2 20

Cook, Timothy E., 1954- Notes for the next epidemic, part one: lessons from the news coverage of AIDS / by Timothy E. Cook. Published/Created: [Cambridge, Mass.]: Joan Shorenstein Barone Center, Press, Politics, Public Policy, Harvard University, John F. Kennedy School of Government, [1991] Description: 16 p.: ill.; 28 cm. Notes: "October 1991." Includes bibliographical references (p. 14-16). Subjects: Journalism, Medical--United States. AIDS (Disease)--Reporting--United States. Mass media--Social aspects--United States. Series: Discussion paper (Joan Shorenstein Barone Center on the Press, Politics, and Public Policy); D-12. Variant Series: Discussion paper; D-12 LC Classification: PN4784.M4 C66 1991

Cormack, Michael J. Ideology / Mike Cormack. Published/Created: Ann Arbor: University of Michigan Press, c1992. Description: 109 p.; 24 cm. ISBN: 0472094912 0472064916 Notes: Errata slip inserted. Includes bibliographical references (p. [104]-106) and index. Subjects: Culture. Ideology. Mass media--Social aspects. Popular culture. Ideology in literature. LC Classification: HM101 .C717 1992 Dewey Class No.: 306.4 20

Corry, John. Global warming and the media / John Corry. Published/Created: Washington, D.C.: Media Institute, c1997. Related Authors: National Journalism Project (U.S.) Description: vi, 50 p.; 26 cm. ISBN: 0937790575 Notes: "A publication of the Media Institute's National Journalism Project." Includes bibliographical references (p. 47-50). Subjects: Global warming--Information services. Mass media policy--United States. Mass media and the environment--United States. LC Classification: QC981.8.G56 C67 1997 Dewey Class No.: 363.738/74 21

Cortés, Carlos E. The children are watching: how the media teach about diversity / Carlos E. Cortés. Published/Created: New York: Teachers College Press, c2000. Description: xxi, 202 p.; 24 cm. ISBN: 0807739383 (cloth: alk. paper) 0807739375 (paper: alk. paper) Notes: Includes bibliographical references (p. 173-189) and index. Subjects: Multiculturalism in mass media. Multicultural education. Mass media and education. Series: Multicultural education series (New York, N.Y.) Variant Series: Multicultural education series LC Classification: P96.M83 C67 2000 Dewey Class No.: 306 21

Coville, Gary, 1949- Jack the Ripper: his life and crimes in popular entertainment / by Gary Coville and Patrick Lucanio. Published/Created: Jefferson, N.C.: McFarland, 1999. Related Authors: Lucanio, Patrick. Description: vii, 193 p.: ill.; 24 cm. ISBN: 078640616X (lib. bdg.: alk. paper) Notes: Includes bibliographical references (p. 177-180) and index. Subjects: Jack, the Ripper--In literature. English literature--20th century--History and criticism. English literature--19th century--History and criticism. English literature--Film and video adaptations. American literature--History and criticism. Popular literature--History and criticism. Popular culture--History--20th century. Serial murders in mass media. Whitechapel (London, England)--In literature. LC Classification: PR478.J34 C68 1999 Dewey Class No.: 820.9/351 21

Crane, Diana, 1933- The production of culture: media and the urban arts / Diana Crane. Published/Created: Newbury Park, Calif.: Sage Publications, c1992. Description: x, 198 p.; 23 cm. ISBN: 0803936931 080393694X (pbk.) Notes: Includes bibliographical references (p. 174-186) and indexes. Subjects: Mass media and the arts--United States. Popular culture--United States. Mass media and the arts--Europe. Popular culture--Europe. Series: Foundations of popular culture; vol. 1 LC Classification: NX180.M3 C7 1992 Dewey Class No.: 700/.1/05 20

Critical studies in media commercialism / edited by Robin Andersen and Lance Strate. Published/Created: New York: Oxford University Press, 2000. Related Authors: Andersen, Robin. Strate, Lance. Description: ix, 341 p.; 25 cm. ISBN: 0198742770 Notes: Includes bibliographical references and index. Subjects: Mass media--Economic aspects. Mass media and culture. Mass media--Influence. LC Classification: P96.E25 C75 2000 Dewey Class No.: 302.23 21

Critical studies of Canadian mass media / edited by Marc Grenier. Published/Created: Toronto: Butterworths, 1992. Related Authors: Grenier, Marc, 1953- Description: xvii, 384 p.: ill.; 23 cm. ISBN: 0409906352: Notes: Includes bibliographical references (p. [341]-376) and index. Subjects: Mass media--Canada. Journalism--Canada. Mass media criticism--Canada. Mass media--Social aspects. LC Classification: P92.C3 C75 1992 Dewey Class No.: 302.23/0971 20

Cubitt, Sean, 1953- Timeshift: on video culture / Sean Cubitt. Published/Created: London; New York: Routledge, 1991. Related Titles: Time shift. Description: x, 206 p.; 23 cm. ISBN: 0415055482 0415016789 (pbk.) Notes: "A Comedia book." Includes bibliographical references (p. [188]-199) and index. Subjects: Video recordings. Video art. Mass media. Popular culture. LC Classification: PN1992.935 .C84 1990 Dewey Class No.: 700/.9/04 20

Cubitt, Sean, 1953- Videography: video media as art and culture / Sean Cubitt. Published/Created: New York: St. Martin's Press, 1993. Description: xix, 239 p.; 23 cm. ISBN: 031210295X (cloth) 0312102968 (pbk.) Notes: Includes bibliographical references (p. 220-232) and index. Subjects: Video recordings. Video art. Mass media. Popular culture. LC Classification: PN1992.935 .C85 1993 Dewey Class No.: 302.23/4 20

Cultivation analysis: new directions in media effects research / edited by Nancy Signorielli and Michael Morgan. Published/Created: Newbury Park, Calif.: Sage Publications, c1990. Related Authors: Signorielli, Nancy. Morgan, Michael, 1953 Apr. 15- Description: 266 p.; 23 cm. ISBN: 0803932952 0803932960 (pbk.) Notes: Includes bibliographical references. Subjects: Mass media--Audiences. Mass media--Psychological aspects. Reality. Variant Series: Sage focus editions; 108 LC Classification: P96.A83 C85 1990 Dewey Class No.: 302.23 20

Cultural difference, media memories: Anglo-American images of Japan / edited by Phil Hammond. Published/Created: London; Herndon, VA: Cassell, 1997. Related Authors: Hammond, Phil, 1962- Description: xxv, 229 p.; 23 cm. ISBN: 0304701106 0304701114 (pbk.) Notes: Includes bibliographical references and index. Subjects: Public opinion--United States. Japan in mass media--United States. Japan in mass media--Great Britain. Japan--Foreign public opinion, American. Japan--Foreign public opinion, British. Public opinion--Great Britain. LC Classification: DS849.U6 C85 1997 Dewey Class No.: 303.3/8/0973 21

Cultural diversity and the U.S. media / edited by Yahya R. Kamalipour, Theresa Carilli; foreword by George Gerbner. Published/Created: Albany: State University of New York Press, c1998. Related Authors: Kamalipour, Yahya R. Carilli, Theresa. Description: xxii, 307 p.; 24 cm. ISBN: 0791439291 (alk. paper) 0791439305 (pbk.: alk. paper) Notes: Includes bibliographical references (p. 293-294) and index. Subjects: Mass media and minorities--United States. Mass media and ethnic relations--United States. Mass media and race relations--United States. Pluralism (Social sciences)--United States. United States--Ethnic relations. Series: SUNY series in human communication processes. Variant Series: SUNY series, human communication processes LC Classification: P94.5.M552 U628 1998 Dewey Class No.: 302.23/089/00973 21

Cultural studies and communications / edited by James Curran, David Morley, Valerie Walkerdine. Published/Created: London; New York: Arnold; New York, NY: Distributed exculsively in the USA by St. Martin's Press, 1996. Related Authors: Curran, James. Morley, David, 1949- Walkerdine, Valerie. Description: x, 371 p.; 24 cm. ISBN: 0340652683 (hardcover): 034061417X (pbk.): Notes: Includes bibliographical references and index. Subjects: Culture. Communication. Postmodernism. Popular culture. Mass media. LC Classification: HM101 .C8925 1996 Dewey Class No.: 306 20

Culture across borders: Mexican immigration & popular culture / edited by David R. Maciel and María Herrera-Sobek. Published/Created: Tucson: University of Arizona Press, c1998. Related Authors: Maciel, David. Herrera-Sobek, María. Description: xiv, 268 p.: ill.; 25 cm. ISBN: 0816518327 (acid-free, archival-quality paper) 0816518335 (pbk.: acid-free, archival-quality paper) Notes: Includes bibliographical references and index. Subjects: Mexican Americans--Social life and customs--Cultural assimilation. Popular culture--United States--History--20th century. Mexican Americans and mass media. Mexico--Emigration and immigration--United States--Emigration and immigration--History--20th century.

LC Classification: E184.M5 C85 1998 Dewey Class No.: 305.868/72073 21

Culture and power: a media, culture & society reader / edited by Paddy Scannell, Philip Schlesinger, and Colin Sparks. Published/Created: London; Newbury Park, Calif.: Sage Publications, 1992. Related Authors: Scannell, Paddy. Schlesinger, Philip. Sparks, Colin, 1947- Description: ix, 357 p.; 24 cm. ISBN: 0803986300: 0803986319 (pbk.) Notes: Includes bibliographical references and index. Subjects: Mass media--Social aspects. Mass media--Political aspects. Popular culture. Series: Media, culture, and society series. Variant Series: The Media, culture & society series LC Classification: HM258 .C8425 1992 Dewey Class No.: 302.23 20

Culture first!: promoting standards in the new media age / edited by Kenneth Dyson and Walter Homolka. Published/Created: London; New York, NY: Cassell, 1996. Related Authors: Dyson, Kenneth H. F. Homolka, Walter. Description: xv, 175 p.; 22 cm. ISBN: 0304337714 (hbk) 0304337722 (pbk) Notes: Includes bibliographical references and index. Subjects: Mass media and culture. Mass media--Moral and ethical aspects. Mass media--Technological innovations. Aesthetics. LC Classification: P94.6 .C854 1996 Dewey Class No.: 302.23 21

Culture, communication, and development: an inquiry into the relationship of culture and development, and the documentation of a roundtable proceedings. Published/Created: Manila: Asian Institute of Journalism, 1994. Related Authors: Asian Institute of Journalism. Description: vii, 67 p.; 28 cm. Subjects: Community development--Philippines--Mass media--Social aspects--Philippines--Communication and culture--Philippines--Cultural policy--Congresses. LC Classification: HN710.Z9 C611286 1994 Dewey Class No.: 307.1/4/09599 20

Dancing in the dark: youth, popular culture, and the electronic media / by Quentin J. Schultze ... [et al.]. Published/Created: Grand Rapids, Mich.: W.B. Eerdmans Pub. Co., c1991. Related Authors: Schultze, Quentin J. (Quentin James), 1952- Calvin Center for Christian Scholarship. Description: xii, 348 p.: ill.; 23 cm. ISBN: 0802805302: Notes: "Calvin Center for Christian Scholarship." Includes bibliographical references (p. 310-341) and index. Subjects: Mass media and youth--United States. Popular culture--United States. Popular culture--Religious aspects--Christianity. LC Classification: HQ799.2.M35 D36 1990 Dewey Class No.: 302.23/083 20

Danesi, Marcel, 1946- Encyclopedic dictionary of semiotics, media, and communications / Marcel Danesi. Published/Created: Toronto: University of Toronto Press, c2000. Description: viii, 266 p.; 26 cm. ISBN: 0802047831 (bound) 0802083293 (pbk.) Notes: Includes bibliographical references (p. [245]-258) and index. Subjects: Communication--Semiotics--Mass media--Dictionaries. Communication--Sémiotique--Médias--Dictionnaires anglais. Series: Toronto studies in semiotics LC Classification: P87.5 .D36 2000 Dewey Class No.: 302.2/03 21 National Bib. No.: C00-930589-0

Daniels, Les, 1943- Batman: the complete history / by Les Daniels; art direction and design by Chip Kidd. Published/Created: San Francisco: Chronicle Books, c1999. Related Authors: Kidd, Chip. Description: 206 p.: ill. (some col.); 27 cm. ISBN: 0811824705 Notes: Includes index. Subjects: Batman (Fictitious character) in mass media--History. LC Classification: P96.B37 D36 1999 Dewey Class No.: 700/.451 21

Daniels, Les, 1943- Superman: the complete history, the life and times of the man of steel / by Les Daniels. Published/Created: San Francisco, Calif.: Chronicle Books, c1998. Description: 192 p.: ill. (some col.); 27 cm. ISBN: 0811821110 Notes: Includes index. Subjects: Superman (Fictitious character) in mass media. LC

Classification: P96.S94 D36 1998 Dewey Class No.: 700/.451 21

Davey, Frank, 1940- Karla's web: a cultural investigation of the Mahaffy-French murders / Frank Davey. Edition Information: Special blackout ed. Published/Created: Toronto: Viking, 1994. Description: 328 p.: ill., ports.; 24 cm. ISBN: 0670861537: Notes: Includes index. Accompanied by customer response card. Accompanied by dust jacket band explaining nature of blacked out passages. Includes bibliographical references: p. 322-325. Subjects: Homolka, Karla. Bernardo, Paul. Homolka, Karla. Bernardo, Paul. Murder--Ontario--Case studies. Trials (Murder)--Social aspects--Murder--Investigation--Social aspects--Criminal justice, Administration of--Mass media and criminal justice--Computer bulletin boards--Social aspects--Procès (Meurtre)--Aspect social--Meurtre--Enquêtes--Aspect social--Justice pénale--Administration-- Médias et justice pénale--Ontario. Tableaux d'affichage électronique--Aspect social--Ontario. LC Classification: HV6535.C32 O573 1994 Dewey Class No.: 364.1/523/0971338 20

Davies, Jude, 1965- Diana, a cultural history: gender, race, nation, and the people's princess / Jude Davies. Published/Created: Houndmills, Hampshire; New York: Palgrave, 2001. Description: viii, 250 p.; 23 cm. ISBN: 0333736885 Notes: Includes bibliographical references (p. 233-244) and index. Subjects: Diana, Princess of Wales, 1961- --In mass media. Mass media and public opinion--Great Britain--History 20th century. Popular culture--Great Britain--History--20th century. Princesses--Great Britain--Biography. National characteristics in mass media. Race relations in mass media. Sex role in mass media. Women in mass media. LC Classification: DA591.A45 D531216 2001 Dewey Class No.: 941.085/092 B 21

Davis, Laurel R., 1961- The swimsuit issue and sport: hegemonic masculinity in Sports illustrated / Laurel R. Davis. Published/Created: Albany: State University of New York Press, c1997. Description: ix, 168 p.; 24 cm. ISBN: 0791433919 (alk. paper) 0791433927 (pbk.: alk. paper) Notes: Includes bibliographical references (p. 147-159) and index. Subjects: Sports illustrated. Sports--Social aspects--United States. Mass media--Social aspects--Mass media and minorities--Sexism--Sex in popular culture--Masculinity--Bathing suits--United States. Developing countries--In mass media. Series: SUNY series on sport, culture, and social relations LC Classification: GV706.5 .D39 1997 Dewey Class No.: 306.4/83/0973 20

Day, Louis A. Ethics in media communications: cases and controversies / Louis A. Day. Edition Information: 3rd ed. Published/Created: Australia; Belmont, CA: Wadsworth Pub. Co., c2000. Description: xvi, 435 p.: ill.; 24 cm. Cancelled ISBN: 0534561787x (pbk.) Notes: Includes bibliographical references and index. Subjects: Mass media--Moral and ethical aspects. LC Classification: P94 .D39 2000 Dewey Class No.: 175 21

Day, Louis A. Ethics in media communications: cases and controversies / Louis A. Day. Edition Information: 2nd ed. Published/Created: Belmont, CA: Wadsworth Pub., c1997. Description: xiv, 450 p.; 24 cm. ISBN: 0534507166 Notes: Includes bibliographical references (p. 429-432) and index. Subjects: Mass media--Moral and ethical aspects. LC Classification: P94 .D39 1997 Dewey Class No.: 174 20

Day, Louis A. Ethics in media communications: cases and controversies / Louis A. Day. Published/Created: Belmont, Calif.: Wadsworth Pub. Co., 1990. Description: xvii, 365 p.; 24 cm. ISBN: 0534147844 Notes: Includes bibliographical references (p. 357-360) and index. Subjects: Mass media--Moral and ethical aspects. Ethics. LC Classification: P94 .D39 1990 Dewey Class No.: 174/.9097 20

Dayan, Daniel, 1943- Media events: the live broadcasting of history / Daniel Dayan, Elihu Katz. Published/Created: Cambridge, Mass.: Harvard University Press, 1992. Related Authors: Katz, Elihu, 1926- Description: xi, 306 p.; 22 cm. ISBN: 067455955X (alk. paper) Notes: Includes bibliographical references (p. 275-293) and index. Subjects: Television broadcasting of news. Mass media--Social aspects. History, Modern--1945- LC Classification: PN4784.T4 D38 1992 Dewey Class No.: 070.1/95 20

Daynes, Gary. Making villains, making heroes: Joseph R. McCarthy, Martin Luther King, Jr. and the politics of American memory / Gary Daynes. Published/Created: New York: Garland Pub., 1997. Description: ix, 273 p.; 23 cm. ISBN: 081532992X (acid-free paper) Notes: Includes bibliographical references (p. 241-270) and index. Subjects: McCarthy, Joseph, 1908-1957. King, Martin Luther, Jr., 1929-1968. Popular culture--United States--History--20th century. Mass media--Social aspects--United States--Historiography. Series: Garland studies in American popular history and culture LC Classification: E169.04 .D39 1997 Dewey Class No.: 973.9 21

De Kerckhove, Derrick. The skin of culture: investigating the new electronic reality / Derrick De Kerckhove; edited by Christopher Dewdney. Published/Created: Toronto: Somerville House Pub., c1995. Related Authors: Dewdney, Christopher, 1951- Description: xxii, 226 p.: ill.; 23 cm. ISBN: 1895897459 Notes: "A Patrick Crean Book." Includes bibliographical references (p. 219-226). Subjects: Mass media--Telecommunication-Technology--Social aspects. Mass media and technology. LC Classification: HM258 .D36 1995 Dewey Class No.: 302.23/4 20

DeAndrea, William L. Encyclopedia mysteriosa: a comprehensive guide to the art of detection in print, film, radio, and television / William L. DeAndrea. Edition Information: 1st ed. Published/Created: New York: Prentice Hall General Reference, c1994. Description: x, 405 p.: ill.; 25 cm. ISBN: 0671850253: Notes: Includes bibliographical references. Subjects: Detective and mystery stories--Detectives in mass media--Dictionaries. LC Classification: PN3448.D4 D34 1994 Dewey Class No.: 809.3/872/03 20

Debray, Régis. Media manifestos: on the technological transmission of cultural forms / Régis Debray; translated by Eric Rauth. Published/Created: London; New York: Verso, 1996. Description: viii, 179 p.; 22 cm. ISBN: 1859849725 1859840876 (pbk.) Notes: Text submitted as part of the viva, or dissertation defense, confirming the candidate's authority to direct research. Presented at the Sorbonne (Paris I) on Jan. 8, 1994. Includes bibliographical references (p. 178-179). Subjects: Mass media--Philosophy--Semiotics. Philosophy, French--20th century. Mass media and technology. LC Classification: P90 .D4313 1996 Dewey Class No.: 302.23/01 20

Dégh, Linda. American folklore and the mass media / Linda Dégh. Published/Created: Bloomington: Indiana University Press, c1994. Description: 217 p.: ill.; 24 cm. ISBN: 0253316774 (cloth: alk. paper) 0253208440 (pbk.: alk. paper) Notes: Includes bibliographical references (p. 194-213) and index. Subjects: Folklore--Mass media--Popular culture--United States. Series: Folklore today LC Classification: GR105 .D44 1994 Dewey Class No.: 398/.0973 20

DeMoss, Robert G. 21 days to better family entertainment / Robert G. DeMoss, Jr. Published/Created: Grand Rapids, Mich.: Zondervan Pub., c1998. Description: 139 p.: ill.; 21 cm. ISBN: 0310217466 (softcover) Notes: Includes bibliographical references (p. 137-139). Subjects: Television and family. Mass media and the family. Family recreation. Family--Religious aspects--Christianity. Series: The 21-day series LC Classification: HQ520 .D45 1998 Dewey Class No.: 302.23 21

DeMoss, Robert G. Learn to discern / Robert G. DeMoss, Jr. Edition Information: Expanded and updated ed. Published/Created: Grand Rapids, Mich.: Zondervan Pub. House, c1997. Description: 235 p.: ill.; 21 cm. ISBN: 0310211344 Notes: Includes bibliographical references (p. 231-235). Subjects: Popular culture--Mass media--Social aspects--United States. Content analysis (Communication)--Handbooks, manuals, etc. LC Classification: E169.12 .D39 1997 Dewey Class No.: 302.23/4/0973 21

DeMoss, Robert G. Learn to discern / Robert G. DeMoss, Jr.; foreword by Josh McDowell. Published/Created: Grand Rapids, Mich.: Zondervan, c1992. Description: xii, 179 p.: ill.; 23 cm. ISBN: 0310518318 (pbk.) Notes: Includes bibliographical references (p. 171-174) and index. Subjects: Popular culture--Mass media--Social aspects--United States. Content analysis (Communication)--Handbooks, manuals, etc. LC Classification: E169.12 .D39 1992 Dewey Class No.: 302.23/4/0973 20

Deppa, Joan. The media and disasters: Pan Am 103 / Joan Deppa, with Maria Russell, Dona Hayes, and Elizabeth Lynne Flocke. Published/Created: New York: New York University Press, c1994. Description: vi, 346 p.; 24 cm. ISBN: 0814718574: 0814718566 (pbk.): Notes: Includes bibliographical references (p. 334-340) and index. Subjects: Disasters--Press coverage. Pan Am Flight 103 Bombing Incident, 1988. Journalistic ethics. Mass media--Moral and ethical aspects. LC Classification: PN4784.D57 D46 1994 Dewey Class No.: 070.4/4936312465/0941483 20

Dickson, Tom, 1946- Mass media education in transition: preparing for the 21st century / Tom Dickson. Published/Created: Mahwah, N.J.: L. Erlbaum, 2000. Description: xi, 282 p.; 24 cm. ISBN: 0805830979 (alk. paper) Notes: Includes bibliographical references (p. 251-270) and index. Subjects: Mass media--Study and teaching (Higher)--United States. Series: LEA's communication series LC Classification: P91.5.U5 D53 2000 Dewey Class No.: 302.23/071/173 21

Donald, James. Sentimental education: schooling, popular culture, and the regulation of liberty / James Donald. Published/Created: London; New York: Verso, 1992. Description: xi, 203 p.: ill.; 24 cm. ISBN: 0860913430 0860915557 (pbk.) Notes: Includes bibliographical references (p. 180-193) and index. Subjects: Education and state--Great Britain. Education--Social aspects--Great Britain. Popular culture--Great Britain. Mass media--Great Britain. Mass media policy--Great Britain. Education--Great Britain--Philosophy. LC Classification: LC93.G7 D66 1992 Dewey Class No.: 379.41 20

Eco, Umberto. Apocalypse postponed / Umberto Eco; edited by Robert Lumley. Published/Created: Bloomington: Indiana University Press; London: British Film Institute, 1994. Related Authors: Lumley, Robert, 1951- Description: vii, 227 p.: ill.; 24 cm. ISBN: 0253318513 (U.S.: cloth) 0851704182 (cloth) 0851704468 (pbk.) Notes: Includes bibliographical references and index. Subjects: Popular culture. Mass media--Social aspects. Popular culture--Italy. Mass media--Social aspects--Italy. Series: Perspectives LC Classification: HM101 .E28 1994 Dewey Class No.: 306 20

Edelstein, Alex S. Total propaganda: from mass culture to popular culture / Alex S. Edelstein. Published/Created: Mahwah, N.J.: L. Erlbaum Associates, 1997. Description: xv, 345 p.; 24 cm. ISBN: 0805808914 (cloth: alk. paper) 0805808922 (pbk.: alk. paper) Notes: Includes bibliographical references and indexes. Subjects: Mass media and culture. Popular culture. Propaganda. LC Classification: P94.6 .E34 1997 Dewey Class No.: 302.23 21

Elias, Tom. The Simpson trial in black and white / by Tom Elias and Dennis Schatzman. Published/Created: Los

Angeles: General Publishing Group, c1996. Related Authors: Schatzman, Dennis. Description: 286 p., [8] p. of plates: ill.; 24 cm. ISBN: 188164992X Notes: Includes index. Subjects: Simpson, O. J., 1947- --Trials, litigation, etc. Trials (Murder)--California--Los Angeles. Crime and the press--United States. Mass media and race relations--United States. Newspaper court reporting--California--Los Angeles. LC Classification: KF224.S485 E43 1996 Dewey Class No.: 070.4/4934573/025230979494 20

Elite media amidst mass culture: a critical look at mass communication in Korea / edited by Chie-woon Kim and Jae-won Lee. Published/Created: Seoul, Korea: NANAM Publishing House, 1994. Related Authors: Kim, Chie-woon. Lee, Jae-won. Description: 331 p.; 23 cm. Cancelled ISBN: 893006017x Notes: Includes bibliographical references. Subjects: Mass media--Korea (South) Popular culture--Korea (South) LC Classification: P92.K6 E45 1994

Ellmore, R. Terry. NTC's mass media dictionary / R. Terry Ellmore. Published/Created: Lincolnwood, Ill., USA: National Textbook Co., c1991. Related Titles: Mass media dictionary. Description: xi, 668 p.; 24 cm. ISBN: 0844231851: Subjects: Mass media--Dictionaries. LC Classification: P87.5 .E45 1990 Dewey Class No.: 302.23/03 20

Embodied rhetorics: disability in language and culture / \edited by James C. Wilson and Cynthia Lewiecki-Wilson. Published/Created: Carbondale: Southern Illinois University Press, 2001.

Englehardt, Elaine E. Media and ethics: principles for moral decisions / Elaine E. Englehardt, Ralph D. Barney; under the general editorship of Robert C. Solomon. Published/Created: [United States]: Wadsworth Thomson Learning, c2002. Related Authors: Barney, Ralph D. Description: xviii, 334 p.; 21 cm. ISBN: 0155082566 Notes: Includes bibliographical references and index Subjects: Mass media--Moral and ethical aspects. Series: The Wadsworth communication ethics series LC Classification: P94 .E53 2002

Entman, Robert M. The black image in the white mind: media and race in America / Robert M. Entman and Andrew Rojecki. Published/Created: Chicago: University of Chicago Press, 2000. Related Authors: Rojecki, Andrew, 1946- Description: xix, 305 p.: ill.; 24 cm. ISBN: 0226210758 (cloth: alk. paper) Notes: Includes bibliographical references (p. 271-292) and index. Subjects: Afro-Americans in mass media. Mass media and race relations--United States. United States--Race relations. Series: Studies in communication, media, and public opinion LC Classification: P94.5.A372 U55 2000 Dewey Class No.: 302.23/089/00973 21

Erastus-Sacharia, Anna. Media training in Namibia / Anna Erastus, Jutta Franz. Published/Created: Ausspanplatz, Windhoek, Namibia: Namibia Economic Policy Research Unit: Media Institute of Southern Africa, [1995] Related Authors: Franz, Jutta. Description: ix, 152 p.; 30 cm. Notes: "December 1995." "A study ..."--Cover. Includes bibliographical references (p. 131-132) and index. Subjects: Mass media--Study and teaching (Higher)--Namibia. Series: NEPRU research report; no. 12 LC Classification: P91.5.N3 E73 1995 Dewey Class No.: 302.23/071/16881 21

Erni, John Nguyet. Unstable frontiers: technomedicine and the cultural politics of "curing" AIDS / John Nguyet Erni. Published/Created: Minneapolis: University of Minnesota Press, c1994. Description: xviii, 166 p.: ill.; 24 cm. ISBN: 0816623805 (acid-free paper) 0816623813 (pbk.: acid-free paper) Notes: Includes bibliographical references (p. 151-160) and index. Subjects: AIDS (Disease)--Social aspects. AIDS (Disease) in mass media. LC Classification: RA644.A25 E76 1994 Dewey Class No.: 362.1/969792 20

Ethical issues in journalism and the media / edited by Andrew Belsey and Ruth Chadwick. Published/Created: London; New York: Routledge, 1992. Related Authors: Belsey, Andrew. Chadwick, Ruth F. Description: xiii, 179 p.; 22 cm. ISBN: 0415069262 0415069270 (pbk.) Notes: Includes bibliographical references (p. [171]-174) and index. Subjects: Journalistic ethics. Journalism--Philosophy. Journalism--Objectivity. Privacy, Right of. Mass media--Moral and ethical aspects. Series: Professional ethics LC Classification: PN4756 .E78 1992 Dewey Class No.: 174/.9097 20

Ethnicity and the media in Trinidad and Tobago: a research report. Published/Created: St. Augustine: University of the West Indies, Centre for Ethnic Studies, 1995. Related Authors: University of the West Indies (Saint Augustine, Trinidad and Tobago). Centre for Ethnic Studies. Description: v, 59 p.; 28 cm. Notes: Includes bibliographical references (p. 9). Subjects: Mass media and minorities--Trinidad and Tobago. Ethnicity--Trinidad and Tobago. LC Classification: P94.5.M552 T714 1995 Dewey Class No.: 302.23/086/930972983 21

Feminism, multiculturalism, and the media: global diversities / edited by Angharad N. Valdivia. Published/Created: Thousand Oaks, Calif.: Sage Publications, c1995. Related Authors: Valdivia, Angharad N. Description: viii, 332 p.: ill.; 24 cm. ISBN: 0803957742 (alk. paper) 0803957750 (pbk.: alk. paper) Notes: Includes bibliographical references and indexes. Subjects: Mass media and women. Feminism. Pluralism (Social sciences) LC Classification: P94.5.W65 F45 1995 Dewey Class No.: 302.23/082 20

Ferguson, Robert, 1941 July 15- Representing "race": ideology, identity, and the media / Robert Ferguson. Published/Created: London; New York: Arnold, c1998. Description: vi, 288 p.: ill.; 24 cm. ISBN: 0340692383 0340692391 (pbk.) Notes: Filmography: p. 273. Includes bibliographical references (p. 275-282) and index. Subjects: Race relations in mass media. Ideology. Ethnicity. LC Classification: P94.5.M55 F47 1998 Dewey Class No.: 305.8 21

Ferraiuolo, Perucci. Disney and the Bible: a scriptural critique of the Magic Kingdom / Perucci Ferraiuolo. Published/Created: Camp Hill, Pa.: Horizon Books, c1996. Description: xv, 156 p.; 21 cm. ISBN: 0889651299 Notes: Includes bibliographical references. Subjects: Walt Disney Company. Mass media--Religious aspects--Christianity. Christian life--Biblical teaching. Series: And the Bible series LC Classification: PN1999.W27 F37 1996 Dewey Class No.: 261.5/7 21

Ferreira, Eleonora Castaño. Making sense of the media: a handbook of popular education techniques / Eleonora Castaño Ferreira and João Paulo Castaño Ferreira. Published/Created: New York: Monthly Review Press, c1997. Related Authors: Ferreira, João Paulo Castaño. Description: 123 p.: ill.; 25 cm. ISBN: 0853458804 (pbk.) Subjects: Mass media--Study and teaching--Handbooks, manuals, etc. LC Classification: P91.3 .F4 1997 Dewey Class No.: 302.23/07 20

Fink, Conrad C. Media ethics / Conrad C. Fink. Published/Created: Boston: Allyn and Bacon, c1995. Description: xv, 351 p.: ill.; 24 cm. ISBN: 0023377534 Notes: Includes bibliographical references and index. Subjects: Mass media--Moral and ethical aspects. Journalistic ethics. Mass media--Social aspects. LC Classification: P94 .F47 1995 Dewey Class No.: 174 20

Fisher, Joseph C. Advertising, alcohol consumption, and abuse: a worldwide survey / Joseph C. Fisher. Published/Created: Westport, Conn.: Greenwood Press, 1993. Description: xiii, 195 p.: ill.; 25 cm. ISBN: 031328959X (alk. paper) Notes: Includes bibliographical references (p. [155]-185) and indexes. Subjects: Advertising--Alcoholic beverages--Bibliography. Drinking of alcoholic beverages--Bibliography.

Alcoholism in mass media--Bibliography. Consumer behavior--Bibliography. Series: Contributions to the study of mass media and communications, 0732-4456; no. 41 LC Classification: Z7164.C81 F397 1993 HF6161.L46 Dewey Class No.: 016.6591/96631 20

Fleming, Dan. Media teaching / Dan Fleming. Published/Created: Oxford, UK; Cambridge [Mass.] USA: Blackwell, 1993. Description: ix, 318 p.; 24 cm. ISBN: 0631187057 Notes: Includes bibliographical references and index. Subjects: Mass media--Study and teaching. LC Classification: P91.3 .F55 1993 Dewey Class No.: 302.23/07 20

Fleras, Augie, 1947- Media and minorities: representing diversity in a multicultural Canada / Augie Fleras and Jean Lock Kunz. Published/Created: Toronto: Thompson Educational, c2001. Related Authors: Kunz, Jean Lock. Description: xiii, 198 p.; 23 cm. ISBN: 155077123X Notes: Includes bibliographical references (p. [181]-188) and index. Subjects: Mass media and minorities--Canada. Multiculturalism--Canada. LC Classification: P94.5.M552 C238 2001 Dewey Class No.: 302.23/086/930971 21

Fletcher, Ronald. Science, ideology, and the media: the Cyril Burt scandal / Ronald Fletcher. Published/Created: New Brunswick, U.S.A.: Transaction Publishers, c1991. Description: xxviii, 419 p.: port.; 24 cm. ISBN: 0887383769 Notes: Includes bibliographical references (p. 405-411) and index. Subjects: Burt, Cyril Lodowic, Sir, 1883-1971. Fraud in science--England--Case studies. Mass media--Influence--Case studies. Science news--Case studies. Psychologists--England. LC Classification: BF109.B88 F44 1990 Dewey Class No.: 150/.92 20

Foerstel, Herbert N. Banned in the media: a reference guide to censorship in the press, motion pictures, broadcasting, and the Internet / Herbert N. Foerstel. Published/Created: Westport, Conn.: Greenwood Press, 1998. Description: xii, 252 p.; 24 cm. ISBN: 0313302456 (alk. paper) Notes: Includes bibliographical references (p. [237]-239) and index. Subjects: Mass media--Censorship--United States. LC Classification: P96.C42 U654 1998 Dewey Class No.: 363.3/1/0973 21

Footlick, Jerrold K. Truth and consequences: how colleges and universities meet public crises / Jerrold K. Footlick. Published/Created: Phoenix, Ariz.: Oryx Press, 1997. Description: viii, 192 p.; 24 cm. ISBN: 0897749707 (alk. paper) Notes: Includes bibliographical references (p. [173]-180) and index. Subjects: Universities and colleges--Public relations--United States Case studies. Education in mass media--Case studies. Series: American Council on Education/Oryx Press series on higher education LC Classification: LB2342.8 .F66 1997 Dewey Class No.: 659.2/97873 21

Ford, Marjorie (Marjorie A.) Mass culture and electronic media / [selected by] Marjorie Ford, Jon Ford. Published/Created: Boston: Houghton Mifflin Co., c1999. Related Authors: Ford, Jon. Description: ix, 110 p.; 24 cm. ISBN: 0395868033 (pbk.) Subjects: Mass media and culture. Mass media--Technological innovations. Series: Streamlines. Selected readings on single topics LC Classification: P94.6 .F68 1999 Dewey Class No.: 302.23 21

Fore, William F. Mythmakers: gospel, culture, and the media / William F. Fore. Published/Created: New York: Friendship Press, c1990. Description: 150 p.; 22 cm. ISBN: 0377002070: Notes: Includes bibliographical references (p. 140-145) and index. Subjects: Communication--Religious aspects--Christianity. Mass media--Religious aspects--Christianity. Christianity and culture. Mass media--United States. United States--Church history--20th century. LC Classification: BV4319 .F67 1990 Dewey Class No.: 261.5/2 20

Fox, James Alan. How to work with the media / James Alan Fox, Jack Levin. Published/Created: Newbury Park, Calif.:

Sage Publications, c1993. Related Authors: Levin, Jack, 1941- Description: viii, 93 p.: ill.; 23 cm. ISBN: 0803950888 (cl.) 0803950896 (pbk.) Subjects: Mass media and educators--United States. Universities and colleges--Public relations--United States. Series: Survival skills for scholars; v. 2 LC Classification: LB2342.8 .F69 1993 Dewey Class No.: 659.2/937878 20

France and the mass media / edited by Brian Rigby, Nicholas Hewitt. Published/Created: Houndmills, Basingstoke, Hampshire: Macmillan, 1991. Related Authors: Rigby, Brian. Hewitt, Nicholas. Description: xi, 238 p.; 23 cm. ISBN: 0333512812: Notes: "Based on papers given at the conference 'L'Avènement des mass-media dans la France de l'après-guerre: culture et culture populaire,' held at the Maison Française d'Oxford from 17 to 19 February 1989, under the auspices of the Maison Française and the European Humanities Research Centre at the University of Warwick"--P. viii. Includes bibliographical references (p. 220-227) and index. Subjects: Popular culture--France--History--20th century Congresses. Mass media--France--Influence--Congresses. France--Civilization--1945- --Congresses. Series: Warwick studies in the European humanities, 0956-5108 LC Classification: DC33.7 .F678 1991

Francis, Daniel. The imaginary Indian: the image of the Indian in Canadian culture / Daniel Francis. Published/Created: Vancouver, B.C.: Arsenal Pulp Press, c1992. Description: xii, 258 p.: ill.; 22 cm. ISBN: 0889782512: Notes: Includes bibliographical references (p. 241-251) and index. Subjects: Indians of North America--Canada--Public opinion. Indian mass media--Canada. Public opinion--Canada. Indians in popular culture--Canada. LC Classification: E78.C2 F713 1992

Freccero, Carla, 1956- Popular culture: an introduction / Carla Freccero. Published/Created: New York: New York University Press, c1999. Description: x, 202 p.; 23 cm. ISBN: 0814726690 (cloth: acid-free paper) 0814726704 (paper: acid-free paper) Notes: Includes bibliographical references (p. 177-191) and index. Discography: p. 175. Filmography: p. 173. Subjects: Popular culture--United States--History--20th century. Mass media--Social aspects--United States--History--20th century. United States--Civilization--1945- LC Classification: E169.12 .F717 1999 Dewey Class No.: 306/.0973 21

Frechette, Julie D., 1971- Developing media literacy in cyberspace: pedagogy and critical learning for the twenty-first century classroom / Julie D. Frechette. Published/Created: Westport, Conn.: Praeger, 2002. Projected Pub. Date: 0206 Description: p. cm. ISBN: 0275975789 (alk. paper) Notes: Includes bibliographical references (p.). Subjects: Computers and literacy. Media literacy. Mass media in education. Internet in education. Critical pedagogy. LC Classification: LC149.5 .F74 2002 Dewey Class No.: 371.33/4 21

Freeman, Robert M. Popular culture and corrections / Robert M. Freeman. Published/Created: Lanham, Md.: American Correctional Association, c2000. Description: viii, 197 p.; 26 cm. ISBN: 1569911266 (pbk.) Notes: Includes bibliographical references and index. Subjects: Corrections--United States. Prisons--United States. Prisons in mass media. Prisoners in popular culture--United States. LC Classification: HV9304 .F74 2000 Dewey Class No.: 365/.973 21

Fuller, Linda K. Media-mediated relationships: straight and gay, mainstream and alternative perspectives / Linda K. Fuller. Published/Created: New York: Haworth Press, c1996. Description: xvi, 324 p.: ill.; 23 cm. ISBN: 1560248769 (hard: alk. paper) 1560238542 (pbk.: alk. paper) Notes: Includes bibliographical references (p. 285-313) and index. Subjects: Mass media. Interpersonal relations. LC Classification: P91 .F82 1996 Dewey Class No.: 302.23 20

Gandy, Oscar H. Communication and race: a structural perspective / Oscar H. Gandy, Jr.

Published/Created: London: Arnold: New York: Oxford University Press, 1998. Description: ix, 286 p.; 25 cm. ISBN: 0340676906 0340676892 (pbk.) Notes: Includes bibliographical references (p. [247]-275) and index. Subjects: Mass media and race relations. Communication--Social aspects. Mass media criticism. Series: Communication and critique LC Classification: P94.5.M55 G36 1998 Dewey Class No.: 305.8 21

Garnham, Nicholas. Emancipation, the media, and modernity: arguments about the media and social theory / Nicholas Garnham. Published/Created: Oxford; New York: Oxford University Press, 2000. Description: vii, 206 p.; 22 cm. ISBN: 0198742258 019874224X (pbk) Notes: Includes bibliographical references (p. 190-198) and index. Subjects: Mass media and culture. Mass media--Social aspects. Social sciences--Philosophy. LC Classification: P94.6 .G37 2000 Dewey Class No.: 302.23 21 National Bib. No.: GB99-U6749

Gaudet, Larry. Media therapy: a novel / by Larry Gaudet. Edition Information: 1st ed. Published/Created: Toronto: Gutter Press, c1999. Description: 276 p.; 24 cm. ISBN: 1896356281 Notes: "A Sam Hiyate book." Subjects: Internet--Fiction. Mass media--Fiction. Prophets--Fiction. Existentialism--Fiction. Genre/Form: Religious fiction. LC Classification: PR9199.3.G3738 M44 1999 Dewey Class No.: 813/.54 21

Genosko, Gary. McLuhan and Baudrillard: the masters of implosion / Gary Genosko. Published/Created: London; New York: Routledge, 1999. Description: x, 140 p.; 24 cm. ISBN: 0415190614 (alk. paper) 0415190622 (pbk.: alk. paper) Notes: Includes bibliographical references (p. 123-133) and indexes. Subjects: McLuhan, Marshall, 1911- --Influence. Baudrillard, Jean. Mass media--Philosophy. France--Intellectual life--20th century. LC Classification: P85.M23 G46 1999 Dewey Class No.: 302.23/092/2 21

Gerbner, George. Against the mainstream: selected works of George Gerbner / George Gerbner; [edited by] Michael Morgan. Published/Created: New York: Lang, 2002. Projected Pub. Date: 0204 Related Authors: Morgan, Michael, 1953 Apr. 15- Description: p. cm. ISBN: 0820441635 (pbk.: alk. paper) Notes: Collection of articles, essays, etc. originally Published 1958-1999. Includes bibliographical references. Subjects: Mass media. Series: Media & culture (New York, N.Y.); vol. 1. Variant Series: Media & culture; vol. 1 LC Classification: P91.25 .G47 2002 Dewey Class No.: 302.23 21

Germany reunified: a five- and fifty-year retrospective / edited by Peter M. Daly ... [et al.]. Published/Created: New York: P. Lang, c1997. Related Authors: Daly, Peter M. (Peter Maurice) Description: xviii, 256 p.: ill.; 24 cm. ISBN: 0820438030 (alk. paper) Notes: Includes bibliographical references and index. Subjects: Art and state--Germany. Art and state--Germany (East) Mass media--Germany. Germany--History--Unification, 1990. Germany--Intellectual life--20th century. Germany (East)--Church history. Germany--Cultural policy. Series: McGill European studies, 1089-4934; vol. 1 LC Classification: DD290.29 .G495 1997 Dewey Class No.: 943.087/9 21

Gilens, Martin. Why Americans hate welfare: race, media, and the politics of antipoverty policy / Martin Gilens. Published/Created: Chicago: University of Chicago Press, 1999. Description: xii, 296 p.; 24 cm. ISBN: 0226293645 (cloth: alk. paper) Notes: Includes bibliographical references (p. [235]-279) and index. Subjects: Public welfare in mass media. Racism in mass media. Mass media and public opinion--United States. Racism--United States. Public welfare--United States. Public opinion--United States. Series: Studies in communication, media, and public opinion LC Classification: P96.P842 U654 1999 Dewey Class No.: 070.4/493616 21

Giroux, Henry A. Channel surfing: race talk and the destruction of today's youth /

Henry A. Giroux. Edition Information: 1st ed. Published/Created: New York: St. Martin's Press, 1997. Description: 248 p.; 22 cm. ISBN: 0312162650 Notes: Includes bibliographical references (p. [217]-244) and index. Subjects: Youth--United States. Mass media--Social aspects--United States. Racism--United States. Popular culture--United States. LC Classification: HQ799.7 .G57 1997 Dewey Class No.: 305.235 21

Giroux, Henry A. Fugitive cultures: race, violence, and youth / Henry A. Giroux. Published/Created: New York: Routledge, 1996. Description: viii, 247 p.; 24 cm. ISBN: 0415915775 (cloth: acid-free paper) 0415915783 (pbk.: acid-free paper) Notes: Includes bibliographical references (p. [205]-238) and index. Subjects: Youth--United States--Social conditions. Mass media and youth--United States. Popular culture--United States. Working class--United States. Multiculturalism--United States. United States--Race relations. LC Classification: HQ796 .G526 1996 Dewey Class No.: 305.2/35/0973 20

Giroux, Henry A. Impure acts: the practical politics of cultural studies / Henry A. Giroux. Published/Created: New York: Routledge, 2000. Description: x, 166 p.; 24 cm. ISBN: 0415926556 (hb) 0415926564 (pb) Notes: Includes bibliographical references (p. 142-160) and index. Subjects: Politics and culture--United States. Culture--Study and teaching--United States. Political culture--United States. Multiculturalism--United States. Popular culture--United States. Mass media--Political aspects--United States. Technological innovations--Social aspects--United States. United States--Civilization--1970- LC Classification: E169.12 .G565 2000 Dewey Class No.: 973.92 21

Glander, Timothy Richard, 1960- Origins of mass communications research during the American Cold War: educational effects and contemporary implications / Timothy Glander. Published/Created: Mahwah, N.J.: L. Erlbaum, 2000. Description: xiv, 237 p.; 23 cm. ISBN: 080582734X 0805827358 (pbk.) Notes: Includes bibliographical references (p.219-232) and index. Subjects: Mass media--Research--United States--History. Mass media in education--United States. Series: Sociocultural, political, and historical studies in education LC Classification: P91.5.U5 G57 2000 Dewey Class No.: 302.23/07/2073 21

Global culture: media, arts, policy, and globalization / edited by Diana Crane, Nobuko Kawashima, and Ken'ichi Kawasaki. Published/Created: New York: Routledge, 2002. Projected Pub. Date: 0202 Related Authors: Crane, Diana, 1933- Kawashima, Nobuko. Kawasaki, Kenichi. Description: p. cm. ISBN: 0415932297 0415932300 (pbk.) Notes: Includes bibliographical references and index. Subjects: Mass media and culture. Mass media--Social aspects. Cultural policy. LC Classification: P94.6 .G57 2002 Dewey Class No.: 302.23 21

Goban-Klas, Tomasz. The orchestration of the media: the politics of mass communications in communist Poland and the aftermath / Tomasz Goban-Klas. Published/Created: Boulder, Colo.: Westview Press, 1994. Description: xiii, 289 p.; 24 cm. ISBN: 0813318688 (alk. paper) Notes: Includes bibliographical references (p. 267-278) and index. Subjects: Mass media--Social aspects--Poland--History--20th century. Communism and mass media--Poland. Series: International communication and popular culture LC Classification: HN539.5.M3 G6 1994 Dewey Class No.: 302.23/09438 20

Goldfarb, Brian. Media pedagogy: the visual cultures of education in and beyond the classroom / Brian Goldfarb. Published/Created: Durham: Duke University Press, 2002. Projected Pub. Date: 0208 Description: p. cm. ISBN: 0822329360 (cloth: alk. paper) 0822329646 (pbk.: alk. paper) Notes: Includes bibliographical references and index. Subjects: Mass media and education. Audio-visual education--Social aspects. Critical pedagogy. LC

Classification: LB1043 .G57 2002 Dewey Class No.: 371.335 21

Goodall, Peter, 1949- High culture, popular culture: the long debate / Peter Goodall. Published/Created: St. Leonards, NSW: Allen & Unwin, 1995. Description: xx, 204 p.; 22 cm. ISBN: 1863738339 Notes: Includes bibliographical references (p. 179-190) and index. Subjects: Popular culture--Australia. Arts, Australian--20th century. Mass media--Australia. Australia--Intellectual life--20th century. Series: Australian cultural studies LC Classification: DU117.14 .G66 1995

Goodwyn, Andrew, 1954- English teaching and media education / Andrew Goodwyn. Published/Created: Buckingham [England]; Philadelphia: Open University Press, 1992. Description: xii, 128 p.; 23 cm. ISBN: 0335097901: Notes: Includes bibliographical references (p. [122]-124) and index. Subjects: English language--Study and teaching (Secondary)--Great Britain. Mass media--Study and teaching (Secondary)--Great Britain. Series: English, language, and education series. Variant Series: English, language, and education LC Classification: LB1631 .G634 1992 Dewey Class No.: 428/.0071/273 20

Gordon, David, 1935- Controversies in media ethics / A. David Gordon, John M Kittross, Carol Reuss; overview and commentary by John C. Merrill. Published/Created: White Plains, N.Y.: Longman, c1996. Related Authors: Kittross, John M., 1929- Reuss, Carol. Merrill, John Calhoun, 1924- Description: xvi, 316 p.; 24 cm. ISBN: 0801310601 Notes: Includes bibliographical references (p. 303-305) and index. Subjects: Mass media--Moral and ethical aspects. LC Classification: P94 .G67 1996 Dewey Class No.: 175 20

Gordon, David, 1935- Controversies in media ethics / A. David Gordon, John Michael Kittross; overview and commentary by John C. Merrill; contributions by Carol Reuss. Edition Information: 2nd ed. Published/Created: New York: Longman, c1999. Related Authors: Kittross, John M., 1929- Merrill, John Calhoun, 1924- Reuss, Carol. Description: xvii, 316 p.; 24 cm. ISBN: 0801330254 Notes: Includes bibliographical references (p. 295-301) and index. Subjects: Mass media--Moral amd ethical aspects. LC Classification: P94 .G67 1999 Dewey Class No.: 175 21

Grandinetti, Fred. Popeye: an illustrated history of E.C. Segar's character in print, radio, television, and film appearances, 1929-1993 / by Fred M. Grandinetti. Published/Created: Jefferson, N.C.: McFarland, c1994. Description: xi, 276 p.: ill.; 23 cm. ISBN: 0899509827 (alk. paper) Notes: Includes indexes. Subjects: Popeye (Fictitious character) in mass media. LC Classification: P96.P65 G73 1994 Dewey Class No.: 741.5/0973 20

Grossberg, Lawrence. Mediamaking: mass media in a popular culture / Lawrence Grossberg, Ellen Wartella, D. Charles Whitney. Published/Created: Thousand Oaks, Calif.: Sage Publications, c1998. Related Authors: Wartella, Ellen. Whitney, D. Charles (David Charles), 1946- Description: xviii, 442p.; 24 cm. ISBN: 0761911766 (acid-free paper) 0761911774 (pbk.: acid-free paper) Notes: Includes bibliographical references (p. 409-421) and index. Subjects: Mass media and culture. LC Classification: P94.6 .G76 1998 Dewey Class No.: 302.23 21

Guido, Michael. Seeds from the sower: the Michael and Audrey Guido story: how God is blessing a couple who dare to take Him at His word / Michael and Audrey Guido; Michael Guido with Sarah Coleman. Published/Created: Nashville: T. Nelson, c1990. Related Authors: Guido, Audrey. Coleman, Sarah Jepson. Description: 212 p., [8] p. of plates: ill.; 22 cm. ISBN: 0840731787 Subjects: Guido, Michael. Guido, Audrey. Guido Evangelistic Association. Evangelists--United States--Biography. Mass media in missionary work. LC Classification: BV3780.G85 A3 1990 Dewey Class No.: 269/.2/0922 B 20

Gupta, V. S. Media policy and nation building: select issues and themes / V.S. Gupta, Bir Bala Aggarwal. Published/Created: New Delhi: Concept Pub., 1996. Related Authors: Aggarwal, Vir Bala. Description: 143 p.; 23 cm. ISBN: 8170225906 Notes: Includes bibliographical references (p. [136]-139) and index. Subjects: Mass media policy--India. Communication--India. Mass media in education--India. LC Classification: P95.82.I4 G87 1996 Dewey Class No.: 302.23/0954 21

Gurevich, Pavel Semenovich. Dialogue of cultures or cultural expansion? / Pavel Gurevich; [translated from the Russian by Joseph Shapiro]. Published/Created: Moscow: Progress Publishers, c1990. Related Titles: Dialog kul'tur ili dukhovnaia ekspansiia. Description: 190 p.; 20 cm. ISBN: 5010020025 Notes: Title on verso t.p: Dialog kul'tur ili dukhovnaia ekspansiia? Includes bibliographical references. Subjects: Mass media. Popular culture--United States. Intercultural communication. United States--Relations--Foreign countries. LC Classification: P91 .G85 1990 Dewey Class No.: 302.23/0973 20

Haldeman, Joe W. The coming / Joe Haldeman. Edition Information: 1st ed. Published/Created: New York: Ace Books, 2000. Description: 216 p.; 24 cm. ISBN: 0441007694 Subjects: Human-alien encounters--Fiction. Life on other planets--Fiction. Astronomy teachers--Fiction. Mass media--Fiction. Genre/Form: Science fiction. Variant Series: Ace science fiction LC Classification: PS3558.A353 C66 2000 Dewey Class No.: 813/.54 21

Hamm, Donald. New opportunities in new media: Saskatchewan's arts and cultural industries / prepared by Donald Hamm for Saskatchewan Municipal Government; in partnership with the Department of Canadian Heritage and Industry Canada; with the participation of Saskfilm. Published/Created: [Saskatchewan?: s.n., 1994] Related Authors: Saskatchewan. Saskatchewan Municipal Government. Arts, Cultural Industries, and Multiculturalism Branch. Canada. Canadian Heritage. Canada. Industry Canada. Saskfilm. Description: 85 p.: ill.; 28 cm. Notes: Cover title. Prepared for the Arts, Cultural Industries, and Multiculturalism Branch of Saskatchewan Municipal Government. "October, 1994"--Cover. Includes bibliographical references (p. 70-72). Subjects: Mass media--Saskatchewan--Marketing. Cultural industries--Saskatchewan. LC Classification: P96.M342 C224 1994 Dewey Class No.: 384/.041 21

Hardt, Hanno. In the company of media: cultural constructions of communication, 1920s-1930s / Hanno Hardt. Published/Created: Boulder, Colo.: Westview Press, c2000. Related Authors: Brennen, Bonnie. Killmeier, Matthew. Description: xii, 186 p.: ill.; 24 cm. ISBN: 0813314224 (alk. paper) Notes: Essays chiefly by the author; includes two essays by Bonnie Brennen and one essay with Matthew Killmeier as collaborator with the author. Includes bibliographical references (p. 163-178) and index. Subjects: Mass media and culture. Series: Critical studies in communication and in the cultural industries LC Classification: P94.6 .H37 2000 Dewey Class No.: 302.23 21

Harmer, John. A war we must win: a frontline account of the battle against the pornography conspiracy / John Harmer. Published/Created: Salt Lake City, Utah: Bookcraft, c1999. Description: xii, 176 p.; 24 cm. Notes: Includes index. Subjects: Pornography--Religious aspects--Mormon Church. Mormon Church--Doctrines. Men--Sexual behavior. Sex in mass media. LC Classification: BX8643.P64 H37 1999 Dewey Class No.: 241/.667 21

Harris, Richard Jackson. A cognitive psychology of mass communication / Richard Jackson Harris. Edition Information: 2nd ed. Published/Created: Hillsdale, N.J.: L. Erlbaum Associates, 1994. Description: xv, 313 p.: ill.; 24 cm. ISBN: 0805812644 (acid-free paper) Notes: Includes bibliographical references (p. 262-298) and indexes. Subjects: Mass media--Psychological aspects. LC Classification: P96.P75 H37 1994 Dewey Class No.: 302.23/01/9 20

Harris, Richard Jackson. A cognitive psychology of mass communication / Richard Jackson Harris. Edition Information: 3rd ed. Published/Created: Mahwah, N.J.: L. Erlbaum Associates, 1999. Description: xvii, 337 p.; 24 cm. ISBN: 080583088X Notes: Includes bibliographical references (p. 271-317) and indexes. Subjects: Mass media--Psychological aspects. Mass media--Social aspects. Series: LEA's communication series LC Classification: P96.P75 H37 1999 Dewey Class No.: 302.23/01/9 21

Harris, Richard Jackson. A cognitive psychology of mass communication / Richard Jackson Harris. Edition Information: 2nd ed. Published/Created: Hillsdale, N.J.: L. Erlbaum Associates, 1994. Description: xv, 313 p.: ill.; 24 cm. ISBN: 0805812644 (acid-free paper) Notes: Includes bibliographical references (p. 262-298) and indexes. Subjects: Mass media--Psychological aspects. LC Classification: P96.P75 H37 1994 Dewey Class No.: 302.23/01/9 20

Hartley, John, 1948- The politics of pictures: the creation of the public in the age of popular media / John Hartley. Published/Created: London; New York: Routledge, 1992. Description: xiii, 240 p.: ill.; 25 cm. ISBN: 0415015413 (hb) 0415015421 (pb) Notes: Includes bibliographical references (p. 234-236) and index. Subjects: Mass media--Audiences. Mass media--Political aspects. Mass media--Influence. Pictures. LC Classification: P96.A83 H37 1992 Dewey Class No.: 302.23 20

High-pop: making culture into popular entertainment / edited by Jim Collins. Published/Created: Malden, MA: Blackwell Publishers, 2002. Projected Pub. Date: 0201 Related Authors: Collins, Jim, 1953- Description: p. cm. ISBN: 0631222103 (alk. paper) 0631222111 (pbk.: alk. paper) Notes: Includes bibliographical references and index. Subjects: Popular culture--United States. Aesthetics--Social aspects--United States. Arts and society--United States. Mass media--Social aspects--United States. Amusements--Social aspects--United States. National characteristics, American. United States--Civilization--1945- LC Classification: E169.12 .H52 2002 Dewey Class No.: 973.92 21

Hilliard, Robert L., 1925- Media, education, and America's counter-culture revolution: lost and found opportunities for media impact on education, gender, race, and the arts / Robert L. Hilliard. Published/Created: Westport, Conn.: Ablex, 2001. Description: xii, 191 p.; 24 cm. ISBN: 1567505120 1567505139 (pbk.) Notes: Includes index. Subjects: Mass media and culture--United States--History--20th century. Mass media--Social aspects--United States--History--20th century. United States--Social conditions--1960-1980. LC Classification: P94.65.U6 H55 2001 Dewey Class No.: 302.23/0973/09046 21

Hills, Matt, 1971- Fan cultures / Matt Hills. Published/Created: London; New York: Routledge, 2002. Projected Pub. Date: 0202 Description: p. cm. ISBN: 0415240247 (HB) 0415240255 (PB) Notes: Includes bibliographical references and index. Subjects: Fans (Persons)--Psychology. Subculture. Television viewers--Psychology. Celebrities in mass media. Motion picture actors and actresses. LC Classification: HM646 .H55 2002 Dewey Class No.: 306.1 21

Hoggart, Richard, 1918- The uses of literacy / Richard Hoggart; introduction by Andrew Goodwin; with a new postscript by John Corner. Published/Created: New Brunswick, N.J., U.S.A.: Transation Publishers, c1998. Description: xliii, 320 p.; 23 cm. ISBN: 0765804212 (pbk.: acid-free paper) Notes: Originally Published: 1992. Includes bibliographical references (p. 310-314) and index. Subjects: Popular culture--Great Britain--History--20th century. Working class--Great Britain--

History--20th century. Mass media--Great Britain--History--20th century. Literacy--Great Britain--History--20th century. Great Britain--Civilization--20th century. Series: Classics in communication and mass culture series LC Classification: DA566.4 .H54 1998 Dewey Class No.: 941.085 21

Hoggart, Richard, 1918- The uses of literacy / Richard Hoggart; with a new introduction by Andrew Goodwin. Published/Created: New Brunswick, N.J., U.S.A.: Transaction Publishers, c1992. Description: xliii, 305 p.; 23 cm. ISBN: 0887388922 Notes: Originally Published: Fair Lawn, N.J.: Essential Books, 1957. Includes bibliographical references (p. 294-298) and index. Subjects: Popular culture--Great Britain--History--20th century. Working class--Great Britain--History--20th century. Mass media--Great Britain--History--20th century. Literacy--Great Britain--History--20th century. Series: Classics in communication and mass culture series LC Classification: DA566.4 .H54 1992 Dewey Class No.: 941.085 20

Holbrook, David. Creativity and popular culture / David Holbrook. Published/Created: Rutherford: Fairleigh Dickinson University Press; London: Associated University Press, c1994. Description: 279 p.; 24 cm. ISBN: 0838634737 (alk. paper) Notes: Includes bibliographical references (p. [268]-272) and index. Subjects: Mass media and children--Moral and ethical aspects. Creative ability. Popular culture. LC Classification: HQ784.M3 H65 1994 Dewey Class No.: 306 20

Holtzman, Linda, 1949- Media messages: what film, television, and popular music teach us about race, class, gender, and sexual orientation / Linda Holtzman. Published/Created: Armonk, N.Y.: M.E. Sharpe, c2000. Description: xiv, 346 p., [16] p. of plates: ill.; 24 cm. ISBN: 0765603365 (hc: alk. paper) Notes: Includes bibliographical references and index. Subjects: Mass media and race relations--United States. Mass media and sex--United States. Mass media--Social aspects--United States. Popular culture--United States. Social classes--United States. United States--Social conditions--1980- LC Classification: P94.5.M552 U646 2000 Dewey Class No.: 302.23 21

Hoover, Dwight W., 1926- Middletown: the making of a documentary film series / Dwight W. Hoover. Published/Created: Chur; Philadelphia: Harwood Academic Publishers, c1992. Description: xvii, 225 p.; 24 cm. ISBN: 3718605430 (hardcover) 3718605422 (softcover) Notes: Filmography: p. [209]-210. Includes bibliographical references (p. [211]-222) and index. Subjects: Middletown Film Project. Documentary films--United States--Production and direction. Documentary mass media. Muncie (Ind.)--History. Series: Visual anthropology (Series); v. 2. Variant Series: Visual anthropology, 0897-1463; v. 2 LC Classification: PN1995.9.D6 H64 1992 Dewey Class No.: 070.1/8 20

Hoover, Stewart M. Religion in the news: faith and journalism in American public discourse / Stewart M. Hoover. Published/Created: Thousand Oaks, Calif: Sage Publications, c1998. Description: xi, 234 p.; 24 cm. ISBN: 0761916776 (hbk.: acid-free paper) 0761916784 (pbk.: acid-free paper) Notes: Includes bibliographical references and index. Subjects: Mass media--Religious aspects. Journalism, Religious. LC Classification: P94 .H657 1998 Dewey Class No.: 302.23/0973 21

Huang, Yunte. Transpacific displacement: ethnography, translation, and intertextual travel in twentieth-century American literature / Yunte Huang. Published/Created: Berkeley: University of California Press, c2002. Description: xv, 209 p.: ill. 24 cm. ISBN: 0520228863 (cloth: alk. paper) 0520232232 (pbk.: alk. paper) Notes: Includes bibliographical references (p. 189-201) and index. Subjects: American literature--Chinese American authors--History and criticism. American literature--20th century--History and criticism. Chinese literature--Appreciation--United States. American literature--Chinese influences. Chinese

Americans--Intellectual life. Chinese Americans in mass media. Chinese Americans in literature. Immigrants in literature. Ethnology in literature. Intertextuality. LC Classification: PS153.C45 H83 2002 Dewey Class No.: 810.9/005 21

Hunt, Darnell M. O.J. Simpson facts and fictions: news rituals in the construction of reality / Darnell M. Hunt. Published/Created: Cambridge, UK; New York: Cambridge University Press, 1999. Description: xii, 350 p.; 23 cm. ISBN: 0521624568 (hb) 0521624681 (pbk.) Notes: Includes bibliographical references (p. 309-343) and index. Subjects: Simpson, O. J., 1947- --Trials, litigation, etc.--Public opinion. Television broadcasting of news--Social aspects--United States. Public opinion--United States. Television viewers--United States--Attitudes. Mass media and race relations. United States--Race relations. LC Classification: PN4888.T4 H855 1999 Dewey Class No.: 302.23/0973 21

Hurst, John. Ethics and the Australian news media / John Hurst and Sally A. White. Published/Created: South Melbourne: Macmillan Education Australia, 1994. Related Authors: White, Sally A. Description: xi, 330 p.; 28 cm. ISBN: 0732919398 (pbk.) Cancelled ISBN: 0732919401 Notes: Includes bibliographical references (p. 298-319) and index. Subjects: Journalistic ethics--Australia. Mass media--Australia. Mass media--Moral and ethical aspects. LC Classification: PN5517.E8 H87 1994 Dewey Class No.: 174/.9097 20

Hutchinson, Earl Ofari. Beyond O.J.: race, sex, and class lessons for America / by Earl Ofari Hutchinson. Published/Created: Los Angeles, CA: Middle Passage Press, c1996. Description: 208 p.; 23 cm. ISBN: 1881032124 Notes: Includes bibliography (p. [201]-203) and index. Subjects: Simpson, O. J., 1947- Racism--Interracial marriage--Social classes--United States. UAfro-Americans and mass media. nited States--Race relations. LC Classification: E185.615 .O32 1996 Dewey Class No.: 305.8/00973 20

Ignatieff, Michael. The warrior's honor: ethnic war and the modern conscience / Michael Ignatieff. Edition Information: 1st American ed. Published/Created: New York: Metropolitan Books, 1998. Description: ix, 207 p.; 22 cm. ISBN: 0805055185 (hc: alk. paper) Notes: Includes bibliographical references (p. 191-195) and index. Subjects: Ethnic relations. Social conflict. Social justice. Mass media and ethnic relations. Humanitarian assistance. LC Classification: GN496 .I55 1998 Dewey Class No.: 305.8 21

Image journeys: audio-visual media and cultural change in India / edited by Christiane Brosius, Melissa Butcher. Published/Created: New Delhi; Thousand Oaks, CA: Sage Publications, 1999. Related Authors: Brosius, Christiane, 1966- Butcher, Melissa, 1966- Description: 338 p.; 23 cm. ISBN: 0761993258 (cloth) 0761993266 (pbk.) Notes: Includes bibliographical references (p. [311]-325) and index. Subjects: Mass media and culture--Social change--India. LC Classification: P94.65.I4 I46 1999 Dewey Class No.: 302.23/0954 21

Images of Africa: stereotypes and realities / edited by Daniel M. Mengara. Published/Created: Trenton, NJ: Africa World Press, 2000.

Images of the U.S. around the world: a multicultural perspective / edited by Yahya R. Kamalipour; foreword by Majid Tehranian. Published/Created: Albany: State University of New York Press, c1999. Related Authors: Kamalipour, Yahya R. Description: xxxi, 359 p.: ill.; 24 cm. ISBN: 0791439712 (alk. paper) 0791439720 (pbk.: alk. paper) Notes: Includes bibliographical references and index. Subjects: Mass media--Political aspects--Foreign countries. Mass media--Social aspects--Foreign countries. United States--Foreign public opinion. United States--Relations--Foreign countries.

Series: SUNY series in human communication processes. Variant Series: SUNY series, human communication processes LC Classification: E840.2 .I55 1999 Dewey Class No.: 303.48/273 21

Images of youth: popular culture as educational ideology / edited by Michael A. Oliker and Walter P. Krolikowski. Published/Created: New York: P. Lang, 2001. Projected Pub. Date: 1111 Related Authors: Oliker, Michael A., 1946- Krolikowski, Walter P. Description: p. cm. ISBN: 0820445193 (pbk.: alk. paper) Notes: Includes bibliographical references. Subjects: Mass media and youth--Motion pictures and youth--Music and youth--Television and youth--Adolescent psychology--Education--Social aspects--United States. Popular culture--United States--History--20th century. Series: Adolescent cultures, school & society; vol. 12. Variant Series: Adolescent cultures, school and society; vol. 12 LC Classification: HQ799.2.M35 I43 2001 Dewey Class No.: 302.23/0835/0973 21

Imaging education: the media and schools in America / edited by Gene I. Maeroff. Published/Created: New York: Teachers College Press, c1998. Related Authors: Maeroff, Gene I. Hechinger Institute on Education and the Media. Description: vii, 232 p.; 24 cm. ISBN: 0807737356 (cloth: alk. paper) 0807737348 (paper: alk. paper) Notes: "Published in collaboration with the Hechinger Institute on Education and the Media"--P. ii. Includes bibliographical references and index. Subjects: Education in mass media. Mass media--United States. LC Classification: P96.E292 U65 1998 Dewey Class No.: 370/.973 21

Impact! Published/Created: New York, NY: Vanguarde Media Inc., c1999- Description: v.: ill.; 37 cm. Vol. 1, issue 1 (Dec. 1999)- Current Frequency: Biweekly Notes: Title from cover. Subjects: African Americans in popular culture--Periodicals. African Americans in the performing arts--Periodicals. African Americans and mass media--Periodicals.

Inform.educate.entertain@sg: arts & media in Singapore. Published/Created: Singapore: Research & Planning Division, Ministry of Information and the Arts, c2000. Related Authors: Singapore. Ministry of Information and the Arts. Research & Planning Division. Description: 225 p.: col. ill.; 24 cm. ISBN: 9971886642 Notes: "Second edition"--P. 2. Subjects: Arts--Singapore. Mass media--Singapore. LC Classification: NX579.A3 S562 2000 Dewey Class No.: 302.23/095957 21

Information society: new media, ethics, and postmodernism / Karamjit S. Gill, ed. Published/Created: London; New York: Springer, c1996. Related Authors: Gill, Karamjit S. Description: xxxii, 390 p.; 24 cm. ISBN: 3540760369 Notes: Based on the proceedings of the international conference on New Visions of the Post-industrial Society, University of Brighton, July 1994. Includes bibliographical references. Subjects: Mass media--Technological innovations--Congresses. Mass media--Moral and ethical aspects--Congresses. Mass media--Social aspects--Congresses. Postmodernism--Congresses. Series: Human-centred systems LC Classification: P96.T42 I55 1996 Dewey Class No.: 302.23 20

Ingebretsen, Ed. At stake: monsters and the rhetoric of fear in public culture / Edward J. Ingebretsen. Published/Created: Chicago: University of Chicago Press, c2001. Description: xvi, 341 p.; 24 cm. ISBN: 0226380068 (alk. paper) 0226380076 (pbk.: alk. paper) Notes: Includes bibliographical references (p. 295-327) and index. Subjects: Monsters in mass media. Mass media--United States. Popular culture--United States. LC Classification: P96.M62 I54 2001 Dewey Class No.: 302.23/0973 21

Interart poetics: essays on the interrelations of the arts and media / edited by Ulla-Britta Lagerroth, Hans Lund, Erik Hedling. Published/Created: Amsterdam; Atlanta, GA: Rodopi, 1997. Related Authors: Lagerroth, Ulla Britta, 1927- Lund, Hans, 1939- Hedling, Erik. Description: 354 p.;

ill.; 25 cm. ISBN: 9042002026 (bd.) 9042002107 (paper) Notes: Papers from a conference held in May 1995, at Lund University. Includes bibliographical references and index. Subjects: Mass media and art--Congresses. Performing arts--Congresses. Art and literature--Congresses. Series: Internationale Forschungen zur allgemeinen und vergleichenden Literaturwissenschaft; 24 LC Classification: N72.M28 I57 1997

International Afro mass media: a reference guide / James Phillip Jeter ... [et al.]. Published/Created: Westport, Conn.: Greenwood Press, 1996. Related Authors: Jeter, James Phillip. Description: xiii, 297 p.: ill.; 25 cm. ISBN: 0313284008 (hardcover: alk. paper) Notes: Includes bibliographical references and index. Subjects: Black mass media. LC Classification: P94.5.B55 I57 1996 Dewey Class No.: 302.23/08996 20

International media monitoring / edited by Kaarle Nordenstreng, Michael Griffin. Published/Created: Cresskill, N.J.: Hampton Press, c1999. Related Authors: Nordenstreng, Kaarle. Griffin, Michael S., 1953- Description: xxvii, 452 p.; 24 cm. ISBN: 1572731834 cl 1572731842 ppb Notes: Includes bibliographical references and indexes. Subjects: Mass media criticism. Mass media--Objectivity. Mass media--Social aspects. Series: Hampton Press communication series LC Classification: P96.C76 I58 1999 Dewey Class No.: 302.23 21

International media research: a critical survey / edited by John Corner, Philip Schlesinger, and Roger Silverstone. Published/Created: London; New York: Routledge, 1998. Related Authors: Corner, John, 1943- Schlesinger, Philip, 1948- Silverstone, Roger. Description: x, 238 p.; 24 cm. ISBN: 0415184967 (pbk) Notes: Includes bibliographical references and index. Subjects: Mass media--Research. Mass media and culture. Mass media policy. LC Classification: P91.3 .I56 1998 Dewey Class No.: 302.23 20

Internships: perspectives on experiential learning: a guide to internship management for educators and professionals / edited by Andrew Ciofalo. Edition Information: Original ed. Published/Created: Malabar, Fla.: Krieger Pub. Co., 1992. Related Authors: Ciofalo, Andrew, 1935- Description: xi, 263 p.; 24 cm. ISBN: 0894645811 (alk. paper) Notes: Collection of thirty articles previously Published between 1976 and 1991. Includes bibliographical references. Subjects: Mass media--Study and teaching (Internship) Business education (Internship) Experiential learning. LC Classification: P91.3 .I57 1992 Dewey Class No.: 302.23/071/1 20

It's show time!: media, politics, and popular culture / edited by David A. Schultz. Published/Created: New York: P. Lang, c2000. Related Authors: Schultz, David A. (David Andrew), 1958- Description: xiv, 277 p.: ill.; 23 cm. ISBN: 082044135X (alk. paper) Notes: Includes bibliographical references and index. Subjects: Mass media and culture--Mass media--Political aspects--United States. United States--Civilization--1970- Series: Politics, media & popular culture, 1094-6225; v. 2 LC Classification: P94.65.U6 I88 2000 Dewey Class No.: 302.23/0973 21

Jayaweera, Neville. Folk media and development communication: myths and realities: a report on experiences in people's communication in Mexico, India, and the Philippines / by Neville Jayaweera; in collaboration with David Briddell ... [et al.]. Published/Created: Manila: Asian Social Institute, 1991. Description: 92 p.; 22 cm. ISBN: 971854321X Notes: A joint publication of the Asian Social Institute, Manila and the ISPCK, Delhi in cooperation with the World Association for Christian Communication." Includes bibliographical references (p. 68-69). Subjects: Mass media--Folklore--Philippines. Mass media--Folklore--India. Mass media--Folklore--Mexico. LC Classification: P92.P5 J39 1991 Dewey Class No.: 302.23/09599 20

Jensen, Joli. Redeeming modernity: contradictions in media criticism / Joli Jensen. Published/Created: Newbury Park, Calif.: Sage Publications, c1990. Description: 221 p.; 23 cm. ISBN: 0803934769 0803934777 (pbk.) Notes: Includes bibliographical references (p. 202-206) and index. Subjects: Mass media. Popular culture. Mass media--Social aspects. Mass media--United States. Series: Communication and human values (Newbury Park, Calif.) Variant Series: Communication and human values LC Classification: P91 .J47 1990 Dewey Class No.: 302.23/0973 20

Jerry, F. L. The framing of who done-it: O.J. Simpson on trial by TV & world news medium / [by F.L. Jerry]. Edition Information: Rev. Published/Created: Detroit, Mich.: Futuramic Pub. Co., 1996. Description: 70 leaves; 21 cm. Subjects: Simpson, O. J., 1947- --Trials, litigation, etc. Trials (Murder)--California--Los Angeles. Free press and fair trial--United States. Mass media and race relations--United States. LC Classification: KF224.S485 J47 1996 Dewey Class No.: 345.73/02523/0979494 21

Johnson, Ann K. (Ann Kathleen), 1946- Urban ghetto riots, 1965-1968: a comparison of Soviet and American press coverage / Ann K. Johnson. Published/Created: Boulder: East European Monographs; New York: Distributed by Columbia University Press, 1996. Description: 209 p.; 24 cm. ISBN: 0880333340 Notes: Based on the author's thesis (Ph. D.--University of Denver, 1994). Includes bibliographical references (p. [126]-179). Subjects: Race relations and the press--United States. Race relations and the press--Soviet Union. Mass media and public opinion--United States. Mass media and public opinion--Soviet Union. Riots--United States. Series: East European monographs; no. 437. Variant Series: East European monographs; 437 LC Classification: PN4888.R3 J64 1996 Dewey Class No.: 070.4/49305813 20

Johnson, Lesley L., 1948- Media, education, and change / Lesley L. Johnson. Published/Created: New York: P. Lang, 2001. Description: xiii, 182 p.; 23 cm. ISBN: 082044281X (pbk.: alk. paper) Notes: Includes bibliographical references (p. [157]-169) and index. Subjects: Mass media in education--United States. Media literacy--United States. Series: Counterpoints (New York, N.Y.); v. 106. Variant Series: Counterpoints; v. 106 LC Classification: LB1043 .J55 2001 Dewey Class No.: 302.23/07 21

Johnson, Melvin L. Junk food in the body of Christ: influences of the entertainment industry / Melvin L. Johnson. Published/Created: Baden, PA: Rainbow's End Co., c1995. Description: 239 p.; 22 cm. ISBN: 1880451107 Subjects: Spiritual life--Christianity. Food--Religious aspects--Christianity. Music--Religious aspects--Christianity. Music and occultism. Mass media--Religious aspects--Christianity. LC Classification: BV4501.2 .J559 1995 Dewey Class No.: 248.4 20

Johnson, Michael L. New westers: the west in contemporary American culture / Michael L. Johnson. Published/Created: Lawrence, Kan.: University Press of Kansas, c1996. Description: xii, 408 p.: ill.; 25 cm. ISBN: 0700607633 (alk. paper) Notes: Includes bibliographical references (p. [385]-390) and index. Subjects: Popular culture--West (U.S.) Popular culture--United States. West (U.S.)--In mass media. West (U.S.)--In literature. LC Classification: F596 .J49 1996 Dewey Class No.: 978 20

Johnston, John, 1953- Information multiplicity: American fiction in the age of media saturation / John Johnston. Published/Created: Baltimore, Md.: Johns Hopkins University Press, 1998. Description: x, 307 p.; 24 cm. ISBN: 080185704X (alk. paper) 0801857058 (pbk.) 0801857058 (pbk.: alk. paper) Notes: Includes bibliographical references (p. 267-296) and index. Subjects: American fiction--20th century--History and criticism. Mass media and literature--Literature and technology--United States--History--20th century. Technology and civilization in literature. Postmodernism

(Literature)--Information technology--Mass media--United States. Information science in literature.LC Classification: PS374.M43 J64 1998 Dewey Class No.: 813/.5409356 21

Jones, Steve, 1961- Rock formation: music, technology, and mass communication / Steve Jones. Published/Created: Newbury Park, Calif.: Sage, c1992. Description: 223 p.; 23 cm. ISBN: 080394442X 0803944438 (pbk.) Notes: Includes bibliographical references (p. 209-216) and index. Subjects: Rock music--History and criticism. Mass media and music. Popular culture--History--20th century. Communication in music. Series: Foundations of popular culture; v. 3 LC Classification: ML3534 .J68 1992 Dewey Class No.: 781.66 20

Joyce, Michael, 1945- Moral tales and meditations: technological parables and refractions / Michael Joyce; afterword by Hélène Cixous. Published/Created: Albany: State University of New York Press, c2001. Description: xvi, 149 p.; 24 cm. ISBN: 0791451550 (alk. paper) Notes: Includes bibliographical references (p. 147-149). Subjects: Technology and civilization--Mass media--Moral and ethical aspects--Fiction. Technology and civilization--Mass media--Moral and ethical aspects. Didactic fiction, American. Parables. LC Classification: PS3560.O885 M6 2001 Dewey Class No.: 813/.54 21

Juhasz, Alexandra. AIDS TV: identity, community, and alternative video / Alexandra Juhasz; videography by Catherine Saalfield. Published/Created: Durham, N.C.: Duke University Press, 1995. Related Authors: Saalfield, Catherine. Description: x, 316 p.: ill.; 24 cm. ISBN: 0822316838 (cloth: alk. paper) 0822316951 (paperback: alk. paper) Notes: Includes bibliographical references (p. [259]-270) and index. Subjects: AIDS (Disease) in mass media. Series: Console-ing passions LC Classification: P96.A39 J84 1995 Dewey Class No.: 362.1/969792 20

Juusela, Pauli. Journalistic codes of ethics in the CSCE countries: an examination / Pauli Juusela. Published/Created: Tampere: University of Tampere, Dept. of Journalism and Mass Communication, 1991. Description: 94 p.: ill.; 26 cm. ISBN: 951442932X Notes: Includes bibliographical references (p. 90-91). Subjects: Journalistic ethics--Europe. Reporters and reporting--Europe. Mass media--Europe. Series: Julkaisuja (Tampereen yliopisto. Tiedotusopin laitos). Sarja B; 31. Variant Series: Julkaisuja. B, 0358-4151 = Publications. Series B; 31/1991 LC Classification: PN4756 .J88 1991

Kamath, M. V., 1921- Professional standards in media: a selection from Mediawatch, the columns of M.V. Kamath, 1987-1990 / edited and introduced by Jane Swamy. Published/Created: Bombay: Xavier Institute of Communications, St. Xavier's College, c1991. Related Authors: Swamy, Jane. Mediawatch. Description: xvi, 140 p.; 24 cm. Notes: Includes bibliographical references (p. 140). Subjects: Mass media--Professional ethics--India. LC Classification: P94 .K362 1987 Dewey Class No.: 174 20

Kanellos, Nicolás. Thirty million strong: reclaiming the Hispanic image in American culture / Nicolás Kanellos. Published/Created: Golden, Colo.: Fulcrum Pub., c1998. Description: x, 166 p.: ill.; 23 cm. ISBN: 1555912656 (pbk.) Notes: Includes bibliographical references (p. 153-160) and index. Subjects: Hispanic Americans--History. Hispanic Americans and mass media. United States--Civilization--Hispanic influences. LC Classification: E184.S75 K38 1998 Dewey Class No.: 973/.0468 21

Kaplar, Richard T. The government factor: undermining journalistic ethics in the information age / Richard T. Kaplar and Patrick D. Maines. Published/Created: Washington, D.C.: Cato Institute, c1995. Related Authors: Maines, Patrick D. Description: xi, 100 p.; 21 cm. ISBN: 1882577256 1882577264 (pbk.) Notes:

Includes bibliographical references and index. Subjects: Journalistic ethics--United States. Freedom of the press--United States. Government and the press--United States. Mass media--United States--Moral and ethical aspects. LC Classification: PN4888.E8 K37 1995 Dewey Class No.: 174/.9097 20

Karamoy, Willy A. (Willy Arnold), 1935- In search of drug information: affinity to prevention abuse: lesson from Indonesia: a book for readings and research / Willy A. Karamoy. Published/Created: [Jakarta]: Social Cooperation Agency for Promoting Noble Citizens of Indonesia, 1996. Description: iv, 109 p.: ill.; 21 cm. ISBN: 9799513308 Notes: Includes bibliographical references (p. 107-109). Subjects: Drugs and mass media--Indonesia. Drug abuse--Indonesia--Prevention. LC Classification: HV5840.I6 K37 1996

Katz, Jon. Virtuous reality: how America surrendered discussion of moral values to opportunists, nitwits, and blockheads like William Bennett / Jon Katz. Edition Information: 1st ed. Published/Created: New York: Random House, c1997. Description: xxvi, 212 p.: ill.; 22 cm. ISBN: 0679449132 Notes: Includes index. Subjects: Mass media--Moral and ethical aspects. Mass media--Technological innovations. LC Classification: P94 .K38 1997 Dewey Class No.: 302.23 20

Kelley, Gordon E., 1934- Sherlock Holmes: screen and sound guide / by Gordon E. Kelley. Published/Created: Metuchen, N.J.: Scarecrow Press, 1994. Description: xiv, 317 p.: ill.; 23 cm. ISBN: 0810828596 (alk. paper) Notes: Includes bibliographical references (p. 274-282) and index. Subjects: Holmes, Sherlock (Fictitious character) in mass media Handbooks, manuals, etc. LC Classification: P96.H59 K45 1994 Dewey Class No.: 791.43/651 20

Kellner, Douglas, 1943- Media culture: cultural studies, identity, and politics between the modern and the postmodern / Douglas Kellner. Published/Created: London; New York: Routledge, 1995. Description: ix, 357 p.: ill.; 24 cm. ISBN: 0415105692 (hbk.): 0415105706 (pbk.): Notes: Includes bibliographical references (p. [342]-351) and index. Subjects: Mass media--United States. Popular culture--United States. LC Classification: P92.U5 K38 1995 Dewey Class No.: 302.23/0973 20

Kelly, Ann Cline. Jonathan Swift and popular culture: myth, media, and the man / by Ann Cline Kelly. Published/Created: New York: Palgrave, 2002. Projected Pub. Date: 0202 Description: p. cm. ISBN: 0312239599 Notes: Includes bibliographical references and index. Subjects: Swift, Jonathan, 1667-1745. Church of Ireland--Clergy--Biography. Popular culture--Great Britain--History--18th century. Mass media--Great Britain--History and criticism. Verse satire, English--History and criticism. Authors, Irish--18th century--Biography. Satire, English--History and criticism. LC Classification: PR3726 .K45 2002 Dewey Class No.: 828/.509 B 21

Key, Wilson Bryan, 1925- Subliminal adventures in erotic art / by Wilson Bryan Key. Published/Created: Boston: Branden Pub. Co., c1992. Related Authors: Key, Wilson Bryan, 1925- Clam-plate orgy. Description: xxiii, 209 p.: ill.; 23 cm. ISBN: 0828319510: Notes: Rev. ed. of: The clam-plate orgy, 1980. Includes bibliographical references and index. Subjects: Mass media and art--United States. Erotic art--United States. Subliminal perception--United States. Commercial art--United States. LC Classification: N72.M28 K49 1992 Dewey Class No.: 701/.05 20

Key, Wilson Bryan, 1925- The age of manipulation: the con in confidence, the sin in sincere / Wilson Bryan Key. Edition Information: 1993 ed. Published/Created: Lanham, Md.: Madison Books: Distributed by National Book Network, 1993. Description: xix, 296 p., [32] p. of plates: ill.; 23 cm. ISBN: 0819186538 (pbk.: alk. paper) Notes: Originally Published: New

York: H. Holt, c1989. Includes bibliographical references (p. [269]-282) and index. Subjects: Mass media--Psychological aspects. Advertising--Psychological aspects. Manipulative behavior. Subliminal projection. Subliminal advertising. LC Classification: P96.P75 K39 1993 Dewey Class No.: 302.23 20

Kieran, Matthew, 1968- Media ethics: a philosophical approach / Matthew Kieran. Published/Created: Westport, Conn.: Praeger, 1997. Description: ix, 168 p.; 24 cm. ISBN: 0275956342 (hardcover: alk. paper) Notes: Includes bibliographical references (p. [153]-160) and index. Subjects: Mass media--Moral and ethical aspects. LC Classification: P94 .K54 1997 Dewey Class No.: 174 21

King, Stephen, 1947- Stephen King's danse macabre. Published/Created: New York: Berkley Books, 2001. Projected Pub. Date: 0109 Description: p. cm. ISBN: 042518160X Notes: Originally Published: New York: Everest House, c1981. Filmography: p. Includes bibliographical references and index. In English. Subjects: Horror in mass media. LC Classification: P96.H65 K5 2001 Dewey Class No.: 700/.4164 21

Kivikuru, Ullamaija. Tinned novelties or creative culture?: a study on the role of mass communication in peripheral nations / Ullamaija Kivikuru. Published/Created: Helsinki: [University of Helsinki, Dept. of Communication], 1990. Description: 1 v. (various pagings): ill.; 25 cm. ISBN: 9514554124 Notes: Includes bibliographical references (p. 489-514). Subjects: Mass media--Finland. Mass media--Tanzania. Communication and culture. Series: Julkaisuja (Helsingin yliopisto. Tiedotusopin laitos). 1F; 10. Variant Series: Publications / University of Helsinki, Department of Communication, 0357-5160; 1F/10/90 = Julkaisuja / Helsingin yliopisto, Tiedotusopin laitos; 1F/10/90 LC Classification: P92.F5 K57 1990 Dewey Class No.: 302.23/094897 20

Klages, Mary. Woeful afflictions: disability and sentimentality in Victorian America / Mary Klages. Published/Created: Philadelphia: University of Pennsylvania Press, c1999. Description: 250 p.: ill.; 24 cm. ISBN: 0812234995 (acid-free paper) Notes: Includes bibliographical references (p. [233]-241) and index. Subjects: People with disabilities--United States--History--19th century. People with disabilities--United States--Public opinion. People with disabilities in mass media--History. People with disabilities in literature--History and criticism. Public opinion--United States. LC Classification: HV1553 .K53 1999 Dewey Class No.: 362.4/0973/09034 21

Kondo, Dorinne K. About face: performing race in fashion and theater / Dorinne Kondo. Published/Created: New York: Routledge, 1997. Description: xiii, 276 p.: ill.; 24 cm. ISBN: 0415911400 0415911419 (pbk.) Notes: Includes bibliographical references (p. 261-270) and index. Subjects: Asian Americans--Ethnic identity. National characteristics, Japanese. Fashion--Japan--Themes, motives. Asian American theater--Social aspects. Stereotype (Psychology) in mass media. Popular culture--United States. LC Classification: E184.O6 K65 1997 Dewey Class No.: 391/.00952 21

Kumar, Keval J. Media education, communication, and public policy: an Indian perspective / Keval J. Kumar. Edition Information: 1st ed. Published/Created: Bombay: Himalaya Pub. House, 1995. Description: xxii, 425 p.: maps; 22 cm. ISBN: 8174931805 Notes: Includes bibliographical references (p. [297]-321). Subjects: Mass media in education--India. Communication in education--India. LC Classification: LB1043.2.I4 K86 1995 Dewey Class No.: 371.3/58 21

Kurian, George Thomas. Encyclopedia of medical media & communications / George Thomas Kurian. Published/Created: Gaithersburg, Md.: Aspen Publishers, 1996. Description: viii, 985 p.; 26 cm. ISBN: 0834206854 Notes:

Includes bibliographical references and index. Subjects: Communication in medicine. Health in mass media. Medicine--Periodicals--Bibliography. LC Classification: R118 .K87 1996 Dewey Class No.: 610/.14 20

Langton, Marcia, 1951- "Well, I heard it on the radio and I saw it on the television": an essay for the Australian Film Commission on the politics and aesthetics of filmmaking by and about Aboriginal people and things / by Marcia Langton. Published/Created: North Sydney, NSW: Australian Film Commission, c1993. Related Authors: Australian Film Commission. Description: 93 p.; 22 cm. ISBN: 0642191794 Notes: Includes bibliographical references (p. 87-89). Subjects: Australian aborigines in mass media. Ethnic mass media--Australia. Mass media and race relations--Australia. LC Classification: P94.5.A85 L36 1993 Dewey Class No.: 791.43/652039915 20

Lasn, Kalle. Culture jam: the uncooling of America / Kalle Lasn. Edition Information: 1st ed. Published/Created: New York: Eagle Brook, c1999. Description: xvii, 251 p.: ill.; 25 cm. ISBN: 0688156568 Notes: Includes bibliographical references (p. 217-234) and index. Subjects: Mass media and culture. Mass media--Influence. Mass media and the environment. Mass media criticism. Popular culture. Social movements. Intercultural communication. LC Classification: P94.6 .L37 1999 Dewey Class No.: 302.23 21

Latin American advertising, marketing and media sourcebook. Published/Created: London: Euromonitor PLC; Chicago, Ill.: Euromonitor International, c1995. Related Authors: Euromonitor PLC. Description: xiii, 182 p.: maps; 31 cm. ISBN: 0863385443 Notes: "Marketing handbooks"--Cover. Includes index. Subjects: Advertising agencies--Latin America--Directories. Marketing--Latin America--Directories. Mass media--Latin America--Directories. Marketing--Latin America--Statistics. Television broadcasting--Latin America--Statistics. LC Classification: HF6182.L29 L38 1995 National Bib. No.: GB95-79082

Latin American media directory plus United States and Canada / International Media Center, School of Journalism and Mass Communication, Florida International University = Guía de medios latinoamericanos incluyendo Estados Unidos y Canadá / Centro de Prensa Internacional, Escuela de Periodismo y Medios de Comunicación, Universidad Internacional de la Florida. Published/Created: North Miami, FL: The Center, c1997- Related Authors: Florida International University. International Media Center. Description: v.: ill., maps; 23 cm. 1997- Current Frequency: Annual Continues: Hispanic media directory of the Americas 1094-2971 (DLC) 97655662 (OCoLC)35653468 ISSN: 1094-298X Cancel/Invalid LCCN: sn 97036359 Notes: In English and Spanish. SERBIB/SERLOC merged record Subjects: Mass media--Latin America--Directories. Hispanic American mass media--Directories. Mass media--Directories. LC Classification: P88.8 .H57 Dewey Class No.: 302.23/025 21

Lauritsen, John. The AIDS war: propaganda, profiteering and genocide from the medical-industrial complex / John Lauritsen. Published/Created: New York: Asklepios, c1993. Description: 479 p.: ill.; 22 cm. ISBN: 0943742080: Notes: Includes bibliographical references and indexes. Subjects: AIDS (Disease)--Political aspects. AIDS (Disease)--Research. AIDS (Disease)--Government policy. AIDS (Disease) in mass media. LC Classification: RA644.A25 L37 1993 Dewey Class No.: 362.1/969792 20

Law in the domains of culture / edited by Austin Sarat and Thomas R. Kearns. Edition Information: 1st pbk. ed. Published/Created: Ann Arbor: University of Michigan Press, 2000. Related Authors: Sarat, Austin. Kearns, Thomas R. Description: 241 p.; 24 cm. ISBN: 0472087010 (pbk.: alk. paper) Notes: Originally Published: 1998. Includes bibliographical references (p. 93-96) and index. Subjects: Culture and law. Popular culture. Mass media. Series: The Amherst series in law, jurisprudence, and social thought LC Classification: K487.C8 L394 2000 Dewey Class No.: 340/.115 21

Law in the domains of culture / edited by Austin Sarat and Thomas R. Kearns . Published/Created: Ann Arbor: University of Michigan Press, c1998. Related Authors: Sarat, Austin. Kearns, Thomas R. Description: 241 p.; 24 cm. ISBN: 047210862X (cloth: acid-free paper) Notes: Includes bibliographical references and index. Subjects: Culture and law. Popular culture. Mass media. Series: The Amherst series in law, jurisprudence, and social thought LC Classification: K487.C8 L394 1998 Dewey Class No.: 340/.115 21

Law, Ian. Race in the news / Ian Law. Published/Created: Hampshire; New York: Palgrave, 2002. Description: ix, 178 p.; 22 cm. ISBN: 0333740742 0333740750 (pbk.) Notes: Includes bibliographical references (p. 167-175) and index. Subjects: Mass media and race relations. LC Classification: P94.5.M55 L38 2002 Dewey Class No.: 305.8 21

Lawrence, John Shelton. The myth of the American superhero / John Shelton Lawrence and Robert Jewett. Published/Created: Grand Rapids, MI: W.B. Eerdmans, 2002. Projected Pub. Date: 0204 Related Authors: Jewett, Robert. Description: p. cm. ISBN: 0802860834 (alk. paper) Notes: Includes bibliographical references and index. Subjects: Popular culture--United States. Heroes in mass media. Heroes--United States--Folklore. National characteristics, American. Heroes--Political aspects--United States. Political culture--United States--Civilization--Intellectual life. LC Classification: E169.12 .L36 2002 Dewey Class No.: 973 21

Leadership in times of change: a handbook for communication and media administrators / edited by William G. Christ Published/Created: Annandale, Va.: National Communication Association; Mahwah, N.J.: Erlbaum, c1999. Related Authors: Christ, William G. Description: xiii, 415 p.: ill.; 24 cm. ISBN: 080582698X (cloth) 0805829113 (pbk.) Notes: Includes bibliographical references and indexes. Subjects: Communication--Study and teaching (Higher)--Management Handbooks, manuals, etc. Mass media--Study and teaching (Higher)--Management Handbooks, manuals, etc. Series: LEA's communication series LC Classification: P91.3 .L39 1998 Dewey Class No.: 302.2/071/173 21

Lee, Jae-won. Seoul Olympics and the global community / edited by Jae-won Lee. Published/Created: Seoul, Korea: Seoul Olympics Memorial Association, c1992. Description: 192 p.; 23 cm. Subjects: Olympic Games (24th: 1988: Seoul, Korea) Mass media and sports. Olympics--Social aspects. LC Classification: GV722 1988 .L44 1992 Dewey Class No.: 796.48 20

Lee, Jong Bom. Intercultural ethos mediation with the mass media: sympathy as the means for the mediation of the Christian ethos in the modern Confucian society / Jong Bom Lee. Published/Created: Frankfurt am Main; New York: P. Lang, c2001. Description: 189 p.; 21 cm. ISBN: 0820443824 Notes: Includes bibliographical references (p. 182-188) Subjects: Sympathy. Sympathy--Religious aspects. Mass media--Moral and ethical aspects. Series: Forum interdisziplinäre Ethik; Bd. 27 LC Classification: BJ1475 .L44 2001 Dewey Class No.: 170 21

Leslie, Larry Z. Mass communication ethics: decision making in postmodern culture / Larry Z. Leslie. Published/Created: Boston: Houghton Mifflin, c2000. Description: xvii, 326 p.: ill.; 24 cm. ISBN: 0395904900 Notes: Includes bibliographical references and index. Subjects: Mass media--Moral and ethical aspects. Mass media and culture. LC Classification: P94 .L47 2000 Dewey Class No.: 175 21

Levine, Michael, 1954- Selling goodness / Michael Levine. Edition Information: 1st ed. Published/Created: Los Angeles, Calif.: Renaissance Books, c1998. Description: ix, 288 p.; 22 cm. ISBN: 158063009X Notes: Includes bibliographical references (p. 279-282) and index. Subjects: Social service--Public relations. Mass media and social service. Special events. Fund raising. Charities. Nonprofit organizations. LC Classification: HV42 .L48 1998 Dewey Class No.: 659.2 21

Levine, Michael, 1954- The princess & the package: exploring the love-hate relationship between Diana and the media / Michael Levine. Published/Created: Los Angeles, Calif.: Renaissance Books, c1998. Description: 352 p.; 24 cm. ISBN: 1580630286 (hc.: alk. paper) Notes: Includes bibliographical references (p. 329-343) and index. Subjects: Diana, Princess of Wales, 1961- --In mass media. Princesses--Great Britain--Biography. Mass media--Great Britain. LC Classification: DA591.A45 D538 1998 Dewey Class No.: 941.085/092 B 21

Lewis, Jeff, 1952- How to get noticed by the national media: your complete guide to high-impact publicity / [Jeff Lewis & Dick Jones]. Edition Information: 1st ed. Published/Created: Duluth, MN: Trellis Pub., c2001. Related Authors: Jones, Dick, 1948- Description: 153 p.; cm. ISBN: 1930650426 (alk. paper) Notes: Includes index. Subjects: Corporations--Public relations--United States. Mass media and publicity--United States. Industrial publicity--United States--Management. LC Classification: HD59.6.U6 L49 2001 Dewey Class No.: 659.2 21

Lindfors, Bernth. Loaded vehicles: studies in African literary media / Bernth Lindfors. Published/Created: Trenton, NJ: Africa World Press, c1996. Description: viii, 216 p.; 23 cm. ISBN: 0865435421 Notes: Includes bibliographical references (p. [185]-194) and index. Subjects: African literature (English)--History and criticism. Periodicals--Publishing--Africa--History--20th century. Literature--Publishing--Africa--History--20th century. Books and reading--Africa--History--20th century. Mass media--Africa--History--20th century. LC Classification: PR9340.5 .L565 1996 Dewey Class No.: 820.9/96 20

Lipsitz, George. Time passages: collective memory and American popular culture / George Lipsitz. Published/Created: Minneapolis: University of Minnesota Press, c1990. Description: xvii, 306 p.; 23 cm. ISBN: 0816618054: 0816618062 (pbk.): Notes: Includes bibliographical references (p. 275-291) and index. Subjects: Popular culture--United States--History--20th century. Mass media--Social aspects--United States. Memory--Social aspects--United States--History--20th century. Series: American culture (Minneapolis, Minn.); 4 Variant Series: American culture; [4] LC Classification: E169.12 .L55 1990 Dewey Class No.: 973.9 20

Literature, markets and media in Germany and Austria today / edited by Arthur Williams, Stuart Parkes, Julian Preece. Published/Created: Oxford; New York: P. Lang, c2000. Related Authors: Williams, Arthur, 1940- Parkes, K. Stuart, 1943- Preece, Julian. Description: vi, 326 p.; 23 cm. ISBN: 3906765156 Notes: Chiefly rev. papers from the Sixth Bradford International Colloquium on Contemporary German-Language Literature held at the University of Bradford in April 1998. Includes bibliographical references (p. [311]-315) and index. Subjects: German literature-Austrian literature-20th century--History and criticism. Literature publishing--Germany--Austria--Mass media and literature--Germany--Austria--Authorship--Economic aspects--Germany--Austria--History--20th century-Congresses. LC Classification: PT405 .L545 2000 Dewey Class No.: 830.9/0091 21

Lloyd-Kolkin, Donna. Media & you / by Donna Lloyd-Kolkin and Kathleen R. Tyner. Published/Created: Englewood Cliffs, N.J.: Educational Technology Publications, c1991. Related Authors: Tyner, Kathleen R. Related Titles: Media and you.

Description: 170 p., [9] leaves of plates: ill.; 28 cm. ISBN: 0877782261: Notes: "An elementary media literacy curriculum." Includes bibliographical references and index. Subjects: Audio-visual materials--Study and teaching (Elementary) Handbooks, manuals, etc. Mass media--Study and teaching (Elementary)--Handbooks, manuals, etc. Media literacy--Handbooks, manuals, etc. LC Classification: LB1043.5 .L56 1991 Dewey Class No.: 372.13/35 20

Lodge, David, 1935- Home truths: a novella / David Lodge. Published/Created: New York: Penguin Books, 2000. Description: 114 p.; 20 cm. ISBN: 0140291806 Subjects: Authors--Fiction. Mass media and publicity--Fiction. London (England)--Fiction. LC Classification: PR6062.O36 H59 2000 Dewey Class No.: 823/.914 21

Loetterle, Bridget C., 1941- Ageless prose: a study of the media-projected images of aging / Bridget C. Loetterle. Published/Created: New York: Garland Pub., 1994. Description: xxii, 305 p.; 24 cm. ISBN: 0815315341 (alk. paper) Notes: Includes bibliographical references (p. 269-290) and index. Subjects: Aged in mass media. Mass media--Denmark. Series: Garland studies on the elderly in America LC Classification: P94.5.A382 U65 1994 Dewey Class No.: 305.26 20

Lofficier, Jean-Marc. French science fiction, fantasy, horror and pulp fiction: a guide to cinema, television, radio, animation, comic books and literature from the middle ages to the present / by Jean-Marc Lofficier and Randy Lofficier; foreword by Stephen R. Bissette. Published/Created: Jefferson, N.C.: McFarland, c2000. Related Authors: Lofficier, Randy. Description: xi, 787 p.: ill.; 28 cm. ISBN: 0786405961 (lib. bdg.: alk. paper) Notes: Includes bibliographical references (p. 755-756) and index. Subjects: Fantasy fiction, French--History and criticism. Mass media--France. LC Classification: PQ637.F3 L64 2000 Dewey Class No.: 700/.415 21

Loriga, Ray, 1967- My brother's gun / Ray Loriga; translated by Kristina Cordero. Edition Information: 1st U.S. ed. Published/Created: New York: St. Martin's Press, 1997. Related Authors: Cordero, Kristina. Description: 119 p.; 22 cm. ISBN: 0312169477 Subjects: Juvenile delinquents--Fiction. Murder--Fiction. Brothers--Fiction. Mass media and culture--Fiction. Genre/Form: Adventure stories. LC Classification: PQ6662.O77 C3513 1997 Dewey Class No.: 863/.64 21

Loss, Archie K. (Archie Krug) Pop dreams: music, movies, and the media in the 1960s / Archie K. Loss. Published/Created: Fort Worth, TX: Harcourt Brace College Publishers, c1999.. Description: viii, 232 p.: ill.; 21 cm. ISBN: 0155041460 (pbk.) Notes: Includes bibliographical references (p. 215-221) and index. Subjects: Mass media--United States--History--20th century. Series: Harbrace books on America since 1945 LC Classification: P92.U5 L67 1999

Louw, P. Eric. The media and cultural production / P. Eric Louw. Published/Created: London; Thousand Oaks: Sage, 2001. Description: x, 229 p.; 24 cm. ISBN: 0761965823 0761965831 (PBK) Notes: Includes bibliographical references (p. [215]-222) and index. Subjects: Mass media and culture. Mass media--Influence. Power (Social sciences) LC Classification: P94.6 .L68 2001 Dewey Class No.: 302.23 21 National Bib. No.: GBA1-44402

Lull, James. Media, communication, culture: a global approach / James Lull. Edition Information: 2nd ed., [fully rev. and updated]. Published/Created: New York: Columbia University Press, 2000. Description: x, 308 p.: ill.; 23 cm. ISBN: 0231120737 (pbk.: alk. paper) Notes: Includes bibliographical references (p. [293]-303) and index. Subjects: Mass media and culture. LC Classification: P94.6 .L85 2000 Dewey Class No.: 302.23 21

Lull, James. Media, communication, culture: a global approach / James Lull. Published/Created: New York: Columbia University Press, c1995. Description: viii, 207 p.: ill.; 24 cm. ISBN: 023110264X 0231102658 (paper) Notes: Originally Published: Cambridge [England]: Polity Press, in association with Blackwell Publishers, 1994. Includes bibliographical references and index. Subjects: Mass media and culture. LC Classification: P94.6 .L85 1995 Dewey Class No.: 302.23 20

Lynch, James J. Cyberethics: managing the morality of multimedia / James J. Lynch. Published/Created: Leighton Buzzard, Bedfordshire: Rushmere Wynne, 1996. Description: 235 p.: ill.; 26 cm. ISBN: 0948035382 Notes: Includes bibliographical references (p. 229) and index. Subjects: Mass media--Moral and ethical aspects. Computer science--Moral and ethical aspects. LC Classification: P94 .L96 1996 Dewey Class No.: 175 21

Ma, Sheng-mei. The deathly embrace: orientalism and Asian American identity / Sheng-mei Ma. Published/Created: Minneapolis: University of Minnesota Press, c2000. Projected Pub. Date: 0010 Description: p. cm. ISBN: 0816637105 (alk. paper) 0816637113 (pbk.: alk. paper) Notes: Includes bibliographical references (p.) and index. Subjects: Asian Americans--Ethnic identity. Asian Americans--Cultural assimilation. Orientalism--United States. Asian Americans and mass media. American literature--Asian American authors--History and criticism. LC Classification: E184.O6 M22 2000 Dewey Class No.: 305.895073 21

MacDonald, Barrie I. Keyguide to information sources in media ethics / Barrie MacDonald and Michel Petheram. Published/Created: Washington, D.C.: Mansell, 1998. Related Authors: Petheram, Michel. Description: x, 373 p.; 25 cm. ISBN: 0720121280 (hardcover) Notes: Includes bibliographical references and index. Subjects: Mass media--Moral and ethical aspects--Information resources. LC Classification: P94 .M22 1998 Dewey Class No.: 016.175 21

Making & selling culture / Richard Ohmann, editor, with Gage Averill ... [et al.]. Published/Created: Hanover, NH: University Press of New England, c1996. Related Authors: Ohmann, Richard M. (Richard Malin), 1931- Description: xxiii, 254 p.; 24 cm. ISBN: 081955300X (cloth: alk. paper) 0819553018 (pbk.: alk. paper) Notes: Includes bibliographical references. Subjects: Culture--Economic aspects--Congresses. Popular culture--Economic aspects--Congresses. Mass media--Marketing--Congresses. LC Classification: HM101 .M23773 1996 Dewey Class No.: 306.3 20

Making the news: modernity & the mass press in nineteenth-century France / edited by Dean de la Motte & Jeannene M. Przyblyski. Published/Created: Amherst: University of Massachusetts Press, c1999. Related Authors: De la Motte, Dean, 1961- Przyblyski, Jeannene M. Description: vii, 386 p.: ill.; 25 cm. ISBN: 1558491767 (cloth: alk. paper) 1558491775 (pbk.: alk. paper) Notes: Includes bibliographical references (p. 377-383). Subjects: Press--France--History--19th century. Popular culture--France--History--19th century. Mass media and culture--France. Women and journalism--France. Women in journalism--France. Series: Studies in print culture and the history of the book. Variant Series: Studies in print culture & the history of the book LC Classification: PN5177 .M35 1999 Dewey Class No.: 074/.09034 21

Malm, Krister, 1941- Media policy and music activity / Krister Malm and Roger Wallis. Published/Created: London; New York: Routledge, 1992. Related Authors: Wallis, Roger. Description: 271 p.: ill.; 24 cm. ISBN: 0415050197 Notes: Includes bibliographical references and index. Subjects: Mass media and music. LC Classification: ML3849 .M27 1992 Dewey Class No.: 780/.0302 20

Manning, Paul, 1955- Spinning for labour: trade unions and the new media environment / Paul Manning. Published/Created: Aldershot, Hants, England; Brookfield, Vt.: Ashgate, c1998. Description: xii, 401 p.; 23 cm. ISBN: 1840143398 Notes: Includes bibliographical references (p. 380-397) and index. Subjects: Labor unions and mass media--Great Britain. LC Classification: P96.T72 G745 1998 Dewey Class No.: 331.88/0941 21

Manuel, Peter Lamarche. Cassette culture: popular music and technology in north India / Peter Manuel. Published/Created: Chicago: University of Chicago Press, 1993. Description: xix, 302 p.: ill.; 24 cm. ISBN: 0226503992 0226504018 (pbk.) Notes: Includes bibliographical references (p. 289-296) and index. Subjects: Popular music--India--History and criticism. Sound recording industry--India. Mass media and music. Music--Social aspects. Audiocassettes. Series: Chicago studies in ethnomusicology LC Classification: ML3502.I4 M36 1993 Dewey Class No.: 306.4/84 20

Martín B., Jesús (Martín Barbero) Communication, culture and hegemony: from the media to mediations / J. Martin-Barbero; translated by Elizabeth Fox and Robert A. White; with an introduction by Philip Schlesinger. Published/Created: London; Newbury Park: SAGE Publications, 1993. Description: 272 p.; 23 cm. ISBN: 080398488X Cancelled ISBN: 0803984988 (pbk.) Notes: Translation of: De los medios a las mediaciones. Includes bibliographical references (p. [246]-260) and index. Subjects: Mass media--Latin America. Mass media--Social aspects--Latin America. Popular culture--Latin America. Series: Communication and human values (Newbury Park, Calif.) Variant Series: Communication and human values LC Classification: P92.L3 M37 1993 Dewey Class No.: 302.2/34/098 20

Martin, Paul E. Black press, Britons, and immigrants: alternative press and society / Paul E. Martin. Published/Created: Kingston, Jamaica: Vintage Communications, 1998. Description: vi, 252 p.: ill.; 22 cm. ISBN: 9768138696 Notes: Includes bibliographical references (p. 225-252). Subjects: Black newspapers--Great Britain. Mass media and race relations--Great Britain. Immigrants--Great Britain. Great Britain--Race relations. LC Classification: PN5124.B55 M37 1998 Dewey Class No.: 072/.08996 21

Mass culture and everyday life / edited by Peter Gibian. Published/Created: New York: Routledge, 1997. Related Authors: Gibian, Peter, 1952- Description: viii, 304 p.; 24 cm. ISBN: 0415916747 0415916755 (pbk.) Notes: Includes bibliographical references and index. Subjects: Popular culture--United States. Mass media--United States. United States--Social life and customs--1971- LC Classification: E169.04 .M367 1997 Dewey Class No.: 306/.0973 20

Mass culture and perestroika in the Soviet Union / Marsha Siefert, editor. Published/Created: New York: Oxford University Press, c1991. Related Authors: Siefert, Marsha, 1949- Description: 200 p.: ill.; 26 cm. ISBN: 0195073657 Notes: Includes bibliographical references. Subjects: Mass media--Soviet Union. Popular culture--Soviet Union. Perestroika. LC Classification: P92.S65 M35 1991 Dewey Class No.: 302.23/0947/09048 20

Mass media / edited by John A. Coleman and Miklós Tomka. Published/Created: London: SCM Press; Maryknoll: Orbis Books, 1993. Related Authors: Coleman, John Aloysius, 1937- Tomka, Miklós. Description: ix, 125 p.; 22 cm. ISBN: 0334030234 0883448742 (US) Notes: "December 1993."--T.p. verso. Includes bibliographical references. Subjects: Mass media. Mass media--Religious aspects--Christianity. Mass media in religion. Series: Concilium (Glen Rock, N.J.); 1993/6. Variant Series: Concilium; 1993/6 LC Classification: P91 .M3427 1993 Dewey Class No.: 302.23 21

Mass media and cultural identity: ethnic reporting in Asia / edited by Anura

Goonasekera and Youichi Ito. Published/Created: Sterling, VA: Pluto Press, 1999. Related Authors: Goonasekera, Anura, 1940- It¯o, Y¯oichi, 1942- Description: x, 305; 24 cm. ISBN: 0745315623 (hbk) Notes: Includes bibliographical references (p. 289-298) and index. Subjects: Mass media and ethnic relations--Asia. Ethnicity--Asia. Asia--Ethnic relations. LC Classification: P96.E752 A844 1999 Dewey Class No.: 305.8/0095 21

Mass media and drug prevention: classic and contemporary theories and research / edited by William D. Crano, Michael Burgoon. Published/Created: Mahwah, N.J.: L. Erlbaum, 2002. Related Authors: Crano, William D., 1942- Burgoon, Michael. Claremont Symposium on Applied Social Psychology. Description: xiv, 303 p.: ill.; 24 cm. ISBN: 080583477X (alk. paper) 0805834788 (pbk.) Notes: "The Claremont Symposium on Applied Social Psychology." Includes bibliographical references and indexes. Subjects: Drugs and mass media--United States. Drug abuse--United States--Prevention. LC Classification: HV5825 .M254 2002 Dewey Class No.: 362.29/17/0973 21

Mass media and free trade: NAFTA and the cultural industries / Emile G. McAnany, Kenton T. Wilkinson, editors. Edition Information: 1st ed. Published/Created: Austin: University of Texas Press, 1996. Related Authors: McAnany, Emile G. Wilkinson, Kenton T. (Kenton Todd) Description: xv, 420 p.: ill.; 24 cm. ISBN: 0292751982 (alk. paper) 0292751990 (pbk.: alk. paper) Notes: Includes bibliographical references and index. Subjects: Canada. Treaties, etc. 1992 Oct 7. Mass media and culture--Mass media--Economic aspects--Free trade--Culture diffusion--Cultural industries--North America. LC Classification: P94.65.N7 M38 1996 Dewey Class No.:302.23/097 20

Mass media and the moral imagination / edited by Philip J. Rossi and Paul Soukup. Published/Created: Kansas City, MO: Sheed & Ward, c1994. Related Authors: Rossi, Philip J. Soukup, Paul A. Description: xii, 304 p.; 23 cm. ISBN: 1556126220: Notes: Includes bibliographical references and index. Subjects: Mass media--Moral and ethical aspects--Religious aspects. Series: Communication, culture & theology LC Classification: P94 .M33 1994 Dewey Class No.: 302.23 20

Mass media in modern society / edited by Norman Jacobs; with a new introduction by Garth S. Jowett. Published/Created: New Brunswick, U.S.A.: Transaction Publishers, c1992. Related Authors: Jacobs, Norman, 1914- Description: v, 242 p.; 23 cm. ISBN: 1560006129 Notes: Previously Published: Culture for the millions? Princeton, N.J.: Van Nostrand, 1959. Subjects: Popular culture--United States. LC Classification: P92.U5 C86 1992 Dewey Class No.: 302.23/0973 20

Mass mediations: new approaches to popular culture in the Middle East and beyond / edited by Walter Armbrust. Published/Created: Berkeley: University of California Press, c2000. Related Authors: Armbrust, Walter. Description: xi, 378 p.; 23 cm. ISBN: 0520219252 (cloth: alk. paper) Notes: Includes bibliographical references (p. 329-353) and index. Subjects: Mass media--Popular culture--Middle East. LC Classification: P94.65.M628 M37 2000 Dewey Class No.: 302.23/0956 21

Massed medias: linguistic tools for interpreting media discourse / Linda Lombardo ... [et al.]. Published/Created: Milano: Edizioni universitarie di lettere economia diritto, c1999. Related Authors: Lombardo, Linda. Description: 315 p.: ill.; 24 cm. ISBN: 8879161237 Notes: Includes bibliographical references (p. [279]-287) and index. Subjects: Mass media and language. Discourse analysis. Series: Lingue di oggi LC Classification: P96.L34 M364 1999 Dewey Class No.: 302.23/01/4 21

May, Kirse Granat. Golden state, golden youth: the California image in popular culture, 1955-1966 / by Kirse Granat May. Published/Created: Chapel Hill: University of North Carolina Press, 2002. Projected Pub. Date: 0205 Description: p. cm. ISBN: 0807826952 (cloth: alk. paper) 0807853623 (pbk.: alk. paper) Notes: Includes bibliographical references and index. Subjects: Popular culture--California--History--20th century. Mass media--Social aspects--California--History--20th century. Youth--California--Social life and customs--20th century. Baby boom generation--California--History. Popular culture--United States--History--20th century. Mass media--Social aspects--United States--History--20th century. Mass media and youth--United States--History--20th century. Baby boom generation--United States--History. California--Civilization--20th century. California--Social life and customs--20th century. LC Classification: F866.2 .M23 2002 Dewey Class No.: 979.4/053 21

McAlister, Melani, 1962- Epic encounters: culture, media, and U.S. interests in the Middle East, 1945-2000 / Melani McAlister. Published/Created: Berkeley: University of California Press, c2001. Description: xv, 358 p.: ill., map; 24 cm. ISBN: 0520214439 (cloth: alk. paper) 0520228103 (pbk.: alk. paper) Notes: Includes bibliographical references (p. 321-346) and index. Subjects: Mass media and public opinion--United States. Public opinion--United States. Middle East--Foreign relations--United States. United States--Foreign relations--Middle East. Middle East--Foreign public opinion, American. United States--Civilization--1945- Series: American crossroads; 6 LC Classification: DS63.2 .M33 2001 Dewey Class No.: 327.56073 21

McAllister, Matthew P. The commercialization of American culture: new advertising, control, and democracy / by Matthew P. McAllister. Published/Created: Thousand Oaks: Sage Publications, c1996. Description: xii, 296 p.; 23 cm. ISBN: 0803953798 (c. alk. paper) 0803953801 (p: alk. paper) Notes: Includes bibliographical references (p. 260-274) and index. Subjects: Advertising--Social aspects--United States. Mass media--Social aspects--United States. Advertising--United States--History--20th century. LC Classification: HF5813.U6 M327 1996 Dewey Class No.: 659.1/042 20

McCoy, Thomas S. Voices of difference: studies in critical philosophy and mass communication / Thomas S. McCoy. Published/Created: Cresskill, N.J.: Hampton Press, c1993. Description: xi, 276 p.; 24 cm. ISBN: 1881303551 188130356X (paper) Notes: Includes bibliographical references and indexes. Subjects: Mass media. Philosophy, Modern--20th century. Series: The Hampton Press communication series LC Classification: P91 .M373 1993 Dewey Class No.: 302.23 20

McDaniel, Drew O. Electronic tigers of Southeast Asia: the politics of media, technology, and national development / Drew McDaniel. Edition Information: 1st ed. Published/Created: Ames: Iowa State University Press, 2001. Projected Pub. Date: 0111 Description: p. cm. ISBN: 0813819075 Notes: Includes bibliographical references (p.) and index. Subjects: Mass media policy--Asia, Southeastern. Mass media and technology--Asia, Southeastern. Mass media--Asia, Southeastern--Audiences. Mass media--Censorship--Asia, Southeastern. Series: International topics in media LC Classification: P95.82.A78 M37 2001 Dewey Class No.: 302.23/0959 21

McGuigan, Jim. Cultural populism / Jim McGuigan. Published/Created: London, [England]; New York: Routledge, 1992. Description: viii, 290 p.; 23 cm. ISBN: 0415062942 0415062950 (pbk.) Notes: Includes bibliographical references (p. [251]-275) and indexes. Subjects: Culture. Popular culture. Populism. Subculture. Mass media and youth. LC Classification: HM101 .M357 1992 Dewey Class No.: 306 20

McIntyre, Joseph. Hausa in the media: a lexical guide: Hausa-English-German, English-Hausa, German-Hausa / Joseph McIntyre, Hilke Meyer-Bahlburg; assisted by Ahmed Tijani Lawal. Published/Created: Hamburg: Helmut Buske Verlag, c1991. Related Authors: Meyer-Bahlburg, Hilke. Lawal, Ahmed Tijani. Description: xx, 289 p.; 25 cm. ISBN: 3875480082 (alk. paper): Subjects: Hausa language--Dictionaries--English. Hausa language--Dictionaries--German. English language--Dictionaries--Hausa. German language--Dictionaries--Hausa. Mass media and language. LC Classification: PL8233 .M4 1991 Dewey Class No.: 493/.72321 20

McLuhan, Marshall, 1911- Media research: technology, art, communication / Marshall McLuhan; edited with commentary, Michel A. Moos. Published/Created: Amsterdam: G&B Arts, c1997. Related Authors: Moos, Michel A. Description: xviii, 178 p., [4] p. of plates: ill. (some col.), port.; 24 cm. ISBN: 9057010917 Notes: Includes bibliographical references (p. 167-178). Subjects: McLuhan, Marshall, 1911- Mass media and culture. Mass media and technology. Series: Critical voices in art, theory and culture LC Classification: P94.6 .M39 1997 Dewey Class No.: 302.23 21

McNair, Brian, 1959- Mediated sex: pornography and postmodern culture / Brian McNair. Published/Created: London; New York: Arnold; New York: Distributed exclusively in the USA by St. Martin's Press, 1996. Description: ix, 195 p.: ill.; 24 cm. ISBN: 034066293X (hardbound) 0340614285 (pbk.) Notes: Includes bibliographical references (p. [176]-187) and index. Subjects: Pornography. Sex in mass media. Mass media and sex. Sex in popular culture. Postmodernism. LC Classification: HQ471 .M385 1996 Dewey Class No.: 363.4/7 20

Measuring psychological responses to media messages / edited by Annie Lang. Published/Created: Hillsdale, N.J.: Erlbaum, 1994. Related Authors: Lang, Annie. Description: x, 244 p.: ill.; 24 cm. ISBN: 0805807179 (acid-free paper) Notes: Includes bibliographical references and indexes. Subjects: Mass media--Psychological aspects. Series: LEA's communication series LC Classification: P96.P75 M33 1994 Dewey Class No.: 302.23/01/9 20

Measuring psychological responses to media messages / edited by Annie Lang. Published/Created: Hillsdale, N.J.: Erlbaum, 1994. Related Authors: Lang, Annie. Description: x, 244 p.: ill.; 24 cm. ISBN: 0805807179 (acid-free paper) Notes: Includes bibliographical references and indexes. Subjects: Mass media--Psychological aspects. Series: LEA's communication series LC Classification: P96.P75 M33 1994 Dewey Class No.: 302.23/01/9 20

Media and cultural regulation / edited by Kenneth Thompson. Published/Created: London; Thousand Oaks, Calif.: Sage Publications; Milton Keynes: Open University, 1997. Related Authors: Thompson, Kenneth. Description: 248 p.: ill.; 25 cm. ISBN: 0761954392 0761954406 (pbk) Notes: Includes bibliographical references and index. Subjects: Mass media and culture. Mass media policy. Multiculturalism Series: Culture, media and identities LC Classification: P94.6 .M42 1997 Dewey Class No.: 302.23 21 National Bib. No.: GB98-13265

Media and cultural studies: keyworks / edited by Meenakshi Gigi Durham and Douglas M.Kellner. Published/Created: Malden, Mass.: Blackwell Publishers, 2001. Related Authors: Durham, Meenakshi Gigi. Kellner, Douglas, 1943- Description: vii, 646 p.; 25 cm. ISBN: 063122095X (alk. paper) 0631220968 (pbk.: alk. paper) Notes: Includes bibliographical references and index. Subjects: Mass media and culture. Popular culture. Series: Keyworks in cultural studies; 2 LC Classification: P94.6 .M424 2001 Dewey Class No.: 302.23 21

Media and environment in Africa: challenges for the future / edited by S.T. Kwame Boafo. Published/Created: Nairobi, Kenya: ACCE, 1993. Related Authors: Boafo, S. T. Kwame. African Council on Communcation Education. Description: vi, 111 p.: ill.; 30 cm. Notes: Includes bibliographical references and index. Subjects: Mass media and the environment--Africa. Environmental education--Africa. LC Classification: GE30 .M44 1993 Dewey Class No.: 363.7/0071/06 20

Media and migration / edited by Russell King and Nancy Wood. Published/Created: London; New York: Routledge, 2001. Projected Pub. Date: 0105 Related Authors: King, Russell, 1945- Wood, Nancy. Description: p. cm. ISBN: 0415229251 (alk. paper) Notes: Includes bibliographical references and index. Subjects: Mass media and immigrants. Series: Routledge research in cultural and media studies; 8 LC Classification: P94.5.I48 M43 2001 Dewey Class No.: 302.23/086/91 21

Media and the marketplace: ethical perspectives / edited by Eoin G. Cassidy, Andrew G. McGrady. Published/Created: Dublin: Institute of Public Administration, 2001. Related Authors: Cassidy, Eoin G. McGrady, Andrew G. Description: xi, 243 p.; 22 cm. ISBN: 1902448529 Notes: "This publication arose out of a European Union SOCRATES post-graduate intensive programme and accompanying public symposium held in Dublin in Frebruary 1999"--Acknowledgements. Includes bibliographical references. Subjects: Mass media--Moral and ethical aspects.

Media and the transformation of religion in South Asia / edited by Lawrence A. Babb and Susan S. Wadley. Published/Created: Philadelphia: University of Pennsylvania Press, c1995. Related Authors: Babb, Lawrence A. Wadley, Susan S., 1943- Joint Committee on South Asia. American Council of Learned Societies. Description: viii, 298 p.: ill.; 24 cm. ISBN: 0812233042 (hardback: alk. paper) 0812215478 (paper: alk. paper) Notes: "This project was sponsored by the Joint Committee on South Asia of the Social Science Research Council and the American Council of Learned Societies." Includes bibliographical references and index. Subjects: Mass media--Religious aspects. Asia, South--Religion--20th century. LC Classification: BL1055 .W33 1995 Dewey Class No.: 291.1/75 20

Media audiences in Ireland: power and cultural identity / edited by Mary J. Kelly, Barbara O'Connor. Published/Created: Dublin, Ireland: University College Dublin Press, 1997. Related Authors: Kelly, Mary J., 1952- O'Connor, Barbara, M.A. Description: vi, 280 p.: ill.; 24 cm. ISBN: 1900621096 Notes: Includes bibliographical references and index. Subjects: Mass media--Ireland--Audiences. Mass media--Social aspects--Ireland. LC Classification: P96.A832 I746 1997 Dewey Class No.: 302.23/09417 21

Media courses UK. Published/Created: London: British Film Institute, 1993- Related Authors: British Film Institute. Description: v.; 20 x 21 cm. 1993- Current Frequency: Annual Notes: SERBIB/SERLOC merged record Subjects: Mass media--Study and teaching--Universities and colleges--Great Britain--Curricula Directories. LC Classification: P91.5.G7 M43

Media cultures: reappraising transnational media / edited by Michael Skovmand and Kim Christian Schrøder. Published/Created: London; New York: Routledge, 1992. Related Authors: Skovmand, Michael. Schrøder, Kim. Description: viii, 222 p.; 22 cm. ISBN: 0415063841 041506385X (pbk.) Notes: Includes bibliographical references and index. Subjects: Popular culture. Communication, International. Intercultural communication. Series: Communication and society (Routledge (Firm)) Variant Series: Communication and society LC Classification: P91 .M379 1992 Dewey Class No.: 302.23 20

Media education across Europe / edited by David French and Michael Richards. Published/Created: London; New York: Routledge, 1994. Related Authors: French, David, 1946- Richards, Michael, 1945- Description: xi, 217 p.; 23 cm. ISBN: 041510016X 0415100178 (U.S.) Notes: "Published in association with the Broadcasting Standards Council." Includes bibliographical references and indexes. Subjects: Communication--Study and teaching--Europe. Mass media--Study and teaching--Europe. LC Classification: P91.5.E85 M43 1993 Dewey Class No.: 302.2/0704 20

Media education across Europe / edited by David French and Michael Richards. Published/Created: London; New York: Routledge, 1994. Related Authors: French, David, 1946- Richards, Michael, 1945- Description: xi, 217 p.; 23 cm. ISBN: 041510016X 0415100178 (U.S.) Notes: "Published in association with the Broadcasting Standards Council." Includes bibliographical references and indexes. Subjects: Communication--Study and teaching--Europe. Mass media--Study and teaching--Europe. LC Classification: P91.5.E85 M43 1993 Dewey Class No.: 302.2/0704 20

Media education assessment handbook / edited by William G. Christ. Published/Created: Mahwah, N.J.: L. Erlbaum, 1997. Related Authors: Christ, William G. Description: xi, 364 p.; 24 cm. ISBN: 0805821856 Notes: Includes bibliographical references and indexes. Subjects: Mass media--Study and teaching (Higher)--Evaluation. Series: LEA's communication series LC Classification: P91.3 .M386 1997 Dewey Class No.: 302.23/071/1 20

Media education: an introduction / edited by Manuel Alvarado and Oliver Boyd-Barrett. Published/Created: London: BFI Pub.; Milton Keynes [England]: Open University, c1992. Related Authors: Alvarado, Manuel, 1948- Boyd-Barrett, Oliver. Description: xiv, 450 p.: ill.; 24 cm. ISBN: 0851702953 Notes: Includes bibliographical references and index. Subjects: Mass media--Study and teaching. LC Classification: P91.3 .M385 1992 Dewey Class No.: 302.23/07 20

Media entertainment: the psychology of its appeal / edited by Dolf Zillmann, Peter Vorderer. Published/Created: Mahwah, N.J.: Lawrence Erlbaum Associates Publishers, 2000. Related Authors: Zillmann, Dolf. Vorderer, Peter. Description: xi, 282 p.: ill.; 24 cm. ISBN: 0805833242 (alk. paper) 0805833250 (pbk.: alk. paper) Notes: Includes bibliographical references and indexes. Subjects: Mass media--Psychological aspects. Series: LEA's communication series LC Classification: P96.P75 M34 2000 Dewey Class No.: 302.23/01/9 21

Media ethics / edited by Matthew Kieran. Published/Created: London; New York: Routledge, 1998. Related Authors: Kieran, Matthew, 1968- Description: xv, 195 p.; 25 cm. ISBN: 0415168376 (alk. paper) 0415168384 (pbk.: alk. paper) Notes: Includes bibliographical references (p. [179]-186) and index. Subjects: Mass media--Moral and ethical aspects. LC Classification: P94 .M358 1998 Dewey Class No.: 175 21

Media ethics: cases and moral reasoning / Clifford G. Christians ... [et al.]. Edition Information: 6th ed. Published/Created: New York: Longman, 2001. Projected Pub. Date: 0007 Related Authors: Christians, Clifford G. Description: p. cm. ISBN: 0801333385 Notes: Includes bibliographical references and index. Subjects: Mass media--Moral and ethical aspects. LC Classification: P94 .M36 2001 Dewey Class No.: 075 21

Media ethics: cases and moral reasoning. Edition Information: 5th ed. / Clifford G. Christians ... [et al.]. Published/Created: New York: Longman, c1998. Related Authors: Christians, Clifford G. Description: xiii, 331 p.: ill.; 24 cm. ISBN: 0801317894 Notes: Rev. ed. of: Media ethics: cases & moral reasoning / Clifford G. Christians, Mark Fackler, Kim B. Rotzoll. 4th ed. c1995. Includes bibliographical references (p. 313-321) and index. Subjects: Mass media--Moral and ethical aspects. LC Classification: P94 .C45 1998 Dewey Class No.: 170 21

Media ethics: cases and moral reasoning. Edition Information: 5th ed. / Clifford G. Christians ... [et al.]. Published/Created: New York: Longman, c1998. Related Authors: Christians, Clifford G. Description: xiii, 331 p.: ill.; 24 cm. ISBN: 0801317894 Notes: Rev. ed. of: Media ethics: cases & moral reasoning / Clifford G. Christians, Mark Fackler, Kim B. Rotzoll. 4th ed. c1995. Includes bibliographical references (p. 313-321) and index. Subjects: Mass media--Moral and ethical aspects. LC Classification: P94 .C45 1998 Dewey Class No.: 170 21

Media ethics: issues & cases / [edited by] Philip Patterson, Lee Wilkins. Edition Information: 4th ed. Published/Created: Boston, Mass.: McGraw Hill, c2002. Related Authors: Patterson, Philip. Wilkins, Lee. Description: xviii, 314 p.: ill.; 23 cm. ISBN: 0072373881 Notes: Includes bibliographical references (p. 296-306) and index. Subjects: Mass media--Moral and ethical aspects. LC Classification: P94 .M36 2002 Dewey Class No.: 175 21

Media ethics: issues and cases / [edited by] Philip Patterson, Lee Wilkins. Edition Information: 2nd ed. Published/Created: Madison, Wis.: Brown & Benchmark, c1994. Related Authors: Patterson, Philip. Wilkins, Lee. Description: xx, 280 p.: ill.; 23 cm. ISBN: 0697170993 Notes: Includes bibliographical references (p. 271-275) and index. Subjects: Mass media--Moral and ethical aspects. LC Classification: P94 .M36 1994 Dewey Class No.: 174 20

Media ethics: issues and cases / [edited by] Philip Patterson, Lee Wilkins. Published/Created: Dubuque, IA: Wm. C. Brown, c1991. Related Authors: Patterson, Philip. Wilkins, Lee. Description: xviii, 238 p.: ill.; 23 cm. ISBN: 0697111725 Notes: Includes bibliographical references (p. 231-234) and index. Subjects: Mass media--Moral and ethical aspects. LC Classification: P94 .M36 1991 Dewey Class No.: 174 20

Media ethics: issues, cases / [edited by] Philip Patterson, Lee Wilkins. Edition Information: 3rd ed. Published/Created: Boston, Mass.: McGraw-Hill, 1998. Related Authors: Patterson, Philip. Wilkins, Lee. Description: xx, 356 p.: ill.; 23 cm. ISBN: 0697327175 (alk. paper) Notes: Includes bibliographical references and index. Subjects: Mass media--Moral and ethical aspects. LC Classification: P94 .M36 1997 Dewey Class No.: 175 21

Media ethics: opening social dialogue / edited by Bart Pattyn. Published/Created: Leuven: Peeters, 2000. Related Authors: Pattyn, Bart, 1962- European Ethics Network. Description: vi, 422 p.; 24 cm. ISBN: 9042909021 Notes: "This book is a result of the core materials project for the development of courses in professional ethics initiated by the European Ethics Network"--Foreword. Includes bibliographical references. Subjects: Mass media--Moral and ethical aspects. Mass media and culture. Mass media--Social aspects. LC Classification: P94 .M3613 2000 Dewey Class No.: 175 21

Media monitors in Asia / compiled by K.S. Venkateswaran. Published/Created: Singapore: Asian Media Information and Communication Centre, c1996. Related Authors: Venkateswaran, K. S. Description: x, 414 p.; 21 cm. ISBN: 9971905620 Notes: Includes bibliographical references. Subjects: Mass media--Moral and ethical aspects--Asia. Mass media criticism--Asia. LC Classification: P94 .M362 1996

Media scandals: morality and desire in the popular culture marketplace / edited by James Lull and Stephen Hinerman. Published/Created: New York: Columbia University Press, 1997. Related Authors: Lull, James. Hinerman, Stephen. Description: ix, 259 p.; 24 cm. ISBN: 0231111649 0231111657 (pbk.) Notes: Includes bibliographical references and index. Subjects: Scandals in mass media. Mass media and culture. Mass media--Moral and ethical aspects. LC Classification: P96.S29 M43 1997 Dewey Class No.: 302.23 21

Media, consciousness, and culture: explorations of Walter Ong's thought / edited by Bruce E. Gronbeck, Thomas J. Farrell, Paul A. Soukup. Published/Created: Newbury Park, Calif.: Sage Publications, c1991. Related Authors: Gronbeck, Bruce E. Farrell, Thomas J. Soukup, Paul A. Description: xviii, 272 p.; 23 cm. ISBN: 0803940254 Notes: Includes bibliographical references (p. 237-252) and index. Subjects: Ong, Walter J. Communication. Rhetoric. Mass media. Consciousness. Series: Communication and human values (Newbury Park, Calif.) Variant Series: Communication and human values LC Classification: P92.5.O54 M42 1991 Dewey Class No.: 302.2 20

Media, consciousness, and culture: explorations of Walter Ong's thought / edited by Bruce E. Gronbeck, Thomas J. Farrell, Paul A. Soukup. Published/Created: Newbury Park, Calif.: Sage Publications, c1991. Related Authors: Gronbeck, Bruce E. Farrell, Thomas J. Soukup, Paul A. Description: xviii, 272 p.; 23 cm. ISBN: 0803940254 Notes: Includes bibliographical references (p. 237-252) and index. Subjects: Ong, Walter J. Communication. Rhetoric. Mass media. Consciousness. Series: Communication and human values (Newbury Park, Calif.) Variant Series: Communication and human values LC Classification: P92.5.O54 M42 1991 Dewey Class No.: 302.2 20

Media, culture, and Catholicism / Paul A. Soukup, editor. Published/Created: Kansas City, MO: Sheed & Ward, c1996. Related Authors: Soukup, Paul A. Description: xviii, 220 p.: ill.; 24 cm. ISBN: 1556127693 (alk. paper) Notes: Includes bibliographical references (p. 201-210) and index. Subjects: Catholic Church--United States. Mass media in religion--United States. Mass media--Religious aspects--Catholic Church. Christianity and culture--United States. Series: Communication, culture & theology LC Classification: BV652.97.U6 M43 1996 Dewey Class No.: 261.5/2/08822 20

Media, culture, and the religious right / Linda Kintz and Julia Lesage, editors. Published/Created: Minneapolis: University of Minnesota Press, c1998. Related Authors: Kintz, Linda, 1945- Lesage, Julia. Description: xviii, 380 p.; 24 cm. ISBN: 0816630844 (hardcover: alk. paper) 0816630852 (pbk.: alk. paper) Notes: Includes bibliographical references and index. Subjects: Evangelicalism--United States. Christianity and culture--United States. Mass media--Religious aspects--Christianity. Conservatism--Religious aspects--Christianity. LC Classification: BR1642.U5 M43 1998 Dewey Class No.: 261/.0973 21

Merck, Mandy. In your face: 9 sexual studies / Mandy Merck. Published/Created: New York: New York University Press, c2000. Description: viii, 245 p.: ill.; 23 cm. ISBN: 0814756387 (cloth: alk. paper) 0814756395 (pbk.: alk. paper) Notes: Includes bibliographical references (p. 201-234) and index. Subjects: Sex in mass media. Sex in popular culture. LC Classification: P96.S45 M47 2000 Dewey Class No.: 306.7 21

Merkushev, Alexander. The Russian and Soviet press: a long journey from suppression to freedom via suppression and glasnost / by Alexander Merkushev. Published/Created: [Cambridge, Mass.]: Joan Shorenstein Barone Center, Press, Politics, Public Policy, Harvard University, John F. Kennedy School of Government, [1991] Description: 14 p.; 28 cm. Notes: "August 1991." Includes bibliographical references (p. 14). Subjects: Press--Mass media--Censorship--Freedom of information--Soviet Union. Glasnost. Series: Discussion paper (Joan Shorenstein Barone Center on the Press, Politics, and Public Policy); D-10. Variant Series: Discussion paper; D-10 LC Classification: PN5274 .M39 1991

Midwinter, Eric C. Out of focus: old age, the press, and broadcasting / Eric Midwinter. Published/Created: London: Centre for Policy on Ageing in association with Help the Aged, 1991. Related Authors: Help the Aged (Organization) Description: viii, 64 p.: ill.; 30 cm. ISBN: 0904139816 Notes: Includes bibliographical references. Subjects: Journalism--Great Britain--Social aspects. Aged in mass media. Aged on television. Mass media--Great Britain. LC Classification: PN5124.S6 M53 1991 Dewey Class No.: 305.26 20

Miller, Michael Nelson, 1942- Red, white, and green: the maturing of Mexicanidad, 1940-1946 / by Michael Nelson Miller. Edition Information: 1st ed. Published/Created: El Paso, Tex.: Texas Western Press, University of Texas at El Paso, c1998. Description: viii, 227 p.; 23 cm. ISBN: 087404278X Notes: Includes bibliographical references (p. 211-222) and index. Subjects: Avila Camacho, Manuel, 1897-1955 --Influence. Mass media--Political aspects--Mexico. Mexico--Cultural policy. Mexico--Politics and government--1910-1946. Series: Southwestern studies (El Paso, Tex.); no. 107. Variant Series: Southwestern studies; no. 107 LC Classification: F1210 .M6195 1998 Dewey Class No.: 972.0825 21

Miller, Toby. Technologies of truth: cultural citizenship and the popular media / Toby Miller. Published/Created: Minneapolis: University of Minnesota Press, c1998. Description: viii, 304 p.: ill.; 27 cm. ISBN: 0816629846 (alk. paper) 0816629854 (alk. paper) Notes: Includes bibliographical references (p. 269-296) and index. Subjects: Popular culture. Mass media--Social aspects. Arts and society. Masculinity in popular culture. Culture conflict. Politics and culture. Prisoners in popular culture. Series: Visible evidence; v. 2 LC Classification: HM101 .M585 1998 Dewey Class No.: 306 21

Mirzoeff, Nicholas, 1962- An introduction to visual culture / Nicholas Mirzoeff. Published/Created: London; New York: Routledge, 1999. Description: xi, 274 p.: ill., map; 24 cm. ISBN: 0415158753 (hbk.) 0415158761 (pbk.) Notes: Includes bibliographic references and index. Subjects: Visual sociology. Popular culture. Visual communication. Mass media. Art and society. Postmodernism. LC Classification: HM500 .M57 1999 Dewey Class No.: 306 21

Mistry, Malika B. (Malika Babasaheb) Fact sheet on the levels of education and exposure to media among Muslim women in India [microform] / Malika B. Mistry. Edition Information: 1st ed. Published/Created: Mumbai: Centre for Study of Society & Secularism, 1998. Related Authors: Centre for Study of Society & Secularism (Bombay, India) Description: ix; 37 p.; 22 cm. Notes: Includes statistical tables. Microfiche. New Delhi: Library of Congress Office; Washington, D.C.: Library of Congress Photoduplication Service, 2001. 1 microfiche. Master microform held by: DLC. Subjects: Muslim women--Education--India. Mass media--India. LC Classification: Microfiche 2000/60494 (L)

Mitroff, Ian I. The unreality industry: the deliberate manufacturing of falsehood and what it is doing to our lives / by Ian I. Mitroff and Warren Bennis. Published/Created: New York: Oxford University Press, 1993. Related Authors: Bennis, Warren G. Description: xxv, 218 p.: ill.; 21 cm. ISBN: 0195083989 (pbk.): Notes: Originally Published: New York: Birch Lane Press, Carol Pub. Group, 1989. Includes bibliographical references (p. [202]-211) and index. Subjects: Mass media--Social aspects--United States. Popular culture--United States. Public opinion--United States. Truthfulness and falsehood. Mass media--United States--Psychological aspects. Knowledge, Theory of. LC Classification: HN90.M3 M58 1993 Dewey Class No.: 306/.0973 20

Moeran, Brian. A Japanese advertising agency: an anthropology of media and markets / Brian Moeran. Published/Created: Honolulu: University of Hawai i Press, c1996. Description: xi, 322 p.: ports; 23

cm. ISBN: 0824818725 (cloth: alk. paper) 0824818733 (pbk.: alk. paper) Notes: "First Published in the United Kingdom by Curzon Press"...T.p. verso. Includes bibliographical references (p. 306-314) and index. Subjects: Advertising agencies--Advertising--Mass media--Japan--Marketing. Series: ConsumAsiaN book series LC Classification: HF6182.J3 M64 1996 Dewey Class No.: 659.1/0952 20

Mohanty, J. (Jagannath), 1937- Child development and education today: literature, art, media, and materials / Jagannath Mohanty. Published/Created: New Delhi: Deep & Deep Publications, c1998. Description: xxiii, 459 p.; 22 cm. ISBN: 8176290955 Notes: Includes bibliographical references (p. [445]-451) and index. Subjects: Child development--India. Literature--Study and teaching--India. Art--Study and teaching--India. Mass media in education--India. LC Classification: LB1115 .M65 1998

Moore, David T. Five lies of the century: how many do you believe? / David T. Moore. Published/Created: Wheaton, IL: Tyndale House, c1995. Description: 321 p.; 21 cm. ISBN: 0842318690 Notes: Includes bibliographical references (p. 305-321). Subjects: Christianity--United States--20th century. Church and social problems--Violence in mass media. Child rearing--United States--Moral conditions. LC Classification: BR526 .M557 1995 Dewey Class No.: 239 20

Moores, Shaun. Interpreting audiences: the ethnography of media consumption / Shaun Moores. Published/Created: London; Thousand Oaks [Calif.]: Sage, 1993. Description: 154 p.; 24 cm. ISBN: 0803984464: 0803984472 (pbk.) Notes: Includes bibliographical references (p. [141]-151) and index. Subjects: Mass media--Audiences. Mass media--Research--History. Audiences Series: Media, culture, and society series. Variant Series: The Media, culture & society series LC Classification: P96.A83 M66 1993 Dewey Class No.: 302.23 20

Morse, Margaret. Virtualities: television, media art, and cyberculture / Margaret Morse. Published/Created: Bloomington: Indiana University Press, c1998. Description: xii, 266 p.: ill.; 24 cm. ISBN: 0253333822 (cloth: alk. paper) 0253211778 (pbk.: alk. paper) Notes: Includes bibliographical references (p. [243]-256) and index. Subjects: Virtual reality--Social aspects. Communication--Social aspects. Television broadcasting--Social aspects. Mass media--Social aspects. Social interaction. Computers and civilization. Series: Theories of contemporary culture; v. 21 LC Classification: HM258 .M689 1998 Dewey Class No.: 302.23 21

Motavalli, John. Bamboozled at the revolution: how big media lost billions in the battle for the internet / John Motavalli. Published/Created: New York: Viking, 2002. Projected Pub. Date: 0208 Description: p. cm. ISBN: 0670899801 (alk. paper) Subjects: Television broadcasting--United States. Interactive television--United States. Mass media--United States. Internet industry--United States. LC Classification: HE8700.8 .M68 2002 Dewey Class No.: 384.3/1 21

Moving the image: independent Asian Pacific American media arts / edited and introduced by Russell Leong; with a preface by Linda Mabalot. Published/Created: Los Angeles: UCLA Asian American Studies Center and Visual Communications, Southern California Asian American Studies Central, c1991. Related Authors: Leong, Russell. University of California, Los Angeles. Asian American Studies Center. Southern California Asian American Studies Central. Visual Communications. Description: xxi, 287 p.: ill.; 26 cm. ISBN: 0934052131 (pbk.) 0934052158 Notes: "A collaborative project of UCLA Asian American Studies Center and Visual Communications, Southern California Asian American Studies Central, Inc." Includes bibliographical references and index. Subjects: Minorities in motion pictures. Motion picture industry--United States. Asian American motion picture producers and directors. Pacific Islander American motion picture producers and directors. Mass media and minorities--United States. LC Classification: PN1995.9.M56 M68 1991 Dewey Class No.: 791.43/089/95073 20

Mueller, Walt, 1956- Understanding today's youth culture / Walt Mueller. Edition Information: Rev. & expanded Published/Created: Wheaton, Ill.: Tyndale House Publishers, c1999. Description: xiv, 461 p.; 23 cm. ISBN: 0842377395 (pbk.: alk. paper) Notes: Includes bibliographical references (p. 403-440) and index. Subjects: Mass media and teenagers--United States. Popular culture--Religious aspects--Christianity. Parent and teenager--Religious aspects. LC Classification: HQ799.2.M35 M84 1999 Dewey Class No.: 261.8/34235/0973 21

Mueller, Walt, 1956- Understanding today's youth culture / Walt Mueller. Published/Created: Wheaton, Ill.: Tyndale, c1994. Description: xii, 392 p.; 23 cm. ISBN: 0842377360 Notes: Includes bibliographical references (p. 347-377) and index. Subjects: Mass media and teenagers--United States. Popular culture--Religious aspects--Christianity. Parent and teenager--Religious aspects. LC Classification: HQ799.2.M35 M84 1994 Dewey Class No.: 261.8/34235/0973 20

Multimedia / First Symposium Multimedia for Architecture and Urban Design; [in cooperation with Universitá di Roma "La Sapienza", Universitá Degli Studi di Firenze]. Published/Created: [Sao Paulo, Brazil]: Universidade de São Paulo, Faculdade de Arquitetura e Urbanismo, 1994. Related Authors: Universidade de São Paulo. Faculdade de Arquitetura e Urbanismo. Universitá degli studi di Roma La Sapienza. Universitá di Firenze. Description: 269 p.: ill., maps; 28 cm. Notes: Includes bibliographical references. Subjects: Mass media and architecture--Congresses. LC Classification: NA2543.M37 S96 1994

Myrick, Roger. AIDS, communication, and empowerment: gay male identity and the politics of public health messages / Roger Myrick. Published/Created: New York: Harrington Park Press, 1996. Description: x, 141 p.; 23 cm. ISBN: 0789060159 (hard: alk. paper) 1560238844 (pbk.: alk. paper) Notes: Includes bibliographical references and index. Subjects: AIDS (Disease)--Social aspects. AIDS (Disease) in mass media. Gays--Identity. Health promotion. Health education. Mass media in health education. Gay men--Public opinion. LC Classification: RA644.A25 M96 1996 Dewey Class No.: 362.1/969792 20

Nelson, Joyce. Sign crimes/road kill: from mediascape to landscape / Joyce Nelson. Published/Created: Toronto: Between the Lines, c1992. Description: 244 p.; 24 cm. ISBN: 0921284543 (pbk.): 0921284535 (bound): Notes: Includes bibliographical references. Subjects: Mass media--Canada. Environmental protection--Canada. Television--Psychological aspects. Business and politics--Canada. LC Classification: P92.C3 N45 1992 Dewey Class No.: 302.23/0971 20

Neuman, W. Russell. The future of the mass audience / W. Russell Neuman. Published/Created: Cambridge [England]; New York: Cambridge University Press, 1991. Description: xiv, 202 p.: ill.; 23 cm. ISBN: 0521413478 0521424046 (pbk.) Notes: Includes bibliographical references (p. 179-193) and index. Subjects: Mass media--Audiences. Mass media--Technological innovations. Mass media--Psychological aspects. LC Classification: P96.A83 N48 1991 Dewey Class No.: 302.23 20

New histories: the Institute of Contemporary Art, Boston / Milena Kalinovska, curator; Lia Gangitano, Steven Nelson, editors. Published/Created: Boston: The Institute, 1996. Related Authors: Kalinovska, Milena. Gangitano, Lia, 1968- Nelson, Steven, 1962- Institute of Contemporary Art (Boston, Mass.) Description: 217 p.: ill. (some col.); 26 cm. ISBN: 0910663313 Notes: Exhibition held Oct. 23, 1996-Jan

5, 1997. Filmography: p. 193. Includes bibliographical references (p. 192-210). Subjects: Mass media and the arts. Art and history. Multiculturalism. Arts and society--History--20th century. LC Classification: NX180.M3 N48 1996 Dewey Class No.: 700/.1/03 20

New horizons in media psychology: research cooperation and projects in Europe / Peter Winterhoff-Spurk, Tom H.A. van der Voort (Eds.). Published/Created: Opladen: Westdeutscher Verlag, c1997. Related Authors: Winterhoff-Spurk, Peter, 1945- Voort, T. H. A. van der. Description: vi, 219 p.: ill.; cm. ISBN: 3531128590 Notes: Papers presented at a workshop held May 21-23, 1995, Otzenhausen, Ger. Includes bibliographical references. Includes one contribution in French. Subjects: Mass media--Psychological aspects--Congresses. LC Classification: P96.P75 N48 1997 Dewey Class No.: 302.23/01/9 21 126 21

New media in the Muslim world: the emerging public sphere / Dale F. Eickelman and Jon W. Anderson, editors. Published/Created: Bloomington: Indiana University Press, c1999. Related Authors: Eickelman, Dale F., 1942- Anderson, Jon W. Description: ix, 213 p.: ill.; 24 cm. ISBN: 0253335752 (cl: alk. paper) 0253213290 (pbk.: alk. paper) Notes: Includes bibliographical references and index. Subjects: Communication--Religious aspects--Islam. Communication--Social aspects--Islamic countries. Communication policy--Islamic countries. Discourse analysis--Social aspects--Islamic countries. Mass media in Islam. Series: Indiana series in Middle East studies LC Classification: BP185.7 .N48 1999 Dewey Class No.: 302.23/0917/671 21

Newfield, Denise. Words & pictures / Denise Newfield. Published/Created: Johannesburg; London: Hodder & Stoughton; Thorold's Africana Books [distributor], 1993. Description: iv, 24 p.: ill.; 30 cm. ISBN: 0947054979 Subjects: Pictures in education. Teaching--Aids and devices. English language--Study and teaching. Mass media Series: Critical language awareness Dewey Class No.: 302.23 20 National Bib. No.: GB95-24853

Ng¯a Kaiwhakap¯umau I Te Reo (N.Z.) M¯aori broadcasting: report to M¯aori by national M¯aori organisations. Published/Created: Wellington, N.Z.: The Ministry, 1997. Related Authors: New Zealand. Ministry of Commerce. Description: 42 p.; 30 cm. Cancelled ISBN: 0478000138 (pbk.) Notes: Cover title. " Published by the Ministry of Commerce on behalf of the national M¯aori organisations and Ng¯a Kaiwhakap¯umai I Te Reo." "June 1997." Subjects: Broadcasting policy--Ethnic television broadcasting--Ethnic radio broadcasting--Maori (New Zealand people)--Mass media. Television broadcasting--Radio broadcasting--New Zealand. LC Classification: HE8689.9.N45 N495 1997

Nightingale, Virginia. Studying audiences: the shock of the real / Virginia Nightingale. Published/Created: London; New York: Routledge, 1996. Description: xi, 172 p.; 24 cm. ISBN: 0415024471 0415143985 (pbk.) Notes: Includes bibliographical references (p. [153]-162) and index. Subjects: Mass media--Audiences--Television viewers--Research--History. Mass media criticism. Mass media and culture. LC Classification: P96.A83 N54 1996 Dewey Class No.: 302.23 21

Njino, Joseph K. (Joseph Kariuki) Communicating the gospel message in Africa today / Joseph K. Njino, Renato Sesana, Jon P. Kirby. Published/Created: Eldoret, Kenya; AMECEA Gaba Publications, c1992. Related Authors: Sesana, Renato Kizito. Kirby, Jon P., 1945- Description: xiv, 69 p.: ill; 21 cm. ISBN: 9966836071: Notes: Includes bibliographical references. Subjects: Mass media in religion--Evangelistic work--Africa. Language and languages--Religious aspects--Christianity. Series: AMECEA Gaba Publications spearhead; 120 LC Classification: BV652.97.A35 N45 1992 Dewey Class No.: 261.5/2/096 20

Norfleet, Barbara P. When we liked Ike: looking for postwar America / Barbara Norfleet. Edition Information: 1st ed. Published/Created: New York: Norton, c2001. Description: 159 p.: ill.; 27 cm. ISBN: 0393019667 Subjects: National characteristics, American. Whites--United States--Social life and customs--20th century. Middle class--United States--History--20th century. Mass media and the family--United States--History--20th century. Mass media and culture--United States--History--20th century. Whites--United States--Social life and customs--20th century--Pictorial works. Middle class--United States--History--20th century Pictorial works. United States--Social life and customs--1945-1970. United States--Social conditions--1945- United States--Social life and customs--1945-1970 Pictorial works. LC Classification: E169.02 .N66 2001 Dewey Class No.: 973.92 21

Not in our character: proceedings of the National Seminar on the Appraisal of the Social and Moral Image of the Nigerian Society: jointly organised by the Kaduna State Government, Nigerian Television Authority and the New Nigerian Newspapers Ltd.: held at State House, Kaduna, on 7th-9th June, 1995 / edited by Lawal Ja'afar Isa. Published/Created: Kaduna, Nigeria: Kaduna State Government, 1995. Description: vii, 297 p.; 23 cm. Cancelled ISBN: 978337104 (paperback) 978337106 (hardback) Subjects: National characteristics, Nigerian--Congresses. Mass media--Moral and ethical aspects--Nigeria Congresses. Nigeria--Foreign public opinion--Congresses. LC Classification: HC1055 .N378 1995

O'Barr, William M. Culture and the ad: exploring otherness in the world of advertising / William M. O'Barr. Published/Created: Boulder, Colo.: Westview Press, 1994. Description: xi, 212 p.: ill.; 26 cm. ISBN: 0813321964 0813321972 (paper) Notes: Includes bibliographical references (p. 208) and index. Subjects: Advertising--Social aspects--United States--History. Minorities in advertising--United States--History. Mass media and race relations--United States--History. Difference (Psychology) Series: Institutional structures of feeling LC Classification: HF5813.U6 O2 1994 Dewey Class No.: 659.1/042 20

Ogan, Christine L. Communication and identity in the Diaspora: Turkish migrants in Amsterdam and their use of media / Christine Ogan. Published/Created: Lanham: Lexington Books, c2001. Description: x, 201 p., [10] p. of plates: ill., maps; 24 cm. ISBN: 0739102699 (cloth: alk. paper) Notes: Includes bibliographical references (p. [191]-196) and index. Subjects: Mass media and minorities--Netherlands--Amsterdam. Turks--Netherlands--Amsterdam--Communication. Turks--Netherlands--Amsterdam--Ethnic identity. Immigrants--Netherlands--Amsterdam. LC Classification: P94.5.M552 N446 2001 Dewey Class No.: 305.89/4350492352 21

Ohman, Jack. Media mania: a collection of mixed media cartoons / Jack Ohman. Published/Created: New York, NY: Macmillan, c1996. Description: 95 p.: chiefly ill.; 16 x 24 cm. ISBN: 0028608496 (pbk.): Subjects: Mass media--Caricatures and cartoons. American wit and humor, Pictorial. LC Classification: NC1429.O36 A4 1996 Dewey Class No.: 741.5/973 20

Ohmann, Richard M. (Richard Malin), 1931- Selling culture: magazines, markets, and class at the turn of the century / Richard Ohmann. Published/Created: London; New York: Verso, 1996. Description: viii, 411 p.: ill.; 25 cm. ISBN: 1859849741 (hardcover) 1859841104 (pbk.) Notes: Includes bibliographical references (p. [365]-400) and index. Subjects: Advertising--Social aspects--United States--History. Advertising, Magazine--Social aspects--United States History. Marketing--Social aspects--United States--History. Popular culture--United States--History. Mass media--Social aspects--United States--History. Variant Series: The Haymarket series LC Classification:

HF5813.U6 O35 1996 Dewey Class No.: 659.1/042/0973 20

Okunna, Chinyere Stella. Ethics of mass communication / by Chinyere Stella Okunna. Published/Created: Enugu, Nigeria: New Generation Books, 1995. Description: ix, 142 p.; 21 cm. ISBN: 9782900184 Notes: Includes bibliographical references and index. Subjects: Mass media--Moral and ethical aspects. Mass media--Moral and ethical aspects--Nigeria. LC Classification: P94 .O37 1995 Dewey Class No.: 175 21

Olson, Scott Robert. Hollywood planet: global media and the competitive advantage of narrative transparency / Scott Robert Olson. Published/Created: Mahwah, N.J.: L. Erlbaum Associates, 1999. Description: xiv, 215 p.; 24 cm. ISBN: 0805832297 (acid-free paper) 0805832300 (pbk.: acid-free paper) Notes: Includes bibliographical references (p. 187-198) and indexes. Subjects: Mass media--United States--Influence. Mass media and culture. Series: LEA's communication series LC Classification: P92.U5 O44 1999 Dewey Class No.: 302.23/0973 21

Ordovensky, Pat. Working with the news media / by Pat Ordovensky and Gary Marx. Published/Created: Arlington, VA: American Association of School Administrators, c1993. Related Authors: Marx, Gary. Description: 32 p.; 23 cm. ISBN: 0876521928 Notes: Cover title. "AASA Stock no.: 21-00374"--T.p. verso. Subjects: Schools--Public relations. Education in mass media. LC Classification: LB2847 .O73 1993 Dewey Class No.: 659.2/9371 20

Paget, Derek, 1946- True stories?: documentary drama on radio, screen, and stage / Derek Paget. Published/Created: Manchester, UK; New York, NY, USA: Manchester University Press: Distributed exclusively in the USA and Canada by St. Martin's Press, c1990. Description: 185 p.; 23 cm. ISBN: 0719029627(hard) 0719029635 (pbk.) Notes: Includes bibliographical references (p. 173-181) and index. Subjects: Documentary mass media. Series: Cultural politics LC Classification: P96.D62 P34 1990 Dewey Class No.: 070.1 20

Pamer, Nan. I will not bow / Nan M. Pamer. Published/Created: Hazelwood, MO: Word Aflame Press, c1997. Description: 56 p.: ill.; 21 cm. ISBN: 156722203X (pbk.) Subjects: Christianity and culture--United States. Christian life--Pentecostal authors. Mass media--United States--Influence. Clothing and dress--Religious aspects--Christianity. Holiness--Christianity. LC Classification: BR115.C8 P32 1997 Dewey Class No.: 243 21

Paquette, Guy. Evaluation de médias régionaux dans le cadre d'une campagne en promotion de la santé / Guy Paquette; en collaboration avec André Chamorel ... [et al.]. Published/Created: [Québec]: Université Laval, Département d'information et de communication, 1995. Description: iii, 229, 36 leaves: ill.; 28 cm. Notes: Includes bibliographical references (leaves 227-229). Subjects: Mass media in health education--Québec (Province) LC Classification: MLCM 97/14328 (R)

Parry-Giles, Shawn J., 1960- Constructing Clinton: hyperreality and presidential image-making in postmodern politics / Shawn J. Parry-Giles & Trevor Parry-Giles. Published/Created: New York: Peter Lang, 2002. Projected Pub. Date: 0202 Related Authors: Parry-Giles, Trevor, 1963- Description: p. cm. ISBN: 0820456950 (pbk.: alk. paper) Notes: Includes bibliographical references and index. Subjects: Clinton, Bill, 1946- --Relations with journalists. Clinton, Bill, 1946- --Public opinion. Mass media--Political aspects--United States--History 20th century. Press and politics--United States--History--20th century. Political culture--United States--History--20th century. Public opinion--United States--History--20th century. Postmodernism--Political aspects--United States. Virtual reality--Political aspects--United States. Public relations and politics--United States--History 20th century. United States--Politics and government--1993-

2001. Series: Frontiers in political communications; vol. 3 LC Classification: E886 .P374 2002 Dewey Class No.: 973.929/092 21

Pavlik, John V. (John Vernon) New media technology: cultural and commercial perspectives / John V. Pavlik; foreword by Everette E. Dennis. Edition Information: 2nd [rev.] ed. Published/Created: Boston: Allyn and Bacon, c1998. Related Authors: Pavlik, John V. (John Vernon). New media technology and the information superhighway. Description: xiv, 400 p.; 23 cm. ISBN: 020527093X Notes: Rev. ed. of: New media technology and the information superhighway. 1996. Includes bibliographical references (p. 379-394) and index. Subjects: Mass media--Technological innovations. Mass media--Social aspects. Mass media--Economic aspects. Mass media--United States. LC Classification: P96.T42 P38 1998 Dewey Class No.: 302.23 21

Pendergast, Tom. Creating the modern man: American magazines and consumer culture, 1900-1950 / Tom Pendergast. Published/Created: Columbia, Mo.: University of Missouri Press, c2000. Description: x, 289 p.: ill.; 24 cm. ISBN: 0826212808 (alk. paper) Notes: Includes bibliographical references (p. 269-283) and index. Subjects: Masculinity--United States--History--20th century. Body image in men--United States. Men in mass media--United States. Men in popular culture--United States. Consumption (Economics)--United States. LC Classification: HQ1090.3 .P45 2000 Dewey Class No.: 305.31/0973 21

Penley, Constance, 1948- NASA/TREK: popular science and sex in America / Constance Penley. Published/Created: New York: Verso, 1997. Projected Pub. Date: 9703 Description: p. cm. ISBN: 0860914054 (hc) 0860916170 (pbk.) Notes: Includes index. Subjects: United States. National Aeronautics and Space Administration. Star trek (Television program) Popular culture--United States--History--20th century. Astronautics and civilization. Astronautics in literature. Astronautics in mass media. Sex customs--United States--History--20th century. LC Classification: E169.04 .P45 1997 Dewey Class No.: 973.91 21

Perloff, Marjorie. Radical artifice: writing poetry in the age of media / Marjorie Perloff. Published/Created: Chicago: University of Chicago Press, 1991. Description: xvi, 248 p.: ill.; 24 cm. ISBN: 0226657337 (cloth: alk. paper) Notes: Includes bibliographical references (p. 217-244) and index. Subjects: American poetry--20th century--History and criticism Theory, etc. Experimental poetry, American--History and criticism. Mass media and literature--United States. Avant-garde (Aesthetics)--United States. Experimental poetry--Authorship. Radicalism in literature. Poetics. LC Classification: PS325 .P38 1991 Dewey Class No.: 811/.5409 20

Perloff, Richard M. The dynamics of persuasion / Richard M. Perloff. Published/Created: Hillsdale, N.J.: L. Erlbaum, 1993. Description: xii, 411 p.: ill.; 25 cm. ISBN: 0805804900 (alk. paper) Notes: Includes bibliographical references (p. 355-394) and indexes. Subjects: Persuasion (Psychology) Mass media--Psychological aspects. Attitude change. Series: Communication textbook series. General communication theory and methodology LC Classification: BF637.P4 P39 1993 Dewey Class No.: 153.8/52 20

Perry, David K. Theory and research in mass communication: contexts and consequences / David K. Perry. Edition Information: 2nd ed. Published/Created: Mahwah, N.J.: Erlbaum, 2002. Description: xi, 319 p.: ill.; 24 cm. ISBN: 0805839372 (cloth: alk. paper) 0805839380 (pbk.) Notes: Includes bibliographical references (p. 278-304) and indexes. Subjects: Mass media--Philosophy. Mass media--Research. Series: LEA's communication series LC Classification: P90 .P378 2002 Dewey Class No.: 302.23/01 21

Perry, David K. Theory and research in mass communication: contexts and consequences / David K. Perry. Published/Created: Mahwah, N.J.: L. Erlbaum Associates, 1996. Description: ix, 230 p.: ill.; 24 cm. ISBN: 0805819231 (cloth: acid-free paper) 080581924X (pbk.: acid-free paper) Notes: Includes bibliographical references (p. 201-219) and indexes. Subjects: Mass media--Philosophy. Mass media--Research. LC Classification: P90 .P378 1996 Dewey Class No.: 302.23/01 20

Perry, Nick, 1942- Hyperreality and global culture / Nick Perry. Published/Created: New York: Routledge, 1998. Description: xii, 194 p.: ill.; 24 cm. ISBN: 0415105145 (hb) 0415105153 (pb) Notes: Includes bibliographical references (p. 173-186) and index. Subjects: Culture. Cultural relations. Mass media--Social aspects. Reality. Imagination. National characteristics. Series: Routledge social futures series Variant Series: Social futures series LC Classification: HM101 .P457 1998 Dewey Class No.: 306 21

Persky, Stan, 1941- Mixed media, mixed messages / Stan Persky; [editor, Audrey McClellan]. Published/Created: Vancouver: New Star Books, 1991. Related Authors: McClellan, Audrey. Description: ii, 206 p.; 22 cm. ISBN: 092158623X Notes: The articles reprinted in this book originally appeared in the Vancouver Sun's Saturday Review, the Globe and Mail, Books in Canada, and the Canadian Forum. Includes index. Subjects: Mass media--Moral and ethical aspects. LC Classification: P94 .P385 1991 Dewey Class No.: 302.23 20

Philip, Marlene Nourbese, 1947- Frontiers: selected essays and writings on racism and culture, 1984-1992 / M. Nourbese Philip. Published/Created: Stratford, Ont., Canada: Mercury Press: Distributed in the U.S. by Inland Book Co. and Bookslinger, c1992. Description: 286 p.; 23 cm. ISBN: 0920544908: Notes: Includes bibliographical references. Subjects: Racism--Canada. Racism--United States. Mass media and race relations--Canada. Mass media and race relations--United States. Racism in language. Canada--Race relations. United States--Race relations. LC Classification: F1035.N3 P48 1992

Phillips, Phil. Dinosaurs: the Bible, Barney & beyond / Phil Phillips. Published/Created: Lancaster, Penn.: Starburst, Inc., c1994. Description: 191 p.; 21 cm. ISBN: 0914984594: Notes: Includes bibliographical references. Subjects: Jurassic Park (Motion picture) Bible and evolution. Creationism. Dinosaurs in mass media. Mass media--Religious aspects--Christianity. Barney (Fictitious character) LC Classification: BS659 .P55 1995 Dewey Class No.: 231.7/65 20

Popular culture and mass communication in twentieth-century France / edited by Rosemary Chapman and Nicholas Hewitt. Published/Created: Lewiston, NY: E. Mellen Press, 1992. Projected Pub. Date: 1111 Related Authors: Chapman, Rosemary, 1951- Hewitt, Nicholas. Description: p. cm. ISBN: 0773494995 Notes: Includes bibliographical references and index. Subjects: Mass media--France. Popular culture--France--History--20th century. LC Classification: P92.F8 P66 1992 Dewey Class No.: 302.23/0944/0904 20

Portales, Marco, 1948- Crowding out Latinos: Mexican Americans in the public consciousness / Marco Portales. Published/Created: Philadelphia: Temple University Press, 2000. Description: xiv, 209 p.: ill.; 24 cm. ISBN: 1566397421 (alk. paper) 156639743X (pbk.: alk. paper) Notes: Includes bibliographical references (p. 187-195) and index. Subjects: Mexican Americans--Public opinion. Mexican Americans--Education. Mexican Americans and mass media. Hispanic Americans--Public opinion. Hispanic Americans--Education. Hispanic Americans and mass media. LC Classification: E184.M5 P67 2000 Dewey Class No.: 305.86872073 21

Quay, Sara E. Westward expansion, 1849-1890 / by Sara E. Quay. Published/Created: Westport, CT: Greenwood Press, 2002. Projected Pub. Date: 0205 Description: p. cm. ISBN: 0313312354 (alk. paper) Notes: Includes bibliographical references and index. Subjects: Pioneers--Pioneers--West (U.S.)--History--19th century--Sources. Frontier and pioneer life--West (U.S.)--Sources. Popular culture--West (U.S.)--History--19th century. Popular culture--United States. West (U.S.)--Civilization--19th century. West (U.S.)--Social life and customs--19th century. West (U.S.)--In mass media. Series: American popular culture through history LC Classification: F593 .Q39 2002 Dewey Class No.: 978/.02 21

Raja, John Joshva. Facing the reality of communication: culture, church, and communication / by John Joshva Raja. Published/Created: Delhi: ISPCK, 2001. Related Authors: I.S.P.C.K. (Organization) Description: xiv, 339 p.; 23 cm. ISBN: 8172146051 Notes: Includes bibliographical references (p. [314]-337). "Webliography": (p. [338]-339). Subjects: Communication--Religious aspects--Christianity. Christian education. Mass media in religion. LC Classification: BV4319+

Readings in mass communication: media literacy and culture / [edited by] Kimberly B. Massey. Published/Created: Mountain View, Calif.: Mayfield Pub., c1999. Related Authors: Massey, Kimberly K. Description: xxi, 295 p.; 24 cm. ISBN: 1559349611 Notes: Includes bibliographical references and index. Subjects: Mass media and culture--Popular culture--United States. Media literacy. LC Classification: P94.65.U6 R39 1999 Dewey Class No.: 302.23/0973 21

Reed, Robert M. The encyclopedia of television, cable, and video / by Robert M. and Maxine K. Reed. Published/Created: New York: Van Nostrand Reinhold, c1992. Related Authors: Reed, Maxine K. Description: xv, 622 p.; 29 cm. ISBN: 0442006276; Notes: "A Reed Gordon book." Includes bibliographical references (p. 619-922). Subjects: Mass media--Encyclopedias. LC Classification: P87.5 .R44 1991 Dewey Class No.: 302.23/03 20

Reeves, Byron, 1949- The media equation: how people treat computers, television, and new media like real people and places / Byron Reeves & Clifford Nass. Published/Created: Stanford, Calif.: CSLI Publications; New York: Cambridge University Press, c1996. Related Authors: Nass, Clifford Ivar. Description: xiv, 305 p.; 25 cm. ISBN: 157586052X Notes: Includes bibliographical references (p. [257]-298) and index. Subjects: Mass media--Audiences--Influence--Psychological aspects. LC Classification: P96.A83 R44 1996 Dewey Class No.: 302.23 20

Reid, Mark (Mark A.) PostNegritude visual and literary culture / Mark A. Reid. Published/Created: Albany: State University of New York Press, c1997. Description: xiv, 146 p.: ill.; 24 cm. ISBN: 0791433013 (hardcover: alk. paper) 0791433021 (pbk.: alk. paper) Notes: Includes bibliographical references (p. 135-140) and index. Subjects: Blacks and mass media. Series: The SUNY series, cultural studies in cinema/video LC Classification: P94.5.B55 R45 1997 Dewey Class No.: 305.8/96073 20

Religion, television, and the information superhighway: a search for a middle way: conference report / compiled by Robert Lewis Shayon & Nash Cox. Published/Created: Philadelphia, Pa.: Waymark Press, c1994. Related Authors: Shayon, Robert Lewis. Cox, Nash. Description: 98 p.; 22 cm. Notes: Based on papers presented at a conference held at Annenberg School of Communication, University of Pennsylvania, Pa., on Apr. 22-23, 1994. Includes bibliographical references. Subjects: Television in religion--Mass media--Religious aspects--Congresses. LC Classification: BV656.3 .R418 1994

Report of the Seminar on Promoting Independent and Pluralistic Asian Media, Alma Ata, Kazakhstan, 5-9 October 1992. Published/Created: [New York]: United Nations; [Paris?]: United Nations Educational, Scientific, and Cultural Organization, [1992] Related Authors: United Nations. Unesco. Description: 64 p.; 28 cm. Subjects: Mass media--Asia--Congresses. LC Classification: P92.A7 S46 1992

Reports on media ethics in Europe / Kaarle Nordenstreng (ed.). Published/Created: Tampere: University of Tampere, Dept. of Journalism and Mass Communication, 1995. Related Authors: Nordenstreng, Kaarle. Description: 129 p.; 25 cm. ISBN: 9514438973 Notes: Includes bibliographical references (p. 124-125). Subjects: Mass media--Moral and ethical aspects. Mass media--Europe. Journalism--Europe. Series: Julkaisuja / Tampereen yliopisto, Tiedotusopin laitos. Sarja B, 0358-4151 = Publications / University of Tampere, Department of Journalism and Mass Communication. Series B; 41/1995 Julkaisuja (Tampereen yliopisto. Tiedotusopin laitos). Sarja B; 41. LC Classification: P94 .R46 1995 Dewey Class No.: 174 21

Rethinking media literacy: a critical pedagogy of representation / Peter McLaren ... [et al.]. Published/Created: New York: P. Lang, c1995. Related Authors: McLaren, Peter, 1948- Description: xvii, 259 p.; 23 cm. ISBN: 0820418021 (pbk.: alk. paper) Notes: Includes bibliographical references. Subjects: Mass media--Study and teaching. Series: Counterpoints (New York, N.Y.); v. 4. Variant Series: Counterpoints; v. 4 LC Classification: P91.3 .R49 1995 Dewey Class No.: 302.23/07 20

Rethinking media, religion, and culture / [edited by] Stewart M. Hoover, Knut Lundby. Published/Created: Thousand Oaks, Calif.: Sage Publications, c1997. Related Authors: Hoover, Stewart M. Lundby, Knut. Description: x, 332 p.: ill.; 24 cm. ISBN: 0761901701 076190171X (pbk.) Notes: "This book grows out of a conference titled Media-religion-culture held at the University of Uppsala, Sweden, in May of 1993"--Acknowledgements. Includes bibliographical references and index. Subjects: Mass media--Religious aspects. Mass media and culture. Religion and culture. LC Classification: P94 .R48 1997 Dewey Class No.: 302.23 21

Rhodes, Chip. Structures of the Jazz Age: mass culture, progressive education, and racial discourse in American modernist fiction / Chip Rhodes. Published/Created: New York: Verso, 1998. Projected Pub. Date: 9809 Description: p. cm. ISBN: 1859848338 (cloth) 1859842003 (pbk.) Subjects: American fiction--20th century--History and criticism. Modernism (Literature)--United States. Progressive education--United States. Popular culture in literature. Race relations in literature. Primitivism in literature. Mass media in literature. Education in literature. Nineteen twenties. Variant Series: The Haymarket series LC Classification: PS374.M535 R48 1998 Dewey Class No.: 810.9/0052 21

Richards, Chris, 1952- Teen spirits: music and identity in media education / Chris Richards. Published/Created: London, UK; Bristol, Pa.: UCL Press, 1998. Description: xiv, 215 p.; 24 cm. ISBN: 1857288580 1857288599 Notes: Includes bibliographical references (p. 199-209) and index. Subjects: Mass media--Study and teaching (Secondary) Popular music--Study and teaching (Secondary) Mass media and teenagers. Series: Media, education and culture LC Classification: P91.3 .R53 1998 Dewey Class No.: 302.23/071/2 21

Rickels, Laurence A. The case of California / Laurence A. Rickels. Published/Created: Minneapolis: University of Minnesota Press, 2001. Projected Pub. Date: 0106 Description: p. cm. ISBN: 0816638780 (pbk.: alk. paper) Notes: Originally Published: Baltimore: Johns Hopkins University Press, c1991. Subjects: Mass media--California--Psychological aspects. California--Civilization--20th century--Psychological aspects. LC Classification:

F866.2 .R53 2001 Dewey Class No.: 979.4/053 21

Riggs, Karen E. Mature audiences: television in the lives of elders / Karen E. Riggs. Published/Created: New Brunswick, N.J.: Rutgers University Press, c1998. Description: xiv, 197 p.; 24 cm. ISBN: 081352539X (alk. paper) 0813525403 (pbk: alk. paper) Notes: Includes bibliographical references (p. 177-190) and index. Subjects: Television and the aged--United States. Mass media and the aged--United States. Aged--United States--Psychology. Aged--Communication--United States. Series: Communications, media and culture LC Classification: HQ1064.U5 R546 1998 Dewey Class No.: 306.4/85/0846 21

Ritual, performance, media / edited by Felicia Hughes-Freeland. Published/Created: London; New York: Routledge, 1998. Related Authors: Hughes-Freeland, Felicia, 1954- Association of Social Anthropologists of the Commonwealth. Conference (1996: University College of Swansea) Description: x, 233 p.: ill.; 25 cm. ISBN: 0415163374 (hbk) 0415163382 (pbk.) Notes: Based on papers first presented at the ASA Conference, held at the University of Wales, Swansea, in Mar. 1996. Includes bibliographical references and index. Subjects: Rites and ceremonies--Congresses. Performing arts--Congresses. Mass media--Congresses. Series: A.S.A. monographs; 35. Variant Series: ASA monographs; 35 LC Classification: GN473 .R593 1998 Dewey Class No.: 306.4 21

Robertson, Pat. The autobiography of Pat Robertson: shout it from the housetops! / by Pat Robertson with Jamie Buckingham. Edition Information: Rev. ed. Published/Created: South Plainfield, NJ: Bridge Pub., 1995. Related Authors: Buckingham, Jamie. Description: xi, 369 p.; 22 cm. ISBN: 0882700979 Subjects: Robertson, Pat. Evangelists--United States--Biography. Mass media in religion. LC Classification: BR1725.R62 A3 1995 Dewey Class No.: 269/.2/092 B 20

Rodowick, David Norman. Reading the figural, or, Philosophy after the new media / D.N. Rodowick. Published/Created: Durham: Duke University Press, 2001. Projected Pub. Date: 0110 Description: p. cm. ISBN: 0822327112 (cloth: alk. paper) 0822327228 (pbk.: alk. paper) Notes: Includes bibliographical references and index. Subjects: Mass media--Philosophy. Visual communication. Semiotics. Aesthetics. Series: Post-contemporary interventions LC Classification: P91 .R626 2001 Dewey Class No.: 302.23/01 21

Rohde, Carl C. Symbol soup / Carl C. Rohde, André Platteel. Published/Created: Amsterdam: BIS Publishers; New York: Thames and Hudson, 1999. Related Authors: Platteel, André. Description: 9 v. in 1: ill. (some col.); 30 cm. ISBN: 0500281270 (set) Notes: Title from slipcase. Subjects: Visual communication. Mass media and popular culture. Signs and symbols. LC Classification: P93.5 .R64 1999 Dewey Class No.: 302.23 21

Rosen, Elana Yonah. Changing the world through media education / Elana Yonah Rosen, Arli Paulin Quesada, Sue Lockwood Summers. Published/Created: Golden, Colo.: Fulcrum Resources, c1998. Related Authors: Quesada, Arli Paulin. Summers, Sue Lockwood. Just Think Foundation. Description: xiv, 194 p.: ill.; 28 cm. ISBN: 1555919715 (pbk.) Notes: "A new media literacy curriculum by the Just Think Foundation." Includes bibliographical references (p. 185-189) and index. Subjects: Audio-visual education--Handbooks, manuals, etc. Audio-visual materials--Handbooks, manuals, etc. Media literacy--Handbooks, manuals, etc. Mass media--Study and teaching (Middle school)--Handbooks, manuals, etc. Critical thinking--Study and teaching (Middle school) Handbooks, manuals, etc. Curriculum planning--Handbooks, manuals, etc. Series: Developing minds; pt. 1 LC Classification: LB1043 .R66 1998 Dewey Class No.: 371.33/5 21

Ross, Jeffrey Ian. Making news of police violence: a comparative study of Toronto and New York City / Jeffrey Ian Ross; foreword by Donna C. Hale. Published/Created: Westport, Conn.: Praeger, 2000. Description: xviii, 174 p.; 25 cm. ISBN: 0275968251 (alk. paper) Notes: Includes bibliographical references (p. [157]-171) and index. Subjects: Police brutality--Public opinion--Case studies. Police in mass media--Case studies. LC Classification: HV8141 .R67 2000 Dewey Class No.: 363.2/32 21

Rovin, Jeff. Adventure heroes: legendary characters from Odysseus to James Bond / Jeff Rovin. Published/Created: New York, NY: Facts on File, c1994. Description: vi, 314 p.: ill.; 29 cm. ISBN: 0816028818 Notes: Includes bibliographical references (p. 289-290) and index. Subjects: Heroes in mass media--Dictionaries. LC Classification: P96.H46 R67 1994 Dewey Class No.: 700 20

Rushkoff, Douglas. Coercion: why we listen to what "they" say / Douglas Rushkoff. Published/Created: New York: Riverhead, c1999. Description: 321 p.; 24 cm. ISBN: 1573221155 (alk. paper) Notes: Includes bibliographical references (p. [309]-315). Subjects: Mass media--Influence. Persuasion (Psychology) LC Classification: P94 .R87 1999 Dewey Class No.: 302.23 21

Rushkoff, Douglas. Media virus!: hidden agendas in popular culture / Douglas Rushkoff. Edition Information: [Rev. and updated ed.]. Published/Created: New York: Ballantine Books, c1996. Description: xv, 344 p.; 21 cm. ISBN: 0345397746 Notes: Includes bibliographical references (p. 329-331) and index. Subjects: Mass media and culture--United States. Popular culture--United States. LC Classification: P94.65.U6 R87 1996 Dewey Class No.: 302.23 20

Rushkoff, Douglas. Media virus!: hidden agendas in popular culture / Douglas Rushkoff. Edition Information: 1st ed. Published/Created: New York: Ballantine Books, 1994. Description: 338 p.; 25 cm. ISBN: 0345382765: Notes: Includes bibliographical references (p. 323-325) and index. Subjects: Mass media and culture--United States. Popular culture--United States. LC Classification: P94.65.U6 R87 1994 Dewey Class No.: 302.23 20

Russell, Nick. Morals and the media: ethics in Canadian journalism / Nick Russell. Published/Created: Vancouver: UBC Press, c1994. Description: xi, 249 p.: ill.; 26 cm. ISBN: 0774804572 Notes: Includes bibliographical references (p. [237]-242) and index. Subjects: Journalistic ethics--Canada. Mass media--Moral and ethical aspects--Canada. LC Classification: PN4914.E8 R87 1994 Dewey Class No.: 174/.9097/0971 20

Ryan, John, 1949- Media and society: the production of culture in the mass media / John Ryan, William M. Wentworth. Published/Created: Boston, Mass: Allyn and Bacon, c1999. Related Authors: Wentworth, William M. Description: xv, 255 p.: ill.; 23 cm. ISBN: 0205174000 Notes: Includes bibliographical references (p. 237-246) and index. Subjects: Mass media and culture. Mass media--Social aspects. LC Classification: P94.6 .R93 1999 Dewey Class No.: 302.23 21

Salminen, Esko. The silenced media: the propaganda war between Russia and the West in Northern Europe / Esko Salminen. Published/Created: New York: St. Martin's Press, 1999. Description: xii, 198 p.: maps; 23 cm. ISBN: 0312217749 (cloth) Notes: Includes bibliographical references (p. 177-189) and index. Subjects: Mass media--Censorship--Finland. Finland--Relations--Soviet Union. Soviet Union--Relations--Finland. Freedom of the press--Finland. Freedom of speech--Finland. LC Classification: P96.C42 F568 1999 Dewey Class No.: 323.44/5/094897 21

Sampat-Patel, Niti. Postcolonial masquerades: culture and politics in literature, film, video, and photography / Niti Sampat-Patel. Published/Created: New York: Garland Pub., 2000. Projected Pub. Date: 0009 Description: p. cm. ISBN: 0815336497 (alk. paper) Notes: Includes bibliographical references and index. Subjects: Mass media and culture. Postcolonialism. Series: Literary criticism and cultural theory LC Classification: P94.6 .S264 2000 Dewey Class No.: 302.23 21

Sanders, Barry, 1938- The private death of public discourse / Barry Sanders. Published/Created: Boston: Beacon Press, c1998. Description: 248 p.; 24 cm. ISBN: 0807004340 Notes: Includes bibliographical references (p. [227]-234) and index. Subjects: Popular culture--United States--History--20th century. Rhetoric--Political aspects--United States. Rhetoric--Social aspects--United States. Freedom of speech--United States. Public speaking--United States. Mass media--United States. United States--Civilization--20th century. LC Classification: E169.1 .S242 1998 Dewey Class No.: 306.2/0973/09045 21

Sanders, Noel. The thallium enthusiasms: and other Australian outrages / Noel Sanders. Published/Created: Newtown, N.S.W.: Local Consumption Publications, c1995. Description: 200 p.: ill.; 24 cm. ISBN: 0949793256 Notes: Includes bibliographical references. Subjects: Crime in mass media. Mass media--Australia. Mass media and culture--Australia. Popular culture--Australia. Crime--Australia. LC Classification: P96.C742 A947 1995 Dewey Class No.: 364 21

Scannell, Paddy. Radio, television, and modern life: a phenomenological approach / Paddy Scannell. Published/Created: Oxford, UK; Cambridge, Mass., USA: Blackwell, 1996. Description: vii, 192 p.; 24 cm. ISBN: 0631198741 063119875X (pbk.) Notes: Includes bibliographical references (p. [179]-184) and index. Subjects: Mass media--Philosophy. Broadcasting--History. LC Classification: P91 .S297 1996 Dewey Class No.: 302.23/01 20

Schenck, Paul C. The extermination of Christianity: a tyranny of consensus / by Paul C. Schenck with Robert Schenck. Published/Created: Lafayette, La.: Huntington House, c1993. Related Authors: Schenck, Robert L. Description: 239 p.; 22 cm. ISBN: 1563840510 Notes: Includes bibliographical references. Subjects: Popular culture--United States--Religious aspects Christianity. Mass Media--Religious aspects--Christianity. United States--Religious life and customs--1981- LC Classification: BR115.C8 S265 1993 Dewey Class No.: 277.3/0829 20

Schiller, Herbert I., 1919- Mass communications and American empire / Herbert I. Schiller. Edition Information: 2nd ed., updated. Published/Created: Boulder: Westview Press, 1992. Description: x, 214 p.; 23 cm. ISBN: 0813314399 0813314402 (pbk.) Notes: Includes bibliographical references and index. Subjects: Communication--United States. Mass media--United States. Communication, International. Series: Critical studies in communication and in the cultural industries LC Classification: P92.U5 S29 1992 Dewey Class No.: 302.2/0973 20

Schirato, Tony. Communication and cultural literacy: an introduction / Tony Schirato and Susan Yell. Published/Created: St. Leonards, NSW: Allen & Unwin, 1996. Related Authors: Yell, Susan. Description: xxi, 252 p.: ill.; 22 cm. ISBN: 1864480408 Notes: Includes bibliographical references (p. 243-249) and index. Subjects: Communication--Social aspects--Australia. Communication and culture--Australia. Popular culture--Australia. Mass media--Social aspects--Australia. Series: Australian cultural studies LC Classification: HM258 .S278 1996 Dewey Class No.: 302.2 21

Schirato, Tony. Communication and culture: an introduction / Tony Schirato and Susan Yell. Published/Created: London; Thousand Oaks, Calif.: Sage Publications, 2000. Related Authors: Yell, Susan. Schirato, Tony. Communication and cultural literacy. Description: xv, 204 p.: ill.; 24 cm. ISBN: 0761968261 (hbk) 076196827X (pbk.) Notes: Rev. ed. of: Communication and cultural literacy. 1996.

Includes bibliographical references (p. [193]-200) and index. Subjects: Communication--Social aspects--Australia. Communication and culture--Australia. Popular culture--Australia. Mass media--Social aspects--Australia. LC Classification: HM1206 .S35 2000 Dewey Class No.: 302.2 21

Schnell, James A., 1955- Perspectives on communication in the People's Republic of China / James A. Schnell. Published/Created: Lanham, MD: Lexington Books, 1999. Projected Pub. Date: 9908 Description: p. cm. ISBN: 0739100130 (alk. paper) Notes: Includes bibliographical references and index. Subjects: Communication--Social aspects--China. Communication--Political aspects--China. Communication in politics--China. Communication in education--China. Intercultural communication--China. Mass media--China. LC Classification: HN733.5 .S36 1999 Dewey Class No.: 302.2 21

Schostak, John F. Dirty marks: the education of self, media, and popular culture / John F. Schostak. Published/Created: London; Boulder, Colo.: Pluto Press, 1993. Description: 247 p.: ill.; 23 cm. ISBN: 0745304303 0745304311 (pbk) Notes: Includes bibliographical references (p. 231-240) and index. Subjects: Sociolinguistics. Communication and culture. Mass media--Social aspects. Educational sociology. LC Classification: P40 .S336 1993 Dewey Class No.: 306.4/4 20

Schwarz, Ted, 1945- Free speech and false profits: ethics in the media / Ted Schwarz. Published/Created: Cleveland, Ohio: Pilgrim Press, 1996. Description: 272 p.; 21 cm. ISBN: 0829811486 (acid-free paper) Notes: Includes bibliographical references (p. 255-264) and index. Subjects: Freedom of the press. Freedom of speech. Mass media--Moral and ethical aspects. LC Classification: PN4736 .S38 1996 Dewey Class No.: 323.44/5 21

Schwoch, James, 1955- Media knowledge: readings in popular culture, pedagogy, and critical citizenship / by James Schwoch, Mimi White, Susan Reilly. Published/Created: Albany: State University of New York Press, c1992. Related Authors: White, Mimi, 1953- Reilly, Susan, 1944- Description: xxxiv, 170 p.; 24 cm. ISBN: 0791408264 (alk. paper) 0791408256 (alk. paper) Notes: Includes bibliographical references (p. 153-166) and index. Subjects: Mass media--United States. Mass media in education--United States. Popular culture--United States. Series: Teacher empowerment and school reform. Variant Series: SUNY series, teacher empowerment and school reform LC Classification: P92.U5 S58 1992 Dewey Class No.: 302.23/0973 20

Scriven, Michael, 1947- Sartre and the media / Michael Scriven. Published/Created: New York: St. Martin's Press, 1993. Description: xiii, 152 p.; 22 cm. ISBN: 0312106173 Notes: Includes bibliographical references (p. 138-148) and index. Subjects: Sartre, Jean Paul, 1905- Mass media--France--Influence. Philosophy, French--20th century. LC Classification: B2430.S34 S37 1993 Dewey Class No.: 194 20

Seabrook, John. NoBrow: the culture of marketing the marketing of culture / John Seabrook. Edition Information: 1st ed. Published/Created: New York: A.A. Knopf, 2000. Description: 215 p.; 22 cm. ISBN: 0375405046 (cloth) 0375704515 (pbk.) Notes: On t.p. the letter 'r' in nobrow is encircled in the second letter 'o'. Subjects: Mass media and culture--United States. Popular culture--United States. LC Classification: P94.65.U6 S4 2000 Dewey Class No.: 302.23/0973 21

Seabrook, John. Nobrow: the culture of marketing, the marketing of culture / John Seabrook. Edition Information: 1st Vintage Books ed. Published/Created: New York: Vintage, c2001. Description: 226 p.; 21 cm. ISBN: 0375704515 Notes: On t.p. the letter 'r' in nobrow is encircled in the second letter 'o'. Originally Published: New York: Knopf, 2000. With new afterword. Subjects: Mass media and culture--United

States. Popular culture--United States. LC Classification: P94.65.U6 S4 2001 Dewey Class No.: 302.23/0973 21

Shaheen, Jack G., 1935- Arab and Muslim stereotyping in American popular culture / Jack G. Shaheen. Published/Created: Washington, D.C.: Center for Muslim-Christian Understanding, History and International Affairs, Edmund A. Walsh School of Foreign Service, Georgetown University, c1997. Description: vii, 91 p.; 23 cm. Notes: Includes bibliographical references (p. 81-91). Subjects: Stereotype (Psychology) in mass media--United States. Arabs in popular culture--United States. Muslims in popular culture--United States. Popular culture--United States. Stereotype (Psychology)--United States. United States--Ethnic relations. Series: Occasional papers series (Georgetown University. Center for Muslim-Christian Understanding) Variant Series: Occasional papers series LC Classification: P96.S74 S53 1997

Shaw, Colin, 1928- Deciding what we watch: taste, decency, and media ethics in the UK and the USA / Colin Shaw. Published/Created: Oxford, Oxfordshire, England: Clarendon Press; New York: Oxford University Press, 1999. Description: xii, 184 p.; 23 cm. ISBN: 0198159366 (pbk.: alk. paper) 0198159374 (alk. paper) Notes: Includes bibliographical references (p. 175-176) and index. Subjects: Mass media--Moral and ethical aspects. Mass media--Great Britain. Mass media--United States. LC Classification: P94 .S53 1999 Dewey Class No.: 175 21

Shields, David. Remote / David Shields. Edition Information: 1st ed. Published/Created: New York: Alfred Knopf: Distributed by Random House, 1996. Description: 203 p.: ill.; 21 cm. ISBN: 0679445919 Subjects: Shields, David. Mass media--United States. Popular culture--United States. LC Classification: P92.U5 S52 1996 Dewey Class No.: 302.23/0973 20

Shoemaker, Pamela J. Gatekeeping / Pamela J. Shoemaker. Published/Created: Newbury Park: Sage Publications, c1991. Description: viii, 88 p.: ill.; 23 cm. ISBN: 0803944365 (c) 0803944373 (p) Notes: Includes bibliographical references (p. 78-84) and index. Subjects: Communication--Philosophy. Mass media--Philosophy. Series: Communication concepts, 1057-7440; 3 LC Classification: P90 .S457 1991 Dewey Class No.: 302.2/01 20

Shomari, Hashim A. From the underground: hip hop culture as an agent of social change / Hashim A. Shomari (William A. Lee, III). Published/Created: Fanwood, NJ: X-Factor Publications, c1995. Description: 50 p.: ill.; 22 cm. ISBN: 0964252309 Notes: Includes bibliographical references. Subjects: Afro-American youth. Afro-American arts. Rap (Music)--History and criticism. Mass media--Social aspects--United States. LC Classification: E185.86 .S585 1995 Dewey Class No.: 305.23/5/08996073 20

Shrader, William K. Media blight and the dehumanizing of America / William K. Shrader. Published/Created: New York: Praeger, 1992. Description: xxiv, 184 p.; 24 cm. ISBN: 0275941191 (alk. paper) Notes: Includes bibliographical references (p. [177]-180) and index. Subjects: Mass media--Social aspects--United states. Mass media--United States--Psychological aspects. Television broadcasting--United States--Influence. United states--Moral conditions. LC Classification: HN90.M3 S47 1992 Dewey Class No.: 302.23 20

Siddiqi, Mohammad Ahmadullah. Islam, Muslims and media: myths and realities / Mohammad Ahmadullah Siddiqi. Published/Created: Chicago: NAAMPS Publications, c1997. Description: x, 182 p.: ill.; 23 cm. ISBN: 0964162415 Notes: Includes bibliographical references. Subjects: Mass media--Religious aspects--Islam. Islam in mass media. Islam--Essence, genius, nature. LC Classification: BP185.7 .S56 1997 Dewey Class No.: 297.2/7 21

Silk, Catherine, 1946- Racism and anti-racism in American popular culture: portrayals of African-Americans in fiction and film / Catherine Silk and John Silk. Published/Created: Manchester; New York: Manchester University Press; New York, NY, USA: Distributed exclusively in the USA and Canada by St. Martin's Press, c1990. Related Authors: Silk, John, 1942- Description: x, 186 p.; 23 cm. ISBN: 0719030706 Notes: Includes bibliographical references and index. Subjects: Afro-Americans in mass media. Popular culture--United States--History--20th century. Mass media--United States--History--20th century. LC Classification: P94.5.A372 U57 1990 Dewey Class No.: 813.009/3520396073 20

Silk, Mark. Unsecular media: making news of religion in America / Mark Silk. Published/Created: Urbana: University of Illinois Press, c1995. Description: xiii, 181 p.; 24 cm. ISBN: 0252019040 (alk. paper) Notes: Includes index. Subjects: Journalism, Religious--United States--History--20th century. Mass media in religion--United States--History--20th century. Mass media--Religious aspects. United States--Religion--1960- Series: Public expressions of religion in America LC Classification: PN4874.S513 A3 1995 Dewey Class No.: 070.4/492 20

Silverstone, Roger. Why study the media? / Roger Silverstone. Published/Created: London; Thousand Oaks, [Calif.]: Sage, 1999. Description: x, 165 p.; 24 cm. ISBN: 0761964533 0761964541 (pbk) Notes: Includes bibliographical references (p. [155]-159) and index. Subjects: Mass media. Mass media--Study and teaching. LC Classification: P91 .S467 1999 Dewey Class No.: 302.23 21 National Bib. No.: GBA0-11596

Simmons, Philip E., 1957- Deep surfaces: mass culture & history in postmodern American fiction / Philip E. Simmons. Published/Created: Athens: University of Georgia Press, c1997. Description: 236 p.; 25 cm. ISBN: 0820318434 (alk. paper) Notes: Includes bibliographical references (p. [217]-227) and index. Subjects: American fiction--20th century--History and criticism. Postmodernism (Literature)--United States. Mass media and literature--United States--History--20th century. Literature and history--United States--History--20th century. Popular culture--United States--History--20th century. Popular culture in literature. History in literature. LC Classification: PS374.P64 S5 1997 Dewey Class No.: 813/.5409 20

Slade, Christina. The real thing: doing philosophy with media / Christina Slade. Published/Created: New York: P. Lang, 2001. Projected Pub. Date: 1111 Description: p. cm. ISBN: 0820455555 (pbk.: alk. paper) Notes: Includes bibliographical references and index. Subjects: Mass media--Philosophy. Philosophy. Series: Popular culture & everyday life; vol. 4 LC Classification: P91 .S54 2001 Dewey Class No.: 302.23/01 21

Sloop, John M., 1963- The cultural prison: discourse, prisoners, and punishment / John M. Sloop. Published/Created: Tuscaloosa: University of Alabama Press, c1996. Description: vii, 244 p.; 24 cm. ISBN: 0817308229 Notes: Includes bibliographical references (p. 221-240) and index. Subjects: Prisoners in popular culture--Mass media and criminal justice--Discourse analysis--United States. Series: Studies in rhetoric and communication LC Classification: HV9466 .S66 1996 Dewey Class No.: 365/.973 20

Sly, Lesley. The power & the passion: a guide to the Australian music industry / by Lesley Sly. Edition Information: 1st ed. Published/Created: North Sydney, NSW: Warner/Chappell Music Aust., 1993. Related Titles: Power and the passion. Description: 392 p.: ill.; 22 cm. ISBN: 1863620699 Notes: Includes bibliographical references (p. 363-373) and index. Subjects: Popular music--Vocational guidance--Music trade--Mass media--Sound recording industry--Australia. LC Classification: ML3790 .S57 1993 Dewey Class No.: 338.4/778164/0994 20

Smith McKoy, Sheila. When whites riot: writing race and violence in American and South African cultures / Sheila Smith McKoy. Published/Created: Madison: University of Wisconsin Press, c2001. Description: xii, 170 p.: ill.; 24 cm. ISBN: 0299173909 (alk. paper) Notes: Includes bibliographical references (p. 149-157) and index. Subjects: Whites--United States--History Riots--United States--History. Racism--Mass media and race relations--United States. Whites--South Africa--History Riots--South Africa--History. Racism--Mass media and race relations--South Africa. United States--South Africa--Race relations. LC Classification: E184.A1 S664 2001 Dewey Class No.: 305.8/00968 21

Smith, Erna. Transmitting race: the Los Angeles riot in television news / by Erna Smith. Published/Created: [Cambridge, Mass.]: Joan Shorenstein Barone Center--Press, Politics, and Public Policy, John F. Kennedy School of Government, Harvard University, c1994. Related Authors: Joan Shorenstein Barone Center on the Press, Politics, and Public Policy. Description: 18 p.: ill.; 28 cm. Notes: "May 1994." Includes bibliographical references (p. 17-18). Subjects: Mass media and race relations. Riots--California--Los Angeles. African Americans--California--Los Angeles. Series: Research paper (Joan Shorenstein Barone Center on the Press, Politics, and Public Policy); R-11. Variant Series: Research paper; R-11 LC Classification: IN PROCESS (UTILITY LOAD)

Smith, Joel, 1925- Unwarranted hopes and unfulfilled expectations: Canadian media policy and the CBC / Joel Smith. Published/Created: Orono, Me.: Canadian-American Center, University of Maine, c1999. Description: 63 p.; 22 cm. ISBN: 1882582284 Notes: "July 1999." Includes bibliographical references (p. 48-58). Subjects: Canadian Broadcasting Corporation. Broadcasting policy--Canada. Mass media policy--Canada. Canada--Cultural policy. Series: Canadian-American public policy, 1047-1073; no. 39. LC Classification: HE8689.9.C3 S63 1999 National Bib. No.: C00-14285-9

Søgaard, Viggo. Media in church and mission: communicating the Gospel / Viggo Søgaard. Published/Created: Pasadena, Calif.: W. Carey Library, c1993. Description: xiv, 287 p.: ill.; 23 cm. ISBN: 0878082425 (pbk.) Notes: Includes bibliographical references (p. 274-283) and index. Subjects: Communication--Religious aspects--Christianity. Mass media--Religious aspects--Christianity. LC Classification: BV4319 .S645 1993 Dewey Class No.: 254/.3 20

SPREP Regional Environmental Media Training Workshop (Apia, Western Samoa, 2-13 July 1990): report / organised by the South Pacific Regional Environment Programme (SPREP) and the South Pacific Commission (SPC) Regional Media Centre; hosted by the Environment Division, Department of Lands and Environment, Government of Western Samoa. Published/Created: Noumea, New Caledonia: The Commission, c1990. Related Authors: South Pacific Regional Environment Programme. South Pacific Commission. Regional Media Centre. Description: iii, 21 p.; 30 cm. ISBN: 9822031866 Notes: "October 1990." Subjects: Environmental education--Mass media and the environment--Oceania--Congresses. LC Classification: QH541.2 .S69 1990

Spring, Joel H. Images of American life: a history of ideological management in schools, movies, radio, and television / Joel Spring. Published/Created: Albany: State University of New York Press, c1992. Description: ix, 306 p.; 24 cm. ISBN: 0791410692 0791410706 (pbk.) Notes: Includes bibliographical references (p. 265-296) and index. Subjects: Mass media--United States--Influence. Education--Intellectual life--United States--History--20th century. Series: SUNY series, education and culture LC Classification: P92.U5 S625 1992 Dewey Class No.: 302.23/0973 20

Springer, Claudia, 1956- Electronic eros: bodies and desire in the postindustrial age / by Claudia Springer. Edition Information: 1st ed. Published/Created: Austin: University of Texas Press, 1996. Description: x, 182 p.: ill.; 23 cm. ISBN: 0292776969 (cloth: alk. paper) 0292776977 (pbk.: alk. paper) Notes: Includes bibliographical references (p. [162]-173) and index. Subjects: Mass media and technology. Cyborgs in mass media. Sex in mass media. Erotica. LC Classification: P96.T42 S67 1996 Dewey Class No.: 302.23 20

Stanovich, Keith E., 1950- How to think straight about psychology / Keith E. Stanovich. Edition Information: 5th ed. Published/Created: New York: Longman, c1998. Description: xix, 234 p.; 24 cm. ISBN: 0321012461 Notes: Includes bibliographical references (p. 209-228) and index. Subjects: Psychology--Research--Methodology. Mass media--Psychological aspects--Objectivity. LC Classification: BF76.5 .S68 1998 Dewey Class No.: 150/.7/2 21

Stanovich, Keith E., 1950- How to think straight about psychology / Keith E. Stanovich. Edition Information: 4th ed. Published/Created: New York, N.Y.: HarperCollinsCollegePublishers, c1996. Description: xiv, 224 p.; 23 cm. ISBN: 0673994392 (alk. paper) Notes: Includes bibliographical references (p. 199-217) and index. Subjects: Mass media--Psychological aspects--Objectivity. LC Classification: BF76.5 .S68 1996 Dewey Class No.: 150/.72 20

Stanovich, Keith E., 1950- How to think straight about psychology / Keith E. Stanovich. Edition Information: 3rd ed. Published/Created: [New York]: HarperCollins, c1992. Description: xv, 208 p.; 24 cm. ISBN: 0673466027 Notes: Includes bibliographical references (p. 191-203) and index. Subjects: Psychology--Research--Methodology. LC Classification: BF76.5 .S68 1992 Dewey Class No.: 150/.72 20

State of the fantastic: studies in the theory and practice of fantastic literature and film: selected essays from the Eleventh International Conference on the Fantastic in the Arts, 1990 / edited by Nicholas Ruddick. Published/Created: Westport, Conn.: Greenwood Press, 1992. Related Authors: Ruddick, Nicholas, 1952- Description: xvi, 210 p.; 25 cm. ISBN: 0313278539 (alk. paper) Notes: Includes bibliographical references and index. Subjects: Fantasy literature--History and criticism--Congresses. Fantasy in mass media--Congresses. Series: Contributions to the study of science fiction and fantasy, 0193-6875; no. 50 LC Classification: PN56.F34 I58 1990 Dewey Class No.: 809/.915 20

Stevenson, Nick. The transformation of the media: globalisation, morality, and ethics / Nicholas Stevenson. Published/Created: London; New York: Longman, 1999. Projected Pub. Date: 9907 Description: p. cm. ISBN: 0582292050 Notes: Includes bibliographical references and index. Subjects: Mass media--Moral and ethical aspects. Communication, International. Mass media and culture. LC Classification: P94 .S74 1999 Dewey Class No.: 175 21

Strinati, Dominic. An introduction to studying popular culture / Dominic Strinati. Published/Created: London; New York: Routledge, 2000. Description: xvi, 288 p.; 23 cm. ISBN: 0415157668 (alk. paper) 0415157676 (pbk.: alk. paper) Notes: Includes bibliographical references (p. 259-278) and index. Subjects: Mass media--United States. Mass media--Great Britain. Popular culture--United States. Popular culture--Great Britain. LC Classification: P92.U5 S827 2000 Dewey Class No.: 302.23/0973 21

Stuber, Robert. Smart parents, safe kids: everything you need to protect your family in the modern world / Robert Stuber and Jeff Bradley. Published/Created: Kansas City, Mo.: Andrews McMeel Pub., c1997. Related Authors: Bradley, Jeff, 1952- Description: 176 p.; 24 cm. ISBN: 0836235339 Subjects: Safety education.

Parenting. Crime prevention. Internet and children. Mass media and the family. LC Classification: HQ770.7 .S78 1997 Dewey Class No.: 649/.1 21

Sumner, David E., 1946- Graduate programs in journalism and mass communications / David E. Sumner. Edition Information: 1st ed. Published/Created: Ames, Iowa: Iowa State University Press, 1996. Description: xvi, 183 p.; 28 cm. ISBN: 0813821878 (alk. paper) Subjects: Mass media--Study and teaching (Graduate)--United States. Journalism--Study and teaching (Graduate)--United States. LC Classification: P91.5.U5 S86 1996

Sylvester, Judith L., 1952- Directing health messages toward African Americans: attitudes toward health care and the mass media / Judith L. Sylvester. Published/Created: New York: Garland Pub., 1998. Description: xv, 292 p.; 23 cm. ISBN: 0815330510 (alk. paper) Notes: Includes bibliographical references (p. 281-290) and index. Subjects: African Americans--Health and hygiene. Health attitudes--Mass media in health education--United States. African Americans--Attitudes. African Americans and mass media. Medical care--United States--Marketing. Blacks--Health Services Accessibility--United States. Marketing of Health Services--methods. Series: Health care policy in the United States LC Classification: RA448.5.N4 S95 1998 Dewey Class No.: 362.1/089/96073 21

Tassew, Admassu. Reporting a pandemic: a comparative study of AIDS news coverage in African and European prestige dailies / Admassu Tassew. Published/Created: [Göteborg]: Institutionen för journalistik och masskommunikation, Göteborgs universitet, 1995. Description: 235 p.: ill.; 23 cm. ISBN: 9188212076 Notes: Added t.p. with thesis statement inserted. Thesis (Ph. D.)--Göteborg University, Sweden, 1995. Includes bibliographical references (p. 203-225). Subjects: AIDS (Disease) in mass media. Diseases--Reporting. Series: Göteborgsstudier i journalistik och masskommunikation; 8. Variant Series: Göteborg studies in journalism and mass communication, 1101-4652; 8 LC Classification: P96.A39 T37 1995 Dewey Class No.: 070.4/493621969792 21

Taylor, Lisa, 1966- Media studies: texts, institutions, and audiences / Lisa Taylor and Andrew Willis. Published/Created: Oxford, UK; Malden, Mass.: Blackwell Publishers, 1999. Related Authors: Willis, Andrew, 1962 Nov. 17- Description: x, 262 p.: ill.; 26 cm. ISBN: 0631200266 (hc.: alk. paper) 0631200274 (pbk.: alk. paper) Notes: Includes bibliographical references (p. [242]-249) and index. Subjects: Television broadcasting. Motion pictures. Mass media. LC Classification: PN1992.5 .T28 1999 Dewey Class No.: 302.23 21

Taylor, Mark C., 1945- Imagologies: media philosophy / Mark C. Taylor, Esa Saarinen. Published/Created: London; New York, NY: Routledge, 1994. Related Authors: Saarinen, Esa, 1953- Description: 1 v. (various pagings): ill.; 25 cm. ISBN: 0415103371 041510338X (pbk.) Subjects: Mass media--Philosophy. LC Classification: P90 .T39 1994 Dewey Class No.: 302.23/01 20

Teaching mass communication: a guide to better instruction / edited by Michael D. Murray and Anthony J. Ferri. Published/Created: New York: Praeger, 1992. Related Authors: Murray, Michael D. Ferri, Anthony J. Description: vi, 269 p.; 25 cm. ISBN: 0275941566 (alk. paper) Notes: Includes bibliographical references (p. [257]-260) and index. Subjects: Mass media--Study and teaching (Higher) LC Classification: P91.3 .T44 1992 Dewey Class No.: 302.23/071/1 20

Tester, Keith, 1960- Compassion, morality, and the media / Keith Tester. Published/Created: Philadelphia: Open University, 2001. Projected Pub. Date: 0104 Description: p. cm. ISBN: 0335205143 0335205135 (pbk.) Notes: Includes bibliographical references and index. Subjects: Mass media--Moral and ethical aspects. Sympathy. Series: Issues in cultural and media studies LC Classification: P94 .T44 2001 Dewey Class No.: 175 21

The celebration of the fantastic: selected papers from the Tenth Anniversary International Conference on the Fantastic in the Arts / edited by Donald E. Morse, Marshall B. Tymn, and Csilla Bertha. Published/Created: Westport, Conn.: Greenwood Press, 1992. Related Authors: Morse, Donald E., 1936- Tymn, Marshall B., 1937- Bertha, Csilla. Description: xv, 309 p.: ill.; 25 cm. ISBN: 0313278148 (alk. paper) Notes: Conference held in 1989 in Dania, Florida. Includes bibliographical references (p. [291]-293) and index. Subjects: Fantasy fiction, English--History and criticism Congresses. Fantasy fiction, American--History and criticism Congresses. Fantasy in mass media--Congresses. Fantasy in art--Congresses. Series: Contributions to the study of science fiction and fantasy, 0193-6875; no. 49 LC Classification: PN56.F34 I58 1989 Dewey Class No.: 823/.0876609 20

The clubcultures reader: readings in popular cultural studies / edited by Steve Redhead, with Derek Wynne and Justin O'Connor; photographs by Patrick Henry. Published/Created: Oxford; Malden, MA: Blackwell, c1998. Related Authors: Redhead, Steve, 1952- Wynne, Derek. O'Connor, Justin. Description: ix, 230 p. [16] p. of plates: ill.; 23 cm. ISBN: 0631212167 (pbk.: alk. paper) Notes: Includes bibliographical references and index. Subjects: Popular music--History and criticism. Music and youth. Mass media and youth. Popular culture. LC Classification: ML3470 .C62 1998 Dewey Class No.: 306.4/84 20

The Future of Latino independent media: a NALIP sourcebook / Chon A. Noriega, editor. Published/Created: Los Angeles, CA: UCLA Chicano Studies Research Center, 2000. Projected Pub. Date: 0004 Related Authors: Noriega, Chon A., 1961- Description: p. cm. ISBN: 0895510960 (pbk.) Notes: Includes bibliographical references and index. Subjects: Hispanic Americans and mass media. Hispanic American mass media. LC Classification: P94.5.H58 F88 2000 Dewey Class No.: 302.23/089/68 21

The International world of electronic media / edited by Lynne Schafer Gross. Published/Created: New York: McGraw-Hill, c1995. Related Authors: Gross, Lynne S. Description: xi, 368 p.: ill., maps; 25 cm. ISBN: 0070251428 (acid-free paper): Notes: Includes bibliographical references and index. Subjects: Broadcasting. Mass media. LC Classification: HE8689.4 .I58 1995 Dewey Class No.: 384.54 20

The mass media and Canadian diversity / edited by Stephen E. Nancoo, Robert Sterling Nancoo. Published/Created: Mississauga: Canadian Educators' Press, 1996. Related Authors: Nancoo, Stephen E. (Stephen Emmanuel), 1939- Nancoo, Robert S., 1971- Description: 288 p.; 25 cm. ISBN: 1896191045 (pbk.) Notes: Includes bibliographical references and index. Subjects: Mass media and minorities--Canada. Ethnic mass media--Canada. Multiculturalism--Canada. Pluralism (Social sciences)--Canada. LC Classification: P94.5.M552 C26 1996 Dewey Class No.: 302.23/086/930971 21

The mass media and environmental issues / edited by Anders Hansen. Published/Created: Leicester; New York: Leicester University Press; New York: Distributed exclusively in the USA and Canada by St. Martin's Press, 1993. Related Authors: Hansen, Anders. Description: xxii, 238 p.; 24 cm. ISBN: 0718514440 Notes: Includes bibliographical references and index. Subjects: Mass media and the environment. Series: Studies in communication and society (Leicester, England) Variant Series: Studies in communication and society LC Classification: P96.E57 M37 1993 Dewey Class No.: 363.7 20

The media & morality / edited by Robert M. Baird, William E. Loges, Stuart E. Rosenbaum. Published/Created: Amherst,

N.Y.: Prometheus Books, 1999. Related Authors: Baird, Robert M., 1937- Loges, William E. Rosenbaum, Stuart E. Description: 393 p.; 23 cm. ISBN: 1573926817 (alk. paper) Notes: Includes bibliographical references. Subjects: Mass media--Moral and ethical aspects. Series: Contemporary issues (Buffalo, N.Y.) Variant Series: Contemporary issues LC Classification: P94 .M348 1999 Dewey Class No.: 175 21

The media and entertainment industries: readings in mass communications / Albert N. Greco, editor. Published/Created: Boston: Allyn and Bacon, c2000. Related Authors: Greco, Albert N. Description: viii, 279 p.: ill.; 23 cm. ISBN: 0205300103 Notes: Includes bibliographical references and index. Subjects: Mass media--United States. Series: Media economics series LC Classification: P92.U5 G74 2000 Dewey Class No.: 302.23/0973 21

The media and religion in American history / editor, Wm. David Sloan. Published/Created: Northport, AL: Vision Press, 1999. Projected Pub. Date: 9910 Related Authors: Sloan, W. David (William David), 1947- Description: p. cm. ISBN: 1885219148 Notes: Includes bibliographical references and index. Subjects: Religion and the press--United States--History. Journalism, Religious--United States--History. Mass media--United States--Religious aspects. LC Classification: PN4888.R44 M43 1999 Dewey Class No.: 070.4/49200973 21

The People's voice: local radio and television in Europe / edited by Nick Jankowski, Ole Prehn & James Stappers. Published/Created: London: J. Libbey, c1992. Related Authors: Jankowski, Nick. Prehn, Ole. Stappers, J. G., 1930- Description: x, 274 p.; 25 cm. ISBN: 0861963229 Notes: Includes bibliographical references and index. Subjects: Radio broadcasting--Europe. Television broadcasting--Europe. Local mass media--Europe. Series: Acamedia research monographs, 6 Variant Series: Acamedia research monograph, 0956-9057; 6 LC Classification: HE8689.9.E9 P46 1992 Dewey Class No.: 384.54/094 20

The Proceedings of the Media Workshop: Msimbazi Centre, Dar es Salaam, Tanzania, 24th-26th August, 1995. Published/Created: Arusha [Tanzania]: AIDS NGOS Network in East Africa, [1995?] Related Authors: AIDS NGOs Network in East Africa. Description: 87 p: ill.; 30 cm. Notes: Includes bibliographical references (p. 32). Subjects: AIDS (Disease)--Patients--Tanzania--Social conditions Congresses. HIV-positive persons--Tanzania--Social conditions Congresses. Human rights--Tanzania--Congresses. AIDS (Disease) in mass media--Congresses. LC Classification: RA643.86.T34 M43 1995

The Screen education reader: cinema, television, culture / edited by Manuel Alvarado, Edward Buscombe, and Richard Collins. Published/Created: New York: Columbia University Press, c1993. Related Authors: Alvarado, Manuel, 1948- Buscombe, Edward. Collins, Richard, 1946- Related Titles: Screen education (1974) Description: vi, 361 p.; 23 cm. ISBN: 0231081103 (cloth: acid-free): 0231081111 (pbk.): Notes: Includes bibliographical references and index. Subjects: Mass media. Mass media in education. Popular culture. LC Classification: P91 .S37 1993 Dewey Class No.: 791.45 20

The virtual and the real: media in the museum / edited by Selma Thomas and Ann Mintz. Published/Created: Washington, DC: American Association of Museums, c1998. Related Authors: Thomas, Selma. Mintz, Ann, 1947- American Association of Museums. Description: xi, 196 p.: ill.; 23 cm. ISBN: 0931201519 Notes: Includes bibliographical references and index. Subjects: Museums--Technological innovations. Mass media and technology. Multimedia systems. Information technology. LC Classification: AM7 .V57 1998 Dewey Class No.: 069 21

Thwaites, Tony. Introducing cultural and media studies: a semiotic approach / Tony Thwaites, Lloyd Davis, and Warwick Mules. Published/Created: New York: Palgrave, 2002. Projected Pub. Date: 0202 Related Authors: Davis, Lloyd, 1959- Mules, Warwick. Thwaites, Tony. Tools for cultural studies. Description: p. cm. ISBN: 0333972481 Notes: Rev. ed. of: Tools for cultural studies, Published in 1994 by Macmillan Education Australia. Includes bibliographical references and index. Subjects: Culture--Study and teaching. Semiotics. Mass media--Social aspects. LC Classification: HM623 .T59 2002 Dewey Class No.: 306/.071 21

Transgression and the cultural industry / guest convenor, Denise Robinson. Critical media: perspectives on new technologies / guest convenor Julianne Pierce. Published/Created: South Yarra: Australian Centre for Contemporary Art, 1996. Related Authors: Australian Centre for Contemporary Art. Related Titles: Critical media. Description: 115 p.; 21 cm. ISBN: 0947220534 Notes: "The Gordon Darling Foundation Seminars 1995"--T.p. Subjects: Mass media and culture--Congresses. Mass media--Technological innovations--Congresses. Mass media--Social aspects--Australia--Congresses. LC Classification: P94.6 .G67 1995 Dewey Class No.: 302.23 21

Treichler, Paula A. How to have theory in an epidemic: cultural chronicles of AIDS / Paula A. Treichler. Published/Created: Durham: Duke University Press, 1999. Description: xi, 477 p.: ill.; 23 cm. ISBN: 0822322862 (cloth: alk. paper) 0822323184 (pbk.: alk. paper) Notes: Includes bibliographical references (p. [387]-451) and index. Subjects: AIDS (Disease)--Social aspects. Culture--Philosophy. AIDS (Disease) in mass media. LC Classification: RA644.A25 T78 1999 Dewey Class No.: 362.1/969792 21

Troeger, Thomas H., 1945- Ten strategies for preaching in a multimedia culture / Thomas H. Troeger. Published/Created: Nashville: Abingdon Press, c1996. Description: 125 p.; 22 cm. ISBN: 0687007011 (pbk.: acid-free paper) Notes: Includes bibliographical references (p. 122-125). Subjects: Preaching. Mass media--Religious aspects--Christianity. LC Classification: BV4211.2 .T7655 1996 Dewey Class No.: 251/.07 20

Turner, Graeme. British cultural studies: an introduction / Graeme Turner. Published/Created: Boston: Unwin Hyman, 1990. Description: 246 p.: ill.; 23 cm. ISBN: 0044454244 0044454252 (pbk.) Notes: Includes bibliographical references (p. 231-239) and index. Subjects: Popular culture--Great Britain--History--20th century. Mass media--Great Britain--History--20th century. Series: Media and popular culture; 7 LC Classification: DA589.4 .T87 1990 Dewey Class No.: 306.4/0941 20

Turner, Patricia A. (Patricia Ann), 1955- Ceramic uncles & celluloid mammies: Black images and their influence on culture / Patricia A. Turner. Edition Information: 1st ed. Published/Created: New York: Anchor Books, c1994. Related Titles: Ceramic uncles and celluloid mammies. Description: xvi, 238 p., [16] p. of plates: ill.; 24 cm. ISBN: 0385467842: Notes: Includes bibliographical references (p. 220-229) and index.index. Subjects: African Americans in mass media. Popular culture--United States--History. Mass media--United States--History. LC Classification: P94.5.A372 U578 1994 Dewey Class No.: 302.23/089/96073 20

Twitchell, James B., 1943- Carnival culture: the trashing of taste in America / James B. Twitchell. Published/Created: New York: Columbia University Press, c1992. Description: vii, 306 p.: ill.; 24 cm. ISBN: 0231078307 (alk. paper) Notes: Includes bibliographical references (p. [275]-288) and index. Subjects: Mass media--United States. Popular culture--United States. LC Classification: P92.U5 T88 1992 Dewey Class No.: 302.23/0973 20

Tyner, Kathleen R. Literacy in a digital world: teaching and learning in the age of information / Kathleen Tyner. Published/Created: Mahwah, N.J.: Erlbaum, 1998. Description: xii, 291 p.: ill.; 24 cm. ISBN: 0805822275 (hardcover: alk. paper) 0805822283 (pbk.: alk. paper) Notes: Includes bibliographical references (p. 258-273) and indexes. Subjects: Computers and literacy. Media literacy. Mass media in education. Educational innovations. Series: LEA's communication series LC Classification: LC149.5 .T96 1998 Dewey Class No.: 302.2/244 21

Van Nostran, William. The media writer's guide: writing for business and educational programs / by William Van Nostran. Published/Created: Boston: Focal Press, c2000. Related Authors: Van Nostran, William. Scriptwriter's handbook. Description: vii, 242 p.: ill.; 28 cm. ISBN: 0240803167 (alk. paper) Notes: Rev. ed. of: The scriptwriter's handbook. 1989. Includes bibliographical references (p. 231-233) and index. Subjects: Television authorship. Industrial television--Authorship. Video recordings--Authorship. Television in education. Mass media--Authorship. Business writing. LC Classification: PN1992.7 .V36 2000 Dewey Class No.: 808.2/25 21

Veciana-Suarez, Ana. Hispanic media: impact and influence / by Ana Veciana-Suarez; with a foreword by Manuel Galvan. Published/Created: Washington, D.C.: Media Institute, c1990. Description: x, 82 p.; 28 cm. ISBN: 0937790419: Notes: Includes bibliographical references (p. 79-82). Subjects: Hispanic American mass media. LC Classification: P94.5.H58 V429 1990 Dewey Class No.: 302.23/08968073 20

Viewing, reading, listening: audiences and cultural reception / edited by Jon Cruz, Justin Lewis. Published/Created: Boulder: Westview Press, 1994. Related Authors: Cruz, Jon. Lewis, Justin, 1958- Description: xii, 275 p.: ill.; 24 cm. ISBN: 0813315379 0813315387 (pbk.) Notes: Includes bibliographical references. Subjects: Mass media--Audiences. Popular culture. Series: Cultural studies LC Classification: P96.A83 V54 1994 Dewey Class No.: 302.23 20

Violence and mediation in contemporary culture / edited by Ronald Bogue and Marcel Cornis-Pope. Published/Created: Albany: State University of New York Press, c1996. Related Authors: Bogue, Ronald, 1948- Cornis-Pope, Marcel. Description: 207 p.: ill.; 24 cm. ISBN: 0791427196 079142720X (pbk.) Notes: Includes bibliographical references and index. Subjects: Popular culture--History--20th century. Popular culture--United States--History--20th century. Violence in literature. Violence in mass media. Series: SUNY series, the margins of literature LC Classification: CB430 .V56 1996 Dewey Class No.: 306/.0973 20

Virilio, Paul. Desert screen: war at the speed of light / Paul Virilio; translated by Michael Degener. Published/Created: New York: Continuum, 2002. Projected Pub. Date: 0201 Description: p. cm. ISBN: 0826458211 082645822X (pbk.) Notes: Includes bibliographical references and index. Subjects: Operation Desert Shield, 1990-1991, in mass media. Series: Athlone contemporary European thinkers LC Classification: DS79.739 .V5713 2002 Dewey Class No.: 956.7044/2 21

Waldby, Cathy. AIDS and the body politic: biomedicine and sexual difference / Catherine Waldby. Published/Created: London; New York: Routledge, 1996. Description: xii, 169 p.: ill.; 24 cm. ISBN: 041514129X (hbk) 0415141303 (pbk) Notes: Includes bibliographical references (p. 154-165) and index. Subjects: AIDS (Disease) AIDS (Disease) in mass media. Masculinity. Acquired Immunodeficiency Syndrome. Human Body. Sex. Sociology, Medical. AIDS Prevention Series: Writing corporealities LC Classification: RC607.A26 W337 1996 Dewey Class No.: 362.1/969792 21

Walker, John Albert, 1938- Art in the age of mass media / John A. Walker. Edition Information: 3rd ed. Published/Created: London, England; Sterling, Va.: Pluto

Press, 2001. Description: viii, 216 p.: ill.; 24 cm. ISBN: 0745317456 (hbk) Notes: Includes bibliographical references (p. [181]-204) and index. Subjects: Mass media and art. Popular culture. LC Classification: N72.M28 W34 2001

Walls, Jeannette. Dish: the inside story on the world of gossip / Jeannette Walls. Edition Information: 1st ed. Published/Created: New York, N.Y.: Spike, 2000. Projected Pub. Date: 0003 Description: p. cm. ISBN: 0380978210 (hardcover) Notes: "An Avon book." Includes bibliographical references and index. Subjects: Gossip in mass media. LC Classification: P96.G65 W35 2000 Dewey Class No.: 302.23 21

Wark, McKenzie, 1961- Virtual geography: living with global media events / McKenzie Wark. Published/Created: Bloomington: Indiana University Press, c1994. Description: xvii, 252 p.: ill.; 24 cm. ISBN: 0253208947 (pbk.: alk. paper) 0253363497 (alk. paper) Notes: Includes bibliographical references (p. [229]-247) and index. Subjects: Mass media--Social aspects. Series: Arts and politics of the everyday LC Classification: HM258 .W37 1994 Dewey Class No.: 302.23 20

Watney, Simon. Policing desire: pornography, AIDS, and the media / Simon Watney. Edition Information: 3rd ed. Published/Created: Minneapolis: University of Minnesota Press, c1996. Description: xvi, 172 p.; 23 cm. ISBN: 0816630240 0816630259 (pbk.) Notes: Includes bibliographical references (p. 157-169) and index. Subjects: AIDS (Disease)--Social aspects. AIDS (Disease) in mass media. Pornography. Series: Media & society. Variant Series: Media and society LC Classification: RC607.A26 W37 1996 Dewey Class No.: 306.4/61 20

Watney, Simon. Policing desire: pornography, AIDS, and the media / Simon Watney. Edition Information: 3rd ed. Published/Created: London; Herndon, VA: Cassell, 1997. Description: xvi, 172 p.; 22 cm. ISBN: 0304337854 (pbk) Notes: Includes bibliographical references (p. 157-170) and index. Subjects: AIDS (Disease)--Social aspects. AIDS (Disease) in mass media. Pornography. LC Classification: RC607.A26 W37 1997b Dewey Class No.: 362.1/969792 21

Watson, James, 1936- A dictionary of communication and media studies / James Watson and Anne Hill. Edition Information: 3rd ed. Published/Created: London; New York: E. Arnold; New York, NY: Distributed by Routledge, Chapman, and Hall, 1993. Related Authors: Hill, Anne, 1952- Related Titles: Dictionary of communication & media studies. Description: x, 205 p.: ill.; 24 cm. ISBN: 0340574259: Notes: Spine A dictionary of communication & media studies. Subjects: Communication--Dictionaries. Mass media--Dictionaries. LC Classification: P87.5 .W38 1993 Dewey Class No.: 302.03 20

Watson, James, 1936- A dictionary of communication and media studies / James Watson, Anne Hill. Edition Information: 4th ed. Published/Created: London; New York: Arnold; New York, NY: Distributed exclusively in the USA by St. Martin's Press, 1997. Related Authors: Hill, Anne, 1952- Description: xii, 251 p.: ill.; 24 cm. ISBN: 0340676353 (pbk.) Subjects: Communication--Dictionaries. Mass media--Dictionaries. LC Classification: P87.5 .W38 1997 Dewey Class No.: 302.2/03 21

Watson, James, 1936- Dictionary of media and communication studies / James Watson and Anne Hill. Edition Information: 5th ed. Published/Created: London: Arnold; New York: Oxford University Press, 2000. Related Authors: Hill, Anne, 1952- Description: xiii, 364 p.: ill.; 24 cm. ISBN: 0340732059 Subjects: Communication--Dictionaries. Mass media--Dictionaries. Series: Arnold student reference

Weber, Samuel M. Mass mediauras: form, technics, media / Samuel Weber; edited by Alan Cholodenko. Published/Created: Stanford, Calif.: Stanford University Press, 1996. Related Authors: Cholodenko, Alan.

Description: 247 p.; 23 cm. ISBN: 0804726752 (cloth) 0804726760 (paper) Notes: Includes bibliographical references and index. Subjects: Mass media criticism. Mass media--Philosophy. LC Classification: P96.C76 W43 1996 Dewey Class No.: 302.23 20

Weimann, Gabriel, 1950- Communicating unreality: modern media and the reconstruction of reality / by Gabriel Weimann. Published/Created: Thousand Oaks, Calif.: Sage Publications, c2000. Projected Pub. Date: 9910 Description: p. cm. ISBN: 0761919856 0761919864 Notes: Includes bibliographical references (p.) and index. Subjects: Mass media--Influence. Mass media--United States. Mass media--Social aspects. Mass media--Psychological aspects. Reality. LC Classification: P94 .W45 2000 Dewey Class No.: 302.23 21

Weiner, Richard, 1927- Webster's New World dictionary of media and communications / Richard Weiner Edition Information: Rev. and updated. Published/Created: New York: Macmillan, c1996. Description: iv, 676 p.; 24 cm. ISBN: 0028606116 Subjects: Mass media--Dictionaries. Communication--Dictionaries. LC Classification: P87.5 .W45 1996 Dewey Class No.: 302.23/03 20

Weiner, Richard, 1927- Webster's New World dictionary of media and communications / Richard Weiner. Edition Information: 1st ed. Published/Created: New York: Webster's New World: Distributed by Prentice Hall Trade Sales, c1990. Related Titles: Dictionary of media and communications. Description: viii, 533 p.; 25 cm. ISBN: 0139697594: Notes: Spine Dictionary of media and communications. Subjects: Mass media--Dictionaries. Communication--Dictionaries. LC Classification: P87.5 .W45 1990 Dewey Class No.: 302.23/03 20

Wellings, Kaye. Stopping AIDS: AIDS/HIV education and the mass media in Europe / Kaye Wellings and Becky Field. Published/Created: London; New York: Longman, 1996. Related Authors: Field, Becky. Description: viii, 263 p.: ill. ISBN: 0582292271 Notes: Includes bibliographical references and index. Subjects: HIV Infections--prevention & control. Health Education--Europe. Mass Media. AIDS (Disease)--Europe--Prevention--Evaluation. HIV infections--Europe. AIDS (Disease) in mass media--Europe. LC Classification: ACQUISITION IN PROCESS (COPIED)

Whannel, Garry. Media sports stars: masculinities and moralities / Garry Whannel. Published/Created: London; New York: Routledge, 2002. Projected Pub. Date: 0112 Description: p. cm. ISBN: 0415170370 0415170389 (pbk.) Notes: Includes bibliographical references and index. Subjects: Mass media and sports. Masculinity in popular culture--Moral and ethical aspects. Athletes--Conduct of life. Celebrities. LC Classification: GV742 .W43 2002 Dewey Class No.: 796/.081 21

What's next in mass communication: readings on media and culture / [compiled by] Christopher Harper. Published/Created: New York: St. Martin's Press, c1998. Related Authors: Harper, Christopher, 1951- Description: xv, 220 p.; 23 cm. ISBN: 0312167431 Notes: Includes a short introd. to each chapter consisting of several readings; discussion questions and exercises follow each reading. Includes index. Subjects: Mass media--United States. LC Classification: P92.U5 W46 1998 Dewey Class No.: 302.23 21

Wheeler, Tom, 1960- Phototruth or photofiction?: ethics and media imagery in the digital age / Tom Wheeler. Published/Created: Mahwah, NJ: Lawrence Erlbaum Associates, 2002. Projected Pub. Date: 0204 Description: p. cm. ISBN: 0805842616 (pbk.: alk. paper) Notes: Includes bibliographical references and index. Subjects: Photojournalism--Image processing--Digital techniques--Moral and ethical aspects. Mass media criticism. LC Classification: TR820 .W4 2002 Dewey Class No.: 174/.9070 21

Whetmore, Edward Jay. Mediamerica, mediaworld: form, content, and consequence of mass communication / Edward Jay Whetmore. Edition Information: Updated 5th ed. Published/Created: Belmont [Calif.]: Wadsworth, c1995. Description: xvii, 492 p.: ill.; 24 cm. ISBN: 0534258182 Notes: Includes bibliographical references and index. Subjects: Mass media--United States. Mass media. Popular culture--United States. Series: Wadsworth series in mass communication and journalism LC Classification: P92.U5 W48 1995 Dewey Class No.: 302.23/0973 20

Whetmore, Edward Jay. Mediamerica, mediaworld: form, content, and consequence of mass communication / Edward Jay Whetmore. Edition Information: 5th ed. Published/Created: Belmont, Calif.: Wadsworth Pub. Co., c1993. Related Authors: Whetmore, Edward Jay. Mediamerica. Description: xvii, 492 p.: ill. (some col.), map; 24 cm. ISBN: 0534179347 Notes: Rev. ed. of: Mediamerica. 4th ed. c1989. Includes bibliographical references (p. 481-483) and index. Subjects: Mass media--United States. Popular culture--United States. Series: Wadsworth series in mass communication and journalism. Variant Series: Wadsworth mass communication and journalism series LC Classification: P92.U5 W48 1993 Dewey Class No.: 302.23/0973 20

Whetmore, Edward Jay. Mediamerica: form, content, and consequence of mass communication / Edward Jay Whetmore. Edition Information: Updated 4th ed. Published/Created: Belmont, Calif.: Wadsworth Pub. Co., c1991. Description: xvi, 411 p.: ill.; 24 cm. ISBN: 0534152821 Notes: Includes bibliographical references and index. Subjects: Mass media--United States. Popular culture--United States. Series: Wadsworth series in mass communication LC Classification: P92.U5 W48 1991 Dewey Class No.: 302.23/0973 20

Who's who in mass communication / edited by Sylwester Dziki, Janina Maczuga, Walery Pisarek; forewords by Walery Pisarek and Jörg Becker; database indexed by Frank-Michael Bahr. Edition Information: 2nd rev. ed. Published/Created: München; New York: K.G. Saur, 1990. Related Authors: Dziki, Sylwester. Maczuga, Janina. Pisarek, Walery. RSW Prasa. O´srodek Bada´n Prasoznawczych. International Association for Mass Communication Research. Bibliographic Section. Description: xi, 191 p.; 31 cm. ISBN: 3598108842 Notes: At head of The Press Research Centre, Cracow on behalf of the International Association for Mass Communication Research, Bibliographic Section. Includes index. Subjects: Mass media specialists--Biography--Dictionaries. LC Classification: P92.5.A1 W45 1990 Dewey Class No.: 302.23/092/2 B 20

Wild West show! / edited by Thomas W. Knowles and Joe R. Lansdale. Published/Created: New York: Wings Books; Avenel: Distributed by Random House Value Publishing, Inc., c1994. Related Authors: Henry, Will, 1912- Knowles, Thomas W. Lansdale, Joe R., 1951- Description: 240 p.: ill. (some col.), 1 map; 29 cm. ISBN: 0517101866: Notes: Includes bibliographical references. Subjects: Popular culture--West (U.S.). West (U.S.)--In literature--In art--In mass media. LC Classification: F596 .W5795 1994 Dewey Class No.: 978 20

Williams, Michael Andrew. Blacks and the media: communications research since 1978 / by Michael Andrew Williams. Published/Created: Washington, D.C. (C.B. Powell Bldg., Washington 20059): Center for Communications Research, School of Communications, Howard University, [1990] Description: 42 leaves; 28 cm. Subjccts: African Americans and mass media--Bibliography. LC Classification: Z5633.A37 W55 1990 P94.5.A37 Dewey Class No.: 016.30223/08996073 20

Willmott, Glenn, 1963- McLuhan, or modernism in reverse / Glenn Willmott. Published/Created: Toronto; Buffalo: University of Toronto Press, c1996. Description: xv, 262 p.; 24 cm. ISBN: 0802008011 0802071635 (pbk.) Notes: Includes bibliographical references (p. [245]-253) and index. Subjects: McLuhan, Marshall, 1911- Mass media--Philosophy. Mass media criticism. Modernism (Aesthetics) Postmodernism. LC Classification: P92.5.M3 W55 1996 Dewey Class No.: 302.23/01 20 National Bib. No.: C95-932946-3

Wilson, Clint C. Race, multiculturalism, and the media: from mass to class communication / Clint C. Wilson II, Félix Gutiérrez. Edition Information: 2nd ed. Published/Created: Thousand Oaks, Calif.: Sage Publications, c1995. Related Authors: Gutiérrez, Félix. Wilson, Clint C. Minorities and media. Description: xvi, 274 p.: ill.; 24 cm. ISBN: 0803946287 (c: alk. paper) 0803946295 (pbk.: alk. paper) Notes: Rev. ed. of: Minorities and media: diversity and the end of mass communication. c1985. Includes bibliographical references (p. 263-264) and index. Subjects: Mass media and minorities--United States. Multiculturalism--United States. LC Classification: P94.5.M552 U69 1995 Dewey Class No.: 305.8/00973 20

Wilson, James R. (James Ross) Mass media, mass culture: an introduction / James R. Wilson, Stan Le Roy Wilson. Edition Information: 5th ed. Published/Created: Boston: McGraw-Hill, c2001. Related Authors: Wilson, Stan Le Roy. Description: xxvii, 484 p.: ill.; 26 cm. ISBN: 0072314621 Notes: Includes bibliographical references and index. Subjects: Mass media and culture. LC Classification: P94.6 .W55 2001 Dewey Class No.: 302.23 21

Wilson, James R. (James Ross) Mass media/mass culture: and introduction. Edition Information: 4th ed. / James R. Wilson, Stan Le Roy Wilson. Published/Created: New York: McGraw-Hill, c1998. Related Authors: Wilson, Stan Le Roy. Wilson, Stan Le Roy. Mass media/mass culture. Description: xx, 458 p.: ill. (some col.); 23 cm. ISBN: 0070708282 (acid-free paper) Notes: Rev. ed. of: Mass media/mass culture / Stan Le Roy Wilson. 3rd ed. c1995. Includes bibliographical references and index. Subjects: Mass media and culture. LC Classification: P94.6 .W55 1998 Dewey Class No.: 302.23 21

Wilson, Stan Le Roy. Mass media/mass culture: an introduction / Stan Le Roy Wilson. Edition Information: 3rd ed. Published/Created: New York: McGraw-Hill, c1995. Description: xvii, 428 p.: ill. (some col.); 24 cm. ISBN: 0070708266: Notes: Includes bibliographical references and index. Subjects: Mass media and culture. Series: McGraw-Hill series in mass communication LC Classification: P94.6 .W55 1995 Dewey Class No.: 302.23 20

Wilson, Stan Le Roy. Mass media/mass culture: an introduction / Stan Le Roy Wilson. Edition Information: Updated 1993 ed. Published/Created: New York: McGraw-Hill, c1993. Description: xvii, 460 p., [8] p. of plates: ill. (some col.); 24 cm. ISBN: 0070708215 Notes: Includes bibliographical references and index. Subjects: Mass media. Communication and culture. Series: McGraw-Hill series in mass communication LC Classification: P90 .W494 1993 Dewey Class No.: 302.23 20

Wilson, Stan Le Roy. Mass media/mass culture: an introduction / Stan Le Roy Wilson. Edition Information: 2nd ed. Published/Created: New York: McGraw-Hill, Inc., c1992. Description: xvii, 460 p.: ill. (some col.); 24 cm. ISBN: 0070708169 Notes: Includes bibliographical references and index. Subjects: Mass media. Communication and culture. Series: McGraw-Hill series in mass communication LC Classification: P90 .W494 1992 Dewey Class No.: 302.23 20

Women in media education: final report on ACCE/FES/WACC Workshop, Harare, Zimbabwe, 4-7 November, 1991 / prepared by S.T. Kwame Boafo & Esther Adagala. Published/Created: Nairobi, Kenya: ACCE, [1991?] Related Authors: Boafo, S. T. Kwame. Adagala, Esther. African Council on Communication Education. Friedrich-Ebert-Stiftung. World Association for Christian Communication. Description: 17 p.; 30 cm. Subjects: Mass media--Study and teaching (Higher)-- Africa Congresses. Mass media and women--Africa--Congresses. LC Classification: P91.5.A35 A25 1991

Wong, Kokkeong. Media and culture in Singapore: a theory of controlled commodification / Kokkeong Wong. Published/Created: Cresskill, NJ: Hampton Press, c2001. Description: x, 159 p.: 1 ill.; 24 cm. ISBN: 157273311X 1572733128 Notes: Includes bibliographical references (p. 139-147) and indexes. Subjects: Mass media policy--Singapore. Mass media-- Government ownership--Singapore. Commodity control--Singapore. Mass media and culture--Singapore. Information services industry--Government policy Singapore. Popular culture--Political aspects--Singapore. Series: The Hampton Press communication series LC Classification: P95.82.S55 W66 2001 Dewey Class No.: 302.23/095957 21

Writer's encyclopedia / from the editors of Writer's digest. Edition Information: 3rd ed. Published/Created: Cincinnati, Ohio: Writer's Digest Books, c1996. Related Titles: Writer's digest. Writing, A to Z. Description: 499 p.; 24 cm. ISBN: 0898797497 (alk. paper) Notes: Rev. ed. of: Writing, A to Z. 1990. Includes bibliographical references (p. [495]-499). Subjects: Authorship--Dictionaries. Mass media--Dictionaries. LC Classification: PN141 .W72 1996 Dewey Class No.: 808/.02/03 20

Writing, A to Z: the terms, procedures, and facts of the writing business defined, explained, and put within reach / edited by Kirk Polking, Joan Bloss, and Colleen Cannon; assistant editor, Debbie Cinnamon. Edition Information: 1st ed. Published/Created: Cincinnati, Ohio: Writer's Digest Books, c1990. Related Authors: Polking, Kirk. Bloss, Joan. Cannon, Colleen. Cinnamon, Debbie, 1952- Related Titles: Writer's encyclopedia. Description: 539, [6] p.: ill.; 24 cm. ISBN: 0898794358 (alk. paper): Notes: Rev. ed. of: Writer's encyclopedia. c1983. Includes bibliographical references (p. [540]-[546]). Subjects: Authorship-- Vocational guidance--Dictionaries. Mass media--Dictionaries. LC Classification: PN141 .W75 1990 Dewey Class No.: 808/.02/03 20

Young, T. R. The drama of social life: essays in post-modern social psychology / T.R. Young. Published/Created: New Brunswick, U.S.A.: Transaction Publishers, c1990. Description: xiii, 367 p.; 24 cm. ISBN: 0887382029 Notes: Includes index. Bibliography: p. 357-363. Subjects: Social interaction. Social psychology. Drama--Psychological aspects. Mass media--Social aspects. Interpersonal Relations. Psychology, Social. LC Classification: HM291 .Y68 1990 Dewey Class No.: 302 20

Politics and Mass Media

A richer vision: the development of ethnic minority media in western democracies / edited by Charles Husband. Published/Created: Paris, France: Unesco Pub.; London, England: J. Libbey, 1994. Related Authors: Husband, Charles. Description: x, 149 p.; 25 cm. ISBN: 0861964500 (pbk) 923102941X (Unesco) Notes: Includes bibliographies. Subjects: Mass media and minorities. Ethnic mass media. Mass media policy. Multiculturalism. Mass media Role of Ethnic groups Series: Communication and development series LC Classification: P96.M5 R53 1994 Dewey Class No.: 302.2308693 20 National Bib. No.: GB94-39805

AbulJobain, Ahmad. Radical Islamic terrorism or political Islam? / Ahmad AbulJobain. Published/Created: Annandale, VA, USA: United Association for Studies and Research, 1993. Related Authors: United Association for Studies and Research (Annandale, Va.) Description: 43 p.; 23 cm. Notes: Includes bibliographical references. Subjects: Islam--Public opinion. Public opinion--United States. Islam in mass media. Series: Islam under siege. Occasional papers series (United Association for Studies and Research (Annandale, Va.)); no. 1. Variant Series: Islam under siege = [Wa-bashshir al-s¯abir¯in] Occasional papers series; no. 1 LC Classification: BP67.U6 A28 1993 Dewey Class No.: 320.5/5/0917671 20

Akins, Ellen. Public life / Ellen Akins. Edition Information: 1st ed. Published/Created: New York, NY: HarperCollins, c1993. Description: 280 p.; 22 cm. ISBN: 006016753X (cloth): Subjects: Presidents--Election--Fiction. Mass media--Political aspects--Fiction. Political campaigns--Fiction. Genre/Form: Political fiction. LC Classification: PS3551.K54 P83 1993 Dewey Class No.: 813/.54 20

Arabi Idid, Syed. Malaysia's general election 1995: people, issues, and media use / by Syed Arabi Idid & Mazni Buyong. Published/Created: Bangi: Jabatan Komunikasi, Universiti Kebangsaan Malaysia & Asia Foundation, Kuala Lumpur, 1995. Related Authors: Mazni Buyong. Universiti Kebangsaan Malaysia. Jabatan Komunikasi. Asia Foundation. Description: xi, 121 p.: ill.; 23 cm. ISBN: 9839152181 Notes: Includes bibliographical references (p. 111-121). Subjects: Elections--Malaysia. Mass media--Political aspects--Malaysia. Malaysia--Politics and government. LC Classification: JQ1062.A95 A728 1995

Bain, George, 1920- Gotcha!: how the media distort the news / George Bain. Published/Created: Toronto, Ont., Canada: Key Porter, c1994. Description: xi, 266 p.; 24 cm. ISBN: 1550135554 1550136011 (pbk.) Notes: Includes index. Subjects: Journalism--Political aspects--Canada. Government and the press--Canada. Reporters and reporting--Canada. Mass media--Canada--Influence. LC Classification: PN4914.P6 B35 1994 Dewey Class No.: 071/.1 20

Bateman, Robert L. No Gun Ri: a military history of the Korean War incident / Robert L. Bateman. Published/Created: Mechanicsburg, PA: Stackpole Books, c2002. Projected Pub. Date: 0204 Description: p.; cm. ISBN: 0811717631 (alk. paper) Notes: Includes bibliographical references and index. Subjects: United States. Army. Cavalry, 7th. Korean War, 1950-1953--Atrocities. Massacres--Korea (South)--Nogun-ni. Korean War, 1950-1953--Campaigns--Korea (South)--Nogun-ni. Korean War, 1950-1953--United States. Korean War, 1950-1953--Mass media and the war. Nogun-ni (Korea)--History. LC Classification: DS920.8 .B27 2002 Dewey Class No.: 951.904/242 21

Bennett, James R., 1932- Control of the media in the United States: an annotated bibliography / James R. Bennett. Published/Created: New York: Garland, 1992. Description: xxviii, 819 p.; 23 cm. ISBN: 082404438X (alk. paper) Notes: Includes indexes. Subjects: Mass media--Censorship--United States--Bibliography. Communication policy--United States--Bibliography. Series: Garland reference library of social science; v. 456. Variant Series: Garland reference library of social science; vol. 456 LC Classification: Z5634.U6 B46 1992 P96.C4 Dewey Class No.: 016.3633/1/0973 20

Berryhill, Dale A. The media hates conservatives: how it controls the flow of information / by Dale A. Berryhill. Published/Created: Lafayette, La.: Huntington House Publishers, c1994. Description: 224 p.; 22 cm. ISBN: 156384060X Subjects: Mass media--Political aspects--United States. Mass media--United States--Influence. Political campaigns--United States. United States--Politics and government--1989-1993. LC Classification: P95.82.U6 B476 1994

Beschloss, Michael R. Presidents, television, and foreign crises / by Michael R. Beschloss. Published/Created: Washington, DC: Annenberg Washington Program, Communications Policy Studies, Northwestern University, c1993. Related Authors: Northwestern University (Evanston, Ill.). Annenberg Washington Program in Communications Policy Studies. Description: 34 p.: ill.; 28 cm. Notes: Includes bibliographical references. Subjects: Television in politics--United States. Mass media--Political aspects--United States. Presidents--United States--Decision making. LC Classification: HE8700.76.U6 B47 1993

Bhaskara Rao, N., 1940- Social effects of mass media in India / N. Bhaskara Rao, G.N.S. Raghavan. Published/Created: New Delhi: Gyan Pub. House, 1996. Related Authors: Raghavan, G. N. S. Description: xi, 315 p.; 22 cm. ISBN: 8121205212 Notes: Includes index. Subjects: Mass media--Political aspects--India. Mass media--Social aspects--India. Public television--India. 92-13 LC Classification: HM259 .B46 1996 Dewey Class No.: 302.23/0954 21

Blumler, Jay G. The crisis of public communication / Jay G. Blumler and Michael Gurevitch. Published/Created: London; New York: Routledge, 1995. Related Authors: Gurevitch, Michael. Description: vi, 237 p.; 24 cm. ISBN: 0415108519 (alk. paper) 0415108527 (pbk.: alk. paper) Notes: Includes bibliographical references (p. [227]-234) and index. Subjects: Mass media--Political aspects. Television in politics--Great Britain. Press and politics. Series: Communication and society (Routledge (Firm)) Variant Series: Communication and society LC Classification: P95.8 .B58 1995 Dewey Class No.: 302.23/0941 20

Borthakur, B. N., 1948- Communication and village development: a study of two villages in Assam / B.N. Borthakur. Published/Created: Calcutta: Institute of Social Research & Applied Anthropology, 1994. Description: ix, 227 p.; 22 cm. Notes: Includes bibliographical references (p. [203]-207) and index. Subjects: Mass media--Social aspects--India--Dinjoy. Mass media--Social aspects--India--Dhemagorh. Mass media--Political aspects--India--Dinjoy. Mass media--Political aspects--India--Dhemagorh. LC

Classification: HN690.Z9 M314 1994 Dewey Class No.: 302.23/0954162 20

Bosnia by television / edited by James Gow, Richard Paterson, Alison Preston. Published/Created: London: British Film Institute, 1996. Related Authors: Gow, James. Paterson, Richard, 1947- Preston, Alison. British Film Institute. Description: ix, 181 p.: ill., map; 23 cm. ISBN: 0851706126 Notes: Includes bibliographical references and index. Subjects: Yugoslav War, 1991-1995--Press coverage. Yugoslav War, 1991-1995--Foreign public opinion. Yugoslav War, 1991-1995--Mass media and the war. War in mass media. Yugoslav War, 1991-1995--Bosnia and Hercegovina. Television broadcasting of news--Bosnia and Hercegovina. Yugoslavia--History--1992- Bosnia and Hercegovina--History--1992- LC Classification: DR1313.7.P73 B67 1996 Dewey Class No.: 949.703 21

Botswana's media and democracy: selected papers from the Seminar on the Media in a Democracy / Methaetsile Leepile, ed. Published/Created: Gaborone, Botswana: Mmegi Pub. House, 1996. Related Authors: Leepile, Methaetsile. Mmegi Publishing Trust. Description: viii, 128 p.: ill.; 21 cm. ISBN: 9991291709 Notes: "... organised by Mmegi Publishing Trust ..."--P. [4] of cover. Includes bibliographical references. Subjects: Mass media--Democracy--Botswana--Congresses. LC Classification: P92.B67 S46 1994 Dewey Class No.: 302.23/096683 21

Brasch, Walter M., 1945- Social foundations of the mass media / Walter M. Brasch, Dana R. Ulloth. Published/Created: Lanham, MD: University Press of America, 2001. Projected Pub. Date: 0101 Related Authors: Ulloth, Dana Royal. Description: p. cm. ISBN: 0761819169 (pbk.: alk. paper) Notes: Includes bibliographical references and index. Subjects: Mass media--Censorship--History. Freedom of speech--Government and the press--History. LC Classification: P96.C4 B7 2001 Dewey Class No.: 323.44/3 21

Bryant, Jennings. Fundamentals of media effects / Jennings Bryant, Susan Thompson. Published/Created: Boston, Mass.: McGraw-Hill, 2002. Projected Pub. Date: 1111 Related Authors: Thompson, Susan, 1957- Description: p. cm. ISBN: 0072435763 (alk. paper) Notes: Includes index. Subjects: Mass media--United States--Psychological aspects. Mass media--Social aspects--United States. Mass media--Political aspects--United States. Mass media--United States--Influence. Series: McGraw-Hill series in mass communication and journalism LC Classification: HN90.M3 B79 2002 Dewey Class No.: 302.23 21

Building the institutions of freedom: report of the International Council Conference III, Washington, D.C., May 1-4, 1990. Published/Created: [Washington, D.C.]: United States Information Agency, [1990] Related Authors: United States Information Agency. Description: 152 p.: ill.; 23 cm. Subjects: World politics--1985-1995--Congresses. Mass media--Political aspects--Congresses. LC Classification: D849 .I5425 1990

Byrnes, Mark Eaton. Politics and space: image making by NASA / Mark E. Byrnes. Published/Created: Westport, Conn.: Praeger, 1994. Description: 212 p.: ill.; 25 cm. ISBN: 0275949508 (alk. paper) Notes: Includes bibliographical references (p. [187]-206) and index. Subjects: United States. National Aeronautics and Space Administration--Public opinion. Mass media--United States--Influence. Astronautics--United States--Public opinion. United States--Politics and government. LC Classification: TL521.312 .B95 1994 Dewey Class No.: 353.0087/8 20

Carruthers, Susan L. (Susan Lisa) The media at war: communication and conflict in the twentieth century / Susan L. Carruthers. Published/Created: New York: St. Martin's Press, 1999. Projected Pub. Date: 9910 Description: p. cm. ISBN: 0312228007 0312228015 (pbk.) Notes: Includes bibliographical references (p.) and index

Subjects: Mass media and war. LC Classification: P96.W35 C37 1999 Dewey Class No.: 070.4/4935502 21

Cavanaugh, John William. Media effects on voters: a panel study of the 1992 presidential election / John William Cavanaugh. Published/Created: Lanham: University Press of America, c1995. Description: xii, 182 p.: ill.; 23 cm. ISBN: 0819199427 (cloth: alk. paper) Notes: Includes bibliographical references (p. [169]-177) and index. Subjects: Presidents--United States--Election--1992. Mass media--Political aspects--United States. Communication in politics--United States. Advertising, Political--United States. LC Classification: JK526 1992n Dewey Class No.: 324.973/0928 20

Chalaby, Jean K. The de Gaulle presidency and the media: statism and public communications / Jean K. Chalaby. Published/Created: New York: Palgrave, 2002. Projected Pub. Date: 0204 Description: p. cm. ISBN: 0333751388 Notes: Includes bibliographical references and index. Subjects: Gaulle, Charles de, 1890-1970 --Views on mass media. Mass media policy--France--History--20th century. Government publicity--France. Press and politics--France. France--Politics and government--1958-1969. Series: French politics, society, and culture series. Variant Series: French politics, society and culture LC Classification: DC420 .C4238 2002 Dewey Class No.: 944.083/6/092 B 21

Chelkowski, Peter J. Staging a revolution: the art of persuasion in the Islamic Republic of Iran / Peter Chelkowski, Hamid Dabashi. Published/Created: London: Booth-Clibborn Editions, 2000. Related Authors: Dabashi, Hamid, 1951- Description: 312 p.: ill. (chiefly col.); 29 cm. ISBN: 1873968272 Notes: Includes bibliographical references and index. Subjects: Iran-Iraq War, 1980-1988--Propaganda. Mass media--Political aspects--Semiotics--Religious aspects--Political culture--Iran. Political psychology. Propaganda, Iranian. Iran--History--Revolution, 1979--Propaganda. LC Classification: DS318.825 .C44 2000 Dewey Class No.: 955.05/42 21

China's media, media's China / edited by Chin-Chuan Lee. Published/Created: Boulder, Colo.: Westview Press, 1994. Related Authors: Li, Chin-ch`üan, 1946- Description: ix, 340 p.; 23 cm. ISBN: 0813388007 (alk. paper) Notes: Includes bibliographical references and index. Subjects: Mass media--Political aspects--China. Mass media policy--China. Foreign correspondents--China. Foreign correspondents--United States. LC Classification: P95.82.C6 C45 1994 Dewey Class No.: 302.23/0951 20

Chomsky, Noam. Media control: the spectacular achievements of propaganda / Noam Chomsky. Edition Information: 1st ed. Published/Created: New York: Seven Stories Press, c1997. Description: 58 p.; 17 cm. ISBN: 1888363495 Subjects: Propaganda. Propaganda--United States. Mass media--Political aspects. Mass media and public opinion. Series: The open media pamphlet series; 2 LC Classification: HM263 .C447 1997 Dewey Class No.: 303.3/75 21

Cole, Bernadette. Mass media, freedom, and democracy in Sierra Leone / Bernadette Cole. Published/Created: [Freetown, Sierra Leone]: Premier Pub. House, [c1995] Description: iii, 83 p.; 22 cm. Notes: Includes bibliographical references (p. 78-83). Subjects: Democracy--Mass media--Political aspects--Sierra Leone--Politics and government. LC Classification: P95.82.S5 C65 1995 Dewey Class No.: 302.23/09664 21

Coles, Robert. Doing documentary work / Robert Coles. Published/Created: New York: New York Public Library: Oxford University Press, 1997. Description: 278 p.: ill.; 22 cm. ISBN: 0195116291 (acid-free) Notes: Based on a series of lectures. Includes index. Subjects: Documentary mass media. LC Classification: P96.D62 C65 1997 Dewey Class No.: 070.1 21

Combelles-Siegel, Pascale. Target Bosnia: integrating information activities in peace operations: NATO-led operations in Bosnia-Herzegovina, December 1995-1997 / Pascale Combelles Siegel. Published/Created: Washington, DC: National Defense University, 1998. Description: 199 p.: map; 23 cm. ISBN: 1579060080 Notes: Includes bibliographical references (p. 193-198). Subjects: North Atlantic Treaty Organization. Yugoslav War, 1991-1995--Press coverage. Yugoslav War, 1991-1995--Mass media and the war. Yugoslav War, 1991-1995--Propaganda. Yugoslav War, 1991-1995--Bosnia and Hercegovina. LC Classification: DR1313.7.P73 C66 1998 Dewey Class No.: 949.703 21

Combelles-Siegel, Pascale. The troubled path to the Pentagon's rules on media access to the battlefield: Grenada to today / Pascale Combelles-Siegel. Published/Created: [Carlisle Barracks, PA]: Strategic Studies Institute, U.S. Army War College, 1996. Related Authors: Army War College (U.S.). Strategic Studies Institute. Description: vi, 53 p.; 23 cm. Notes: "May 15, 1996" Includes bibliographical references (p. 42-53). Subjects: War in the press--Government policy--United States. Armed Forces and mass media--United States. Persian Gulf War, 1991--Press coverage. Grenada--History--American invasion, 1983--Press coverage. LC Classification: P96.A752 U54 1996 Dewey Class No.: 070.4/4935502 21

Committee to Protect Journalists. Bouch pe: the crackdown on Haiti's media since the overthrow of Aristide / written by Kim Brice; edited by Greg Victor. Published/Created: New York, NY: Committee to Protect Journalists, [1992] Related Authors: Brice, Kim. Victor, Greg. Related Titles: Crackdown on Haiti's media since the overthrow of Aristide. Description: 63 leaves; 29 cm. ISBN: 0944823092 Notes: Report of a fact-finding mission sent to Haiti in May 1992. Subjects: Government and the press--Haiti. Freedom of the press--Haiti--History--20th century. Journalists--Crimes against--Haiti. Foreign correspondents--Haiti--Crimes against. Censorship--Mass media--Haiti--History--20th century. Haiti--Politics and government--1986- LC Classification: PN4748.H3 C66 1992 Dewey Class No.: 079/.7294/09048 20

Committee to Protect Journalists. Bouch pe: the crackdown on Haiti's media since the overthrow of Aristide / written by Kim Brice; edited by Greg Victor. Published/Created: New York, NY: Committee to Protect Journalists, [1992] Related Authors: Brice, Kim. Victor, Greg. Related Titles: Crackdown on Haiti's media since the overthrow of Aristide. Description: 63 leaves; 29 cm. ISBN: 0944823092 Notes: Report of a fact-finding mission sent to Haiti in May 1992. Subjects: Government and the press--Haiti. Freedom of the press--Haiti--History--20th century. Journalists--Crimes against--Haiti. Foreign correspondents--Haiti--Crimes against. Censorship--Haiti--History--20th century. Mass media--Haiti--History--20th century. Haiti--Politics and government--1986- LC Classification: PN4748.H3 C66 1992 Dewey Class No.: 079/.7294/09048 20

Communicating democracy: the media and political transitions / edited by Patrick H. O'Neil. Published/Created: Boulder: Lynne Rienner, 1998. Related Authors: O'Neil, Patrick H., 1966- Description: vi, 225 p.; 24 cm. ISBN: 1555876692 (hardcover: alk. paper) Notes: Includes bibliographical references (p. 209-213) and index. Subjects: Communication in politics. Mass media--Political aspects. Democracy. LC Classification: JA85 .C66 1998 Dewey Class No.: 302.23 21

Communication and democracy: exploring the intellectual frontiers in agenda-setting theory / edited by Maxwell McCombs, Donald L. Shaw, David Weaver. Published/Created: Mahwah, NJ: Lawrence Erlbaum Associates, 1997. Related Authors: McCombs, Maxwell E. Shaw, Donald Lewis. Weaver, David H. (David Hugh), 1946- Description: xiii, 272 p.: ill.; 24 cm. ISBN: 0805825541 (c: alk. paper)

080582555X (p: alk. paper) Notes: Includes bibliographical references (p. 231-253) and index. Subjects: Mass media--Political aspects. Press and politics. Mass media and public opinion. LC Classification: P95.8 .C559 1997 Dewey Class No.: 302.23 21

Communication in Eastern Europe: the role of history, culture, and media in contemporary conflicts /edited by Fred L. Casmir. Published/Created: Mahwah, N.J.: Erlbaum, c1995. Related Authors: Casmir, Fred L., 1928- Description: xii, 350 p.; 24 cm. ISBN: 0805816259 (lib. bdg.: alk. paper) Notes: Includes bibliographical references and indexes. Subjects: Mass media--Communication--Political aspects--Communication policy--Europe, Eastern. Europe, Eastern--Politics and government--1989- Series: LEA's communication series LC Classification: HN380.7.Z9 M365 1995 Dewey Class No.: 302.23/0947 20

Conner, Judson, 1925- Meeting the press: a media survival guide for the defense manager / by Judson Conner. Published/Created: Washington, DC (Fort Lesley J. McNair, Washington DC 20319-6000): National Defense University: For sale by U.S. G.P.O., 1993. Description: xii, 103 p.: ill.; 21 cm. ISBN: 0160404789 Subjects: Government and the press--United States. Armed forces and mass media--United States. United States--Armed Forces--Public relations. LC Classification: UH703 .C66 1993 Dewey Class No.: 355.3/42/0973 20

Converging media? Converging regulation? / edited by Richard Collins. Published/Created: London: Institute for Public Policy Research, IPPR, c1996. Related Authors: Collins, Richard, 1946- Description: 70 p.: ill.; 22 cm. ISBN: 186030026X Notes: Includes bibliographical references. Subjects: Mass media policy--Communication policy--Great Britain. Series: Media (London, England) Variant Series: Media LC Classification: P95.82.G7 C66 1996 Dewey Class No.: 302.23/0941 21

Creating a free press in Eastern Europe / Al Hester & Kristina White, eds.; The James M. Cox, Jr., Center for International Mass Communication Training and Research, The Henry W. Grady College of Journalism and Mass Communication, The University of Georgia, Athens, Georgia, U.S.A. Published/Created: Athens, Ga.: University of Georgia, c1993. Related Authors: Hester, Albert L., 1932- White, Kristina, 1952- James M. Cox, Jr., Center for International Mass Communication Training and Research. Description: xiii, 487 p.: ill.; 22 cm. ISBN: 0943089042: Notes: Includes bibliographical references. Subjects: Freedom of the press--Europe, Eastern. Journalism--Europe, Eastern. Mass media--Europe, Eastern. LC Classification: Z658.E852 C74 1993 Dewey Class No.: 323.44/5 20

Crocombe, R. G. The Pacific Islands and the USA / Ron Crocombe. Published/Created: Rarotonga [Fiji]: Institute of Pacific Studies, University of the South Pacific; Honolulu: Pacific Islands Development Program, East-West Center, 1995. Description: xxx, 418: ill., maps; 21 cm. ISBN: 9820201160 Notes: Includes bibliographical references (p. 381-401) and index. Subjects: Economic assistance, American--Oceania. Education and state--Oceania. Mass media--Oceania. Oceania--Foreign economic relations--United States. United States--Foreign economic relations--Oceania. Oceania--Emigration and immigration. Oceania--Foreign relations--United States. United States--Foreign relations--Oceania. LC Classification: HF1642.55.Z4 U635 1995

Crosstalk: citizens, candidates, and the media in a presidential campaign / Marion R. Just ... [et al.]. Published/Created: Chicago: The University of Chicago Press, c1996. Related Authors: Just, Marion R. Description: xiv, 307 p.: ill.; 24 cm. ISBN: 0226420205 (cloth) 0226420213 (paper) Notes: Includes bibliographical references (p. 279-291) and indexes. Subjects: Presidents--United States--Election--1992. Political campaigns--United States. Voting--United States. Mass media--

Political aspects--United States. Mass media and public opinion--United States. Series: American politics and political economy LC Classification: JK526 1992o Dewey Class No.: 324.9730928 20

Croteau, David. By invitation only: how the media limit political debate / David Croteau and William Hoynes. Published/Created: Monroe, ME: Common Courage, c1994. Related Authors: Hoynes, William. Description: 218 p.: ill.; 20 cm. ISBN: 1567510450: 1567510442 (pbk.): Notes: Includes bibliographical references (p. 197-207) and index. Subjects: Mass media--Political aspects--United States. Television and politics--United States. United States--Politics and government--1989-1993. LC Classification: P95.82.U6 C76 1994 Dewey Class No.: 302.23/0973 20

Croteau, David. Media/society: industries, images, and audiences / David Croteau, William Hoynes. Edition Information: 2nd ed. Published/Created: Thousand Oaks, Calif.: Pine Forge Press, c2000. Related Authors: Hoynes, William. Description: xx, 399 p.: ill.; 25 cm. ISBN: 0761986847 (cloth: acid-free paper) 0761986375 (pbk.: acid-free paper) Notes: Includes bibliographical references (p. 371-383) and index. Subjects: Mass media--Social aspects--United States. Mass media--Political aspects--United States. LC Classification: HN90.M3 C76 2000 Dewey Class No.: 302.23 21

Croteau, David. Media/society: industries, images, and audiences / David Croteau, William Hoynes. Published/Created: Thousand Oaks, Calif.: Pine Forge Press, c1997. Related Authors: Hoynes, William. Description: xix, 344 p.: ill.; 24 cm. ISBN: 0803990650 (acid-free paper) Notes: Includes bibliographical references (p. 321-331) and index. Subjects: Mass media--Social aspects--United States. Mass media--Political aspects--United States. LC Classification: HN90.M3 C76 1997 Dewey Class No.: 302.23 21

Curry, Jane Leftwich, 1948- Poland's journalists: professionalism and politics / Jane Lefwich Curry. Published/Created: Cambridge; New York: Cambridge University Press, 1990. Description: x, 302 p.; 24 cm. ISBN: 0521362016 Notes: Includes index. Bibliography: p. 289-293. Subjects: Journalists--Poland--Biography. Journalism--Political aspects--Poland. Journalism--Social aspects--Poland. Journalistic ethics--Poland. Mass media--Political aspects--Poland. Series: Soviet and East European studies; 66 LC Classification: PN5355.P6 C8 1990 Dewey Class No.: 070.92/2438 B 20

Davies, Matt, 1960- International political economy and mass communication in Chile: national intellectuals and transnationsl hegemony / Matt Davies. Published/Created: New York: St. Martin's Press, 1999. Description: xvii, 206 p.: map; 22 cm. ISBN: 0312220014 (cloth) Notes: Includes bibliographical references (p. 169-199) and index. Subjects: Mass media--Research--Chile--History. Mass media--Political aspects--Chile. Communication--International cooperation. Communication and culture. Series: International political economy series LC Classification: P91.5.C5 D38 1999 Dewey Class No.: 302.23/0983 21

Davis, Richard, 1955- New media and American politics / Richard Davis, Diana Owen. Published/Created: New York: Oxford University Press, 1998. Related Authors: Owen, Diana Marie. Description: ix, 304 p.; 24 cm. ISBN: 0195120604 (alk. paper) 0195120612 (pbk.: alk. paper) Notes: Includes bibliographical references (p. 263-295) and index. Subjects: Mass media--Political aspects--United States. Mass media--Technological innovations. United States--Politics and government--1993-2001. LC Classification: P95.82.U6 D38 1998 Dewey Class No.: 302.23/0973 21

Davis, Richard, 1955- The press and American politics: the new mediator / Richard Davis. Edition Information: 2nd ed. Published/Created: Upper Saddle River,

N.J.: Prentice Hall, c1996. Description: xxv, 357 p.: ill., maps; 24 cm. ISBN: 0131859439 Notes: Includes bibliographical references and index. Subjects: Press and politics--United States. Mass media--Political aspects--United States. United States--Politics and government--1989- LC Classification: PN4888.P6 D37 1996 Dewey Class No.: 071/.3 20

Davis, Richard, 1955- The press and American politics: the new mediator / Ricahrd Davis. Edition Information: 3rd ed. Published/Created: Upper Saddle River, NJ: Prentice Hall, c2001 Description: x, 358 p.; 24 cm. ISBN: 0130264040 Notes: Includes bibliographical references and index. Subjects: Press and politics--United States. Mass media--Political aspects--United States. United States--Politics and government--1989- LC Classification: PN4888.P6 D37 2001 Dewey Class No.: 071/.3 21

Day, Holliday T. Power: its myths and mores in American art, 1961-1991 / Holliday T. Day; with essays by Brian Wallis, Anna C. Chave, and George E. Marcus; artists' profiles by Catsou Roberts, and a photographic essay by Christopher Scoates and Debra Wilbur. Published/Created: Indianapolis, Ind.: Indianapolis Museum of Art in cooperation with Indiana University Press, c1991. Related Authors: Indianapolis Museum of Art. Akron Art Museum. Virginia Museum of Fine Arts. Description: 159 p.: ill. (some col.); 29 cm. ISBN: 0253316588 0936260572 (pbk.) Notes: Catalog of an exhibition held at the Indianapolis Museum of Art, September 5-November 3, 1991, Akron Art Museum, January 18-March 21, 1992, and the Virginia Museum fo Fine Arts, May 11-July 12, 1992. Includes bibliographical references and index. Subjects: Art, American--20th century--Exhibitions. Art--Political aspects--Art and society--Mass media and art--United States--Exhibitions. LC Classification: N72.P6 D38 1991 Dewey Class No.: 709/.73/07477252 20

Dearing, James W. Agenda-setting / James W. Dearing, Everett M. Rogers. Published/Created: Thousand Oaks, Calif.: Sage, c1996. Related Authors: Rogers, Everett M. Description: x, 139 p.: ill.; 22 cm. ISBN: 0761905626 (cloth) 0761905634 (pap.) Notes: Includes bibliographical references (p. 101-128) and indexes. Subjects: Mass media and public opinion--United States. Mass media--Political aspects--United States. Mass media--United States--Influence. Mass media--Social aspects--United States. Public opinion--United States. Political planning--United States. Series: Communication concepts; 6 LC Classification: P96.P832 U636 1996 Dewey Class No.: 302.23/0973 21

Dearing, James W. Agenda-setting / James W. Dearing, Everett M. Rogers. Published/Created: Thousand Oaks, Calif.: Sage, c1996. Related Authors: Rogers, Everett M. Description: x, 139 p.: ill.; 22 cm. ISBN: 0761905626 (cloth) 0761905634 (pap.) Notes: Includes bibliographical references (p. 101-128) and indexes. Subjects: Mass media and public opinion--United States. Mass media--Political aspects--United States. Mass media--United States--Influence. Mass media--Social aspects--United States. Public opinion--United States. Political planning--United States. Series: Communication concepts; 6 LC Classification: P96.P832 U636 1996 Dewey Class No.: 302.23/0973 21

Defence and the media in time of limited war / edited by Peter R. Young. Published/Created: Portland, Or.: Frank Cass, 1992. Related Authors: Young, Peter R. Description: 281 p.: ill.; 23 cm. ISBN: 0714634786(HB) 0714640859 (PB) Notes: "This group of studies first appeared in a special issue on 'Defence and the media in time of limited war' of Small wars & insurgencies, vol. 2, no. 3 (Dec. 1991)"--T.p. verso. Includes bibliographical references and index. Subjects: Press and politics--History--20th century--Congresses. Freedom of the press--20th century--Congresses. Government and the press--20th century--Congresses. War--Press coverage--History--20th century--Congresses. Armed Forces and mass media--History--20th century Congresses. LC Classification: PN4751 .D43 1992 Dewey Class No.: 323.44/5 20

DeLuca, Anthony R. Politics, diplomacy, and the media: Gorbachev's legacy in the West / Anthony R. DeLuca. Published/Created: Westport, Conn.: Praeger, 1998. Description: x, 165 p.; 25 cm. ISBN: 0275959686 (alk. paper) Notes: Includes bibliographical references (p. [155]-158) and index. Subjects: Gorbachev, Mikhail Sergeevich, 1931- Communication in politics--Soviet Union. Public relations and politics--Soviet Union. Mass media and public opinion--Soviet Union. Soviet Union--Politics and government--1985-1991. LC Classification: DK288 .D45 1998 Dewey Class No.: 947.085 21

Dembour, Marie-Bénédicte, 1961- Recalling the Belgian Congo: conversations and introspection / Marie-Bénédicte Dembour. Published/Created: New York: Berghahn Books, 2000. Description: xx, 235 p.: ill., maps; 22 cm. ISBN: 1571819452 (hardback: alk. paper) Cancelled ISBN: 1571817562 (pb: alk. paper) Notes: Includes bibliographical references (p. 214-230) and index. Subjects: Ethnology--Congo (Democratic Republic) Colonial administrators--Congo (Democratic Republic) History. Congo (Democratic Republic)--In mass media. Belgium--Colonies--Africa--Administration. Congo (Democratic Republic)--History. Congo (Democratic Republic)--Politics and government. Congo (Democratic Republic)--Social life and customs. Series: New directions in anthropology; v. 9 LC Classification: GN654 .D37 2000 Dewey Class No.: 306/.096751 21

Democracy and the media: a comparative perspective / edited by Richard Gunther, Anthony Mughan. Published/Created: Cambridge; New York: Cambridge University Press, 2000. Related Authors: Gunther, Richard. Mughan, Anthony Description: xv, 496 p.; 24 cm. ISBN: 0521771803 0521777437 (pbk.) Notes: Includes bibliographical references (p. 449-485) and index. Subjects: Mass media--Political aspects. Democracy. Series: Communication, society, and politics LC Classification: P95.8 .D394 2000 Dewey Class No.: 302.23 21

Democratization and the media / edited by Vicky Randall. Published/Created: London; Portland, OR: F. Cass, 1998. Related Authors: Randall, Vicky. Related Titles: Democratization. Description: 258 p.; 23 cm. ISBN: 0714648949 0714644463 (pbk.) Notes: Originally appeared as a special issue of Democratization, summer 1998. Includes bibliographical references and index. Subjects: Mass media--Political aspects. Democratization. LC Classification: P95.8 .D427 1998 Dewey Class No.: 321.8/09/045 21

Der Derian, James. Virtuous war: mapping the military-industrial-media-entertainment network / James Der Derian. Published/Created: Boulder, CO: Westview Press, 2001. Projected Pub. Date: 0105 Description: p. cm. ISBN: 0813397944 (alk. paper) Notes: Includes index. Subjects: War--Simulation methods. War games. Imaginary wars and battles. War--Moral and ethical aspects. Military-industrial complex--United States. Mass media--United States. World politics--1989- United States--Military policy. LC Classification: U21.2 .D347 2001 Dewey Class No.: 355.02 21

Desert Storm and the mass media / editors, Bradley S. Greenberg, Walter Gantz. Published/Created: Cresskill, N.J.: Hampton Press, c1993. Related Authors: Greenberg, Bradley S. Gantz, Walter. Description: xiv, 447 p.: ill.; 24 cm. ISBN: 1881303349 1881303357 (pbk.) Notes: Includes bibliographical references (p. 415-435) and indexes. Subjects: Persian Gulf War, 1991--Journalists. Persian Gulf War, 1991--Mass media and the war. Series: The Hampton Press communication series LC Classification: DS79.739 .D47 1993 Dewey Class No.: 956.704/42 20

Diamond, Edwin. The media show: the changing face of the news, 1985-1990 / Edwin Diamond. Published/Created: Cambridge, Mass.: MIT Press, c1991. Description: xiv, 230 p.; 22 cm. ISBN: 0262041251: Notes: Includes index. Subjects: Television broadcasting of news--United States. Mass media--Political aspects--United States. Mass media--Social aspects--United States. LC Classification: PN4888.T4 D478 1991 Dewey Class No.: 302.23/45/0973 20

Diamond, Edwin. White House to your house: media and politics in virtual America / Edwin Diamond and Robert A. Silverman. Published/Created: Cambridge, Mass: MIT Press, c1995. Related Authors: Silverman, Robert A., 1971- Description: xiii, 178 p.; 21 cm. ISBN: 0262041502 (hc: alk. paper) Notes: Includes bibliographical references (p. [161]-168) and index. Subjects: Presidents--United States--Election. Communication in politics--United States. Communication--Political aspects--United States. Mass media--Political aspects--United States. LC Classification: JK528 .D53 1995 Dewey Class No.: 324.7/3/0973 20

Do the media govern?: politicians, voters, and reporters in America / Shanto Iyengar, Richard Reeves, editors. Published/Created: Thousand Oaks, Calif.: Sage Publications, c1997. Related Authors: Iyengar, Shanto. Reeves, Richard, 1936- Description: xx, 463 p.: ill.; 24cm. ISBN: 0803956053 (cloth: acid-free paper) 0803956061 (pbk.: acid-free paper) Notes: Includes bibliographical references and indexes. Subjects: Mass media--Political aspects--United States. Press and politics--United States. Journalism--Political aspects--United States. LC Classification: P95.82.U6 D64 1997 Dewey Class No.: 302.23/0973 20

Dunnigan, James F. Digital soldiers: the evolution of high-tech weaponry and tomorrow's brave new battlefield / James F. Dunnigan. Edition Information: 1st ed. Published/Created: New York: St. Martin's Press, 1996. Description: xxi, 309 p.; 24 cm. ISBN: 0312145888 Notes: "A Thomas Dunne book." Includes index. Subjects: Weapons systems--Technological innovations. Military-industrial complex . Armed Forces and mass media. LC Classification: UF500 .D87 1996 Dewey Class No.: 355/.07 20

Dye, Thomas R. American politics in the media age / Thomas R. Dye, Harmon Zeigler, S. Robert Lichter. Edition Information: 4th ed. Published/Created: Pacific Grove, Calif.: Brooks/Cole Pub. Co., c1992. Related Authors: Zeigler, L. Harmon (Luther Harmon), 1936- Lichter, S. Robert. Description: xiv, 352 p.: ill. (some col.), map; 24 cm. ISBN: 0534167764 Notes: Includes bibliographical references and indexes. Subjects: Mass media--Political aspects--United States. United States--Politics and government. LC Classification: JK274 .D97 1991 Dewey Class No.: 320.973 20

Edwards, Lee. Mediapolitik: how the mass media have transformed world politics / Lee Edwards. Published/Created: Washington, D.C.: Catholic University of America Press, c2001. Description: 364 p.; 24 cm. ISBN: 0813209919 (alk. paper) 0813209927 (pbk.) Notes: Includes bibliographical references (p. 339-345) and index. Subjects: Mass media--Political aspects. Mass media policy. Mass media--Influence. World politics--1989- LC Classification: P95.8 .E34 2001 Dewey Class No.: 302.23 21

Elections '97: media watch, August 1997. Published/Created: Nairobi, Kenya: Kenya Human Rights Commission; London: Article 19, [1997] Related Authors: Kenya Human Rights Commission. Article 19 (Organization) Media Monitoring (Project: Kenya) Description: iv, 20 p.: ill.; 30 cm. Notes: "Media Monitoring in Kenya, August 1997 report"--Cover. Includes bibliographical references. Subjects: Radio in politics--Kenya. Television in politics--Kenya. Mass media--Objectivity--Kenya. Elections--Kenya. LC Classification: HE8689.7.P6 E39 1997

El-Nawawy, Mohammed, 1968- The Israeli-Egyptian peace process in the reporting of western journalists / Mohammed el-Nawawy. Published/Created: Westport, CT: Ablex Pub., 2002. Projected Pub. Date: 0202 Description: p. cm. ISBN: 1567505449 (alk. paper) 1567505457 (pbk.: alk. paper) Subjects: Arab-Israeli conflict--Mass media and the conflict. Arab-Israeli conflict--Press coverage. Foreign correspondents--Israel. Foreign correspondents--Egypt. Mass media--Political aspects. Government and the press--Israel. Government and the press--Egypt. Series: Civic discourse for the third millennium LC Classification: DS119.7 .N385 2002 Dewey Class No.: 956 21

Engaging the public: how government and the media can reinvigorate American democracy / edited by Thomas J. Johnson, Carol E. Hays, Scott P. Hays. Published/Created: Lanham, Md.: Rowman & Littlefield, c1998. Related Authors: Johnson, Thomas J., 1960- Hays, Carol E., 1963- Hays, Scott P., 1962- Description: xiii, 281 p.: ill.; 24 cm. ISBN: 0847688895 (cloth: alk. paper) 0847688909 (pbk.: alk. paper) Notes: Includes bibliographical references and index. Subjects: Political participation--United States. Mass media--Political aspects--United States. Voting--United States. United States--Politics and government--1993-2001. LC Classification: JK1764 .E54 1998 Dewey Class No.: 324.973 21

European Institute for the Media. Media Monitoring Unit. The 1992 national elections in Romania: coverage by radio and television / report by the Media Monitoring Unit of the European Institute for the Media. Published/Created: Manchester: European Institute for the Media, [1992] Description: 67 leaves: map, tables; 30 cm. Notes: "November 1992." Subjects: Television in politics--Romania. Radio in politics--Romania. Elections--Romania. Mass media--Political aspects--Romania. LC Classification: HE8689.9.R9 E88 1992

Exoo, Calvin F. The politics of the mass media / Calvin F. Exoo. Published/Created: Minneapolis/St. Paul: West Pub. Co., c1994. Description: xvi, 332 p.: ill.; 23 cm. ISBN: 0314028919 (alk. paper) Notes: Includes bibliographical references (p. 313-319) and index. Subjects: Mass media--Political aspects--United States. United States--Politics and government--1989-1993. LC Classification: P95.82.U6 E95 1994 Dewey Class No.: 302.23/0973 20

Faringer, Gunilla L. Press freedom in Africa / Gunilla L. Faringer. Published/Created: New York: Praeger, 1991. Description: xii, 144 p.; 22 cm. ISBN: 0275937712 (alk. paper) Notes: Includes bibliographical references (p. [133]-136) and index. Subjects: Freedom of the press--South Africa--History--20th century. Press and politics--South Africa--History--20th century. Mass media--Political aspects--South Africa. Communication--Political aspects--South Africa. Mass media--Political aspects--Developing countries. Communication--Political aspects--Developing countries. South Africa--Politics and government--20th century. LC Classification: PN4748.S58 F37 1991 Dewey Class No.: 323.44/5/0968 20

Fiske, John. Media matters: everyday culture and political change / John Fiske. Published/Created: Minneapolis, Minn.: University of Minneota Press, c1994. Description: xxviii, 282 p.: ill.; 24 cm. ISBN: 0816624623 (acid-free paper) Notes: Includes bibliographical references (p. 269-273) and index. Subjects: Popular culture--United States. Mass media--Political aspects--United States. Politics and culture--United States. United States--Politics and government--1989-1993. United States--Politics and government--1993-2001. LC Classification: E169.04 .F574 1994 Dewey Class No.: 306/.0973 20

Fiske, John. Media matters: race and gender in U.S. politics / John Fiske. Edition Information: Rev. ed. Published/Created: Minneapolis: University of Minnesota Press, c1996. Description: xi, 304 p.: ill.;

23 cm. ISBN: 0816624631 (pb: acid-free paper) Notes: Includes bibliographical references (p. 291-295) and index. Subjects: Popular culture--United States. Mass media--Political aspects--United States. Politics and culture--United States. United States--Politics and government--1989-1993. United States--Politics and government--1993-2001. LC Classification: E169.04 .F574 1996 Dewey Class No.: 306/.0973 20

Foreign and security policy in the information age / edited by Frank P. Harvey and Ann L. Griffiths. Published/Created: Halifax, N.S.: Centre for Foreign Policy Studies, Dalhousie University c1999. Related Authors: Harvey, Frank P. Griffiths, Ann Lynn, 1960- Description: vi, 192 p.; 22 cm. ISBN: 1896440150 Notes: Includes bibliographical references. Subjects: National security--Congresses. Mass media--Congresses. Information warfare--Congresses. Canada--Military policy--Congresses. Canada--Foreign relations--1945---Congresses. LC Classification: UA10.5 .F67 1999 Dewey Class No.: 327.1 21

Forlizzi, Lori. The boundaries of free speech: how free is too free? Edition Information: Abridged ed. / [writer, Lori Forlizzi]. Published/Created: Dubuque, Iowa: Kendall/Hunt Pub. Co., [c1991] Related Authors: Piazza, Thomas Leonard. Boundaries of free speech. Description: 28 p.: ill.; 28 cm. ISBN: 0840369271 Notes: Cover title. Abridged ed. of: The boundaries of free speech by Tom Piazza and Keith Melville. Includes bibliographical references (p. 27). Subjects: Freedom of speech--United States. Censorship--United States. Mass media--Censorship--United States. Series: National issues forum. Variant Series: National issues forums LC Classification: KF4772.Z9 F67 1991 Dewey Class No.: 342.73/0853 347.302853 20

Foundation for Democracy in Zaire: proposal 1991/1992. Published/Created: [Brooklyn, N.Y.: Fondation pour la democratie au Zaire, 1991] Related Authors: Foundation for Democracy in Zaire. Description: 1 v. (various pagings): ill., maps; 28 cm. Subjects: Political participation--Congo (Democratic Republic) Democracy--Congo (Democratic Republic) Civics, Congolese (Democratic Republic) Mass media--Political aspects--Congo (Democratic Republic) LC Classification: JQ3616 .F68 1991

Fox, Claire F. The fence and the river: culture and politics at the U.S.-Mexico border / Claire F. Fox. Published/Created: Minneapolis: University of Minnesota Press, c1999. Description: x, 188 p.: ill.; 26 cm. ISBN: 0816629986 (acid-free paper) 0816629994 (pbk.: acid-free paper) Notes: Includes bibliographical references (p. 169-182) and index. Subjects: Mexican-American Border Region--In art. Popular culture--United States--History--20th century. Mexican-American Border Region--Civilization. Mexican-American Border Region--In literature. Mexican-American Border Region--In mass media. Mexican-American Border Region--Politics and government. United States--Relations--Mexico. Mexico--Relations--United States. Series: Cultural studies of the Americas; v. 1 LC Classification: F787 .F69 1999 Dewey Class No.: 972/.1 21

France at war in the twentieth century: propaganda, myth and metaphor / edited by Valerie Holman and Debra Kelly. Published/Created: New York: Berghahn, 2000. Related Authors: Holman, Valerie. Kelly, Debra. Description: x, 164 p.: ill.; 23 cm. ISBN: 1571817018 1571817700 (PBK.) Notes: Includes bibliographical references and index. Subjects: Propaganda, French--History--20th century. Mass media and public opinion--France--History--20th century. France--Politics and government--20th century. France--History, Military--20th century. Series: Contemporary France (Providence, R.I.); v. 1. Variant Series: Contemporary France; v. 3 National Bib. No.: GBA0-Z8336

Franklin, Bob, 1949- Packaging politics: political communications in Britain's media democracy / Bob Franklin. Published/Created: London; New York: E. Arnold; New York: Distributed in the USA by Routledge, Chapman, and Hall, 1994. Description: viii, 257 p.: ill.; 23 cm. ISBN: 0340555963: Notes: Includes bibliographical references (p. [227]-246) and index. Subjects: Government publicity--Great Britain. Communication in politics--Great Britain. Mass media--Political aspects--Great Britain. LC Classification: JN329.P8 F73 1994 Dewey Class No.: 306.2 20

Freeman, Laurie Anne, 1957- Closing the shop: information cartels and Japan's mass media / Laurie Anne Freeman. Published/Created: Princeton, N.J.: Princeton University Press, c2000. Description: xix, 256 p.; 25 cm. ISBN: 0691059543 (cloth: alk. paper) Notes: Includes bibliographical references (p. [199]-245) and index. Subjects: Mass media--Political aspects--Japan. Press and politics--Japan. Mass media--Censorship--Japan. LC Classification: P95.82.J3 F74 2000 Dewey Class No.: 302.23/0952 21

Fried, Amy. Muffled echoes: Oliver North and the politics of public opinion / Amy Fried. Published/Created: New York: Columbia University Press, c1997. Description: xii, 308 p.; 24 cm. ISBN: 0231108206 (acid-free paper) 0231108214 (pbk.) Notes: Includes bibliographical references (p. [275]-293) and index. Subjects: North, Oliver--Public opinion. Iran-Contra Affair, 1985-1990--Public opinion. Public opinion--United States. Mass media--United States--Influence. Series: Power, conflict, and democracy. Variant Series: Power, conflict, and democracy series LC Classification: E876 .F78 1997 Dewey Class No.: 973.927 21

From Loren to Marimar: the Philippine media in the 1990s / edited by Sheila S. Coronel. Published/Created: Quezon City, Philippines: Philippine Center for Investigative Journalism, c1999. Related Authors: Coronel, Sheila S. Philippine Center for Investigative Journalism. Description: ix, 193 p.: ill.; 23 cm. ISBN: 971060621X Subjects: Mass media Philippines. Freedom of the press--Philippines. LC Classification: P92.P5 F76 1990 Dewey Class No.: 302.23/09599 21

From massacres to genocide: the media, public policy, and humanitarian crises / Robert I. Rotberg, Thomas G. Weiss, editors. Published/Created: Washington, D.C.: Brookings Institution, c1996. Related Authors: Rotberg, Robert I. Weiss, Thomas George. Description: x, 203 p.; 24 cm. ISBN: 0815775903 (alk. paper) 081577589X (pbk.: alk. paper) Notes: Includes bibliographical references and index. Subjects: Disaster relief. International relief. Disasters--Press coverage. Mass media. Disaster relief--Public relations. Human rights. LC Classification: HV553 .F76 1996 Dewey Class No.: 363.3/4526 20

Gabriel, John, 1951- Whitewash: racialized politics and the media / John Gabriel. Published/Created: London; New York: Routledge, 1998. Description: vii, 219 p.; 25 cm. ISBN: 0415149703 (HB) 041514969X (PB) Notes: Includes bibliographical references (p. 192-213) and index. Subjects: Mass media and race relations--Mass media--Political aspects--United States. Mass media and race relations--Mass media--Political aspects--Great Britain. United States--Politics and government--1993-2001. Great Britain--Politics and government--1979- LC Classification: P94.5.M552 U634 1998 Dewey Class No.: 302.23/0973 21

Gadzekpo, Audrey. Is there a place for the state media in a constitutional democracy? / Audrey Gadzekpo. Published/Created: Accra, Ghana: Institute of Economic Affairs, c1998. Description: 30 p.; 23 cm. ISBN: 9988584482 Notes: Includes bibliographical references (p. 28-30). Subjects: Mass media policy--Ghana. Ghana--Politics and government--1979- Series: Occasional papers (Institute of Economic Affairs (Ghana)); no. 17. Variant Series: Occasional papers, 0855-3238; no. 17 LC Classification: P95.82.G4 G33 1998 Dewey Class No.: 320/.01/4 21

Ganley, Gladys D. Mikhail and the multiplying media / Gladys D. Ganley. Published/Created: Cambridge, Mass.: Program on Information Resources Policy, Harvard University, Center for Information Policy Research, c1994. Related Authors: Harvard University. Program on Information Resources Policy. Description: 223 p.; 28 cm. ISBN: 1879716097 Notes: "June 1994"--T.p. verso. "P-94-3"--T.p. verso. Includes bibliographical references. Subjects: Communication policy--Soviet Union. Freedom of information--Soviet Union. Glasnost. Telecommunication--Soviet Union. Press--Soviet Union. Mass media policy--Soviet Union. Soviet Union--History--Attempted coup, 1991--Mass media and the coup. Soviet Union--Politics and government--1985-1991. LC Classification: P92.S65 G36 1994 Dewey Class No.: 302.2/0947 20

Ganley, Gladys D. The exploding political power of personal media / Gladys D. Ganley. Published/Created: Norwood, N.J.: Ablex Pub., c1992. Description: xvi, 181 p.; 24 cm. ISBN: 0893917567 Notes: Includes bibliographical references and indexes. Subjects: Mass media--Political aspects. Mass media--Technological innovations. Series: The Communication and information science series LC Classification: P95.8 .G35 1991 Dewey Class No.: 302.23 20

Ganley, Gladys D. Unglued empire: the Soviet experience with communications technologies / Gladys D. Ganley; with foreword by Marshall I. Goldman. Published/Created: Norwood, N.J.: Ablex Pub. Corp., c1996. Description: xvii, 234 p.; 24 cm. ISBN: 1567501974 (cloth) 1567501982 (pbk.: alk. paper) Notes: Includes bibliographical references and indexes. Subjects: Mass media--Soviet Union. Communication and traffic--Soviet Union. Glasnost. Soviet Union--Politics and government--1985-1991. Series: Ablex Communication, culture, & information series LC Classification: HN530.Z9 M345 1996 Dewey Class No.: 302.23/0947 20

Garnham, Nicholas. Capitalism and communication: global culture and the economics of information / Nicholas Garnham; edited by Fred Inglis. Published/Created: London; Newbury Park: Sage Publications, 1990. Related Authors: Inglis, Fred. Description: 216 p.; 24 cm. ISBN: 0803982585 (pbk.) Cancelled ISBN: 0803992577 Notes: Includes bibliographical references and index. Subjects: Mass media--Economic aspects. Mass media--Political aspects. Marxian economics. Series: Media, culture, and society series. Variant Series: The Media, culture & society series LC Classification: P96.E25 G3 1990 Dewey Class No.: 338.4/730223 20

Gehrke, Gernot. Europe without the Europeans: a question of communication? / Gernot Gehrke. Published/Created: Düsseldorf, Germany: European Institute for the Media, c1998. Related Authors: European Institute for the Media. Description: viii, 78 p.; 30 cm. Notes: "July 1998." Includes bibliographical references (p. 72-78). Subjects: Mass media--Political aspects--Europe. European federation. European Union. Series: Mediafact LC Classification: P95.82.E85 G44 1998 Dewey Class No.: 302.23/094 21

Genest, Marc A., 1958- Negotiating in the public eye: the impact of the press on the intermediate-range nuclear force negotiations / Marc A. Genest. Published/Created: Stanford, Cal.: Stanford University Press, c1995. Description: xi, 189 p.: ill.; 23 cm. ISBN: 0804724393 (acid-free paper): Notes: Includes bibliographical references (p. 176-186) and index. Subjects: Soviet Union. Treaties, etc. United States, 1987 Dec. 8. North Atlantic Treaty Organization. Nuclear arms control--United States. Nuclear arms control--Soviet Union. Intermediate-range ballistic missiles. Mass media--Influence. Europe--Defenses. LC Classification: JX1974.7 .G4286 1995 Dewey Class No.: 327.1/74/0947 20

Getting the real story: censorship and propaganda in South Africa / edited by

Gerald B. Sperling and James E. McKenzie. Published/Created: Calgary, Alta.: Detselig Enterprises, c1990. Related Authors: Sperling, Gerald B. McKenzie, James E. University of Regina. School of Journalism and Communications. Description: vi, 168 p.: ports.; 23 cm. ISBN: 155059009X Notes: Based on papers presented in March 1989 at a conference organized by the School of Journalism and Communications, University of Regina. Subjects: Freedom of the press--South Africa--Congresses. Mass media--Censorship--South Africa--Congresses. Propaganda, South African--Congresses. Journalism--Political aspects--South Africa--Congresses. Mass media--Political aspects--South Africa--Congresses. LC Classification: PN4748.S58 G48 1990 Dewey Class No.: 323.44/5/0968 20

Gibbs, Joseph, 1965- Gorbachev's glasnost: the Soviet media in the first phase of perestroika / Joseph Gibbs. Edition Information: 1st ed. Published/Created: College Station: Texas A & M University Press, c1999. Description: xiii, 147 p.; 25 cm. ISBN: 0890968926 (cloth: alk. paper) Notes: Includes bibliographical references (p. [131]-137) and index. Subjects: Gorbachev, Mikhail Sergeevich, 1931- Mass media--Political aspects--Soviet Union. Glasnost. Freedom of information--Soviet Union. Soviet Union--Politics and government--1985-1991. Series: Eastern European studies (College Station, Tex.); no. 9. Variant Series: Eastern European studies; no. 9 LC Classification: P95.82.S65 G53 1999 Dewey Class No.: 302.23/0947/09048 21

Ginsberg, Benjamin. Politics by other means: politicians, prosecutors, and the press from Watergate to Whitewater / Benjamin Ginsberg, Martin Shefter. Edition Information: Rev. and updated ed. Published/Created: New York: W. W. Norton, c1999. Related Authors: Shefter, Martin, 1943- Description: 224 p.; 21 cm. ISBN: 039331877X (pbk.) Notes: Includes bibliographical references and index. Subjects: Political participation--United States. Political parties--United States. Elections--United States. Governmental investigations--United States. Mass media--Political aspects--United States. United States--Politics and government--1945-1989. United States--Politics and government--1989- LC Classification: JK1764 .G56 1999 Dewey Class No.: 323/.042/0973 21

Ginsberg, Benjamin. Politics by other means: politicians, prosecutors, and the press in the post-electoral era / Benjamin Ginsberg, Martin Shefter. Edition Information: 3rd ed. Published/Created: New York: Norton, 2002. Projected Pub. Date: 0202 Related Authors: Shefter, Martin, 1943- Description: p. cm. ISBN: 0393977633 (pbk.) Notes: Includes bibliographical references and index. Subjects: Political participation--United States. Political parties--United States. Elections--United States. Governmental investigations--United States. Mass media--Political aspects--United States. United States--Politics and government--1945-1989. United States--Politics and government--1989- LC Classification: JK1764 .G56 2002 Dewey Class No.: 320.973 21

Gonzenbach, William J. The media, the president, and public opinion: a longitudinal analysis of the drug issue, 1984-1991 / William J. Gonzenbach. Published/Created: Mahwah, N.J.: Erlbaum, c1996. Description: xvi, 117 p.: ill.; 24 cm. ISBN: 0805816895 (acid-free paper) 0805816909 Notes: Includes bibliographical references (p. 110-113) and indexes. Subjects: Drug abuse--Government policy--United States--Public opinion. Narcotics, Control of--United States--Public opinion. Public opinion--United States. Drugs and mass media--United States. Presidents--United States. United States--Politics and government--1981-1989. United States--Politics and government--1989- Series: LEA's communication series LC Classification: HV5825 .G623 1996 Dewey Class No.: 362.29/12/097309048 20

Government media, autonomy and after / edited by G.S. Bhargava. Published/Created: New Delhi: Institute of Social Sciences and Concept Pub. Co., 1991. Related Authors: Bhargava, G. S., 1925- Institute of Social Sciences (New Delhi, India) Description: xii, 134 p.; 22 cm. ISBN: 8170223660: Notes: Papers presented at a seminar organized by the Institute of Social Sciences, on 28 April 1990, at the Parliament House Annexe, New Delhi. Includes index. Includes bibliographical references. Subjects: Mass media policy--India--Congresses. LC Classification: P95.82.I4 G68 1991 Dewey Class No.: 302.23/0954 20

Graber, Doris A. (Doris Appel), 1923- Mass media and American politics / Doris A. Graber. Edition Information: 4th ed. Published/Created: Washington, D.C.: CQ Press, c1993. Description: xv, 448 p.: ill.; 23 cm. ISBN: 087187699X: Notes: Includes bibliographical references and index. Subjects: Mass media--Social aspects--United States. Mass media--Political aspects--United States. LC Classification: HN90.M3 G7 1993 Dewey Class No.: 302.23/0973 20

Graber, Doris A. (Doris Appel), 1923- Processing the news: how people tame the information tide / Doris A. Graber. Edition Information: 2nd ed. Published/Created: Lanham, Md.: University Press of America, [1993] Description: x, 300 p.: ill.; 23 cm. ISBN: 0819190985 (acid-free paper) Notes: Originally Published: New York: Longman, 1988. Includes bibliographical references (p. 269-293) and index. Subjects: Public opinion--United States--Case studies. Human information processing--Case studies. Political socialization--United States--Case studies. Mass media--Political aspects--United States--Case studies. Democracy. LC Classification: HM261 .G78 1993 Dewey Class No.: 306.2 20

Graham, Tim. Pattern of deception: the media's role in the Clinton presidency / by Tim Graham. Edition Information: 1st ed. Published/Created: Alexandria, Va.: Media Research Center, c1996. Related Authors: Bozell, L. Brent, 1925- Media Research Center. Description: x, 271 p.; 23 cm. ISBN: 0962734837 (pbk.) Notes: Foreword by L. Brent Bozell, III. Includes bibliographical references. Subjects: Clinton, Bill, 1946- --Relations with journalists. Mass media--Political aspects--United States. Journalism--Mass media--Objectivity--United States. Journalism--Political aspects--United States. United States--Politics and government--1993-2001. LC Classification: P95.82.U6 G73 1996 Dewey Class No.: 070.4/49324/097309049 21

Gross, Peter. Mass media in revolution and national development: the Romanian laboratory / Peter Gross. Edition Information: 1st ed. Published/Created: Ames, Iowa: Iowa State University Press, 1996. Description: xiii, 206 p.; 24 cm. ISBN: 0813826705 Notes: Includes bibliographical references (p. 171-194) and index. Subjects: Mass media--Political aspects--Romania. Press and politics--Romania. Journalism--Romania--History. Romania--Politics and government--1989- LC Classification: P95.82.R6 G76 1996 Dewey Class No.: 302.23/09498 20

Gruner, Elliott. Prisoners of culture: representing the Vietnam POW / by Elliott Gruner. Published/Created: New Brunswick, N.J.: Rutgers University Press, c1993. Description: x, 245 p.: ill.; 24 cm. ISBN: 0813519306: 0813519314 (pbk.): Notes: Includes bibliographical references (p. 225-231) and index. Includes filmography (p. 231-235). Subjects: Vietnamese Conflict, 1961-1975--Mass media and the conflict. Prisoners of war in mass media. Prisoners of war--United States. Prisoners of war--Vietnam. Series: Communications, media, and culture LC Classification: P96.V46 G78 1993 Dewey Class No.: 303.6/6 20

Gustainis, J. Justin. American rhetoric and the Vietnam War / J. Justin Gustainis. Published/Created: Westport, Conn.: Praeger, 1993. Description: xvii, 169 p.; 25 cm. ISBN: 027593361X (alk. paper)

Notes: Includes bibliographical references (p. [159]-163) and index. Subjects: Vietnamese Conflict, 1961-1975--Propaganda. Vietnamese Conflict, 1961-1975--Protest movements--United States. Vietnamese Conflict, 1961-1975--Mass media and the conflict. United States--Politics and government--1945-1989. Series: Praeger series in political communication, 1062-5623 LC Classification: DS559.8.P65 G87 1993 Dewey Class No.: 959.704/3373 20

Hammond, William M. Public affairs: the military and the media, 1968-1973 / by William M. Hammond. Published/Created: Washington,D.C.: Center of Military History, United States Army, 1996. Description: xix, 659 p.: ill., maps; 25 cm. ISBN: 0160485428 (pbk.) Notes: Includes bibliographical references and index. Subjects: Vietnamese Conflict, 1961-1975--Press coverage. Armed Forces and mass media--United States--History. Series: United States Army in Vietnam LC Classification: DS559.46 .H37 1996 Dewey Class No.: 070.4/4995970434 20

Hammond, William M. Reporting Vietnam: media and military at war / William M. Hammond. Published/Created: Lawrence, Kan.: University Press of Kansas, c1998. Description: xi, 362 p.: ill., maps; 24 cm. ISBN: 0700609113 (cloth: alk. paper) Notes: Includes bibliographical references and index. Subjects: Vietnamese Conflict, 1961-1975--Press coverage--United States. Armed Forces and mass media--United States--History. Series: Modern war studies LC Classification: DS559.46 .H38 1998 Dewey Class No.: 959.704/38 21

Hartley, John, 1948- The indigenous public sphere: the reporting and reception of aboriginal issues in the Australian media / John Hartley and Alan McKee. Published/Created: Oxford; New York: Oxford University Press, 2000. Related Authors: McKee, Alan. Description: xvii, 369 p.: ill.; 23 cm. ISBN: 0198159994 (alk. paper) Notes: Includes bibliographical references (p. 341-362) and index. Subjects: Australian aborigines in mass media. Mass media--Australia. Australian aborigines--Politics and government. LC Classification: P94.5.A852 A85 2000 Dewey Class No.: 302.23/089/9915 21

Hartley, John, 1948- The politics of pictures: the creation of the public in the age of popular media / John Hartley. Published/Created: London; New York: Routledge, 1992. Description: xiii, 240 p.: ill.; 25 cm. ISBN: 0415015413 (hb) 0415015421 (pb) Notes: Includes bibliographical references (p. 234-236) and index. Subjects: Mass media--Audiences. Mass media--Political aspects. Mass media--Influence. Pictures. LC Classification: P96.A83 H37 1992 Dewey Class No.: 302.23 20

Harvey, Lisa St. Clair, 1957- Stolen thunder: the cultural roots of political communication / Lisa St. Clair Harvey. Published/Created: New York: Peter Lang, 1994. Description: vii, 116 p.; 24 cm. ISBN: 0820423394 (alk. paper) Notes: Includes bibliographical references Subjects: Presidents--United States--Election. Presidents--United States--Election--1988. Television in politics--United States. Mass media--Political aspects--United States. Public opinion--United States. Series: American university studies. Series XV. Communications; v. 4. Variant Series: American university studies, Series XV, Communications; vol. 4 LC Classification: JK524 .H37 1994 Dewey Class No.: 324.973/0927 20

Hayden, Joseph. Covering Clinton: the president and the press in the 1990s / Joseph Hayden. Published/Created: Westport, Conn.: Praeger, 2001. Projected Pub. Date: 0111 Description: p. cm. ISBN: 0275970345 (alk. paper) Notes: Includes bibliographical references and index. Subjects: Clinton, Bill, 1946- --Relations with journalists. Presidents--United States--Press coverage. Journalism--Political aspects--United States--History 20th century. Press and politics--United States--History--20th century. Mass media--Political aspects--United States--History 20th century. United States--Politics and government--1993-2001. Series: Praeger series in presidential studies, 1062-0931 LC Classification: E886.2 .H39 2001 Dewey Class No.: 973.929/092 21

Heinke, Rex S. Media law / Rex S. Heinke. Published/Created: Washington, D.C.: BNA Books, c1994. Description: xx, 610 p.; 26 cm. ISBN: 087179800X Notes: Includes index. Subjects: Press law--United States. Freedom of the press--United States. Mass media--Law and legislation--United States. LC Classification: KF2750 .H45 1994 Dewey Class No.: 342.73/0853 347.302853 20

Herman, Edward S. Manufacturing consent: the political economy of the mass media / Edward S. Herman and Noam Chomsky; with a new introduction by the authors. Published/Created: New York: Pantheon Books, 2002. Projected Pub. Date: 0201 Related Authors: Chomsky, Noam. Description: p. cm. ISBN: 0375714499 Notes: Updated ed. of: Manufacturing consent. 1st ed. c1988. Includes bibliographical references and index. Subjects: Mass media--Ownership. Mass media and propaganda. LC Classification: P96.E25 H47 2002 Dewey Class No.: 381/.4530223 21

Herman, Edward S. The global media: the new missionaries of corporate capitalism / Edward S. Herman and Robert W. McChesney. Published/Created: London; Washington, D.C.: Cassell, 1997. Related Authors: McChesney, Robert Waterman, 1952- Description: viii, 262 p.; 223 cm. ISBN: 0304334332 (hardback) 0304334340 (pbk.) Notes: Includes bibliographical references (p. [206]-254) and index. Subjects: Communication, International. Mass media--Economic aspects. Mass media--Political aspects. LC Classification: P96.I5 H46 1997 Dewey Class No.: 302.2 21

Herman, Edward S. Triumph of the market: essays on economics, politics, and the media / Edward S. Herman. Published/Created: Boston: South End Press, c1995. Description: ix, 276 p.; 22 cm. ISBN: 0896085228: 089608521X (pbk.): Notes: A majority of the essays were originally Published in Z magazine between Dec. 1989 and Dec. 1994. Includes bibliographical references (p. 239-266) and index. Subjects: Capitalism. Post-communism. Mass media--Political aspects. Political participation. Economic history--1990- LC Classification: HB501 .H466 1995 Dewey Class No.: 330.12/2 20

Human rights and the media /edited by Robert Haas. Edition Information: 1st ed. Published/Created: Kuala Lumpur, Malaysia: Asian Institute for Development Communication; Singapore: Friedrich Naumann Foundation, 1996. Related Authors: Haas, Robert, Dr. Asian Institute for Development Communciation. Friedrich-Naumann-Stiftung. Description: v, 87 p.; 23 cm. ISBN: 9839981749 Notes: Includes bibliographical references. Subjects: Human rights--Asia, Southeastern--Congresses. Mass media--Asia, Southeastern--Congresses. LC Classification: JC599.A785 H86 1996

Hunt, W. Ben (William Ben) Getting to war: predicting international conflict with mass media indicators / W. Ben Hunt. Published/Created: Ann Arbor: University of Michigan Press, c1997. Description: 304 p.: ill.; 24 cm. ISBN: 0472107518 (cloth: acid-free paper) Notes: Includes bibliographical references (p. 289-299) and index. Subjects: War--Forecasting. Mass media and war. War in mass media. Political indicators. LC Classification: U21.2 .H83 1997 Dewey Class No.: 355.02 21

Hutchison, David, 1944- Media policy: an introduction / David Hutchison. Published/Created: Oxford, UK; Malden, Mass.: Blackwell Publishers, 1999. Description: viii, 248 p.; 24 cm. ISBN: 0631204334 (alk. paper) 0631204342 (alk. paper) Notes: Includes bibliographical references (p. [216]-238) and index. Subjects: Mass media policy. LC Classification: P95.8 .H88 1999 Dewey Class No.: 302.23 21

In "media" res: readings in mass media and American politics / edited by Jan P. Vermeer. Published/Created: New York: McGraw-Hill, c1995. Related Authors: Vermeer, Jan Pons. Description: xv, 198 p.; 24 cm. ISBN: 0070674671 Notes: Includes bibliographical references and index. Subjects: Mass media--Political aspects--United States. Government and the press--United States. Communication in politics--United States. Public opinion--United States. United States--Politics and government--1993-2001. LC Classification: P95.82.U6 I5 1995 Dewey Class No.: 320.973 20

International Colloquium "Interaction of Mass Media, Public, and Power Institutions in Democratization Process": materials (27-30 November 1991) / Byelorussian State University, Department of Sociology, Scientific Centre for Sociological Studies, Byelorussian Research Service "Public Opinion." Published/Created: Minsk: [s.n.], 1991. Related Authors: Belaruski dziarzhauny universitet. Dept. of Sociology. Belaruski dziarzhauny universitet. Scientific Centre for Sociological Studies Byelorussian Research Service "Public Opinion." Description: 150 p.; 20 cm. Notes: Includes bibliographical references. English and Russian. Subjects: Mass media--Political aspects--Congresses. Mass media--Social aspects--Congresses. Mass media--Economic aspects--Congresses. Democracy--Congresses. Democratization--Congresses. LC Classification: P95.8 .I58 1991 Dewey Class No.: 302.23 20

Jackson, David J. (David James), 1969- Entertainment and politics: the influence of pop culture on young adult political socialization / David J. Jackson. Published/Created: New York: Peter Lang, 2002. Projected Pub. Date: 0204 Description: p. cm. ISBN: 0820457469 (pbk.: alk. paper) Notes: Includes bibliographical references and index. Subjects: Popular culture--Political aspects--United States. Young adults--United States--Political activity. Mass media and youth--United States. Mass media--Political aspects--United States. Political socialization--United States. United States--Social life and customs--1971- Series: Politics, media & popular culture; v. 6. Variant Series: Politics, media, and popular culture; v. 6 LC Classification: E169.12 .J25 2002 Dewey Class No.: 306/.0973 21

Jacobsen, John Kurt, 1949- Dead reckonings: ideas, interests, and politics in the "information age" / John Kurt Jacobsen. Published/Created: Atlantic Highlands, N.J.: Humanities Press, 1997. Description: xv, 238 p.; 24 cm. ISBN: 0391040073 (cloth: alk. paper) 0391040308 (pbk.: alk. paper) Notes: Includes bibliographical references and index. Subjects: Policy sciences. Ideology. Mass media--Political aspects. LC Classification: H97 .J33 1997 Dewey Class No.: 320/.6 20

Jamieson, Kathleen Hall. The interplay of influence: news, advertising, politics, and the mass media / Kathleen Hall Jamieson, Karlyn Kohrs Campbell. Edition Information: 4th ed. Published/Created: Belmont, CA: Wadsworth Pub., c1997. Related Authors: Campbell, Karlyn Kohrs. Description: xvi, 352 p.; 24 cm. ISBN: 0534514316 Notes: Includes bibliographical references and index. Subjects: Mass media--Influence. Mass media--Audiences. Advertising. Mass media--Political aspects. Mass media--United States. Series: Wadsworth series in mass communication and journalism LC Classification: P94 .J34 1997 Dewey Class No.: 302.23 20

Jamieson, Kathleen Hall. The interplay of influence: news, advertising, politics, and the mass media / Kathleen Hall Jamieson, Karlyn Kohrs Campbell. Edition Information: 5th ed. Published/Created: Belmont, CA: Wadsworth, 2000. Projected Pub. Date: 0007 Related Authors: Campbell, Karlyn Kohrs. Description: p. cm. ISBN: 0534533647 (alk. paper) Notes: Includes bibliographical references and index. Subjects: Mass media--Influence. Mass media--Audiences. Advertising. Mass media--Political aspects. Mass media--United States. LC Classification: P94 .J34 2000 Dewey Class No.: 302.23 21

Jamieson, Kathleen Hall. The interplay of influence: news, advertising, politics, and the mass media / Kathleen Hall Jamieson, Karlyn Kohrs Campbell. Edition Information: 3rd ed. Published/Created: Belmont, Calif.: Wadsworth Pub., c1992. Related Authors: Campbell, Karlyn Kohrs. Description: xvi, 304 p.: ill.; 24 cm. ISBN: 0534141064 Notes: Includes bibliographical references and index. Subjects: Mass media--Influence. Mass media--Audiences. Mass media--United States. LC Classification: P94 .J34 1992 Dewey Class No.: 302.23 20

Jibo, Mvendaga. Politics, mass media & national development / Mvendaga Jibo. Published/Created: Lagos: Malthouse Press, 1996. Description: 181 p.; 21 cm. ISBN: 9780230319 Notes: Includes bibliographical references (p. [170]-174) and index. Subjects: Mass media--Political aspects--Nigeria. Nigeria--Politics and government--1984-1993. Nigeria--Politics and government--1993- Nigeria--Economic conditions. LC Classification: DT515.842 .J53 1996

Johns, Christina Jacqueline. State crime, the media, and the invasion of Panama / Christina Jacqueline Johns and P. Ward Johnson. Published/Created: Westport, Conn.: Praeger, 1994. Related Authors: Johnson, P. Ward. Description: vi, 157 p.; 25 cm. ISBN: 0275943143 (alk. paper) Notes: Includes bibliographical references (p. [135]-147) and index. Subjects: Noriega, Manuel Antonio, 1934- Mass media--Political aspects--United States. Press and politics--United States. Political ethics--United States. Political ethics--Panama. Panama--History--American Invasion, 1989. United States--Foreign relations--Panama. Panama--Foreign relations--United States. Series: Praeger series in criminology and crime control policy, 1060-3212 LC Classification: F1567 .J64 1994 Dewey Class No.: 972.8705/3 20

Johnson, Ann K. (Ann Kathleen), 1946- Urban ghetto riots, 1965-1968: a comparison of Soviet and American press coverage / Ann K. Johnson. Published/Created: Boulder: East European Monographs; New York: Distributed by Columbia University Press, 1996. Description: 209 p.; 24 cm. ISBN: 0880333340 Notes: Based on the author's thesis (Ph. D.--University of Denver, 1994). Includes bibliographical references (p. [126]-179). Subjects: Race relations and the press--United States. Race relations and the press--Soviet Union. Mass media and public opinion--United States. Mass media and public opinion--Soviet Union. Riots--United States. Series: East European monographs; no. 437. Variant Series: East European monographs; 437 LC Classification: PN4888.R3 J64 1996 Dewey Class No.: 070.4/49305813 20

Johnson, Douglas V. The impact of the media on national security policy decision making / Douglas V. Johnson II. Published/Created: [Carlisle Barracks, Pa.]: Strategic Studies Institute, U.S. Army War College, 1994. Related Authors: Army War College (U.S.). Strategic Studies Institute. Description: vi, 33 p.; 23 cm. Notes: "October 7, 1994" Includes bibliographical references (p. 25-33). Subjects: Mass media--Political aspects--United States. National security--United States--Decision making. Government and the press--United States. Press and politics--United States. United States--Military policy--Decision making. LC Classification: P95.82.U6 J665 1994 Dewey Class No.: 302.23/0973 20

Kahan, Michael. Media as politics: theory, behavior, and change in America / Michael Kahan. Published/Created: Upper Saddle River, N.J.: Prentice Hall, c1999. Description: xv, 267 p.; 23 cm. ISBN: 0138760535 Notes: Includes bibliographical references (p. 255-260) and index. Subjects: Mass media--Political aspects--United States. United States--Politics and government--1993-2001. LC Classification: P95.82.U6 K35 1999 Dewey Class No.: 302.23/0973 21

Katz, Jon. Media rants: postpolitics in the digital nation / Jon Katz; [with an afterword by Wendy Kaminer]. Edition Information: 1st ed. Published/Created: San Francisco, CA: Hardwired, 1997. Description: ix, 152 p.; 23 cm. ISBN: 1888869127 (pbk.) Notes: Includes index. Subjects: Katz, Jon. Mass media and technology--United States. Mass media--Political aspects--United States. Discourse analysis--Social aspects--United States. Internet. World Wide Web. United States--Politics and government--1993-2001. LC Classification: P96.T422 U635 1997 Dewey Class No.: 302.23/0973 21

Kauffman, James Lee, 1958- Selling outer space: Kennedy, the media, and funding for Project Apollo, 1961-1963 / James L. Kauffman. Published/Created: Tuscaloosa: University of Alabama Press, c1994. Description: x, 190 p.; 24 cm. ISBN: 0817307478 (alk. paper) Notes: Revision of author's thesis (Ph. D.)--Indiana University, 1989, originally presented under the Selling space. Includes bibliographical references (p. 175-185) and index. Subjects: Project Apollo (U.S.) Communication in politics--United States. Mass media--United States--Influence. United States--Politics and government--1961-1963. Series: Studies in rhetoric and communication LC Classification: TL789.8.U6 A5428 1994 Dewey Class No.: 387.8/0973 20

Kellner, Douglas, 1943- Grand theft 2000: media spectacle and a stolen election / Douglas Kellner. Published/Created: Lanham, Md.: Rowman & Littlefield Publishers, c2001. Description: xxi, 242 p.; 24 cm. ISBN: 0742521028 (alk. paper) 0742521036 (pbk.: alk. paper) Notes: Includes bibliographical references (p. 221-223) and index. Subjects: Presidents--United States--Election--2000. Contested elections--United States--History--20th century. Press and politics--United States--History--20th century. Mass media--Political aspects--United States Political corruption--United States--History--20th century. United States--Politics and government--1993-2001. LC Classification: E889 .K45 2001 Dewey Class No.: 324.973/0929 21

Kennedy, William V. The military and the media: why the press cannot be trusted to cover a war / William V. Kennedy. Published/Created: Westport, Conn.: Praeger, c1993. Description: xii, 167 p.; 25 cm. ISBN: 0275941914 (alk. paper) Notes: Includes bibliographical references (p. [159]-161) and index. Subjects: Armed Forces and mass media--United States. War--Press coverage--United States. LC Classification: P96.A752 U65 1993 Dewey Class No.: 070.4/49355 20

Kerbel, Matthew Robert, 1958- Remote & controlled: media politics in a cynical age / Matthew Robert Kerbel. Edition Information: 2nd ed. Published/Created: Boulder, Colo.: Westview Press, 1998. Projected Pub. Date: 9811 Description: p. cm. ISBN: 0813368693 (alk. paper) Notes: Includes bibliographical references (p.) and index. Subjects: Mass media--Political aspects--United States. United States--Politics and government--20th century. Series: Dilemmas in American politics LC Classification: P95.82.U6 K47 1998 Dewey Class No.: 302.23/0973 21

Kurian, George Thomas. Political market place, USA / by George Thomas Kurian and Jeffrey D. Schultz. Published/Created: Phoenix, Ariz.: Oryx Press, c1999. Related Authors: Schultz, Jeffrey D. Description: vii, 345 p.; 28 cm. ISBN: 1573562262 (pbk.: alk. paper) Notes: Includes indexes. Subjects: Politics, Practical--United States. Mass media--Political aspects--United States. United States--Politics and government. LC Classification: JK271 .K87 1999 Dewey Class No.: 323/.042/02573 21

Lachapelle, Guy, 1955- Polls and the media in Canadian elections: taking the pulse / Guy Lachapelle. Published/Created: Ottawa: Royal Commission on Electoral Reform and Party Financing and Canada Communications Group, Supply and Services Canada and Dundurn Press, 1991. Related Authors: Canada. Royal

Commission on Electoral Reform and Party Financing. Description: xix, 182 p.; 23 cm. ISBN: 1550021125: Notes: Issued also in French under Les sondages et les médias lors des élections au Canada. Subjects: Political campaigns--Canada. Elections--Canada. Mass media--Political aspects--Canada. Public opinion--Canada. Public opinion polls--Law and legislation--Canada. Public opinion polls--Law and legislation. Series: Research studies (Canada. Royal Commission on Electoral Reform and Party Financing); no. 16. Variant Series: Research studies; 16 LC Classification: JL193 .L28 1991 Dewey Class No.: 324.7/3/0971 20 National Bib. No.: C91-90528-2

Lapham, Lewis H. Lights, camera, democracy! / Lewis Lapham. Published/Created: New York: At Random, 2001. Projected Pub. Date: 0103 Description: p. cm. ISBN: 0679647139 0812991621 (alk. paper) Subjects: Political culture--United States. Mass media--Political aspects--United States Mass media--Social aspects--United States. Popular culture--United States. United States--Politics and government--1989- United States--Politics and government--1945-1989. United States--Social conditions--1980- LC Classification: E839.4 . L37 2001 Dewey Class No.: 973.92 21

Latin politics, global media / Elizabeth Fox and Silvio Waisbord, editors. Edition Information: 1st ed. Published/Created: Austin: University of Texas Press, 2002. Projected Pub. Date: 0204 Related Authors: Fox, Elizabeth (Fox de Cardona) Waisbord, Silvio R. (Silvio Ricardo), 1961- Description: p. cm. ISBN: 0292725361 (alk. paper) Cancelled ISBN: 029272527X (alk. paper) Notes: Includes bibliographical references and index. Subjects: Mass media--Political aspects--Latin America. Mass media policy--Latin America. Latin America--Politics and government--1980- LC Classification: P95.82.L29 L38 2002 Dewey Class No.: 302.23/098 21

Lauritsen, John. The AIDS war: propaganda, profiteering and genocide from the medical-industrial complex / John Lauritsen. Published/Created: New York: Asklepios, c1993. Description: 479 p.: ill.; 22 cm. ISBN: 0943742080: Notes: Includes bibliographical references and indexes. Subjects: AIDS (Disease)--Political aspects. AIDS (Disease)--Research. AIDS (Disease)--Government policy. AIDS (Disease) in mass media. LC Classification: RA644.A25 L37 1993 Dewey Class No.: 362.1/969792 20

Lenart, Silvo. Shaping political attitudes: the impact of interpersonal communication and mass media / Silvo Lenart. Published/Created: Thousand Oaks, Calif.: Sage Publications, c1994. Description: vii, 150 p.: ill.; 24 cm. ISBN: 0803957084 0803957092 (pbk.) Notes: Includes bibliographical references (p. 140-145) and index. Subjects: Public opinion. Communication in politics. Mass media--Political aspects. Interpersonal communication. LC Classification: HM261 .L497 1994 Dewey Class No.: 303.3/8 20

Levine, Allan Gerald, 1956- Scrum wars: the prime ministers and the media / Allan Levine. Published/Created: Toronto; Niagara Falls, N.Y., U.S.A.: Dundurn Press, c1993. Description: xxiv, 389 p.: ill.; 24 cm. ISBN: 1550021915 (cloth) 1550022075 (pbk.) Notes: Includes bibliographical references (p. [365]-382) and index. Subjects: Mass media--Political aspects--Canada. Government and the press--Canada. Prime ministers--Canada. Canada--Politics and government--1867- LC Classification: P95.82.C2 L48 1993 Dewey Class No.: 302.23/0971 20

Lewis, Justin, 1958- Constructing public opinion: how political elites do what they like and why we seem to go along with it / Justin Lewis. Published/Created: New York: Columbia University Press, c2001. Description: xiv, 250 p.; 24 cm. ISBN: 0231117663 (alk. paper) 0231117671 (pbk.: alk. paper) Notes: Includes bibliographical references (p. [221]-234) and index. Subjects: Public opinion. Public opinion--United States. Mass media and public opinion--United States. Political psychology. LC Classification: HM1236 .L48 2001 Dewey Class No.: 303.3/8 21

Liebovich, Louis. Bylines in despair: Herbert Hoover, the Great Depression, and the U.S. news media / Louis W. Liebovich. Published/Created: Westport, Conn.: Praeger, 1994. Description: xv, 223 p.: ill.; 25 cm. ISBN: 0275948439 (alk. paper) Notes: Includes bibliographical references (p. [213]-216) and index. Subjects: Hoover, Herbert, 1874-1964. Depressions--1929--United States. Presidents--Press coverage--United States--History--20th century. Mass media--Political aspects--United States--History 20th century. United States--Politics and government--1929-1933. LC Classification: E802 .L52 1994 Dewey Class No.: 973.91/6/092 20

Limburg, Val E. Electronic media ethics / Val E. Limburg. Published/Created: Boston: Focal Press, c1994. Description: x, 188 p.: ill.; 24 cm. ISBN: 0240801458 (acid-free paper) Notes: Includes bibliographical references and index. Subjects: Mass media--Moral and ethical aspects--United States. LC Classification: P94 .L56 1994 Dewey Class No.: 174 20

Lusane, Clarence, 1953- Race in the global era: African Americans at the millennium / by Clarence Lusane. Published/Created: Boston: South End Press, 1997. Projected Pub. Date: 9710 Description: p. cm. ISBN: 0896085732 (alk. paper) 0896085740 Notes: Includes bibliographical references. Subjects: Racism--Political aspects--United States. Afro-Americans--Politics and government. Afro-Americans--Social conditions--1975- Afro-Americans in mass media. United States--Race relations. LC Classification: E185.615 .L93 1997 Dewey Class No.: 305.896/073 21

Maherzi, Lotfi. World communication report: the media and the challenge of the new technologies / [author Lotfi Maherzi]. Published/Created: Paris: Unesco, 1997. Related Authors: Unesco. Description: 298 p.: ill., maps; 30 cm. ISBN: 9231034286 Notes: Includes bibliographical references. Subjects: Communication--Technological innovations. Communication, International. Mass media--Political aspects. Freedom of information. LC Classification: P96.T42 M34 1997

Malovi´c, Stjepan. The people, press, and politics of Croatia / Stjepan Malovic and Gary W. Selnow. Published/Created: Westport, Conn.: Praeger, 2001. Related Authors: Selnow, Gary W. Description: xi, 245 p.; 24 cm. ISBN: 0275965430 (alk. paper) Notes: Includes bibliographical references (p. [235]-238) and index. Subjects: Mass media--Political aspects--Croatia. Press and politics--Croatia. Croatia--Politics and government--1990- LC Classification: P95.82.C87 M35 2001 Dewey Class No.: 302.23/094972 21

Manufacturing consent: Noam Chomsky and the media: the companion book to the award-winning film by Peter Wintonick and Mark Achbar / [edited by Mark Achbar]. Published/Created: Montréal; New York: Black Rose Books, c1994. Related Authors: Achbar, Mark. Institute of Policy Alternatives (Montréal, Québec) Related Titles: Noam Chomsky and the media. Description: 264 p.: ill.; 22 x 24 cm. ISBN: 1551640031 (bound): 1551640023 (pbk.): Notes: "A publication of the Institute of Policy Alternatives of Montreal (IPAM)"--T p. verso. 18 "Philosopher All-Stars" trading cards affixed to p. 3 of cover. Includes bibliographical references and index. Subjects: Chomsky, Noam--Political and social views. Chomsky, Noam--Pensée politique et sociale. Mass media--Political aspects. Médias--Aspect politique. United States--Politics and government. United States--Foreign relations. États-Unis--Relations extérieures. LC Classification: P85.C47 M36 1994 Dewey Class No.: 302.23 20 National Bib. No.: C94-900195-3

Mass communication and political information processing / edited by Sidney Kraus. Published/Created: Hillsdale, N.J.: L. Erlbaum Associates, 1990. Related

Authors: Kraus, Sidney. Description: xv, 227 p.: ill.; 24 cm. ISBN: 0805803890 Notes: Papers presented at a symposium on "political information processing" held during a congress entitled "Communication and Cognition--Applied Epistemology" held Dec. 6-8, 1987, in Gent, Belgium. Includes bibliographical references and indexes. Subjects: Mass media--Political aspects--Congresses. Series: Communication (Hillsdale, N.J.) Variant Series: Communication LC Classification: P95.8 .M377 1990 Dewey Class No.: 302.23 20

Mass communication, democracy, and civil society in Africa: international perspectives / edited by Luke Uka Uche. Published/Created: Lagos: Nigerian National Commission for Unesco, 1999. Related Authors: Uche, Luke Uka, 1947- Description: xxi, 557 p.: ill.; 24 cm. ISBN: 9780416838 Notes: Includes bibliographical references and indexes. Subjects: Mass media--Social aspects--Political aspects--Africa. Telecommunication--Social aspects--Political aspects--Africa. Civil society--Democratization--Africa. LC Classification: HN780.Z9 M35 1999 Dewey Class No.: 302.23/096 21

Mass media and democratization: a country study on Nepal. Published/Created: Kathmandu, Nepal: Institute for Integrated Development Studies, c1996. Related Authors: Institute for Integrated Development Studies (Kathmandu, Nepal) Description: 259 p.: ill.; 23 cm. Notes: Includes bibliographical references (p. 187-189). Subjects: Mass media--Social aspects--Political aspects--Nepal. Democratization--Nepal. LC Classification: HN683.5 .M369 1996 Dewey Class No.: 302.23/095496 21

Mass media and society / edited by James Curran and Michael Gurevitch. Edition Information: 3rd ed. Published/Created: London: Arnold; New York: Oxford University Press, 2000. Related Authors: Curran, James. Gurevitch, Michael. Description: vi, 408 p.: ill.; 24 cm. ISBN: 0340732016 (pb) Notes: Includes bibliographical references and index. Subjects: Mass media--Social aspects. Mass media--Political aspects. LC Classification: HM1206 .M37 2000 Dewey Class No.: 302.23 21

Mass media and society / edited by James Curran and Michael Gurevitch. Edition Information: 2nd ed. Published/Created: London; New York: Arnold; New York: Distributed exclusively in the USA by St Martin's Press, 1996. Projected Pub. Date: 9605 Related Authors: Curran, James. Gurevitch, Michael. Description: p. cm. ISBN: 0340614188 (pbk.) Notes: Includes bibliographical references and index. Subjects: Mass media--Social aspects. Mass media--Political aspects. LC Classification: HM258 .M185 1996 Dewey Class No.: 302.23 20

Mass media and society / edited by James Curran and Michael Gurevitch. Published/Created: London; New York: E. Arnold; New York: Distributed in the USA by Routledge, Chapman and Hall, 1991. Related Authors: Curran, James. Gurevitch, Michael. Description: 350 p.: ill.; 25 cm. ISBN: 0340559470: 034051759X (pbk.): Notes: Includes bibliographical references and index. Subjects: Mass media--Social aspects--Political aspects. LC Classification: HM258 .M26578 1992 Dewey Class No.: 302.23 20

Mass media in Vietnam / David Marr, editor. Published/Created: Canberra: Department of Political and Social Change, Research School of Pacific and Asian Studies, Australian National University, 1998. Related Authors: Marr, David G. Australian National University. Dept. of Political and Social Change. Description: vi, 166 p.; 22 cm. ISBN: 0909524327 Notes: Includes bibliographical references and index. Subjects: Mass media--Vietnam. Series: Political and social change monograph; 25 LC Classification: P92.V46 M37 1998 Dewey Class No.: 302.23/09597 21

Mass media, politics, and society in the Middle East / edited by Kai Hafez. Published/Created: Cresskill, N.J.: Hampton Press, c2001. Related Authors: Hafez, Kai, 1964- Description: x, 249 p.; 24 cm. ISBN: 1572733039 1572733047 (pbk.) Notes: Includes bibliographical references and indexes. Subjects: Mass media--Middle East. Series: The Hampton Press communication series. Political communication LC Classification: P92.M5 M374 2001 Dewey Class No.: 302.23/0956 21

Masud, Enver. The war on Islam / Enver Masud. Published/Created: Arlington, VA: Madrasah Books, 2000. Description: 173 p.; 22 cm. ISBN: 097000110X (paperback: alk. paper) Subjects: Islam in mass media. Mass media--Religious aspects--Islam. Mass media--Objectivity--United States. LC Classification: P96.I84 M37 2000 Dewey Class No.: 297 21

Mazzocco, Dennis W. Networks of power: corporate TV's threat to democracy / Dennis W. Mazzocco; foreword by Herbert I. Schiller. Published/Created: Boston, MA: South End Press, c1994. Description: xiv, 208 p.; 23 cm. ISBN: 0896084736 0896084728 (pbk.) Notes: Includes bibliographical references (p. 195-198) and index. Subjects: ABC Television Network. Mass media--Ownership--United States. Mass media--Political aspects--United States. Communication, International. Broadcast journalism--Political aspects--United States. United States--Politics and government--1981-1989. United States--Foreign relations--1981-1989. LC Classification: P96.E252 U655 1994 Dewey Class No.: 302.23/0973 20

McChesney, Robert Waterman, 1952- Corporate media and the threat to democracy / Robert W. McChesney. Published/Created: New York: Seven Stories Press, c1997. Description: 79 p.; 18 cm. ISBN: 1888363479 (alk. paper) Notes: Includes bibliographical references (p. 75-79). Subjects: Communication, International. Mass media--Economic aspects. Communication, International cooperation. Democracy. Series: The Open media pamphlet series LC Classification: P96.I5 M337 1997 Dewey Class No.: 302.2 21

McChesney, Robert Waterman, 1952- Rich media, poor democracy: communication politics in dubious times / Robert W. McChesney. Published/Created: Urbana: University of Illinois Press, c1999. Description: xii, 427 p.; 25 cm. ISBN: 0252024486 (cloth: alk. paper) Notes: Includes bibliographical references (p. [321]-394) and index. Subjects: Mass media--Political aspects--United States. Mass media--United States--Social aspects. Democracy--United States. Series: The history of communication LC Classification: P95.82.U6 M38 1999 Dewey Class No.: 302.23/0973 21

McGuinness, P. P. (Padraic Pearse) The media crisis in Australia: ownership of the media and democracy / Padraic P. McGuinness. Published/Created: Melbourne, Vic.: Schwartz & Wilkinson, c1990. Description: 110 p.; 22 cm. ISBN: 1863370366: Subjects: Mass media--Australia--Ownership. Mass media policy--Australia. LC Classification: P96.E252 A86 1990 Dewey Class No.: 302.23/0994 20

Media and democracy in Latin America and the Caribbean. Published/Created: Paris: Unesco Pub., 1996. Related Authors: González, Rosa M. Unesco. Description: 250 p.; 22 cm. ISBN: 9231031880 (pbk.) Notes: Prepared by the Communication Division of UNESCO and edited by Rosa M. González. Includes bibliographical references. Subjects: Mass media--Latin America. Mass media--Caribbean Area. Freedom of the press--Latin America. Freedom of the press--Caribbean Area. Series: Communication and development series LC Classification: P92.L3 M43 1996 Dewey Class No.: 302.23/098 21

Media and democracy in South Africa / edited by Jane Duncan, Mandla Seleoane. Published/Created: Pretoria: HSRC and FXI, 1998. Related Authors: Duncan, Jane.

Seleoane, Mandla. Description: 253 p.; 22 cm. ISBN: 0796918546 Notes: Includes bibliographical references (p. 247-253). Subjects: Mass media--Political aspects--South Africa. Democracy--South Africa. South Africa--Politics and government--1989- LC Classification: P95.82.S6 M43 1998 Dewey Class No.: 302.23/0968 21

Media and politics in Asia: trends, problems, and prospects / edited by Carolina G. Hernandez, Werner Pfennig. Published/Created: [Diliman, Quezon City, Philippines]: U.P. Center for Integrative and Development Studies; [Manila]: National Institute for Policy Studies: Friedrich Naumann Foundation, c1991. Related Authors: Hernandez, Carolina G. Pfennig, Werner, 1944- University of the Philippines. Center for Integrative and Development Studies. National Institute for Policy Studies (Philippines) Friedrich-Naumann-Stiftung. Description: ix, 236 p.: ill.; 23 cm. ISBN: 9718797009 Notes: Based on a conference of the same name held Mar. 1990, Manila, Philippines. Subjects: Mass media--Political aspects--Asia--Congresses. LC Classification: P92.A7 M42 1991 Dewey Class No.: 302.23/095 20

Media and politics in Japan / edited by Susan J. Pharr and Ellis S. Krauss. Published/Created: Honolulu: University of Hawai'i Press, c1996. Related Authors: Pharr, Susan J. Krauss, Ellis S. Description: xv, 389 p.; 25 cm. ISBN: 0824816986 (alk. paper) 0824817613 (pbk.) Notes: Includes bibliographical references and index. Subjects: Mass media--Political aspects--Japan. Japan--Politics and government--1945- LC Classification: P95.82.J3 M43 1996 Dewey Class No.: 302.23/0952 20

Media and politics in transition: cultural identity in the age of globalization / Jan Servaes & Rico Lie (eds.). Edition Information: 1st ed. Published/Created: Leuven: Acco, 1997. Related Authors: Servaes, Jan, 1952- Lie, Rico. Description: 240 p.: ill.; 24 cm. ISBN: 9033438356 Notes: Papers presented at the international conference "Media & Politics", held at the Katholieke Universiteit Brussel from 27 February to 1 March 1997. Includes bibliographical references (p. [223]-234) and index. Subjects: Mass media--Political aspects. Mass media and culture. Mass media--Social aspects. Communication in politics. LC Classification: P95.8 .M385 1997 Dewey Class No.: 302.23 21

Media and public policy / edited by Robert J. Spitzer. Published/Created: Westport, Conn.: Praeger, 1993. Related Authors: Spitzer, Robert J., 1953- Description: xi, 235 p.; 25 cm. ISBN: 0275943038 (alk. paper) Notes: Includes bibliographical references (p. [213]-228) and index. Subjects: Mass media--Political aspects--United States. United States--Politics and government--1989-1993. United States--Foreign relations--1989-1993. Series: Praeger series in political communication, 1062-5623 LC Classification: P95.82.U6 M46 1993 Dewey Class No.: 302.23/0973 20

Media and voters in Canadian election campaigns / Frederick J. Fletcher, editor. Published/Created: Toronto: Dundurn Press, c1991. Related Authors: Fletcher, Frederick J. Canada. Royal Commission on Electoral Reform and Party Financing. Description: xxiii, 258 p.: ill.; 23 cm. ISBN: 1550021141: Notes: "... commissioned as part of the research program of the Royal Commission on Electoral Reform and Party Financing"--P. ii. Includes bibliographical references. Subjects: Canada. Parliament--Elections. Mass media--Political aspects--Canada. Communication in politics--Canada. Political campaigns--Canada. Campaign management--Canada. Series: Research studies (Canada. Royal Commission on Electoral Reform and Party Financing); v. 18. Variant Series: Research studies; v. 18 LC Classification: JL193 .M37 1991 Dewey Class No.: 324.7/3/0971 20

Media effects: advances in theory and research / edited by Jennings Bryant, Dolf Zillmann. Published/Created: Hillsdale, N.J.: Erlbaum, 1994. Related Authors: Bryant,

Jennings. Zillmann, Dolf. Description: ix, 505 p.: ill.; 24 cm. ISBN: 0805809171 (cloth: alk. paper) 080580918X (pbk.: alk. paper) Notes: Includes bibliographical references and indexes. Subjects: Mass media--United States--Psychological aspects. Mass media--Social aspects--United States. Mass media--Political aspects--United States. Mass media--United States--Influence. Series: Lea's communication series LC Classification: HN90.M3 M415 1994 Dewey Class No.: 302.23 20

Media effects: advances in theory and research / Jennings Bryant & Dolf Zillmann, editors. Edition Information: 2nd ed. Published/Created: Mahwah, NJ: Lawrence Elbaum Associates, 2002. Projected Pub. Date: 0202 Related Authors: Bryant, Jennings. Zillmann, Dolf. Description: p. cm. ISBN: 0805838635 (case: alk. paper) 0805838643 (pbk.: alk. paper) Notes: Includes bibliographical references and index. Subjects: Mass media--United States--Psychological aspects. Mass media--Social aspects--United States. Mass media--Political aspects--United States. Mass media--United States--Influence. Series: LEA's communication series LC Classification: HN90.M3 M415 2002 Dewey Class No.: 302.23 21

Media in transition: from totalitarianism to democracy / [edited by Oleg Manaev and Yuri Pryliuk; preface by Cees J. Humelink; introduction by Oleg Manaev and Yuri Pryliuk; translated by Mikhail Sobutsky]. Published/Created: Kyïv [Ukraine]: Abris, 1993. Related Authors: Manaev, Oleg. Pryliuk, Yuri. Description: xi, 291 p.; 21 cm. Cancelled ISBN: 0586828113 Notes: Includes bibliographical references and index. Subjects: Mass media--Political aspects. Mass media--Social aspects. Democracy. Democratization. Multiculturalism. LC Classification: P95.8 .M393 1993 Dewey Class No.: 302.23 20

Media polls in American politics / Thomas E. Mann and Gary R. Orren, editors. Published/Created: Washington, D.C.: Brookings Institution, c1992. Related Authors: Mann, Thomas E. Orren, Gary R. Joan Shorenstein Barone Center on the Press, Politics, and Public Policy. Description: ix, 172 p.; 24 cm. ISBN: 0815754566: 0815754558 (pbk.): Notes: "A study produced jointly with the Joan Shorenstein Barone Center on the Press, Politics, and Public Policy, John F. Kennedy School of Government, Harvard University." Includes bibliographical references and index. Subjects: Public opinion polls. Public opinion--United States. Election forecasting--United States. Mass media--Political aspects--United States. Press and politics--United States. LC Classification: HM261 .M44 1992 Dewey Class No.: 303.3/8 20

Media, crisis, and democracy: mass communication and the disruption of social order / edited by Marc Raboy and Bernard Dagenais. Published/Created: London; Newbury Park: SAGE, 1992. Related Authors: Raboy, Marc, 1948- Dagenais, Bernard. Description: vii, 199 p.; 24 cm. ISBN: 0803986394 (cased) 0803986408 (pbk): Notes: Bibliography: p. 181-189. - Includes index. Subjects: Mass media--Political aspects. Mass media--Social aspects. Crises. Series: Media, culture, and society series. Variant Series: The Media, culture & society series LC Classification: P95.8 .M39 1992 Dewey Class No.: 302.23 20 National Bib. No.: GB92-27770

Media, crisis, and democracy: mass communication and the disruption of social order / edited by Marc Raboy and Bernard Dagenais. Published/Created: London; Newbury Park: SAGE, 1992. Related Authors: Raboy, Marc, 1948- Dagenais, Bernard. Description: vii, 199 p.; 24 cm. ISBN: 0803986394 (cased) 0803986408 (pbk): Notes: Bibliography: p. 181-189. - Includes index. Subjects: Mass media--Political aspects. Mass media--Social aspects. Crises. Series: Media, culture, and society series. Variant Series: The Media, culture & society series LC Classification: P95.8 .M39 1992 Dewey Class No.: 302.23 20

Media, democracy and renewal in Southern Africa / editors, Keyan Tomaselli and Hopeton Dunn. Published/Created: Denver, CO: International Academic Publishers, 2001. Projected Pub. Date: 0112 Related Authors: Tomaselli, Keyan G., 1948- Dunn, Hopeton S. Description: p. cm. ISBN: 1588681513 (pbk.) Notes: Includes bibliographical references. Subjects: Mass media--Political aspects--Africa, Southern. Mass media--Social aspects--Africa, Southern. Democracy--Africa, Southern. Africa, Southern--Politics and government--1994- LC Classification: P95.82.A4156 M43 2001 Dewey Class No.: 302.23/0968 21

Media, elections, and democracy / Frederick J. Fletcher, editor. Published/Created: Toronto: Dundurn Press, c1991. Related Authors: Fletcher, Frederick J. Canada. Royal Commission on Electoral Reform and Party Financing. Description: xxi, 234 p.: ill.; 23 cm. ISBN: 155002115X Notes: "... commissioned as part of the research program of the Royal Commission on Electoral Reform and Party Financing"--P. ii. Includes bibliographical references. Subjects: Mass media--Political aspects. Communication in politics. Elections. Democracy. Series: Research studies (Canada. Royal Commission on Electoral Reform and Party Financing); v. 19 Variant Series: Research studies, 1188-2743; v. 19 LC Classification: P95.8 .M38 1991 Dewey Class No.: 302.23 20

Mermin, Jonathan, 1966- Debating war and peace: media coverage of U.S. intervention in the post-Vietnam era / Jonathan Mermin. Published/Created: Princeton, N.J.: Princeton University Press, c1999. Description: xii, 162 p.; 24 cm. ISBN: 0691005338 (alk. paper) 0691005346 (pbk.: alk. paper) Notes: Includes bibliographical references and index. Subjects: War in mass media. Mass media--United States. United States--Military policy. United States--Foreign relations. LC Classification: P96.W352 U556 1999 Dewey Class No.: 070.4/49355/033073 21

Meyer, Thomas, 1943- Media democracy: how the media colonize politics / Thomas Meyer. Published/Created: Cambridge, UK: Polity Press; Malden, MA: Blackwell, c2002. Projected Pub. Date: 0211 Description: p. cm. ISBN: 0745628435 0745628443 (pbk.) Notes: Includes bibliographical references and index. Subjects: Mass media--Political aspects. LC Classification: P95.8 .M493 2002 Dewey Class No.: 302.23 21

Michigan. Civil Rights Commission. The role and responsibility of the media in the community: final report / [Michigan Civil Rights Commission]. Published/Created: [Lansing, Mich.: The Commission, 1996] Description: xi, 49 p.; 28 cm. Notes: "Cover title". "Adopted September 30, 1996"--Cover. Includes bibliographical references (p. 48-49). Subjects: Mass media and minorities--Michigan. Minorities--Press coverage--Michigan. Stereotype (Psychology) in mass media. Mass media policy--Michigan. Freedom of the press--Michigan. LC Classification: P94.5.M552 U66 1996 Dewey Class No.: 302.23/086/9309774 21

Mickler, Steve. The myth of privilege / Steve Mickler. Published/Created: Fremantle, W.A.: Fremantle Arts Centre Press, 1998. Description: 346 p.: ill.; 21 cm. ISBN: 186368249X Notes: Includes bibliographical references (p. 331-338) and index. Subjects: Australian aborigines in mass media. Mass media and minorities--Australia. Mass media and race relations--Australia. Australia--Ethnic relations--Political aspects. LC Classification: P94.5.A85 M53 1998 Dewey Class No.: 302.23/089/9915 21

Miller, Arthur, 1915- On politics and the art of acting / Arthur Miller. Published/Created: New York: Viking, 2001. Description: 87 p.: ill.; 19 cm. ISBN: 0670030422 (alk. paper) Subjects: Miller, Arthur, 1915- --Political and social views. Acting--Political aspects--United States--History--20th century. Mass media--Political aspects--United States--History 20th century. Presidents--United States--History--20th century. Politicians--United States--History--20th century. Presidents--United States--Psychology. Politicians--United States--Psychology. Political culture--United States--History--20th century. United States--Politics and government--1945-1989. United States--Politics and government--1989- LC Classification: E743 .M547 2001 Dewey Class No.: 320.973/01/4 21

Miller, Edward D. The Charlotte project: helping citizens take back democracy / by Edward D. Miller. Published/Created: St. Petersburg, Fla. (801 Third Street, St. Petersburg, Fla. 33701): Poynter Institute for Media Studies, 1994. Related Titles: Charlotte observer (Charlotte, N.C.: 1916) Description: 93 p.: ill.; 23 cm. Notes: At head of How The Charlotte observer reinvented its democratic role by reaching out to its readers. Subjects: Charlotte observer (Charlotte, N.C.: 1916) Press and politics--North Carolina. Mass media--Political aspects--North Carolina. Political campaigns--North Carolina. Series: The Poynter papers; no. 4 LC Classification: PN4751 .M55 1994 Dewey Class No.: 071/.56 20

Miller, Michael Nelson, 1942- Red, white, and green: the maturing of Mexicanidad, 1940-1946 / by Michael Nelson Miller. Edition Information: 1st ed. Published/Created: El Paso, Tex.: Texas Western Press, University of Texas at El Paso, c1998. Description: viii, 227 p.; 23 cm. ISBN: 087404278X Notes: Includes bibliographical references (p. 211-222) and index. Subjects: Avila Camacho, Manuel, 1897-1955 --Influence. Mass media--Political aspects--Mexico. Mexico--Cultural policy. Mexico--Politics and government--1910-1946. Series: Southwestern studies (El Paso, Tex.); no. 107. Variant Series: Southwestern studies; no. 107 LC Classification: F1210 .M6195 1998 Dewey Class No.: 972.0825 21

Miller, William Lockley, 1943- Media and voters: the audience, content, and influence of press and television at the 1987 general election / William L. Miller. Published/Created: Oxford: Clarendon Press; Oxford; New York: Oxford University Press, 1991. Description: xvii, 231 p.: ill.; 23 cm. ISBN: 0198273770: Notes: Includes bibliographical references (p. [223]-227) and index. Subjects: Great Britain. Parliament--Elections,--1987. Elections--Great Britain. Mass media--Political aspects--Great Britain. LC Classification: JN956 .M54 1991 Dewey Class No.: 324.941/0858 20

Milton, Andrew K. The rational politician: exploiting the media in new democracies / Andrew K. Milton. Published/Created: Aldershot; Brookfield, Vt.: Ashgate, c2000. Description: viii, 197 p.; 23 cm. ISBN: 0754611701 Notes: Includes bibliographical references (p. 191-194) and index. Subjects: Mass media--Political aspects--Europe, Eastern. Decommunization--Europe, Eastern. Democracy--Europe, Eastern. Europe, Eastern--Politics and government--1989- LC Classification: P95.82.E852 M55 2000 Dewey Class No.: 302.23/0947 21

Milton, Andrew K. The rational politician: exploiting the media in new democracies / Andrew K. Milton. Published/Created: Aldershot; Brookfield, Vt.: Ashgate, c2000. Description: viii, 197 p.; 23 cm. ISBN: 0754611701 Notes: Includes bibliographical references (p. 191-194) and index. Subjects: Mass media--Political aspects--Europe, Eastern. Decommunization--Europe, Eastern. Democracy--Europe, Eastern. Europe, Eastern--Politics and government--1989- LC Classification: P95.82.E852 M55 2000 Dewey Class No.: 302.23/0947 21

Mitchell, Greg, 1947- The campaign of the century: Upton Sinclair's race for governor of California and the birth of media politics / Greg Mitchell. Edition Information: 1st ed. Published/Created: New York: Random House, 1992. Description: xx, 665 p.; 24 cm. ISBN: 0871134675: Notes: Includes bibliographical references (p. [623]-633) and index. Subjects: Sinclair, Upton, 1878-1968. Governors--California--Election--History--20th century. Mass media

Political aspects--California--History--20th century. California--Politics and government--1850-1950. LC Classification: F866 .M65 1992 Dewey Class No.: 979.4/05 20

Mughan, Anthony. Media and the presidentialization of parliamentary elections / Anthony Mughan. Published/Created: Houndmills, Basingstoke, Hampshire; New York: Palgrave, 2000. Description: xiv, 179 p.: ill.; 23 cm. ISBN: 0333800184 Notes: Includes bibliographical references (p. 167-175) and index. Subjects: Elections--Great Britain. Political parties--Great Britain. Political leadership--Great Britain. Mass media--Political aspects--Great Britain. Great Britain--Politics and government--1945- LC Classification: JN956 .M82 2000 Dewey Class No.: 324.941/0858 21

Mutz, Diana Carole. Impersonal influence: how perceptions of mass collectives affect political attitudes / Diana C. Mutz. Published/Created: Cambridge; New York: Cambridge University Press, 1998. Description: xx, 334 p.: ill.; 25 cm. ISBN: 0521631327 Notes: Includes bibliographical references (p. 301-326) and index. Subjects: Mass media--Political aspects. Mass media and public opinion. Series: Cambridge studies in political psychology and public opinion LC Classification: P95.8 .M88 1998 Dewey Class No.: 302.23 21

Naylor, R. T., 1945- Bankers, bagmen, and bandits: business and politics in the age of greed / R.T. Naylor. Published/Created: Montreal; New York: Black Rose Books, c1990. Description: 166 p.; 23 cm. ISBN: 0921689764 (pbk.: alk. paper) 0921689772 (hard: alk. paper) Subjects: International economic relations. International finance. Mass media--Political aspects. Business and politics. Corporations--Political activity. LC Classification: HF1359 .N39 1990 Dewey Class No.: 332.1/5 20

Nazer, Hisham M., 1932- Power of a third kind: the Western attempt to colonize the global village / Hisham M. Nazer. Published/Created: Westport, Conn.: Praeger, 1999. Description: xxv, 167 p.; 24 cm. ISBN: 0275964892 (acid-free paper) Notes: Includes bibliographical references (p. [147]-160) and index. Subjects: Mass media--Political aspects. Ideology. Power (Social sciences) LC Classification: P95.8 .N35 1999 Dewey Class No.: 302.23 21

Negrine, Ralph M. Parliament and the media: a study of Britain, Germany, and France / Ralph Negrine. Published/Created: London: Royal Institute of International Affairs, 1998. Description: viii, 164 p.: ill.; 23 cm. ISBN: 1855675552 (hardcover) 1855675560 (pbk.) Notes: Includes bibliographical references (p. 136-138). Subjects: Mass media--Political aspects--Great Britain. Mass media--Political aspects--Germany. Mass media--Political aspects--France. Great Britain--Politics and government--1979-1997. Germany--Politics and government--1945- France--Politics and government--1981-1995. Series: Chatham House papers (Unnumbered) Variant Series: Chatham House papers LC Classification: P95.82.G7 N43 1998 Dewey Class No.: 302.23/0941 21

Negrine, Ralph M. Politics and the mass media in Britain / Ralph Negrine. Edition Information: 2nd ed. Published/Created: London; New York: Routledge, 1994. Description: x, 235 p.: ill.; 24 cm. ISBN: 0415094682 (acid-free paper) Notes: Includes bibliographical references (p. 215-231) and index. Subjects: Mass media--Political aspects--Great Britain. Great Britain--Politics and government--1979-1997. LC Classification: P95.82.G7 N44 1994 Dewey Class No.: 302.23/0941 20

Negrine, Ralph M. The communication of politics / Ralph Negrine. Published/Created: London; Thousand Oaks: Sage, 1996. Description: xiii, 192 p.: ill.; 24 cm. ISBN: 0803977387 0803977395 (pbk.) Notes: Includes bibliographical references (p. [181]-188) and index. Subjects: Communication in politics--Great Britain--United States.

Mass media--Political aspects--Great Britain--United States. LC Classification: JA85.2.G7 N44 1996

Nesbitt-Larking, Paul W. (Paul Wingfield), 1954- Politics, society, and the media: Canadian perspectives / Paul Nesbitt-Larking. Published/Created: Peterborough, Ont.: Broadview Press, c2001. Description: 423 p.; 23 cm. ISBN: 1551111810 Notes: Includes index. Includes bibliographical references: p. 399-413. Subjects: Mass media--Political aspects--Canada. Médias--Aspect politique--Canada. LC Classification: P95.82.C2 N47 2001 Dewey Class No.: 302.23/0971 21 Nat'l Bib. Agency No.: 20019303742

Neuman, Johanna. Lights, camera, war: is media technology driving international politics / Johanna Neuman. Edition Information: 1st ed. Published/Created: New York: St. Martin's Press, 1996. Description: 327 p.: ill.; 22 cm. ISBN: 0312140045 Notes: Includes bibliographical references (p. 283-309) and index. Subjects: Broadcast journalism. Television broadcasting of news. Journalism--Political aspects. War in mass media. LC Classification: PN4784.B75 N48 1996 Dewey Class No.: 070.1/9 20

News media and foreign relations: a multifaceted perspective / edited by Abbas Malek. Published/Created: Norwood, N.J.: Ablex Pub., c1997. Related Authors: Malek, Abbas. Description: xiv, 268 p.: ill.; 24 cm. ISBN: 1567502725 (cloth) 1567502733 (paper) Notes: Includes bibliographical references and indexes. Subjects: Mass media--Political aspects. Press and politics. International relations. Series: The Ablex communication, culture & information series LC Classification: P95.8 .N48 1997 Dewey Class No.: 302.23 20

Niblo, Stephen R., 1941- Mexico in the 1940s: modernity, politics, and corruption / Stephen R. Niblo. Published/Created: Wilimington, Del.: Scholarly Resources, 1999. Description: xxv, 408 p.: ill.; 24 cm. ISBN: 0842027047 (cloth: alk. paper) Notes: Includes bibliographical references (p. 369-385) and index. Subjects: Political corruption--Mexico--History--20th century. Mass media--Political aspects--Mexico. Mexico--Politics and government--1910-1970. Series: Latin American silhouettes. Variant Series: Latin American silhouettes: studies in history and culture LC Classification: F1234 .N495 1999 Dewey Class No.: 972.08/2 21

Nigeria: the mass media and democracy / edited by Ismail Ibrahim & Tunde Akanni. Published/Created: Lagos, Nigeria: Civil Liberties Organisation, 1996. Related Authors: Ibrahim, Ismail, 1968- Akanni, Tunde. Description: xix, 171 p.; 23 cm. ISBN: 9783218867 Notes: Includes bibliographical references. Subjects: Mass media--Political aspects--Freedom of the press--Press and politics--Democracy--Nigeria. LC Classification: P85.82.N6 N547 1996 Dewey Class No.: 302.23/09669 21

Nimmo, Dan D. Mediated political realities / Dan Nimmo, James E. Combs. Edition Information: 2nd ed. Published/Created: New York: Longman, c1990. Related Authors: Combs, James E. Description: xiv, 242 p.; 23 cm. ISBN: 080130220X Notes: Includes bibliographical references and indexes. Subjects: Mass media--Political aspects--United States. LC Classification: P95.82.U6 N56 1990 Dewey Class No.: 302/.12 20

Nimmo, Dan D. Political commentators in the United States in the 20th century: a bio-critical sourcebook / Dan Nimmo, Chevelle Newsome. Published/Created: Westport, Conn.: Greenwood Press, 1997. Related Authors: Newsome, Chevelle. Description: xxii, 424 p.; 24 cm. ISBN: 0313295859 (hardcover: alk. paper) Notes: Includes bibliographical references (p. [411]-412) and index. Subjects: Mass media--Political aspects--Journalists--United States--Biography. United States--Politics and government--20th century. LC Classification: P95.82.U6 N57 1997 Dewey Class No.: 302.23/092/273 20

Nimmo, Dan D. The political pundits / Dan Nimmo, James E. Combs. Published/Created: New York: Praeger, 1992. Related Authors: Combs, James E. Description: xx, 195 p.; 24 cm. ISBN: 0275935418 (alk. paper) 0275935450 (pbk.: alk. paper) Notes: Includes bibliographical references (p. [177]-184) and index. Subjects: Mass media--Political aspects. Communication in politics. Mass media criticism. Series: Praeger series in political communication LC Classification: P95.8 .N56 1992 Dewey Class No.: 302.23 20

Nyamnjoh, Francis B., 1961- Mass media and democratisation in Cameroon / by Francis B. Nyamnjoh. Published/Created: Yaoundé, Cameroun: Fondation Friedrich Ebert, c1996. Related Authors: Friedrich-Ebert-Stiftung. Description: 181 p.; 21 cm. Notes: At head of Friedrich Ebert Foundation in Cameroon. Includes bibliographical references (p. 177-181). Subjects: Mass media--Political aspects--Cameroon. Democracy--Cameroon. Cameroon--Politics and government--1982- LC Classification: P92.82.C17 N93 1996 Dewey Class No.: 302.23/096711 21

Ó Siochrú, Seán, 1955- Global media governance: a beginner's guide / Seán Ó Siochrú and W. Bruce Girard with Amy Mahan. Published/Created: Lanham, MD: Rowman & Littlefield, 2002. Projected Pub. Date: 0203 Related Authors: Girard, W. Bruce, 1955- Mahan, Amy. Description: p. cm. ISBN: 0742515656 (alk. paper) 0742515664 (pbk.: alk. paper) Notes: Includes bibliographical references and index. Subjects: Communication--International cooperation. Mass media--Political aspects. Series: Critical media studies LC Classification: P96.I5 O17 2002 Dewey Class No.: 302.2 21

O'Heffernan, Patrick. Mass media and American foreign policy: insider perspectives on global journalism and the foreign policy process / Patrick O'Heffernan. Published/Created: Norwood, NJ: Ablex Pub., c1991. Description: xvi, 262 p.; 24 cm. ISBN: 0893917281 0899391729X (pbk.) Notes: Includes bibliographical references (p. 233-249) and indexes. Subjects: Mass media--Political aspects--United States. United States--Foreign relations--1977-1981. United States--Foreign relations--1981-1989. Series: Communication and information science LC Classification: E872 .O37 1991 Dewey Class No.: 327.73 20

O'Rourke, William. Campaign America '96: the view from the couch / William O'Rourke. Published/Created: New York: Marlowe & Co., c1997. Description: viii, 516 p.; 24 cm. ISBN: 1569247587 Notes: Includes bibliographical references (p. 494-506) and index. Subjects: Presidents--United States--Election--1996. Presidential candidates--United States. Mass media--Political aspects--United States. Voting--United States. United States--Politics and government--1993-2001. LC Classification: E888 .O76 1997 Dewey Class No.: 324.973/0929 21

O'Rourke, William. Campaign America '96: the view from the couch / William O'Rourke. Edition Information: 2nd ed. Published/Created: Notre Dame, IN: University of Notre Dame Press, 2000. Description: viii, 551 p.; 23 cm. ISBN: 0268022518 (pbk.: alk. paper) Notes: Includes bibliographical references (p. 529-541) and index. Subjects: Presidents--United States--Election--1996. Presidential candidates--United States. Mass media--Political aspects--United States. Voting--United States. United States--Politics and government--1993-2001. LC Classification: E888 .O76 2000 Dewey Class No.: 324.973/0929 21

Page, Benjamin I. Who deliberates?: mass media in modern democracy / Benjamin I. Page. Published/Created: Chicago: University of Chicago Press, 1996. Description: ix, 167 p.; 23 cm. ISBN: 0226644723 (alk. paper) 0226644731 (pbk.: alk. paper) Notes: Includes bibliographical references (p. [135]-144) and index. Subjects: Mass media--Political aspects--United States. Communication in politics--United States. Mass media--

Objectivity--United States. Democracy. United States--Politics and government--1993-2001. Series: American politics and political economy LC Classification: P95.82.U6 P34 1996 Dewey Class No.: 302.23/0973 20

Paletz, David L., 1934- The media in American politics: contents and consequences / David L. Paletz. Edition Information: 2nd ed. Published/Created: New York: Addison-Wesley, 2001. Projected Pub. Date: 0107 Description: p. cm. ISBN: 0321077776 Notes: Includes bibliographical references and index. Subjects: Mass media--Political aspects. United States--Politics and government--20th century. LC Classification: HE8689.7.P6 P35 2001 Dewey Class No.: 302.23/0973 21

Pearce, David D. Wary partners: diplomats and the media / David D. Pearce. Published/Created: Washington, D.C.: Congressional Quarterly, c1995. Description: xiii, 205 p.; 24 cm. ISBN: 1568020678 (cl: alk. paper) 156802066X (p: alk. paper) Notes: "An Institute for the Study of Diplomacy book." Includes bibliographical references (p. 197) and index. Subjects: Mass media--Political aspects. International relations. Journalism--Political aspects. LC Classification: P95.8 .P43 1995 Dewey Class No.: 302.23/0883522 20

Petersson, Bo. The Soviet Union and peacetime neutrality in Europe: a study of Soviet political language / Bo Petersson. Published/Created: Lund: MH Pub., c1990. Description: 164 p.; 22 cm. ISBN: 9197145807 Notes: Includes bibliographical references (p. 141-164). Subjects: Russian language--Political aspects. Mass media and language--Soviet Union. Communication--Political aspects--Soviet Union. Neutrality--Europe. Soviet Union--Foreign relations--1945-1991. Series: Lund political studies; 65 LC Classification: PG2074.73 .P48 1990 Dewey Class No.: 491.7 20

Piazza, Thomas Leonard. The boundaries of free speech: how free is too free? / [writers, Tom Piazza, Keith Melville]. Published/Created: Dubuque, Iowa: Kendall/Hunt Pub. Co., [c1991] Related Authors: Melville, Keith. Description: 24, [7] p.: ill.; 28 cm. ISBN: 0840369247 Notes: Cover title. Includes bibliographical references (p. 23). Subjects: Freedom of speech--United States. Censorship--United States. Mass media--Censorship--United States. Series: National issues forum. Variant Series: National issues forums LC Classification: KF4772.Z9 P5 1991 Dewey Class No.: 342.73/0853 347.302853 20

Poggioli, Sylvia. The media in Europe after 1992: a case study of La repubblica / by Sylvia Poggioli. Published/Created: [Cambridge, Mass.]: John F. Kennedy School of Government, Harvard University, Joan Shorenstein Barone Center, [1991] Description: 23 p.; 28 cm. Notes: Cover title. "September 1991." Includes bibliographical references (p. 21-23). Subjects: Repubblica (Rome, Italy) Journalism--Italy. Press and politics--Italy. Mass media--Italy. Series: Discussion paper (Joan Shorenstein Barone Center on the Press, Politics, and Public Policy); D-11. Variant Series: Discussion paper / Harvard University, John F. Kennedy School of Government, The Joan Shorenstein Barone Center; D-11 LC Classification: PN5249.R6 R466 1991

Political communication: engineering visions of order in the socialist world / edited by Sarah Sanderson King and Donald P. Cushman. Published/Created: Albany: State University of New York Press, c1992. Related Authors: King, Sarah Sanderson, 1932- Cushman, Donald P. Description: xiii, 212 p.: map; 23 cm. ISBN: 0791412016 (alk. paper): 0791412024 (alk. paper: pbk.): Notes: Includes bibliographical references and index. Subjects: Mass media--Social aspects--Communist countries. Mass media--Political aspects--Communist countries. Communication in politics--Communist countries. World politics 1989- Communist countries. Politics and government. Series: SUNY series in human communication processes Variant Series: SUNY series, human communication processes LC Classification: HN962.M3 P65 1992 Dewey Class No.: 302.23/09171/7 20

Politics in familiar contexts: projecting politics through popular media / Robert L. Savage and Dan Nimmo, editors. Published/Created: Norwood, N.J.: Ablex Pub., c1990. Related Authors: Savage, Robert L. Nimmo, Dan D. Description: ix, 278 p.; 24 cm. ISBN: 0893915084 Notes: Includes bibliographical references and indexes. Subjects: Mass media--Political aspects. Series: Communication, the human context LC Classification: P95.8 .P65 1990 Dewey Class No.: 302.23 20

Ponder, Stephen, 1942- Managing the press: origins of the media presidency, 1897-1933 / Stephen Ponder. Edition Information: 1st ed. Published/Created: New York: St. Martin's Press, 1999. Description: xviii, 233 p.; 22 cm. ISBN: 0312213840 Notes: Includes bibliographical references (p. [215]-229) and index. Subjects: Presidents--United States--History--20th century. Government and the press--United States--History--20th century. Press and politics--United States--History--20th century. Mass media--Political aspects--United States--History 20th century. United States--Politics and government--1897-1901. United States--Politics and government--1901-1953. LC Classification: E176.1 .P816 1999 Dewey Class No.: 352.23/02748/0973 21

Purvis, Hoyt H. Media, politics, and government / Hoyt Purvis. Edition Information: 1st ed. Published/Created: Fort Worth: Harcourt College Publishers, c2001. Description: xviii, 376 p.: ill.; 24 cm. ISBN: 0155036432 Notes: Includes bibliographical references (p. 345-350) and index. Subjects: Mass media--Political aspects--United States. United States--Politics and government. LC Classification: P95.82.U6 P87 2001 Dewey Class No.: 302.23/0973 21

Rajagopal, Arvind. Politics after television: religious nationalism and the reshaping of the Indian public / Arvind Rajagopal. Published/Created: Cambridge, UK; New York: Cambridge University Press, c2001. Description: viii, 393 p.; 24 cm. ISBN: 0521640539 Notes: Includes bibliographical references (p. 372-389) and index. Subjects: Television in politics--India. Elections--India. Mass media--Political aspects--India. Nationalism--Religious aspects--India. Immigrants--United States. LC Classification: HE8700.76.I4 R34 2001 Dewey Class No.: 306.2/0954 21

Reader, Keith. Regis Debray: a critical introduction / Keith Reader. Published/Created: London; Boulder, Colo.: Pluto Press, 1995. Description: x, 93 p.; 22 cm. ISBN: 074530821X 0745308228 (pbk.) Notes: Includes bibliographical references (p. 85-86) and index. Subjects: Debray, Régis--Political and social views. Ex-Communists--France--Attitudes. Mass media--Political aspects--France. Intellectuals--France--Attitudes. World politics--1989- France--Politics and government--1981-1995. France--Cultural policy. Series: Modern European thinkers LC Classification: HX264 .R43 1995 Dewey Class No.: 335.43 20

Retter, James D. Anatomy of a scandal: an investigation into the campaign to undermine the Clinton presidency / James D. Retter. Published/Created: Los Angeles: General Pub. Group, c1998. Description: 320 p.: ill.; 23 cm. ISBN: 1575440636 (hc) Notes: Includes bibliographical references and index. Subjects: Clinton, Bill, 1946- --Public opinion. Clinton, Hillary Rodham--Public opinion. Mass media--Political aspects--United States. Press and politics--United States. Hate--Political aspects--United States. Conservatism--United States--History--20th century. United States--Politics and government--1993-2001. LC Classification: E885 .R48 1998 Dewey Class No.: 302.23/0973/09045 21

Ricks, Charles W. The military-news media relationship: thinking forward / Charles W.

Ricks. Published/Created: [Carlisle Barracks, PA]: Strategic Studies Institute, U.S. Army War College, [1993] Related Authors: Army War College (U.S.). Strategic Studies Institute. Related Titles: Military news media relationship. Description: vii, 40 p.; 23 cm. Notes: "December 1, 1993." Includes bibliographical references (p. 36-40). Subjects: Journalism, Military--United States. Armed Forces and mass media--United States. United States--Armed Forces--Public relations. LC Classification: P96.A75 R53 1993 Dewey Class No.: 355.3/42/0973 20

Robinson, Gertrude Joch. Constructing the Quebec referendum: French and English media voices / Gertrude J. Robinson. Published/Created: Toronto; Buffalo: University of Toronto Press, c1998. Description: x, 262 p.; 24 cm. ISBN: 0802009093 (bound): 0802078907 (pbk.): Notes: Includes bibliographical references and index. Subjects: Mass media--Political aspects--Québec (Province) Mass media and public opinion--Québec (Province) Referendum--Québec (Province)--Press coverage. Public opinion--Québec (Province) Québec (Province)--Politics and government--1960- LC Classification: P95.82.C2 R6 1998 Dewey Class No.: 070.4/49971404 21 National Bib. No.: C98-930966-5

Ronning, Helge. Media and democracy: theories and principles with reference to an African context / Helge Ronning. Published/Created: Harare: SAPES Books, 1994. Related Authors: SAPES Trust. Description: 20 p.; 21 cm. ISBN: 1779050151 Notes: "SAPES Trust"--P. [4] of cover. Includes bibliographical references (p. 19-20). Subjects: Mass media--Political aspects--Africa. Democracy. Freedom of speech--Africa. Freedom of information--Africa. Free enterprise--Africa. Africa--Politics and government--1960- Series: Seminar paper series; no. 8 LC Classification: P95.82.A4 R66 1994

Rosenstiel, Tom. Strange bedfellows: how television and the presidential candidates changed American politics, 1992 / by Tom Rosenstiel. Edition Information: 1st ed. Published/Created: New York: Hyperion, c1993. Description: xiii, 368 p.: ill.; 25 cm. ISBN: 1562828592: Notes: Includes bibliographical references (p. 355-358) and index. Subjects: Television in politics--United States. Presidents--United States--Election--1992. Mass media--Political aspects. LC Classification: HE8700.76.U6 R67 1993 Dewey Class No.: 324.7/3/097309049 20

Ross, BevAnne. Presidential campaigns and the media: with special emphasis upon the 1988 campaigns / BevAnne Ross. Edition Information: 1st ed. Published/Created: [Novato, Calif.]: BAR Publications, c1991. Description: v, 732 p.; 23 cm. Notes: Includes bibliographical references (p. 600-632) and index. Subjects: Presidents--United States--Election--1988. Press and politics--United States--History--20th century. Mass media--Political aspects--United States--History 20th century. United States--Politics and government--1981-1989. LC Classification: E880 .R67 1991

Ruggles, Myles Alexander. The audience reflected in the medium of law: a critique of the political economy of speech rights in the United States / by Myles Alexander Ruggles. Published/Created: Norwood, N.J.: Ablex Pub. Corp., c1994. Description: xx, 185 p.; 23 cm. ISBN: 0893918814 (cloth) 0893919934 (pbk.) Notes: Includes bibliographical references (p. 165-174) and index. Subjects: Freedom of speech--United States. Mass media--Law and legislation--United States. Freedom of speech--Economic aspects. LC Classification: KF4772 .R84 1994 Dewey Class No.: 342.73/0853 347.302853 20

Rusike, E. T. The politics of the mass media: a personal experience / by E.T.M. Rusike. Published/Created: [Harare, Zimbabwe: Roblaw Publishers, 1990] Description: 111 p., 8 p. of plates: ill.; 19 cm. ISBN: 0908309090 Notes: Includes bibliographical references (p. 104-106). Subjects: Rusike, E. T. Mass media--Political aspects--Zimbabwe. Government and the press--Zimbabwe. Zimbabwean newspapers. LC Classification: P95.82.Z55 R88 1990

Russomanno, Joseph. Speaking our minds: conversations with the people behind landmark First Amendment cases / Joseph Russomanno. Published/Created: Mahwah, NJ: Lawrence Erlbaum Associates, 2002. Projected Pub. Date: 0202 Description: p. cm. ISBN: 0805837671 (cloth: alk. paper) 080583768X (pbk.: alk. paper) Subjects: Freedom of speech--United States--Cases. Freedom of the press--United States--Cases. Mass media--Law and legislation--United States--Cases. LC Classification: KF4770.A7 R87 2002 Dewey Class No.: 342.73/0853

Ryan, Charlotte, 1949- Prime time activism: media strategies for grassroots organizing / by Charlotte Ryan; foreword by William A. Gamson. Edition Information: 1st ed. Published/Created: Boston, MA: South End Press, c1991. Description: xiv, 295 p.: ill.; 22 cm. ISBN: 0896084019 (pbk.): 0896084027: Notes: Includes bibliographical references (p. 259-288) and index. Subjects: Public relations and politics. Mass media--Political aspects. LC Classification: JF2112.P8 R93 1991 Dewey Class No.: 659.2/932 20

Sadkovich, James J., 1945- The U.S. media and Yugoslavia, 1991-1995 / James J. Sadkovich. Published/Created: Westport, Conn.: Praeger, 1998. Description: xx, 272 p.; 25 cm. ISBN: 0275950468 (alk. paper) Notes: Includes bibliographical references (p. [247]-262) and index. Subjects: Yugoslav War, 1991-1995--Press coverage--United States. Yugoslav War, 1991-1995--Mass media and the war. Yugoslav War, 1991-1995--Foreign public opinion, American. War in mass media. LC Classification: DR1313.7.P73 S23 1998 Dewey Class No.: 949.703 21

Salminen, Esko. The silenced media: the propaganda war between Russia and the West in Northern Europe / Esko Salminen. Published/Created: New York: St. Martin's Press, 1999. Description: xii, 198 p.: maps; 23 cm. ISBN: 0312217749 (cloth) Notes: Includes bibliographical references (p. 177-189) and index. Subjects: Mass media--Censorship--Finland. Finland--Relations--Soviet Union. Soviet Union--Relations--Finland. Freedom of the press--Finland. Freedom of speech--Finland. LC Classification: P96.C42 F568 1999 Dewey Class No.: 323.44/5/094897 21

Sanders, James, 1963- South Africa and the international media, 1972-1979: a struggle for representation / James Sanders. Published/Created: London; Portland, OR: F. Cass, 2000. Description: xvi, 270 p.; 24 cm. ISBN: 0714649791 0714680419 (pbk.) Notes: Based on the author's doctoral dissertation. Includes bibliographical references (p. [238]-260) and index. Subjects: Mass media--Political aspects--Anti-apartheid movements--South Africa. South Africa--In mass media--Race relations--Political aspects. South Africa--Politics and government--1961-1978. LC Classification: P96.S68 S26 2000 Dewey Class No.: 070.4/49968 21

Schechter, Danny. The more you watch the less you know: news wars/(sub)merged hopes/media adventures / Danny Schechter; foreword by Charlayne Hunter-Gault. Published/Created: New York: Seven Stories Press, 1997. Projected Pub. Date: 9703 Description: p. cm. ISBN: 1888363401 Subjects: Schechter, Danny. Mass media. LC Classification: P90 .S337 1997 Dewey Class No.: 302.23 21

Schmuhl, Robert. Demanding democracy / Robert Schmuhl. Published/Created: Notre Dame: University of Notre Dame Press, c1994. Description: vii, 149 p.; 23 cm. ISBN: 0268008728 (alk. paper) Notes: Includes bibliographical references (p. 139-142). Subjects: Mass media--Political aspects--United States--Politics and government--1989-1993. LC Classification: P95.82.U6 S347 1994 Dewey Class No.: 302.23/0973 20

Schmuhl, Robert. Statecraft and stagecraft: American political life in the age of personality / Robert Schmuhl. Published/Created: Notre Dame, Ind.: University of Notre Dame Press, c1990. Description: ix, 113 p.: ill.; 23 cm. ISBN: 0268017379: Notes: Includes bibliographical references (p. 103-106). Subjects: Mass media--Political aspects--United States. United States--Politics and government--1981-1989. LC Classification: P95.82.U6 S35 1990 Dewey Class No.: 302.23/0973 20

Schmuhl, Robert. Statecraft and stagecraft: American political life in the age of personality / Robert Schmuhl. Edition Information: 2nd ed. Published/Created: Notre Dame, IN: University of Notre Dame Press, 1992. Projected Pub. Date: 1111 Description: p. cm. ISBN: 0268017441 (pbk.) Notes: Includes bibliographical references. Subjects: Mass media--Political aspects--United States. United States--Politics and government--1981-1989. United States--Politics and government--1989-1993. LC Classification: P95.82.U6 S35 1992 Dewey Class No.: 302.23/0973 20

Schnell, James A., 1955- Perspectives on communication in the People's Republic of China / James A. Schnell. Published/Created: Lanham, MD: Lexington Books, 1999. Projected Pub. Date: 9908 Description: p. cm. ISBN: 0739100130 (alk. paper) Notes: Includes bibliographical references and index. Subjects: Communication--Social aspects--China. Communication--Political aspects--China. Communication in politics--China. Communication in education--China. Intercultural communication--China. Mass media--China. LC Classification: HN733.5 .S36 1999 Dewey Class No.: 302.2 21

Schudson, Michael. Watergate in American memory: how we remember, forget, and reconstruct the past / Michael Schudson. Published/Created: New York: BasicBooks, c1992. Description: xii, 282 p.; 23 cm. ISBN: 0465090842: Notes: Includes bibliographical references (p. 223-267) and index. Subjects: Watergate Affair, 1972-1974--Public opinion. Public opinion--United States. Mass media--Political aspects--United States. LC Classification: E860 .S38 1992 Dewey Class No.: 364.1/32/0973 20

Schultz, Julianne, 1956- Reviving the fourth estate: democracy, accountability, and the media / Julianne Schultz. Published/Created: Cambridge, UK; New York, NY, USA: Cambridge University Press, 1998. Description: xi, 304 p.; 24 cm. ISBN: 0521620422 0521629705 (pbk.) Cancelled ISBN: 052001629705 (pbk.) Notes: Includes bibliographical references (p. 277-292) and index. Subjects: Mass media--Political aspects. Journalism--Political aspects. Mass media--Ownership. Democracy. Series: Reshaping Australian institutions LC Classification: P95.8 .S377 1998 Dewey Class No.: 302.23 21

Schulz, Dorothea Elisabeth. Perpetuating the politics of praise: jeli singers, radios, and political mediation in Mali/ Dorothea E. Schulz. Published/Created: Köln: R. Köppe, 2001. Description: 293 p.; 24 cm. Notes: Includes bibliographical references (p. [270]-293). Subjects: Political culture--Mali. Mass media--Political aspects--Mali. Communication--Political aspects--Mali. Mali--Politics and government--1991- Series: Studien zur Kulturkunde; 118. Bd. LC Classification: DT551.8 .S38 2001 Dewey Class No.: 306.2/096623 21

Schwartz, Stephen, 1948- A strange silence: the emergence of democracy in Nicaragua / Stephen Schwartz. Published/Created: San Francisco, Calif.: ICS Press; Lanham, Md.: National Book Network [distributor], c1992. Description: xvii, 156 p.; 24 cm. ISBN: 1558150714 (alk. paper) Notes: Includes bibliographical references (p. 141-145). Subjects: Government, Resistance to--Nicaragua--History--20th century. Democracy--Nicaragua--History--20th century. Press and politics--United States--History--20th century. Journalism--Objectivity--United States--History--20th century. Mass media--Objectivity--United States--History--20th century. Journalism

Political aspects--United States--History 20th century. Nicaragua--Politics and government--1979-1990. LC Classification: F1528 .S4 1992 Dewey Class No.: 320.97285 20

Segell, Glen. Electronic democracy and the UK 2001 elections / Glen Segell. Published/Created: London: G. Segell, c2001. Description: 149 p.; 30 cm. ISBN: 190141423X Subjects: Great Britain. Parliament. House of Commons--Elections, 2001. Elections--Great Britain--Computer network resources. Mass media--Political aspects--Great Britain. Elections--Great Britain--Statistics. Dewey Class No.: 324.941086 21 National Bib. No.: GBA1-X8809

Semetko, Holli A. Germany's unity election: voters and the media / Holli A. Semetko, Klaus Schoenbach. Published/Created: Cresskill, N.J.: Hampton Press, c1994. Related Authors: Schoenbach, Klaus. Description: xvii, 151 p.; 24 cm. ISBN: 1881303756 1881303764 (pbk.) Notes: Includes bibliographical references (p. 133-144) and indexes. Subjects: Germany. Bundestag--Elections, 1990. Political campaigns--Germany. Political campaigns--Germany (East) Mass media--Political aspects--Germany. Mass media--Political aspects--Germany (East) Elections--Germany. Elections--Germany (East) LC Classification: JN3972.A95 S46 1994 Dewey Class No.: 324.943/0879 20

Sen, Krishna. Media, culture, and politics in Indonesia / Krishna Sen, David T. Hill. Published/Created: Melbourne; New York: Oxford University Press, 2000. Related Authors: Hill, David. Description: x, 245 p.; 22 cm. ISBN: 0195537033 Notes: Includes bibliographical references (p. 224-239) and index. Subjects: Mass media--Political aspects--Indonesia. Mass media--Social aspects--Indonesia. Indonesia--Politics and government--1966-1998. Indonesia--Intellectual life. Indonesia--Social conditions--20th century. LC Classification: P95.82.I5 S46 2000 Dewey Class No.: 302.23/09598 21

Senadhira, Sugeeswara P. Under siege: mass media in Sri Lanka / by Sugeeswara P. Senadhira. Published/Created: New Delhi: Segment Books, 1996. Description: 165 p.; 23 cm. ISBN: 8185330336 Notes: Includes bibliographical references (p. [151]-153) and index. Subjects: Mass media--Sri Lanka. Mass media--Political aspects--Sri Lanka. Mass media--Social aspects--Sri Lanka. Public television--Sri Lanka. 92-05 LC Classification: P92.S75 S46 1996 Dewey Class No.: 302.23/5493 21

Seymour-Ure, Colin, 1938- The British press and broadcasting since 1945 / Colin Seymour-Ure. Published/Created: Oxford, OX, UK; Cambridge, Mass.: Basil Blackwell, 1991. Description: xi, 269 p.; 22 cm. ISBN: 063116443X: 0631164448 (pbk.): Notes: Includes bibliographical references (p. 258-263) and index. Subjects: Press--Great Britain. Broadcasting--Great Britain. Mass media--Political aspects--Great Britain. Series: Making contemporary Britain LC Classification: PN5118 .S39 1991 Dewey Class No.: 302.23/0941 20

Shaw, Tony, writer on history. Eden, Suez, and the mass media: propaganda and persuasion during the Suez crisis / Tony Shaw. Published/Created: London; New York: Tauris Academic Studies, I.B. Tauris; New York: In the U.S.A. and Canada distributed by St. Martin's, 1996. Description: xi, 268 p.: map; 22 cm. ISBN: 1850439559 Notes: Includes bibliographical references (p. 252-260) and index. Subjects: Eden, Anthony, Earl of Avon, 1897- Mass media--Great Britain--History--20th century. Egypt--History--Intervention, 1956. Great Britain--Politics and government--1945-1964. LC Classification: DT107.83 .S483 1996

Sherrow, Victoria. Image and substance: the media in U.S. elections / Victoria Sherrow. Published/Created: Brookfield, Conn.: Millbrook Press, c1992. Description: 128 p.: ill.; 24 cm. ISBN: 1562940759 (lib. bdg.) Summary: Examines the critical role played by the print and broadcasting media in American politics; the history and impact of this relationship; and the use and abuse of the media in a democratic society. Notes: Includes bibliographical references (p. 123-124) and index. Subjects: Advertising, Political--United States--Juvenile literature. Political campaigns--United States--Juvenile literature. Mass media--Political aspects--United States--Juvenile literature. Advertising, Political. Mass media--Political aspects. Politics, Practical. Elections. Series: Issue and debate LC Classification: JK1978 .S48 1992 Dewey Class No.: 324.7/3/0973 20

Siegel, Arthur. Politics and the media in Canada / Arthur Siegel. Edition Information: 2nd [rev.] ed. Published/Created: Toronto; New York: McGraw-Hill Ryerson, c1996. Description: xiv, 272 p.; 23 cm. ISBN: 0075515334 Notes: Includes bibliographical references and index. Subjects: Mass media--Political aspects--Canada. Communication in politics--Canada. Series: McGraw-Hill Ryerson series n Canadian politics LC Classification: P95.82.C2 S54 1996 Dewey Class No.: 302.23/0971 21

Sinclair, Upton, 1878-1968. I, candidate for governor: and how I got licked / Upton Sinclair; introduction by James N. Gregory. Published/Created: Berkeley: University of California Press, c1994. Description: xxi, 249 p.: ill.; 22 cm. ISBN: 0520081978 (hbk.: alk. paper) 0520081986 (pbk.: alk. paper) Notes: Originally Published: New York: Farrar & Rinehart, c1935. Includes bibliographical references (p. xxi). Subjects: Sinclair, Upton, 1878-1968. Governors--California--Election--History--20th century. Mass media--Political aspects--California--History--20th century. California--Politics and government--1865-1950. LC Classification: F866 .S59 1994 Dewey Class No.: 324.9794/05 20

Small, Melvin. Covering dissent: the media and the anti-Vietnam War movement / Melvin Small. Published/Created: New Brunswick, N.J.: Rutgers University Press, c1994. Description: x, 228 p., [16] p. of plates: ill.; 24 cm. ISBN: 0813521068: 0813521076 (pbk.): Notes: Includes bibliographical references (p. [207]-216) and index. Subjects: Vietnamese Conflict, 1961-1975--Protest movements--United States. Vietnamese Conflict, 1961-1975--Mass media and the conflict. Series: Perspectives on the sixties LC Classification: DS559.62.U6 S64 1994 Dewey Class No.: 959.704/3373 20

Smith, Andrew F., 1946- International conflict and the media / by Andrew F. Smith. Published/Created: New York: The American Forum for Global Education, 1997. Description: 179 p.: ill.; 28 cm. ISBN: 094467562X Notes: Includes bibliographical references (p. 175-175). Subjects: Mass media and war--United States. Press and politics--United States. Press and propaganda--United States. Persian Gulf War, 1991--Mass media and the war. LC Classification: P96.W352 U557 1997 Dewey Class No.: 070.4/4935502/00973 21

Smith, Desmond, 1943- Democracy and the Philippine Media, 1983-1993 / Desmond Smith. Published/Created: Lewiston, N.Y.: Edwin Mellen Press, c2000. Description: xix, 382 p.; 24 cm. ISBN: 0773478167 Notes: Includes bibliographical references (p. 357-374) and index. Subjects: Mass media--Political aspects--Democracy--Philippines--Politics and government--1986- LC Classification: P95.82.P6 S64 2000 Dewey Class No.: 302.23/09599 21

So this is democracy?: report on state of the media in southern Africa, 1996 / compiled by David Nthengwe & David Lush; edited by Daniel Sibongo & David Lush. Published/Created: Windhoek, Namibia: Media Institute of Southern Africa, c1997. Related Authors: Nthengwe, David. Lush, David. Sibongo, Daniel. Media Institute of Southern Africa. Description: xx, 116 p.: ill.; 21 cm. ISBN: 9991672826 Subjects: Mass media policy--Freedom of the press--Africa, Southern--Politics and government--1994- LC Classification: P95.82.A4156 S644 1997 Dewey Class No.: 302.23/0968 21

Sorenson, John, 1952- Imagining Ethiopia: struggles for history and identity in the Horn of Africa / John Sorenson. Published/Created: New Brunswick, N.J.: Rutgers University Press, 1993. Description: xii, 216 p.: map; 24 cm. ISBN: 0813519721: 081351973X (pbk.) Notes: Includes bibliographical references (p. [193]-207) and index. Subjects: Famines--Ethiopia--History--20th century. Famines in mass media--History--20th century. Ethiopia--Politics and government--1889-1974--Public opinion. Ethiopia--Politics and government--1974-1991--Public opinion. Ethiopia--Foreign public opinion. LC Classification: DT387 .S67 1993 Dewey Class No.: 963/.05 20

Sparrow, Bartholomew H., 1959- Uncertain guardians: the news media as a political institution / Bartholomew H. Sparrow. Published/Created: Baltimore: Johns Hopkins University Press, c1999. Description: xxi, 277 p.; 24 cm. ISBN: 0801860350 (alk. paper) 0801860369 (pbk.: alk. paper) Notes: Includes bibliographical references (p. [205]-266) and index. Subjects: Journalism--Political aspects--United States. Mass media--Political aspects--United States. Press and politics--United States. Press--United States--Influence. Series: Interpreting American politics LC Classification: PN4888.P6 S68 1999 Dewey Class No.: 070.4/49324/0973 21

Splichal, Slavko. Media beyond socialism: theory and practice in East-Central Europe / Slavko Splichal. Published/Created: Boulder: Westview Press, 1994. Description: xiv, 177 p.; 23 cm. ISBN: 081331819X Notes: Includes bibliographical references (p. 153-163) and index. Subjects: Mass media--Political aspects--Europe, Eastern. Mass media--Political aspects--Europe, Central. Series: International communication and popular culture LC Classification: P95.82.E852 S66 1994 Dewey Class No.: 302.23/0947 20

Sproule, J. Michael, 1949- Propaganda and democracy: the American experience of media and mass persuasion / J. Michael Sproule. Published/Created: Cambridge, U.K.; New York, NY: Cambridge University Press, 1997. Description: x, 332 p.: ill.; 24 cm. ISBN: 0521470226 Notes: Includes bibliographical references (p. 272-309) and indexes. Subjects: Propaganda--United States--History--20th century. Mass media--Political aspects--United States. Government and the press--United States--History--20th century. Series: Cambridge studies in the history of mass communications LC Classification: HM263 .S648 1997 Dewey Class No.: 302.23/0973 20

Sreberny, Annabelle. Small media, big revolution: communication, culture, and the Iranian revolution / Annabelle Sreberny-Mohammadi, Ali Mohammadi. Published/Created: Minneapolis: University of Minnesota Press, c1994. Related Authors: Mohammadi, Ali. Description: xxiii, 225 p.: ill.; 23 cm. ISBN: 0816622167 (alk. paper) 0816622175 (pbk.: alk. paper) Notes: Includes bibliographical references (p. 201-211) and index. Subjects: Mass media--Political aspects--Iran. Communication--Political aspects--Iran. Islam and state--Iran. Freedom of information--Iran. Iran--History--Revolution, 1979. LC Classification: P95.82.I7 S68 1994 Dewey Class No.: 302.23/0955 20

Taylor, Philip M. Global communications, international affairs and the media since 1945 / Philip M. Taylor. Published/Created: London; New York: Routledge, 1997. Description: xx, 248 p.; 24 cm. ISBN: 0415116783 0415116791 (pbk.) Notes: Includes bibliographical references (p. 229-241) and index. Subjects: Communication, International. Mass media--Political aspects. World politics--1945- Series: The new international history series LC Classification: P96.I5 T39 1997 Dewey Class No.: 302.2 21

The 1996 presidential campaign: a communication perspective / edited by Robert E. Denton, Jr. Published/Created:

Westport, Conn.: Praeger, 1998. Related Authors: Denton, Robert E., Jr. Description: xx, 299 p.: ill.; 25 cm. ISBN: 0275956814 (hc: alk. paper) 0275961524 (pbk.: alk. paper) Notes: Includes bibliographical references (p. [285]-290) and index. Subjects: Presidents--United States--Election--1996. Political campaigns--United States. Communication in politics--United States. Mass media--Political aspects--United States. Series: Praeger series in political communication, 1062-5623 LC Classification: JK526 1996e Dewey Class No.: 324.7/0973/09049 21

The celling of America: an inside look at the U.S. prison industry / edited by Daniel Burton-Rose with Dan Pens and Paul Wright. Edition Information: 1st ed. Published/Created: Monroe, Me.: Common Courage Press, c1998. Related Authors: Burton-Rose, Daniel. Pens, Dan. Wright, Paul, 1965- Description: v, 263 p.; 20 cm. ISBN: 1567511406 1567511414 (alk. paper) Notes: "A Prison legal news book." Includes bibliographical references and index. Subjects: Prisons--Government policy--United States. Criminal justice, Administration of--United States. Prisoners--United States--Social conditions. Prisoners--Legal status, laws, etc.--United States. Convict labor--United States. Prisons in mass media. Prison administration--United States. LC Classification: HV9469 .C46 1998 Dewey Class No.: 365/.973 21

The FAIR reader: an Extra! review of press and politics in the '90s / edited by Jim Naureckas and Janine Jackson. Published/Created: Boulder, Colo.: Westview Press, 1996. Related Authors: Naureckas, Jim. Jackson, Janine. Related Titles: Extra! (New York, N.Y.: 1987) Description: xviii,254 p.; 25 cm. ISBN: 0813328020 0813328039 (pbk.) Notes: Articles appeared originally in Extra! or Extra! update. Includes bibliographical references and index. Subjects: Press and politics--Mass media--Objectivity--Reporters and reporting--United States--Politics and government--1989- Series: Critical studies in communication and in the cultural industries LC Classification: PN4888.P6 F35 1996 Dewey Class No.: 302.23/0973 20

The Gulf War as popular entertainment: an analysis of the military-industrial media complex / edited by Paul Leslie. Published/Created: Lewiston, NY: E. Mellen Press, 1997. Related Authors: Leslie, Paul, 1955- Description: ix, 56 p.; 24 cm. ISBN: 0773486666 (hardcover: alk. paper) Notes: Includes bibliographical references and index. Subjects: Persian Gulf War, 1991--United States. Persian Gulf War, 1991--Mass media and the war. Military-industrial complex. Series: Symposium series (Edwin Mellen Press); v. 42. Variant Series: Symposium series; v. 42 LC Classification: DS79.724.U6 G86 1997 Dewey Class No.: 956.7044/2 21

The Gulf War: implications for global business and media / [edited by] Dilnawaz A. Siddiqui, Abbass F. Alkhafaji. Published/Created: Apollo, Penn.: Closson Press, c1992. Related Authors: Siddiqui, Dilnawaz A. (Dilnawaz Ahmed), 1937- Alkhafaji, Abbass F. Description: 216 p.: ill.; 23 cm. ISBN: 155856103X (pbk.) Notes: Includes bibliographical references and index. Subjects: Persian Gulf War, 1991--Miscellanea. Islam--Economic aspects. Middle East--In mass media. Middle East--Economic conditions--1979- . LC Classification: DS79.72 .G844 1992 Dewey Class No.: 959.7044/2 20

The mad cow crisis: health and the public good / edited by Scott C. Ratzan. Published/Created: Washington Square, N.Y.: New York University Press, c1998. Related Authors: Ratzan, Scott C. Description: xii, 247 p.: ill.; 24 cm. ISBN: 0814775101 (hbk.) 081477511X (pbk.) Notes: Includes bibliographical references and index. Subjects: Bovine spongiform encephalopathy--Social aspects--Political aspects. Mass media in health education. Creutzfeldt-Jakob disease--Social aspects--Political aspects. LC Classification: RA644.P93 M33 1998 Dewey Class No.: 362.1/9683 21

The Media and foreign policy / edited by Simon Serfaty. Edition Information: 1st U.S. pbk. ed. Published/Created: New York: St. Martin's Press in association with Foreign Policy Institute, Paul H. Nitze School of Advanced International Studies, Johns Hopkins University, 1991. Related Authors: Serfaty, Simon. Description: xx, 265 p.; 21 cm. ISBN: 0312064985 (pbk.): Notes: Includes bibliographical references and index. Subjects: Mass media--Political aspects--United States. International relations. United States--Foreign relations--1945- LC Classification: P95.82.U6 M43 1991 Dewey Class No.: 327.1 20

The Media and foreign policy / edited by Simon Serfaty. Published/Created: New York: St. Martin's Press in association with Foreign Policy Institute, Paul H. Nitze School of Advasnced International Studies, Johns Hopkins University, 1990. Related Authors: Serfaty, Simon. Description: xx, 249 p.; 23 cm. ISBN: 031204528X Notes: Includes bibliographical references and index. Subjects: Mass media--Political aspects--United States. International relations. United States--Foreign relations--1945-1989. LC Classification: P95.82.U6 M43 1990 Dewey Class No.: 327.1 20

The Media and foreign policy / edited by Simon Serfaty. Published/Created: Houndmills, Basingstoke, Hampshire: Macmillan in association with Foreign Policy Institute, Paul H. Nitze School of Advanced International Studies, Johns Hopkins University, 1990. Related Authors: Serfaty, Simon. Johns Hopkins University. Foreign Policy Institute. Description: xx, 249 p.; 23 cm. ISBN: 0333541634 Notes: Includes bibliographical references and index. Subjects: Mass media--Political aspects--United States. International relations. United States--Foreign relations--1945- LC Classification: P95.82.U6 M43 1990b

The Media and international security / edited by Stephen Badsey. Published/Created: London; Portland, OR: F. Cass, 2000. Related Authors: Badsey, Stephen. Description: xxxii, 264 p.; 25 cm. ISBN: 0714648485 0714644064 (pbk.) Notes: Based on a meeting which was held at the Royal Military Academy, Sandhurst, Sept. 27-29, 1995. Includes bibliographical references and index. Subjects: Armed Forces and mass media--Great Britain. Security, International. Series: The Sandhurst conference series, 1483-1153 LC Classification: P96.A752 G76 2000 Dewey Class No.: 302.23/0941 21

The media and politics / Paul A. Winters, book editor. Published/Created: San Diego, Calif.: Greenhaven Press, c1996. Related Authors: Winters, Paul A., 1965- Description: 80 p.; 24 cm. ISBN: 1565103831 (alk. paper) 1565103823 (pbk.: alk. paper) Notes: Includes bibliographical references (p. 75-76) and index. Subjects: Mass media--Political aspects--United States. United States--Politics and government--1989- Series: At issue (San Diego, Calif.) Variant Series: At issue LC Classification: P95.82.U6 M45 1996 Dewey Class No.: 302.23/0973 20

The politics of news: the news of politics / edited by Doris Graber, Denis McQuail, Pippa Norris. Published/Created: Washington, D.C.: CQ Press, c1998. Related Authors: Graber, Doris A. (Doris Appel), 1923- McQuail, Denis. Norris, Pippa. Description: xii, 268 p.; 24 cm. ISBN: 1568024134 (cloth) 1568024126 (paper) Notes: Includes bibliographical references and index. Subjects: Mass media--Political aspects. Press and politics. LC Classification: P95.8 .P655 1998 Dewey Class No.: 302.23 21

The role of the media in a democracy: the case of Jordan: proceedings of a seminar organised by the University of Jordan in cooperation with the Konrad Adenauer Foundation, 27-28 September, Amman / [editor, George Hawatmeh] Published/Created: Amman: Center for Strategic Studies, University of Jordan, 1995. Related Authors: Hawatmeh, George. J¯ami`ah al-Urdun¯iyah. Markaz al-Dir¯as¯at al-Istir¯at¯ij¯iyah. Konrad-Adenauer-Stiftung. Description: 147 p.; 25 cm. Notes: Proceedings of a conference held in 1994. Subjects: Mass media--Political aspects--Jordan--Congresses. Journalism--Political aspects--Jordan--Congresses. Press and politics--Jordan--Congresses. Government and the press--Jordan--Congresses. Broadcast journalism--Jordan--Congresses. Political participation--Jordan--Congresses. LC Classification: P95.82 .R65 1994 Dewey Class No.: 302.23/095695 21

The Silent revolution: media, democracy, and the free trade debate / edited by James P. Winter. Published/Created: Ottawa: University of Ottawa Press, c1990. Related Authors: Winter, James P. Description: xvii, 196 p.: ill.; 23 cm. ISBN: 0776602969 Notes: Includes bibliographical references (p. 142-145). Subjects: Mass media--Political aspects--Canada. Mass media and business--Canada. Free trade--Canada. Canada--Politics and government--1980- LC Classification: P95.82.C2 S55 1990 Dewey Class No.: 302.23/0971 20

Thompson, John B. (John Brookshire) Political scandal: power and visibility in the media age / John B. Thompson. Published/Created: Cambridge: Polity Press; Malden, MA: Blackwell, 2000. Description: xiii, 324 p.: ill.; 23 cm. ISBN: 0745625495 0745625509 (pbk.) Notes: Includes bibliographical references (p. [272]-307) and index. Subjects: Scandals in mass media. Mass media--Political aspects. LC Classification: P96.S29 T49 2000 Dewey Class No.: 306.2 21

Thompson, Mark, 1959- Forging war: the media in Serbia, Croatia and Bosnia-Hercegovina / [Mark Thompson]. Published/Created: London: Article 19, [1994] Related Authors: Article 19 (Organization) Description: xii, 271 p.: maps; 23 cm. ISBN: 1870798228 (pbk) Notes: "May 1994." Includes bibliographical references. Subjects: Mass media--Political aspects--Yugoslavia. Yugoslav War, 1991-1995--Mass media and the war. Journalism--Political aspects--Yugoslavia. Freedom of information--Yugoslavia. Yugoslavia--Politics and government--1992- Propaganda Serbia Croatia Bosnia and Herzegovina LC Classification: P92.82.Y8 T48 1994 Dewey Class No.: 303.3/75/09497 21

Thrall, A. Trevor. War in the media age / A. Trevor Thrall. Published/Created: Cresskill, N.J.: Hampton Press, c2000. Description: vi, 277 p.; 24 cm. ISBN: 1572732466 1572732474 (pbk.) Notes: Includes bibliographical references and indexes. Subjects: Mass media and war--United States. Government and the press--United States. Series: The Hampton Press communication series. Political communication LC Classification: P96.W352 U558 2000 Dewey Class No.: 070.4/4935502/0973 21

Tiffen, Rodney. Scandals: media, politics & corruption in contemporary Australia / Rodney Tiffen. Published/Created: Sydney, Australia: UNSW Press, 1999. Description: ix, 291 p.; 22 cm. ISBN: 0868406015 Notes: Includes bibliographical references (p. [274]-281) and index. Subjects: Political corruption--Australia. Scandals--Australia. Scandals in mass media--Australia. Scandals--Press coverage--Australia. Australia--Politics and government--1945- LC Classification: JQ4029.C6 T54 1999 Dewey Class No.: 994.06 21

Truesdell, Matthew. Spectacular politics: Louis-Napoleon Bonaparte and the Fête impériale, 1849-1870 / Matthew Truesdell. Published/Created: New York: Oxford University Press, 1997. Description: x, 238 p.: ill.; 25 cm. ISBN: 019510689X (acid-free paper) Notes: Includes bibliographical references (p. 193-228) and index. Subjects: Napoleon III, Emperor of the French, 1808-1873 Influence. Symbolism in politics. Mass media and public opinion--France--History--19th century. Rites and ceremonies--France--History--19th century. France--Politics and government--1848-1870--Social aspects. France--Cultural policy. LC Classification: DC278 .T78 1997 Dewey Class No.: 944.07 20

Turpin, Jennifer E. Reinventing the Soviet self: media and social change in the former Soviet Union / Jennifer Turpin. Published/Created: Westport, Conn.: Praeger, c1995. Description: x, 154 p.: ill.; 24 cm. ISBN: 0275950433 (alk. paper) Notes: Includes bibliographical references (p. [134]-144) and index. Subjects: Mass media--Soviet Union. Propaganda, Soviet--United States. Soviet Union--Social conditions--1970-1991. Soviet Union--Politics and government--1953-1985. Soviet Union--Politics and government--1985-1991. LC Classification: HN530.Z9 M388 1995 Dewey Class No.: 306/.0973 20

Twentieth Century Fund. Task Force on Television and the Campaign of 1992. 1-800-PRESIDENT: the report of the Twentieth Century Fund Task Force on Television and the Campaign of 1992 / with background papers by Kathleen Hall Jamieson, Ken Auletta, Thomas E. Patterson. Published/Created: New York: Twentieth Century Fund Press; [Washington, D.C.]: Distributed by the Brookings Institution, 1993. Related Authors: Jamieson, Kathleen Hall. Auletta, Ken. Patterson, Thomas E. Related Titles: One eight hundred president. Description: xiv, 119 p.; 23 cm. ISBN: 0870783491: Notes: Includes bibliographical references and index. Subjects: Television in politics--Presidents--United States--Election--1992. Mass media--Political aspects. LC Classification: HE8700.76.U6 T94 1993 Dewey Class No.: 324.7/3/0973 20

Vachnadze, Georgii Nikolaevich. Secrets of journalism in Russia: mass media under Gorbachev and Yeltsin / by G.N. Vachnadze. Published/Created: Commack, N.Y.: Nova Science Publishers, c1992. Description: x, 437 p.; 25 cm. ISBN: 1560720816: Notes: Includes indexes. Subjects: Mass media policy--Government and the press--Soviet Union--Politics and government--1985-1991. LC Classification: P95.82.S65 V3 1992 Dewey Class No.: 302.23/0947/09048 20

Vijaya Lakshmi, K. P. Communications across the borders: the U.S., the non-aligned and the new information order / K.P. Vijaya Lakshmi. Published/Created: New Delhi, India: Radiant Publishers, c1993. Description: xii, 202 p.; 22 cm. ISBN: 8170272041: Notes: Includes bibliographical references (p. [180]-197) and index. Subjects: Communication--Developing countries. Mass media policy--Developing countries. Communication--United States--International cooperation. Communication--Political aspects. LC Classification: P92.2 .V55 1993

Visions of the First Amendment for a new millennium: Americans speak out on the future of free expression / Robert Bennett ... [et al.]. Published/Created: Washington: Annenberg Washington Program, Communications Policy Studies, Northwestern University, c1992. Related Authors: Bennett, Robert (Robert W.) Northwestern University (Evanston, Ill.). Annenberg Washington Program in Communications Policy Studies. Description: 143 p.; 26 cm. Notes: Includes bibliographical references. Subjects: Freedom of speech--United States. Mass media--Political aspects--United States. Freedom of the press--United States. Censorship--United States. LC Classification: JC591 .V57 1992 Dewey Class No.: 323.44/3/0973 20

Wanta, Wayne. The public and the national agenda: how people learn about important issues / Wayne Wanta. Published/Created: Mahwah, N.J.: Lawrence Erlbaum Associates, 1997. Description: viii, 122 p.; 24 cm. ISBN: 080582460X (cloth: alk. paper) 0805824618 (pbk.: alk. paper) Notes: Includes bibliographical references (p. 111-116) and indexes. Subjects: Mass media--Political aspects. Press and politics. Mass media--Audiences. Mass media and public opinion. LC Classification: P95.8 .W36 1997 Dewey Class No.: 302.23 21

Ward, Ian, 1950- Politics of the media / Ian Ward. Published/Created: South Melbourne: Macmillan, 1995. Description: x, 322 p.: ill.; 22 cm. ISBN: 0732927900 (cloth) 0732927897 (pbk.) Notes: Includes index. Includes bibliographical references (p. 302-318). Subjects: Mass media--Political aspects. Mass media--Influence. LC Classification: P95.8 .W37 1995 Dewey Class No.: 302.23 20

Washington, Sally. Consultation and communications: integrating multiple interests into policy, managing media relations. Published/Created: Paris: Organisation for Economic Co-operation and Development; Washington, D.C.: OECD Washington Center [distributor], c1997. Description: 39 p.; 27 cm. ISBN: 9264155708 (pbk.): Notes: Prepared by Sally Washington. Includes bibliographical references (p. 38-39). Subjects: Political participation--OECD countries. Government publicity--OECD countries. Government and the press--OECD countries. Mass media--Government policy--OECD countries. Series: Public management occasional papers; no. 17 LC Classification: JF799 .W37 1997 National Bib. No.: GB97-63061

Wilkin, Peter. The political economy of global communication: an introduction / Peter Wilkin. Published/Created: London; Sterling, Va.: Pluto Press, 2001. Projected Pub. Date: 0109 Description: p. cm. ISBN: 0745314066 Subjects: Telecommunication--Mergers. Mass media--Mergers. Consolidation and merger of corporations. Globalization--Economic aspects. Telecommunication--Political aspects. Series: Human security in the global economy LC Classification: HE7631 .W535 2001 Dewey Class No.: 384/.041 21

Williams, Keith, 1958- British writers and the media, 1930-45 / Keith Williams. Published/Created: Houndmills, Basingstoke, Hampshire: Macmillan Press; New York: St. Martin's Press, 1996. Description: xi, 284 p.; 22 cm. ISBN: 0333638956 (cloth) 0333638964 (pbk.) 0312158203 (cloth) Notes: Includes bibliographical references (p. 241-273) and index. Subjects: English literature--20th century--History and criticism. Mass media and literature--Great Britain--History--20th century. Politics and literature--Great Britain--History--20th century. Authors, English--20th century--Political and social views. World War, 1939-1945--Great Britain. Right and left (Political science) Great Britain--Politics and government--1936-1945. Great Britain--Politics and government--1910-1936. LC Classification: PR478.M37 W55 1996 Dewey Class No.: 820.9/00912 20

Winebrenner, Hugh, 1937- Iowa precinct caucuses: the making of a media event / by Hugh Winebrenner. Edition Information: 4th ed. Published/Created: Ames: Iowa State University Press, 1998. Related Titles: Southeastern political review. Description: xiv, 281 p.: ill.; 24 cm. Notes: "Portions of this book were previously Published as The Iowa precinct caucuses ... in the Southeastern political review 13 (1985): 99-132"--T.p. verso. Includes bibliographical references and index. Subjects: Presidents--United States--Nomination. Mass media--Political aspects--United States. Press and politics--United States. Political parties--Iowa. Iowa--Politics and government. LC Classification: JK521 .W55 2000

Winebrenner, Hugh, 1937- Iowa precinct caucuses: the making of a media event / by Hugh Winebrenner. Edition Information: 2nd ed. Published/Created: Ames: Iowa State University Press, 1998. Related Titles: Southeastern political review. Description: xiv, 281 p.: ill.; 24 cm. ISBN: 0813824893 (acid-free paper) Notes: "Portions of this book were previously Published as The Iowa precinct caucuses ... in the Southeastern political review 13 (1985): 99-132"--T.p. verso. Includes bibliographical references and index. Subjects: Presidents--United States--Nomination. Mass media--Political aspects--United States. Press and politics--United States. Political parties--Iowa. Iowa--Politics and government. LC Classification: JK521 .W55 1998 Dewey Class No.: 324.2777/0152 21

Winter, James P. Common cents: media portrayal of the Gulf War and other events / James Winter. Published/Created: Montréal; New York: Black Rose Books, c1992. Related Authors: Institute of Policy Alternatives (Montréal, Québec) Description: xxi, 274 p.; 23 cm. ISBN: 1895431247 (pbk.) 1895431255 (hardcover) Notes: "A publication of the Institute of Policy Alternatives of Montréal (IPAM)"--T.p. verso. Includes bibliographical references and indexes. Subjects: Mass media--Political aspects--Canada. Mass media--Objectivity--Canada. Persian Gulf War, 1991--Mass media and the war. Canada--Politics and government--1980- LC Classification: P95.82.C2 W56 1992 Dewey Class No.: 302.23/0971/09048 21

Wolfsfeld, Gadi. Media and political conflict: news from the Middle East / Gadi Wolfsfeld. Published/Created: Cambridge [England]; New York, NY, USA: Cambridge University Press, 1997. Description: xiv, 255 p.: ill.; 24 cm. ISBN: 0521580455 0521589673 (pbk.) Notes: Includes bibliographical references (p. 240-246) and index. Subjects: Mass media--Political aspects. Press and politics. LC Classification: P95.8 .W65 1997 Dewey Class No.: 302.23 20

Woodward, Gary C. Perspectives on American political media / Gary C. Woodward. Published/Created: Boston: Allyn and Bacon, c1997. Description: xii, 256 p.: ill.; 23 cm. ISBN: 0205262503 Notes: Includes bibliographical references (p. 241-246) and index. Subjects: Mass media--Political aspects--United States. United States--Politics and government--1989- LC Classification: P95.82.U6 W66 1997 Dewey Class No.: 302.23/0973 20

Yeric, Jerry L. Mass media and the politics of change / Jerry L. Yeric. Published/Created: Itasca, Ill.: F.E. Peacock Publishers, c2001 Description: xii, 280 p.: ill.; 23 cm. ISBN: 0875814344 Notes: Includes bibliographical references and index. Subjects: Mass media--Political aspects--United States. Mass media--Influence. United States--Politics and government. LC Classification: P95.82.U6 Y47 2001 Dewey Class No.: 302.23/0973 21

Young, Peter R. The media and the military: from the Crimea to Desert Strike / Peter Young and Peter Jesser. Published/Created: New York: St. Martin's Press, 1997. Related Authors: Jesser, Peter. Description: viii, 391 p.; 23 cm. ISBN: 0312210116 (cloth) 0312210124 (paper) Notes: Includes bibliographical references (p. 365-381) and index. Subjects: Armed Forces and mass media--History. LC Classification: P96.A75 Y68 1997 Dewey Class No.: 355.3/42 21

Zaffiro, James J. (James Joseph), 1955- From police network to station of the nation: a political history of broadcasting in Botswana, 1927-1991 / James J. Zaffiro. Published/Created: Gaborone, Botswana: The Botswana Society, 1991. Related Titles: Political history of broadcasting in Botswana, 1927-1991. Description: 108 p.; 23 cm. ISBN: 9991260145 Notes: Includes bibliographical references. Subjects: Radio broadcasting--Political aspects-History--Mass media policy--Botswana. LC Classification: PN1991.3.B65 Z34 1991

Zasurskii, Ivan. Media and power in post-Soviet Russia / by Ivan Zasoursky. Published/Created: Armonk, N.Y.: M.E. Sharpe, 2002. Projected Pub. Date: 0205 Description: p. cm. ISBN: 0765608634 (alk. paper) Notes: "Published in cooperation with the Transnational Institut, Amsterdam". Includes bibliographical references and index. Subjects: Mass media--Political aspects--Russia (Federation) Russia (Federation)--Politics and government--1991- LC Classification: P95.82.R9 Z3713 2002 Dewey Class No.: 302.23/0947 21

Children and Mass Media

Armstrong, Louise. Rocking the cradle of sexual politics: what happened when women said incest / Louise Armstrong. Published/Created: Reading, Mass.: Addison-Wesley, c1994. Description: 305 p.; 25 cm. ISBN: 0201624710 Notes: Includes bibliographical references (p. [279]-296) and index. Subjects: Incest. Child sexual abuse. Mass media--Social aspects. LC Classification: HQ71 .A753 1994 Dewey Class No.: 306.877 20

Axelrod, Lauryn. TV-proof your kids: a parent's guide to safe and healthy viewing / Lauryn Axelrod; with a foreword by Renee Hobbs. Published/Created: Secaucus, N.J.: Carol Pub. Group, c1997. Description: xv, 272 p.: ill.; 23 cm. ISBN: 1559724080 (pbk.) Notes: "A Citadel Press book." Includes bibliographical references (p. 265) and index. Subjects: Television and children--United States. Television and family--United States. Mass media and children. Media literacy. Parenting--United States. LC Classification: HQ784.T4 A94 1997 Dewey Class No.: 302.23/45/083 21

Barson, Michael. Teenage confidential: an illustrated history of the American teen / Michael Barson & Steven Heller. Published/Created: San Francisco: Chronicle Books, 1998. Related Authors: Heller, Steven. Description: 132 p.: ill. (some col.); 28 cm. ISBN: 0811815846 (pbk.) Notes: Includes bibliographical references (p. 132) Subjects: Teenagers in motion pictures--United States. Teenagers in mass media--United States. Teenagers in literature. LC Classification: PN1995.9.Y6 B37 1998 Dewey Class No.: 791.43/652055 21

Beckelman, Laurie. Media violence / by Laurie Beckelman. Edition Information: 1st ed. Published/Created: New York: Crestwood House, 1999.

Best, Joel. Threatened children: rhetoric and concern about child-victims / Joel Best. Published/Created: Chicago: University of Chicago Press, 1990. Description: xii, 232 p.: ill.; 23 cm. ISBN: 0226044254 (alk. paper) Notes: Includes bibliographical references and index. Subjects: Child abuse--United States. Missing children--United States. Mass media--Social aspects--United States. LC Classification: HV6626.52 .B47 1990 Dewey Class No.: 362.7/6/0973 20

Calvert, Sandra L. Children's journeys through the information age / Sandra L. Calvert. Edition Information: 1st ed. Published/Created: Boston: McGraw-Hill College, c1999. Description: xxii, 298 p.: ill.; 24 cm. ISBN: 0070116644 Notes: Includes bibliographical references (p. 258-282) and indexes. Subjects: Television and children--Computers and children--Internet and children--Mass media and children--Sex role in mass media--Violence in mass media--United States. Series: McGraw Hill series in developmental psychology LC Classification: HQ784.T4 C24 1999 Dewey Class No.: 303.48/33/083 21

Children's publishing, media & entertainment. Published/Created: New York, N.Y.: Primary Research, c1994. Related Authors: Primary Research (Firm: New York, N.Y.) Description: 250 p.; 27 cm. Subjects: Children's literature--Publishing--United States. Mass media and children--United States. LC Classification: Z479 .C455 1994 Dewey Class No.: 070.5/0973 20

Considine, David M., 1950- Visual messages: integrating imagery into instruction / David M. Considine and Gail E. Haley. Published/Created: Englewood, Colo.: Teacher Ideas Press, 1992. Related Authors: Haley, Gail E. Description: xv, 267 p.: ill.; 28 cm. ISBN: 0872879127: Notes: Includes bibliographical references and index. Subjects: Visual literacy--United States. Mass media and children--United States. Activity programs in education--United States. LC Classification: LB1068 .C66 1992 Dewey Class No.: 371.3/35 20

Considine, David M., 1950- Visual messages: integrating imagery into instruction / David M. Considine and Gail E. Haley. Edition Information: 2nd ed. Published/Created: Englewood, Colo.: Teacher Ideas Press, 1999. Related Authors: Haley, Gail E. Description: xxiii, 371 p.: ill.; 28 cm. ISBN: 1563085755 (softbound) Notes: "A media literacy resource for teacher." Includes bibliographical references and index. Subjects: Visual literacy--United States. Mass media and children--United States. Activity programs in education--United States. LC Classification: LB1068 .C66 1999 Dewey Class No.: 371.33/5 21

Cooper, Alison, 1967- Media power? / Alison Cooper. Edition Information: 1st American ed. Published/Created: New York: F. Watts, 1997. Description: 32 p.: ill. (some col.); 27 cm. ISBN: 0531144526 Summary: Discusses the influence that such means of communication as movies, television, radio, and newspapers have on the way people think and behave. Notes: Includes index. Subjects: Mass media--Juvenile literature. Mass media. Series: Viewpoints (Franklin Watts, inc.) Variant Series: Viewpoints LC Classification: P91.2 .C665 1997 Dewey Class No.: 302.23 21

Cronström, Johan. Bibliography: research on pornography and sex in the media: a selection (1970-) / comp. by Johan Cromström. Published/Created: [Göteborg]: The UNESCO International Clearinghouse on Children and Violence on the Screen, 2000. Description: 30 p.; 25 cm. ISBN: 9189471032 Subjects: Children in pornography--Bibliography. Mass media and children--Bibliography. Sex in mass media--Bibliography.

Czerneda, Julie. Great careers for people interested in communications technology / [Julie Czerneda, Victoria Vincent] Published/Created: Detroit, MI: UXL, c1996. Related Authors: Vincent, Victoria. Description: 48 p.: ill. (some col.); 26 cm. ISBN: 0787608599: Notes: Includes index "First Published in Canada by Trifolium Books Inc. and Weigl Educational Publishers Limited"--T.P. Verso. Subjects: Communication and traffic--Vocational guidance--Juvenile literature. Telecommunication--Vocational guidance--Juvenile literature. Mass media--Vocational guidance--Juvenile literature. Telecommunication--Vocational guidance. Vocational guidance. Series: Career connections (Detroit, Mich.) Variant Series: Career connections LC Classification: HE152.5 .C95 1996 Dewey Class No.: 384/.023/73 21

Davies, John (John P.) Educating students in a media-saturated culture / John Davies. Published/Created: Lancaster, Pa.: Technomic Pub. Co., c1996. Description: xvii, 311 p.: ill.; 23 cm. ISBN: 1566763657 Notes: Includes bibliographical references (p. 261-294) and index. Subjects: Mass media--Study and teaching. Mass media and youth. LC Classification: LB1043 .D38 1996

Day, Nancy. Sensational TV: trash or journalism? / Nancy Day. Published/Created: Springfield, N.J.: Enslow, c1996. Description: 112 p.: ill.; 24

cm. ISBN: 0894907336 (alk. paper) Summary: Questions whether the mass media, especially television, present an accurate representation of the news or whether it is more concerned with the sensational story. Notes: Includes bibliographical references (p. 100-109) and index. Subjects: Sensationalism on television--Magazine format television programs--Talk shows--Reality television programs--Sensationalism in journalism--Juvenile literature. Television programs. Talk shows. Series: Issues in focus (Hillside, N.J.) Variant Series: Issues in focus LC Classification: PN1992.8.S37 D38 1996 Dewey Class No.: 791.45/653 20

DeGaetano, Gloria. Screen smarts: a family guide to media literacy / Gloria DeGaetano and Kathleen Bander. Published/Created: Boston: Houghton Mifflin Co., 1996. Related Authors: Bander, Kathleen. Description: xvi, 206 p.: ill.; 21 cm. ISBN: 0395715504 (alk. paper) Notes: Includes bibliographical references (p. [193]-198) and index. Subjects: Mass media and the family. Mass media and children. Media literacy. LC Classification: P94.5.F34 D44 1996 Dewey Class No.: 306.85 20

Dewing, Martha. Beyond TV: activities for using video with children / Martha Dewing. Published/Created: Santa Barbara, Calif.: ABC-CLIO, c1992. Description: xix, 186 p.: ill.; 23 cm. ISBN: 0874366011 Notes: Includes bibliographical references and index. Subjects: Video recording. Libraries--Special collections--Video recordings. Children's libraries--Activity programs. School libraries--Activity programs. Audio-visual library service. Video tapes in education. Mass media and children. LC Classification: Z692.V52 D49 1992 Dewey Class No.: 027.62/5 20

Doppelt, Jack C. Guilt by allegation: lessons from the Cardinal Bernardin case: rapporteur summary / by Jack C. Doppelt; cosponsored by Northwestern University's Annenberg Washington Program, Medill School of Journalism, and School of Law, May 24, 1994. Published/Created: Washington, D.C. (1455 Pa. Ave., N.W., Suite 200, Washington, D.C. 20004-1008): Annenberg Washington Program, c1994. Related Authors: Northwestern University (Evanston, Ill.). Annenberg Washington Program in Communications Policy Studies. Medill School of Journalism. Northwestern University (Evanston, Ill.). School of Law. Description: iii, 24 p.; 28 cm. Subjects: Bernardin, Joseph Louis, 1928- --Trials, litigation, etc. Sex crimes--Press coverage--United States. Mass media--Objectivity--United States--Congresses. Child sexual abuse by clergy--Ohio--Cincinnati. LC Classification: KF228.B45 D57 1994

Edgar, Kathleen J. Everything you need to know about media violence / Kathleen J. Edgar. Edition Information: Rev. ed. Published/Created: New York: Rosen Pub. Group, 2000. Description: 64 p.: ill,; 25 cm. ISBN: 0823931080 Notes: Includes bibliographical references (p. 62) and index. Subjects: Violence in mass media--Juvenile literature. Series: The need to know library LC Classification: P96.V5 E34 2000 Dewey Class No.: 303.6 21

Feilitzen, Cecilia von. Outlooks on children and media: child rights, media trends, media research, media literacy, child participation, declarations / compiled and written by Cecilia von Feilitzen & Catharina Bucht. Published/Created: Göteborg, Sweden: UNESCO International Clearinghouse on Children and Violence on the Screen, NORDICOM, 2001. Related Authors: Bucht, Catharina. UNESCO International Clearinghouse on Children and Violence on the Screen. World Summit on Media for Children (3rd: 2001: Thessaloniki, Greece) Description: 130 p.; 30 cm. ISBN: 9189471075 Notes: "The 3rd World Summit on Media for Children, Thessaloniki, Greece, 23-26 March 2001." Includes bibliographical references (p. 119-122) and index. Subjects: Mass media and children--Congresses. LC Classification: P94.5.C55 F45 2001 Dewey Class No.: 302.23/083 21

Gauntlett, David. Video critical: children, the environment and media power / David Gauntlett. Published/Created: Luton, Bedfordshire, UK: University of Luton Press , c1996. Description: viii, 176 p.: ill.; 24 cm. ISBN: 1860205135 (pbk) Notes: Includes bibliographical references (p. [155]-168). Subjects: Television and children. Mass media and children--Research. Video recordings for children. Environment and children. Mass media and the environment. LC Classification: HQ784.T4 G35 1996 Dewey Class No.: 302.23/45/083 21

Gause, Val. A beginner's guide to media communications / Val Gause. Published/Created: Lincolnwood, Ill., USA: National Textbook Co., 1997. Description: xi, 144 p.: ill.; 29 cm. ISBN: 0844259373 Summary: An introduction to writing for the media, focusing on school-related publications, radio, and television, and covering such topics as newswriting, photojournalism, media ethics, and new technologies. Notes: Includes index. Subjects: Mass media--Authorship--Juvenile literature. LC Classification: P96.A86 G38 1997 Dewey Class No.: 808/.066302 20

Germany. Media and the protection of young persons / [editor, Sigrid Born]. Published/Created: Bonn: Inter Nationes, 1999. Related Authors: Born, Sigrid. Description: 64 p.; 21 cm. Notes: "Information from the Federal Republic of Germany." Includes bibliographical references (p. 64). Subjects: Children--Legal status, laws, etc.--Germany. Mass media--Law and legislation--Germany--Criminal provisions. Child welfare--Germany. Series: Legal texts LC Classification: KK3567 .A28 1999

Grossman, Dave. Stop teaching our kids to kill: a call to action against TV, movie & video game violence / Dave Grossman and Gloria DeGaetano. Edition Information: 1st ed. Published/Created: New York: Crown Publishers, c1999. Related Authors: DeGaetano, Gloria. Description: viii, 196 p.: ill.; 22 cm. ISBN: 0609606131 Notes: Includes bibliographical references (p. 183-185) and index. Subjects: Mass media and children. Television and children. Violence on television. Children and violence. LC Classification: HQ784.M3 G76 1999 Dewey Class No.: 302.23/083 21

Gurian, Michael. What stories does my son need?: a guide to books and movies that build character in boys / Michael Gurian with Terry Trueman. Published/Created: New York: Jeremy P. Tarcher/Putnam, c2000. Related Authors: Trueman, Terry. Description: 142 p.; 19 cm. ISBN: 1585420409 (alk. paper) Notes: Includes indexes. Subjects: Boys--Psychology. Boys--Books and reading. Motion pictures for children. Mass media and children. Child rearing. LC Classification: HQ775 .G824 2000 Dewey Class No.: 028.1/6241 21

Hagell, Ann. Young offenders and the media: viewing habits and preferences / Ann Hagell and Tim Newburn. Published/Created: London: Policy Studies Institute, c1994. Related Authors: Newburn, Tim. Policy Studies Institute. Description: xvi, 105 p.: ill.; 23 cm. ISBN: 0853746141 Notes: Includes bibliographical references. Subjects: Juvenile delinquents--Great Britain--Attitudes. Mass media and youth--Great Britain. Mass media--Great Britain--Influence. Television and youth--Great Britain. Mass media surveys--Great Britain. Series: Research report (Policy Studies Institute); 763. Variant Series: PSI research report; 763 LC Classification: HV9145.A5 H365 1994 National Bib. No.: GB95-8276

Handbook of children and the media / Dorothy G. Singer, Jerome L. Singer, editors. Published/Created: Thousand Oaks, Calif.: Sage Publications, c2001. Related Authors: Singer, Dorothy G. Singer, Jerome L. Description: xvii, 765 p.: ill.; 27 cm. ISBN: 0761919546 (cloth: alk. paper) Notes: Includes bibliographical references and index. Subjects: Television and children--United States. Mass media and children--

United States. Video games--Psychological aspects. LC Classification: HQ784.T4 S533 2001 Dewey Class No.: 302.23/45/083 21

Holbrook, David. Creativity and popular culture / David Holbrook. Published/Created: Rutherford: Fairleigh Dickinson University Press; London: Associated University Press, c1994. Description: 279 p.; 24 cm. ISBN: 0838634737 (alk. paper) Notes: Includes bibliographical references (p. [268]-272) and index. Subjects: Mass media and children--Moral and ethical aspects. Creative ability. Popular culture. LC Classification: HQ784.M3 H65 1994 Dewey Class No.: 306 20

Images of the child / edited by Harry Eiss. Published/Created: Bowling Green, OH: Bowling Green State University Popular Press, c1994. Related Authors: Eiss, Harry Edwin. Description: 358 p.: ill.; 24 cm. ISBN: 0879726539 0879726547 Notes: Includes bibliographical references. Subjects: Mass media and children. Children in popular culture. Children in literature. Youth in literature. Children in advertising. Toys--Social aspects. Popular culture. LC Classification: HQ784.M3 I48 1994

Interacting with video / edited by Patricia M. Greenfield and Rodney R. Cocking. Published/Created: Norwood, N.J.: Ablex Pub. Corp., c1996. Related Authors: Greenfield, Patricia Marks. Cocking, Rodney R. Description: xii, 218 p.: ill. ISBN: 1567501311 (cl) 1567501524 (pp) Notes: Includes bibliographical references and indexes. Subjects: Mass media and children. Television and children. Video games--Psychological aspects. Interactive video--Psychological aspects. Child psychology. Child Development. Video Games--psychology. Series: Advances in applied developmental psychology (1993); v. ii. Variant Series: Advances in applied developmental psychology; vol. 11 LC Classification: HQ784.M3 I57 1996 Dewey Class No.: 305.231 21

Investing in our nation's youth: National Youth Anti-Drug Media Campaign: phase II (final report). Published/Created: Washington, DC: Executive Office of the President, Office of National Drug Control Policy: For sale by the U.S. G.P.O., Supt. of Docs., [1999] Related Authors: United States. Office of National Drug Control Policy. Description: 1 v. (various pagings): ill.; 28 cm. 1 appendix. ISBN: 0160500591 (main v.) Notes: Shipping list no.: 99-0290-P (main v.), 99-0293-P (appendix). "June 1999." Includes bibliographical references. Subjects: Children--Drug use--United States--Prevention. Youth--Drug use--United States--Prevention. Drug abuse--United States--Prevention. Drugs and mass media--United States. Advertising, Public service--United States. LC Classification: HV5824.C45+

Joly, Dominique. On TV, in newspapers / written by Dominique Joly ... [et al.]; translated and adapted by Scott Steedman ... [et al.]. Published/Created: Mankato, MN: Creative Education, 1997. Projected Pub. Date: 9708 Description: p. cm. ISBN: 0886828465 Summary: Explains how newspapers, television news programs, and theatrical shows are produced. Notes: Includes index. Subjects: Mass media--Juvenile literature. Performing arts. LC Classification: P91.2 .J6513 1997 Dewey Class No.: 791.43/72 20

Kids' media culture / edited by Marsha Kinder. Published/Created: Durham, [NC]: Duke University Press, c1999. Related Authors: Kinder, Marsha. Description: viii, 338 p.: ill.; 24 cm. ISBN: 0822323508 (cloth: alk. paper) 0822323710 (pbk.: alk. paper) Notes: Includes bibliographical references (p. [317]-322) and index. Subjects: Mass media and children--United States. Child consumers--United States. Series: Console-ing passions LC Classification: HQ784.M3 K54 1999 Dewey Class No.: 302.23/083 21

Lane, Christopher A. Parenting by remote control: how to make the media work for, rather than against your family / Christopher and Melodie Lane.

Published/Created: Ann Arbor, Mich.: Vine Books/Servant Publications, c1991. Related Authors: Lane, Melodie, 1961- Description: 243 p.; 21 cm. ISBN: 0892837411 Notes: Includes bibliographical references (p.227-243). Subjects: Mass media and children--United States. Mass media--Religious aspects--Christianity. LC Classification: HQ784.M3 L35 1991 Dewey Class No.: 302.2/34/088054 20

Lee, Mary Price. Drugs and the media / Mary Price Lee, Richard S. Lee. Edition Information: 1st ed. Published/Created: New York: Rosen Pub. Group, 1994. Related Authors: Lee, Richard S. (Richard Sandoval), 1927- Description: 64 p.: ill. (some col.); 25 cm. ISBN: 0823915379 Notes: Includes bibliographical references (p. 62) and index. Subjects: Drugs and mass media--United States--Juvenile literature. Substance abuse--United States--Juvenile literature. Series: The Drug abuse prevention library LC Classification: HV5825 .L434 1994 Dewey Class No.: 070.4/4936229/0973 20

Levine, Madeline. See no evil: a guide to protecting our children from media violence / Madeline Levine. Published/Created: San Francisco: Jossey-Bass Publishers, c1998. Description: xi, 290 p.; 23 cm. ISBN: 0787943479 (pbk.: alk. paper) Notes: Originally Published: Viewing violence. New York: Doubleday, 1996. Includes bibliographical references (p. 251-267) and index. Subjects: Mass media and children. Mass media and teenagers. Violence in mass media. LC Classification: HQ784.M3 L48 1998 Dewey Class No.: 302.23/083 21

Luke, Carmen. Constructing the child viewer: a history of the American discourse on television and children, 1950-1980 / Carmen Luke. Published/Created: New York: Praeger, 1990. Description: ix, 331 p.; 24 cm. ISBN: 0275935167 (alk. paper) Notes: Includes bibliographical references (p. [297]-318) and indexes. Subjects: Television and children--United States--History. Mass media and children--United States--History. Discourse analysis. LC Classification: HQ784.T4 L85 1990 Dewey Class No.: 302.23/45/083 20

Mazor, Barry. New media and multimedia developer / Barry Mazor. Edition Information: 1st ed. Published/Created: New York Rosen Central, 2000. Description: 45 p.: ill.; 23 cm. ISBN: 0823931021 Summary: Describes the various types of jobs available in the field of new media development and the education and training required. Notes: Includes bibliographical references and index. Subjects: Mass media--Technological innovations--Interactive multimedia--Mass media--Computer science--Vocational guidance. Series: Coolcareers.com LC Classification: P96.T42 M375 2000 Dewey Class No.: 302.23/024 21

Media communication in everyday life: interpretative studies on children's and young people's media actions / edited by Michael Charlton and Ben Bachmair. Published/Created: München; New York: K.G. Saur, 1990. Related Authors: Charlton, Michael, 1948- Bachmair, Ben. Description: 224 p.: ill.; 21 cm. ISBN: 3598202083: Notes: Includes translation of articles from German. Includes bibliographical references. Subjects: Mass media and children--Germany (West) Television and children--Germany (West) Series: Communication research and broadcasting; no. 9 LC Classification: HQ784.M3 M42 1990

Media, children, and the family: social scientific, psychodynamic, and clinical perspectives / edited by Dolf Zillmann, Jennings Bryant, Aletha C. Huston. Published/Created: Hillsdale, N.J.: Erlbaum, 1994. Related Authors: Zillmann, Dolf. Bryant, Jennings. Huston, Aletha C. Description: xiii, 351 p.: ill.; 24 cm. ISBN: 0805812105 (alk. paper) 0805814159 (pbk.: alk. paper) Notes: Includes bibliographical references and indexes. Subjects: Mass media--Social aspects. Mass media and the family. Mass media and children Television broadcasting

Pornography--Social aspects. Series: LEA's communication series LC Classification: HM258 .M3743 1994 Dewey Class No.: 302.23 20

Medved, Michael. Saving childhood: protecting our children from the national assault on innocence / Michael Medved and Diane Medved. Edition Information: 1st ed. Published/Created: New York, NY: HarperCollinsPublishers, c1998. Related Authors: Medved, Diane. Description: xii, 324 p.; 25 cm. ISBN: 0060173726 Notes: Includes bibliographical references (p. 293-311) and index. Subjects: Children--United States. Children and adults--United States. Mass media and children--United States. Child rearing--United States. Innocence (Psychology) LC Classification: HQ792.U5 M43 1998 Dewey Class No.: 305.23/0973 21

Mohanty, J. (Jagannath), 1937- Child development and education today: literature, art, media, and materials / Jagannath Mohanty. Published/Created: New Delhi: Deep & Deep Publications, c1998. Description: xxiii, 459 p.; 22 cm. ISBN: 8176290955 Summary: With reference to India. Notes: Includes bibliographical references (p. [445]-451) and index. Subjects: Child development--Literature--Study and teaching--Art--Study and teaching--Mass media in education--India. LC Classification: LB1115 .M65 1998

Molen, Julie Henriëtte Walma van der, 1967- Children's recall of television and print news / door Julie Henriëtte Walma van der Molen. Published/Created: [The Netherlands: s.n., 1998?] Description: viii, 141 p.: ill.; 24 cm. Notes: "Stellingen" (1 leaf) inserted. Thesis (doctoral)--Rijksuniversiteit te Leiden, 1998. Includes bibliographical references and index. Summary in Dutch. Subjects: Mass media and children. Mass media--Psychological aspects. Press, Juvenile. Memory in children. LC Classification: P94.5.C55 M65 1998

Njau, Wangui. A mid-term report of the content analysis of media reports pertaining to adolescent reproductive health issues in Kenya, July to December, 1994 / by Wangoi Njau (Centre for the Study of Adolescence (CSA)). Published/Created: [Nairobi: s.n., 1995] Related Authors: Centre for the Study of Adolescence (Nairobi, Kenya) Kenya Youth Initiative Project. Description: viii, 80 leaves: ill.; 30 cm. Notes: At head of Kenya Youth Initiative Project. "January 1995." Newspaper cuttings on 9 folded leaves inserted. Subjects: Teenagers--Kenya--Sexual behavior. Hygiene, Sexual--Kenya. Teenage pregnancy--Kenya. Teenagers in mass media. Sex in mass media. LC Classification: HQ27 .N55 1995

Parker, Steve. 20th century media / by Steve Parker. Published/Created: Milwaukee: Stevens Pub., 2002. Projected Pub. Date: 0207 Description: p. cm. ISBN: 0836831829 (v. 1: lib. bdg.) 0836831837 (v. 2: lib. bdg.) 0836831845 (v. 3: lib. bdg.) 0836831853 (v. 4: lib. bdg.) 0836831861 (v. 5: lib. bdg.) 083683187X (v. 6: lib. bdg.) Incomplete Notes: Includes indexes. Subjects: Mass media--History--20th century--Juvenile literature. Mass media--History--20th century. LC Classification: P91.2 .P37 2002 Dewey Class No.: 302.23/09/04 21

Patterson, Philip D., 1954- Stay tuned: what every parent should know about media / Philip D. Patterson. Published/Created: Webb City, Mo.: Covenant Pub., c2002. Projected Pub. Date: 0204 Description: p. cm. ISBN: 1892435217 (pbk.) Notes: Includes bibliographical references. Subjects: Mass media and children--Moral and ethical aspects--United States. Mass media--United States. Child rearing--Religious aspects--Christianity. LC Classification: HQ784.M3+ Dewey Class No.: 302.23/083/0973 21

Petley, Julian. Media: the impact on our lives / Julian Petley. Published/Created: Austin, TX: Raintree Steck-Vaughn, c2001. Description: 61 p.: ill. (some col.); 25 cm. ISBN: 0739831755 Subjects: Mass media--

Social aspects--Juvenile literature. Mass media--Influence--Juvenile literature. Mass media. Series: 21st century debates LC Classification: HM1013 .P47 2001 Dewey Class No.: 302.23 21

Phillips, Phil. The truth about Power Rangers / Phil Phillips. Published/Created: Lancaster, Pa.: Starburst Publishers, c1995. Description: 107, [4] p.: ill.; 21 cm. ISBN: 0914984675 Notes: "An in-depth look at the Mighty Morphin Power Rangers, revealing the violence and philosophy behind the #1 toy and kids' TV show in America"--Cover. Includes bibliographical references (p. [109]). Subjects: Mighty Morphin Power Rangers (Television program) Television and children. Violence on television. Mass media and children. Toys--Social aspects. Parenting. Parenting--Religious aspects--Christianity. LC Classification: HQ784.T4 P46 1995 Dewey Class No.: 302.23/45/083 20

Robie, Joan Hake. Teenage Mutant Ninja Turtles exposed! / Joan Hake Robie. Published/Created: Lancaster, Pa.: Starburst Publishers, c1991. Description: 77 p.: ill.; 21 cm. ISBN: 0914984314 Notes: "TimeLee books." Includes bibliographical references (p. 76-77). Subjects: Mass media and children--United States. Violence in mass media. Teenage Mutant Ninja Turtles (Fictitious characters) LC Classification: HQ784.M3 R52 1991 Dewey Class No.: 302.23/083 20

Sanders, Barry, 1938- A is for ox: violence, electronic media, and the silencing of the written word / Barry Sanders. Edition Information: 1st ed. Published/Created: New York: Pantheon Books, c1994. Description: xiii, 269 p.; 22 cm. ISBN: 0679417117: Notes: Includes bibliographical references (p. 245-256) and index. Subjects: Oral communication--Social aspects. Literacy. Mass media and youth. Mass media--Social aspects. Children and violence. LC Classification: P95 .S26 1994 Dewey Class No.: 302.2/242 20

Schissel, Bernard, 1950- Blaming children: youth crime, moral panic and the politics of hate / Bernard Schissel. Published/Created: Halifax, N.S.: Fernwood, c1997. Description: 133 p.: ill.; 23 cm. ISBN: 1895686830: Notes: Includes bibliographical references: p. 129-133. Subjects: Juvenile delinquency--Canada. Juvenile delinquency--Canada--Public opinion. Mass media and public opinion--Canada. Youth in mass media. Public opinion--Canada. LC Classification: HV9108 .S35 1997 Dewey Class No.: 364.36/0971 21

Schrank, Jeffrey Understanding mass media / Jeffrey Schrank. Edition Information: 4th ed. Published/Created: Lincolnwood, Ill.: National Textbook Co., 1991. Description: xi, 372 p.: ill.; 26 cm. Summary: A textbook examining the importance of the mass media as means of communication and as shapers of the environment. Notes: Includes index. Subjects: Mass media--Juvenile literature Mass media LC Classification: P91.2 .S38 1991 Dewey Class No.: 302.2/3 19

Schultze, Quentin J. (Quentin James), 1952- Winning your kids back from the media / Quentin J. Schultze. Published/Created: Downers Grove, Ill.: InterVarsity Press, c1994. Description: 168 p.; 21 cm. ISBN: 0830813985 (alk. paper) Notes: "Saltshaker books"--P. [4] of cover. Includes bibliographical references (p. [163]-168). Subjects: Mass media and children--United States. Communication in the family--United States. Mass media--Religious aspects--Christianity. LC Classification: HQ784.M3 S37 1994 Dewey Class No.: 302.23/083 20

Sherrow, Victoria. Image and substance: the media in U.S. elections / Victoria Sherrow. Published/Created: Brookfield, Conn.: Millbrook Press, c1992. Description: 128 p.: ill.; 24 cm. ISBN: 1562940759 (lib. bdg.) Summary: Examines the critical role played by the print and broadcasting media in American politics; the history and impact of this relationship; and the use and abuse of the media in a democratic society.

Notes: Includes bibliographical references (p. 123-124) and index. Subjects: Advertising, Political--Political campaigns--Mass media--Political aspects--United States--Juvenile literature. Advertising, Political. Mass media--Political aspects. Politics, Practical. Elections. Series: Issue and debate LC Classification: JK1978 .S48 1992 Dewey Class No.: 324.7/3/0973 20

Shomari, Hashim A. From the underground: hip hop culture as an agent of social change / Hashim A. Shomari (William A. Lee, III). Published/Created: Fanwood, NJ: X-Factor Publications, c1995. Description: 50 p.: ill.; 22 cm. ISBN: 0964252309 Notes: Includes bibliographical references. Subjects: Afro-American youth. Afro-American arts. Rap (Music)--History and criticism. Mass media--Social aspects--United States. LC Classification: E185.86 .S585 1995 Dewey Class No.: 305.23/5/08996073 20

Shuker, Roy. Youth, media, and moral panic in New Zealand: (from hooligans to video nasties) / Roy Shuker and Roger Openshaw, with Janet Soler. Published/Created: Palmerston North, N.Z.: Dept. of Education, Massey University, c1990. Related Authors: Openshaw, Roger. Soler, Janet. Description: iv, 109 p.: ill.; 27 cm. Notes: Includes bibliographical references. Subjects: Juvenile delinquents--New Zealand. Mass media and teenagers--New Zealand. Deviant behavior. Subculture--New Zealand. Popular culture--New Zealand. Series: Delta research monograph, 0110-4748; no. 11 LC Classification: HV9230.4.A5 S57 1990 Dewey Class No.: 364.2/54 20

Strasburger, Victor C., 1949- Adolescents and the media: medical and psychological impact / Victor C. Strasburger. Published/Created: Thousand Oaks: Sage Publications, c1995. Description: xi, 137 p.: ill.; 23 cm. ISBN: 0803954999 (alk. paper) 0803955006 (pbk.: alk. paper) Notes: Includes bibliographical references (p. 101-123) and indexes. Subjects: Mass media and teenagers. Series: Developmental clinical psychology and psychiatry; v. 33 LC Classification: HQ799.2.M35 S87 1995 Dewey Class No.: 302.23/0935 20

Strasburger, Victor C., 1949- Children, adolescents, and the media / Victor C. Strasburger, Barbara J. Wilson; with contributions by Jeanne B. Funk, Edward Donnerstein, Bob McCannon. Published/Created: Thousand Oaks Calif.: Sage Publications, c2002. Projected Pub. Date: 0203 Related Authors: Wilson, Barbara J. Description: p. cm. ISBN: 0761921249 (cloth) 0761921257 (pbk.) Notes: Includes bibliographical references and index. Subjects: Mass media and children--United States. Mass media and teenagers--United States. LC Classification: HQ784.M3 S78 2002 Dewey Class No.: 302.23/083 21

Tobin, Joseph Jay. "Good guys don't wear hats": children's talk about the media / Joseph Tobin. Published/Created: New York: Teachers College Press, c2000. Description: x, 166 p.: ill.; 24 cm. ISBN: 0807738867 (pbk.) 0807738875 (cloth) Notes: Includes bibliographical references (p. 153-157) and index. Subjects: Mass media and children. Children--Attitudes. Children--Language. LC Classification: HQ784.M3 T63 2000 Dewey Class No.: 302.23/083 21

Walsh, David Allen. Selling out America's children: how America puts profits before values-- and what parents can do / David Walsh. Published/Created: Minneapolis: Fairview Press, [1995] Description: xi, 172 p.; 23 cm. ISBN: 0925190276 Notes: Originally Published: Minneapolis: Deaconess Press, c1994. Includes index. Subjects: Mass media and children--Moral and ethical aspects. Children--United States--Attitudes. Child consumers--Parenting--United States. LC Classification: HQ784.M3 W35 1995 Dewey Class No.: 305.23/0973 20

Weiss, Ann E., 1943- Who's to know?: information, the media, and public awareness / Ann E. Weiss

Published/Created: Boston: Houghton Mifflin, 1990. Description: 182 p.; 22 cm. ISBN: 0395497027: Summary: Does the public have a right to know? Discusses factors that may interfere with that right and limit public knowledge, using examples from current events which dramatize the complex issues of media censorship. Notes: Includes bibliographical references (p. [163]-168) and index. Subjects: Mass media--Censorship--Freedom of information--Mass media--Objectivity--Privacy, Right of--Juvenile literature. Mass media--Censorship. Freedom of information. Privacy, Right of. LC Classification: P96.C64 W4 1990 Dewey Class No.: 363.3/1 20

Wilson, Wayne, 1953- Careers in publishing and communications / Wayne Wilson. Published/Created: Bear, Del.: Mitchell Lane Publishers, 2001. Projected Pub. Date: 1111 Description: p. cm. ISBN: 1584150882 Summary: Surveys a variety of career opportunities in the world of newspapers, magazines, book publishing, radio, television, films, and the Internet and profiles Hispanic Americans who have succeeded in these fields. Notes: Includes bibliographical references and index. Subjects: Communication--Mass media--Publishers and publishing---Vocational guidance--Juvenile literature. Hispanic Americans in mass media--Vocational guidance for minorities--Juvenile literature. Communication--Mass media--Publishers and publishing--Hispanic Americans Vocational guidance. Series: Latinos at work LC Classification: P91.6 W55 2001 Dewey Class No.: 302.2/023 21

Wright, Randal A. Protecting your family in an X-rated world / Randal A. Wright. Published/Created: Salt Lake City, Utah: Deseret Book Co., [1992] Description: ix, 144 p.; 22 cm. ISBN: 0875796176 (pbk.): Notes: Previously Published as: Families in danger. c1988. Includes bibliographical references and index. Subjects: Child rearing--Religious aspects--Mormon Church. Mass media and children--Moral and ethical aspects. Mass media and children--United States. LC Classification: HQ769.3 .W74 1992 Dewey Class No.: 649/.1 20

York, Frank. Protecting your child in an X-rated world / by Frank York and Jan LaRue. Published/Created: Wheaton, Ill.: Tyndale House Publishers, c2002. Projected Pub. Date: 0104 Related Authors: LaRue, Jan. Description: p. cm. ISBN: 1561799076 Notes: Includes bibliographical references and index. Subjects: Children and sex. Mass media and children. Pornography. Internet and children. LC Classification: HQ784.S45 Y67 2002 Dewey Class No.: 363.4/7 21

AUTHOR INDEX

C

D

E

F

G

H

N

O

P

Q

R

S

Y

Z

TITLE INDEX

#

A

B

C

D

E

F

G

H

I

J

K

L

M

N

O

P

Q

R

S

U

V

W

Y

Z

Subject Index

#

A

B

C

D

G

H

I

N

O

P

Q

R

S

T

U

V

W

Y

Z